THE HANDBOOK OF GLOBALISATION, SECOND EDITION

The Handbook of Globalisation, Second Edition

Edited by

Jonathan Michie

Director, Department for Continuing Education and President, Kellogg College, University of Oxford, UK

Edward Elgar
Cheltenham, UK • Northampton, MA, USA

Published by
Edward Elgar Publishing Limited
The Lypiatts
15 Lansdown Road
Cheltenham
Glos GL50 2JA
UK

Edward Elgar Publishing, Inc.
William Pratt House
9 Dewey Court
Northampton
Massachusetts 01060
USA

A catalogue record for this book
is available from the British Library

Library of Congress Control Number: 2010939211

FSC www.fsc.org MIX Paper from responsible sources FSC® C018575

ISBN 978 1 84980 369 4 (cased)
ISBN 978 1 84980 376 2 (paperback)

Typeset by Manton Typesetters, Louth, Lincolnshire, UK
Printed and bound by MPG Books Group, UK

Contents

PART IV LABOUR STANDARDS

PART V EUROPE AND NORTH AMERICA

PART VI GOVERNANCE

PART VII INTERNATIONAL ECONOMIC INSTITUTIONS

PART VIII POLICY IMPLICATIONS AND RESPONSES

Contributors

Philip Arestis, Cambridge Centre for Economic and Public Policy, Department of Land Economy, University of Cambridge, UK; and Department of Applied Economics, University of the Basque Country, Spain

Elissa Braunstein, Associate Professor, Department of Economics, Colorado State University, USA

Peter Brosnan, Emeritus Professor of Industrial Relations, Griffith University, Australia

Ha-Joon Chang, Faculty of Economics, University of Cambridge, UK

The late Charles Craypo, formerly Professor Emeritus, Economics Department, University of Notre Dame, USA

George DeMartino, Professor, Josef Korbel School of International Studies, University of Denver, USA

Gary Dymski, Department of Economics, University of California, USA

Gerald Epstein, Professor of Economics and Co-Director, Political Economy Research Institute, University of Massachusetts Amherst, USA

The late Andrew Glyn, formerly Fellow in Economics at Corpus Christi College, Oxford, UK

James Heintz, Associate Research Professor, Political Economy Research Institute, University of Massachusetts

Colin Hines, Co-Director of Finance for the Future, former head of Greenpeace International's Economics Unit

The late Paul Hirst, formerly Professor of Social Theory, Birkbeck College, University of London, UK

Geoffrey M. Hodgson, Research Professor in Business Studies at the University of Hertfordshire, UK

Jeremy Howells, Eddie Davies Chair in Entrepreneurship and Innovation and Executive Director, Manchester Institute of Innovation Research, Manchester Business School, UK

Grazia Ietto-Gillies, Emeritus Professor of Applied Economics, London South Bank University; Visiting Research Professor, Birkbeck, University of London, UK

Mathias Koenig-Archibugi, Senior Lecturer in Global Politics, London School of Economics and Political Science, London, UK

Simon Lee, Centre for Democratic Governance, Department of Politics and International Studies, University of Hull, UK

Photis Lysandrou, Professor of Global Political Economy, London Metropolitan Business School, UK

Jonathan Michie, Director, Department for Continuing Education and President, Kellogg College, University of Oxford, UK

José Gabriel Palma, Faculty of Economics, Cambridge University, UK

Mića Panić, Emeritus Fellow of Selwyn College, University of Cambridge, UK and former Vice Chairman of the United Nations Committee for Development Policy

Jonathan Perraton, Department of Economics and Political Economy Research Centre, University of Sheffield, UK

Joseph Plasmans, Emeritus Professor of Econometrics, Department of Economics, University of Antwerp, Belgium and CentER, Tilburg University, the Netherlands

Malcolm Sawyer, Professor of Economics, Leeds University Business School, University of Leeds, UK

Scott Sinclair, Senior Research Fellow, Canadian Centre for Policy Alternatives, Canada

Ajit Singh, Emeritus Professor of Economics, University of Cambridge, and Life Fellow, Queens' College, Cambridge, UK; Tun Ismail Ali Chair in International Economics and Finance, University of Malaya, Kuala Lumpur, Malaysia

Jim Stanford, Economist for the Canadian Auto Workers, Toronto, Canada, and author, *Economics for Everyone* (Pluto, 2008)

Bob Sutcliffe, University of the Basque Country, Bilbao, Spain (retired)

Grahame Thompson, Emeritus Professor of Political Economy, Open University, UK and Visiting Professor, Copenhagen Business School, Denmark

John Toye, Department of International Development, University of Oxford, UK

Frank Wilkinson, Centre for Business Research, University of Cambridge; also Visiting Professor, Birkbeck College, University of London, UK

Richard Woodward, Department of Politics and International Studies, University of Hull, UK

Ann Zammit, Independent consultant, formerly Senior Staff member, South Centre Geneva, Switzerland

Globalisation: introduction and overview

Jonathan Michie

Since the 1980s it had been fashionable to suggest that there was little that individual countries could do in the face of global economic forces, and any attempt to pursue independent policies would be doomed to failure. 'Even China', it was often said, was embracing the global free market. The idea that developing countries, such as India, could promote their own developmental interests by sheltering behind exchange controls or national planning had been swept away along with the Berlin Wall. In the globalised economy of the twenty-first century, it was argued, national governments had to go with the flow of global markets.

As the 2008 credit crunch was breaking, the global strategy firm Oxford Analytica held one of its usual daily analysis sessions, but open to those attending its annual conference. The chair briefly summarised the unfolding global crisis, and then went round the table asking the various national experts to report. Despite the consensus referred to above, the reports did not paint a picture of a uniform globalised market to which each country related in the same way. The US and UK had been referred to in the opening statement, being very much at the centre of whatever it was that had caused the worst economic crisis since the 1930s. But when the expert on Brazil was called, he reported that the socialist President Lula had kept its financial sector rather independent of the global markets. Next India, and here too it was reported that it actually hadn't opened itself up to the global market quite as much as might have been thought. Then China, where, it was reported, the Communist Party had maintained rather a firm grip.

Of course, no one can escape a world economic crisis, and Brazil, India and China suffered along with the rest. But it was clear that those countries had developed a rather different relation to the global market economy than had the US and the UK. Brazil, India and China had not caused the crisis, and to some extent, at least, their own economic strategies and policies did enable them to survive the global recession in better shape than if they had fully joined in the orgy of free market globalisation that the UK and US had been championing through the 1980s and 1990s.

So, the continued globalisation of economic activities is certainly of major significance for the prosperity – or otherwise – of the world's population; it has been accompanied by major policy debates and developments; and this 'globalisation' has been the subject of wide-ranging cross-disciplinary academic research for the past several years – some would say for the past several decades, a point discussed below. But the resulting academic debates are far from being resolved. In this, they reflect the continued policy debate and action, and the continuously changing contours of the globalisation process itself.

The purpose of the current volume is to bring together the key strands of this wide-ranging research agenda, and to report the latest state of play in the resulting academic debates. This literature is one that I have been involved in myself with various co-authors from a series of research projects. However, rather than include anything from these projects, or with my co-authors, within the body of this volume, I have instead referred liberally to various of these contributions within this introductory chapter, in which I also give an overview of the subsequent 28 chapters.[1]

Part I: Globalisation in question?

First is the question of how radical a break the current state of globalisation is from previous developments. The title of this first part of the book is taken from Hirst and Thompson (1996), who are sceptical of such claims. Chapter 1 of the current volume is reproduced from the previous edition, since Paul Hirst had, sadly, died before this updated version was commissioned; in that chapter, Hirst and Thompson had brought their arguments up to date from their 1996 book for the 2003 edition of this volume, continuing though to question how unprecedented the globalisation developments of the 1990s really had been. Grahame Thompson then brings this analysis right up to date with a new Chapter 2 for this edition, on financial globalisation and the 2008–10 global credit crunch and recession, in which he challenges the notion that the 2008 financial crisis was global in scope. Rather, he argues, the international financial system is quite differentiated, even though it is, of course, characterised by contagion, to which he argues the best regulatory response is to develop what he describes as 'distributed preparedness for resilience', rather than top-down global rules that would rely on the same institutions of global economic governance that have failed us in the past.

Such scepticism is challenged by Jonathan Perraton in Chapter 3, who argues that globalisation is a process and so cannot be dismissed simply because it has not arrived at some pre-imagined 'state'. The question remains, however, of just how different the current globalisation process is from previous globalisation processes. Scepticism about this had been expressed by other authors before Hirst and Thompson, including the late Andrew Glyn, who in the previous edition had reported the latest state of play with his co-author Bob Sutcliffe, arguing that globalisation is widely misinterpreted, and that in particular its quantitative extent and novelty are exaggerated. Their chapter, Chapter 4, criticises the use of inappropriate statistical measures, conclusions drawn from little data and the failure to make historical comparisons, or to see counter-globalisation tendencies and limits to globalisation. The best measures suggest that globalisation is neither so new nor so great as is often supposed. The political implications of this argument are then briefly explored.[2]

Similarly, Costello et al. (1989) had argued that these globalisation trends 'have been with us for some time, and they need to be seen in historical context' (p. 38), and in particular need to be seen for what they are, namely an attempt to reconstruct the conditions for profitable growth internationally. As to whether the resulting globalisation would prevent national governments from pursuing any alternative paths, they argue (p. 55) that:

> National economic management is only an anachronism if it is seen as operating in an international vacuum. Instead, the nation state should be recognized for what it is: the single most powerful mechanism of legal and organizational powers for economic intervention.

As for whether such intervention is necessary, Michie (1995, p. xx) argues that:

> The global economy can be imagined to be a self-equilibrating mechanism of the textbook variety, or it can be recognized as subject to processes of cumulative causation whereby if one or more countries fall behind the pack, there may be dangers of them falling further behind rather than enjoying an automatic ticket back to the equilibrium solution path. These two alternative, conflicting views of real world economic processes have very different implications regarding institutional needs and arrangements.

There are, then, two interrelated issues. First, how radically different are current processes from previous ones? And second, what are the policy implications? Michie (1996, p. 124) argued that of the variety on offer, the following description of the globalisation of economic activity is apposite:

> All old-established national industries have been destroyed or are daily being destroyed. They are dislodged by new industries, whose introduction becomes a life and death question for all nations, by industries that no longer work up indigenous raw material, but raw material drawn from the remotest zones; industries whose products are consumed, not only at home, but in every quarter of the globe. In place of the old wants, satisfied by the productions of the country, we find new wants, requiring for their satisfaction the products of distant lands. We have universal interdependence of nations. And as in material, so also in intellectual production.

This characterisation of globalisation processes was written more than 160 years ago.[3] Likewise, the difficulties faced by national governments attempting to pursue policies in the face of globalisation have been discussed in detail for decades, and the actual difficulties have been faced up to and tackled, with varying degrees of both commitment and success, for decades as well:

> The real question, then, is not whether is it best to act at the national or international level; it is how best to secure international action. For all to remain frozen until such time as everyone else moves is inadequate, however eloquent the calls for movement being made might be. Action at the local, regional, national or bloc level, far from being a utopian alternative to the real international stage, might in reality prove a prerequisite to cooperation. (Michie, 1996, p. 125)

Part II: Analysing the global economy

Globalisation is sometimes interpreted or presented as resulting from technological innovation, and certainly such innovation has fuelled globalisation processes. Likewise there have no doubt been demand–pull pressures from globalisation on new technologies, hastening their advent, adoption, diffusion and development. Jeremy Howells has been analysing such processes for many years, and he opens Part II in Chapter 5 by considering 'systems of innovation' within a global economy, both as a theoretical construct and as influencing how successfully economies can adapt and perform within an ever-changing global economic environment.

In Chapter 6, Gary Dymski reviews recent historical experience with international debt crises, with an emphasis on how economists have answered two core questions about these episodes – namely, why do they occur, and what should be done about them? He concludes that:

> For economists who operate on the premise that "there is no alternative" to market-driven flows of credit and capital, these crises present opportunities for fine-tuning. This is the only way of moving ever closer to the idea of economic efficiency set out in the textbooks. But for economists who regard the structure of global financial flows as flawed, the costs of each crisis episode are cumulative: each crisis leads to more international and intranational inequality, and to the further dismantling of national development-oriented institutions (Baker et al., 1998). For these economists, the subprime crisis represents the culmination of several decades in which debt crises led to borrowers being punished, while creditors were given an ever freer scope for action.
>
> The draconian efforts required to restore order in global financial markets in response to the subprime crisis have by no means addressed the root causes of international debt crises. To the contrary, since the steps taken to salvage the global financial architecture have bailed out firms and market participants that precipitated these crises, future crises – possibly in still new forms – become still more likely. Further, these asymmetric resolutions of international debt crises leave the world ever farther from an alternative set of financial relations in which the gains of financial integration are more evenly shared, and the costs of crises no longer fall most heavily on the most vulnerable nations and people.

The inequality to which Dymski refers is then analysed, in Chapter 7, by José Gabriel Palma, who subjects the relevant data to rigorous scrutiny, producing new findings on the distribution of income within countries. The situation in Latin America is, he reports, quite striking in terms of the degree of inequality, to the extent that it is not immediately obvious why this has, up until now, proved sustainable – as Palma puts it, since political oligarchies the world over would no doubt like to appropriate as high a share of national income as possible, 'the key question that still needs to be answered is why is it that it is only in Latin America that they manage to get away with it?'.

Part III: Transnational corporations

Part III analyses the role of transnational corporations within the global economy. Grazia Ietto-Gillies in Chapter 8 provides a comprehensive overview of the role played within the current globalisation processes by transnational corporations. She argues that the dominant drivers of globalisation are first, technological innovation in the field of communication and information together with advances in the field of transportation, and second, organisational innovation and in particular the organisation of production across countries.

Gerry Epstein in Chapter 9 also provides data on the role of transnational corporations, and discusses the effect that the operation of transnational corporations has on the economy, and on specific economies that experience either outward or inward investment:

> Despite the fact that there has been a great deal of research during the last several decades on MNCs, there is no consensus on their effects. Still, the evidence that does exist suggests the following: though foreign direct investment can have positive impacts on home and host countries, the likelihood that these positive effects will materialise and be widely shared is greatly diminished by the 'neo-liberal' policy framework that is dominant in much of the world today. I conclude that what is needed instead of more deregulation and 'free' capital mobility, is a more democratic framework of multinational investment regulation to help countries and their citizens reap the benefits that can be associated with international investment. If this was done properly, the tensions that arise between the interests of southern and northern workers might be significantly reduced.

In Chapter 10, Elissa Braunstein reviews the literature dealing with gender and foreign direct investment. This literature covers a variety of topics, such as how women's roles outside the formal market sector can impact upon the profitability of multinational investment. The chapter focuses in particular on the implications of such work for a country's overall development strategy; for any government that is seeking to gain the maximum benefit from such inward investment, understanding the role of gender is key.

Part IV: Labour standards

In its first decade of operation, the International Labour Organization adopted a convention on minimum wages – Convention 26 'Concerning the Creation of Minimum Wage-Fixing Machinery', 1928. Its concern was to ensure that global trade was not based on cheap labour. In Chapter 11, Peter Brosnan discusses the operation of minimum wage legislation within the context of globalisation – which makes the enforcement of such legislation more difficult but also, perhaps, more necessary.

The impact that this sort of labour standards legislation is discussed by Ajit Singh and Ann Zammit in Chapter 12 within the context of economic development more generally. They point to various difficulties, such as the limited proportion of the population for whom such legislation might actually impact, through to the more general problem, that if such legislation hampers economic development, the losers in the long run may include those whom such legislation sets out to protect.

These various factors and arguments are considered and discussed by James Heintz in Chapter 13. He evaluates the danger of negative consequences, and discusses, within this context, current developments in implementation strategies, concluding that:

> Regardless of the implementation strategy, the limitations of any scheme along these lines to introduce global labor standards should be explicitly recognized. Most significantly, only a subset of the world's workforce would receive any benefits, since the standards are aimed at workers who produce goods for export. Workers producing non-traded goods and services would not be directly affected by interventions such as a standardized code of conduct or a social clause. In these cases, the ongoing mission of the ILO to encourage states to implement and enforce better domestic standards remains invaluable. Furthermore, adopting expansionary macroeconomic policies could be more strategic for improving the well-being of all workers than a targeted set of labor standards. A coordinated approach involving a range of interventions – both macroeconomic and in terms of international regulation – would also reduce the tensions between better standards and job creation.
>
> Despite the limitations of global labor standards, the potential that such interventions have for improving the working lives of a significant number of people should not be underestimated. Furthermore, the possible impact of such a system extends well beyond the benefits generated by its core policies. The development of an appropriate regulatory scheme for enforcing basic standards of decency could serve as a model for governing multinational economic activities more generally. Because of these possible contributions, striving to create an effective framework for global labor standards represents an important policy goal in this era of the new international division of labor.

Part V: Europe and North America

One of the reasons for being sceptical of generalised claims about globalisation having created a global market in which individual countries no longer matter, is that much of the supposedly 'global' activities of multinational corporations and international financial markets is actually within and between Europe and North America. In both cases, institutional developments have created new regional structures – the North American Free Trade Area, and the European Union. The rhetoric within the EU has been explicit about productivity and competitiveness. In Chapter 14, Joseph Plasmans considers relative productivity within Europe and North America within the context of globalisation, and concludes that local and regional factors are still of great importance in determining relative productivity levels and growth. The conscious effort to create a single European market, with a single currency, is analysed by Philip Arestis and Malcolm Sawyer in Chapter 15.[4] They stress that this has not been simply a technical exercise, nor a politically neutral one:

> The establishment of the euro and the European Monetary Union has been undertaken within a specific institutional and policy framework. The institutional framework gives prominence in policy formulation to an undemocratic and unaccountable European Central Bank. It is a policy framework that emphasises the control of inflation over the reduction of unemployment, although it provides a weak instrument (monetary policy) for the control of inflation and generates macroeconomic policies. The latter tend to increase rather than diminish the level and disparity of unemployment. Economic performance with the euro has been disappointing, and the eurozone is facing very considerable pressures, which put its future in doubt.

The equivalent processes within North America are analysed by Jim Stanford in Chapter 16 in his discussion of NAFTA, where he argues that:

> The relatively simple task of eliminating tariffs on intra-NAFTA merchandise trade constitutes a modest portion of the overall NAFTA package. More important has been the NAFTA's attempt to establish a continent-wide regime of deregulated, market-oriented economic development. Indeed, the Mexican government's primary interest in the NAFTA may have been precisely to commit itself publicly and permanently to a broadly neoliberal development strategy, thus winning the confidence and approval of both international investors and domestic wealth-holders. The NAFTA has had a significant impact on trade and direct investment flows within North America, but the overall impact of NAFTA on aggregate economic variables (such as investment, growth, productivity and incomes) has been disappointing, including for Mexico (which was expected by economists to benefit dramatically from its integration within the continental market). The prospects for the expansion of NAFTA (to include other countries in the Western Hemisphere), or for its deepening (to address topics such as monetary integration or migration) seem dim. Meanwhile, the broader relative decline of the US economy (most dramatically visible in the financial crisis and recession of 2009) has imposed spillover consequences on its NAFTA partners, and on the long-run vitality of the continental market generally. Without a substantial revitalization of both North American economic leadership, and initiatives to further intensify and deepen economic links between the three NAFTA partners, it would seem that NAFTA's long-run economic and political importance is likely to fade.

In Chapter 17, Charles Craypo and Frank Wilkinson analyse the way in which the US economy relates to the global, in particular through exporting jobs via FDI, and importing labour into the US.[5] Such an analysis is not common, which is surprising given how common and important are the processes being analysed – both to the economy in question, and to the citizens of that country, as well as for the citizens of other countries. This is undoubtedly a weakness of mainstream economics, that it does not even ask the right questions, let alone attempt to answer them. Frank Wilkinson's work, on the other hand, is based on the idea of productive systems:

> Where neoclassical theory reifies the market and loosens it from its institutional moorings in civil society, the legal system and the organizations of the state, the productive systems approach sees these institutions as playing a central role in the constitution and development of productive forces. Systems of production exist at a number of levels: the workplace; the enterprise or firm; the industrial sector or inter-firm network; nation states; and transnational trading blocs. (Rubery et al., 2002, p. 2)

Craypo and Wilkinson detail and analyse the way in which US corporations make use of immigrant labour in the US, while at the same time relocating production from the US to other countries:

> Deregulated markets, short-term corporate performance objectives and overriding shareholder and executive claims on resources, now dominate the US productive system. These, together with the increasing globalisation of this system, encourage corporations to cut pay and worsen conditions of work – moves that workers are increasingly powerless to resist. When dominant firms drive down labour costs in this way, others are forced to follow suit or risk operating at considerable disadvantage. This builds on a long historical tradition of wage cost competition based on cutting the pay of existing workforces, recruiting other workers who will work for less, or by simply relocating production to more employer-friendly sites. Within the global productive system, US employers increasingly resort to importing low-wage labour and exporting production processes to low-wage countries. Immigrant labour and emigrant jobs have thus become the hallmark of US labour relations and production strategies.

Part VI: Governance

In Chapter 18, Richard Woodward argues that globalisation points to aspects of both continuity and change in world politics. Similarly, in Chapter 19, Mathias Koenig-Archibugi reviews the substantial body of research:

> which shows that the performance of governance functions is not limited to the actions of governments exercising sovereign powers over their jurisdictions, but occurs also at supranational and transnational levels. Governance – understood as the establishment and operation of rule systems facilitating the coordination and cooperation of social actors – is conceptually distinct from government – understood as an organisation in charge of administering and enforcing those rules (Young, 1999). The literature discussed in this chapter (originating mostly from political scientists and international relations scholars) maintains that governance is not co-extensive with government, and that government should not be seen as a necessary condition of governance. More specifically, it shows that the absence of a world government does not mean that governance is impossible beyond the level of individual states. Global issues such as ozone depletion, the spread of financial crises and the prohibition of certain kinds of weapons are managed by governance structures that do not conform

to the hierarchical model of rule-setting and enforcement that is typical of states. The combination of these structures can be said to form a system of global governance.

The key question, of the relationship between globalisation and national economic policy, is then confronted by Simon Lee in his analysis in Chapter 20 of the UK's Labour governments of 1997–2010 and its 'third way' – often presented as a response to the constraints of globalisation:

> The third way has not reconciled UK domestic economic policy choices with globalisation in a manner that has been able to insulate domestic modernisation from the consequences of increasing volatility and contagion in global financial markets. Following the global financial crisis, during 2009 the UK experienced a fall in GDP of 4.8 per cent, a bigger fall than any year of the Great Depression and the UK's biggest contraction since 1921 (NIESR, 2010, p. 1). The demise of the political economy of the third way has demonstrated that long-term stability in monetary and fiscal policy cannot be guaranteed in a world of liberalised financial markets and volatile short-term capital flows, without effective regulation (United Nations, 2009). Under the political economy of the third way, the sources of imprudence, debt, risk and instability emanated from the private sector and liberalised markets overseas rather than solely from the public sector. The provision of an initially prudent (and latterly imprudent) framework for national macroeconomic policy was not sufficient to guarantee economic stability in the face of a 'risk-based' approach to the governance of financial markets, which empowered speculation and irresponsible risk-taking, at the expense of the taxpayer and manufacturing industry (Lee, 2009).

Tackling these underlying issues will require not just specific policy reforms, such as the introduction of a Tobin tax,[6] but also the reform of the current international economic institutions.

Part VII: International economic institutions

The penultimate part looks at the existing international economic institutions, with Scott Sinclair in Chapter 21 considering the World Trade Organization and its General Agreement on Trade in Services (GATS), which is exerting constant pressure on national governments to open services to foreign commercial providers. The role of the International Monetary Fund and the World Bank are then discussed by John Toye in Chapter 22.[7] Toye considers the pressures that have arisen given the criticisms of these institutions following their damaging roles in the Asian financial crisis.[8]

Mića Panić then analyses the global economic institutions and considers how best they might be reformed in response both to criticisms that they have failed, and more generally to meet the challenges ahead:

> Given the extent of global economic interdependence at the beginning of the twenty-first century, it is increasingly apparent that the world needs urgently a new international institutional framework capable of helping individual countries solve

their most pressing economic problems under these conditions. The objective of achieving global public goods through improvements in national economic security and social well-being is as relevant now as it was in the 1940s. However, without the spirit of 'Bretton Woods' – the absence of which is equally obvious at present – it would be virtually impossible to convene another 'Bretton Woods' conference, let alone to agree on a common course of action and implement it. Much more likely, the realities of interdependence may force an increasing number of countries to organise regional 'Bretton Woods' systems or, following the example of Western Europe, create economic and monetary unions.

Globally, however, the most that one can hope for at present is an improvement in the work of the existing institutions along *some* of the lines suggested in this chapter. Unfortunately, the attitude and actions of the world's largest economies in particular, especially since the 1980s, make even the objective of such modest improvements look positively utopian.

Part VIII: Policy implications and responses

The chapter by Mića Panić concludes that the policies that are necessary in face of global developments appear to have little chance of being implemented at present because of the political opposition from those who consider the current arrangement beneficial to their own economic interests. In Chapter 24, Ha-Joon Chang examines in detail the policy pronouncements from the world economic institutions, the leading industrialised countries who in any case call the shots within those institutions, and the academic economists and other experts within those countries.[9] The developing countries are, of course, being told that they must follow the free-market prescriptions espoused by the leading industrialised economies. It could, of course, be questioned just how far the leading industrialised economies themselves practise what they preach. But more to the point is to consider what they practised when they were at the same stage of development as the developing countries are today. And here there is absolutely no doubt. Today's rich countries grew rich behind protective barriers and domestic intervention. Those who gain a competitive advantage through such policies are, of course, the first to propose – or demand, if they have the power – free trade. This, Chang argues, is what we are witnessing today. The leading economies, which have manoeuvred themselves into a position of being able to do well in a straight commercial competition with the less developed economies, are now demanding precisely that – the sort of commercial competition in which the rich will become richer, and in which the poorer countries whose industries and firms may not be able to survive such competition will see those industries and firms go to the wall. This will leave those economies no alternative but to import goods from the advanced economies instead – or else invite the multinational corporations from those economies into their countries, to produce domestically.

In Chapter 25, Colin Hines makes the case for rejecting such demands – along with the whole global free-market logic – and instead campaign for an equitable international economic system, along with a proper appreciation of what can be done locally:

> The widespread resistance to globalisation can be built upon to fashion a viable localist alternative. There are already countless people and groups strengthening their local economies from the grassroots up. The greatest spur to consideration of such radical local alternatives at the governmental level will be the need to respond to global economic upheavals and the deflation, the job losses and inadequate consumer demand that will come in its wake. Equally crucial in shaping a different localist imperative amongst politicians will be the pressure that the politically active can bring to bear. This must shift from just fighting separate issue-specific aspects of globalisation to realising that their individual successes can only be secured as part of an overarching change to localisation, but in an internationally supportive manner.

In Chapter 26, George DeMartino also challenges the current drive towards a global free-market – what he describes as global neo-liberalism – but focuses on the international trading system and how it might best be reformed. By global neo-liberalism he means the policy regime created during the last quarter of the twentieth century in which 'largely unregulated market forces override the state in directing international trade and investment flows'; this therefore includes 'free trade, the liberalization of international financial markets, the global protection of property rights, and so forth'. DeMartino argues that the resulting system is unstable and unsustainable, and that governments will be forced to intervene: the important question is 'What will come next, after the current experiment with free trade has been abandoned?'

DeMartino considers the various alternatives, including the labour standards arguments that are surveyed in Chapters 11–13. From this he argues for a new policy that would create incentives for such standards to be adopted by all trading nations, with good standards rewarded by the tariff structure and poor standards penalised. He deals with the various objections that have been raised to such standard-setting, and recognises also that such measures would only tackle one part of the system that at present is generating such inequalities and instability globally. The other areas in which action is needed are discussed by several of the other authors in the current volume: tackling the international debt crisis (Dymski), dealing with inequality through domestic policy (Palma), encouraging transnational corporations to operate in ways that would provide economic benefit to those areas in which they operate (Ietto-Gillies, Epstein, Braunstein), setting labour standards nationally and internationally (Brosnan, Heintz), reforming NAFTA (Stanford), the European single currency system (Arestis and Sawyer), the international economic institutions (Sinclair, Toye, Panić), reasserting the legitimacy of government (Lee), allowing developing economies to pursue the sort of industrial policies that proved successful for the currently leading countries (Chang) and encouraging local and regional economic development (Hines). For DeMartino, his proposal for reforming the international trading system – to encourage a ratcheting up of standards in place of the sort of social dumping that can lock all into a downward spiral – would be a supportive contribution to such an alternative agenda.

The 2007–08 credit crunch and the global recession of 2009, which saw the first decline in global national income since the 1930s, is analysed by Photis Lysandrou in Chapter 27. Lysandrou pinpoints a key factor that has been generally overlooked by other accounts of the causes of the credit crunch, namely the huge increase in inequality, both within and between countries. This process created a large number of high net worth individuals who drove the demand for new financial instruments in which to invest and with which to speculate. To create a new era of sustainable development will require these gross inequalities to be tackled and overcome.

In the concluding Chapter 28, Geoff Hodgson reflects on what lessons have been learned by the fact that the economics profession appeared to have done such a poor job over the past 30 years in analysing and describing how the economy functions, and in advising on how economies should be regulated and governed to secure sustainable development. That failure of mainstream neoclassical economics needs to be recognised and tackled.

Conclusion

One of the most important conclusions that emerges clearly from a number of the authors is that it is wrong to consider 'globalisation' as representing some natural or technical development that can be then judged as either welcome or otherwise, and reformed accordingly. The facts that international capital markets have been given a free leash to move into unregulated speculation, that the international institutions have been imposing pro-Western policies on the rest of the world and that multinational corporations have been given increasingly free reign, have been the result of policy design and have been pursued by Western governments and the financial and other corporations involved. At each stage, a range of other options has been available for designing and constructing the international trading, financial and productive systems. Indeed:

> At this juncture, the overriding virtue of the productive systems approach is to re-emphasize the diversity of institutional forms which are present in capitalist systems and the potential solutions to the problem of societal cooperation to coexist. A systems approach cautions against the assumption that changes in national and global trading regimes can in any way be separated from what is happening at the level of the regulatory framework. An emphasis on 'spontaneous' convergence between systems can only obscure the important policy choices to be made in national and global governance. (Rubery et al., 2002, p. 9)

That is, there is an alternative. History has not come to an end; it is still being made. The question is, in whose interests? There is no doubt that over the past

30 years or so, policy has been driven by the interests of the international financial system and the transnational corporations. This has at times been recognised by those responsible, even as they acted, with talk therefore of balancing these imbalances through the introduction of the 'social chapter' to the European Union's Maastricht Treaty on monetary union, and environmental and labour standards clauses in NAFTA. But the main drive has remained a free-market one, despite the inequalities and instabilities that this inevitably generates.

Why has policy taken such a turn, following the much more successful 25 years up to the mid-1970s? In part the answer is, of course, that there have been powerful interests that have benefited, and in the struggle between economic interests, these have gained the upper hand. It may also be partly due, though, to the inability of mainstream economics to even recognise the above factors, let alone analyse them and propose alternative policies. In the world of textbook neoclassical economics, the free market outcome will maximise economic welfare. It may be acknowledged that there will be losers as well as winners when markets are deregulated, but, the theory goes, the winners could compensate the losers, so all would become better off. And in theory, perhaps they could.

In practice, however, the world works rather differently. The textbook model may provide a useful analytical tool, but it is not a description of reality, and the attempts to change reality to fit the model are misguided and destructive of the sort of social, political and economic institutions that historically have actually created economic growth and social progress. This needs to be recognised for appropriate policy to be generated and pursued. Of course, there would still be powerful interests that would prefer the current free-for-all. But at least such behaviour could be seen for what it is – an attempt by those with economic power to enjoy more of the spoils.

The alternative to mainstream, neoclassical economics has, of course, continued to analyse the world as it is, and the large literature on alternative economic analysis and policy discussion can only be touched on by the various authors below.[10] Baker et al. (1998) set out a comprehensive approach to progressive economic policy in the era of globalisation.[11] And many of the chapters in this volume themselves build upon large literatures. Howells (Chapter 5) discusses the importance of innovation systems, and the policy implications are set out elsewhere (for example, Howells and Michie, 1997; Archibugi, et al., 1999). Ietto-Gillies (Chapter 8) has set out in detail the role of transnational corporations in the global economy (for example, Ietto-Gillies, 2001, 2002). And in particular, Chapters 24–26 on policy implications and responses all draw on work that was developed more fully by the authors' own books: Chang (2002), Hines (2002) and DeMartino (2000).

A 1999 collection on *Global Instability* – with many of the same authors as in this collection – was introduced in the following terms, which applies just as much today, and to the chapters contained in the current volume:

> The problems witnessed in today's global economy are not just technical, economic ones. They are also political. Devising new structures of World Economic Governance requires, as a starting point, that this be recognised. This means that to be successful, any alternative needs to not only spell out appropriate policy and institutional developments, it also needs to win sufficient political support to force through the necessary change of course.
>
> In this context, ideological issues also play a role. It is thus necessary to expose the current complacent orthodoxy in mainstream economics, and challenge the fatalistic belief that the new globalised economy rules out any change of course. As many of the chapters that follow demonstrate, the fact that the economy is becoming increasingly internationalised does not dictate the form that this process is taking. The free market, *laissez-faire* agenda is one being pursued by those who benefit from such a deregulated, winner-take-all environment. It is not the only choice. And for the majority of the world's population, it is an inappropriate one. (Michie, 1999, p. 6)

In the face of the 2008 credit crunch, UK Prime Minister Gordon Brown acknowledged 'the collapse of a failed laissez-faire dogma'. The University of Oxford held an online debate on whether the crisis sounded the death knell of laissez-faire capitalism – with 54 per cent voting in favour of the motion (University of Oxford, 2008). In that debate I argued that coordinated international action, including nationalisation, fiscal deficits and regulation had indeed replaced the previous laissez-faire approach, but asked whether laissez-faire capitalism would seek to make a comeback once the mess it created had been cleared up. The answer, I argued, is that if we let it, yes it will; that there are vast private fortunes to be had; that we must ensure that the lessons learned from the global banking crisis are not lost; that we need a sustainable future in economic as well as environmental terms; and that laissez-faire capitalism would endanger both – unleashing another era of unsustainable speculative activity, while ignoring the environmental consequences:

> Regulation can ensure environmental effects are factored into decision-making. This need not be a cost – on the contrary, it can act as a spur for industry to invest in green growth, knowing that the alternatives will be increasingly outlawed. That way, directors can justify long-term investments in green technologies to their shareholders – because regulation will make this the only way of enjoying sustainable profits in the future. Otherwise, their fiduciary duty is to make short-term financial returns by speculating on the markets along with everyone else. It is a question of what sort of system we design and maintain – one of laissez-faire capitalism, where short-term financial returns are maximised, or one where activities are regulated to take account of the environmental and economic costs that society would otherwise have to bear. (Michie, 2008)

Notes

1. The topic of globalisation – and the accompanying literature – is also critically analysed and discussed in the University of Oxford's online course on Globalisation, from which the opening paragraphs above are taken: see www.conted.ox.ac.uk, and also in the University of Oxford's iTunes U podcast series by Michie and Yueh, http://itunes.ox.ac.uk/

2. Because Andrew Glyn passed away before this updated edition was prepared, this chapter is reprinted from the previous edition.
3. Written in 1847 (published 1848) by Marx and Engels, *The Communist Manifesto*.
4. There is, of course, a huge literature on the development of the EU and single currency; see, for example, Healey (1995), Amin and Tomaney (1995) and Moss and Michie (1998).
5. Chuck Craypo passed away before this updated edition was prepared, so this chapter is reprinted from the previous edition.
6. On which, see, for example, Arestis and Sawyer (1999).
7. On the World Bank, see also Wade (2002).
8. On which, see Stiglitz (2002).
9. Ha-Joon Chang was unable to update his chapter for this edition; however, his chapter summarised his own book, which continues to represent a substantive contribution to the literature (Chang, 2002), so this chapter is reprinted from the previous edition.
10. For a critique of the mainstream neoclassical approach, see Kitson and Michie (2000), Chapter 1; this book also includes an analysis of globalisation (Chapter 2) and trade theory (Chapters 3 and 4).
11. The literature on globalisation is also surveyed from the various disciplinary approaches by Power (2001) for economics; Lukens-Bull (2001), human geography; Williams (2001), management and business; Lee (2001), politics; Hills (2001), sociology; Hines (2001), 'critiques and alternatives'; and Archibugi (2001), innovation studies.

References

Amin, A. and J. Tomaney (eds) (1995), *Behind the Myth of European Union: Prospects for Cohesion*, London: Routledge.

Archibugi, D. (2001), 'Globalization of technology', in J. Michie (ed.), *Reader's Guide to the Social Sciences*, London: Fitzroy Dearborn/Routledge.

Archibugi, D., J. Howells and J. Michie (eds) (1999), *Innovation Policy in a Global Economy*, Cambridge: Cambridge University Press.

Arestis, P. and M. Sawyer (1999), 'What role for the Tobin tax in world economic governance?', in J. Michie and J. Grieve Smith (eds), *Global Instability: The Political Economy of World Economic Governance*, London: Routledge.

Baker, D., G. Epstein and R. Pollin (eds) (1998), *Globalization and Progressive Economic Policy*, Cambridge: Cambridge University Press.

Chang, H.-J. (2002), *Kicking Away the Ladder – Development Strategy in Historical Perspective*, London: Anthem Press.

Costello, N., J. Michie and S. Milne (1989), *Beyond the Casino Economy*, London: Verso.

DeMartino, G.F. (2000), *Global Economy, Global Justice: Theoretical Objections and Policy Alternatives to Neoliberalism*, London: Routledge.

Healey, N.M. (ed.) (1995), *The Economics of the New Europe*, London: Routledge.

Hills, M. (2001), 'Globalization, sociology', in J. Michie (ed.), *Reader's Guide to the Social Sciences*, London: Fitzroy Dearborn/Routledge.

Hines, C. (2001), 'Globalization, critiques and alternatives', in J. Michie (ed.), *Reader's Guide to the Social Sciences*, London: Fitzroy Dearborn/Routledge.

Hines, C. (2002), *Localization: A Global Manifesto*, London: Earthscan.

Hirst, P. and G. Thompson (1996), *Globalization in Question*, Cambridge: Polity Press.

Howells, J. and J. Michie (eds) (1997), *Technology, Innovation and Competitiveness*, Cheltenham, UK and Lyme, USA: Edward Elgar.

Ietto-Gillies, G. (2001), *Transnational Corporations. Fragmentation amidst Integration*, London: Routledge.

Ietto-Gillies, G. (2002), 'How internationalised are EU transnationals?', *The Journal of Interdisciplinary Economics*, **13**(1–3), 13–49.

Kitson, M. and J. Michie (2000), *The Political Economy of Competitiveness: Essays on Employment, Public Policy and Corporate Performance*, London: Routledge.

Lee, S. (2001), 'Globalization, politics', in J. Michie (ed.), *Reader's Guide to the Social Sciences*, London: Fitzroy Dearborn/Routledge.

Lee, S. (2009), *Boom to Bust: The Politics and Legacy of Gordon Brown*, Oxford: Oneworld.
Lukens-Bull, R. (2001), 'Globalization, human geography', in J. Michie (ed.), *Reader's Guide to the Social Sciences*, London: Fitzroy Dearborn/Routledge.
Michie, J. (1995), 'Introduction', in J. Michie and J. Grieve Smith (eds), *Managing the Global Economy*, Oxford: Oxford University Press.
Michie, J. (1996), 'Creative destruction or regressive stagnation?', *International Review of Applied Economics*, **10**(1), 121–6.
Michie, J. (1999), 'Introduction', in J. Michie and J. Grieve Smith (eds), *Global Instability: The Political Economy of World Economic Governance*, London: Routledge.
Michie, J. (2008), 'Closing Statement', in University of Oxford, 2008.
Moss, B.H. and J. Michie (eds) (1998), *The Single European Currency in National Perspective: A Community in Crisis?*, London: MacMillan.
NIESR (2010), 'Biggest contraction since 1921', *NIESR Monthly Estimates of GDP*, 13 January.
Power, D. (2001), 'Globalization, economic', in J. Michie (ed.), *Reader's Guide to the Social Sciences*, London: Fitzroy Dearborn/Routledge.
Rubery, J., B. Burchell, S. Deakin and J. Michie (2002), 'Productive systems: introduction and overview', in B. Burchell, S. Deakin, J. Michie and J. Rubery (eds), *Systems of Production: Markets, Organisations and Performance*, London: Routledge.
Stiglitz, J. (2002), *Globalization and its Discontents*, London: Penguin.
United Nations (2009), *Report of the Commission of Experts of the President of the United Nations General Assembly on Reforms of the International Monetary and Financial System*, New York: United Nations.
University of Oxford (2008), 'The current financial crisis sounds the death knell for laissez-faire capitalism', online debate, www.ox.ac.uk/oxford_debates/past_debates/michaelmas_2008_laissezfaire_capitalism/index.html; accessed 4 October 2010.
Young, Oran, R. (1999), *Governance in World Affairs*, Ithaca and London: Cornell University Press.
Wade, R.H. (2002), 'US hegemony and the World Bank: the fight over people and ideas', *Review of International Political Economy*, **9**(2), 201–29.
Williams, A. (2001), 'Globalization, management and business', in J. Michie (ed.), *Reader's Guide to the Social Sciences*, London: Fitzroy Dearborn/Routledge.

PART I

GLOBALISATION IN QUESTION?

1 The future of globalisation*

Paul Hirst and Grahame Thompson

Before we consider the future of 'globalisation' we must define its nature and outline its past. This is a complex and contested concept. If we take growing international interconnectedness – increasing flows of trade, investment and communications between nations – to be what most people mean by the term, then 'globalisation' has been happening for the last 50 years. Moreover, new technologies – long distance jets, satellites, IT, fibre optic cables – have made international travel, media and financial exchanges far easier, enabling dramatic increases in traffic volumes. The key questions are threefold. First, are these economic and social processes linking nations since 1945 unprecedented? Second, are these processes developing at the expense of state and national governance, that is, are national economies dissolving into a global marketplace and relations between states becoming secondary to more complex interactions between a variety of economic, social and political agencies? Third, is international economic interconnectedness set to increase or decrease?

The history of globalisation

Naturally these questions are almost impossible to answer in the scale of a short chapter. We are sceptical about many of the claims in the literature, in particular that national economies are dissolving. We refer readers to what we judge to be the best presentations of both sides of the debate (Held et al., 1999; Hirst and Thompson, 1999).

Here we shall focus on two primary issues: the future of international governance and the likely limits to economic globalisation. The first thing to note is that although we have had a long period of growing international interconnectedness there is no reason to assume that such processes will continue indefinitely or that they have an inherent dynamic that prevails over all countervailing forces. Globalisation has a history. The 50 years between 1950–2000 are not remarkable when compared with the period 1850–1914 – in that period flows of merchandise trade, capital investment and labour migration were all comparable to or greater than those of today (Hirst and Thompson, 1999, ch. 2). Technological change in the form of international telegraph cables unified markets and led to price and interest rate convergence of a kind that has never been equalled since. Financial integration was far greater, and levels of capital export from the major lender countries unprecedented. Economic convergence in prices and wages across the Atlantic was largely achieved by vast flows of surplus labour from Europe to the New World (O'Rourke and Williamson, 1999). This process is not operating on the same scale today. Migration flows are relatively smaller and the pressure in all developed countries is to further restrict migration. If the key engine of international convergence in the first great phase of globalisation no longer operates, that is because it was one of the first targets of an anti-globalisation public policy backlash. Most major recipient countries followed the lead of the USA in the early twentieth century in restricting migration. Globalisation processes were under challenge well before 1914. Many countries introduced protective tariffs, seeking to protect farmers against the competition of American wheat or to shelter emerging manufacturing sectors (James, 2001).

Thus 1914 shattered a world order that was slowly unravelling under the pressure of competing national policies. In the inter-war period attempts to re-create the institutions of the *belle époque*, including the Gold Standard, failed. The result was a period of intense antagonistic competition to monopolise markets and raw materials. The experience of the 1930s confirmed that if free trade has its problems then generalised competitive protectionism is a disaster. This should be borne in mind when 'anti-globalisers' criticise the WTO and favour the 'localisation' of trade. The world order created by the USA after 1945 attempted to address the sources of the earlier crisis and to institutionalise international economic liberalism. One should remember that this was only possible because of the Allied military victory and the unassailable economic dominance of the USA. Globalisation was restored by military force and national policy; it was not a 'natural' state of affairs. It also rested on a huge asymmetry; in that the new dominant power, the USA, was willing to accept the costs of creating the new regime and to tolerate national protectionist strategies on the part of its clients like Japan and South Korea. This was similar to British policy during the Pax Britannica.

The situation is now different. The USA is militarily dominant in a way no power has been in modern history. North America is the world's largest economy, but the USA is no longer willing to act as it did in the immediate post-1945 period. The USA is a major capital importer, it treats the value of the dollar as a matter of national economic management, (though it can also afford to operate a policy of 'benign neglect' in respect to the international value of the dollar because its exports still only comprise about 15 per cent of GDP), its foreign aid is derisory, and it promotes trade liberalisation in areas where it has a huge competitive advantage, but is unwilling either to open its own markets in key sectors or to allow national strategies of protection for emerging competing industries in developing countries. All the major industrial powers, with the partial exception of the UK, created their manufacturing sectors under a protectionist regime; Germany, Japan and the USA included. Current WTO rules prohibit such strategies and force most developing countries into manufacturing for export markets in relatively low value niches. The implication is that current processes of 'globalisation' are unlikely radically to diminish the gap between the developed and the developing worlds.

If 'globalisation' is conceived as a process that promotes cross-border exchanges and transterritorial agencies at the *expense* of nation states then it would be deeply problematic. If all states, including the most powerful, were to cease to be the primary political actors across borders, being displaced by companies, NGOs, regional governments, networks, international agencies, and so on, then one could anticipate a severe anti-globalisation 'backlash' as nationally-rooted publics experience a loss of the benefits of domestic governance and increased exposure to international pressures. If the majority of states cease to be effective actors, but the G7 still dominate in terms of economic governance and the USA alone dominates militarily, then Western and American dominance will be resented, resisted and challenged both nationally and transnationally in an increasingly unequal and conflictual world. This shows that there are inherent limits to globalisation conceived as a process that leads to the decline of national economies and state power. A truly global market system, in which international competitive pressures and market forces subsume national economies, and in which transnational agencies and networks reduce states to the equivalent of local authorities, would be vulnerable to multiple political and social threats that it had no means to counter: international terrorism, commercial piracy, crime, protest movements and national backlash strategies of local withdrawal from the global system. The complete victory of extreme economic liberalism in both policy and fact would most likely spell the end of the system, not as in 1914 in inter-state war, but in a series of terrorist outrages, local economic crises – like that in Argentina – major crises in the financial markets, and the re-politicisation of national governance, leading to the restoration of distinctive local policy regimes.

The open international economy is not a 'natural' state of affairs, to which the world reverts by economic logic when the distorting influences of politics on markets are removed. Rather it depends on state power; economic liberalism has to be instituted and defended. If it is to survive then its negative effects have to be ameliorated by public policy. Economists have had to learn this the hard way, but few really understood the extreme fragility of markets and the dependence of economics on state power before September 11. Globalisation can go backwards: it can be impeded – as the backlash policies of the late nineteenth century showed; and it can be reversed – as the inter-war years demonstrated. The current 'anti-globalisation movement' is a noisy sign of widespread dissatisfaction, but the real backlash would come from conventional politicians and would start to show in new state policies. Such policies would include both national measures and the advocacy of changed policies in international forums like the WTO by states and groups of states. Such policies may be difficult to distinguish in the first instance from the re-regulation that is necessary to counter the negative consequences of excessive economic liberalism. A major backlash against international openness by states, and by legitimate and non-legitimate non-state and transnational actors, can only be prevented by a judicious mixture of appropriate force and governance measures that stabilise markets and protect citizens against unacceptable insecurity and risk. Both dimensions of policy are necessary, and both will be expensive – military action and social solidarity need to go together; the latter is essential to underpin and legitimate the former. The future of the open international trading system in the immediate future (the next 25 years) thus rests on appropriate political policies and in the actions of the major nation states, and the USA in particular.

The future of global governance

However, it would be foolish to look at immediate events alone, and not also long-term trends (Hirst, 2001). The threats to global stability are multiplying and are likely to become more severe as the twenty-first century progresses. The most serious are only indirectly connected to the current open international economy but create a context in which at worst it could fail and break down. Many of these threats are unlikely to become critical in the next 30 years, and so are beyond the scope of normal political calculation, yet they require action now if there is to be any prospect of forestalling or even mitigating them.

The most serious is climate change, which is likely to become progressively worse as the century unfolds and to have destabilizing effects by mid-century and catastrophic consequences by 2080.[1] The consequences – turbulent weather, inundations due to rising sea levels, desertification and water shortages, loss of farm land, and the spread of disease – are likely to develop in chaotic and unpredictable ways that will not be amenable to adaptation by the kind of incremental action policy makers are used to. This will affect both developed and developing countries, but the latter are likely to suffer more, as they have fewer resources to respond to the consequences, and they have large populations. A worsening environment is likely to be associated with the displacement of large numbers of climatic refugees, adding to the existing and growing migratory pressures from poorer countries. It is also possible that current UN estimates that the world's population will peak in 2040 and then decline may prove to be wrong, not least because they are based upon optimistic assumptions about economic development. Insecurity and persistent poverty will lead to people having more children rather than fewer – thus population pressures may well be another source of turbulence, making the effects of climate change on the displacement of peoples worse.

The odds are that the current extreme inequality of global income distribution will continue (Wade and Wolf, 2002). That for the majority of the world's poor this will be the result of a failure of domestic economic development rather than direct exploitation by the rich will not make their lot easier to bear. It is prudent to assume that the normal economic processes will not transform the bulk of the world from developing to developed status without the need for other forms of intervention. Most of the population of Africa, and the majority in East and South Asia and Latin America will remain poor – part of the 80 per cent who share just 14 per cent of world GDP. It is highly unlikely that the major developing nations – Brazil, China, India, Indonesia or Nigeria – will effect the same transition to advanced industrialism as Japan or South Korea (Hirst and Thompson, 1999, ch. 5). Uneven industrialisation heavily oriented toward export markets will leave huge populations in excluded rural areas and urban slums.

Such problems, and more immediate ones like transnational crime syndicates or AIDS, are frequently cited by advocates of greater global governance as demonstrating the inherent limitations of the nation state. Yet they are also beyond the scope of action by any foreseeable global or transnational institutions. To cope with climate change or global inequality in a serious way, supranational institutions would require coercive powers over states and the ability to command resource redistribution, chiefly at the expense of the top 20 per cent of the world's population represented by the countries of the OECD. Yet these countries, singly in the case of the USA, collectively in the case of the rest, have the power to resist such coercion and to refuse redistribution. Far from legitimating a move toward cosmopolitan governance and a new international order these emerging global threats all but paralyse political will. If anything they focus political and business elites on the short-term, because to confront the long-term consequences of doing little now is almost unthinkable. For example, the Kyoto accords on climate change, if implemented, would have the effect merely of modestly offsetting the impact and onset of global warming. Hence the resistance in the USA of having to bear the short-term costs of an emissions reduction policy.

Power in governing the international economy is likely to remain in the hands of the wealthy nations and the supranational bodies that they control and fund, like the IMF or the World Bank. It is also likely that the exercise of that power will be challenged by major non-OECD states like China, India and Russia, and by protest movements and NGO coalitions across the globe. It is obvious that the actions of the major powers and the supranational agencies that they control will be less legitimate and that wider forums, like the WTO, will become more conflictual as the less developed nations vigorously defend their interests.

The agenda for global governance is thus constrained by the inherent limits of truly authoritative global institutions, by the perceptions and interests of state elites in the G7, and by the mass attitudes of the populations of the OECD countries. A real world government would quickly become a tyranny – conservative in the defence of entrenched privilege in the hands of the rich, and confiscatory in the hands of the poor, and thus resisted and thwarted by the losers of either policy. The nation states, however powerful, cannot act alone, whilst nothing can be accomplished without their active support, legitimation and funding. That means that the agenda for strengthening international governance and mitigating those threats to stability that can be addressed in the short-term involves three dimensions. First, reinforcing those international institutions that can function effectively, and redirecting their policies. Institutions like the IMF are not inherently defective and it, for example, has a necessary role as an international lender of last resort. It is also necessary to expand the scope and power of other less headline-catching international institutions so that they are able to perform extended regulatory tasks, for example, beefing up the Bank for International Settlements' role in supervising national financial regulators so that the supervision of banks and other financial institutions is enhanced, and strengthening the ILO to negotiate new conventions on migration and international labour mobility and raising the floor of international labour standards. Second, promoting coordinated state action, whether by treaty or intergovernmental cooperation, for example, to tackle problems like international criminal and terrorist networks, to promote disease prevention and containment strategies, to pursue measures to combat global warming that can in fact be agreed (such as research and subsidies for non-fossil and renewable energy sources) and to raise the level of development aid. Third, to commit the major powers, and the USA in particular, to seek solutions where possible in a multilateral framework and for the powers to seek the widest legitimacy for their actions by strategies of consultation and coalition building.

Such measures would mean that when major global crises do occur, such as a sudden escalation of climate change or a major epidemic, then the states of the developed world can cooperate with others and that at least a minimum regulatory framework to ensure market stability and physical security is in place. Such measures amount to an extended version of 'business as usual', renewing the regulatory framework of multilateral international governance created after 1945. It would also mean a return to a policy of 'embedded liberalism', that is, market openness coupled with strong governance and social protection rather than contemporary economic liberal doctrine which is a mere use of political power to enhance the scope of market forces (Ruggie, 1998, ch. 2).

The prospect of such a policy of enlightened multilateralism on the part of the advanced countries, and the USA in particular, is poor. The main reason for such narrowly self-interested policies is that the present state of affairs is quite unlike 1945. The anti-globalisation movement and the terrorist threat are not a direct challenge to the system like that represented by the USSR and its allied communist parties. The former can still be dismissed as confused protest and indeed the movement does not have coherent alternatives to current institutions and their policies. The terrorist threat is a matter for police and military action. The international economy in 1945 was at a virtual standstill and thus could be re-built from the ground up. Moreover, the major state elites are in fact satisfied with the high level of control they do in fact have, whilst often preaching impotence in the face of the forces of globalisation to their domestic publics. Global markets are not all-powerful; the scope of action by international agencies, inter-state cooperation and governance by states remains considerable. So far major financial crises have been contained. Concerted action by governments, central banks, financial market authorities and major companies prevented a disastrous panic in the aftermath of September 11. Even in recession, the G7 economies are not faced by immediate economic and social crisis.

One could thus conclude that 'globalisation' in the sense conceived by extreme economic liberals and their radical critics has not happened. The world, far from being an integrated system dominated by ungovernable market forces, is divided into three major trading blocs, dominated by nation states: NAFTA is centred in the USA, Japan is a bloc-sized national economy, and the EU is an association of states. Each bloc follows distinctive policies, and has distinctive problems and institutions of economic management. Most major companies hail from one of the three main blocs, and most companies have the bulk of their assets and the majority of their sales within one of the blocs.

International interconnectedness has not subsumed the distinctive national economies of, for example, Germany, or Japan or the USA. Hence the central powers in the system are neither likely to initiate a backlash against it nor are they likely to act on the scale necessary to counter the emerging global crisis and the current difficulties of the mass of the world's population outside the OECD. One might conclude that the current system is well enough governed and sufficiently beneficial to those on whose behalf it is governed that it will persist until problems accumulate that cause it to fail and a crisis that is beyond governance overwhelms the system. Unlike the 1930s or the period before 1914 the backlash against the international economy is not likely to start with the core states of the G7, but at the periphery.

This may seem pessimistic but it is highly likely that a crisis stemming from climate change, mass poverty in the developing world, and intense migratory pressures will overwhelm global institutions of governance and cooperation in the distant but foreseeable future, sometime in the second half of this century. Before then difficulties and conflicts will accumulate, weakening the will to cooperate and undermining any prospect of solidarity between rich and poor, developed and developing nations. In this context governance will be asserted at the level where the public can put pressure on leaders, in nation states. International agencies will be harder to sustain and transnational politics and institutions will decline in favour of state-based ones. States will seek to protect their populations and to monopolise and control the distribution of key resources. Faced with climate change political processes, rather than markets, will allocate scarce goods like food, shelter for the displaced, water and energy. States will seek to obtain these things by force, as will political movements. Those displaced by climate change are unlikely to be passive. At least some major states will fight over access to water and oil.

This is a bleak prospect, but it emphasises the continued relevance of classic international relations as a discipline, and of realism in particular. The military power of the West is overwhelming. The USA and its allies dominate the seas and international airspace. They thus control the major trade routes and access to the world trading system. The already overwhelming military capacity of the USA is set to increase in the immediate future as the military exploit emergent technologies and utilise space as a new environment for intelligence, communications and weapons directed at earth. However, such power has its limits. The advanced economies are vulnerable to terrorism and will remain so, even if they adopt draconian measures that restrict the liberties of their own populations. Masses of migrants would be hard to contain, even with brutal and repressive policies of exclusion and frontier control. Advanced weapons may be ineffective against determined enemies with strong national cohesion and an effective military leadership with clear objectives. The USA, for all its recent victories, has not really faced such an enemy since Vietnam. Thus the bulk of the Iraqi army was ill-trained and poorly motivated, the Serbs increasingly hostile to Milosevic, and the Taliban a hollow regime based on savage repression. Moreover, at least some of the emerging technologies will be easy to copy and adapt by the less sophisticated powers. Intelligent mines and small remotely-piloted vehicles, for example, may make defensive strategies easier and counter Western offensive dominance, making it difficult for advanced armies to occupy territory without heavy casualties (Hirst, 2001).

One should thus assume a highly conflictual world: with constant police action against terrorists, migrants and protestors, low grade wars and incursions by the USA and its allies in failed states and terrorist havens, conflicts between less developed states (increasingly over access to resources), the involvement of the great powers on behalf of their clients, and increasingly conflictual relations between major states over resources and trade. In this world order international norms and legal standards will most likely come under increasing pressure in matters of human rights, conflict and war. This will be a process similar to the widespread violation of the Hague Conventions during World War I. States will repudiate human rights conventions and international legal regulation, even as international lawyers attempt to complete the edifice they have been building since 1945. The USA already will not submit to the International Criminal Court, and without it the whole project of subjecting national political actors to common international norms is gravely weakened. Faced with terrorist outrages and masses of displaced persons, many states will be unwilling to continue to subscribe to international conventions and will slip into authoritarian regimes against outsiders, supported by their frightened citizens. Rules that only apply to some, the unlucky and defeated in the case of war criminals, or the lucky who happen to find one of the few liberal havens in the case of refugees, will cease to have general effect or credibility (Krasner, 1999).

If political norms increasingly cease to be accepted or followed, by contrast rules-based economic governance will remain strong. Indeed, this is the most likely dimension of global governance and re-regulation. The WTO is a rules-based organisation and it is impossible to open markets without common standards that apply to all and that are justifiable. Equally, tightening financial regulation and banking supervision, partly to prevent financial crises and partly to control terrorism and money laundering, will extend the scope of regulatory and rules-based supervision by national and international agencies. Companies are increasingly using international arbitration and supranational standards of commercial conduct to resolve disputes that span national jurisdiction. Thus in the short term we may see both more conflict in the political sphere and greater regulation and normalisation in the economic (Weiner, 1999).

Any argument about global governance must allow for the extreme variability of global processes and the variety of global institutions. It is clear that on different dimensions and at different locations governance practices and outcomes can vary widely. We should, therefore, expect combined phenomena of integration and disintegration, increasingly effective governance on some dimensions and retreat on others, different mechanisms for different problems, both localisation and internationalisation. Unless this is recognised, the complexity of short-term outcomes may hide long-term trends toward conflict, localisation and chaos.

The future of the global economy

Even well before the events of September 2001 there were several indications that the rapid globalisation of economic activity experienced during the 1980s and the 1990s may have begun to stall. The rate of growth of the US economy was slowing, Japan's intractable economic problems were no nearer solution, and there was unease in Europe about its future economic prospects as the adoption of the euro loomed and growth faltered. But these essentially cyclical uncertainties were being bolstered by some potentially longer-term structural changes. Thus the world may be experiencing the final years of one of those periodic explosions in internationalisation that throw so much into confusion and seem to herald the complete transformation in the way societies are organised. There is beginning to emerge a serious questioning of the ability of the global economic system to sustain its seemingly as rapid integrationist trajectory.

In this section we examine the potential cyclical and structural constraints on the future growth of economic globalisation. We ask the question 'Are there any limits to economic globalisation?'. The strong globalisation thesis would seem to imply an ever-expanding universe of economic interdependency and integration between national economies, so that the significance of national borders for economic activity eventually disappears. The issues for us here are first, why should this be the case? and, second, is it happening?

Globalisation is here defined in strictly economic terms, basically as increasing trade interdependency and investment integration. The strong globalisation thesis contends that macroeconomic and industrial policy intervention by national governments can only distort and impede the rational process of resource allocation by corporate decisions and consumer choices, which are now made on a global scale. All corporate players need to do to prosper is to shake off their nationally orientated bureaucratic style of management, and the government intervention that goes along with it, and enter the new world of open global marketing and production networks. International markets provide coordinating and governance mechanisms in and of themselves: national strategies and policy intervention are likely merely to distort them. The era of effective national economies, and state policies corresponding to them, is over. The market will, and should, decide (Ohmae, 1990; 1995).

We have challenged this conception and we do not think the international economy looks anything like this (Hirst and Thompson, 1999; 2000), but it offers a powerful imagery and should not be ignored. It is thus worth confronting it in its own terms.

A key element in this challenge is to question the extent of contemporary trade globalisation. If we look at merchandise trade flows between the main economic blocs expressed as a proportion of the originating country or bloc GDP then, for the most part, quite low percentages of GDP seem to have been traded in 1998 (see Table 1.1).

Only Western Europe appears anywhere close to being an integrated trading zone, with 18 per cent of its combined GDP traded between the countries of Western Europe. Yet this is an artefact of national accounting and the EEA should be treated as a single quasi autarchic trade bloc. The only other relationship that appears significant is that between the East Asian traders and North America, where the former exported just under 11 per cent of their GDP to North America, mostly to the USA. However, look at the relationship between North America and Japan. Only 0.7 per cent of North American GDP was ex-

Table 1.1 Merchandise trade flows as a percentage of originating Triad bloc/country GDP (1998)

To	North America	Western Europe[a]	Japan (J)	East Asian Traders[b] (EAT)	J + EAT
From					
North America	3.8	2.0	0.7	1.1	1.8
European Economic Area[a] (EEA)	2.3	18.0	0.4	1.0	1.4
Japan (J)	3.3	2.0	–	3.0	3.0
East Asian Traders[b] (EAT)	10.7	6.9	4.1	na	na
J + EAT	14.0	8.9	4.1	na	na

Notes:
a. European Economic Area (EEA) = EU + Switzerland, Turkey, Norway, Malta, Liechtenstein and the states of the former Yugoslavia.
b. East Asian Traders (EAT): China, Hong Kong, Taiwan, Korea, Malaysia, Thailand and Singapore.
na = not available.

Sources: *WTO Annual Report 2000, Volume II, International Trade Statistics*, derived from various tables; *World Economic Indicators 2000*, World Bank, Table 4.2; *Taiwan Statistical Data Book 2000*.

ported to Japan, while Japan exported 3.3 per cent of its GDP to North America. These are still quite small numbers.

Of course there are many objections that could be mounted to this way of measuring the extent of trade 'globalisation', and these are dealt with elsewhere (Hirst and Thompson, 2000; Thompson, 2001). Comparing merchandise trade and total GDP is not comparing like with like as total GDP is made up of many sectors, some of which have been expanding at a faster rate than the merchandise sector. But even when a proper comparison is made, only Western Europe displays a highly integrated trade environment (nearly 81 per cent of merchandise trade relative to merchandise GDP is inter-Western European trade). The other main trading blocs still remain surprisingly un-integrated on this traditional and long established measure of globalisation.

For economists these figures raise the question of the 'missing trade'. Why isn't there more trade in the international system? Broadly, the answer is that the lack of trade is because of the continued significance of national territories and national borders, a point we come back to in a moment.

In economics, national borders are viewed as an impediment and an obstacle to trade. They are an impediment to the development of market forces, so the advent of modern globalisation and a 'borderless world' would be a triumph from the point of view of those supporting the strong globalisation position mentioned earlier. The problem is to overcome these 'barriers' to trade.

How is international trade analysed in economics? When economic modelling techniques are applied to the specifics of international trade, these produce disappointing results in terms of explaining the amount, composition and direction of international trade flows. As just mentioned, these models would predict much higher levels of international trade. This has led to a great deal of soul searching amongst economists, and a resort to analysing 'what is in the data' rather than constructing further theoretical models. Thus despite the seeming sophistication of much international trade theory, when it comes to the empirical side of things the approach is still fairly simple. At heart it relies on operationalising a 'gravity' model.

Empirically, trade is traditionally modelled as positively related to some measure of the 'size' of the communities between which it takes place and negatively related to the distance between them. This is known as a 'gravity model'. But what has interested economists recently is a series of institutional, cultural or political and geographical variables that are also very important in determining trade. These can be expressed as a series of 'control' variables designed to capture other relationships between countries that might stimulate trade between them. These can include such aspects as whether countries share a common border, whether they share a common language, whether they have had colonial connections, whether they belong to a common trade bloc (for example, the EU, ASEAN, NAFTA), what the position is in respect to common jurisdictional standards and the legal enforceability of contracts between them, and finally whether they share a common currency.

The distance variable is the most consistent and significant of the variables explaining international trade (Leamer and Storper, 2001). Indeed, one of the most obvious constraints on an infinitely expanding international division of labour and a 'complete' globalisation is that the effects of distance cannot be entirely eliminated. Although there have been several 'communication revolutions' which have significantly reduced the costs of transporting over distance, eventually these will come up against the basic physical impossibility of total transport cost elimination, so here is one (fairly obvious) 'limit to globalisation' (see Obstfeld and Rogoff, 2001). Table 1.2 expresses the effects of distance on economic interactions for a range of variables: trade, FDI, equity flows and technology flows. Economic interactions fall away dramatically with distance. For instance, if you add 7000 km distance between any nodal points, 97 per cent of trade disappears.

But an interesting feature of recent trade empirics is the central importance that has emerged for the 'cultural' or 'political' determinants of trade specified by the control variables just mentioned. For instance, once the contributions

Table 1.2 The effect of distance on economic interactions. Percentage reductions in the value of magnitudes relative to 1000 km

	Trade	FDI	Equity Flows	Technology Flows (R&D Stock)
1000 km	0	0	0	0
2000 km	58	25	45	35
4000 km	82	44	69	72
8000 km	97	58	83	95

Source: Calculated from Venables (2001).

of, say, migration (which can be approximated by variables such as sharing a border, a common language or colonial experience), and different legal cultures have been accounted for in regression analyses, the specific contribution of GDP as such as a determinant of trade levels is severely limited, and indeed becomes less than 1 in many cases. We stress the significance of this in a moment.

The specific effect of national borders on trade and the globalisation debate can be taken up in the context of these empirical gravity model equations. There has recently been something of a test case analysis of this involving the border between the USA and Canada (McCallum, 1995; Engel and Rogers, 1996; Helliwell, 1998; 2000). If globalisation has emerged, then surely this border would have been one of the first to have lost its pertinence as far as trade, investment and migration is concerned. But it has not. Careful analyses have demonstrated the continued central importance of this border as an 'obstacle' to trade (and other flows) between the USA and Canada. This is the case as tariffs and quotas have been eliminated, NAFTA established, and other barriers removed. What these analyses do is begin to confront the mysteries of the 'missing trade' at the international level. Far from there being an 'excess' of international trade as many critics of globalisation believe from the economists' perspective, there is not 'enough' of it (and this goes for capital flows as well which, whilst not discussed here, are addressed in Hirst and Thompson, 2000 and Thompson, 2001).

What most analyses of the growth of international trade do is to look only at international trade without comparing it with what is going on in the home territory at the same time. International trade is expanding but so too is domestic trade, and it looks as though domestic trade is expanding at a similar rate to, or at a more rapid rate than its international equivalent (after accounting for the other control variables). We might need to be a little more cautious here, however, since these analyses were conducted for the very early years of NAFTA. Recent evidence suggests that cross-border US–Canada trade has grown considerably. Also, the full implementation of NAFTA does not take effect until 2008.

But overall, this particular border continues to be a remarkable 'barrier' to trade in and of itself, even after taking account of all the usual variables that might determine trade. What is more, there is evidence that the state boundaries *within* the US act as a 'barrier to trade' (Wolf, 1997), so the idea that it is tariffs and quotas or other at-border international impediments to trade which represent the main obstacles to international integration is further put into question. Moreover, differences in cultural and legal systems between these two countries – which might be thought to inhibit trade, as suggested earlier – also appear small in this particular case. What is more, these results are confirmed in the case of the other OECD countries though admittedly on the basis of less appropriate and reliable data (Wei, 1996; Helliwell, 1998).

In addition, there is good evidence that migration is a significant stimulus to trade (Casella and Rauch, 1997; Rauch, 1999). It is very significant, for instance, in the case of imports into the USA. Migration sets up networks of relationships across borders, making it easier to establish a low transaction cost mechanism for the conduct of international trade (we come back to this in a moment). As long as countries maintain their commitment to regulate their populations in some sense (which is almost a defining feature of the notion of geographical 'territoriality'), then this situation will continue. In particular, in so far as countries continue to clamp down on international migration this could inhibit the further growth of international trade. So here is another potential 'limit to globalisation' and one that shows a major difference between integration processes today and those of the nineteenth century.

It seems that this particular point is crucial in the context of the jurisdictional consequences of borders; the fact that any movement across a national frontier involves the movement from one legal, regulatory and cultural jurisdiction to another. These jurisdictions proscribe, adjudicate and enforce a wide range of norms, rules, habits, networks and similar features, which involve much more than just the 'obstacles' to trade found at the point of the frontier. It is 'behind border' characteristics that are crucial. An interesting suggestion here is that it may be the state of the legal and administrative certainty associated with the enforcement of contracts (with respect to both trade and capital flows) that is the key to the OECD bias in international economic transactions. When a measure to represent this was introduced into the gravity model formulation this was found to account for such a significant proportion of the level of international trade that the impact of income *per se* was less than 1 (Anderson and Marcouiller, 1999). Thus the implication here is that GDP growth has a less than proportionate impact on international trade growth; the bulk of the growth in international trade over the post-World War II period being accounted for by the 'one-off' impact of legal enforceability. This thereby points to a potential optimal level of international trade as this one-off boost to trade eventually exhausts itself.

Another important area of discussion involving gravity model type approaches to international trade revolves around the effects of common currencies on trade. An additional variable that can be included in the gravity model equations is one for countries sharing a common currency. There are 193 independent countries recognised by the UN but only about 120 different currencies operate. Many countries share a currency; and some have done so for a very long time. Under current circumstances, however, the issues are European Monetary Union and 'dollarisation'. In January 2002 12 EU member states adopted the euro. In addition there are a number of countries that have experimented with abandoning their own currency in favour of the US dollar, mainly in Latin America, or who have established a 'hard currency board' approach to monetary management. What are the effects of these policies on trade?

There seem to be very large trade gains to be made by adopting common currencies, as those countries that have done so trade with each other to a much greater extent than those with their own currency (other things remaining equal) (Rose, 2000; Rose and Wincoop, 2001). This has led to a number of suggestions for further dollarisation and even the adoption of a single world currency (Alesina and Barro, 2001; Dornbusch, 2001; Rogoff, 2001). The beneficial effects have to do with the macroeconomic discipline and stability that 'dollarisation' is supposed to instill in (mainly) small and wayward countries. However, these gains are disputed (Persson, 2001; Rose, 2001). On close scrutiny there is little evidence that the suggested welfare and growth benefits have actually materialised (though inflation has been lower) from these policies and we should remain very sceptical about such policy initiatives (Edwards, 2000; 2001). The recent case of Argentina should reinforce this vary cautious attitude towards currency boards and talk of full dollarisation. As the US dollar appreciated in value, the Argentine peso also appreciated in value because it was linked to it via a currency board. This made Argentine exports very internationally uncompetitive independently of what was actually going on in Argentina itself, which was one of the reasons undermining the stability of the Argentinian economy.

But independently of these disputes, as long as countries continue to maintain their own currencies – which for the foreseeable future looks highly likely for most countries – again there will be an added limit to the extension of 'trade globalisation' (Rodrik et al., 2004).

Let us now consider another way trade is analysed in respect to borders and the long-term impediments to ever greater globalisation, which can be illustrated by the schema of different types of trade shown in Box 1.1.

BOX 1.1 TYPES OF TRADE

1. **THOSE GOODS EXCHANGED ON 'ORGANISED MARKETS'** (e.g. minerals, raw materials, primary agricultural products)
2. **THOSE GOODS EXCHANGED ACCORDING TO 'REFERENCE PRICES'** (e.g. processed raw materials, chemicals, basic standardized components)
3. **THOSE DIFFERENTIATED GOODS AND SERVICES EXCHANGED ON THE BASIS OF 'NETWORKS'** (e.g. complex manufactured goods and services)

Note: This schema is based upon Rauch (1999).

International trade can be divided into three categories. The first is that traded on organised exchanges, like primary products such as minerals and agricultural products, where price is established according to classic market mechanisms. Here one might think of markets like the Chicago grain markets, the London metal exchanges, and the Rotterdam spot market for oil.

The second category is intermediate goods that are traded according to 'reference prices' quoted in specialist publications and the like, such as chemicals and processed raw materials. For the prices of these goods you would consult a reference manual or trade price book. These are readily available in an openly published form.

The third type of trade is differentiated manufactured goods and services where there is no organised market or quoted reference prices. Here we do not find a uniform standard price but rather more 'one-off' pricing, differentiated according to complex networks of supply.

Unlocking the complex determinants of trade with respect to each of these categories is not easy (Rauch, 1999). Although the first, and to a lesser extent the second, of these categories display a high international trade to production ratio so that a high proportion of their output is exported, these are declining in importance as components of total international trade. These categories of trade are also less sensitive to the 'cultural variables' mentioned earlier in the context of the gravity model, so they are more closely correlated with the growth of wealth and income. But what has expanded rapidly is the third category, particularly complex manufactured goods. And this has a relatively low production to trade ratio, when all the other variables that determine trade have been accounted for. The key here is these other cultural, political or geographical influences, which act at the expense of income growth as such. There is a great deal of production but relatively lower levels of it are exported abroad as a pure consequence of income growth, rather than as a consequence of other variables like distance, migration and legal similarities, and so on.

Thus we have a situation where those categories of trade with high income elasticity related production propensity to export are declining in significance, while that category with a lower income elasticity related production propensity for export is increasing in importance. Perhaps this is at least one of the reasons for the relative lack of international trade, as opposed to domestic trade within a country.

The reasons for these different propensities are interesting and important. Where there is an organised market for exchange, as in the case of the first category, the organisation of the exchange is relatively easy and cheap. Transaction costs are low. However, with sophisticated manufactured goods there are no organised markets to facilitate exchanges. Rather they are traded in the context of often one-off, lengthy and complex networks of supply and distribution. Manufacturers have to set up webs of distribution systems, which are often singular and unique for each particular category of good. They require the seeking out of trading partners and the securing of a network of participants, something, it might be added, that migration makes easier. Above all these systems are costly to set up and maintain – transaction costs are high. This may account for the lack of trading in these goods across frontiers relative to their trading at home, and put a limit on the extent of their expansion. It is just too costly, for instance, for US manufacturers to secure distribution systems for their goods in Japan, so there are low levels of US exports to Japan, as shown in Table 1.1 above.

An obvious question here is whether there is any empirical evidence to support these remarks.

Whilst there was a rapid growth in world trade for all the categories of trade mentioned in Box 1.1 over the 1970s and 1980s, there was a downturn in the growth of agricultural exports in the second half of the 1990s. But after a slowdown in manufacturing exports in the same period, these recovered in 1999–2000, mainly as a result of a rapid growth of exports from the emerging economies.

In case this seems deliberately to concentrate upon merchandise trade and leave out trade in services, which are thought to be growing at a faster rate, this latter claim is not in fact true. Trade in cultural goods, for instance, was also falling off in the late 1990s. Trade in services has remained at about 20 per cent of total world trade ever since 1975, so by concentrating only on merchandise trade we have covered the bulk of total world trade.

In this section we have argued three things. First, that far from market exchange sweeping unhindered across the globe there are likely to continue to be real limits to the further expansion of global trade, limits largely established by the continuing salience of national territories and borders.

Second, we have argued that the real constraints on any further development of global trade are more likely to be the institutional, cultural and political variables, or the geographical ones analysed above, rather than straightforward economic ones.

Third, there is some limited indication that overall world trade growth has slowed in recent years. Of course this may be mainly for cyclical reasons, but the analysis has also demonstrated that there are a potential set of more structural constraints that even in the medium term could undermine an ever expanding international division of labour and trade integration.

If nothing else, these remarks indicate that there are good and interesting reasons still to take the issues of borders seriously in economics, despite the fashionable insistence that they are no longer significant in an age of globalisation.

Conclusion

In this chapter we have tried to look forward to the future of global governance and the future of the global economy. We have tried to demonstrate three things. That the current state of international interconnectedness is not unprecedented and that previous episodes of integration have generated a backlash and have ended in the regression of international trade and investment. That national states are not being overwhelmed and the future of extended multilateral governance does not look promising. In a turbulent physical and international environment the nation state may become more salient as a means of protection against global forces beyond supranational governance. That there may be inherent limits to the growth of international trade, that borders do matter, and that we may be approaching those limits. These messages are comforting neither to the advocates of the 'Washington Consensus' nor to their 'anti-globalisation' critics.

Notes

* Reprinted by permission of Sage Publications Ltd (© *Cooperation & Conflict*, NISA – Nordic International Studies Association, 2002).

1. The evidence and probable consequences considered in the 2001 report of the UN Intergovernmental Panel on Climate Change and the 2002 report of the US National Academy of Sciences are compelling and disturbing.

References

Alesina, A. and R.J. Barro (2001), 'Dollarization', *American Economic Review, Papers and Proceedings*, **91**, May, 381–5.

Anderson, J.E. and D. Marcouiller (1999), 'Trade, insecurity, and home bias: An empirical investigation', *NEBR Working Paper No. 7000*, Cambridge, MA.

Casella, A. and J.E. Rauch (1997), 'Anonymous market and group ties in international trade', *NBER Working Paper No. 6186*, Cambridge, MA.

Dornbusch, R. (2001), 'Fewer monies, better monies', *American Economic Review, Papers and Proceedings*, **91**, May, 238–42.

Edwards, S. (2000), 'Exchange rate regimes, capital flows and crisis prevention', unpublished mimeo, University of California, LA, August.
Edwards, S. (2001), 'Dollarization and economic performance: an empirical investigation', *NEBR Working Paper No. 8274*, May.
Engel, C. and J.H. Rogers (1996), 'How wide is the border?', *The American Economic Review*, **86**(5), 1112–25.
Held, D. and P. Hirst (2002), *Globalization: the Argument of our Time*, opendemocracy.net.
Held, D., A. McGrew, D. Goldblatt and J. Perraton (1999), *Global Transformations*, Cambridge: Polity Press.
Helliwell, J.F. (1998), *How Much do National Borders Matter?*, Washington, DC: Brookings Institution.
Helliwell, J.F. (2000), *Globalization: Myths, Facts and Consequences*, Toronto: C.D. Howe Institute.
Hirst, P. (2001), *War and Power in the 21st Century*, Cambridge: Polity Press.
Hirst, P.Q. and G.F. Thompson (1999), *Globalization in Question: The International Economy and the Possibilities of Governance* (2nd edn; 1st edn 1996), Cambridge: Polity Press.
Hirst, P.Q. and G.F. Thompson (2000), 'Globalization in one country: the peculiarities of the British', *Economy and Society*, **29**(3), August, 335–56.
James, H. (2001), *The End of Globalization: Lessons from the Great Depression*, Cambridge MA: Harvard University Press.
Krasner, S.D. (1999), *Sovereignty, Organised Hypocrisy*, Princeton, NJ: Princeton University Press.
Leamer, E. and M. Storper (2001), 'The economic geography of the internet age', *Journal of International Business Studies*, **32**(4), 641–65.
McCallum, J. (1995), 'National borders matter: Canada–US regional trade patterns', *The American Economic Review*, **85**(3), 615–23.
Obstfeld, M. and K. Rogoff (2001), 'The six major puzzles in international macroeconomics: is there a Common Cause?', in B. Bernanke and K. Rogoff (eds), *NEBR Macroeconomics Annual 2000*, Cambridge, MA: MIT Press.
Ohmae, K. (1990), *The Borderless World*, London and New York: Collins.
Ohmae, K. (1995), *The End of the Nation State*: *The Rise of Regional Economies*, London: Harper Collins.
O'Rourke, K.H. and J.G. Williamson (1999), *Globalization and History: The Evolution of the Nineteenth Century Atlantic Economy*, Cambridge MA: MIT Press.
Parsley, D.C. and S-J. Wei (1999), 'Border, border, wide and far, how I wonder what you are', *World Bank Policy Working Paper No. 2217*, Washington, DC: World Bank.
Persson, T. (2001), 'Currency unions and trade: how large is the treatment effect?', *Economic Policy*, No. 33, pp. 435–48.
Rauch, J.E. (1999), 'Networks versus markets in international trade', *Journal of International Economics*, **48**, 7–35.
Rodrik, D. (1999), *The New Global Economy and Developing Countries: Making Openness Work*, Policy Essay No. 24, Washington, DC: The Overseas Development Council.
Rodrik, D. (2000), 'How far will international economic integration go?', *Journal of Economic Perspectives*, **14**(1), Winter, 177–86.
Rodrik, D. with A. Subramanian and F. Trebbi (2004), 'Institutions rule: the primacy of institutions over geography and integration in economic development', *Journal of Economic Growth*, **9**(2), June, 131–65.
Rogoff, K. (2001), 'Why not a global currency?', *American Economic Review, Papers and Proceedings*, **91**, May, 243–7.
Rose, A.K. (2000), 'One money, one market: estimating the effect of common currencies on trade', *Economic Policy*, No. 30 (April), pp. 7–73.
Rose, A.K. (2001), 'Currency unions and trade: the effect is large', *Economic Policy*, No. 33, pp. 449–61.
Rose, A.K. and E. van Wincoop (2001), 'National money as a barrier to international trade: the real case of currency union', *American Economic Review, Papers and Proceedings*, **91**, 386–90.
Ruggie, J.G. (1998), *Constructing the World Polity*, London: Routledge.

Rugman, A. (2000), *The End of Globalization*, London: Random House Business Books.
Thompson, G.F. (2001), 'Are there any limits to globalization? International trade, capital flows and borders', mimeographed, Open University.
Van Wincoop, E. (2000), 'Borders and trade', *Federal Reserve Bank of New York*, April.
Venables, A.J. (2001), 'Geography and international inequalities: the impact of new technologies', background paper for *Globalization, Growth and Poverty*, World Bank, Washington, 2002.
Wade, R. and M. Wolf (2002), 'Are global poverty and inequality getting worse?', *Prospect*, March, pp. 1–8.
Wei, S-J. (1996), 'Intra-national versus international trade: how stubborn are nations in global integration?', *NBER Working Paper No. 5531*, Cambridge, MA.
Wei, S-J. (2000), 'Local corruption and global capital flows', *Brookings Papers on Economic Activity*, No. 2, pp. 303–56.
Weiner, J. (1999), *Globalization and the Harmonization of Law*, London: Pinter.
Wolf, H.C. (1997), 'Patterns of intra- and inter-state trade', *NBER Working Paper No. 5939*, Cambridge, MA.

2 Financial globalization? History, conditions and prospects

*Grahame Thompson**

Do we have a genuine global financial system? This chapter challenges the strong notion that the recent financial crisis was global in scope. It examines and troubles several key aspect of the recent events, asking whether the international financial system is a genuinely 'global' one, whether the crisis itself was 'global' in its characteristics, and what the nature of the term 'crisis' means. It argues that the international financial system is quite differentiated, being made up of domestic-national, supra-national regional and inter-national aspects. The system is characterized by contagion, however, and the chapter goes on to consider the role of this in generating slipovers into the wider economic mechanism. And given this characterization of the financial system the implications for how to organize a regulatory response are pursued. Here the argument is that the principle of 'distributed preparedness for resilience' should guide this response, not a new set of top-down global rules and norms organized once again by the institutions of global economic governance.

Financial globalization?

Strictly speaking, financial globalization would involve a set of financial markets, exchanges and institutions that trade in financial instruments and channel global savings (wherever they are generated) to investment wherever the risk-adjusted rate of return is the greatest. In this way, financial institutions and markets intermediate between agents irrespective of their location or that of the institution or market. Such liberalization of trade in financial assets would make countries irrelevant; asset prices, portfolios and firm financial policies would no longer be in any way country dependent or necessarily tethered to domestic financial markets (Stulz, 2005). But the reality is that these conditions are not met by the current international financial system, and are unlikely to be so for the foreseeable future (Hirst et al., 2009, Chapter 6). The rest of this section provides evidence for this and suggests that there is no truly 'globalized' financial system despite recent events that seem to have confirmed that the crisis took a quintessentially global form. The apparent paradox of there being no truly global financial system at the same time as there seems to have been a global crisis and slowdown will be addressed in a later section. Subsequently the chapter develops an alternative assessment and explores some of its consequences. This is important because unless the key characteristics of the international financial system are fully recognized it is difficult to suggest sensible measures that might be employed to address its shortcomings and deal with its failings.

A key element in this assessment relates to the way conventional economics goes about analysing the international economic system and globalization.[1] Although there are many alternative specifications and nuances, the basic approach continues to be one that models global economic welfare in a perfectly competitive world (though there are models of the kind considered in a moment that work with oligopoly). As the above outline of financial globalization indicates, many presumptions that are controversial and unrealistic would need to be built into such a modelling environment. Nevertheless, such a modelling framework continues to drive the conventional understanding of the financial system as it operates in an international context. One of the specific approaches is to develop a computable general equilibrium model (or C-GEM), the characteristics of which can be used to illustrate many of the difficulties and misunderstandings associated with globalization as conventionally analysed.[2] Although such C-GEMs are too mathematically sophisticated and complex to be fully considered here, at their heart is an expression such as the one shown in square brackets in equation (2.1) immediately below, which can be used to illustrate the basic approach (though this is not meant to be systematic):

$$\Delta W_G = \bullet\bullet\bullet\bullet\bullet\bullet\ [P_x^i - P_w^{i(e)}]\ \bullet\bullet\bullet\bullet\bullet\bullet\ [P_N^n - P_w^{n(e)}]. \qquad (2.1)$$

Supposing we were interested in assessing the consequences for 'global welfare' (W_G) of the development of a truly barrier-less global economy – that is, full global liberalization. This would involve comparing and then aggregating all the differences in actual prices of goods and services operating in different markets and countries with those prices prevailing in such a barrier-less, perfectly competitive world. For any particular price (P) of a good or service i in country X, (P_x^i), the comparison is with the single price that would prevail for that good or service under conditions of perfect equilibrium at the world level ($P_w^{i(e)}$). These comparisons would be made for every good and service in each country (P_N^n) and the differences aggregated to compute the change in global welfare (ΔW_G) consequent upon the 'introduction' of a truly barrier-less global market. In very simple terms this is what a C-GEM does and it provides the basis justification for considering the beneficial welfare effects of liberalization and globalization, one where there are no impediments to trade or financial flows.

But herein lies the rub, so to speak. In contrast to the formation and use of C-GEM, the actual empirics of modelling international trade and investment *flows* usually involves the operationalization of a gravity model as specified in general terms by the second equation given below. Again this is used for illustrative purposes only.[3] What it shows are all the elements that keep the two main variables in equation (2.1) apart, so to speak (i.e., $P^i_x - P^{i(e)}_w$): what goes on in between these two variables and accounts for their differences:

$$\begin{aligned} Iij = a + b\left(\frac{GDPi}{Pi}\right) + c\left(\frac{GDPj}{Pj}\right) - d(Dij) \\ + e(BDRij) + f(LANij) + g(COLij) \\ + h(BLOCij) + k(LAWij) + l(CURij) + u \end{aligned} \tag{2.2}$$

The first line of equation (2.2) gives the basic gravity model variables. In this case investment flows (like FDI) between countries *i* and *j* (I_{ij}) – but this could alternatively be trade flows – are a positive function of the per capita income of the two countries and a negative function of the distance between them. But that is not the end of the matter because a series of control variables are added to account for institutional, cultural and geographic differences between countries that can also (partially) account for the amount of investment (or trade) flows between them. Only the most common and important of these are used in this illustrative exercise. The variables on the second line indicate whether the two countries share a common border (*BDR*), whether they share a common language (*LAN*), and whether there is some colonial history between them (*COL*). On the following line added dummy variables indicate whether the countries belong to a common trading bloc (*BLOC*), whether there is a common legal framework (*LAW* – so that contracts can be confidently enforced) and finally whether the two countries share a common currency (*CUR*). All these have been shown to significantly contribute to investment (and trade) flows between countries (Hirst et al., 2009). Other variables could be added and some subtracted as suits the analytical purpose or issue being confronted.[4]

The point about this discussion is that the cultural, institutional and geographical variables shown in equation (2.2) cannot just be wished away via a process of 'liberalization'. The barriers they produce to international economic interactions (trade and financial) are real. They constitute part of the 'structure' of the system, and inhibit the full realization of 'global' welfare benefits. Indeed, the continued existence of countries with borders, territories and jurisdictions implies modelling the international system in a different manner, one that does not presume that a single global market could somehow be conjured into existence: differences between P^i_xs will always remain pertinent, even in the context of financial markets.[5]

Global or supra-national regional?

One of the problems with existing dominant approaches towards the analysis of the financial system is indicated by the data plotted in Figures 2.1 and 2.2.

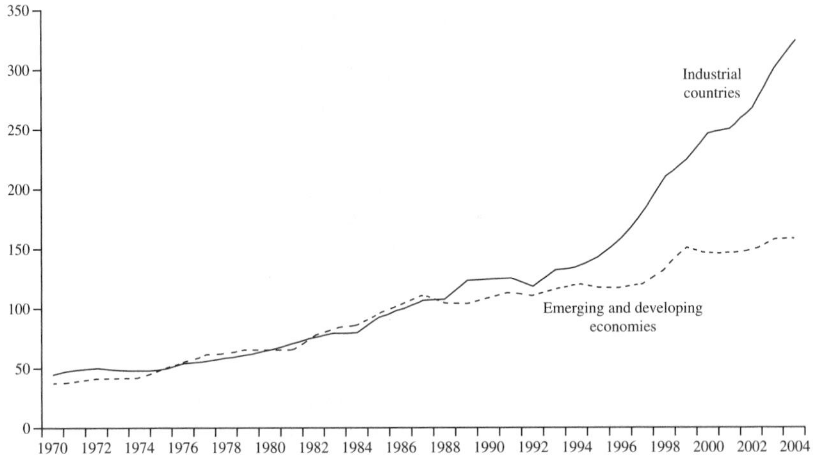

Note: Ratio of sum of foreign assets and liabilities to GDP, 1970–2004.

Source: P. Lane and G.M. Milesi-Ferretti (2006). 'The External Wealth of Nations (Mark II)', CEPR Discussion Paper.

Figure 2.1 Foreign assets and liabilities as share of GDP (industrial group and emerging markets/developing countries group, 1970–2004)

These show typical measures of financial globalization: foreign assets and liabilities as a proportion of GDP and the external assets and liabilities of the banking sector only. In each case there seems to be an unproblematic growth of 'financial globalization'. But the question to ask is exactly *where* is all this activity taking place? As presented the data is too aggregated (though the differentiation between the industrial economies and the emerging markets and developing economies shown in Figure 2.1 begins to unpack the issue).

Figure 2.3 breaks up the 'global' into the patterns of flows between geographical areas for 1999 and 2007 respectively (expressed as a percentage of world GDP) and shows the size of domestic financial assets in each area. What are we to make of this data?

Clearly between 1999 and 2007 there was a growth in the complexity of financial integration. But there is also a certain continuity. As might be expected – though this should be stressed – it is the US and greater Europe (Western Europe, UK, Russia and Eastern Europe) that dominate in terms of both flows and the size of domestic financial assets. And this position did not change much between 1999 and 2007. Even in 2007 – the eve of the crisis – just these two areas accounted for over 70 per cent of global domestic assets and global flows.[6] This is why the *financial* crisis could legitimately be described as a North At-

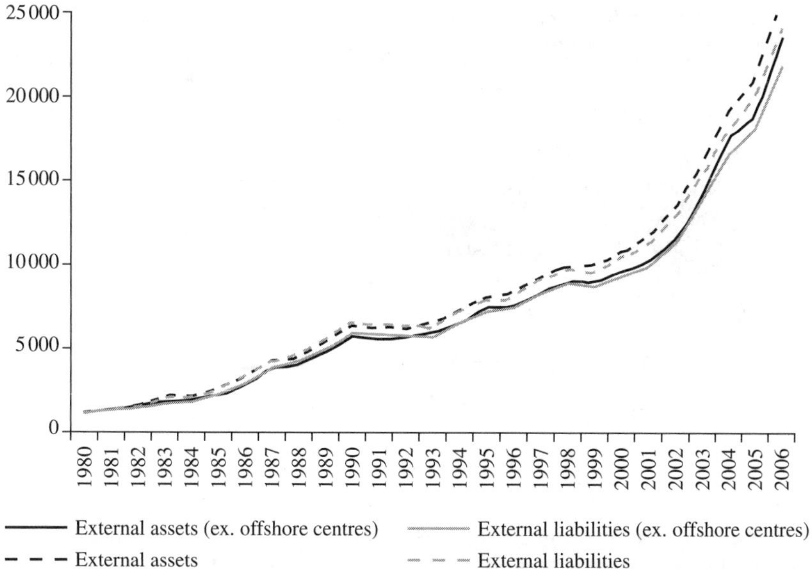

Notes: External assets/liabilities 'ex. off shore centres' exclude financial centres (Bahamas, Bermuda, Cayman Islands, Isle of Man, Jersey and Netherlands Antilles). The data cover banks' unconsolidated gross international on-balance sheet assets and liabilities. They are based on the residence of the reporting institution and measure the activities of all banking offices residing in each reporting country. Such offices report exclusively on their own unconsolidated business, which thus includes international transactions with any of their own affiliates. BIS reporting banks include banks residing in Australia, Austria, the Bahamas, Bahrain, Bermuda, Brazil, the Cayman Islands, Chile, Denmark, Finland, Greece, Guernsey, Hong Kong SAR, India, Ireland, Isle of Man, Jersey, Korea, Luxembourg, Macao SAR, Mexico, the Netherlands Antilles, Norway, Panama, Portugal, Singapore, Spain, Taiwan and Turkey. Detailed information on breaks in series is available on the BIS website under http://www.bis.org.

Source: *The International Role of the Euro: A Status Report*, Economic Papers No. 317, April 2008, The European Commission, Figure 4, p. 6, originally credited to Ferguson et al. (2007).

Figure 2.2 External bank assets and liabilities

lantic crisis not a global one (e.g., Nesvetailova and Palan, 2009; Gowan, 2009). And this description is reinforced by the data included in Figure 2.4, which shows where financial write-downs of the banking sector happened over the crisis period. These were almost entirely accounted for by the Americas and Europe.

Asia was hardly affected. Thus, for all intents and purposes the financial crisis was not a truly global one. It was an *inter-national* one centred on the North Atlantic economies with only very few exceptions. And the reasons are clear from the analysis of what a truly global financial system would look like, and

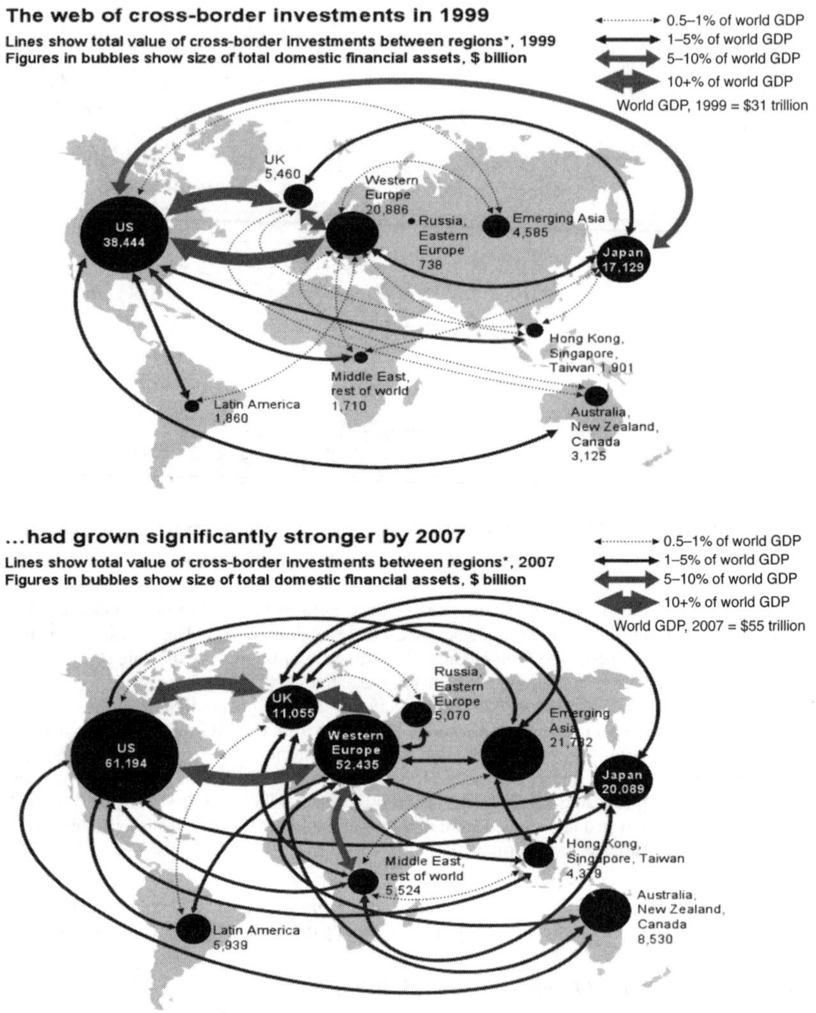

Note: * Includes total value of cross-border investments in equity and debt securities, lending and deposits, and foreign direct investment.

Source: *Mapping Global Financial Flows: Fifth Annual Report*, McKinsey Global Institute, October 2008, Figure 11, p. 24.

Figure 2.3 Financial flows between major economies 1999 and 2007

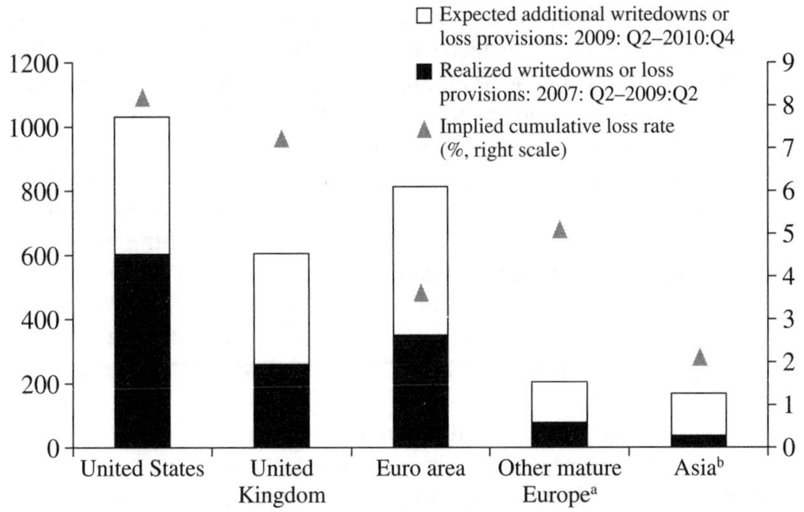

Notes:
a. Includes Denmark, Iceland, Norway, Sweden, and Switzerland.
b. Includes Australia, Hong Kong SAR, Japan, New Zealand and Singapore.

Source: 'The Road to Recovery', Ch. 1 in *Global Financial Stability Report*, IMF, October 2009, Figure 1.9, p. 8.

Figure 2.4 Realized and expected write-downs or loss provisions for banks by region (in billions of US dollars unless shown)

the data shown in Figure 2.3. If the financial system were truly global then losses of this magnitude would already have had a devastating impact 'globally' on commercial banks in many other countries, but this has not happened.[7]

So we need to draw an important analytical distinction here: between an inter-nationalized economic structure (note the hyphen – not an 'international' one) and a globalized economic structure (Hirst et al., 2009, Chapter 1). An *inter-nationalized economy* is an economy made up of a series of individual national economies that interact between themselves mainly via activities like trade interdependency, investment integration and migration (trade, investment and labour flows across borders). The most significant feature of this – though not the only one – would still be these separated national economies that interact between themselves.

On the other hand, a *globalized economy* would be an economy that existed as a single economic entity in its own right somewhat beyond the interacting individual national economies. This economy would be driven by market forces and competition between 'footloose' economic agents (companies, banks, financial institutions, individuals) that are not clearly tethered to any single national economy but which would take the global arena as their sphere of operations: producing, sourcing, marketing and so on, and moving their operations across the globe according to the profitable opportunities that present themselves anywhere. This mirrors the description of financial globalization outlined above. These two types of economy are 'ideal types' – a kind of conceptual model – that do not exist as such in practice or on the ground, so to speak. They provide an abstract image of two different possible types of economy. A difficulty is that traditional discussions of the 'international economy' or 'global economy' do not draw this crucial distinction between the two forms of economic mechanism just outlined. But it is important for the analysis that follows, as will become clear.

Contagion between markets and economies

In the context of the recent economic crisis how do we account for the fact that although the financial crisis may have been centred on just a few countries stretching across the North Atlantic, this escalated into a seemingly more global economic crisis involving many more countries and regions? Here we need to recognize the importance of contagion between different markets and national economies. Such contagion is shown for equity markets in Figure 2.5.

But a preliminary difficulty is that contagion could be a feature of either the two ideal types of economy just outlined – its existence does not act as a discriminator between them. There has been large-scale contagion during the crisis, and there is little doubt that the international economy has experienced a deepening recession. But contagion – the degree of volatility between different markets and between markets in different countries – has been a feature of all financial crises ever since the Tulip speculative bubble of 1637.[8] There is nothing particularly novel about this, so it is not just a feature of a globalized economic structure as defined above. However, measuring the extent of contagion during financial crises is complex and controversial (Allen and Gale, 2000; Forbes and Rigobon, 2002; Dungey, 2008a). There are several approaches. All estimate correlation coefficients between different markets in different countries. But correlation coefficients do not necessarily say anything about causation, so further analysis is needed to isolate the transmission shock associated with an international disturbance from that associated with a purely domestic disturbance (to establish the degree of 'international contagion' only). But this could be caused by there being 'underlying' macroeconomic variances between countries, or trade disturbances, or simply because of 'news shocks' (see Fernández-Izquierdo and Lafuente, 2004; Serwa and Bohl, 2005; Nikkinen et al., 2006 for representative examples of these approaches). So contagion – the transmission of shocks – should not be confused with interdependency – the existence of high correlations (Eichengreen et al., 1996, though see also Forbes and Rigobon, 2002).

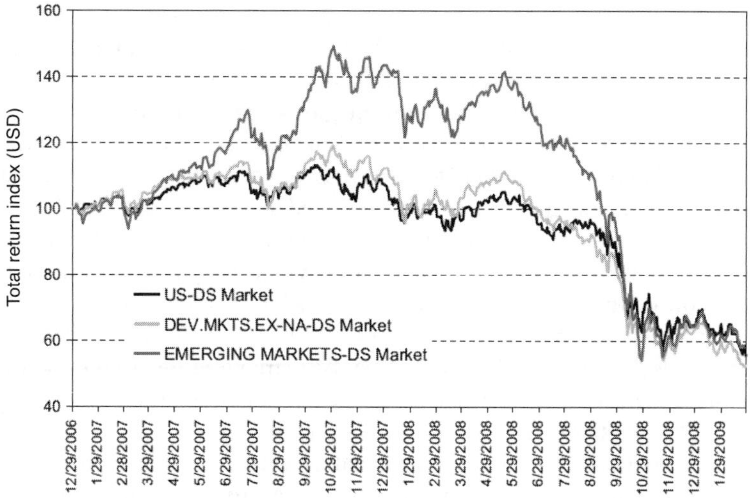

Note: Total return index (USD) for major component markets: US developed markets ex North America, and emerging markets.

Source: Bartram and Bodnar (2009), Figure 2, p. 1250.

Figure 2.5 Contagion in stock markets, 2006–09

In the context of the recent crisis, preliminary evidence shows that there does not seem to have been a growth in the capacity of contagion to translate such volatility between markets and countries as between the periods 2000–07 and 2007–08 (Dungey, 2008b). The volatility was the same in each period – it is just that the initial shock was bigger for the 2007–08 period, hence the greater magnitude of the impact. So this does not mean that 'globalized' interdependency at the international level had increased, only that the initial shock was greater.

But how did such contagion happen? One might look towards 'financial networks' to address this question (Babus, 2007; Pistor, 2008; Allen and Babus, 2009; Haldane, 2009). Financial networks are building up 'connections' that increase the vulnerability to systemic shock, although they could also reduce susceptibility to these if they were to spread the risks and dissipate the initial shock (as expected by conventional opinion about risk management – and as echoed by the natural disasters literature considered in a moment). However, Brunnermeier (2009) has shown that network effects of so-called risk-sharing do not necessarily work in a networked financial system, rather they can exacerbate it.[9] Thus, one needs to map these networks and assess the vulnerabilities within them. This is taken up below. But contagion as such is quite compatible with either an inter-nationalized economic structure or a globalized one as defined above; it is not necessarily associated just with 'globalization'.

The impossible conditions for a genuine global financial system

The bottom line in respect to this consideration of the extent of financial integration and globalization is to stress the structural limits to this process once again. As long as there remain different currencies tied to different domestic financial systems, that is, no single global currency; no proper global central bank to act as lender of last resort for this single currency; and only a few countries that can borrow on the international markets in their own currency to finance their economic activity while the vast majority of other countries must borrow in someone else's currency, there is a necessary structural disjuncture between domestic and international financial systems that cannot be bridged (Arestis and Basu, 2003; Arestis et al., 2005). This is the structural basis of all the uncertainties and risks in the international financial system, and these conditions will hardly disappear in the foreseeable future. These structural constraints inhibit the formation of a genuinely global financial system, leaving a much more differentiated system of national domestic, international financial and supra-national regional relationships and interactions that need to be viewed in their specificity and singularity rather than as a single coherent 'global system'.

And this serves to raise a very important point about the future of financial globalization and the consequences for the renewed global regulatory standard-setting debate, particularly in the case of financial globalization. The consequence of the remarks above is to suggest that full financial globalization is impossible without such a single global currency, and given that such a single currency is most unlikely (indeed, for the foreseeable future politically impossible), then there will be no full 'global' financial internationalization. This looks like an impossible dream.

Of course, there are many calls for a single global currency, mainly by US economists who see this as a way of further bolstering the international position of the US dollar (e.g., Rogoff, 2001; Cooper, 2006). And it is also important to recognize that the call for a single global currency is not a new phenomenon. In the previous period of globalization during the second half of the nineteenth century there were feverish discussions about the possibility of inaugurating a single 'global' currency, originally based upon the Latin Monetary Union of 1865 (Einaudi, 2001). There were conferences in the 1860s: in Berlin in 1863 though the debate began in earnest as Napoleon III called an international monetary conference in 1867. But the vision of the 1860s was never realized (Bordo and James, 2006) as the proposals foundered upon incompatible political differences as to exchange rate conversion procedures and administrative means to 'manage' monetary policy and banking activity. The lesson of this episode should not be lost on the current debate, however. It demonstrates that money involves matters of sovereignty, indeed political issues are at the core of both the creation and the operation of money (Knapp, 1924; Keynes, 1930; Goodhart, 1998; Ingham, 2004, 2006). Without getting into a long historical analysis, the definition of money, the creation of money and the operation of money require a political authority to issue it and provide for its credibility. The implications of this is that there is a need for a 'big government' with a 'strong central bank', and clear 'lender of last resort' facilities, to manage the financial cycle by constraining the boom and softening the slump. This is as necessary in an international setting as it is in a national one. Without all of these conditions, money and finance will not operate 'efficiently', let alone optimally.

Under these circumstances the introduction of new global banking and creditworthiness standards may be desirable – even necessary – but they are also impossible under a regime of financial liberalization and floating exchange rates. Whilst there are different currencies, not all of which are used as either international transaction currencies or as the standard of prices and asset values, uncertainty rules in financial markets, which necessitates the introduction of various creditworthiness standards to try to govern this. However, these standards are inherently unstable given the need for the less developed and emergent market countries (the vast bulk in fact) to earn foreign currency and finance their commercial activity through the issue of assets not denominated in their own currencies. As we have seen above, this opens up a necessary structural 'rupture' or 'separation', (1) between the 'domestic' and the 'international' financial systems of countries, and (2) between those able to finance their activity in their own currency and those who cannot. Such an inherent instability means that there are great pressures to opt for some kind of regional response. This provides for the big government, strong central bank and lender of last resort facilities so necessary for some form of financial stability.

A final point to make in this section is that the 'global' character of the crisis was largely a media-constructed event, though it was aided by politicians who have bought into the globalization story for basically domestic political reasons: it provides an excuse when necessary for them to offload blame and to discipline their citizens in the name of continued 'international competitiveness'. In addition, almost every 'City commentator' has a vested interest in claiming a global aspect to the crisis since this bolsters the scope of their activities. But also – and perhaps most disappointingly – many academic commentators fell for this story since they are themselves mesmerized by the prospects and spectacle of a new epochal rupture, one that allows them to indulge their skills as critical analysts of profoundly changing events (Thompson, 2009). Never ones to miss an opportunity for hyperbole and exaggeration, for all of these parties a 'global crisis' sounds so much better than an ordinary and boring multi-domestic or inter-national one.

The crisis

Crises always expose the underlying character of situations and events. They are intriguing – even attractive – occasions since they provide a glimpse into the very structure of the system. Indeed, there is probably a subliminal desire for crises: they enable decisive action to be taken, leadership to be exercised, hands to be rung, mistakes to be exposed, blame to be apportioned. They break the normal pattern of the mundane.[10]

Crises are also periodic 'events'. But what exactly is an event? Things are always happening but events seem something more, something beyond the ordinary – an unexpected eruption. In the social world, events display two related aspects: first they break ongoing processes by establishing 'differences' between before and after; second they draw together 'dispersions', seemingly creating a momentary unity amongst a range of different instances and contexts – but at the same time precisely preserving that dispersion by exposing its distribution. Summing up, events might be described as an occasion for the 'dispersed unity of differences'.[11]

How are any of these remarks pertinent from the point of view of the recent (and ongoing) financial crisis? First the crisis exposed the real nature of the monetary system. The extreme measures adopted by the authorities – the 'nationalization' of large sections of the financial system – indicates to a basic structural truth of capitalism. The only way to gain control of the money supply is for there to be a socialized financial system. This may sound paradoxical but in a capitalist system where credit is the basic form of money, controlling the money supply is always crucial but also highly problematical. The money supply (credit) is crucial because that economic agent who has money has command over resources. As a result there is always an intense political struggle over controlling the money supply; between the 'public authorities' on the one hand and private economic actors in the financial system on the other. This was exposed very acutely during the debate about 'monetarism' in the 1970s and 1980s. The monetarist argued that the authorities could 'manage' the economy simply by controlling the money supply. But central bankers knew differently. Though they never quite couched it in these terms, the central bankers knew they could not control the money supply. That was in the hands of private economic agents – who, of course, jealously guard this capacity at all costs.[12] To control the money supply would have meant socializing the financial system, the complete opposite of the monetarist's policy prescription of liberalization and de-regulation. But therein lies the paradox. Instead, the central bankers tried to manage the financial system, and influence private economic actors – and the economy beyond – via an interest rate policy. But interest rates affect the demand for money in the first instance, not its supply. Thus, the authorities never implemented 'monetarism' proper because they knew they could not. Rather they adopted an interest-rate-based policy, which was clearly only partially successful.[13] As we have seen subsequently, however, private economic agents relished their renewed capacity to 'control the money supply' by indulging in an orgy of credit creation as interest rates were pushed lower and lower.

This orgy of credit creation was brought to a sudden halt by the 'credit crunch'. Indeed, credit creation (money supply) almost stopped. This provided the opportunity – and indeed the very necessity – for the authorities to confirm the basic truth of the above remarks by nationalizing large sections of the financial system so as to try to kickstart the money supply process again. In extremis deep structural characteristics are revealed. And as a consequence of this nationalization, administrative means of distributing credit have emerged. Indeed, this administrative mechanization was written into the very terms of the nationalization moves. The commercial banks and other financial institutions involved were instructed to allocate credit in various ways: to existing mortgagees (delay or abandon foreclosures) or to lend to small businesses.[14] And many more claims along these lines – for administrative allocation of credit in a very general sense – subsequently emerged. Thus, we have seen other vulnerable financial institutions seeking help, and large industrial companies radically undermined by the recession to claim their share of support. All this is a consequence of nationalizing the financial system; administrative methods for the creation and allocation of credit take over from the market.

Second, this was a genuine event in that it galvanized all parties into action. And in a 'period of the exception' the location of sovereign power was once again (ex)posed.[15] So it was nation-states that came to the rescue of *their* financial systems, not some general global response. And this also exposed the basic dispersion of the international financial system. These responses were different and particular: specific to the characteristics of each national financial system.[16] At its basic level the international financial system remains just that – still an *inter*-nationalized one organized between national economies. It is towards the implication of this different reading of the nature of the financial system and its crises for regulatory reform that the next section explores.

What is to be done?

As John Kay has reminded us, national economies, international financial markets and businesses are complex, dynamic, non-linear systems, about which it is almost impossible to make specific predictions (Kay, 2009). It is foolish to pretend otherwise. Thus, the argument here is that if financial crises are fundamentally 'irrational' – driven by 'excessive exuberances', 'animal spirits', 'bandwagon effects', 'bubbles', Ponzi schemes, exotic calculative technologies, and the like – then we should prepare ourselves in quite a different manner than so far for the next crisis – because there will be one.[17]

Given the analysis so far, the first lesson to be learned is that further 'global' rules to try to tame the financial system are very unlikely to be fully successful.

This is not an argument against strong regulatory rules but only against these always being conceived as necessarily global in scope because the financial system is thought to be global. If it is not – and indeed will continue not to be so – then a different response is called for. Analysis of the financial system conducted elsewhere – and of the 'real' economy beyond – suggests the trajectory of development is largely supra-nationally regional in organization and not global, and with continued strong nationally based characteristics (e.g., Glick and Rose, 1999; Agur, 2008; Hirst et al., 2009, Chapter 6). If this is so, supra-national regional and nationally based responses would be more sensible. This would allow for these to be tailored to the specific conditions and features of such regional or national financial confutations; it would enable agreement on what to do to be reached more easily since fewer players are involved; and it would encourage 'regulatory innovation' since different regulatory frameworks would arise. Some (managed) regulatory competition is no bad thing. In a moment we address what could be thought to be one of the major drawbacks of this structure: it might allow or further encourage clever financial operators to find and exploit the gaps left within it, precisely the problem experienced with past regulatory structures. But as a first step a thorough 'audit' of what the main financially affected countries have done in their individual responses to the crisis should be conducted. This would provide a necessary information base on what each country had already installed in terms of domestic regulatory structures before the crisis hit, how robust they proved to be and what has since been done to reform them. The objective here would be to initiate a period of 'mutual learning' – not in some top-down manner driven by the (now largely discredited) global institutions of financial governance but from a bottom-up one, by listening to the range of different responses that were extant and later introduced at the national level.

Clearly, the recent financial crisis was deep and very serious – indeed for the banking sector in particular it may have been the worst crisis since the 1930s, and it has spilled over into the real economy of those countries most closely affected. But financial crises come and go – this is not the first such crisis and nor will it be the last. And here we need to reflect upon the typical 'financial crisis cycle' as it could be termed. It is a little difficult to know where exactly to analytically break into this cycle but for convenience we do this with the phase involving 'financial innovation' since this is a central part of the existing concerns. Financial innovation always raises many fears as it takes hold, which are well documented and discussed at the time. Warnings are offered as to their likely downside effects but these warnings are, of course, never properly heeded by authorities or regulators (for reasons outlined in a moment). But this leads to a second phase as the crisis largely brought about by these innovations hit the system. This results in a great deal of fire-fighting (as recently and at present) to try to gain control of the crisis and prevent it spreading. It leads to a lot of hand-wringing, immediate soul-searching, recriminations, and so on ('Why didn't we see this happening or heed the warnings, etc.?'). As the crisis subsides this is followed by a longer analytical diagnostic and post-mortem phase. What were the reasons for the crisis? Who or what was to blame? What lessons can be learned and what done to prevent a further crisis? This is a difficult phase because there is never agreement about causes or consequences. However, alongside this, or just behind it, the 'authorities' begin to act, putting into place a discussion about measures needed to prevent another crisis of this type. This phase requires a political mobilization to gather momentum amongst the affected parties. And this is the most difficult and lengthy phase because getting a consensus about what to do is never easy. Eventually, some consensus is reached, however, which usually means a very watered down and minimalist set of regulatory responses are agreed and gradually implemented. But meanwhile, of course, the system has moved on and a new set of financial innovations have taken hold, so the responses to the previous crisis now being gradually implemented look as though they are unnecessary or addressing yesterday's problem. And the fact that the authorities are still grappling with the regulatory consequences of that previous round of innovations means their focus is not on the existing round or the threats these now pose. So the cycle continues.[18]

I was once at a conference where I asked a panel of regulators and central bank governors what could be done, if anything, to break this cycle and their response was intriguing. The chair of the session replied that this was an 'existential question' and that such existential questions could not be answered! On reflection, however, I think this answer should be taken seriously. Perhaps the mind-set of such bank governors and regulators is so focused on traditional responses that they cannot jump out of that mind-set and see that the system is actually 'existential' in the sense that it is 'irrational'.[19] It is not, therefore, fully amenable to systematic and calculative responses where the IMF's Financial Stability Forum, BIS Basel Committee or the G20 simply begins another round of negotiations for a comprehensive and consistent set of new global regulatory norms and rules to be adhered to by everyone. Rather, what is needed is a realization that financial insecurity is going to continue to be a fact of life; involving as it does 'excessive exuberances', 'animal spirits', 'bandwagon effects', Ponzi schemes, and so on. If this is so what is needed is to organize a highly flexible regulatory regime of 'distributed preparedness for resilience', one that does not presume a single centre from which a new elaborate global regulatory regime emanates (Collier and Lakoff, 2008).[20] This approach would have to pay particular attention to the necessarily fragmented nature of financial regulation – given the range of initiatives as suggested earlier – in an attempt to forestall any exploitation of the gaps within it (Perrow, 2007). But it would need to recognize that the crisis represented only a *temporary* dispersed unity of differences as suggested above, not a permanent one, so that the underlying distribution of differences continues. To address this would involve a lot of contingency planning and attempts to coordinate the disparate array of 'local' (supra-nationally regional or national in our case) organizational and partial initiatives, requiring the application of improvisational skills and ingenuity. This approach – which Collier (2008) terms enactment based assessment – is contrasted to the traditional archival-statistical approach, which relies on assembling knowledge from already known risks and past patterns of events. The task would be to map the vulnerabilities and network the relationship between them. And this regulatory world would always need to expect the unexpected (Weick and Sutcliffe, 2007; Lentzos and Rose, 2009).

And whilst it will be difficult for those states that have socialized large sections of their financial systems to return these to private ownership quickly, this is not necessarily a priority. It may be that a newly formulated regulatory regime will require a continued presence of public ownership of significant parts of the financial system, if nothing else because of the analysis above indicating the difficulty of kickstarting the credit/money production process without it. And this may be the only effective way to deal with the continued dispersed character of the international financial system and to prepare for the resilience necessary to deal with new unexpected eruptions as they happen, because these will happen whatever is done.

Of course, such a response along these lines is unlikely. More likely is for the traditional financial crisis cycle to kick in once again (and 'business as usual' to re-emerge – Thompson, 2009). But imaginative thinking about the future to try to create a robust alternative conception is absolutely necessary, even if the precise terms of what has been suggested here proves wanting. However, this can hardly be worse than the recent debacle.

Conclusions

The argument of this chapter is that the 'global' financial crisis was not really global at all, but one confined to relatively few countries centred across the North Atlantic (between North America and greater Europe). But this did not stop the spillover from this area to much of the rest of the world in terms of a wider economic contagion and downturn. Contagion proved rife, though such contagion is not new in the international economic system, so, of itself, it cannot be used as an indicator for the onset of a new specific phase of international capitalism called globalization. But do these linguistic differences matter much? In fact, they are conceptual differences, not just linguistic ones. The chapter has argued that getting the conceptual terminology right is important because it indicates to the policy conclusions that might be drawn from any analysis. If the international economic system is not a globalized one in the terminology developed above, but rather an inter-nationalized one, where there are strong elements of irrationality, then the regulatory response should be centred on national economies (or supra-national regional configurations) rather than necessarily at the global level. This led to suggestions of how to develop a 'bottom-up' regulatory response based upon catastrophe management and a distributed preparedness for resilience.

Notes

* This chapter draws heavily on my article, Thompson (2010a).

1. Many of the themes developed here were first outlined in Thompson (2004).
2. For particular application of this technique by the World Bank see Essama-Nssah (2006).
3. For a thorough analysis of the use of gravity equations in modelling international trade see Rauch (1999).
4. In the equations for investment flows (FDI, equity) the distance variable (*D*) is a highly significant one (see Hirst et al., 2009, Table 6.8, p. 175, and Hirst and Thompson, Chapter 1, this book).
5. This is referred to as the 'home bias' effect. In the case of trade see Disdier and Head (2008), Nitsch and Wolf (2009); and for financial markets see Bong-Chan et al. (2006) and Cai and Warnock (2004).
6. Again, as might have been expected, cross-border investment activity weakened in 2008, with reductions in flows between most areas, but particularly for the 'North America–UK–Western Europe' triangle (McKinsey *Global Investment Report 2009*, Exhibit 13).
7. For instance, after an initial shock China and India emerged more or less unscathed.
8. On the first 'global financial bubble' (of 1720) see Frehen et al. (2009). On the tulip bubble, and its limited significance, see Goldgar (2007).
9. Brunnermeier suggests an interesting measure to cope with contagion in these settings designed to indicate to the 'value at risk' of any organization's balance sheet that is co-varied with other organizations in the network ('CoVaR'). This is designed as part of a better assessment of systemic network stress (Adrian and Brunnermeier, 2009). Haldane (2009) constructs various measures of network characteristics based upon the extent of foreign assets and liabilities between the main financial centres.
10. Thus, echoing a point made above, the media loves them; it chases them, helps construct them, and revels in them: 'breaking news', 'global tremors', 'the worst day on Wall Street since …', and so on. Crises are enthusiastically embraced by the media when they erupt.
11. An additional – and related – aspect of 'events' would be to stress their specific *political* character. According to Badiou (2001) and Rancière (1999) genuinely political events are those that declare a radical equality. They announce an equality where there had previously been a deep inequality. They right a wrong (Thompson, 2007). In the context of the financial crisis being discussed here, this would manifest itself in the way such events seem to demonstrate a unity in the diversity they display, and the way they open up an opportunity to put right things that had, up until then, been going very much awry.
12. In the contemporary crisis the emphasis on the private control of the money supply was signalled by the call from several leading UK monetarists for the government to once again borrow from the commercial banks to create money (to prevent a potential deflationary spiral from emerging): 'Money being destroyed by the collapse in bank lending to the private sector must be made good by bank lending to the public sector. … If banks' claims on the private sector fall, the initial effect on the other side of the balance sheet is a matching decline in their deposit liabilities (ie, the quantity of money). In these circumstances there is a risk of a debt-deflationary spiral. If so, the right policy response is for the government itself to borrow from the banks. … If the government borrows from the banks on an appropriate scale … we believe that a wider recovery can be reconciled with reductions in the private sector's indebtedness to the banks' ('Government must borrow from banks to create money', *Financial Times* letters, 31 December 2008, p. 10). The clear objective was to avoid at all cost the direct creation of money for use by the public sector. This would have involved the government selling Treasury Bills (TBs) to the Bank of England (not the private commercial banking sector), which would then become assets of the Bank. The Bank could then create liabilities to match these assets

in the form of expanding the monetary base (printing money). That cash could be used to purchase the TBs, so the government would have money directly to hand to use as it wished (substitute for tax cuts, give away, use to purchase resources, etc.). This would locate the creation of an addition to the money supply firmly with the public authorities in the first instance (because the Bank of England is a joint stock company whose shares are all owned by the Treasury). But the 'success' of the quantitative easing arranged by the Bank and the financial institutions in the UK was celebrated by the same monetarists who proposed it earlier as the crises eased in mid-2009 ('Keep the money flowing to stave off deflation', Tim Congdon, *Financial Times*, 9 July 2009, p. 13). However, the actual way quantitative easing was arranged by the Bank was quite different from the monetarist's immediate prescription, though it still essentially relied upon handing augmentation of the money supply to the private sector. It operated through the non-bank private financial institutions in the first instance (Chadha, 2010; Dale, 2010). The Bank purchased gilts for the pension funds and insurance companies, thus altering the balance of their portfolios and pushing up yields. This would encourage these institutions to buy equities and commercial bonds, which would mean commercial banks' deposits rose, on the basis of which those banks could create additional credit for the private sector. Whether this quite worked in the manner suggested is another matter, of course.

13. Thus, the authorities in effect conducted a 'Keynesian' monetary policy not a 'monetarist' monetary policy. Indeed, in the 2009 crisis, interest rates have been forced down to almost zero, where monetary policy stops. In principle this enables the government to purchase anything at zero cost to itself (since it can borrow at zero cost) and to spend as much as it likes. But, as indicated in footnote 12, the authorities chose not to exercise this option. Instead they went for a conventional route of borrowing from the private sector, hence encumbering the public sector with significant amounts of debt, which could have been avoided.
14. However, one of the problems more generally has been whether the nationalized banks – let alone the non-nationalized ones – have acted to pass on any easing of credit condition to their customers. Generally they failed to do this – a consequence of having ownership but not full control in the case of the nationalized banks, which may be an emergent pattern in the financial system. Some form of further nationalization *plus* the exercise of control (or 'governance') may be an answer.
15. Thus, Gordon Brown almost became a 'Schmittian sovereign' for a while ('Sovereign is he who decides on the exception', Schmitt, 1998; in his *New York Times* column on 12 October Paul Krugman described Brown's decisive action in the UK as the potential saviour of the world financial system!). This is somewhat of an exaggeration, of course, since the very existence of the UK state was not in question (though it might have been more the case for Iceland's Geir Haarde).
16. And these basic differences re-emerged as the reform packages promoted by the G20 or the Basel Committee took shape in early 2010. Some countries supported a 'bank tax' proposed by the G20 (UK, US, Switzerland – who had experienced significant runs on their banks) while others were against it (Canada, Australia, Spain – where banks had been more resilient because of different domestic regulatory arrangements). And in the case of more stringent bank capital adequacy ratios suggested by the Basel Committee, Germany, France and Japan were against this (because their domestic banking systems relied more on networked relationships to firms, which they considered more resilient to 'over-exposure') while the Anglo-American economies were in favour (because these economies had allowed the equity base of their banking system to deteriorate).
17. In part this 'irrationality' can be illustrated by the way that options contracts (which are important in the derivatives markets) are priced – in fact necessarily 'mis-priced'. Two key assumptions for valuing options are that the volatility of returns is constant and their distribution is log-normal (Black and Scholes, 1973; Merton, 1973; Brooks et al., 1994). In practice neither of these assumptions is likely other than by pure chance: usually returns are volatile and unexpected combinations of events disrupt their distribution. This means that strictly speaking, options can only be 'correctly' priced ex-post; when the contact has matured (because then the actual volatility and distribution would be known). These problems have given rise to a complex debate about options pricing (e.g., Mehrling, 2005; MacKenzie, 2006). Elsewhere I discuss this issue of 'irrationality' at length (Thompson, 2010b).

18. See Reinhart (2008) and Reinhart and Rogoff (2008) for the way the 'financial crisis cycle' has reproduced itself over many centuries, and the failure of the regulatory authorities to come to terms with this. At the time of preparing this chapter another round of crises was just in the making, this time associated with sovereign debt.
19. An existential moment in this context would be a crisis that lacks purpose, meaning or authentication, leading to anxiety, disorientation and confusion in the face of the seeming randomness, absurdity and volatility of events.
20. Here the lessons from natural disaster planning are introduced. And although in its own terms this has been problematic (e.g., in the case of the flooding in New Orleans in 2007) in principle it provides an important alternative conceptual apparatus for thinking about crisis management (Grossi and Kunreuther, 2005).

References

Adrian, T. and Brunnermeier, M.J. (2009), 'CoVaR', available at http://www.princeton.edu/~markus; accessed 6 October 2010.

Agur, I. (2008), 'The US trade deficit, the decline of the WTO and the rise of regionalism', *Global Economy Journal*, **8**(3), 1–32.

Allen, F. and Babus, A. (2009), 'Networks in finance', in P. Kleindorfer and J. Wind (eds) *Network-based Strategies and Competence*, Philadelphia: Wharton School Publishing.

Allen, F. and Gale, D. (2000), 'Financial contagion', *Journal of Political Economy*, **108**(1), 1–33.

Arestis, P. and Basu, S. (2003), 'Financial globalization: some conceptual problems', *Eastern Economic Journal*, **29**(3), 183–9.

Arestis, P., Basu, S. and Mallik, S. (2005), 'Financial globalization: the need for a single currency and a global central bank', *Journal of Post Keynesian Economics*, **27**(3), 507–31.

Babus, A. (2007), 'The formation of financial networks', Discussion Paper No. 06-093, Rotterdam: Tinbergen Institute.

Badiou, A. (2001), *Ethics: An Essay on the Understanding of Evil*, London: Verso.

Bartram, S.M. and Bodnar, G.M. (2009), 'No place to hide: the global crisis in equity markets 2008/2009', *Journal of International Money and Finance*, **28**(9), 1246–92.

Black, F. and Scholes, M. (1973), 'The pricing of options and corporate liabilities', *Journal of Political Economy*, **81**(3), 637–54.

Bong-Chan, K., Stulz, R.-M. and Warnock, F.E. (2006), 'Financial globalization, governance and the evolution of the home bias', *BIS Working Paper* No. 220, December, Basel: Bank of International Settlements.

Bordo, M. and James, H. (2006), 'One world money, then and now', *International Economics and Economic Policy*, **3**(3/4), 395–407.

Brooks, R., Corson, J. and Wales, J.D. (1994), 'The pricing of index options when the underlying assets all follow a lognormal diffusion', in D.M. Chance and R.P. Trippi (eds) *Advances in Futures and Options Research*, Vol. 7, Stamford CT: JAI Press Inc.

Brunnermeier, M.K. (2009), 'Deciphering the liquidity and credit crunch 2007–2008', *Journal of Economic Perspectives*, **23**(1), 7–100.

Cai, F. and Warnock, F.E. (2004), 'International diversification at home and abroad', *International Finance Discussion Paper* No. 2004-793, Washington, DC: Federal Reserve Board.

Chadha, J (2010), 'Quantitative easing – a mid-term review', available at http://www.york.ac.uk/res/mmf/documents/QE.pdf; accessed 6 October 2010.

Collier, S.J. (2008), 'Enacting catastrophe: preparedness, insurance, budgetary rationalization', *Economy and Society*, **37**(3), 224–50.

Collier, S.J. and Lakoff, A. (2008), 'Distributed preparedness: the spatial logic of domestic security in the US', *Environment and Planning D: Society and Space*, **26**, 7–28.

Cooper, R.N. (2006), 'Proposal for a common currency amongst rich democracies', *International Economics and Economic Policy*, **3**(3/4), 387–94.

Dale, S. (2010), 'QE – One year on', Bank of England speech, available at http://www.bankofengland.co.uk/publications/speeches/2010/speech428.pdf; accessed 6 October 2010.

Disdier, A.-C. and Head, K. (2008), 'The puzzling persistence of the distance effect on bilateral trade', *The Review of Economics and Statistics*, February, **90**(1), 37–48.

Dungey, M. (2008a), 'Contagion in currency markets: what do we mean?', Australia: La Trobe University.
Dungey, M. (2008b), 'The tsunami: measures of contagion in the 2007–2008 credit crunch', *CESinfo Forum*, **9**(4), 33–43.
Eichengreen, B., Rose, A.K. and Wyplosz, C. (1996), 'Contagious currency crises', *NBER Working Paper* No. W5681, July.
Einaudi, L. (2001), *Money and Politics: European Monetary Unification and the International Gold Standard (1865–1873)*, Oxford: Oxford University Press.
Essama-Nssah, B. (2006), 'Building an Applied General Equilibrium Model', Poverty Reduction Group (PRMPR), The World Bank, teaching material for PAMS 15–19 May, 2006, available at http://siteresources.worldbank.org/INTPSIA/Resources/490023-1121114603600/1413109-1135026571018/CGE_Modeling_052206.pdf; accessed 8 October 2010.
Fernández-Izquierdo, A. and Lafuente, J.A. (2004), 'International transmission of stock exchange volatility: empirical evidence from the Asian crisis', *Global Finance Journal*, **15**(2), 125–37.
Forbes, K.J. and Rigobon, R. (2002), 'No contagion, only interdependence: measuring stock market comovements', *Journal of Finance*, **57**(5), 2223–61.
Frehen, R.G.P., Goetzmann, W.N. and Rouwenhorst, K.G. (2009), 'New evidence on the first financial bubble', *NBER Working Paper* No.15332, September, Cambridge MA: NBER.
Glick, R. and Rose, A.K. (1999), 'Contagion and trade: why are currency crises regional?', *Journal of International Money and Finance*, **18**(4), 603–17.
Goldgar, A. (2007), *Tulipmania: Money, Honor and Knowledge in the Dutch Golden Age*, Chicago, IL: University of Chicago Press.
Goodhart, C.A.E. (1998), 'Two concepts of money: implications for the analysis of optimal currency areas', *European Journal of Political Economy*, **14**(3), 407–32.
Gowan, P. (2009), 'Crisis in the heartland: consequences of the new Wall Street system', *New Left Review*, **II**(55), 2–29.
Grossi, P. and Kunreuther, H. (eds) (2005), *Catastrophe Modeling: A New Approach to Managing Risk*, New York: Springer.
Haldane, A.G. (2009), 'Rethinking the financial network' Bank of England speech, London, April.
Hirst, P.Q., Thompson, G.F. and Bromley, S. (2009), *Globalization in Question*, 3rd edn, Cambridge: Polity Press.
Ingham, G. (2004), *The Nature of Money*, Cambridge: Polity Press.
Ingham, G. (2006), 'Further reflections on the ontology of money', *Economy and Society*, **35**(2), 259–78.
Kay, J. (2009), *The Long and the Short of It*, London: The Erasmus Press.
Keynes, J.M. (1930), *A Treatise on Money*, London: Macmillan.
Knapp, G. (1924), *The State Theory of Money*, New York: Augustus M. Kelly.
Lentzos, F. and Rose, N. (2009), 'Governing insecurity: contingency planning, protection, resilience', *Economy and Society*, **38**(2), 230–54.
MacKenzie, D. (2006), *An Engine, Not a Camera: How Financial Models Shape Markets*, Cambridge MA: MIT Press.
Mehrling, P. (2005), *Fischer Black and the Revolutionary Idea of Finance*, New York: John Wiley.
Merton, R.C. (1973), 'Theory of rational option pricing', *Bell Journal of Economics and Managerial Science*, **4**(1), 141–83.
Nesvetailova, A. and Palan, R. (2009), 'A very North Atlantic credit crunch: geopolitical implications of the global liquidity crisis', *International Affairs*, Autumn 2008/Winter 2009.
Nikkinen, J., Omran, M., Sahlstrom, P. and Aijo, J. (2006), 'Global stock market reactions to scheduled US macroeconomic news announcements', *Global Finance Journal*, **17**(1), 92–104.
Nitsch, W. and Wolf, N. (2009), 'Tear down this wall: on the persistence of borders in trade', *Warwick Economic Research Papers*, No. 919.
Perrow, C. (2007), *The Next Catastrophe*, Princeton, NJ: Princeton University Press.
Pistor, K. (2008), 'Global network finance: organizational hedging in times of uncertainty', *Columbia Law School Working Paper* No. 339, October.
Rancière, J. (1999), *Dis-Agreement: Politics and Philosophy*, Minneapolis: University of Minnesota Press.

Rauch, J.E. (1999), 'Networks versus markets in international trade', *Journal of International Economics*, **48**(1), 7–35.

Reinhart, C.M. (2008), 'Eight hundred years of financial folly', *MPRA Paper* No. 11864, December 2008 available at: http://mpra.ub.uni-muenchen.de/11864/; accessed 5 October 2010.

Reinhart, C.M. and Rogoff, K.S. (2008), 'This time it's different: a panoramic view of eight centuries of financial crises', *National Bureau of Economic Research Working Paper* No. 13882, March 2008.

Rogoff, K. (2001), 'Why not a global currency?', *American Economic Review, Papers and Proceedings*, **91**, May, 243–47.

Schmitt, C. (1998), *Political Theology: Four Chapters on the Concept of Sovereignty*, Cambridge, MA: MIT Press.

Serwa, D. and Böhl, M.T. (2005), 'Financial contagion vulnerability and resistance: a comparison of European stock markets', *Economic Systems*, **29**(3), 344–62.

Stulz, R.M. (2005), 'The limits of financial globalization', *The Journal of Finance*, **60**(4), 1595–1638.

Thompson, G.F. (2004), 'Are there any limits to globalization? International trade, capital flows and borders', in N. Karagiannis and M. Witter (eds) *The Caribbean Economies in an Era of Free Trade*, Hampshire: Ashgate.

Thompson, G.F. (2007), 'The fate of territorial engineering: mechanisms of territorial power and post-liberal forms of international governance', *International Politics*, **44**(5), 487–512.

Thompson, G.F. (2009), 'What's in the frame? How the financial crisis is being packaged for public consumption', *Economy and Society*, **38**(3), 520–24.

Thompson, G.F. (2010a), '"Financial globalization" and the "crisis": a critical assessment and "what is to be done"?', *New Political Economy*, **15**(1), 127–45.

Thompson, G.F. (2010b), 'The global regulatory consequences of an irrational crisis: examining "animal spirits" and "excessive exuberances"', *Globalizations*, **7**(1/2), 87–103.

Weick, K.E. and Sutcliffe, K.M. (2007), *Managing the Unexpected: Resilient Performance in an Age of Uncertainty*, San Francisco, CA: John Wiley and Sons.

3 The scope and implications of globalisation

Jonathan Perraton

During the 1990s and early 2000s 'globalisation' became arguably *the* buzzword of the times. For all its resonance in academic and popular discourse, 'globalisation' often remained a vague and elusive concept. Globalisation has been widely used to refer to sharp increases in levels of international economic flows since the 1970s. Using various definitions, authors have typically claimed either that it heralds the demise of the nation state or that it amounts to nothing new. A growing academic school – ably represented by Paul Hirst and Grahame Thompson in their contribution to this volume in Chapter 1 and elsewhere (Hirst et al. 2009) – argues that there is less than meets the eye to this phenomenon. However, these conceptions of globalisation are typically inadequate and their analysis of empirical evidence consequently misleading. Further, much has changed since earlier debates, with the 2008– financial crisis illustrating the interconnectedness of the global economy, including the evolving relationship between developed and emerging economies. The crisis has also undermined claims that globalisation will ensure generalised prosperity. This chapter proposes an analytic approach to globalisation, argues that available evidence does point to a fundamental transformation in the world economy, which in key respects is unprecedented, and draws implications for nation states and the welfare of their citizens.

Conceptions of globalisation

Broadly speaking there are three approaches to globalisation, referred to here as the hyper-globalist, the sceptical and the transformationalist views (Held et al., 1999). For the hyper-globalists contemporary globalisation has created a single global economy transcending and integrating the world's major economic regions. Technological changes and market integration in this interpretation create an imperative towards the de-nationalisation of strategic economic activities so that it is global finance and corporate capital, rather than nation states, that exercise decisive influence over the organisation, location and distribution of economic power and wealth. Since the authority of states is territorially bound, global markets can escape effective political regulation. In this borderless economy, states have no option other than to accommodate global market forces, whilst multilateral economic institutions, notably the IMF, World Bank and WTO, effectively function to further this globalisation. New information and communication technologies (ICTs) are crucial here for breaking down barriers of distance and leading to the global diffusion of technological know-how. Whether celebrated in neo-liberal business and journalistic literature (notably Friedman, 2006)[1] or deplored in radical literature (for example Greider, 1997; Gray, 2009), globalisation is taken to spell the end of national management of economies and, particularly, of the welfare state.

In academic circles this hyper-globalist school has relatively few adherents, but this business school view of the world is highly influential in policy circles and popular discourse. In a weaker form it underlay arguments for the 'Washington Consensus', asserting that increased integration raises gains from pursuing laissez-faire microeconomic policies and conservative macroeconomic policies, and also raises the costs of departing from such policies. This view became prevalent amongst international economic agencies and in more academic versions claimed that embracing globalisation offers the prospect of income convergence for emerging economies (Sachs and Warner, 1995; Lucas, 2000; Dollar and Kraay, 2004).

The sceptical view, by contrast, sees contemporary integration instead as 'inter-nationalisation', where recent growth of international flows represents rising interactions between well-defined national economies, rather than the emergence of global economic activity. National economic policy therefore at least potentially remains coherent and effective. Putting this in an historical perspective, this view sees current levels of global flows as not unprecedented but comparable to – in some respects, lower than – those during the classical Gold Standard period before World War I. The emergence of global financial markets in the classical Gold Standard period with the telegraph – the 'Victorian Internet' (Standage, 1999) – undermines notions that new ICTs are crucial. Hyper-globalisation reports of the 'death of distance' are found to be exaggerated – even with ICTs geographical distance and the influence of historic and cultural links still affect levels and patterns of international flows of goods, service, finance and technology. Further, rather than being global, the sceptics argue that increased international economic activity is primarily a phenomenon largely confined to developed countries, with these states having been the very architects of a more open international economy. Dismissing the idea of a unified global economy, the sceptical position concludes that the world displays distinct economic and political blocs, within which different forms of capitalism continue to flourish. Sceptics test the claims of the hyper-globalists and find them wanting as an account of contemporary developments – economic activity remains significantly more nationally based than would be the case under a model globalised economy, geographical factors continue to have a significant impact on international economic flows. Often the hyper-globalist view is taken as representative of analyses of globalisation more generally.

The transformationalist view of globalisation proposed here differs from both these approaches in viewing globalisation as a process rather than an end-state.

The historical context of globalisation is examined in more detail elsewhere;[2] but the evidence presented below does point to levels of integration that are qualitatively higher than in earlier periods. Globalisation can be conceived as a process, or set of processes, that embodies a transformation in the spatial organisation of social relations, engendering a shift in the spatial reach of networks and systems of social relations to transcontinental patterns of human organisation, activity and the exercise of social power. More specifically here we focus on the emergence of global product and financial markets and the international organisation of business. This entails a stretching of economic activity across frontiers, regions and continents. The growing extensity[3] of economic activity is combined with an intensification or growing magnitude, of interconnectedness and flows of trade, investment, finance and so on so that domestic economic activity is increasingly enmeshed with activity elsewhere. This growing extensity and intensity deepens their impact such that the effects of distant events can be highly significant elsewhere and specific local developments can have global consequences. In this sense, the boundaries between domestic matters and global affairs become increasingly fluid. Networks and infrastructures have emerged to facilitate these interactions, and institutions have emerged to regulate them. Such developments are rarely uniform and typically display clear patterns of hierarchy and unevenness. Globalisation is not a singular condition, a linear process or a final end-point of social change. Although the impact of globalisation processes is affected by the extensity and intensity of the processes, it cannot simply be read off from them. Globalisation theory should not be seen as a substitute for established social science approaches to assessing the impact of social relations, but instead it complements them by illuminating the specific role played by the intercontinental dimension of social relations and indicating how established tools should be modified and applied to understanding these relations. Globalisation does not simply denote a shift in the extensity or scale of social relations and activity. Fundamentally, argue the transformationalists, it also involves the spatial reorganisation of economic, political, military and cultural power. Globalisation can thus be understood as involving a shift or transformation in the scale of human social organisation that extends the reach of power relations across the world's major regions and continents. It implies a world in which developments in one region can come to shape the life chances of communities in distant parts of the globe.

Herein lies the key contrast with the hyper-globalisation and sceptical approaches. Both these views share a remarkably similar conception of globalisation as an end-state, the sceptics testing this notion against the evidence and finding it wanting. Conceiving globalisation as an end-state is problematic for two reasons. First, this all too often leads to conflating global markets with perfect markets so that when global markets do not operate as textbook perfect markets this is erroneously taken as evidence against globalisation. On the contrary, global markets may lead to global market failures; indeed, these may be aggravated by the absence of effective global economic governance. Second, there seems little reason to think that processes of social change like globalisation have a single putative end-point. This leads to the analysis above where it is assumed that globalisation inexorably leads to one outcome and cannot be altered by policy choices. Both the hyper-globalist and sceptical approaches use similar conceptions of economic globalisation in terms of perfectly integrated international markets, the sceptics claiming to test the assertion of the hyper-globalisation school that such markets have arisen. It is not simply that reality by definition does not conform to this ideal type – it is also the wrong model. This is a concept of an equilibrium end-state. However, an equilibrium of frictionless international capital mobility would be expected to produce very low, not very high, cross-border financial flows and transactions. Such a model is therefore unhelpful in explaining the huge volume of cross-border transactions and periodic turbulence in international financial markets. Focusing on perfect international markets fails to explain non-market integration by multinational corporations (MNCs), since MNCs exist precisely because of imperfections in international markets. This concept is severely limited as an analytical tool. Fundamentally, it is unhelpful to study economic processes in terms of a single implied end-point, given the likelihood of multiple equilibria. The end-point concept of globalisation implies a unilinear, even inexorable, process. Rather, globalisation can be seen as a process of emergence of global product markets and global organisation of production. This both covers several areas of economic activity and also has multiple causes. Market dynamics are important, but globalisation cannot simply be reduced to this. Nor can it simply be explained in terms of new technology: but modern technology has been central to moving the volume of goods traded and to processing the vast level of transactions on contemporary international financial markets as well as providing the communications infrastructure for organising international business.

The sceptics are right to point out that markets are not protean entities but require a legal framework, and that global markets have emerged as the result of deliberate political decisions by key states to liberalise. These observations do not, though, mean that globalisation is a myth, for several reasons. Continuing regulation of markets by governments does not mean that they can control the outcomes of these markets; regulators themselves are often playing catch-up with developments in the markets, particularly in global finance. The response of regulators to financial innovation in the years before the 2008 crisis vividly demonstrated this. Nor does the fact that governments deliberately deregulated mean that it would be a simple task to change this. Whilst in an important sense deregulation entailed *re*regulation – regulations were not simply removed but new ones devised and implemented – the national dimension to this is often over-stated in sceptical accounts. There is evidence of growing uniformity in business regulation, at least across developed countries (Braithwaite and Drahos, 2000). In part this is due to links between national regulators and the emergence of an international epistemic community amongst them, in part it is the result of formal integration agreements either regionally (for example, the Single European Market or NAFTA) or globally through the WTO, and in part it reflects regulatory arbitrage from international competition. Thus, a global architecture for international markets is emerging. Politically how this architecture is developed remains open, as global debates on international financial regulation following the financial crisis show.

Globalisation as a multidimensional process with multiple causes can be expected to have multiple possible outcomes. The limitations of the unilinear conception of globalisation can be seen in the use of convergence measures to 'test' globalisation trends. Typically such analysis is either naive – assorted variables are presumed to converge with globalisation for no clear theoretical reason and anything less is taken as evidence against globalisation – or predicated upon models assuming perfect competition. Even modern neoclassical models of globalisation assuming imperfect competition and scale economies show that integration can result in agglomeration and spatial unevenness, and inequality in processes that imply multiple equilibria, and they do not propose simple convergence stories or that gains will necessarily be equitably distributed (Krugman and Venables, 1995; Gomory and Baumol, 2000; Venables, 2001). Less orthodox accounts based on the pioneering work of Stephen Hymer on MNCs make similar predictions on the basis of profit-seeking activity by oligopolistic MNCs (for example, Kozul-Wright, 1995). Globalisation processes do not necessarily imply homogenisation or convergence in conditions across countries – international transactions are often driven precisely by differences in countries' domestic conditions. Moreover, hierarchy and unevenness in the nature of global systems may be perpetuated, accentuated or modified by globalisation. Whether incomes, growth rates and other economic conditions and policies are expected to converge as a result of globalisation depends on the theoretical approach adopted and the nature of the globalisation process.

Empirical evidence

One key indication of globalisation has been that international trade, finance and production have consistently grown faster than income in the post-war period, and these are considered below. One omission here is international migration, which was a key component of globalisation processes in the classical Gold Standard period. The forces leading towards globalisation of product and financial markets, particularly improvements and cost reductions in transport and communications, may have a similar impact on international labour movements (Stalker, 2000). In the classical Gold Standard period migration is estimated to have contributed more to international income convergence than trade or capital flows (Hatton and Williamson, 2005, ch. 6); the more limited levels and patterns of contemporary migration have meant that this has not produced convergence in the contemporary period with the migrant share of world population having only grown slowly over the past 50 years and South to North migration only accounts for around a third of contemporary migration (UNDP, 2009, ch. 2). Trade and/or capital flows can in principle substitute for migration, and if globalisation leads to income convergence across nations this might be expected to reduce pressures for migration. In practice these trends are more likely to lead to increased migration. Trends towards income convergence are considered further below, but there is no immediate prospect of a major erosion of international wage differentials between North and South. Further, there appears to be a non-linear relationship between global income differentials and migration pressures. Some domestic industrial development is often necessary to provide potential migrants with internationally marketable skills. Increased international economic integration spreads information more widely about global opportunities so that international labour flows have become more responsive to demand shifts in recipient countries. Thus, development through international economic integration seems more likely to increase migration than to reduce it. Globalisation of product and financial markets reflects political decisions to liberalise as well as falls in transport costs, although the determinants of liberalisation differ across policy areas (Garrett, 2000). By contrast, recipient countries largely can and do control labour inflows; policy-makers face conflicting pressures with demographic changes to develop migration regimes.

International trade

Historically, trade has often played a profound role in economic and social change (Findlay and O'Rourke, 2007). International trade has reached unprecedented levels relative to output, leading to global goods and services markets and the transformation of labour markets as transport costs have fallen and protectionist barriers have been reduced. Trade has grown to unprecedented levels in the post-war period, as shown by Table 3.1, so that it is clearly higher relative to output than during the classical Gold Standard period. More detailed evidence also points to structural breaks in many countries' trade–GDP ratios in the 1970s (Ben-David and Papell, 1997). These figures are for merchandise trade only. Figures for trade in services are more patchy and only available more recently – but they too show a clear upward trend. Trade in goods and services grew more rapidly than GDP over the 1990s and is now equivalent to about 29 per cent of world GDP from around 19 per cent in 1990 (WTO, 2001, p. 1).[4]

Given the post-war growth in non-tradable services, much of it in the public sector, it is useful to compare these figures more directly to value-added in the goods sectors as Table 3.2 does for selected countries. Except for the slightly

Table 3.1 Export–GDP ratios, 1870–1998

	Merchandise Exports as % of GDP (1990 prices)					
	1870	1913	1929	1950	1973	1998
France	4.9	7.8	8.6	7.6	15.2	28.7
Germany	9.5	16.1	12.8	6.2	23.8	38.9
Japan	0.2	2.4	3.5	2.2	7.7	13.4
UK	12.2	17.5	13.3	11.3	14.0	25.0
United States	2.5	3.7	3.6	3.0	4.9	10.1
World	4.6	7.9	9.0	5.5	10.5	17.2

Source: Maddison (2000, p. 363).

Table 3.2 Merchandise trade as percentage of merchandise value-added, 1890–2000

	1890	1913	1960	1970	1980	1990	2000
France	18.5	23.3	16.8	25.7	44.0	53.5	68.0
Germany	22.7	29.2	24.6	31.3	48.5	57.8	78.5
Japan	10.2	23.9	15.3	15.7	25.8	18.9	27.5[a]
Sweden	42.5	37.5	39.7	48.8	72.9	73.1	87.5[b]
UK	61.5	76.3	33.8	40.7	52.6	62.8	63.5
United States	14.3	13.2	9.6	13.7	30.9	35.8	48.3[c]

Note: a: 1999; b: 1998; c: 1997.

Sources: Feenstra (1998); World Bank, World Development Indicators database; US *Economic Report to the President*, 1999.

anomalous case of the UK, there is a clear increase in goods trade relative to goods output. The integration of the United States into the world economy is particularly notable.

These figures should be interpreted with care as they compare gross trade figures relative to measures of value-added. Indeed, firms are increasingly able to divide the production process into different stages and locate them according to comparative advantage, thus increasing trade in inputs and semi-finished manufactures (Krugman, 1995, 2008; Feenstra, 1998). This has significantly increased the import content of manufactured goods in developed countries, leading to the development of interdependent production processes across countries. The fall in transport costs may have bottomed out for shipping but continued to fall for air transport (Hummels, 2007). Falling protectionist trade barriers and transport costs only explain part of this growth of trade (Baier and Bergstrand, 2001). Instead, the changes in the nature of production process detailed have been central to the growth of trade: intermediates accounted for around 40 per cent of non-fuel trade in 2008 (WTO, 2009, p. 2), relatively modest falls in trade costs can induce large rises in trade volumes by allowing for increased vertical specialisation internationally (Hummels et al., 2001; Yi, 2003). This has led to the development of complex international production processes. Figures 3.1 and 3.2 show that whilst this has risen relative to output and trade, latterly these trends appear to have stabilised.

Transport costs and protectionist barriers fell through the post-war period, but a series of key qualitative changes in the 1980s and 1990s have paved the way towards a global free trade regime. Developing countries abandoned protectionist policies, partly as a result of pressure from multilateral institutions; the collapse of the Comecon system and liberalisation in China and Vietnam brought former command economies into the world trading system; the completion of the Uruguay Round of the General Agreement on Tariffs and Trade (GATT) led to the establishment of the World Trade Organization. Most countries and, on some measures, a majority of the world's population are now

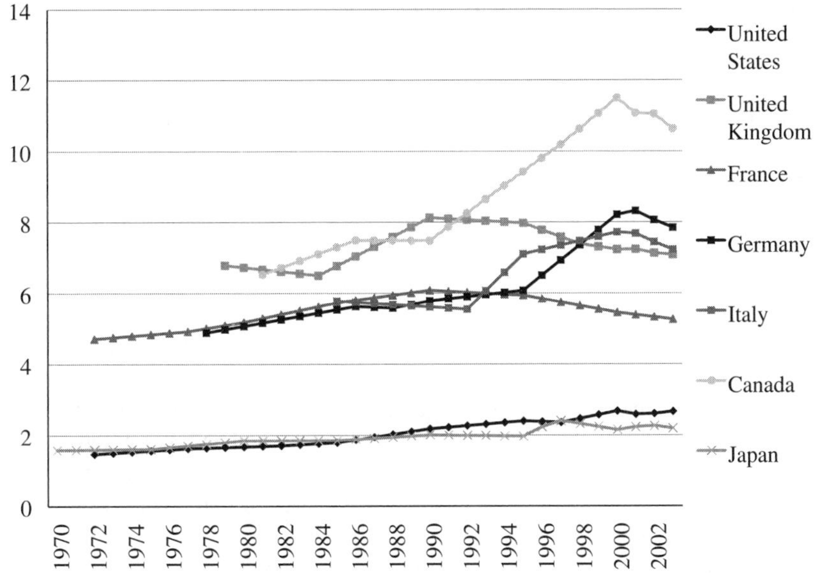

Source: IMF (2007).

Figure 3.1 Total offshoring in G7 economies (% output)

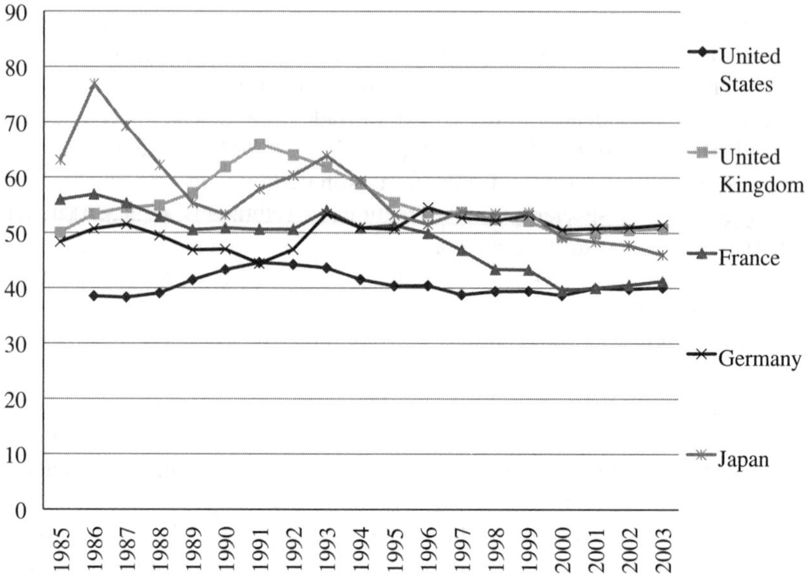

Source: IMF (2007).

Figure 3.2 Total offshoring in G5 economies (% imports)

operating free trade regimes – the share depends critically on the classification of China and India (Sachs and Warner, 1995; Wacziarg and Welch, 2008).[5] Within the picture of global trade liberalisation there are important exceptions, particularly in agricultural goods in which the least developed countries have a comparative advantage.

An extensive trading system has thus developed since World War II. Although there are some regional patterns to trade, interregional trade has grown alongside intra-regional trade. Regional trading arrangements generally appear to be reducing rather than increasing global barriers to trade. The result of this is that trade has led to national markets for goods and services becoming increasingly enmeshed and to global ones emerging. As Estevadeordal and Suominen (2009) show, the emergence of 'spaghetti' trade agreements, increasingly involving countries geographically dispersed and diverse in income, has created a complex web of trading relations, but DeRosa (2007) finds that in general, preferential trading arrangements are trade-creating. Since homogeneous products form a diminishing proportion of trade, price data provides only limited evidence for global markets; Arribas et al. (2009) find that global trading networks have emerged that have been underestimated in earlier studies.

There are two main qualifications that sceptics raise about such figures. First, with much of post-war growth taking place in relatively non-tradable services this represents a case of increasing internationalisation of sectors with falling shares of national income. However, the tradable sector of the economy is not disconnected from the rest: external balance needs to be maintained, it is often central to productivity growth and much of the services sector is not free-standing, but directly connected to goods production. Further, wage rates are often closely related to developments in the tradable sector.

The second main qualification raised by sceptics is that there are persistent distance effects in patterns of trade. It is certainly true that reports of the 'death of distance' have been exaggerated: estimates appear to show a stubborn and largely unchanging effect of geographical distance on trade flows despite falling transport costs and protectionist barriers (Venables, 2001); even recent estimates that directly incorporate transport costs found that evidence for a declining distance effect was largely confined to developed economies with poor, distant economies continuing to face significant apparent barriers (Brun et al., 2005). However, Coe et al. (2007) find evidence for declines in coefficients for distance and other geographical indicators. Indeed, the effect may be subtler than this: Melitz (2007) notes that although distance raises the costs of trade it is also correlated with differences in endowments that drive trade based upon resource differences. Differences in latitude do appear to have significant positive effects on trade, but the decline in resource-based trade relative to manufacturing trade over the post-war period has meant that this positive impact of distance has diminished over time so that some of the continued negative estimated effect of distance is partly picking up the relative decline of resource-based trade.

For much of the post-war period the growth of trade was largely driven by the growth of intra-industry trade as developed countries' markets for manufactures became increasingly enmeshed. However, since the mid-1980s, developing countries' share of world trade has risen continuously largely due to increased manufactured exports. Export growth through their incorporation into the world economy has been central to the development of these newly industrialising economies (NIEs). The growth of these NIEs has led to increased differentiation between developing countries in terms of income levels, wages and the products they export – the spread of industrialisation has been highly uneven. The emergence of new economic giants, notably China and India, has had profound consequence for the world economy as these economies have developed their own independent dynamics (Akin and Kose, 2008). Their major export thrust not only has major competitive implications for the already industrialised economies, but also for export competition with other would-be industrialising economies, which may undermine their development efforts (Coleman, 2007).

Whilst global markets have emerged for many products, the nature of these markets remains under-researched. Some, particularly in primary commodities, are clearly organised on exchanges. Even these are often less perfect than often supposed, with degrees of cartelisation, and some manufactures markets are cartelised too. But other markets, particularly for manufactures, are not so clearly instituted. Intra-industry trade by its very nature entails imperfect, often oligopolistic, competition. The limits to international price convergence – partly due to fluctuations in the exchange rate from financial globalisation – are sometimes taken as evidence against global markets, but this can be analysed in terms of pricing behaviour of oligopolistic companies in international markets (Brinkman, 1999).

The growing extensity and intensity of trade has been matched by the establishment of the WTO, providing an institutional architecture for world trade. Whilst the GATT provided a skeleton framework for governing trade, the WTO is both more invasive as it moves into harmonisation of trade in services, intellectual property rights and investment measures, and has greater powers over national governments. The WTO operates quite clear and stringent rules in its thrust towards global trade liberalisation. Further, by a two-thirds majority the WTO can vote to bring any new subject into its ambit. Although formally a one member–one vote institution, in practice the operation of dispute panels between countries through the WTO has revealed asymmetries of power and resources between developed and developing economies (Narlikar, 2005). Developing countries have been able to negotiate through various coalitions, but the Doha Round of WTO negotiations focused on development issues remains effectively stalled at the time of writing. At the level of industrial policy, the institutionalising of free trade through the WTO has profound effects on national policy options. Many of the trade and industrial policies that were operated by developed countries during their industrialisation – and several newly industrialising economies like Korea and Taiwan in the post-war period – are now no longer permissible under WTO rules – as Ha-Joon Chang points out in his chapter in this volume (Chapter 24) and elsewhere (Chang, 2002).

The impact on macroeconomic policy is considered below as an ensemble with the other aspects of economic globalisation. Textbook trade theory predicts that product market integration would lead to some convergence of factor incomes, although not necessarily to the point of factor price equalisation, and such effects were seen during the classical Gold Standard period (O'Rourke and Williamson, 1999). Increased specialisation in production, so that as industrialised countries have lost markets for low-skill-intensive products demand for their high-skill-intensive products has risen, has led to large falls in demand for, particularly, male manufacturing workers in developed countries, whilst wages for highly skilled workers have tended to rise and differentials widen. Fragmentation of production globally is likely to increase these effects. Many, but by no means all, earlier studies of the shift in demand away from low-skilled labour in developed countries concluded that trade played a secondary role relative to skill-biased technical change; however, other evidence points to significant effects through trade and possible biases that are likely to reduce estimates of its effects (Wood, 1994, 2002). Further, since the initial estimates, exports from developed countries have, as noted, grown considerably in magnitude but also in sophistication, which makes assessing the impact more complex (Krugman, 2008); it may not simply be the lowest skilled that are most vulnerable. As differentiation between developing countries has grown, the effects of trade on their labour markets has become more complex, with less skilled labour not necessarily gaining from trade depending on the relative global position of their country.

Further, focusing on the effects of developed–developing country trade overlooks the effects of trade in general. As Rodrik (1997) points out, increased trade acts to raise the elasticity of demand for labour; similar effects would be expected from foreign direct investment, considered in the next section. Whilst the North–South trade effects flow from orthodox trade theory of comparative advantage determined by relative factor supplies, the increased elasticity of demand for labour result does not assume such trade and can also be derived from a post-Keynesian approach (Galbraith and Berner, 2001). The large effective increase in the global labour force means that labour faces greater competitive pressure, and this has been associated with a decline in labour's share of national income as well as greater wage inequality (IMF, 2007, ch. 5). Increased elasticity of demand for labour has a number of key consequences: it reduces the ability of labour to extract rents in production processes and increases the incidence of taxes and other measures on labour (and other immobile factors). This doesn't mean that welfare states or environmental measures become unaffordable because they make the country 'uncompetitive'. Indeed, amongst developed countries, more open economies tend to have larger welfare states (Rodrik, 1997). This is perhaps not surprising: whilst openness offers the standard gains from trade it also exposes citizens to greater risks. A functioning welfare state financed by progressive taxation can cushion citizens against external fluctuations and, in a rough-and-ready way, ensure that the gainers partially compensate the losers. However, this integration does tend to shift the costs of welfare states onto labour at a time when the demands placed upon them are increasing.

Multinational corporations and foreign direct investment

Foreign direct investment by multinational corporations has grown faster than trade, let alone income, over the post-war period and sales by foreign affiliates of MNCs are now more than double global exports (see Table 3.3). MNCs account for a significant minority of private GDP, particularly in manufactur-

Table 3.3 Sales and output of foreign affiliates of MNCs, 1982–2007

	1982	1990	2000	2007
Foreign affiliates' sales/world exports ratio	1.16	1.25	2.23	1.82
Sales of foreign affiliates/world GDP (%)	23.2	25.5	49.2	57.2
Gross production of foreign affiliates/world GDP (%)	5.3	6.6	9.9	11.0
Exports of foreign affiliates/world exports (%)	30.0	26.6	50.8	33.3

Source: UNCTAD, *World Investment Report*, 2001, p. 10; 2008, p. 10.

Table 3.4 FDI flows as a percentage of gross fixed capital formation, 1982–99

	1982	1989–94 average	1995	1997	1999
World					
Inward	2.5	4.1	5.3	7.5	16.3
Outward	1.7	4.9	5.7	7.4	15.4
Developed countries					
Inward		3.7	4.4	6.1	17.0
Outward		5.5	6.7	8.9	19.4
Developing countries					
Inward		5.2	7.7	10.9	13.8
Outward		2.4	3.3	3.9	3.3

Source: UNCTAD (2001, pp. 10, 312–13).

ing, and, on some estimates, a majority of world trade (with a quarter or more of world trade being between branches of the same company). As major international borrowers and savers, MNCs have been central to the development of global finance. Although FDI remains a minority of total investment, it is growing and significant, as Table 3.4 shows. These figures are partially misleading as the majority of the FDI between developed countries is in the form of mergers and acquisitions, but this is much less true for investment in (and from) developing and transition economies. These figures are by their nature guesstimates; data at the national level indicate that in the manufacturing sector foreign affiliates now account for around a quarter of output in the EU and around 18 per cent in the US, although foreign investment in Japan remains very low.[6] Figures on MNC production of services is patchy, although the tertiary sector now accounts for around 42 per cent of FDI stocks (UNCTAD, 2001, p. 257).

Following economic liberalisation, FDI in transition economies has often accounted for a significant proportion of their national investment. Most FDI flows to developed countries, but the share of developing economies has risen to 21.4 per cent now from 17.1 per cent a decade ago (UNCTAD, 2001, p. 256); inflows to China account for around half of this increase and ten economies account for three-quarters of all FDI inflows to developing countries (ibid., p. 52). In some developing and transition economies MNCs play a key role in production, investment and technology transfer and have played a key role in embryonic industrial clusters and in facilitating export growth. Nevertheless, distribution of FDI stocks is highly uneven, Sutcliffe (2004) finding that stocks are more unevenly distributed globally than income per head. Flows to developing countries remain highly concentrated and typically flow to countries where the developmental process is already established and the conditions for sustained growth are in place rather than playing a catalytic role in development.

Scepticism over the significance of these developments has been expressed on several grounds. Globalisation sceptics stress that MNCs often have the majority of their sales and assets in their home country, along with their core operations, and argue that they remain essentially national companies with international operations (for example, Hirst et al., 1999, ch. 3). Amongst the largest 100 MNCs, foreign operations are substantial, accounting in 1999 for 41.7 per cent of their assets, 49.2 per cent of sales and 45.6 per cent of employment (calculated from UNCTAD, 2001, p. 94). Overseas operations are hardly marginal or peripheral to many MNCs. There are several comments that can be made here. As we have noted, FDI flows continue to grow rapidly; there is no overall slowdown in the growth of MNCs' overseas operations. Part of the trend identified can be attributed to companies aiming to focus on their core competencies; this will not necessarily result in lower international production, but may lead to foreign affiliate production being replaced by outsourcing. A retreat from diversified global production to more focused operations has not necessarily meant a departure from a global strategy (OECD, 2001). Inward FDI is a key source of international competitive pressure; MNCs have both created and are subject to global competition. Focusing on individual companies tends to miss the wider picture: whilst individual MNCs vary in their capacity and strategy for operating production internationally, overall they have increased the responsiveness of output to changes in national conditions. FDI continues to grow and MNCs continue to expand their overseas operations. MNC activity and intra-firm trade remain central to the production and trade of many key industries (OECD, 1996).

The growth and power of MNCs is examined further elsewhere in this volume. The growth of international production has several key consequences. As noted above, increased FDI generally, not just to low-wage countries, has similar effects to increased trade on raising the elasticity of demand for labour (Hatzius, 2000; Molnar et al., 2008). This is beyond simply the effects of outsourcing and relocation of production to low-wage, developing and transition economies. International production tends to undermine national industrial policies and wider social arrangements. Part of this is formal: although attempts to negotiate a global regime for MNCs have so far failed, several WTO measures act to limit countries' policy autonomy. In particular WTO agreements over Trade in Intellectual Property Rights (TRIPS) and Trade-Related Investment Measures (TRIMs) act to limit countries' ability to ensure technology transfer from inward investment and impose performance requirements on MNCs – tools that were used successfully by countries in their post-war development (Lall, 2002). Liberalisation of the inward investment regime has largely proceeded through bilateral agreements: during the 1990s between 80 and 150 regulatory changes to FDI regimes were introduced annually; the vast majority of these made the regime more liberal (UNCTAD, 2001, ch. 4). Governments have fewer policy levers over MNCs.

Arguably the key issue is the generation and diffusion of technology. In Chapter 5 of this volume Jeremy Howells discusses the various forms of globalisation of technology. MNCs have often dominated the most technologically dynamic industries and accounted for the majority of private R&D expenditure, including a growing proportion abroad by foreign affiliates. This has been central to their growth. Companies undertake overseas production where they possess a specific advantage best exploited within the firm through multinational production, rather than exporting from the home base or licensing the technology. Multinationals' growth *qua* multinationals has been based on their ability to generate and exploit technological advantage internationally: not merely did they generate specific advantages through technology creation, their multinational nature enabled them to exploit this advantage around the globe. For much of the post-war period this advantage was typically generated by innovation networks in the company's home country and then diffused world-wide. Increasingly, however, MNCs cannot rely solely on their domestic base for generating technological advantage and have responded by diversifying their innovatory capacity internationally. Rising costs of innovation and the need to tap into overseas innovation networks have led to increasing numbers of joint-ventures and strategic alliances between MNCs for the generation and diffusion of technology. Such developments are particularly common in industries with high levels of recurrent R&D expenditure. Cross-border strategic alliances grew rapidly in the 1980s and continued to grow in the 1990s, often between companies from different continents (OECD, 2001). One key result of globalisation is that for all but the G7 countries foreign R&D had a greater impact on productivity than domestic R&D (Frantzen, 2000); FDI, as well as trade, is an important conduit for this. The international dispersion of technology undermines national industrial and technology strategies.

MNC activity acts to erode the corporate tax base. Differences in corporate tax rates do appear to have significantly affected FDI flows, and corporate tax rates (both headline and effective rates) have declined whilst the cross-country variance has fallen over the past decade amongst advanced countries (Bretschger and Hettich, 2002; Clausing, 2007). In part, governments have responded by broadening the corporate tax base but cutting rates on the most mobile capital. However, these developments do not make welfare states unviable or mean that a low tax/limited welfare regime is necessary to attract FDI (Görg et al., 2009).

Global strategies increase the exit options of MNCs, without necessarily making them footloose. Since technological advantage is necessarily temporary, these developments do not necessarily make national industrial policy ineffective; indeed, by attracting FDI it may enhance them. Nevertheless, MNC activity appears to have led to a shift in industrial policy away from national industrial development strategies and towards an emphasis on offering inducements for inward FDI. For example, Cowling and Tomlinson (2002) find that outward FDI by Japanese corporations hollowed out the home base and undermined Japanese development strategies.

Both the hyper-globalisation and sceptical schools postulate one ideal form of a globalised MNC and compare this with specific firms. This ignores the overall effect of global production and competition arising from MNC activity. Multinationals' ability to produce abroad and response to global competition continues to place constraints upon national economic and industrial strategies.

The globalisation of finance

For many, the most potent example of globalisation is the extraordinary level of international financial transactions. Particularly since the demise of the Bretton Woods system, international finance has grown exponentially to almost astronomical levels for some products. The 2008– crisis illustrated the interconnections of global financial markets as complex derivative products transmitted a crisis originating in the US sub-prime loans market across the world.

The level of transactions is extraordinary, as Table 3.5 shows.[7] Whereas in the early 1970s the ratio of foreign exchange trading to world trade was around 2:1, by the early 1990s this ratio had risen to 50:1 and is around 70:1 today (Eatwell and Taylor, 2000, pp. 3–4); the majority of these foreign exchange positions are held for less than a week. The gross flows are less dramatic, the difference being indicative of the degree of volatility in international financial markets, but Table 3.6 shows a general rise in cross-border capital movements.

A range of evidence points to financial globalisation on an unprecedented scale (Obstfeld and Taylor, 2004, part II; Eichengreen, 2008). External assets

Table 3.5 Cross-border transactions in bonds and equities (% GDP)

	1975	1980	1985	1990	1995	1998
US	4	9	35	89	135	230
Japan	2	8	62	119	65	91
Germany	5	7	33	57	172	334
France	–	5	21	54	187	415
Italy	1	1	4	27	253	640
Canada	3	9	27	65	187	331

Source: Bank for International Settlements, *Annual Report*, 1999, p. 118.

Table 3.6 Gross foreign direct investment plus portfolio investment flows

	Annual Average % of GDP					
	1970–74	1975–79	1980–84	1985–89	1990–95	1996–2000
Canada	1.7	3.4	3.6	6.1	7.2	12.6
France	–	1.3	2.1	4.1	7.2	19.4
Germany	1.2	1.3	1.7	5.2	6.3	17.7
Italy	0.9	0.3	0.6	1.7	5.7	15.6
Japan	–	0.6	2.6	5.9	3.7	4.6
Sweden	1.0	1.2	1.7	5.0	7.0	27.3
UK	3.6	4.0	5.4	14.4	11.9	28.6
US	1.0	1.5	1.4	2.9	3.3	9.3

Sources: 1970–95: IMF, *World Economic Outlook*, May 1997; 1996–2000: calculated from IMF, *Balance of Payments Statistics Yearbook* and *International Financial Statistics Yearbook*, 2002.

and liabilities have grown relative to GDP not just for developed countries, but also amongst emerging economies (Lane and Milesi-Ferretti, 2007). The close correlations between national savings and investment rates, taken by sceptics as evidence of the continued importance of national capital markets, have declined as international payments imbalances have grown. Further, a high correlation between national savings and investment shares can still be consistent with high international capital mobility if the two are jointly determined and/or the government targets the current account. High net capital mobility would only be expected if there were significant differentials in rates of return between countries and these have largely been eliminated, in part due to past capital flows. Whilst investors still retain a home bias towards domestic assets, gross flows of capital have grown, consistent with a high degree of enmeshment between national capital markets. Moreover, this is consistent with much of these flows being speculative: the variance of national current accounts is estimated to be excessive for consumption smoothing amongst developed countries (Ghosh, 1995; Shibata and Shintani, 1998).

Similarly, price evidence points to convergence in interest rates (Obstfeld and Taylor, 2004, part II). When currency can be sold forward, any difference between rates is exactly offset by the difference between the current and forward exchange rate for the period the asset is held, so that returns are equalised when expressed in a common currency (covered interest rate parity holds). Outside of this condition, returns are not equalised so that exchange rates do not exactly move to offset differences in interest rates (uncovered interest rate parity does not hold). Over the longer term there is evidence of convergence of real interest rates amongst the major advanced economies, implying some convergence in the costs of capital. The failure of exchange rates to move to offset differences in interest rates, at least in the short run, is due both to variations over time in the premium over standard interest rates that the markets demand for holding assets denominated in particular currencies, and to operational features of the foreign exchange markets. Market operators use forecasts of exchange rates based both on an analysis of economic fundamentals and trend spotting in data series ('chartism'). Since there is a range of opinions amongst traders this creates the conditions for high volumes of trading and possibilities for speculation. In particular, chartism can lead to speculative bubbles that drive the exchange rate away from its equilibrium value, the short-term focus of most traders leading to a relative concentration on such movements. Convergence of interest rates and integration of capital markets has led to narrowing of differences in the cost of capital although key differences remain because of the difficulties of enforcing claims across borders (Stulz, 2005). Overall we may conclude:

> The world still does not fit the traditional model of perfect capital mobility, in which all national savings flow into one global 'pool' of savings, with equalized real interest rates and domestic investment completely uncorrelated with national saving in each country. This, however, is not due to a lack of integration of financial markets, but rather to other features of the contemporary global economy which were ignored in the traditional model. (Blecker, 2002, p. 136)

The position of developing countries is more complex and the integration of their financial systems with global markets is often lower. Developing countries would be expected to pay a premium on developed country interest rates to reflect their greater default risk, but this becomes counter-productive when it simply increases the probability of default and thus decreases the expected return; at this point credit rationing operates to prevent further lending. Since debtors continue to repay past loans at rates determined in the global market and agents within them can move funds to international markets, developing countries remain part of global financial markets. After effectively being excluded from international financial markets after the debt crisis in the 1980s (see further Gary Dymski's Chapter 6), flows to developing countries resumed on a significant scale in the 1990s. The 1997 East Asian currency crisis disrupted these flows again, although there are clear signs of a resumption since; the flows remain concentrated on leading economies in Asia and Latin America and the leading transition economies.

What are the policy implications of these developments? The sanguine view is that the only restrictions global finance imposes on national governments is to stop them pursuing policies that are unsustainable, or at least harmful, anyway. This view is hard to sustain after the exchange rate crises since the late 1990s.

Standard economic analysis since Mundell–Fleming indicates that, in the absence of capital controls, countries can choose between fixing their exchange rate or pursuing an independent monetary policy. Capital controls were largely abolished amongst industrialised countries by the 1990s and there has been widespread capital account liberalisation amongst developing and transition economies under pressure from international agencies and in an attempt to attract private finance. However, the Mundell–Fleming dichotomy is ceasing to be an accurate representation of policy choices available to national authorities. Financial globalisation rendered fixed exchange rate systems increasingly unsustainable.

Earlier crises were typically caused by unsustainable policies, but the 1990s saw the emergence of 'second generation' crises where a speculative attack raises the output and employment costs of maintaining a currency peg so that governments are forced to abandon otherwise sustainable pegs. With 'third generation' crises it is a build-up of foreign debt that becomes unsustainable; whereas 'second generation' crises are typically triggered during an economic downturn (as with European Monetary System countries over 1992–93), 'third generation' crises can occur with booming economic activity and sound fiscal and monetary positions (as with the East Asian countries in 1997). Furthermore, whereas the effects of 'second generation' crises are largely benign – countries' output and employment rise following post-crisis devaluation – 'third generation' crises tend to be contractionary since the post-crisis devaluation raises the domestic currency debt burden and can lead to widespread business bankruptcy. In either case, even if there are imbalances in the economy's fundamentals the question remains as to why the markets provide large inflows of capital for years before suddenly and sharply reversing these flows. As Obstfeld and Taylor (2004, p. 10) note:

> Unfortunately, market discipline often seems insufficient to deter misbehaviour. Capital markets may tolerate inconsistent policies too long and then abruptly reverse course, inflicting punishment far harsher than the underlying policy 'crimes' would seem to warrant. And in some cases, capital-market openness has constrained the pursuit of arguably desirable economic goals.

The emergence of financial crisis across the developed world and beyond has shown the potential for systemic risk, the high cost of bank bailouts and the scale of potential losses of output (cf. IMF, 2009, esp. ch. 4).

The logic of these has been taken to imply that countries' choice is now limited to floating rates or full monetary union (Eichengreen, 2008). Whilst increased capital mobility (and openness to trade) has acted to reduce national policy autonomy in the expected ways, it has also weakened countries' ability to pursue independent monetary policies with floating exchange rates. Financial innovations and global flows have weakened both national authorities' control over monetary aggregates and their ultimate relationship to target variables. Turbulent capital flows lead to exchange rates diverging from values consistent with either interest rate differentials or the relative costs of producing goods and services. The result of this is that exchange rates cease to be an effective equilibrating mechanism or an effective policy tool (UNCTAD, 2007, ch. 1). Even monetary union does not necessarily provide immunity from speculation, as several euro-area countries have found recently.

Whilst variations in government spending, taxation and general macroeconomic policy point to a continued range of national policy options, the response of markets increases the uncertainty policy-makers face in the response to macro-policies. Markets' response to government policies depends on their assessment of the economic credibility of the government; as such there is no set market response to particular policies (Mosley, 2003). Rather than global financial markets imposing particular policies on national governments, they have significantly changed the costs associated with particular policies and instruments through their effects on interest rate risk premia and exchange rate movements; at times these costs may be so high as to make the policy prohibitively expensive. Moreover, governments do not face clear policy rules, but uncertainty over market reactions as markets have periodically supported policies before turning suddenly and sharply against them. This induces policy caution amongst governments and tends to lead to a deflationary bias in macroeconomic policy (see also Blecker, 2002). With developing countries this is accentuated by the IMF's bias towards deflationary policies, which after the 1997 East Asian crisis even drew criticism from the World Bank (Stiglitz, 2002). The instability of contemporary financial integration inhibits rational planning for firms and governments and raises systemic risks; Eatwell and Taylor (2000) point to a number of possible policy responses to reduce this instability. The aftermath of the East Asian crisis has put capital controls back onto the agenda and whilst national regulatory authorities have largely played catch-up with international financial integration, potential leverage remains: banks remain dependent on national central banks to act as crisis managers and lenders of last resort as the 2008– crisis has dramatically shown.

The effects of financial globalisation go beyond its impact on macroeconomic policy. State direction of finance, a key policy tool of developmental states and several industrial countries, is sharply undermined. Grahl (2002) argues that the level of international financial transactions observed is not simply speculative, but indicative of the emergence of a global financial system. Whilst much finance may still be raised nationally, global finance provides the key alternative source and use for funds and as such sets benchmark rates of return. The exit possibilities offered by global financial markets undermine the 'voice'-based systems of national finance often claimed to underlie continental and East Asian alternative forms of capitalism to the Anglo-Saxon variant.

By starting from a conception of a perfect international capital market under which there would be few, if any, speculative flows, both the hyper-globalisation and sceptical views miss key features of contemporary financial globalisation and its differences from earlier episodes. Interest rates are now determined globally, and although national differences remain in other financial markets they are increasingly affected by global developments. Above all, the speculative nature of much of these flows not merely severely limits government freedom for manoeuvre, but does so in a manner that is unpredictable.

Consequences and policy implications

Economic globalisation has been interpreted here as both a rise in economic activity that is world-wide in scope and a growing intensification of economic flows and activities across societies and between people, a process of both growing extensity and intensity. Global product and financial markets have emerged. Multinational corporations operate global business strategies and have created global competition. This has had a profound effect on growth, labour markets and incomes and the macro- and microeconomic policies that governments can pursue. These changes are driven by a combination of technological change, deliberate policy choice – albeit often under pressure from regulatory competition and/or multilateral agencies – and market processes and entrepreneurial activity: it is the market processes that are important here more than particular states of competition. These processes do not necessarily lead to convergence in incomes.

The evidence presented so far indicates that globalisation processes and their institutionalisation, particularly through the WTO, have weakened the effectiveness of national governments' traditional macroeconomic and microeconomic policy instruments. Furthermore, increased trade and factor mobility have increased the elasticity of demand for labour and thereby reduced labour's bargaining power. Cross-country differences remain important but globalisation has contributed to a general rise in inequality amongst developed countries (Alderson and Nielsen, 2002).

The benign view of globalisation sees it as boosting growth and development throughout the world. Openness to trade and investment boosts growth, and growth raises the income of the poor and thereby reduces poverty, the argument runs (for example, Dollar and Kraay, 2004). As Milanovic (2003, pp. 667–8) notes:

> It is only a slight caricaturization of this naïve view to state that its proponents regard globalization as a *deus ex machina* for many of the problems, such as poverty, illiteracy or inequality, that beset the developing world. The only thing that a country needs to do is to open up its borders, reduce tariff rates, attract foreign investment and in a few generations if not less the poor will become rich, the illiterate will learn how to read and write, and inequality will vanish as poor countries catch up with the rich.

There are several grounds for some scepticism here. The link between growth and economic openness and liberalisation is weaker than this account suggests (cf. Mosley, 2000). Moreover, the widespread shift amongst developing countries to greater openness noted above has coincided with a slowdown in their growth rates compared with earlier in the post-war period (Weisbrot et al., 2007); this may in part be due to deflationary biases in the global economy. Gains from trade openness may be lower than in earlier periods and the link between growth and poverty reduction is not as automatic as this account implies. Accounts of this sort typically assume a simple catch-up or convergence story where poorer countries are expected to grow faster than richer ones so that income differentials will narrow over time (usually conditional on countries maintaining open, liberalised economies). However, as noted above, work in the 'new economic geography' has shown how integration under external scale economies can lead to spatial inequalities. Other evidence indicates that apparent estimated income convergence processes may actually be leading to a 'twin peaks' distribution of income levels with the emergence of two (or more) groups of countries at different income levels (Quah, 1997). This is at the level of countries; at the level of individuals, claims that global poverty and inequality fell between the 1980s and 1990s as a result of globalisation – and particularly the growth of China and India – are problematic (Wade, 2004; Milanovic, 2005).

The emergence of the 2008– crisis illustrates the processes and downsides of contemporary globalisation (Turner, 2008). Although the causes of it remain to be determined fully, global capital imbalances saw major inflows to the US and other economies fuelling asset price bubbles. Downward pressure on prices from the rise in emerging country exports kept inflation rates low, which led to inappropriate monetary policy that fuelled the asset price boom. Whilst globalisation pressures limited the growth of real wages, households maintained their consumption levels by borrowing against expected house price inflation. Globalisation thus fuelled the unsustainable processes that led up to the crisis.

This is not, however, to endorse the radical version of the hyper-globalisation position. Whilst this highlights inequities in global exchange – notably, developed country governments preaching trade liberalisation whilst maintaining barriers to products (particularly in agriculture) – it is too limited a perspective. Trade and international capital flows do provide important potential gains, even though these have often been exaggerated, and their distribution – both between countries and within them – remains uneven. Despite the pressures of globalisation, countries are still able to maintain welfare states, whilst globalisation does offer possibilities for growth by developing countries even though this is much less automatic than triumphalist accounts suggest. The global problems this perspective highlights – notably, environmental degradation and persistent poverty – are just that: global. They would not cease if globalisation processes were reversed; nor is the record of autarchic societies encouraging. The 'take-it-or-leave-it' view of globalisation informs many politicians, opinion-makers and activists in a way that is misleading and unhelpful in its prescriptions. Conceiving globalisation as either an inexorable force we must live with or something to be resisted as we retreat to small-scale local economies does not provide useful guides as to how we might manage market failures on a global scale.

The key problem here is the perspective that globalisation processes necessarily entail a particular trajectory of free market liberalisation. It is here that the sceptical position, whilst significantly underestimating the scope and impact of globalisation processes, makes several key points. National governments do retain key powers. In some respects states, especially developed countries, have more power than ever before, but the demands placed upon them are also unprecedented. The sceptical position recognises that markets are not protean entities but require governance. The key limitation of their position here is an under-emphasis on the global pressures that transform markets and an overemphasis on the efficacy of national governance of markets.

Increasingly, what is needed is imaginative proposals for governance of global markets to deal with inequalities and global market failures. Although the main international economic agencies have been seen as operating to promote 'Washington Consensus' policies, there are signs that the World Bank at least is shifting (Stiglitz, 2002) in part as a result of external pressure from governments and citizens' groups. It is notable that recent success stories – China, India and others – have operated active policies that differ significantly from 'Washington Consensus' prescriptions (Rodrik, 2007). Economic globalisation is a contested process and it has been accompanied by a significant internationalisation of both political authority (as governments cooperate with others in decision-making) and a corresponding globalisation of political activity. This multilateral system institutionalises a process of political coordination amongst governments, intergovernmental and transnational agencies – public and private – designed to realise common purposes or collective goods through making or implementing global or transnational rules, and managing trans-border problems, for example the WTO. Of course, it is scarred by enormous inequalities of power, and remains a product of the inter-state system. But it has, nevertheless, created the infrastructure of a global polity and new arenas through which globalisation itself is promoted, contested or regulated. Further reform and integration of institutions is desirable; in this context the decoupling of trade issues from environmental and labour issues may be helpful. The late twentieth century has seen the emergence of global economic processes of an unprecedented scale becoming deeply enmeshed with national and local economic processes. The nature of these processes has radically changed the costs and benefits of particular economic activities and national economic strategies. The task of political economy in an era of globalisation is to adapt existing theoretical tools to explain these developments and to suggest what policy tools may be effective for managing them.

Notes

1. On Friedman's thesis see the symposium: 'The world is not flat: Putting globalisation in its place', *Cambridge Journal of Regions, Economy and Society*, **1**(3) (2008).
2. See Baldwin and Martin (1999), Held *et al.* (1999), Bordo *et al.* (2000), Perraton (2001).
3. An explanation of the term 'extensity' is located in Chapter 8 (p. 174) of this volume.
4. These figures are just for recorded trade; the United Nations (UNDP, 1999, p. 5) estimated that the global illegal drugs trade alone was equivalent to 8 per cent of world trade in 1995. More generally, global links and technologies have aided the 'dark side' of globalisation with the emergence of global criminal networks.
5. Wacziarg and Welch (2008) reclassify both countries as closed in 2001, although the basis for characterising China in particular as a closed economy is questionable.
6. OECD, *Measuring Globalisation: The Role of Multinationals in OECD Economies*, 2001 volume (Paris: OECD).
7. Figures for the UK are probably even higher (cf. Held et al., 1999, p. 224).

References

Akin, C. and M. Kose (2008), 'Changing nature of North–South linkages: stylized facts and explanations', *Journal of Asian Economics*, **19**(1), 1–28.

Alderson, A. and F. Nielsen (2002), 'Globalization and the great U-Turn: income inequality trends in 16 OECD countries', *American Journal of Sociology*, **107**(5), 1244–99.

Arribas, I., F. Pérez and E. Tortosa-Ausina (2009), 'Measuring globalization of international trade', *World Development*, **37**(1), 127–45.

Baier, S. and J. Bergstrand (2001), 'The growth of world trade: tariffs, transport costs, and income similarity', *Journal of International Economics*, **53**(1), 1–27.

Baldwin, R. and P. Martin (1999), 'Two waves of globalisation: superficial similarities, fundamental differences', in H. Siebert (ed.), *Globalisation and Labour*, Tubingen: Mohr, pp. 3–58.

Ben-David, D. and D. Papell (1997), 'International trade and structural change', *Journal of International Economics*, **43**(3–4), 513–23.

Blecker, R. (2002), 'International capital mobility, macroeconomic imbalances, and the risk of global contraction', in J. Eatwell and L. Taylor (eds), *International Capital Markets*, Oxford: Oxford University Press, pp. 127–76.

Bordo, M., B. Eichengreen and D. Irwin (2000), 'Is globalization today really different than globalization a hundred years ago?', in M. Richardson (ed.), *Globalisation and International Trade Liberalisation*, Cheltenham, UK and Northampton, MA, USA: Edward Elgar.

Braithwaite, J. and P. Drahos (2000), *Global Business Regulation*, Cambridge: Cambridge University Press.

Bretschger, L. and F. Hettich (2002), 'Globalisation, capital mobility and tax competition: theory and evidence for OECD countries', *European Journal of Political Economy*, **18**(4), 695–716.

Brinkman, H.-J. (1999), *Explaining Prices in the Global Economy*, Cheltenham, UK and Northampton, MA, USA: Edward Elgar.

Brun, J.-F., C. Carrère, P. Guillaumont and J. de Melo (2005), 'Has distance died? Evidence from a panel gravity model', *World Bank Economic Review*, **19**(1), 99–120.

Chang, H.-J. (2002), *Kicking Away the Ladder: Development Strategy in Historical Perspective*, London: Anthem Press.

Clausing, K. (2007), 'Corporate tax revenues in OECD countries', *International Tax and Public Finance*, **14**(2), 115–33.

Coe, D., A. Subramanian and N. Tamirisa (2007), 'The missing globalization puzzle: evidence of the declining importance of distance', *IMF Staff Papers*, **54**(1), 34–58.

Coleman, W. (2007), 'Accommodating emerging giants', mimeographed, Duke University.

Cowling, K. and P. Tomlinson (2002), 'Revisiting the roots of Japan's economic stagnation: the role of the Japanese corporation', *International Review of Applied Economics*, **16**(4), 373–90.

DeRosa, D. (2007), 'The trade effects of preferential arrangements', Working Paper No. 0 7–1, Washington DC: Peterson Institute for International Economics.

Dollar, D. and A. Kraay (2004), 'Trade, growth and poverty', *Economic Journal*, **114**(493), F22–F49.

Eatwell, J. and L. Taylor (2000), *Global Finance at Risk: The Case for International Regulation*, Cambridge: Polity Press.

Eichengreen, B. (2008), *Globalizing Capital: A History of the International Monetary System*, Princeton, NJ: Princeton University Press.

Estevadeordal, A. and K. Suominen (2009), *The Sovereign Remedy? Trade Agreements in a Globalizing World*, Oxford: Oxford University Press.

Feenstra, R. (1998), 'Integration of trade and disintegration of production in the global economy', *Journal of Economic Perspectives*, **12**(4), 31–50.

Findlay, R. and K. O'Rourke (2007), *Power and Plenty: Trade, War, and the World Economy in the Second Millennium*, Princeton, NJ: Princeton University Press.

Frantzen, D. (2000), 'Innovation, international technological diffusion and the changing influence of R&D on productivity', *Cambridge Journal of Economics*, **24**(2), 193–210.

Friedman, T. (2006), *The World is Flat: The Globalized World in the Twenty-First Century*, London: Penguin.

Galbraith, J. and M. Berner (eds) (2001), *Inequality and Industrial Change: A Global View*, Cambridge: Cambridge University Press.

Garrett, G. (2000), 'The determinants of globalization', *Comparative Political Studies*, **33**(6–7), 941–91.

Ghosh, A. (1995), 'International capital mobility amongst the major industrialised countries: too little or too much?', *Economic Journal*, **105**(428), 107–28.

Gomory, R. and W. J. Baumol (2000), *Global Trade and Conflicting National Interests*, Cambridge, MA: The MIT Press.

Görg, H., H. Molana and C. Montagna (2009), 'Foreign direct investment, tax competition and social expenditure', *International Review of Economics and Finance*, **18**(1), 31–7.

Grahl, J. (2002), 'Globalized finance', *New Left Review*, **8**, Mar/Apr, 23–47.

Gray, J. (2009), *False Dawn: The Delusions of Global Capitalism*, London: Granta.

Greider, W. (1997), *One World, Ready or Not*, London: Penguin Books.

Hatton, T. and J. Williamson (2005), *Global Migration and the World Economy*, Cambridge, MA: The MIT Press.

Hatzius, J. (2000), 'Foreign direct investment and factor demand elasticities', *European Economic Review*, **42**(1), 117–43.
Held, D., A. McGrew, D. Goldblatt and J. Perraton (1999), *Global Transformations: Politics, Economics and Culture*, Cambridge: Polity Press.
Hirst, P., G. Thompson and S. Bromley (2009), *Globalization in Question*, Third Edition, Cambridge: Polity Press.
Hummels, D. (2007), 'Transportation costs and international trade in the second era of globalization', *Journal of Economic Perspectives*, **21**(3), 131–54.
Hummels, D., J. Ishii and K.-M. Yi (2001), 'The nature and growth of vertical specialization in world trade', *Journal of International Economics*, **54**(1), 75–96.
IMF (2007), *World Economic Outlook: Spillovers and Cycles in the Global Economy*, Washington DC: International Monetary Fund.
IMF (2009), *World Economic Outlook: Sustaining the Recovery*, Washington DC: International Monetary Fund.
Kozul-Wright, R. (1995), 'Transnational corporations and the nation state', in J. Michie and J. Grieve Smith (eds), *Managing the Global Economy*, Oxford: Oxford University Press.
Krugman, P. (1995), 'Growing world trade: causes and consequences', *Brookings Papers on Economic Activity*, 1, 327–62.
Krugman, P. (2008), 'Trade and wages, reconsidered', *Brookings Papers on Economic Activity*, **1**, 103–54.
Krugman, P. and A. Venables (1995), 'Globalization and the inequality of nations', *Quarterly Journal of Economics*, **110**(4), 857–80.
Lall, S. (2002), 'Transnational corporations and technology flows', in D. Nayyar (ed.), *Governing Globalization*, Oxford: Oxford University Press.
Lane, P. and G. Milesi-Ferretti (2007), 'The external wealth of nations mark II: revised and extended estimates of foreign assets and liabilities, 1970–2004', *Journal of International Economics*, **73**(2), 223–50.
Lucas, R.E. (2000), 'Some macroeconomics for the 21st century', *Journal of Economic Perspectives*, **14**(1), 159–68.
Maddison, A. (2000), *The World Economy: A Millennial Perspective*, Paris: OECD.
Melitz, J. (2007), 'North, south and distance in the gravity model', *European Economic Review*, **51**(4), 971–91.
Milanovic, B. (2003), 'The two faces of globalization', *World Development*, **31**, 667–83.
Milanovic, B. (2005), *Worlds Apart: Measuring International and Global Inequality*, Princeton, NJ: Princeton University Press.
Molnar, M., N. Pain and D. Taglioni (2008), 'Globalisation and employment in the OECD', *OECD Economic Studies*, **44**(1), 1–34.
Mosley, L. (2003), *Global Capital and National Governments*, Cambridge: Cambridge University Press.
Mosley, P. (2000), 'Globalisation, economic policy and convergence', *World Economy*, **23**(5), 613–34.
Narlikar, A. (2005), *The World Trade Organization*, Oxford: Oxford University Press.
Obstfeld, M. and A.M. Taylor (2004), *Global Capital Markets: Integration, Crisis, and Growth*, Cambridge: Cambridge University Press.
OECD (1996), *Globalisation of Industry: Overview and Sector Reports*, Paris: Organisation for Economic Co-operation and Development.
OECD (2001), *New Patterns of Industrial Globalisation: Cross-Border Mergers and Acquisitions and Strategic Alliances*, Paris: Organisation for Economic Co-operation and Development.
O'Rourke, K. and J. Williamson (1999), *Globalization and History*, Cambridge, MA: MIT Press.
Perraton, J. (2001), 'The global economy – myths and realities', *Cambridge Journal of Economics*, **25**(5), 669–84.
Quah, D. (1997), 'Empirics for growth and distribution: stratification, polarization, and convergence clubs', *Journal of Economic Growth*, **2**, 27–59.
Rodrik, D. (1997), *Has Globalization Gone Too Far?*, Washington, DC: Institute for International Economics.

Rodrik, D. (2007), *One Economics, Many Recipes: Globalization, Institutions, and Economic Growth*, Princeton, NJ: Princeton University Press.
Sachs, J. and A. Warner (1995), 'Economic reform and the process of global integration', *Brookings Papers on Economic Activity*, **26**(1), 1–118.
Shibata, A. and M. Shintani (1998), 'Capital mobility in the world economy', *Journal of International Money and Finance*, **17**(5), 741–56.
Stalker, P. (2000), *Workers without Frontiers: The Impact of Globalization on International Migration*, London: Lynne Rienner.
Standage, T. (1999), *The Victorian Internet: The Remarkable Story of the Telegraph and the Nineteenth Century's Online Pioneers*, London: Phoenix.
Stiglitz, J. (2002), *Globalization and its Discontents*, London: The Penguin Press.
Stulz, R. (2005), 'The limits of financial globalization', *Journal of Finance*, **60**(4), 1595–1638.
Sutcliffe, B. (2004), 'World inequality and globalization', *Oxford Review of Economic Policy*, **20**(1), 15–37.
Turner, G. (2008), *The Credit Crunch: Housing Bubbles, Globalisation and the Worldwide Economic Crisis*, London: Pluto Press.
UNCTAD (2001), *World Investment Report 2001*, New York: United Nations.
UNCTAD (2007), *Trade and Development Report 2007*, New York: United Nations.
UNCTAD (2008), *World Investment Report 2008*, New York: United Nations.
UNDP (1999), *Human Development Report 1999*, New York: Oxford University Press.
UNDP (2009), *Human Development Report 2009*, New York: Oxford University Press.
Venables, A. (2001), 'Geography and international inequalities: the impact of new technologies', *Journal of Industry, Competition and Trade*, **1**(2): 135–89.
Wacziarg, R. and K. Welch (2008), 'Trade liberalization and growth: new evidence', *World Bank Economic Review*, **22**(2), 187–231.
Wade, R.H. (2004), 'Is globalization reducing poverty and inequality?', *World Development*, **32**(4), 567–89.
Weisbrot, M., D. Baker and D. Rosnick (2007), 'The scorecard on development: 25 years of diminished progress', in K.S. Jomo (ed.), *Flat World, Big Gaps: Economic Liberalization, Globalization, Poverty and Inequality*, London: Zed Books, pp. 24–47.
Wood, A. (1994), *North–South Trade, Employment and Inequality*, Oxford: Oxford University Press.
Wood, A. (2002), 'Globalization and wage inequalities: a synthesis of three theories', *Review of World Economics*, **138**(1), 54–82.
WTO (2001), *International Trade Statistics 2001*, Geneva: World Trade Organization.
WTO (2009), *International Trade Statistics 2009*, Geneva: WTO.
Yi, K.-M. (2003), 'Can vertical specialization explain the growth of world trade?', *Journal of Political Economy*, **111**(1), 52–102.

4 Measures of globalisation and their misinterpretation*

Bob Sutcliffe and Andrew Glyn

Almost everybody seems to believe that globalisation is happening at a headlong pace, and is the defining characteristic of contemporary capitalism. Some like it; others see it as the source of all evil. But most see it as both unprecedented and irresistible. In an earlier paper (Glyn and Sutcliffe, 1992) we analysed indicators of economic internationalisation in their historical perspective and found reason for serious scepticism with regard to the image of world capitalism presented by those who believe that it has been unprecedentedly transformed by globalisation; similar points have been made by a variety of authors from various perspectives (Sachs and Warner, 1995; Hirst and Thompson, 1996). This chapter seeks to reinforce this 'globalo-scepticism', paying particular attention to why different statistical measures of recent trends suggest alternative conclusions and to which of them are the most meaningful.

We do not question that globalisation in one of its meanings – the world-wide spread of capitalist relations in production and distribution – has been a major feature of the last 50 years. This has taken the form of the decline in peasant production, the absorption of domestic workers, mainly women, into the paid labour force and most recently the decline of state productive activity in both communist and non-communist countries.

The globalisation debate, however, is mainly couched in terms of another concept: the increasing international integration of economic activity. This is seen to have been the central event of the current epoch of world social and economic development. Some see it as the whole process of post-World War II development, others more as a phase in that development which has been especially marked since the late 1970s and is associated with other features of that period such as the growth of neo-liberal economic ideology.

It is our opinion that the degree of globalisation in this sense, as well as its novelty, has been greatly exaggerated. Consider the following two paragraphs:

1. An ever-increasing proportion of the world's production is sold outside the countries where it was produced. International trade has grown more than production in every year since 1945. And over the whole period since then

foreign investment has grown even more rapidly than trade. Capitalist corporations operate increasingly in more than one country; and the value of the world-wide sales of MNCs and of their associated companies comes to more than one third of the gross product of the world. The number of MNCs has risen from 7000 in the early 1960s to more than 60 000 in the year 2000.

2. The immense majority of what is produced in the world is consumed in its country of production, as it was in 1913. This percentage may grow because services, which are traded less than goods, are increasing disproportionately. The largest MNCs now produce a lower percentage of output in the USA than they did in 1977. The value of the sales of branches of US and Japanese MNCs is growing more slowly than the world economy as a whole. No more than 12 per cent of the world's capital stock is foreign-owned; foreign investment is not much greater in relation to world output than it was in 1913.

Which of these two cameos corresponds to the real face of capitalism today? The answer is that this question is like the famous optical illusion puzzles in which one line looks longer than the other when they are really exactly the same length. Both the sentences are based on exactly the same body of information. They simply select and present it in a different way. To reach the right answer you have to use the right technique for looking. When assessing quantitative indicators, there can be differences of opinion over whether some measure is large or small, whether some trend shows an important or an unimportant change. But a precondition for such debate is an analysis of what indicators are most appropriate. Many people seem to have an exaggerated impression of the present degree of globalisation, in most of its dimensions, and of its rate of increase, in at least some respects. Our objective in what follows is to lay out as clearly as we can what seem to us to be the best measures of globalisation, focusing on trade, foreign direct investment and importance of multinationals (the internationalisation of financial flows is less contentious).

International trade in goods and services

Probably the most widely known 'fact' about the world economy today is that never has so much of world output been exported to other countries, in other words trade as a proportion of production is unprecedentedly high. In his authoritative overview of historical trends Maddison (1995, pp. 37–8) measures the degree of trade integration by the ratio of merchandise exports to GDP at constant prices. This gives dramatic results for Europe in particular – the export ratio declining from 16 per cent in 1913 to 9 per cent in 1950 before rising to 21 per cent in 1973 and 30 per cent in 1992. It appears that the importance of trade has tripled since 1950 and now far exceeds its weight in the economy reached at the end of the classical free trade period, and such figures are widely quoted in discussions of globalisation (see Rodrik, 2000 and Bourguignon et al., 2002).

A rising share of exports, measured in constant prices, implies that the volume of exports has grown faster than the volume of production overall, a comparison frequently made to demonstrate the growing importance of trade. For example exports grew by 5.1 per cent per year for the EU-15 over the period 1970–99 against the 2.4 per cent per year growth rate for GDP (OECD 2001: tables 3.1 and 4.8). Such constant price comparisons, however, exaggerate changes in the weight of exports in the economy.

This is because the prices of exports rise systematically more slowly than do prices for output as a whole. For the EU-15 over the period 1970–99 the deflator for exports rose by 4.3 per cent per year whilst the GDP deflator rose by 5.8 per cent per year. So over this period around half of the discrepancy between export and GDP volume growth was offset by a slower growth of export prices. The fall in the relative export prices reflects the faster than average growth of labour productivity in the export sector compared to the economy as a whole. For example, over the period 1960–94 labour productivity in EU manufacturing, where exports are concentrated, grew at 4.1 per cent per year whilst GDP per person employed increased at only 2.7 per cent per year. This relatively rapid productivity growth in the export sector means that the share of employment devoted to exports grew systematically more slowly than the share of exports in output at constant prices. It is the share of export at current prices which most closely reflects productivity gains and thus the share of resources devoted to exporting activity. This measure shows a less dramatic change than the constant price figures.

In fact, in 1999 the shares of exports in GDP at current prices exceeded the levels of 1913 by a comparatively modest degree (Table 4.1). This is true for the OECD countries in total and for the USA, Europe and Japan taken separately. Whilst such an historical perspective is interesting its relevance to discussions about constraints on post-1945 systems of national economic management may seem limited (see Bairoch and Kozul-Wright, 1996 for discussion of the pre-1914 period). Much more significant from that point of view is the post-war period experience. Despite the recovery of world trade in volume terms, trade shares recovered quite slowly in the 1950s and 1960s when manufacturing productivity was growing very fast and thus the relative prices of exports were falling. Export shares then increased markedly in the early 1970s as OECD countries exported more to oil producers and developing countries to pay for the higher cost of oil. In the last quarter century, with globalisation apparently in full spate, export shares have risen only by one quarter in the USA and the EU and in Japan have actually fallen.

Table 4.1 Exports as percentage of GDP, 1913–94

Current Prices	1913	1950	1960	1974	1989	1999
USA	6	4.6	5.2	8.5	9.4	10.7
EU	22	16.7	19.1	25.9	28.0	32.1
Japan	20	11.8	10.7	13.6	10.6	10.4
OECD	16	10.5	12.3	17.0	18.0	22.1

Source: OECD (2001) for 1974 and later years; linked to OECD, *National Accounts of Member Countries*; figures for 1913 assume that the differences as compared to 1950 are equal to those estimated by Maddison for Merchandise Exports only (1991: Table F7).

Whilst the ratio of current price exports to GDP is the best measure of the trend in the importance of production for overseas markets it is subject to one upward bias. Exports include an import content so that their value exaggerates the value-added contributed to them by the domestic economy. Thus before comparing exports to GDP the import content should really be subtracted. A crude adjustment suggests that some 26 per cent of European GDP was devoted to export production in 1999 rather than 32 per cent in the unadjusted data.

The upshot is that the best simple measure of the trend in the direct importance of trade for the domestic economy is the export share at current prices. This shows a relatively modest rise over the past 25 years, contrary to the exaggerated impression derived from constant price series. Even the current price export shares exaggerate the level of trade dependence because of the inclusion of the import content of exports.

The export share shows the proportion of economic activity which has to compete internationally on world markets. In a developed country with a classical structure of imports – raw materials, food and fuel – they represent interdependence but are complementary to domestic production, not in competition with it. But now imported manufactures represent an additional competitive pressure on substantial sections of the economy over and above that derived from export markets. Table 4.2 shows that the classic division of labour has been unwinding for OECD countries as the share of imported food and materials slipped down; over the past decade falling oil prices have even reduced the share of imported energy to below that of 1964. Thus the share of manufactures in total OECD imports grew over the past 40 years from one half to four-fifths. As Feenstra (1998) has emphasised many of these manufactured imports are intermediate goods – semi-finished and components.

The impact of international competition within domestic economies is most clearly displayed in the degree of import penetration of the domestic market for manufactures (Table 4.3).

Table 4.2 Product composition of OECD imports

	Food	Materials	Energy	Machinery	Other Manufacturing
1964	18	16	11	19	34
1974	12	11	22	21	34
1989	9	6	10	34	41
1998	8	4	7	40	41

Source: OECD (2001): Tables 12 and 13.

Table 4.3 Import penetration of domestic markets for manufactures, 1913–99

	1913	1950	1963	1974	1989	1999	From 'South' 1999
USA	3	2	3	6	14	21	9
Japan	34	3	4	5	5	6	5
Europe	13	6	11	17	21	29	8

Note: The figures represent imports as a percentage of apparent consumption (production plus imports less exports). Data for Europe are simple averages of UK, Germany, France and Italy.

Source: 1913–63 Batchelor et al. (1980): Table 3.3; 1974–1999 authors' calculations from OECD Stan Database, 1998 and 2001 editions. There are minor breaks in the series after 1950 and after 1963 and for Germany after 1989. The figure for imports from South (non-OECD plus Korea and Mexico) are derived from totals for 1999 and share of South in 1996 reported in Landesmann et al. (2000).

Increasing import competition was noticeable even in the 1950s and, with the important exception of Japan, it has continued unabated with import market shares doubling in Europe after 1974 and rising more than threefold in the USA. Most of this competition comes from other OECD countries. Imports from the 'South', however, have grown rapidly and now take nearly one tenth of domestic markets in the USA and Europe.

The basis for the general impression of sharply increasing international integration through trade surely lies in this growing penetration by imports of domestic manufacturing markets. But manufacturing only constituted 18 per cent of OECD employment in 1999 (ranging from 15 per cent in USA to 24 per cent in Germany); for OECD this represents a decline of one third as compared to 1974. Does globalisation amount, therefore, to increasingly fierce competition about a diminishing and relatively small, but publicly highly visible, sector?

The significance of manufacturing is underplayed by its share of employment since other sectors contribute substantially to manufactured commodities. So part of the output of agriculture, mining, energy, construction, transport and finance and business services is dependent on the success of domestic manufacturing. Thus bits of these sectors are, at one remove, subject to the international competition within manufacturing markets. Data for the UK in the mid-1990s suggest that the inclusion of intermediate inputs increases the weight of manufacturing by one half as compared to its contribution to value-added or employment. If we extended the calculation to include the value of agricultural and mining output (which is extensively, if far from freely traded internationally) it would seem that around 30 per cent of the UK economy is directly or indirectly contributing to the production of internationally traded goods.

Of course some services are traded directly as well. In the mid-1990s OECD exports of commercial services were about 25 per cent of exports of goods and for the USA the figure was 35 per cent. But these are concentrated in a narrow range of specialised services (international transport, international finance, consulting and so forth) and are irrelevant for the mass of domestic service producers (tourism is one exception, being in competition with a broad range of domestic services). There is no obvious way of quantifying what part of services is seriously internationalised; but any plausible estimate would leave a majority of employment in OECD countries, possibly a substantial and probably a growing majority, largely untouched by international competition. Outside agriculture, mining and manufacturing only a small proportion of workers are subject to international competition directly or indirectly through services provided to traded goods sectors. Wholesale and retail trade, community, personal and social services, utilities and construction together employ some 60 per cent of employment in the OECD as a whole, rather more in the USA (calculations from OECD *Labour Force Statistics*). These sectors are almost wholly insulated from international competition through trade; in Japan where the proportions employed in these sectors is rather less, there is exceptionally little import competition in manufacturing.

The impact of internationalisation through trade, therefore, is quite complicated. For one section of the economy, manufacturing production and its suppliers, together with some specialised enclaves in the services sector, internationalisation has intensified considerably in the USA (from a very low level) and in Europe, but much less in Japan. For the rest of the economy, covering probably a growing majority of those in employment, international competition is of little direct relevance, though even the ‘sheltered sector’ is affected by the macroeconomic consequences of the success or otherwise of the traded goods sectors.

One reason for the impression of pervasive internationalisation is that a substantial part of the sheltered sectors deals with imports even if it does not compete with them. Thus the retail sector, for whom international competition is largely irrelevant, sells an increasing proportion of imported products (or products which copy foreign products – witness the croissantification and bagelisation of UK supermarkets), garages service imported cars, insurance companies cover imported VCRs and so on. Many services deal with and are ancillary to goods even if they are not involved in their production, so that the increasing internationalisation of goods production may be highly relevant to them. Their position on the domestic market may even be threatened if they do not keep as abreast of information on new overseas sources of supply as their domestic rivals. This overseas competition in the goods in which they deal increases both the informational complexity and unpredictability of their business. But the economic consequences of this relationship to the world economy are shallower than when maintenance of their position on the domestic market depends on their costs relative to those of overseas producers.

Foreign direct investment

Foreign direct investment (FDI) rose rapidly in the final decades of the twentieth century. UNCTAD's *World Investment Report 2002* calculates that the inward stock of FDI in developed countries increased from 4.8 per cent of GDP in 1980 to 8.1 per cent in 1990 and jumped to 17.1 per cent in 2000 (for outward FDI the figures are 6.2 per cent, 9.6 per cent and 22.1 per cent). Although the increase seems impressive, comparing a stock of FDI to GDP does not directly measure its significance. For the OECD countries the ratio of non-residential capital stock to GDP lies in the range 2–3. In order to allow for historic cost valuation of FDI (meaning its undervaluation in current cost terms), we will take the minimum figure of 2 as a rule of thumb, thus assuming that the share of FDI in the domestic capital stock is about one half its ratio to GDP. This suggests that foreign ownership of productive capital does not amount to much more than 10 per cent of the total for the OECD countries. Using the same rule of thumb, the figure for the developing countries would give a higher figure of about 15 per cent. According to these estimates less than 10 per cent of the world's non-residential capital stock is foreign-owned (UNCTAD, 2001, Annex Table B6).

Another, probably more reliable, method of arriving at this result is by looking at the figures for flows of FDI compared to the corresponding flow of domestic investment (Table 4.4). These figures are not subject to the accounting biases caused by historic cost valuation. They show what the share of the capital stock represented by FDI would be if the flow continued at that rate.

In recent years the proportions of capital expenditure represented by FDI, as shown in Tables 4.4a and 4.4b, have varied within the range of 3–22 per cent: at first higher in developing than developed countries, though now the reverse and lower in Japan than in the rest of the OECD. The relative size of FDI was generally less in the early 1990s than it had been in the late 1980s, but then, as

Table 4.4a Foreign direct investment, 1990–2000

% of Gross Domestic Investment	WORLD		Developed Countries		USA		Japan		European Union	
	90–95	96–2000	90–95	96–2000	90–95	96–2000	90–95	96–2000	90–95	96–2000
Inward	4.1	12.6	3.6	12.8	4.3	12.4	0.1	0.5	5.5	21.8
Outward	4.8	10.2	5.5	15.2	6.1	8.8	2.2	2.1	7.7	30.5

Source: UNCTAD (2002): Annex Table B5.

Table 4.4b Foreign direct investment, 1990–2000

% of Gross Domestic Investment	DEVELOPED						DEVELOPING					
	1990–95	96	97	98	99	2000	1990–95	96	97	98	99	2000
Inward	3.6	4.8	7.4	11.0	16.5	22.0	5.7	9.1	11.1	11.4	13.4	13.4
Outward	5.5	7.3	8.9	13.9	20.1	25.0	2.5	3.8	4.0	3.1	3.5	5.8

Source: UNCTAD (2002): Annex Table B5.

the tables show, rose very rapidly in the second half of the decade. In the year 2001 FDI once again experienced a sudden collapse, the value of the flow being less than a half of the previous year; only a small part of this fall has been attributed to the effect of the September 11 attack (UNCTAD, 2002, Chapter 1). These figures are consistent with the previous rough estimate that FDI as a proportion of capital stock world-wide cannot be more than 10 per cent and is almost certainly less than this: the foreign share of current investment in developed countries has only exceeded this level in the latest three available years.

Is 10 a large or small percentage? It has certainly grown over the last three decades and especially rapidly in the second half of the 1990s. But it is still a good deal smaller than is commonly supposed. It is now probably greater than its previous historical peak, though not by a large margin. Estimates of the size of foreign direct investment before its collapse after 1913 suggest that it amounted to between 7 and 9 per cent of world output, somewhat below today's figure (Maddison, 1995; Bairoch and Kozul Wright, 1996).

There are a number of reasons why the weight of foreign investment may be still less than these figures suggest. One is that the recent flow of FDI to developing countries has been concentrated in very few countries. Over one third of the higher figure for inward FDI to developing countries during the 1990s is accounted for by China alone. And most FDI into China comes not from developed countries but from other overseas Chinese capitalists in other Asian developing countries so it does not correspond to the common image of FDI as Western multinationals expanding throughout the world.[1] In addition, not all FDI consists of the construction of new production facilities by overseas companies, thus generating a clear increase in competition through internationalisation. Well over half of FDI inflows into OECD countries represent cross-border mergers and acquisitions. In the year 2000 the estimated value of cross-border mergers and acquisitions was over 90 per cent of the value of the total FDI flow. Some, but by no means all, of these mergers and acquisitions result in international intrusion into the competitive structure of the industry, just like a new plant or office. Other acquisitions are closer to portfolio investments, involving a change in ownership but with relatively little impact on industry behaviour. So that is another reason why FDI does not always have the results which are commonly ascribed to it. In addition, a considerable part of the acquisitions were the result of privatisation policies which must tail off as state sectors decline; so the relative amount of FDI for this reason is likely to flag.

The sectoral composition of FDI is less biased towards manufacturing than foreign trade. In the 1990s around one half of outward FDI from major home countries was in the services sector (two thirds in the case of Japan). Obviously FDI can reach into parts of the service sector immune from direct competition from imports (for example McDonald's) and this represents some qualification to the remarks above about the insulation of large parts of the services sector.

As yet, however, the impact on services overall is still very much smaller than for manufacturing.

Firms

Both popular and scholarly perceptions about globalisation are based to a great extent on perceptions about firms. It is the multinational corporation (MNC), as agent of globalisation, which plays a starring role in nearly all the theoretical approaches to the contemporary world economy. The MNC, however, can be hero or villain. By some it is regarded as the modern incarnation of the finance capital which the classical Marxist writers on imperialism regarded as so important and by others as the confirmation that the age of which Hilferding, Bukharin and Lenin wrote has been superseded.

Firms are seen as the centrepiece of globalisation either because they are large and getting larger relative to the world economy or because they are multinational and becoming more so. As to the size of firms and their concentration it remains extremely difficult to find satisfactory estimates of the degree of concentration of national (let alone world) output by numbers of firms. Firms are usually ranked in terms of the size of their turnover. This is not the same as their contribution to the value of production since it is a gross and not a net (value-added) figure. Companies in which raw materials or semi-finished goods constitute a large part of costs, and that buy these inputs from other firms will have a turnover greatly in excess of their net contribution to such aggregates as the GNP. But, despite this elementary fact, most assessments of the relative size of large firms or MNCs in the world economy are carried out by comparing turnover with GNP. This is not comparing like with like and will give us an exaggerated number. One often quoted conclusion is that the world is 'controlled' by the largest 200 companies (defined by total sales) which had a turnover equal to 24.2 per cent of World Product in 1982, rising to 31.2 per cent by 1995 (Clairmonte and Kavanagh, 1994; Clairmonte, 1997). This calculation is misleadingly presented as the 'share of the 200 in world GNP' and is often referred to with such misleading phrases as 'the large MNCs control more than a third of the world's production'. Such figures are based on double-counting: the sales of one corporation include the value of those products and materials which it has bought from suppliers. But an estimate of a firm's contribution to the national product is a much more difficult figure to obtain and, in the absence of a large amount of research, the only way to calculate it is by means of another rule of thumb, this time relating value-added to sales. We will probably not be far wrong if we take a ratio of 3:1 as the average ratio of sales to value-added.[2] Applying this to the estimates of the importance of the 200 largest firms we would arrive at the conclusion that they accounted for about 10 per cent or less of World Product instead of the frequently heard estimate of nearly one third. This figure is broadly consistent with the estimate that in the year 2000 the 100 largest firms ranked by value of foreign assets (almost all of which are included in the top 200 firms ranked by turnover) owned (at home and abroad) assets worth about $6300 billion (UNCTAD, 2002) which amounts to a little under 10 per cent of the world's capital stock (estimated by the rule of thumb mentioned in the previous section).[3] Even this figure must be an upper limit since it includes the assets of affiliates which are not wholly owned by the parent companies.

In the debate about globalisation large firms and multinational corporations have become virtually interchangeable concepts. But figures for the concentration of world production in a certain number of firms do not in themselves imply anything at all about the multinationality of those firms. All the firms could in principle be purely national in their operations. So it is necessary to look at data specifically about multinationality.

A corporation could be classified as an MNC according to where it sells, where it produces, whom it employs, who owns it, where it has its offices and so on. There is no official definition and so one source may be using completely divergent criteria from another. What is most nearly coming to be an official definition of an MNC is that which is used by UNCTAD's annual *World Investment Report (WIR)*. In a series of annual reports on international production and investment the *WIR* has come to use the following very inclusive criterion: a firm which has at least one foreign subsidiary (defined as a firm in another country with more than 10 per cent of the equity owned by the parent company). This means that a company with only one marketing subsidiary of which it owns only 10 per cent of the equity is regarded as a multinational.

It is not surprising to learn that on the basis of that broad definition there are no fewer than 64 592 MNCs in the world at the last count, having between them at least 851 167 foreign affiliates, an average of 13 each (UNCTAD, 2001); many of these MNCs would not have enough affiliates to put them in the category of multinational as alternatively defined by the Harvard Business School (subsidiaries in at least six countries). If the *WIR* definition is far too inclusive to define an entity which many say is qualitatively changing the world, it is still important that the number of firms that are thus weakly defined as MNCs rose from around 7000 in 1960 to nearly 65 000 in 2001. There is no doubt that in some sense that is a sign of more international or globalised times, although a high proportion of this growing number of affiliates cannot be more than marketing agencies for the products of the parent.

Most of the MNCs defined in this way are not giant companies. The *WIR* figures do not allow any estimate of the average size of the parent companies. The average turnover of their foreign subsidiaries, however, is just under $22 million, and on average they each produce value-added of about $4 million and employ 62 people (UNCTAD, 2002, Table 1.1, p. 4 and Annex Table A.1.3, p. 272). Since nearly 60 per cent of the subsidiaries are in developing countries which account for only 30 per cent of the stock of foreign capital this implies that the above world average figures should be roughly halved for the developing countries and multiplied by about six for subsidiaries in the developed countries, which account for 12 per cent of the subsidiaries and nearly 70 per cent of the investments. (The missing figures are accounted for by Central and Eastern Europe.)

The *WIR* estimates (generalising from US and Japanese data) that the gross output produced by these subsidiaries (in GDP terms) was equal to a little under 11 per cent of the world's GDP in the year 2000. The World Bank (1997a), using a different methodology, reached the compatible estimate of 7.5 per cent for 1995. The distribution of this output by sectors is shown in Table 4.5. Employment in their subsidiaries amounts to 1.5–2 per cent of the world's active population, which probably means about 4 per cent of employed labour.

Table 4.5 National and 'global' production (percentage of total world GDP)

Sector	Agriculture	Industry	Services	Total
Location of output:				
National	5	26	61	92
Global	0	5	2	7
Total	5	31	63	100

Note: National production is production by enterprises in their own country; 'global' production is production of foreign-owned enterprises. Totals do not equal 100 due to rounding.

Source: World Bank (1997a and 1997b).

These numerical estimates of the importance of multinational corporations are neither large nor small in themselves. They are large in relation to recent past experience, much less so in a longer-term comparison, and quite small in relation to presumptions common in discussions of globalisation.

A common perception about multinational firms is that they are increasingly developing globally integrated production in which the firm produces final products from components which it manufactures in plants in many different countries. There are a number of widely publicised examples of this and a number of spectacular failures of such a strategy. The spread of integrated production implies a rising proportion of international trade taking the form of intra-trade between branches of the same firm. Despite this common view it is extraordinarily difficult to find satisfactory estimates of the importance of this trade. The only authoritative figures seem to be for the USA and Japan between 1983 and 1999 (UNCTAD, 1997; OECD, 2002). The *World Investment Report* has estimated that intra-trade in the USA rose between 1983 and 1992 from 33 to 36 per cent of exports and from 35 to 40 per cent of imports; and in Japan intra-trade rose from 22 to 28 per cent of exports and fell from 15 to 14 per cent of imports. A more recent survey by the OECD calculates that between 1990 and 1999 US intra-trade rose for exports (from 33 to 36 per cent) and fell for imports (from 44 to 39 per cent); for Japan there was a sharp rise, however, during the 1990s (from 17 to 31 per cent for exports and from 15 to 24 per cent for imports). The OECD report speculates that the intra-firm percentage has risen especially fast in trade between a few middle-income countries and richer countries (especially Mexico and the USA due to the *maquiladoras*). While intra-trade is important and growing, it is much smaller than is claimed by widely read writers on globalisation who frequently quote much higher figures (up to 92 per cent for US trade) with no basis in fact (Reich, 1993, p. 114). The figures quoted above suggest that intra-firm transactions may account for about one third of international trade, a figure which has been circulating for at least 30 years, though with very little empirical backing. The figures for the USA are fairly stable, though those for Japan are rising. This fact is connected with the nature of intra-firm transactions. The bulk of this intra-trade is almost certainly not the result of globally integrated production but of the increasing use of marketing subsidiaries by multinational corporations, especially in industries such as electronics, computers and vehicles; for example, two-thirds of US imports by foreign-based multinationals are of this kind (OECD, 2002, p. 163).

All the figures quoted above do not tell us very much qualitatively about the institution of the MNC which so many people think defines our age. The history of the species depends on how it is defined. Observations about MNCs are based on many different definitions. If the MNC is a company that sells its product in foreign markets then there are hundreds of thousands of them and they have been common for centuries. If it is one with marketing subsidiaries abroad, then there are tens of thousands of them and they have existed for many decades. If it is one with production subsidiaries abroad then there are thousands of them and they have existed for many decades. If it is one that practises international integration of production then there are probably a few dozen of them, though they are so often remarked upon and described that you would think that there were more. If it is one with significant ownership in more than one nation then there may also be a few dozen at the most. If it is a company with more than one basic national origin, then there are probably two (Royal Dutch Shell and Unilever) and they have both existed for many decades. If it is a company that is so international in ownership, production and management that it no longer has a basic nation state then we are not convinced that there are yet any: such a beast would be a future mutation (Ruigrok and van Tulder, 1995).

There is in our view rather little evidence here for the view that the multinational corporation has suddenly transformed the world. Rather there is the continuation of very long-term tendencies towards industrial concentration going on at a speed of 'glacial drift',[4] and considerable evidence that more and more firms, especially medium and small ones, are beginning to operate at an international level. Despite general perceptions to the contrary, the tendency is not so much that some predefined beast – the largest and most famous of the multinational corporations, such as Shell, Nestlé, Unilever or General Motors – has been controlling very much more of the world economy, but that the nature of the beast has been changing; globalisation has meant more that a growing number of companies have global interests rather than that a given number of companies directly control more of the globe.

Finance

Our review of the facts about globalisation has concentrated on issues of production. There is less dispute about the huge expansion of international financial flows; cross-border bank lending and transactions in bonds and equities have grown spectacularly (BIS, 1997). The daily turnover of the foreign exchange market, now more than $1500 billion, is six times the total gross central bank intervention during the 1992 ERM crisis (Eichengreen and Wyplosz, 1993). Such explosive growth of international financial transactions renders exchange rates wholly dependent on shifts in market expectations.

However, many such transactions represent reshuffling of existing portfolios and do not increase the degree of internationalisation of ownership of financial assets. The UK case is interesting as a medium sized country with a highly developed, and internationally very integrated capital market. By the end of 2001 37 per cent of UK company equities were owned abroad as were 18 per cent of UK government bonds. UK life assurance and pension funds held 22 per cent of the assets in the form of foreign equities and bonds. In each case the percentages had increased very sharply over the past 20 years, though households still hold virtually no overseas financial assets. It is still the case, however, that the majority of portfolios are invested in financial assets emanating from the domestic economy and that the majority of domestic financial liabilities are due to domestic residents. It is possible to envisage a situation where ownership of financial capital is so internationalised, and portfolios are so diversified, that clearly identifiable national blocs of capital will cease to be very significant. We are certainly not there yet.

Conclusions

Historical economic trends are often exaggerated. Globalisation is one. We do not mean that there has been no important process of globalisation going on in the last 50 years. But we are certain that at the present time its extent and significance have been misinterpreted; and in general the misinterpretation has leaned in the direction of exaggeration. The exaggeration has resulted from a number of interpretive tendencies:

- inappropriate statistical measures have been used (for instance, the use of constant price data to measure the importance of trade, or comparison of the turnover of firms with national output figures);
- upward trends have been assumed for variables where very few reliable observations exist (such as the percentage of intra-trade of multinationals in total trade);
- recent and present measures of globalisation have been taken to indicate a situation that is historically unprecedented, whereas the world economy might be better seen as restoring normality after a long mid-century global crisis rather than changing itself into something completely new;
- the growth of some variables has seemed remarkable in absolute terms while relatively they are much less impressive (as in the case of foreign direct investment);
- little attention has been paid to the analytical reasons for limits to globalisation (such as the growing importance of services);
- counter-globalisation tendencies have been ignored (such as the growing restriction on human migration);
- insufficient argument has been made that recent quantitative changes have resulted in qualitative ones.

This short chapter has left aside the qualitative questions in order to examine critically some of the commonly held quantitative notions about international economic integration, in the hope that this will do something to clarify what is today surely the central debate in international political economy. We do not wish to suggest that globalisation is neither large nor important. But we do wish to say that a look at the quantitative evidence shows that it is a gradual rather than a sudden process and that it has not in general reached unprecedented levels. Exaggeration on both these scores will lead to inappropriate interpretations and political reactions to globalisation.

We do not believe that any specific political conclusions follow from this chapter. But it does suggest some very general points. The main one is that the exaggeration of the degree of globalisation has given rise to (or has been used to justify) a sense of impotence among many on the left. Globalisation seems to explain why national political plans always go wrong: it is because the national state has lost independence due to globalisation. The future of left politics, therefore, seems to depend uniquely on the possibility of building an international political movement to combat globalised capital and the de facto international state. And since to many that prospect seems very difficult and distant, the implication is political impotence for the foreseeable future. In our opinion this fatalistic perspective would be wrong even if globalisation has advanced much further than we believe it has. It is not true that the consolidation of the national state rendered local institutions powerless and local politics redundant. No more should globalisation render redundant the politics of smaller units including the national state. But changing global structures will tend to alter the political areas in which local or national autonomy exists. There is no reason to suppose that it will eliminate their importance.

Nonetheless, any degree of globalisation (including that which existed before it became a buzzword) does seem to us to demand greater internationalisation of political perspectives and action, whether it be international trade union action in relation to multinational corporations or international cooperation of progressives over human and civil rights, especially when these have a clear international dimension, such as questions of asylum rights, immigration rights and so on. There is a marked imbalance between the globalisation of the movement of money and things and the opposite tendency in the movement of people. It seems to demand some redress: people should be able to move more freely, and at the same time they should find it easier to acquire democratic rights when they do move. Globalisation demands now (as it always has done) that the concept of citizenship, both from the point of view of rights and from the point of view of participation in the political process, also be globalised. The concept of international citizenship has begun to be discussed but it lags far behind the development of the ideological justification for the globalisation of money and capital markets. None of this seems to us new but globalisation at any pace makes it more urgent. It is not an alternative to national or local political action but a complement to it.

Notes

* This is an extensively updated and slightly abridged version of our article 'Still underwhelmed: indicators of globalization and their misinterpretation' which appeared in the *Review of Radical Political Economics*, **31** (1), 1999.

1. Newspaper reports suggest that substantial inflows of FDI into China actually originate within China itself, masquerading as FDI in order to obtain tax breaks.
2. This is intermediate between an estimate for the USA of 2.8:1 (Laffer, 1969) and a ratio of 5:1 given implicitly by UNCTAD (2002) (Table 1.1, p. 10) for all foreign affiliates). DeGrauwe and Camerman have directly calculated this ratio for several large firms and find it to be between 3.5 and 4.5:1 for manufacturing and about 3:1 for services (de Grauwe and Camerman, 2002).
3. These figures plainly refute many common exaggerated impressions and claims such as the one that '[s]ome 400 multinational corporations own two-thirds of the planet's fixed assets…' (Robinson, 1996, p. 20).
4. The phrase was the conclusion of M.A. Adelman writing in 1951 ('The measurement of industrial concentration', *Review of Economics and Statistics*, **33**, November 1951: pp. 295–6), and was still regarded as appropriate by F.M. Sherer and David Ross in 1990 (*Industrial Market Structure and Economic Performance*, Boston: Houghton Mifflin Co., 1990).

References

Bairoch, P. and R. Kozul-Wright (1996), 'Globalization myths: some historical reflections on integration, industrialisation and growth in the world economy', in R. Kozul-Wright and R. Rowthorn (eds), *Multinational Corporations and the Global Economy*, Basingstoke: Macmillan.

Bank of International Settlements (BIS) (1997), *Annual Report,* Basle: BIS.

Batchelor, R., R. Major and A. Morgan (1980), *Industrialisation and the Basis for Trade*, Cambridge: Cambridge University Press.

Bourguignon, F. et al. (2002), *Making Sense of Globalisation*, CEPR Policy Paper No. 8.

Clairmonte, Fréderic F. (1997), 'Ces deux cents sociétés qui contrôlent le monde', *Le Monde Diplomatique*, April.

Clairmonte, Fréderic F. and John Kavanagh (1994), 'Sous les ailes du capitalisme planetaire', *Le Monde Diplomatique*, March.

De Grauwe, P. and M Camerman (2002), 'How big are the big multinationals?', available at http://www.econ.kuleuven.be/ew/academic/intecon/degrauwe.

Eichengreen, B. and C. Wyplosz (1993), 'The unstable EMS', *Brookings Papers on Economic Activity 1.*

Feenstra, R. (1998), 'Integration of trade and disintegration of production in the global economy', *Journal of Economic Perspectives*, **12**, 31–50.

Glyn, A. and B. Sutcliffe (1992), 'Global but leaderless', in Ralph Milliband and Leo Panitch (eds), *The Socialist Register 1992*, London: Merlin Press, pp. 76–95.

Gordon, D. (1988), 'The global economy: new edifice or crumbling foundations', *New Left Review*, **168**, 24–65.

Hirst, P. and G. Thompson (1996), *Globalization in Question*, Cambridge: Polity Press.

Laffer, Arthur 1969, 'Vertical integration by corporations, 1929–1965', *Review of Economics and Statistics*, **LI**, 91–3.

Landesmann, M., R. Stehrer and S. Leitner (2000), 'Trade Liberalisation and Labour Markets', *WIIW Working Paper 20*, October, Vienna.

Maddison, A. (1991), *Dynamic Forces in Capitalist Development*, Oxford: Oxford University Press.

Maddison, A. (1995), *Monitoring the World Economy, 1820–1992*, Paris: OECD.

OECD (2001), *Historical Statistics 1970–1999*, Paris: OECD.

OECD (2002), 'Intra-industry and intra-firm trade and the internationalisation of production', *Economic Outlook*, **2002/1** (71), June, 159–70.

Reich, Robert B. (1993), *The Work of Nations: Preparing Ourselves for 21st Century Capitalism*, London: Simon and Schuster.

Robinson, William I. (1996), 'Globalization: nine theses on our epoch', *Race and Class*, **38** (2), 13–31.

Rodrik, D. (2000), 'How far will international economic integration go?', *Journal of Economic Perspectives*, **14** (1), Winter, 177–86.

Ruigrok, Winifred and Rob van Tulder (1995), *The Logic of International Restructuring*, London and New York: Routledge.

Sachs J. and A. Warner (1995), 'Economic Reform and the Process of Global Integration', *Brookings Papers on Economic Activity. Macroeconomics 1.*

UNCTAD (1997), *World Investment Report 1997*, Geneva: UNCTAD.

UNCTAD (2001), *World Investment Report 2001*, Geneva: UNCTAD.

UNCTAD (2002), *World Investment Report 2002*, Geneva: UNCTAD.

World Bank (1996), *World Development Report 1996*, Washington, DC: World Bank.

World Bank (1997a), *Global Economic Prospects and the Developing Countries 1997*, Washington, DC: World Bank.

World Bank (1997b), *World Development Report 1997*, Washington, DC: World Bank.

PART II

ANALYSING THE GLOBAL ECONOMY

5 Innovation and globalisation: a systems of innovation perspective

Jeremy Howells

1 Introduction

The systems of innovation approach has proved valuable in exploring the role of geographical scale and different scalar levels in relation to the innovation process and as a way of analysing wider socioeconomic processes and institutional arrangements in innovative activity that have been so often neglected in the past. From a nationally based starting point, in terms of national systems of innovation (NSI: see Freeman, 1987, 1988; Lundvall, 1988; Edquist, 1997a), the systems of innovation approach has been considerably extended as a conceptual construct. Thus, Chris Freeman (1987, 1) originally defined the systems of innovation concept (from a national perspective) as 'the network of institutions in the public and private sectors whose activities and interactions initiate, import, modify and diffuse new technologies'. The concept has widened and developed over time (see reviews by Lundvall, 1992b; Nelson, 1992; Nelson and Rosenberg, 1993; McKelvey, 1994; Freeman, 1995; Edquist, 1997b; Archibugi et al., 1999), but it is these institutional and infrastructural settings (which were initially reviewed at a national level) that frame the search, exploration and learning processes involved in innovation, that remain the foundations of the approach and its perspective (Lundvall, 1992b, 12; Galli and Teubal, 1997, 351–3) at whatever scale. Thus, in spatial terms the application and conceptualisation of the approach has moved in terms of its exploration and development as a concept, both 'up', to global systems of innovation (see, for example, Spencer, 2000; Carlsson, 2006), and 'down', both to regional systems of innovation (RSI; see Cooke et al., 1997; Howells, 1999) and to local systems of innovation (see, for example, Acs et al., 1998). It has also been applied within a more non-spatial, 'localised' sense via a sectoral perspective in terms of a sectoral systems of innovation framework (SSI; Breschi and Malerba, 1997; see also Carlsson and Stankiewicz, 1991; and Carlsson, 1995 regarding technological systems).

From a global perspective all these developments of the systems of innovation model serve to suggest that innovation, far from taking a uniform, rootless and spaceless nature, is influenced by its context and will remain highly uneven, distinctive and differentiated in form. Thus, 'Innovations are not evenly distributed over the whole economic system at random, but tend to concentrate in certain sectors and their surroundings' Schumpeter (1939, 111). This has been acknowledged at a geographical level where it has been long recognised that innovation and its processes are highly differentiated across space (see, for example, Ullman, 1958, 193).

This chapter explores the special attributes of the systems of innovation approach, how the approach has developed over time and what contribution it provides in terms of aiding our understanding of the global economy. The analysis will conclude by highlighting the development of the concept and the remaining gaps that still remain in our conceptual and analytical frameworks both in terms of the approach itself and in relation to the issue of globalisation more generally.

2 Systems of innovation: development of a concept

What insights and attributes does the systems of innovation approach bring to the study of globalisation and innovation? It is argued here that the systems of innovation approach brings five attributes that are useful and insightful to the study of innovation in a globalising world. These five qualities are briefly outlined below.

2.1 Context

First, as noted earlier, the development of the systems of innovation approach has been important in highlighting the context of the innovation process and in turn factors that shape local innovation contexts (Carlsson and Jacobsson, 1997, 268). Certain environments are conducive to innovation, others not (Tödtling, 1995). The systems of innovation approach has sought to identify those elements of the system, such as institutions and the technical infrastructure, that are significant factors in helping to shape the innovation process. However, in evolutionary terms there is also the Darwinian issue of selection processes at work here. On the one hand, good innovation environments make it more likely that innovations will be generated and succeed, leading to a strong process of cumulative causation and positive feedback processes. On the other, though, certain system attributes (associated with the emergence and growth of institutional rigidities; Hodgson, 1989, 89–91), may stagnate and ossify, leading to negative 'lock-in' effects and thus negative feedback processes within national or regional systems (Staber, 1996, 299).

2.2 Scale

Innovation context is therefore an important issue that has been highlighted by the approach, but also as the approach has been developed it has highlighted different system levels or scales (Oinas and Malecki, 1999). Although national systems of innovation still remain the most significant level at which such institutional contexts operate (Nelson, 1993, 518), other levels, international, regional and local, are also important foci for certain aspects of the innovation process and are worthy of study (Metcalfe, 1995, 41; McKelvey, 1997, 202; Cantwell and Iammarino, 1998, 403; Cantwell and Janne, 2000, 245; Verspagen and Schoenmakers, 2004, 40). No single systems 'level' is necessarily the 'best' to view the whole innovation process. It is therefore useful to consider a variety of different system levels in helping to understand and explain innovation activity.

2.3 Interaction and inter-connectedness

Important in the innovation process, too, is interaction within the system (Lundvall, 1988, 1992c; Johnson and Gregersen, 1995) and the inter-connectedness of the different systems (Bunnell and Coe, 2001, 577). In this latter respect, the appropriate level at which different elements of the innovation process interact in relation to its overall task environment (associated with its geographical, sectoral, technological contexts) is an important consideration. Different national systems of innovation will increasingly trade on their particular strengths and specialities within the global economy (Niosi and Bellon, 1994; Shin, 2002). As such, different innovation systems will become more integrated and inter-dependent of each other over time, although many will still remain marginalised and largely detached from the global economy.

2.4 Dynamic and evolutionary nature

The systems of innovation approach can be firmly rooted in evolutionary traditions (Andersen, 1996; Saviotti, 1997; McKelvey, 1997). McKelvey (1997, 219) argues that three evolutionary elements should exist in a properly functioning system of innovation, namely: a retention and transmission of information; a generation of novelty leading to diversity; and a selection process amongst alternatives. These evolutionary functions in turn shape – but are also shaped by – individual and collective innovative activities (ibid., 201). Thus, the decisions and actions of agents within the system are enabled as well as limited by other agents and institutions in the innovation system (Lundvall, 1992b, 10).

2.5 Variation, diversity and unevenness

In combination with its emphasis on context and acknowledgement of evolutionary change, the systems of innovation approach, by its nature, acknowledges that there will be variation and diversity within and between systems. Indeed, innovation is a central element in creating this diversity, with the generation of novelty leading to such diversity (McKelvey, 1997, 209). However, not only is diversity evident between national innovation systems, for example, it is also a desirable feature and manifestation of economic development and international specialisation (Patel and Pavitt, 1994, 92). Institutions play a clear and pivotal role in creating such diversity by enhancing (or diminishing) the ability of the system to generate and exploit new ideas (Carlsson and Jacobsson, 1997, 272). Diversity between systems therefore occurs, although within an innovation system a strong selection process in terms of technological trajectory or sectoral specialisation may 'lock in' a system (Wijnberg, 1994) and through this inertia actually reduce its variety (Metcalfe, 1995, 29).

3 Systems of innovation and the global economy: conceptual and empirical insights

The previous section outlined what particular insights the systems of innovation concept has contributed to the study of innovation, but how does it contribute to our knowledge and understanding of the global economy?

In a world that is continually changing and raising critical questions for development and growth (Dicken, 1998), the systems of innovation approach has, early on, sought to provide key answers and solutions. The systems of innovation approach has always had a strong policy focus and has sought to identify and suggest policy mechanisms that can help develop and enhance national and local system capabilities for this purpose – see especially the contributions in Lundvall (1992a) and Edquist (1997a).

However, the approach also warns against providing generic solutions to the problems of performance and developments within systems of innovation. The issue of variety and context suggests that although generic sets of policy mechanisms should be made available and considered for particular innovation systems, their selection, structure and application should vary. Strong socio-cultural, institutional and regulatory differences still remain between national systems (Bartholomew, 1997). As such, it is often misleading to assume that there is a single ('best-practice') ensemble of policies to deploy for particular nation states or regions (see Gertler's [2001, 6] discussion of this in the context of firm-level strategy). It is dangerous trying to transpose policies into different system environments. This point is emphasised by Wijnberg (1994, 319), who notes that: 'A crucial element of every systemic approach is to question the utility of copying particular elements of systems without having other elements in place that interact in an essential way with the elements copied.'

Second, the emphasis in the approach on diversity within and between innovation systems argues against the neoclassical, 'hyperglobalist' hypothesis of globalisation (see Shin, 2002, 419). Instead it supports a more uneven, partial (indeed sometimes reversible) 'transformational' process of the globalisation of innovation, which is highly variable over space and time. Individual systems of innovation will experience highly different forms of globalisation, whilst some systems may be largely excluded from the process of globalisation. Much of the variability in the state and condition of innovation systems has been seen with respect to national systems of innovation. However, at least in more developed parts of the world, variance at the regional level may be even more significant and persistent over time (Oughton et al., 2002, 99).

Third, the systems of innovation approach has been successful in recognising and evaluating the 'negative'; namely, the *lack* of certain agents and intermediaries (Howells, 2006), resources and competencies and the identification of system *failures* and *obstacles* within the innovation system. This is compared with other agglomeration and economic development models, associated with industrial clusters and districts, which have tended to focus on highly successful, but fairly unique high-technology districts and regions (which in turn have been difficult, if not impossible, to copy and replicate elsewhere). In part this respect of the 'negative', or what is lacking, may be because there has been a focus on what elements there should be for a system to exist and be successful. It has therefore been used in a diagnostic sense to identify system failures (Patel and Pavitt, 1994, 90–92) and obstacles that are hindering the overall innovative performances of national economies.

Missing elements, in terms of key agents or institutions, and the lack of links between them, suggest a partial or deformed system prone to failure or poor performance. This has obviously received attention in relation to developing or transitional economies (see, for example, Chang and Kozul-Wright, 1994; Radosevic, 1997), but is of particular interest at the *sub-national* level. Here the question is not only what elements and links within the innovation system are missing, but more fundamentally what elements and links should a regional or local innovation system possess if it is to be considered a functioning innovation system compared with the more comprehensive national innovation system arrangement. More specifically, 'What is the irreducible minimum of a system of innovation, below which it cannot be considered to exist or operate?' (Howells, 1999, 81). Paradoxically, 'proper', fully functioning sub-national systems of innovation may actually be much rarer occurrences than generally supposed (Evangelista et al., 2002, 184). This may have conceptual implications in terms of what elements and links a regional or local innovation system should be expected to possess, but also suggests the practical qualities of the approach in highlighting what needs to be done in these regions or localities if they are to reap the full benefits of innovation and economic development.

4 Conclusions and prospective view

It has been argued above that the systems of innovation approach has had a great capacity to evolve and be extended over time. The approach has proved flexible and has been able to accommodate other emerging areas of interest in innovation research, for example, in networks and distributed innovation processes (although see below), which have clear systemic elements to them. However, challenges remain to the approach and its utility in analysing the changing global economy. Critics would argue that these qualities of flexibility in interpretation and ability to encompass other conceptual developments are also weaknesses, in making the approach too opaque and lacking in specificity and testability.

In part this weakness is reflected in the ongoing problems of measurement and empirical analysis within the approach (Archibugi et al., 1999, 7–9). In terms of analysis and measurement there have been some shifts in the foci of analysis within the study of systems of innovation. In terms of the 'objects' (see Archibugi and Michie, 1995) of innovation, what empirical analyses there have been remain largely centred on R&D and patent activity (Frost, 2001; Verspagen and Schoenmakers, 2004), although a wider set of indicators is now starting to be introduced and used (Evangelista et al., 2002). Similarly, although the firm remains the most important 'subject' of systems of innovation analysis, due to its coordinating role in organising search and innovation processes (McKelvey, 1997, 205), there have been few empirical attempts to analyse networks within an innovation system context. This remains an important omission as a much more thorough understanding of the relationships, communities and networks in innovation systems need to be undertaken if the process of innovation is to be fully understood within such systems (Saxenian, 1998, 29; Bunnell and Coe, 2001, 578).

Equally, for an approach that espouses a dynamic and evolutionary perspective, the study of systems of innovation remains fundamentally rooted in nodes or points, rather than in links or flows. This means that in a geographical sense it is much harder to map innovation *processes* and that the analysis tends towards a static rather than a dynamic analytical framework (although changes in node patterns over time can provide a partial perspective on system dynamics). This introduces a further weakness of the approach in its treatment of knowledge and with it, the role of individuals. There has been a continuing confusion over the difference between information and knowledge, in that knowledge requires individuals to receive, absorb and understand information (McKelvey, 1997, 207) and in this sense it is only individuals that can possess knowledge (Howells, 2000, 2002). All too often the interaction between knowledge and innovation has been considered heroically at much more aggregate levels. The mobility of individuals and the extra-local transfer of knowledge (see Audretsch and Stephan, 1996; Zucker and Darby, 1996; Zucker et al., 1997; Almedia and Kogut, 1997) is one field of inquiry that has gradually developed over time. Nonetheless, a number of studies have sought to explore in greater depth, at an organisational level, the nature of knowledge 'flows' and organisational learning between multinational enterprises and in particular the role that subsidiaries play in knowledge transfer from particular countries and regions (Frost, 2001; Lam, 2003; Sanna-Randaccio and Veugelers, 2007; Driffield et al. 2010; Birkinshaw et al., 2010). Such studies show that there is a complex interplay of tapping, interacting and absorbing knowledge by subsidiaries that co-evolve and adapt with the 'local' nation or region within which they are based. A second strand of enquiry examining flows centred on the phenomenon of innovation offshoring has only just begun to emerge. Although there has now been a considerable analysis of general offshoring activities by companies, in the field of innovation this has remained limited until recently (Massini and Miozzo, 2010). In particular, offshoring innovative activities has been revealed as a way of tapping into increasingly scarce scientific and engineering talent in dispersed overseas locations with companies entering a 'global race for talent' (Lewin et al., 2009).

Despite these remaining weaknesses and gaps, the systems of innovation approach has remained both robust and flexible in it ability to absorb conceptual developments and empirical findings from the wider literature of innovation, multinational and organisational studies and to ground this within a more holistic development framework. However, it may be in its more pragmatic and applied qualities (Archibugi and Iammarino, 1999), especially in highlighting the 'negatives' in innovation systems where the contribution of the systems of innovation approach to the global economy may be truly felt in terms of helping the poorer and more marginalised systems and peoples of the world to overcome their problems.

References

Acs, Zolton J., F.R. Fitzroy and I. Smith (1998), 'Contrasting US metropolitan systems of innovation', in J. De La Mothe and G. Paquet (eds), *Regional Systems of Innovation*, Boston: Kluwer, pp. 111–24.

Almedia, P. and B. Kogut (1997), 'The exploration of technological diversity and the geographic localization of innovation', *Small Business Economics*, **9**(1), 21–31.

Andersen, Esben S. (1996), 'From static structures to dynamics: specialization and innovative linkages', in Christian De Bresson (ed.), *Economic Interdependence and Innovative Activity: An Input–Output Analysis*, Cheltenham, UK and Brookfield, USA: Edward Elgar, pp. 333–55.

Archibugi, D. and S. Iammarino (1999), 'The policy implications of globalisation of innovation', *Research Policy*, **28**(2/3), 317–36.

Archibugi, D. and J. Michie (1995), 'The globalisation of technology: a new taxonomy', *Cambridge Journal of Economics*, **19**(1), 121–40.

Archibugi, Daniele, Jeremy Howells and Jonathan Michie (1999), 'Innovation systems and policy in a global economy', in Daniele Archibugi, Jeremy Howells and Jonathan Michie (eds), *Innovation Systems in a Global Economy*, Cambridge: Cambridge University Press, pp. 1–16.

Audretsch, D.B. and P.E. Stephan (1996), 'Company scientist locational links: the case of biotechnology', *American Economic Review*, **86**(3), 641–52.

Bartholomew, Sarah (1997), 'The globalization of technology: a socio-cultural perspective', in Jeremy Howells and Jonathan Michie (eds), *Technology, Innovation and Competitiveness*, Cheltenham, UK and Lyme, USA: Edward Elgar, pp. 37–62.

Birkinshaw, J., H. Bresman and R. Nobel (2010), 'Knowledge transfer in international acquisitions: a retrospective', *Journal of International Business Studies*, **41**(1), 21–6.

Breschi, Stefano and Franco Malerba (1997), 'Sectoral innovation systems: technological regimes, Schumpeterian dynamics, and spatial boundaries', in Charles Edquist (ed.), *Systems of Innovation: Technologies, Institutions and Organizations*, London: Pinter, pp. 130–56.

Bunnell, T.G. and N.G. Coe (2001), 'Spaces and scales of innovation', *Progress in Human Geography*, **25**(4), 569–89.

Cantwell, J. and S. Iammarino (1998), 'MNCs, technological innovation and regional systems in the EU: some evidence in the Italian case', *International Journal of the Economics of Business*, **5**(3), 383–407.

Cantwell, J. and O. Janne (2000), 'The role of multinational corporations and national states in the globalization of innovatory capacity: the European perspective', *Technology Analysis and Strategic Management*, **12**(2), 243–62.

Carlsson, Bo (ed.) (1995), *Technological Systems and Economic Performance: The Case of Factory Automation*, Dordrecht: Kluwer.

Carlsson, B. (2006), 'Internationalization of innovation systems: a survey of the literature', *Research Policy*, **35**(1), 56–67.

Carlsson, Bo and Staffan Jacobsson (1997), 'Diversity creation and technological systems: a technology policy perspective', in Charles Edquist (ed.), *Systems of Innovation: Technologies, Institutions and Organizations*, London: Pinter, pp. 266–94.

Carlsson, B. and R. Stankiewicz (1991), 'On the nature, function and composition of technological systems', *Journal of Evolutionary Economics*, **1**(2), 93–118.

Chang, H.-J. and R. Kozul-Wright (1994), 'Organising development: comparing the national systems of entrepreneurship in Sweden and South Korea', *Journal of Development Studies*, **30**(4), 859–91.

Cooke, P.M., G. Uranga and G. Etxebarria (1997), 'Regional innovation systems: institutional and organisational dimensions', *Research Policy*, **26**(4/5), 475–91.

Dicken, Peter (1998), *Global Shift: Transforming the World Economy*, London: Paul Chapman.

Driffield, N., J.H. Love and S. Menghinello (2010), 'The multinational enterprise as a source of international knowledge flows: direct evidence from Italy', *Journal of International Business Studies*, **41**, 350–59.

Edquist, Charles (ed.) (1997a), *Systems of Innovation: Technologies, Institutions and Organizations*, London: Pinter.

Edquist, Charles (1997b), 'Systems of innovation approaches – their emergence and characteristics', in Charles Edquist (ed.), *Systems of Innovation: Technologies, Institutions and Organizations*, London: Pinter, pp. 1–35.

Evangelista, R., S. Iammarino, V. Mastrostefano and A. Silvani (2002), 'Looking for regional systems of innovation: evidence from the Italian innovation survey', *Regional Studies*, **36**(2), 174–86.

Freeman, Christopher (1987), *Technology Policy and Economic Performance: Lessons from Japan*, London: Pinter.

Freeman, Christopher (1988), 'Japan: a new national system of innovation?', in Giovanni Dosi, Christopher Freeman, Richard Nelson, Gerald Silverberg and Luc Soete (eds), *Technological Change and Economic Theory*, London: Pinter, pp. 330–48.

Freeman, C. (1995), 'The national system of innovation in historical perspective', *Cambridge Journal of Economics*, **19**(1), 5–24.

Frost, T.S. (2001), 'The geographic sources of foreign subsidiaries' innovations', *Strategic Management Journal*, **22**(2), 101–21.

Galli, Ricardo and Morris Teubal (1997), 'Paradigmatic shifts in national innovation systems', in Charles Edquist (ed.), *Systems of Innovation: Technologies, Institutions and Organizations*, London: Pinter, pp. 342–70.

Gertler, M.S. (2001), 'Best practice? Geography, learning and the institutional limits to strong convergence', *Journal of Economic Geography*, **1**(1), 5–26.

Hodgson, G. (1989), 'Institutional rigidities and economic growth', *Cambridge Journal of Economics*, **13**(1), 78–101.

Howells, Jeremy (1999), 'Regional systems of innovation?', in Daniele Archibugi, Jeremy Howells and Jonathan Michie (eds), *Innovation Systems in a Global Economy*, Cambridge: Cambridge University Press, pp. 67–93.

Howells, J. (2000), 'Knowledge, innovation and location', in John R. Bryson, Peter W. Daniels, Nick Henry and Jane Pollard (eds), *Knowledge, Space, Economy*, London: Routledge, pp. 50–62.

Howells, J. (2002), 'Tacit knowledge, innovation and economic geography', *Urban Studies*, **39**(5/6), 871–84.

Howells, J. (2006), 'Intermediation and the role of intermediaries in innovation', *Research Policy*, **35**(5), 715–28.

Johnson, B. and B. Gregersen (1995), 'Systems of innovation and economic integration', *Journal of Industry Studies*, **2**(2), 1–18.
Lam, A. (2003), 'Organizational learning in multinationals: R&D networks of Japanese and US MNEs in the UK', *Journal of Management Studies*, **40**(3), 673–703.
Lewin, A.Y., S. Massini and C. Peeters (2009), 'Why are companies offshoring innovation? The emerging global race for talent', *Journal of International Business Studies*, **40**(2), 901–25.
Lundvall, Bengt-Åke (1988), 'Innovation as an interactive process – from user–producer interaction to national systems of innovation', in Giovanni Dosi, Christopher Freeman, Richard Nelson, Gerald Silverberg and Luc Soete (eds), *Technological Change and Economic Theory*, London: Pinter, pp. 349–69.
Lundvall, Bengt-Åke (ed.) (1992a), *National Systems of Innovation: Towards a Theory of Innovation and Interactive Learning*, London: Pinter.
Lundvall, Bengt-Åke (1992b), 'Introduction', in Bengt-Åke Lundvall (ed.), *National Systems of Innovation: Towards a Theory of Innovation and Interactive Learning*, London: Pinter, pp. 1–19.
Lundvall, Bengt-Åke (1992c), 'User–producer relationships, national systems of innovation and internationalization', in Bengt-Åke Lundvall (ed.), *National Systems of Innovation: Towards a Theory of Innovation and Interactive Learning*, London: Pinter.
Massini, Silvia and Marcela Miozzo (2010), 'Outsourcing and offshoring of knowledge-intensive business services: implications for innovation', in Faiz Gallouj and Faridah Djellal (eds), *The Handbook of Innovation and Services: A Multi-Disciplinary Perspective*, Cheltenham, UK and Northampton, MA, USA: Edward Elgar, pp. 469–500.
McKelvey, Maureen (1994), 'How do national systems of innovation differ? A critical analysis of Porter, Freeman, Lundvall and Nelson', in Geoffrey Hodgson and E. Screpanti (eds), *Rethinking Economics – Markets, Technology and Market Evolution*, Aldershot, UK and Brookfield, USA: Edward Elgar, pp. 117–37.
McKelvey, Maureen (1997), 'Using evolutionary theory to define systems of innovation', in Charles Edquist (ed.), *Systems of Innovation: Technologies, Institutions and Organizations*, London: Pinter, pp. 200–222.
Metcalfe, J.S. (1995), 'Technology systems and technology policy in an evolutionary framework', *Cambridge Journal of Economics*, **19**(1), 25–46.
Nelson, R.R. (1992), 'National innovation systems: a retrospective on a study', *Industrial and Corporate Change*, **1**(2), 347–74.
Nelson, Richard R. (1993), 'A retrospective', in Richard R. Nelson (ed.), *National Innovation Systems: A Comparative Analysis*, New York: Oxford University Press, pp. 505–23.
Nelson, Richard R. and Nathan Rosenberg (1993), 'Technical innovation and national systems', in R.R. Nelson (ed.), *National Innovation Systems: A Comparative Analysis*, New York: Oxford University Press, pp. 3–21.
Niosi, J. and B. Bellon (1994), 'The global interdependence of national innovation systems: evidence, limits and implications', *Technology in Society*, **16**(2), 173–97.
Oinas, Paul and Edward J. Malecki (1999), 'Spatial innovation systems', in Edward J. Malecki and Paul Oinas (eds), *Making Connections: Technological, Learning and Regional Economic Change*, Aldershot: Avebury, pp. 7–34.
Oughton, C., M. Landabaso and K. Morgan (2002), 'The regional innovation paradox: innovation policy and industrial policy', *Journal of Technology Transfer*, **27**(1), 97–110.
Patel, P. and K. Pavitt (1994), 'National innovation systems: why they are important, and how they might be measured and compared', *Economics of Innovation and New Technology*, **3**(1), 77–95.
Radosevic, Slavo (1997), 'Systems of innovation in transformation: from socialism to post-socialism', in Charles Edquist (ed.), *Systems of Innovation: Technologies, Institutions and Organizations*, London: Pinter, pp. 371–94.
Sanna-Randaccio and R. Veugelers (2007), 'Multinational knowledge spillovers with decentralised R&D: a game theoretic approach', *Journal of International Business Studies*, **38**(1), 47–63.
Saviotti, Paulo P. (1997), 'Innovation systems and evolutionary theories', in Charles Edquist (ed.), *Systems of Innovation: Technologies, Institutions and Organizations*, London: Pinter, pp. 180–99.

Saxenian, AnnaLee (1998), 'Regional systems of innovation and the blurred firm', in John De La Mothe and George Paquet (eds), *Local and Regional Systems of Innovation*, Boston: Kluwer, pp. 29–43.

Schumpeter, Joseph A. (1939), *Business Cycles: A Theoretical, Historical and Statistical Analysis of the Capitalist Process*, New York: McGraw-Hill (2 volumes).

Shin, M.E. (2002), 'Measuring economic globalization: spatial hierarchies and market topologies', *Environment and Planning A*, **34**(3), 417–28.

Spencer, J.W. (2000), 'Knowledge flows in the global innovation system: do US firms share more scientific knowledge than their Japanese rivals?', *Journal of International Business*, **31**(3), 521–30.

Staber, U. (1996), 'Accounting for variations in the performance of industrial districts: the case of Baden-Württemburg', *International Journal of Urban and Regional Research*, **20**, 299–316.

Tödtling, F. (1995), 'The innovation process and local environment', in Stephen Conti, Edward J. Malecki and Paul Oinas (eds), *The Industrial Enterprises and its Environment: Spatial Perspectives*, Aldershot: Avebury, pp. 171–93.

Ullman, E.L. (1958), 'Regional development and the geography of concentration', *Chapters and Proceedings, Regional Science Association*, **4**, 179–98.

Verspagen, B. and W. Schoenmakers (2004), 'The spatial dimension of patenting by multinational firms in Europe', *Journal of Economic Geography*, **4**(1), 23–42.

Wijnberg, N. (1994), 'National systems of innovation: selection environments and selection processes', *Technology in Society*, **16**(3), 313–20.

Zucker, L.G. and M.R. Darby (1996), 'Star scientists and institutional transformation: patterns of invention and innovation in the formation of the biotechnology industry', *Proceedings of the National Academy of Science*, **93**(23), 12709–16.

Zucker, L.G., M.R. Darby and M.B. Brewer (1997), 'Intellectual human capital and the birth of US biotechnology enterprises', *American Economic Review*, **88**(1), 290–306.

6 The international debt crisis

*Gary Dymski**

Introduction

This chapter reviews recent historical experience with international debt crises, with an emphasis on how economists have answered two core questions about these episodes: why do they occur? And what should be done about them? The last three decades, a period of increasingly unregulated cross-border financial flows, witnessed numerous international debt and currency crises – among them, the 1982 Latin American debt crisis, the 1994–95 Mexican 'tequila' crisis, the 1997 Asian financial crisis, the 1998–99 Russian ruble/Long-Term Capital Management crisis, and the 2001–02 meltdown of the Argentine economy – even before the 2007–08 subprime crisis shook the global financial system to its foundations. International debt crisis has become a defining feature of the contemporary world economy (Eatwell and Taylor, 2000).

Until the subprime crisis, international debt crisis could be defined as ruptures in market relations that arise when the sum of a borrower nation's cross-border repayment obligations cannot be met without radically altering expenditure levels or renegotiating repayment terms. Because both parties to cross-border debt contracts are not covered by a common contract law, lenders expect that borrowers' national governments bear residual repayment responsibility. Cross-border debt also typically involves exchange risk. If the debt contract is denominated in the lender's currency, then the borrower takes on exchange risk, and vice versa. A currency crisis arises when overseas payment obligations cannot be met at prevailing exchange rates. Most cross-border debt contracts are written in lenders' currencies, so international debt and currency crises often coincide.

The subprime crisis of 2007–08 emerged as a new kind of international debt crisis, whose impacts on borrower and lender nations are very different than in previous experience. This chapter unfolds the history of international debt crisis, including the evolution of thinking regarding the causes of debt crises and what to do about them. The chapter concludes with an analysis of the subprime crisis and the global crisis that followed on its heels, focusing on how this crisis is different, and on its implications for the future of cross-border lending and borrowing.

From the inter-war period to the end of Bretton Woods

International debt crises have a history nearly as long as international debt flows. Bordo et al. (1998) argue that financial integration has followed a U-shaped pattern: it was at very high levels until the early twentieth century, collapsed between the wars and then has gradually returned to pre-1914 levels. The breakdown of cross-border financial obligations and the collapse of banking systems in the 1930s' Depression generated numerous studies – notably those of Charles Kindleberger. His 1937 volume identified four motivations for cross-border capital movements, of which three are potentially destabilizing. He observes that shifts in perceptions about exchange rate stability can lead to changes in motives and hence to capital flow reversals. Kindleberger emphasizes the link between fear and capital flight, which he terms 'abnormal capital movements': 'the same forces that induce people to attempt to expatriate their capital make them unwilling to lend freely at home' (p. 157). Abnormal capital movements pose a problem for borrower nations: 'the balance sheet position of the country may be weakened if short-term liabilities are acquired in exchange for assets not readily available' (p. 157). The key to limiting fear and speculative pressure is a hegemonic global financial center willing and able to serve as an issuer of reserve currency and lender of last resort (Kindleberger, 1973, 1974).

The United States became the financial hegemon with the 1944 establishment of the Bretton Woods system of fixed exchange rates. Initially, tight regulation of banks combined with central bank vigilance minimized worries about the destabilizing consequences of cross-border lending. Indeed, the 1950s Marshall Plan demonstrated the benefits of international lending.

By the late 1960s, financial crises emerged as regular characteristics of business cycle dynamics (Wolfson, 1994). These events led Minsky (1975) to set out his financial instability hypothesis, which asserted that agents are led by a combination of uncertainty and competitive forces to overvalue assets and become overleveraged in upswings; they take on excessive debt, which makes them financially fragile. Cashflow precommitments for debt repayment reduce the economy's margin for error, eventually leading to a downturn.

The end of the Bretton Woods dollar standard system in 1973 exposed nations and firms to exchange risk for the first time in four decades. With the re-emergence of exchange rate volatility, economists also renewed their attention to financial disruptions across borders. Kindleberger (1978) demonstrated that historically, Minskian financial instability often crossed national borders. Krugman and Taylor (1978) developed a cross-border Minsky model. Krugman's 1979 paper gave rise to a literature on currency crises. His 'first generation model' (FGM) suggests that if a nation's macroeconomic structure is unsustainable in the medium run, speculators can start a currency crisis in the short run by making payment demands that precipitate a currency collapse. If cross-border lending had occurred, international debt crisis follows. The Minsky/Kindleberger model suggests the opposite course of events: an international debt crisis can trigger a currency crisis. Which triggers depends on which market (currency or debt) moves first.

The Latin American debt crisis

These theoretical speculations were soon put to the test. The end of the Bretton Woods system coincided with the first of two oil price shocks in the 1970s. These events generated stagflation and high interest rates, forcing some bank borrowers into market-based financing. Banks had to seek out new loan customers. Meanwhile, national restrictions on international capital movements were lifted: floating exchange rates created 'the overwhelming need to hedge against the costs that fluctuating exchange rates imposed upon the private sector' (Eatwell and Taylor, 2000, p. 2). The banks found their new loan customers by recycling the revenues of oil exporters, especially to oil importing nations. A key component of this 'petrodollar' recycling was large-scale bank lending to Latin America. In an era attuned to the 'limits to growth' (Meadows, 1981), this lending seemed eminently justified by these nations' resources and growth prospects. As Citibank's Walter Wriston (1982) put it, countries don't go bankrupt.

Competitive pressures among megabanks, together with these lenders' 'disaster myopia' (Guttentag and Herring, 1984), led to a rapid build-up of bank loans to Latin America. This lending momentum came to a stop when Mexico's August 1982 debt moratorium triggered the first international debt crisis in 50 years. The unprecedented nominal interest rates of this period, combined with global stagnation, generated debt moratoria, renegotiations and adjustment programs throughout Latin America.[1]

The Latin American debt crisis occurred just as principal/agent theory based on asymmetric information was coming into fashion, as were microfoundational explanations of macroeconomic phenomena.[2] Asymmetric information models of the credit market assert that borrowers may have informational advantages of two kinds over lenders: information concerning their competency, which affects their probability of success (their 'type'); and their plans for using and repaying the loans they receive, which affect the likelihood of repayment (their 'effort'). Lenders' optimal response is to ration credit and/or to use signaling mechanisms to screen borrowers.

The paradigmatic microfoundational model of the non-payment of Latin American loans is Eaton et al. (1986). These authors argue that debt repudiation is a feasible outcome because of the lack of a common contract law. They also accept Wriston's view, writing that 'the resources of the debtor are likely to be adequate to repay the loans regardless' (p. 485). The borrower country, conceptualized as a unitary agent, compares the relative utility of repaying its debt and of defaulting on its debt; as a rational agent, it defaults when the utility from default is larger. The debt 'crisis' of non-payment is thus due to inadequate debtor 'effort' (not 'type'), that is, to realized moral hazard. The solution is to increase the penalty for not repaying until it exceeds the value of the principal lent; and improve oversight of lending to developing countries. These authors conclude, 'it is surprising that there has been as much lending to developing countries as there has been, not that there is not more' (p. 512).

This model illuminates some aspects of the Latin American debt crisis, but obscures others. First, the underassessment of risk – 'disaster myopia' – is dismissed out of hand, since lenders and borrowers are viewed as fully rational. Second, to operationalize rationality, credit risk is treated in a simplified way, ignoring its institutional and historical precedents (why didn't this crisis arise in 1979?). Third, the 'enforceability' model also has overly simple depictions of the 'agents' in this principal/agent game. On the lenders' side, the focus on one lender ignores the competitive pressures among banks. The borrowers, in turn, were not unitary agents with complete control over national wealth (their 'collateral'); instead, they were firms, state enterprises and political leaders, all with different objectives and time horizons. Modeling a unitary 'borrower' precludes any attention to the evolving roles of various 'sub-agents' in determining each borrower country's 'moves'.

Some alternative explanations addressed these limitations. As noted above, the 'disaster myopia' explanation of overborrowing emerges once the postulate of rationality is relaxed. This view constitutes the microfoundational side of the Minsky/Kindleberger model. Indeed, Kindleberger developed his own account of what had happened (1989). Darity and Horn (1988) developed an overlending model in which developing nations are locked out of primary markets, except in periods of excess liquidity. The late 1970s and early 1980s were such a period; during that time the multinational banks 'pushed' credit onto less developed countries because of their competition for market share (Joint ECLAC, 1989). So the root of the Latin American debt crisis is uneven global development and market segmentation, not borrower recalcitrance.

Dymski and Pastor (1990a, 1990b), in turn, develop a model that replaces the 'unitary agent' borrower nation with several 'players' in borrower countries. In their account, repayment to external lenders may be problematic because it requires the regressive redistribution of national income, threatening political leaders' legitimacy and also the continued worker effort on which national output depends. Repaying debt amidst a crisis can have longer-run costs in political legitimacy and economic productivity.

Other authors have developed alternative explanations that put this crisis into historical perspective. Vos (1994) observes that overlending tends to arise because of the oligopolistic nature of overseas lending markets, competitors' goal of enhancing their market share and lenders' tendency to under-assess risks. Most current LDC borrowers have defaulted in the past, more than once. Eichengreen and Lindert (1989) found that credit markets learn nothing: when lending resumes, former defaulters are treated the same as are those who made payments. This volume also finds (as does Vos) that lending tends to be clustered among certain borrowers, leading to undue concentrations of risk.

From the Latin American debt crisis to the East Asian financial crisis

Concern with the causes of the Latin American debt crisis soon gave way to scholarship on sovereign debt renegotiation and the pricing of securitized sovereign debt. Aggarwal (1996) summarizes this vast literature and interprets it using bargaining models. This literature identified several problems associated with debt 'overhang'. Claessens and Diwan (1990) showed that an overhang of external public debt can generate illiquidity and disincentive effects. Making payments on existing debt can restrict investment and dampen growth, due to a liquidity shortage. This shortage arises, in turn, because expectations of a continuing future debt burden reduce incentives for current investment and dissuade external lenders from new financing. Cohen (1990) noted that when existing debt is offloaded by lenders into a secondary market (as happened from 1987 onward with the Latin American crisis), any primary market (new) debt can be obtained only at the price prevailing in the secondary market. That is, lenders cannot be more optimistic than whichever wealth owners already hold a borrower nation's pre-existing debt. Borrowers in this circumstance are subject to double market discipline.

By the end of the 1980s, Latin America itself was in the midst of its 'lost decade', with stagnation accompanied by hyperinflation, devaluation and regressive redistribution. Still, a reevaluation of international capital and credit flows to the developing world was underway. Sachs (1989), for example, asserted that developing countries could avoid renewed debt crisis by adopting proper macroeconomic policies.

Large-scale financial flows resumed. Cross-border lending to East Asia increased: from \$161 billion in 1985, to \$204 billion in 1990, to a peak of \$534 billion in 1997. Lending to the transition economies of Europe grew next: from \$134 billion in 1990 to a high of \$275 billion in 2000.[3] After 1990, cross-border lending to Latin America also recovered: the nominal value of claims on Latin America grew in every year except one (1999) after 1990 – from \$250 billion in 1990 to \$746 billion in 2001.

The character of cross-border financial flows was evolving. Between 1985 and 1995, about 45 percent of cross-border claims on developing countries were held by banks; after 1995, bank share plummeted, reaching 20 percent in 2000. By contrast, banks' share of developed country cross-border claims has climbed from 16 percent in 1985 to 33 percent in 2000. Banks' reduced role in cross-border lending was paralleled by an increasing role of non-bank private sector lending, much of it taking the form of bonds.[4] Bank lending also shifted toward short-term commitments, and away from long-term lending. Foreign direct investment in developing countries has moved away from greenfield development and toward privatizations and portfolio investments.[5] A final significant shift involves the entry of many large overseas banks into developing economies (Dymski, 2002).

The Mexican 'tequila' crisis of 1994–95, involving a run on the peso, came as a rude shock. Mexico had become a favored locus for capital inflows because of its financial liberalization, its improving macroeconomic fundamentals and its investment prospects, all linked to the 1992 North American Free Trade Agreement. This crisis exposed and, to some extent, triggered many credit-related problems in Mexican banks; the Mexican government was forced to subsidize sell-offs of leading Mexican banks to offshore owners. Since it was such a surprise, this crisis created substantial interest in what was termed the second generation model (SGM) of currency crises (Obstfeld, 1994). The SGM showed that non-linearities in the behaviors and beliefs of agents in capital, credit and currency markets could in themselves give rise to currency crises, especially when a nation's macroeconomic fundamentals fell into a 'gray area'.[6] The SGM thus raised the possibility, commonly observed in non-linear systems, that small changes in beliefs and fundamentals could unleash cumulative cascades and also set off contagion effects in other countries.

Reflecting on this episode, Calvo et al. (1996) emphasized the need for policies protecting borrower countries – especially the maintenance of adequate reserves and provisions for orderly workouts. Stronger measures, such as exchange and capital controls, are rejected. Goldstein and Reinhart (1996), in turn, argued for 'early warning systems' for investors and creditors. Both suggestions anticipate that enhancing information and guarantees will suffice to limit contagion and bandwagon effects.

This calming prognosis was amplified in a World Bank report on capital flows to developing nations (World Bank, 1997), which reviews both the 1980s Latin American debt crisis and the 1994–95 Mexican currency crisis. This report admits that financial opening and cross-border financial flows entail macroeconomic and financial risks, but argues that these risks are manageable and are outweighed by prospective efficiency and output gains. This volume takes as given that 'there is no alternative' to financial liberalization: developing nations' governments can monitor and oversee financial risk; but blocking financial opening would only distort incentives and worsen riskiness in the longer run.

A more troubling interpretation based on Minsky was available, though it did not sway many in this period: the volatility and reversibility of capital flows make economies receiving systematic capital inflows increasingly vulnerable to bad news, downturns, or shifts of investor opinion. So the Mexican crisis is not anomalous, but instead prefigures problems in other nations receiving capital inflows. FGM models of currency crisis indicated that speculators are expected to attack the currencies of nations with non-viable macroeconomic structures. Having current account deficits is one signal of such 'non-viability'. However, these deficits are often linked to capital account inflows. This happens, for example, when a nation favored by overseas investors has many unfinished investment projects, has a politically influential (and financially flighty) upper class interested in conspicuous consumption, and must import many intermediate and consumer goods. But then, virtually any developing nation that becomes a favored offshore investment/loan target will, by virtue of accepting capital inflows, create the macroeconomic circumstances that will later justify speculative runs on its currency.

The Asian financial crisis and its aftermath

East and Southeast Asia became favored venues for cross-border debt flows through the 1990s. The Asian financial crisis, like the tequila crisis, was a surprise: as Obstfeld (1998) wrote, the free flow of capital across borders should induce macro-discipline and reduce the likelihood of policy mistakes. Instead the opposite seemed the case, as this crisis hit the global financial system like an iceberg. The slowmotion detonation began in Indonesia and Thailand, then moved northeasterly to South Korea and the Philippines; longer-run effects then followed, including growth slowdowns in Taiwan, price declines in global equity markets and speculative attacks on Brazil, Russia and Turkey.

The Asian crisis unleashed vigorous and unresolved debates in the realms of both policy and economic research. Turning first to policy, the International Monetary Fund (IMF, 1998; Guitián, 1998) argued that while borrower nations caught in this crisis may have had sound macroeconomic strategies, they were vulnerable because of their improperly supervised banking systems. Specifically, developing countries are especially vulnerable to financial instability because they lack a fully developed set of financial instruments and institutions: information on borrowers is incomplete, so overseas' investors uncertainty is higher than elsewhere (Knight, 1998). The solution is tighter regulation and further financial system development and opening.

The World Bank (1999) took a far more skeptical view of market forces.[7] This report attributes the global financial crisis in the developing world not just to weaknesses in domestic financial systems and oversight but also to international capital market imperfections, which can lead to contagion effects, liquidity crises and panics. This report advocated a rethinking of global financial architecture. Other policy voices went further. For example, UNCTAD (1998) argued that slow global macroeconomic growth combined with unstable 'hot money' flows were at the root of the East Asian crisis. UNCTAD (2000, Chapter 4) challenged both the appropriateness of the IMF's orthodox policies and the advisability of financial liberalization.

This crisis also profoundly shook economists' ideas about international debt crises. For neither the FGM or the SGM fit the East Asian case (Bustelo, 1998) and economists had before 1998 frequently cited the Asian economies' success in using government-led arrangements to asymmetric-information-related incentive problems (Stiglitz and Uy, 1996 and Stiglitz, 1996) and achieve high growth rates (Singh, 1996). Indeed, one of the first reactions to the Asian crisis, by Krugman (1998), argued that rampant moral hazard in Asia's state-controlled banking systems was at its root cause.[8] Numerous analysts (Chang et al., 1998; Crotty and Dymski, 1998; Wade, 1998; Wade and Veneroso, 1998) objected that external factors – such as the stagnant global macroeconomy, unstable global financial markets, the power of Wall Street, and IMF policies – had played the key role. Stiglitz himself reacted immediately in a speech (Stiglitz, 1998) defending the prerogative of developing nations to regulate markets and maintain independent (including non-neoliberal) strategies (and see Stiglitz, 2000). Kregel (1998) showed that the Asian crisis can be understood as an outbreak of Minskyan financial instability. Corsetti et al. (1999) acknowledged speculation and contagion effects, but asserted that these, in turn, were triggered by moral hazard and poorly designed economic policies.

The Asian crisis launched much new empirical and theoretical research, much of it focused on the empirical importance of FGM and SGM factors. This research has verified the empirical significance of contagion effects. For example, Demirgüç-Kunt and Detragiache (1998) find that financial liberalization increases the probability of banking crisis, and that financial crises' contagion effects are large and costly. And since much of the lending in Asia involved intermediation by domestic banking systems, some research has focused on this link in the international lending chain. For example, Hardy and Pazarbasioglu (1998) find that variables capturing the vulnerability of the banking and corporate sector predict subsequent crises, but macroeconomic variables do not. An historical investigation by Williamson and Mahar (1998) also finds that financial liberalization and financial crises coincide.

As in the years after the Latin American crisis, debt repayment attracted attention. Krueger (2002) points out that debt repayment has to be rethought because of the shift away from lending by a few large banks, and toward nonbank financing of cross-border debt. There are also more complex interactions among sovereign and private sector obligations; indeed, sovereign bankruptcy has even been discussed (White, 2002).

The continuing experiences of debt and currency crises (Brazil, Russia, and so on) undoubtedly affected researchers. Increasingly, even market-oriented economists came to skeptical conclusions about the liberalization of financial flows.[9] For example, Espinosa-Vega et al. (2000) argued that developing economies might grow faster if they imposed restrictions on cross-border capital movements; and Calvo (2000) demonstrated that opening up derivatives markets for developing economies may reduce economic welfare. Agénor's survey (2001) found that financial integration is generating many efficiency losses: undue concentration of lending, while some nations are credit-starved; procyclical access to global financial markets; and procyclicality in short-term flows.[10]

Because principal/agent conflicts and asymmetric information exist at several levels of the global economy, models have often shown that any policy that fixes one set of problems may generate others. For example, Vives (2002) argued that while dollarization and short-term debt exert discipline over borrower nations' macroeconomic policies, these measures may lead to excessive liquidation of otherwise viable projects. Chang and Majnoni (2002), in turn, showed that whether contagion effects or fundamentals generate financial crises (that is, whether FGM or SGM factors dominate) depends on whether the fundamentals are 'weak'.

This research by market-oriented economists reached no conclusion. Since these economists use Walrasian equilibrium as an index of how markets are *supposed* to work, they were reluctant to drop it as a benchmark (Crotty and Dymski, 1998). At the same time, recent experience made them uneasy about this reference point. In consequence, debate proceeded uncertainly, with participants sometimes talking past each other. An example is banks' self-assessments of risk: the notion that regulatory standards are inadequate guides to bank safety because of proliferating off-balance sheet commitments and regulatory capture. Barth et al. (2001) and Caprio and Honohan (2002), among others, advocated cross-border mergers and bank self-assessment of risk as means of promoting financial and macroeconomic stability. But then a special issue of *Journal of Banking and Finance* (edited by Szegö, 2002) demonstrated the infeasibility of bank risk self-assessments.[11]

Economists not operating from neoliberal premises have increasingly regarded cross-border debt crises as one element of a global trap for developing nations. Eatwell and Taylor (2000) pointed out the inescapability of the 'trilemma', wherein liberalized capital markets, a fixed exchange rate and an independent monetary or fiscal policy are not mutually consistent. In the neoliberal story, in which an 'alert private sector chastises an inept government' (p. 106), the trilemma can be avoided because floating exchange rates are a viable means of achieving equilibrium (Reinhart, 2000). When the viability of floating rates is rejected, then the trilemma looms as an inescapable obstacle to development once financial markets are liberalized. Crises cannot be traced to inadvisable fiscal or monetary policies in any simple way. Eatwell and Taylor (2000) argued that capital inflows spill over to the macroeconomy via the financial system; this worsens the current account, and the interest rate is raised, and financial fragility and risks grow. As the authors observed, fiscal deficits and moral hazard play no significant role in these dynamics.

So under capital inflows, the trilemma takes a special form: as noted, the very fact of these inflows creates the preconditions for a panic. In many cases, domestic policy cannot erase the problem. Uncovered interest parity becomes a trap for nations with continuing external debt obligations (such as Brazil).[12] Leaving domestic interest rates at current levels will do nothing to stop creditors who are pulling their funds away. But widening the world/local interest rate spread to hold funds or attract new capital only signals the greater likelihood of exchange rate collapse. Under the current rules of the game, there may be no alternative to domestic stagnation and regressive redistribution as the price of inflows of overseas capital and credit.

The subprime crisis and its antecedents

The skepticism of more and more economists about open capital flows as the twenty-first century began was paralleled by shifts in cross-border financial relations, and ultimately in the form of the international debt crisis that exploded across the global financial system in 2007. As noted, cross-border lending by large multinational banks has been declining. While this form of cross-border financial linkage has receded in importance, however, new linkages have grown explosively, leading to the global 'subprime' crisis of 2007.

In the neoliberal era, financial contracts known as derivatives became a key part of the financial system. These contracts resembled loans in that they represented promises to pay; but payment was contingent on the realization of particular prices on particular commodities or financial instruments during particular timeframes. Financial market participants could use derivatives either to insure against enterprise risk or to place bets. New kinds of financial funds emerged in this period as well – among them hedge funds. Hedge funds, structured to evade domestic financial regulation, used market leverage well in excess of what commercial banks were permitted, to seek above-market profits. A favorite strategy involved arbitrage – taking advantage of minute differences in the current and future prices of financial instruments (such as government bonds), using derivatives to either insure against or double-down on the risks associated with such position-taking. In September 1998, Long-Term Capital Management (LTCM), one of the largest and most aggressive hedge funds, collapsed when its aggressive position on Russian currency and securities was undercut by Russia's default on its government bonds.[13] A run on the ruble resulted, damaging currency values and growth rates not just in Russia but in other nations, notably Brazil and Turkey. The Federal Reserve resolved this crisis by orchestrating a 'lender of last resort' response with the cooperation of Wall Street money-center banks, especially the large investment banks.

The LTCM episode signaled the dawn of a new era of international debt crises. The debt burdens of the countries whose currencies plunged worsened significantly due to this crisis; but this worsening of circumstance had nothing to do with changes in their own cross-border borrowing. In effect, this was the SGM squared – financial crisis could occur not only because of belief-driven fluctuations in the beliefs of one's lenders, but also because of failures in risk-taking in completely unrelated markets.

The LTCM crisis apparently proved that the Wall Street megabank complex had sufficient capacity, when coordinated by the Federal Reserve, to handle the failure of even a huge highly leveraged fund. Certainly, this crisis announced the dawn of the age when traditional bank position-taking could be swamped by off-balance-sheet commitments made with unregulated instruments whose core characteristics were poorly understood even by their creators. Despite the risks, those operating in these markets could make huge returns. Consequently, large banks soon got into these markets themselves – especially the large, lightly regulated Wall Street investment banks. Regulators proposed new global rules (under the 'Basel Accord') for limiting global banking risk, which basically involved megabanks running their own 'stress tests' to insure they had sufficient capital to survive various sorts of market shocks.

Meanwhile, the large megabanks continued charging ahead, competing fiercely for market share and fees by expanding into virtually every area of financial market activity. Megabanks drove into new markets by both exploiting the removal of some barriers to non-traditional banking activity and forcing others aside. This was one of the root causes of the 2007 subprime crisis.[14] What set the process in motion was banks' and non-banks' emerging interest in the financial services markets of lower-income and minority areas. In the mid-1990s, lenders came up with new credit instruments, aimed at 'high risk' – initially lower-income and minority – customers. Credit was provided at high rates of interest, with high penalty costs, and high collateral requirements. The options ranged from short-term 'payday' loans to consumer-durable financing to first or second mortgages for homeowners. These 'subprime' mortgage loans were launched in the early 1990s, and then grew at a frenetic pace in neighborhoods historically subject to financial exclusion.

The growth of these 'predatory lending' markets was facilitated by the availability of intermediaries willing to buy securities created by bundling these high-risk loans. Crucial to this demand were hedge funds and private equity funds; unburdened by reporting and oversight requirements, these entities provide a launching pad for high-risk, high-leverage investment strategies. The existence of outlets for subprime paper transformed the landscape of strategic possibility for banks. Previously, only 'conforming' (or 'plain vanilla') mortgages could be securitized – that is, mortgages whose risk parameters (20 percent down payment, due diligence about borrower income, etc.) met Fannie Mae guidelines. Now, non-conforming mortgages were underwritten and securitized, outside Fannie Mae's orbit. Banks could make high-risk loans and then sell off the resulting credit risk.[15]

In the 1990s and early 2000s, subprime loan practices heavily impacted the elderly, people of color and minority neighborhoods in the US.[16] The 2000s witnessed the build-up of a housing market bubble in several countries – particularly the US, the UK and Spain. The gathering housing boom caused home prices in some places to rise beyond the ranges of what homebuyers could afford using conventional mortgages and historical loan–income benchmarks. Subprime mortgages provided the solution: they broadened the pool of home-buyers in overheating markets by emphasizing the dynamic price potential of the housing asset, not the solvency of the borrower. As housing prices rose further and more mortgage suppliers and bundlers crowded in, financial innovations that were viable only with continued home-price appreciation came into common use.

Financial markets were awash in liquidity, so prime and subprime mortgages were often bundled into structured investment vehicles (SIVs) financed by short-term (asset-backed) commercial paper. Competition for return led to indifference about risk. Soon mortgage-backed securities were seen as one component of a broader class of collateralized debt obligation (CDO): securitization was expanded to include bank bridge loans for acquisitions, credit card debt, educational loans and so on. Concerns about downside risk were assuaged by the use of credit-default swaps, a huge proportion of which were issued by AIG.

By the mid-2000s, SIVs representing claims on mortgage and other debt were held throughout the world. In the other post-war episodes of international debt crisis, claims on borrowers in developing nations were held largely by banks in financial centers. In the 2000s, claims were also held by banks and funds in financial centers, augmented by the holdings of nations with large current-account surpluses. The debt in question, by contrast, originated in several high-income nations.

So systemic risk grew in the heart of global financial markets, not, as so often before, on these markets' peripheries. This risk was generated in largely deregulated global markets, by firms and funds who were notorious 'copy cats'. Imitation drove down margins, and firms seeking fee-based earnings on risks insured by third parties gave little thought to their own potential exposures. The growing volume of securitized debt and of SIVs, cross-sold and insured across national borders, increasingly interlocked participants throughout advanced global financial markets.[17]

The housing bubble began to collapse in early 2007 when many homeowners – especially those holding subprime mortgages – could not support mortgage-finance commitments made in the late stages of the boom. As the crisis went on, however, and housing prices fell precipitously, homeowners with more traditional mortgages began to default in large numbers. The cross-border, cross-market liquidity that had financed SIVs and CDOs evaporated in September

2007, as players throughout the global markets found themselves completely uncertain about the extent of default risk, and hence about securitized assets' market value and their own risk exposure. Massive interventions by central banks, especially in nations whose banks had emitted or held large volumes of subprime paper, were required to bring the semblance of order to global markets. Several large investment and commercial banks were dissolved.

The crisis in financial markets and in the world economy continues running its course as these words are written.[18] We might close by noting the irony that whereas the severe international debt crises of the neoliberal era wreaked great havoc on nations, people and banks in the developing world, the high-income countries with the most sophisticated financial markets have provided the locus for the greatest of the international debt crises of this historical time period. How the costs of the subprime crisis will ultimately be borne, and the full implications of this crisis for global economic growth, remains to be seen.

Conclusion

Economists have suggested five answers to the question of what causes international debt crises: perverse macroeconomic policies; problems in cross-border creditor–debtor contracts; problems in creditor–debtor relations within borrower countries; perverse interactions among cross-border creditors; problems in the global structure of cross-border financial flows and commitments. These five causes lead to five parallel responses to the question of what should be done: fix macroeconomic policies; fix the rules governing cross-border financial contracts; fix the rules governing creditor–borrower relations within borrower countries; improve information; or fix the rules governing cross-border financial flows in the global economy.

In the Latin American debt crisis, economists who were broadly sympathetic to market forces focused on the first two causes (and solutions), while those skeptical of such forces emphasized the fifth. In the Asian crisis, market-oriented economists emphasized the third and fourth factors, since the first two were largely resolved. Market skeptics, whose ranks increased in relative terms, pointed to the fifth cause, the overall structure of the global system. With the subprime crisis, some economists focused on the fourth cause, but an even larger share of economists again fingered the fifth cause.

For economists who operate on the premise that 'there is no alternative' to market-driven flows of credit and capital, these crises present opportunities for fine-tuning. This is the only way of moving ever closer to the idea of economic efficiency set out in the textbooks. But for economists who regard the structure of global financial flows as flawed, the costs of each crisis episode are cumulative: each crisis leads to more international and intranational inequality, and to the further dismantling of national development-oriented institutions (Baker et al., 1998). For these economists, the subprime crisis represents the culmination of several decades in which debt crises led to borrowers being punished, while creditors were given an ever freer scope for action.

The draconian efforts required to restore order in global financial markets in response to the subprime crisis have by no means addressed the root causes of international debt crises. To the contrary, since the steps taken to salvage the global financial architecture have bailed out firms and market participants that precipitated these crises, future crises – possibly in still new forms – become still more likely. Further, these asymmetric resolutions of international debt crises leave the world ever farther from an alternative set of financial relations in which the gains of financial integration are more evenly shared, and the costs of crises no longer fall most heavily on the most vulnerable nations and people.

Notes

* Published as Chapter 5 (pp. 90–103) in *The Handbook of Globalisation*, edited by Jonathan Michie (Edward Elgar, 2003) and revised for this edition.

1. Cline (1984, 1996) provides valuable overviews of this crisis. The academic literature on the Latin American debt crisis is surveyed by Eaton and Taylor (1986).
2. The most important of these articles was Stiglitz and Weiss (1983).
3. These statistics were calculated by the author from data series published by the Bank for International Settlements, and are available on request.
4. The shift to bonds represents a return to the historical pattern of the 1920s (Vos, 1994).
5. For Latin America and the Caribbean, see ECLAC (2001).
6. Masson and Agénor (1996) suggest the peso crisis was generated more by SGM-like than FGM-like factors.
7. To see this, compare this document with World Bank (1997).
8. Krugman (1994) previously registered his skepticism of the Asian 'model'. Chang (2000) is a thoughtful rejoinder to the idea that moral hazard characterizes this model. Bustelo et al. (1999) is the most comprehensive review of the literature on the Asian financial crisis.
9. This distinction between 'market-oriented' and 'market-skeptical' economists is arbitrary; in practice, there is a continuum of opinion among economists about how well markets work.
10. These characteristics of contemporary cross-border lending, which reflect lenders' risk aversion, are precisely those against which Kindleberger warned in 1937.
11. For example, Daníelsson argues: 'since market data is endogenous to market behavior, statistical analysis made in times of stability does not provide much guidance in times of crisis … the empirical properties of current risk forecasting models are found to be lacking in robustness while being excessively volatile' (2002, p. 1273).
12. Under uncovered interest parity, the domestic interest rate should in equilibrium equal the world interest rate plus any expected currency devaluation. This is a commonly cited criterion for assessing the soundness of national economic policy.
13. The LTCM story is told in depth by Lowenstein (2000).
14. On the causes and implications of the subprime crisis, see Demyanyk and Van Hemert (2008) and Dymski (2009).
15. Lenders would have done well to remember the experience of the savings-and-loan crisis of the 1980s regarding the selling of risky loans. That episode established the principle of recourse risk: when a lender originates and then sells a loan that falls short of the rate of return promised to its buyer, the buyer has recourse to the seller for the difference. Allowing more adequately for recourse risk would have reduced either the return offered or the seller's leverage, putting the seller at a competitive disadvantage vis-à-vis more aggressive sellers.
16. A nationwide study of 2000 HMDA data (Bradford, 2002) found that African Americans were more than twice as likely as whites to receive subprime loans, and Latinos more than 40–220

percent more likely. The symposium edited by Aalbers (2009) presents an in-depth analysis of the links between racial inequality and the subprime crisis.

17. Among the many valuable 'insider' accounts of reactions on Wall Street as the subprime crisis unfolded are Cohan (2008) and Sorkin (2009).
18. On the magnitude and ramifications of the 2007 global financial crisis, see Blankenburg and Palma (2009).

References

Aalbers, Manuel B. (2009), 'Symposium – The Sociology and Geography of Mortgage Markets: Reflections on the Financial Crisis,' *The International Journal of Urban and Regional Research*, **33**(2), June, 281–442.

Agénor, Pierre-Richard (2001), 'Benefits and Costs of International Financial Integration: Theory and Facts,' Policy Research Working Paper No. 2699, Washington, DC: The World Bank, October.

Aggarwal, Vinod (1996), *Debt Games: Strategic Interaction in International Debt Rescheduling*, Cambridge: Cambridge University Press.

Baker, Dean, Gerald Epstein and Robert Pollin (eds) (1998), *Globalization and Progressive Economic Policy*, Cambridge: Cambridge University Press.

Barth, James R., Gerard Caprio Jr. and Ross Levine (2001), 'Bank Regulation and Supervision: What Works Best?', Working Paper No. 2725, Washington, DC: World Bank, November.

Blankenburg, Stephanie and José Gabriel Palma (eds) (2009), 'The Global Financial Crisis,' *Cambridge Journal of Economics*, **33**(4), 531–839.

Bordo, Michael, Barry Eichengreen and Jongwoo Kim (1998), 'Was There Really an Earlier Period of International Financial Integration Comparable to Today?', Cambridge, MA: National Bureau of Economic Research, Working Paper No. 6738.

Bradford, Calvin (2002), 'Risk or Race? Racial Disparities and the Subprime Refinance Market: A Report of the Center for Community Change,' Washington, DC: Center for Community Change, May.

Bustelo, P. (1998), 'The East Asian Financial Crisis: An Analytical Survey,' ICEI Working Paper No. 10/1998, Instituto Complutense de Estudios Internacionales, Madrid.

Bustelo, Pablo, Clara Garcia and Iliana Olivié (1999), 'Global and Domestic Factors of Financial Crises in Emerging Economies: Lessons from the East Asian Episodes (1997–1999),' ICEI Working Paper No. 16, Complutense Institute for International Studies, Complutense University of Madrid, Spain, November.

Calvo, Guillermo A. (2000), 'Betting against the State: Socially Costly Financial Engineering,' *Journal of International Economics*, **51**(1), 5–19.

Calvo, Guillermo, Morris Goldstein and Eduard Hochreiter (1996), *Private Capital Flows to Emerging Markets after the Mexican Crisis*, Washington, DC: Institute for International Economics.

Caprio, Gerard and Patrick Honohan (2002), 'Banking Policy and Macroeconomic Stability: An Exploration,' Working Paper No. 2856, Washington, DC: World Bank: June.

Chang, Ha-Joon (2000), 'The Hazard of Moral Hazard: Untangling the Asian Crisis,' *World Development*, **28**(4), April, 775–88.

Chang, Ha-Joon, Hong-Jae Park and Chul Gyue Yoo (1998), 'Interpreting the Korean Crisis: Financial Liberalisation, Industrial Policy, and Corporate Governance,' *Cambridge Journal of Economics*, **22**(6), August.

Chang, Roberto and Giovanni Majnoni (2002), 'Fundamentals, Beliefs, and Financial Contagion,' *European Economic Review*, **46**(4/5), 801–8.

Claessens, S. and I. Diwan (1990), 'Investment Incentives – New Money, Debt Relief, and the Critical Role of Conditionality in the Debt Crisis,' *World Bank Economic Review*, **4**(1), 21–41.

Cline, William R. (1984), *International Debt: Systemic Risk and Policy Response*, Washington, DC: Institute for International Economics.

Cline, William (1996), *International Debt Reexamined*, Washington, DC: Institute for International Economics.

Cohan, William D. (2008), *House of Cards: A Tale of Hubris and Wretched Excess on Wall Street*, New York: Doubleday.

Cohen, Daniel (1990), 'Debt Relief – Implications of Secondary Market Discounts and Debt Overhangs,' *World Bank Economic Review*, **4**(1), 43–53.
Corsetti, Giancarlo, Paolo Presenti and Nouriel Roubini (1999), 'What Caused the Asian Currency and Financial Crisis?', *Japan and the World Economy*, **11**(3), 305–73.
Crotty, James and Gary Dymski (1998), 'Can Global Neoliberalism Survive Victory in Asia? The Political Economy of the Korean Crisis,' *International Papers in Political Economy*, **1998**(2), (reprinted in *Money, Finance, and Capitalist Development* in 2001, edited by Philip Arestis and Malcolm Sawyer, Cheltenham, UK and Northampton, MA, USA: Edward Elgar).
Daníelsson, Jón (2002), 'The Emperor Has No Clothes: Limits to Risk Modelling,' *Journal of Banking and Finance*, **26**(7), 1273–96.
Darity, William, Jr. and Bobbie L. Horn (1988), *The Loan Pushers: The Role of Commercial Banks in the International Debt Crisis*, Cambridge, MA: Ballinger Pub, Co.
Demirgüç-Kunt, Asli and Enrica Detragiache (1998), 'Financial Liberalization and Financial Fragility,' IMF Working Paper No. 98/83, Washington, DC: International Monetary Fund, June.
Demyanyk, Yuliya and Otto Van Hemert (2008), 'Understanding the Subprime Mortgage Crisis,' Federal Reserve Bank of Cleveland, published online in *The Review of Financial Studies*, 2009.
Dymski, Gary A. (2002), 'The Global Bank Merger Wave: Implications for Developing Countries,' *The Developing Economies*, **40**(4), 435–66.
Dymski, Gary A. (2009), 'Racial Exclusion and the Political Economy of the Subprime Crisis,' *Historical Materialism*, **17**(2), 149–79.
Dymski, Gary A. and Manuel Pastor, Jr. (1990a), 'Debt Crisis and Class Conflict in Latin America,' *Review of Radical Political Economics*, **22**(1), 155–78.
Dymski, Gary A. and Manuel Pastor, Jr. (1990b), 'Misleading Signals, Bank Lending, and the Latin American Debt Crisis,' *International Trade Journal*, **6**(2), 151–91.
Eaton, Jonathan and Lance Taylor (1986), 'Developing Country Finance and Debt,' *Journal of Development Economics*, **22**(1), 209–65.
Eaton, Jonathan, Mark Gersovitz and Joseph Stiglitz (1986), 'The Pure Theory of Country Risk,' *European Economic Review*, **30**(3), 481–513.
Eatwell, John and Lance Taylor (2000), *Global Finance at Risk*, New York: New Press.
Economic Commission on Latin America and the Caribbean (ECLAC) (2001), *Foreign Investment in Latin America and the Caribbean – 2000 Report*, Santiago: Chile.
Eichengreen, Barry and Peter H. Lindert (eds) (1989), *The International Debt Crisis in Historical Perspective*, Cambridge, MA: MIT Press.
Espinosa-Vega, Marco A., Bruce D. Smith and Chong K. Yip (2000), 'Barriers to International Capital Flows: When, Why, How Big, and for Whom?', Federal Reserve Bank of Atlanta Working Paper No. 2000–16, October.
Goldstein, Morris and Carmen Reinhart (1996), *Forecasting Financial Crises: Early Warning Signals for Emerging Markets*, Washington, DC: Institute for International Economics.
Guitián, Manuel (1998), 'The Challenge of Managing Capital Flows,' *Finance and Development*, **35**(2), IMF.
Guttentag, Jack and Richard Herring (1984), 'Commercial Bank Lending to Less Developed Countries: From Overlending to Underlending to Structural Reform,' *Brookings Discussion Papers in International Economics* No. 16, Washington DC: Brookings Institution.
Hardy, Daniel C. and Ceyla Pazarbasioglu (1998), 'Leading Indicators of Banking Crises: Was Asia Different?' IMF Working Paper No. 98/91, Monetary and Exchange Affairs Department, International Monetary Fund, Washington DC, June.
International Monetary Fund (1998), 'The IMF's Response to the Asian Crisis,' Washington DC: International Monetary Fund, 15 June.
Joint ECLAC/United Nations Centre on Transnational Corporations (1989), *Transnational Bank Behavior and the International Debt Crisis*. Estudios e Informes de la CEPAL, Santiago, Chile: Economic Commission for Latin America and the Caribbean, United Nations.
Kindleberger, Charles P. (1973), *The World in Depression, 1929–1939*, Berkeley: University of California Press.
Kindleberger, Charles P. (1974), *The Formation of Financial Centers: A Study in Comparative Economic History*, Princeton, NJ: International Finance Section, Princeton University.

Kindleberger, Charles P. (1937), *International Short-term Capital Movements*, New York: Columbia University Press.

Kindleberger, Charles P. (1978), *Manias, Panics, and Crashes*, New York: Basic Books.

Kindleberger, Charles P. (1989), *The 1930s and the 1980s: Parallels and Differences*, Singapore: ASEAN Economic Research Unit, Institute of Southeast Asian Studies.

Knight, Malcolm (1998), 'Developing Countries and the Globalization of Financial Markets,' Working Paper No. 98/105, Washington, DC: Monetary and Exchange Affairs Department, International Monetary Fund.

Kregel, Jan (1998), 'Yes, "It" Did Happen Again – A Minsky Crisis Happened in Asia,' Jerome Levy Economics Institute Working Paper No. 234, April.

Krueger, Anne (2002), 'Preventing and Resolving Financial Crises: The Role of Sovereign Debt Restructuring,' Speech at the Latin American Meeting of the Econometric Society, São Paolo, Brazil. Washington, DC: International Monetary Fund, 26 July.

Krugman, Paul (1979), 'A Model of Balance of Payments Crises,' *Journal of Money, Credit, and Banking*, **3**(1/2), 311–25.

Krugman, Paul (1994), 'The Myth of Asia's Miracle,' *Foreign Affairs*, **73**(6), November/December, 62–78.

Krugman, Paul (1998), 'What Happened to Asia?,' Working Paper, MIT Department of Economics, January.

Krugman, Paul and Lance Taylor (1978), 'Contractionary Effects of Devaluation,' *Journal of International Economics*, **8**(3), 445–56.

Lowenstein, Roger (2000), *When Genius Failed: The Rise and Fall of Long-Term Capital Management*, New York: Random House.

Masson, Paul R. and Pierre-Richard Agénor (1996), 'The Mexican Peso Crisis – Overview and Analysis of Credibility Factors,' Working Paper No. 96/6. Washington, DC: International Monetary Fund.

Meadows, Donella H. et al. (1981), *The Limits to Growth: A Report for the Club of Rome's Project on the Predicament of Mankind*, Second Edition, New York: Universe.

Minsky, Hyman P. (1975), *John Maynard Keynes*, New York: Columbia University Press.

Obstfeld, Maurice (1994), 'The Logic of Currency Crises,' Working Paper No. 4640, Cambridge, MA: National Bureau of Economic Research.

Obstfeld, Maurice (1998), 'The Global Capital Market: Benefactor or Menace?', *Journal of Economic Perspectives*, **12**(4), 9–30.

Reinhart, Carmen M. (2000), 'The Mirage of Floating Exchange Rates,' *American Economic Review*, **90**(2), May, 65–70.

Sachs, Jeffrey (ed.) (1989), *Developing Country Debt and the World Economy*, Chicago: University of Chicago Press for the National Bureau of Economic Research.

Singh, Ajit (1996), 'Savings, Investment and the Corporation in the East Asian Miracle,' *East Asian Development: Lessons for a New Global Environment*, Study No. 9, Geneva: United Nations Conference on Trade and Development, March.

Sorkin, Andrew Ross (2009), *Too Big to Fail: The Inside Story of How Wall Street and Washington Fought to Save the Financial System – and Themselves*, New York: Viking.

Stiglitz, Joseph E. (1996), 'Some Lessons from the East Asian Miracle,' *World Bank Research Observer*, **11**(2), 151–77.

Stiglitz, Joseph E. (1998), 'Sound Finance and Sustainable Development in Asia,' Washington DC: The World Bank, 12 March.

Stiglitz, Joseph E. (2000), 'Capital Market Liberalization, Economic Growth, and Instability,' *World Development*, **28**(6), 1075–86.

Stiglitz, Joseph E. and Marilou Uy (1996), 'Financial Markets, Public Policy, and the East Asian Miracle,' *World Bank Research Observer*, **11**(2), 249–76.

Stiglitz, Joseph E. and Andrew Weiss (1983), 'Credit Rationing in Markets with Imperfect Information,' *American Economic Review*, **71**(3), 393–410.

Szegö, Giorgio P. (2002), 'Special Issue: Statistical and Computational Problems in Risk Management: VaR and Beyond VaR,' *Journal of Banking and Finance*, **26**(7), July.

UNCTAD (2000), *Trade and Development Report, 2000*, New York: United Nations.

United Nations Conference on Trade and Development (UNCTAD) (1998), *Trade and Development Report*, Geneva: United Nations.

Vives, Xavier (2002), 'External Discipline and Financial Stability,' *European Economic Review*, **46**(4/5), 821–8.

Vos, Rob (1994), *Debt and Adjustment in the World Economy*, New York: St. Martin's.

Wade, Robert (1998), 'Gestalt Shift: From "Miracle" to "Cronyism" in the Asian Crisis,' *Cambridge Journal of Economics*, **22**(6), August.

Wade, Robert and Frank Veneroso (1998), 'The Asian Crisis: The High Debt Model vs. the Wall Street–Treasury–IMF Complex,' *New Left Review* No. 228, March–April.

White, Michelle (2002), 'Sovereigns in Distress: Do They Need Bankruptcy?', *Brookings Papers on Economic Activity*, **2002**/1.

Williamson, John and Molly Mahar (1998), 'A Survey of Financial Liberalization,' *Essay in International Finance* No. 211, Princeton: Princeton University, November.

Wolfson, Martin H. (1994), *Financial Crises: Understanding the Postwar U.S. Experience*, Second Edition. Armonk, NY: M.E. Sharpe.

World Bank (1997), *Private Capital Flows to Developing Countries: The Road to Financial Integration*, Oxford: Published for the World Bank by Oxford University Press.

World Bank (1999), *Global Economic Prospects for Developing Countries 1998/99: Beyond Financial Crisis*, Washington DC: World Bank.

Wriston, Walter (1982), 'Banking Against Disaster,' *New York Times*, 14 September.

7 National inequality in the era of globalisation: what do recent data tell us?*

José Gabriel Palma

1 Introduction

The issue of the effect of greater international economic and financial integration on national and international income distribution has always been particularly controversial in economic theory. For example, as soon as Samuelson developed his trade-related factor-price-equalisation theorem (1948–49) – that an increase in trade should have a positive effect on both international and national distribution of income (the latter because an export expansion should increase the relative income of the [cheap] abundant factor and reduce that of the [expensive] scarce factor in each country) – it immediately became one of the most debated hypotheses in trade and development economics. And now, many years later, the issues addressed in the Samuelson theorem are again at the core of the globalisation debate on the effects that the globalisation-induced increase in trade and international economic and financial integration would have on national and international income distribution and factor movements.[1] In fact, of all of Samuelson's economic hypotheses, there is probably none that has influenced US foreign policy today as much as the one that postulates that an increased level of trade between countries should reduce the incentive for labour to move across frontiers. In the case of its relationship with Mexico, for example, following the 1982 'debt crisis' the US – always frightened that worsening economic problems in Mexico could turn the usual flow of Mexican immigrants into a tidal wave – gave Mexican exports increasingly preferential access to its market, a process that led to the creation of NAFTA.[2]

As is well known, one of the main problems with the debate on trade and income distribution has been the difficulty of testing alternative hypotheses, especially in their time series formulation, due to the low quality of the available income distribution data. However, at least from a cross-sectional point of view, recent developments in household surveys have improved data substantially. Moreover, over the last decade, some institutions like the OECD (LIS), the World Bank (WB), the Inter-American Development Bank (IADB) and World Institute for Development Economics Research (WIDER) have made sustained efforts to collect and process these surveys.[3] The WB World Development Indicators (WDI) (2010), for example, provide a relatively homogeneous set of data on personal income distribution for 142 countries. However, there are still some significant problems with the WDI data set. For example, although most data refer to income distribution, some still refer to consumption expenditure (particularly in Sub-Saharan Africa). This mix of data makes regional comparison more difficult, as the distribution of consumption tends to be more equal than that of income (usually by a difference of about 3 percentage points on the Gini scale). The degree of accuracy of these surveys is still a problem too.[4]

Another problem is that, rather surprisingly, the WDI data set still reports income (or consumption) distribution only in terms of quintiles; for deciles, it only reports the shares of deciles 1 and 10. Although this is a marked improvement over traditional data sets, it is clearly unsatisfactory; as will be discussed in detail below, crucial distributional information is lost when data are aggregated in quintiles (particularly at the top). Meanwhile, the Research Department of the IADB has constructed a slightly modified data set for several Latin American countries; it uses the same methodology (primary household survey data) and data aggregation (quintiles and deciles 1 and 10) as the WDI.[5] And WIDER has collected information on income inequality for many developed, developing and transition countries in its 'World Income Inequality Database, V2.0c'.[6]

The main aim of this chapter is to use the WDI data set to take another look at national income inequalities in this era of globalisation. Throughout this chapter, unless otherwise stated, the WDI data set will be used for all countries. The total number of countries included in this study is 134.[7]

2 Inequality ranking

Figure 7.1 illustrates how these 134 countries are ranked according to their Gini indices of inequality in (or as close as possible to) 2005.

Among the many issues arising from this graph, there are two that stand out. First, around 2005, there was a particularly wide range of inequality across countries – from a very low Gini index of 24.7 (Denmark) to a huge 74.3 (Namibia). Second, all Latin American countries are clearly grouped at the very top end of the inequality ranking – with a median Gini of 53.7, their degree of inequality is almost half as much again as the overall median value for the rest of the sample (115 countries), and one-third higher than that for the 'developing-non-Latin-American' group of countries (69 countries; this group excludes ex-communist countries). In addition, within the whole group of 134 countries, the median-country-inequality ranking for the 19 Latin American countries is 122.[8] Another important issue arising from this ranking is the difference between Anglophone and non-Anglophone OECD countries, with the latter including continental Europe and Japan – with median Ginis of 36 and 30.9, respectively. The same contrast is found between the ex-communist countries of the former Soviet Union and those of Central Europe – with median Ginis of 36 and 30.6, respectively.

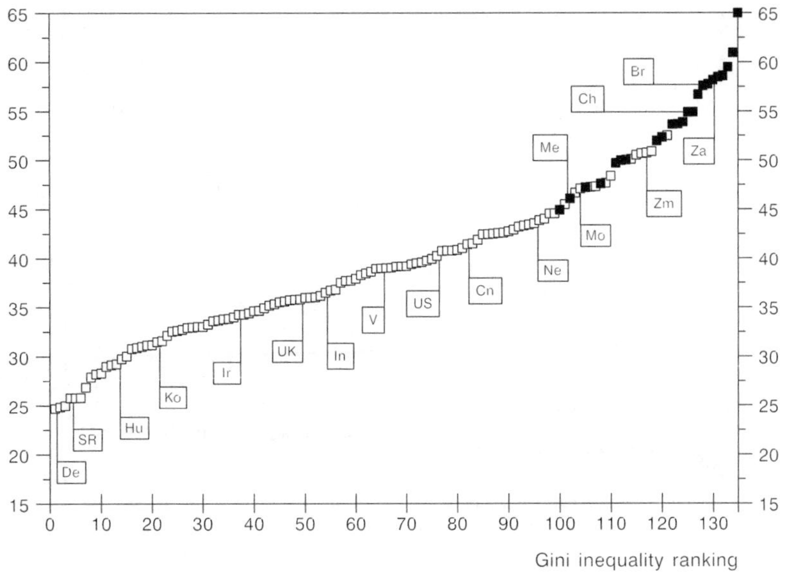

Notes: Countries are ranked according to their degree of inequality (1 to 134); Latin American and Southern African countries are shown in black (this will also be the case in similar graphs below). Throughout this chapter, Gini indices are reported on a scale from 1 to 100. The last country in the ranking is Namibia, with a Gini of 74.3!
Br=Brazil; Cn=China; Ch=Chile; De=Denmark; Hu=Hungary; In=India; Ir=Ireland; Ko=Korea; Me=Mexico; Mo=Mozambique; Ne=Niger (median Sub-Saharan African country, excluding South Africa, and the three 'diamond-rich' countries of Southern Africa – Angola, Botswana and Namibia); SR=Slovak Republic; US=United States; UK=United Kingdom; V=Vietnam; ZA=South Africa; and Zm=Zambia.

Figure 7.1 Gini indices of personal income distribution in 134 countries, c. 2005

However, Figure 7.2 shows an equally important but often ignored fact: the contrasting shares of deciles 9 and 10.[9]

While the range for the income share of decile 9 in these 134 countries only extends across 4.5 percentage points (from 13.3 per cent in Namibia to 17.7 per cent in South Africa – oddly enough, the two extreme observations are both located in Southern Africa), decile 10 has a range 10 times larger (from 20.8 per cent in the Slovak Republic, to 65 per cent in Namibia). This extraordinary difference between the dispersion of these two deciles is also reflected in their standard deviations – while that of decile 9 is just 0.8 percentage points (around a mean of 15.3 per cent), that of decile 10 is 7.2 percentage points (and a mean of 31.9 per cent); hence, the coefficient of variation of decile 10 is more than four times larger than that of decile 9.

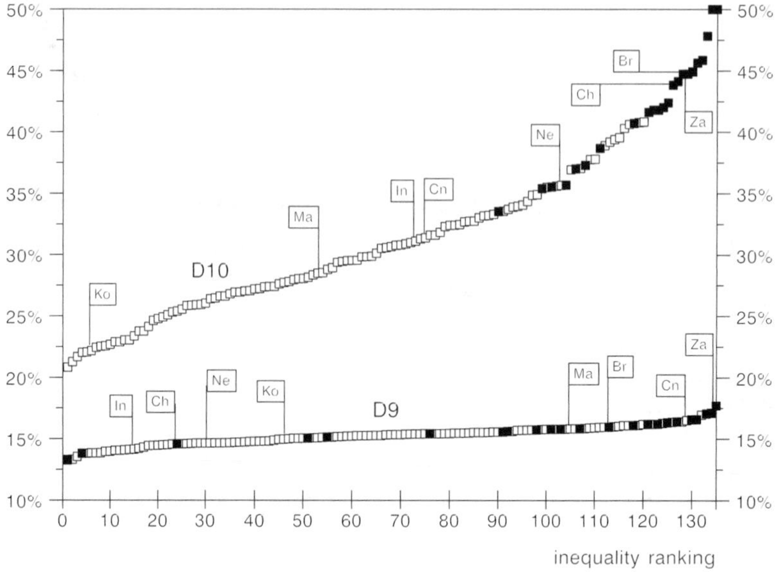

Notes: Both rankings are made independently from the other. Unless otherwise stated, this will be the case for all similar graphs in this chapter.
Br=Brazil; Ch=Chile; Ko=Korea; Cn=China; In=India; Ma=Malaysia; Ne=Niger (median Sub-Saharan Africa country, excluding South Africa, Angola, Botswana and Namibia); and Za=South Africa.
The last two observations in D10 are Botswana (51%), and Namibia (65%).

Figure 7.2 Income share of deciles 9 and 10 in 134 countries, c. 2005

This phenomenon is also corroborated by the fact that while the median values for the share of decile 9 in the Latin American and non-Latin American groups are quite similar (15.8 per cent and 15.3 per cent, respectively), those for decile 10 are very different, with the Latin American share almost half as much again as the median value for the rest of the sample (41.8 per cent and 29.5 per cent respectively). In other words, one of the key elements – if not the key one – needed to be deciphered in order to understand cross-country distributional diversity (and the effects of globalisation on national income distribution) is the determinant of the share of decile 10.[10]

However, there are also some interesting issues in decile 9; for example, while China and India have almost identical rankings in their income share of decile 10 (right in the middle of the distribution), their rankings in decile 9 are different – with India having one of the lowest shares while China is one of the largest.

Figure 7.2 also gives a first indication that the key characteristic of the income distribution of many Latin American countries is its 'winner-takes-all' nature. In

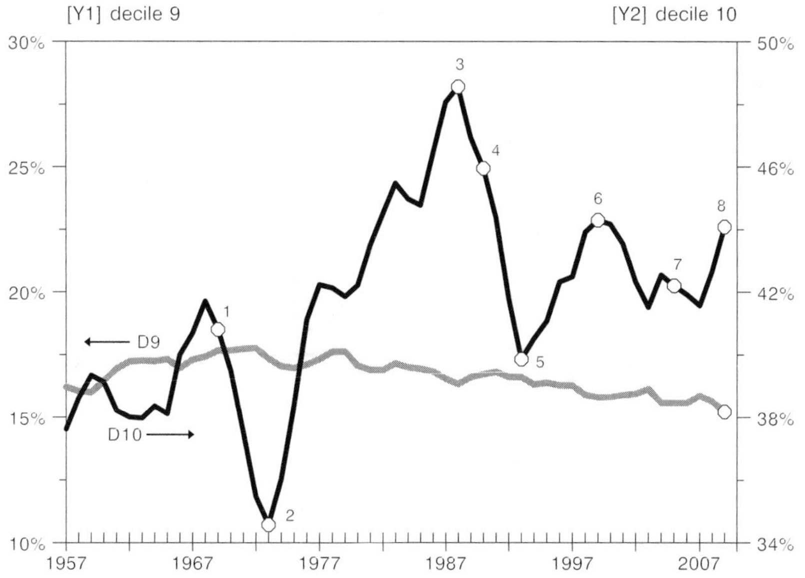

Notes: [Y1]=left-hand vertical axis (showing decile 9), and [Y2]=right-hand axis (showing decile 10). 1=election of Allende; 2=Pinochet's coup d'état; 3=the year Pinochet calls a plebiscite seeking a mandate to remain in power for another eight years; 4=first democratic government (centre-left coalition, the 'Concertación') after Pinochet lost his plebiscite (and had to call for presidential elections); 5=second democratic government (same political coalition, but a return to more 'market-led' distributed policies); 6 and 7=next two governments by the same centre-left coalition; 8=centre-left coalition is defeated in its attempt to win a fifth consecutive presidential election.

Source: Calculations made by Pamela Jervis and author using the FACEA (2010) database. Unless otherwise stated, this will be the source of all historical data for Chile.[11] Three-year moving averages.

Figure 7.3 Chile: income shares of deciles 9 and 10, 1957–2009

the case of Chile, for example, while its decile 10 is ranked as the 128th most unequal among these 134 countries, its decile 9 is ranked as low as 23rd. Figure 7.3 and Figure 7.4 clearly illustrate this phenomenon: after the 1973 coup d'état (which also marked the beginning of neo-liberal reforms and the rapid integration of Chile into the world economy), while income distribution had one of the fastest deteriorations ever recorded, it was only decile 10 that benefited from it.

While the income share of decile 10 increased by 51 per cent between 1973 and 1987 (from 34.2 per cent of national income to no less than 51.7 per cent), that of decile 9 actually fell from 17.5 per cent to 16.3 per cent.[12]

As there are well-known problems with data reporting in decile 1, Figure 7.5 looks at income polarisation across countries by reporting the multiples of

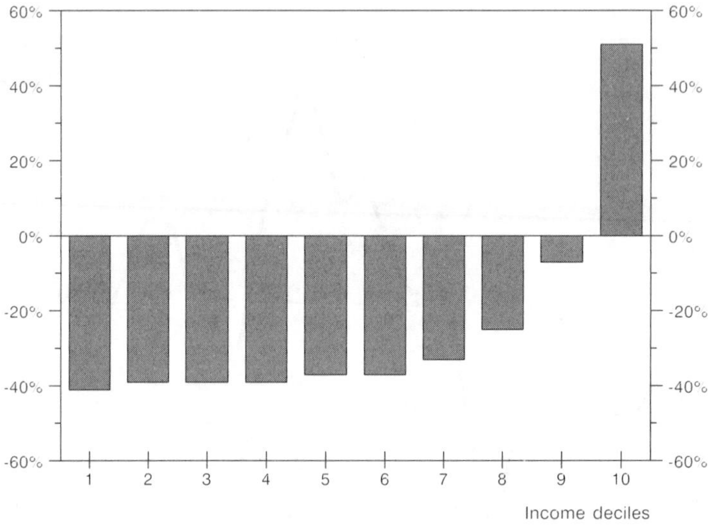

Source: As Figure 7.3.

Figure 7.4 Chile: changes in income shares between 1973 and 1987

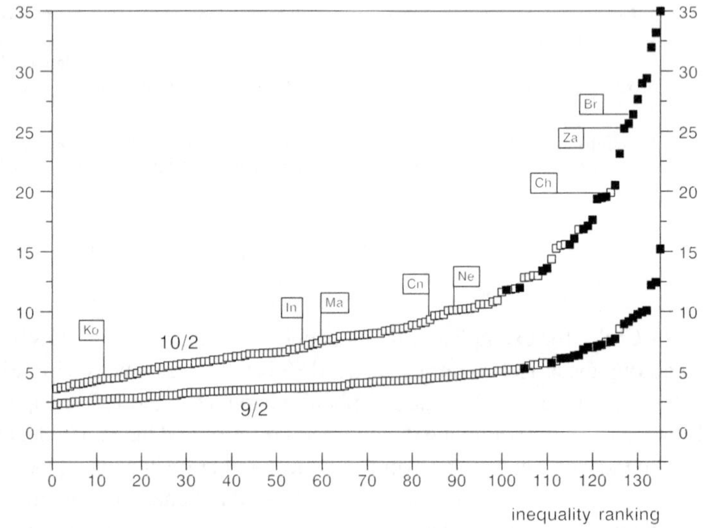

Note: As Figure 7.2. The last observation in D10/D2 is Namibia (with a multiple of 75)!

Figure 7.5 Income shares of D10 as a multiple of that of D2, and D9 as a multiple of that of D2 in 134 countries, c. 2005

deciles 10 over 2, and 9 over 2 – ratios that highlight again the extreme inequality found in Latin America and Southern Africa.

Figure 7.5 shows the remarkable difference in terms of income polarisation when looked at by the ratio of deciles 10 to 2 and by deciles 9 to 2. The ranges for both rankings are very different: while D10/D2 extends from 3.6 to 75 (33.2 without Namibia), that of deciles 9 and 2 only extends from 2.3 to 15 (12.5 without Namibia). However, in both cases income polarisation only really kicks in in the last third of the sample – exactly where Latin American countries start reporting.

Of the more straightforward statistics for measuring inequality, D10/D2 probably best reflects the extreme degree of income inequality found in Latin America.[13] At a median value of 19.4, the Latin American multiple for D10/D2 is more than twice the median value for the 69 non-Latin-American LDCs. These statistics also differentiate most Latin American inequality from that of (non-Southern-mineral-rich) Sub-Saharan Africa – the latter's median value, at 10.3, is about half Latin America's (see Table 7.1).

Table 7.1 *Region median values for different income ratios*

	D10/D1	D10/D2	D9/D2	D10/Q1+Q2	Q4/Q2	Q3/Q2
Latin America	37.2	19.4	7.1	4.0	2.7	1.4
Non-LA LDCs	(13.1)	(8.9)	(4.3)	(2.0)	(2.1)	(1.4)
Caribbean	16.6	10.5	4.9	2.3	2.2	1.5
Sub-Saharan Africa	15.7	10.3	4.8	2.3	2.2	1.5
NICs-2	11.0	7.8	4.2	1.8	2.1	1.5
North Africa	11.1	7.6	3.8	1.7	2.0	1.4
South Asia	8.6	7.0	3.2	1.6	1.8	1.3
OECD-1	12.5	6.6	3.8	1.6	2.0	1.4
Ex-USSR	9.9	6.6	3.6	1.5	1.9	1.4
European Union	9.2	5.6	3.3	1.3	1.8	1.3
Eastern Europe	7.3	5.1	3.0	1.2	1.7	1.3
NICs-1	7.8	4.5	3.0	1.0	1.7	1.3
Nordic countries	6.1	4.0	2.5	1.0	1.6	1.2
Japan	4.5	3.7	2.4	0.9	1.5	1.2
All	11.7	8.1	4.1	1.8	2.0	1.4
LDCs	15.5	10.2	4.7	2.2	2.2	1.5

Notes: Regions as in Appendix 1. With the exception of 'Non-LA LDCs' (which is placed next to Latin America for comparison purposes), regions are ranked according to the multiple of decile 10 over decile 2. Non-LA LDCs=non-Latin American developing countries (69 countries; excludes ex-communist countries). OECD-1=Anglophone OECD; South Asia=India, and NICs-1=Korea. D10/D1=income shares of decile 10 as a multiple of that of D1; D9/D2=income shares of decile 9 as a multiple of that of D2; Q4/Q2=income shares of quintile 4 as a multiple of that of Q2; and Q3/Q2=income share of quintile 3 as a multiple of that of Q2.

As Table 7.1 indicates, Latin America's greater inequality vis-à-vis other regions of the world decreases rapidly for the income groups closer to the middle of the distribution (i.e., between deciles 8 and 3). Yet, oddly enough, many theories purporting to explain Latin America's greater inequality refer to phenomena in this *middle* of the distribution; for example, the 1960s' import-substituting-industrialisation-related 'labour aristocracy' hypothesis, and the 1990s' trade-liberalisation-related 'asymmetric demand for labour' proposition.

The first hypothesis, widely invoked during the 1960s and 1970s, particularly by those connected with the WB, and later on with the emerging 'Washington Consensus', argued that one of the main causes of inequality in Latin America during that period was the price distortions associated with import-substituting industrialisation (ISI). These distorted the values of sectoral marginal productivities, causing artificially higher real wages in manufacturing; that is, producing higher *wage differentials* than would otherwise exist in the economy.[14] However, there was little then (as now) to differentiate Latin America from the rest of the world – developing and developed, ISI and non-ISI – in terms of the income distribution among groups that would include 'aristocratic' and 'non-aristocratic' labour (found in say quintiles 4 and 2, or 3 and 2).

The second proposition basically recycled the 'labour aristocracy' hypothesis for the globalisation era, as a way of explaining the increase in inequality in many developing countries (and especially Latin American countries) implementing trade and financial liberalisation. The increase in inequality, following greater integration with the world economy, contrasts with the predictions of the 'Washington Consensus' before the implementation of these reforms.[15] Hence, it is now argued that this (previously unforeseen) trade-related increase in inequality took place because trade liberalisation has introduced new production techniques intensive in the use of (scarce) skilled workers, therefore increasing wage differentials.[16] However, as is obvious from previous graphs and Table 7.1, what really differentiates Latin American income inequality is located at the poles of the distribution of income – hardly where either skilled or unskilled workers are located. Therefore, even if trade liberalisation introduced new production techniques with 'skill-asymmetrical' demand for labour, it is unlikely that this would account for much of the region's increased inequality. Again, the case of Chile provides a good example of this issue.

Even though Chile implemented one of the most radical trade and financial liberalisation policies in the developing world, and in spite of the fact that this policy has now been in place for nearly four decades, it seems to have had little effect on the relative income distribution of skilled and unskilled labour (proxied in Figure 7.6 by the multiple of deciles 9 to 2, or by 5 to 3, depending on what is understood by these two categories of workers). This graph suggests that massive political upheavals, radical economic reforms and greater integration

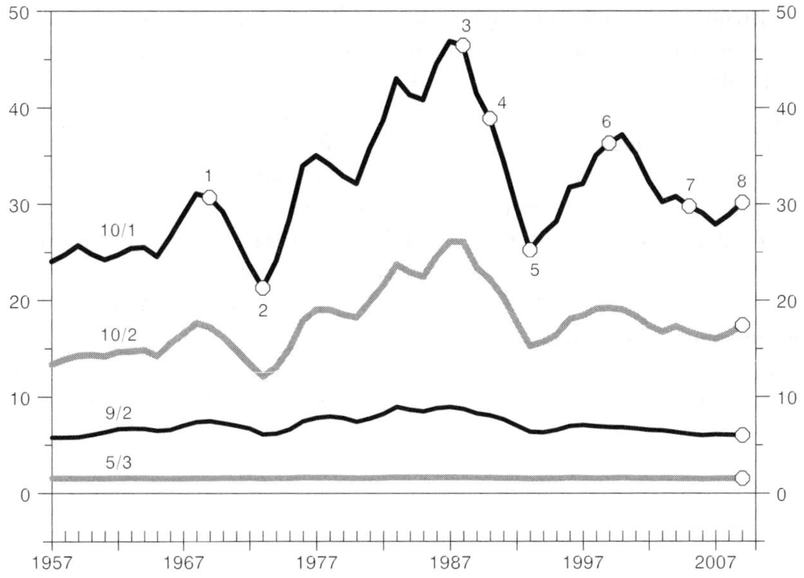

Source: As Figure 7.3. Three-year moving averages.

Figure 7.6 Chile: income shares of D10 as a multiple of that of D1 and D2, of D9 as a multiple of that of D2, and D5 as a multiple of that of D3, 1957–2009

with the world economy have tended to have significant effects at the extreme ends of the income distribution, but little effect in between.

Moreover, the Chilean experience also indicates that 'policy matters'. Income distribution did improve significantly with the progressive distributional policies of the first post-Pinochet democratic government (1990–94), even though it continued the process of greater integration into the world economy; but when the second democratic government (1994–2000, formed by the same political coalition) abandoned these progressive distributional policies for more 'market-oriented' ones, the ratio of deciles 10 to 1 nearly returned to where Pinochet had left it in 1990.

In fact, what happened in Chile clearly indicates what is probably the most significant distributional stylised fact in Latin America, its asymmetric 'ratchet' effect: improvement in income distribution tends to be temporal, while increases in inequality tend to leave more permanent effects – that is, the well-known restrained ability of human processes to be reversed once certain things have happened seems to apply only to increases in inequality.

3 Income inequality and income per capita

The most common (and probably most meaningful) way of comparing income distribution across countries is relative to the level of income per capita. This approach started with Kuznets in 1955 and has dominated distributional debates ever since (although this debate has often confused the statistical evidence for an 'inverted-U' path, with Kuznets' hypothesis regarding its nature). Figure 7.7 shows the regional averages for the whole sample.

This graph suggests four 'layers' of inequality across countries. First, a more equal layer containing the ex-communist countries of Central Europe, the Nordic countries and Japan; a second layer containing a great variety of regions; a third one including Sub-Saharan Africa, China, the Caribbean countries and the US; and fourth, Latin America (and 'mineral-rich' Southern Africa, not shown in the graph), well above every other region in the world – including those with

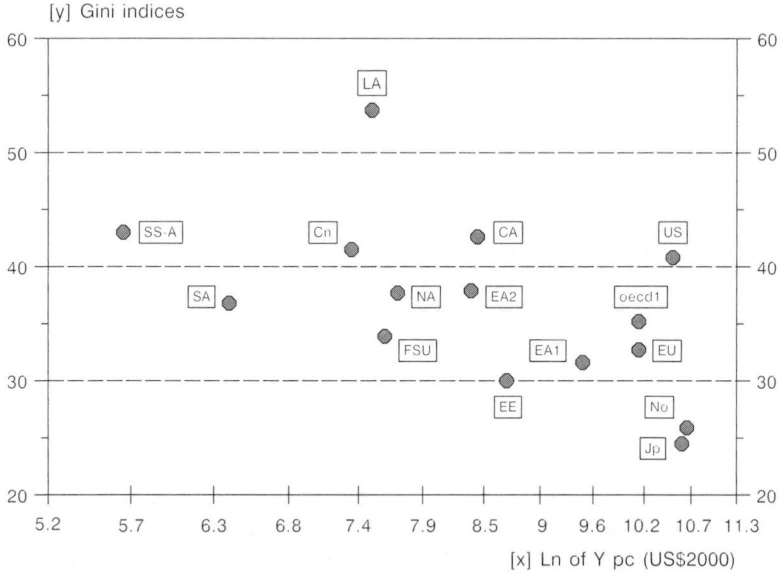

Notes: [Y]=vertical axis; and [X]=horizontal axis (natural logarithm of income per capita). Regions as in Table 7.1 and Appendix 1. CA=Caribbean countries; Cn=China; EA1=East Asia 1 (as NICs-1 in Table 7.1); and EA2=East Asia 2 (as NICs-2 in Table 7.1); EE=Eastern Europe; EU=non-Anglophone European Union; FSU=Former Soviet Union (ex-USSR in Table 7.1); Jp=Japan; LA=Latin America; NA=North Africa; No=Nordic countries; SA=South Asia (as in table 7.1); and SS-A=Sub-Saharan Africa (as in Table 7.1). Regional figures are median values.

Sources: WB (2010). This will also be the case for the remaining graphs in this chapter.

Figure 7.7 Gini indices and log of income per capita, c. 2005

similar income per capita, like North Africa, the 'second-tier' NICs, the Caribbean and the countries of the former USSR.

However, as discussed above, it is also important to look 'inside' this Gini ratio (see Figure 7.8).

As we might have expected, Figure 7.8 shows a particularly close correlation between regional Ginis and the income shares of decile 10 – in part, the result of the way the Gini index is calculated. However, in D10 we are now down to three 'layers' of inequality across countries. Figure 7.9, in turn, shows the regional distributional structure of deciles 1 to 4.

Figure 7.9 shows that the regional distributional structure of deciles 1 to 4 is the mirror image of that of decile 10. Therefore, the Ginis for regional inequality are reflected rather well both at the very top and at the bottom of the regional distribution of income. However, when one looks at the other 50 per cent of the world's population, the 'middle and upper-middle classes' (sometimes called the 'administrative' classes in institutional economics), located between deciles

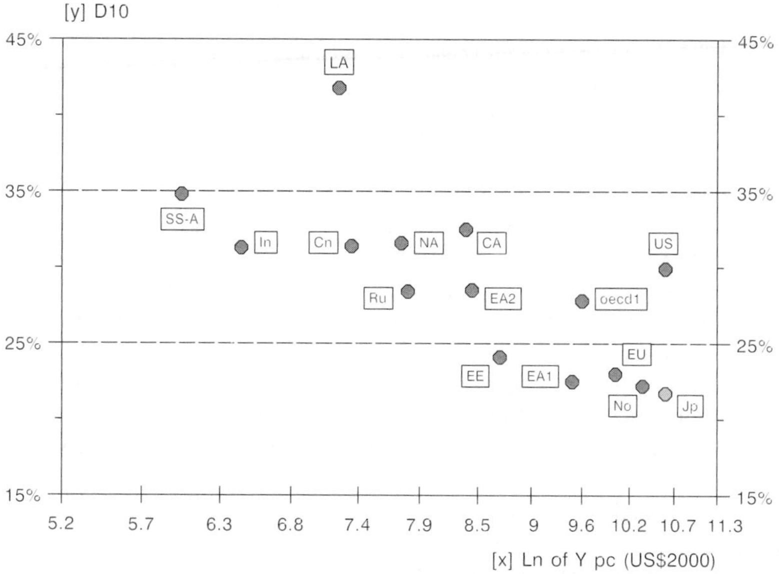

Notes: [Y]=vertical axis; and [X]=horizontal axis. D10=decile 10.
As Figure 7.7, except that from now on Russia (Ru) will be highlighted instead of the median value for the countries of the formers USSR (FSU), and India for SA.
Note that in some regions the median countries for D10 is different from that of the Gini in Figure 7.7.

Figure 7.8 Income share of D10 and log of income per capita, c. 2005

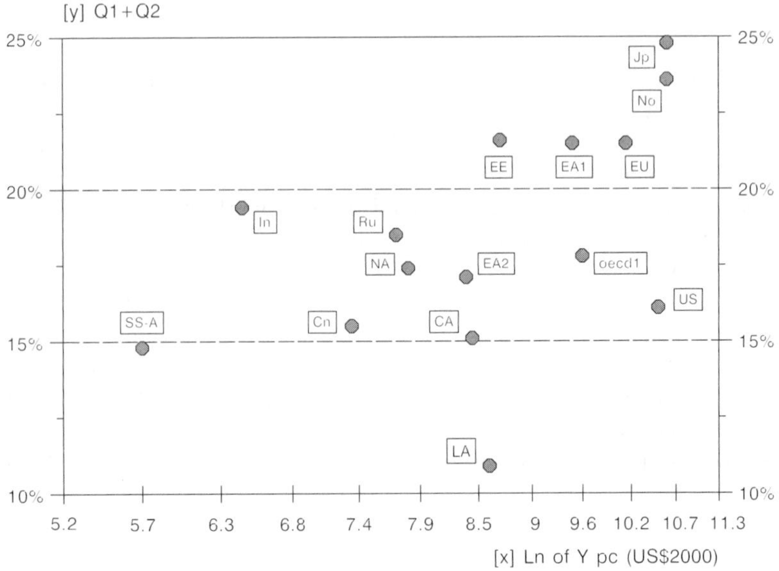

Note: [Y]=vertical axis; and [X]=horizontal axis. As Figure 7.7.

Figure 7.9 Income shares of the bottom 40 per cent and log of income per capita, c. 2005

5 to 9, the regional distributional picture changes completely: from huge disparity to remarkable similarity (see Figure 7.10).

Furthermore, this similarity in the income shares of deciles 5 to 9 is even more extreme in the 'upper-middle' 30 per cent of the population (deciles 7, 8 and 9) (see Figure 7.11).

Table 7.2 presents a set of statistics for the whole sample, which emphasise the extraordinary contrast between the world distributional heterogeneity at the top and bottom of the income distribution and the homogeneity in the middle.

Of all the statistics in Table 7.2, the coefficient of variation best shows the distributional contrast between the homogeneous middles and the heterogeneous tails – the figures for both decile 10 and deciles 1 to 4 are four and five times greater than that for deciles 5 to 9. Furthermore, they are about *six* times larger than that for deciles 7 to 9. This suggests that 'middle classes' across the world (particularly the 'upper-middle classes') seem to be able to benefit from a distributional safety net – that is, regardless of the per capita income level of the country, the characteristics of the political regimes, the economic policies implemented, the structure of property rights, or whether or not they belong to

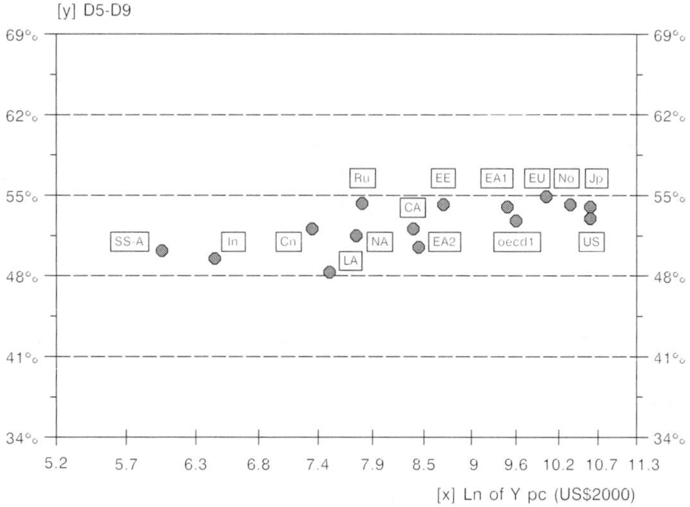

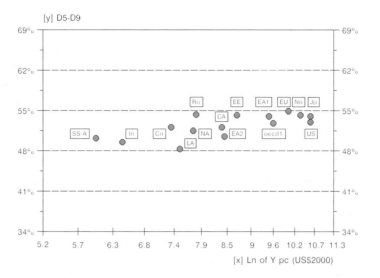

Note: [Y]=vertical axis; and [X]=horizontal axis. As Figure 7.7.

Figure 7.10 Income shares of the 50 per cent of the population located in D5 to D9 and log of income per capita, c. 2005

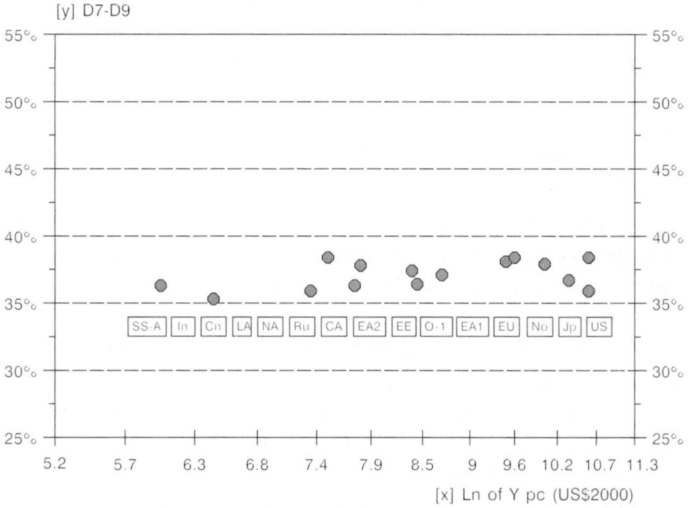

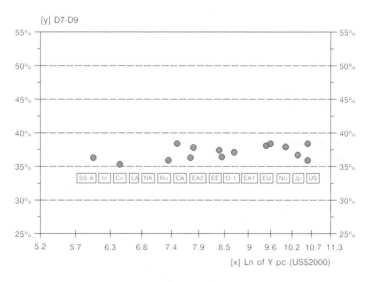

Note: [Y]=vertical axis; and [X]=horizontal axis. As Figure 7.7.

Figure 7.11 Income shares of the 30 per cent of the population located in D7 to D9 and log of income per capita, c. 2005

Table 7.2 Measures of centrality and spread for income groups (132 countries)

	Range	Median	Mean	Variance	St Dev	C o Var*
D10	27.0	30.8	32.0	41.3	7.1	**22**
D1–D4	17.1	17.0	16.6	16.4	4.2	**25**
D5–D9	13.0	52.2	51.7	12.2	2.9	**5**
D7–D9	6.6	37.0	36.7	3.2	1.4	**4**

Notes: st dev=standard deviation; c o var*=coefficient of variation (figures shown are multiplied by 100); D10=decile 10; D1–D4=deciles 1 to 4; D5–D9=deciles 5 to 9; and D7–D9=deciles 7 to 9.
Botswana and Namibia are excluded from the sample for these statistics.

countries that managed to get their prices 'right', their institutions 'right', or their social capital 'right', the 50 per cent of the population located between deciles 5 to 9 seems to have the capacity to appropriate about half the national income. In other words, despite the remarkable variety of political-institutional settlements in the world, the resulting distributional outcomes have one major thing in common: half of the population in each country are able to acquire a 'property right' on about half the national income.[17]

There's no such luck for the bottom 40 per cent of the population. For them, such issues as those mentioned above can make the difference between getting as much as one-quarter of national income (as in Japan, or the Nordic countries), or as little as 10 per cent or less (as in Latin America, South Africa, Botswana and Angola, let alone the meagre 4.3 per cent in Namibia). As far as the top income decile is concerned, the sky is (almost) the limit.

In other words, what is crucial to remember is that the regional distributional structure suggested by the Gini index only reflects the income disparities of *half* the world's population – that is, those at the very top and at the bottom of the distribution; but it does not reflect *at all* the remarkable distributional homogeneity of the other half. This is a rather peculiar phenomenon from a statistical point of view, raising serious questions regarding how useful the Gini index is as an indicator of overall income inequality. Analytically, recent political and economic developments (including globalisation) seem to have been associated with two very different distributional movements across regions in the world: a (better known) 'centrifugal' one in terms of the income shares of the top and bottom deciles (decile 10 and deciles 1 to 4), and a (lesser known) 'centripetal' movement in terms of the income share of deciles 5 to 9. Basically, rather than a 'disappearing middle', what one finds is an increasingly 'homogeneous middle' (see Figure 7.12).

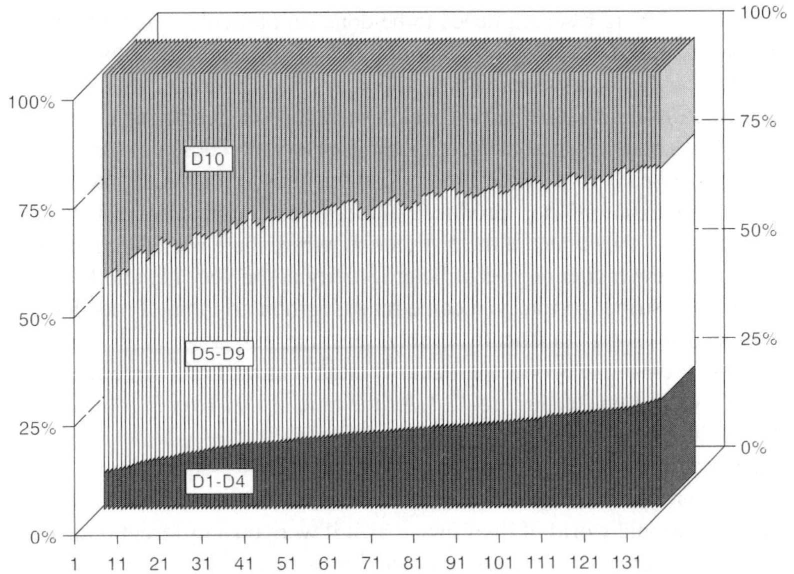

Notes: D10=income share of decile 10; D5–D9=income share of the half of the population between deciles 5 and 9; and D1–D4=income share of deciles 1 to 4.
Countries are ranked according to the income share of D1–D4.[18]

Figure 7.12 The homogeneous middle vs. the heterogeneous tails in 134 countries, c. 2005

Regional distributional homogeneity in the middle and upper-middle of the distribution also casts doubts on the well-known role of mainstream 'human capital' theory on income distribution. According to this theory, the level of education is a crucial variable (if not *the* most crucial variable) in the determination of income inequality.[19] However, in all regions of the world (developed and developing, Latin American and non-Latin American), the top income decile is made up of individuals with relatively high levels of education, while those in the bottom four deciles have relatively low levels of education – that is, either relatively little schooling, or (in the more advanced countries), schooling of a very doubtful quality. So why do these two (relatively homogeneously 'highly-educated' or 'little-educated') groups have the greatest distributional diversity? In turn, if real world educational diversity is found among the population in deciles 5 to 9 – for example, in terms of the share of the population with secondary and (especially) tertiary education – why does one find extraordinary *similarity* in the shares of national income of this educationally highly *heterogeneous* group?

Obviously, more research needs to be done (in particular one that does not confuse increased 'equality of opportunities' with increased 'distributional equality') on the forces shaping the national income shares of different deciles along such different paths (particularly in such opposite 'centrifugal' and 'centripetal' directions). Remarkably, this simple observation does not seem to have been emphasised before. Also, it seems odd that most of the recent literature on income 'polarisation' has produced indices that emphasise distributional changes around the *middle* of the distribution, where there is greater homogeneity.[20] In fact, the higher degree of heterogeneity at the very top and bottom of the income distribution makes income ratios, particularly that of 'deciles 10 to 2' and '10 to 1–4', statistically highly sensitive indicators of distributional disparities across the world, particularly highlighting Latin America's huge income polarisation (see Figure 7.13; for the ratio of D10 over D1–4 see Figure 7.19 below).

The most remarkable feature from this perspective is that Latin America, and the four Southern African countries mentioned above, seem to be living in a distributional world of their own – as if it were on a different planet… In fact, this is such an analytically challenging issue that its subject requires a

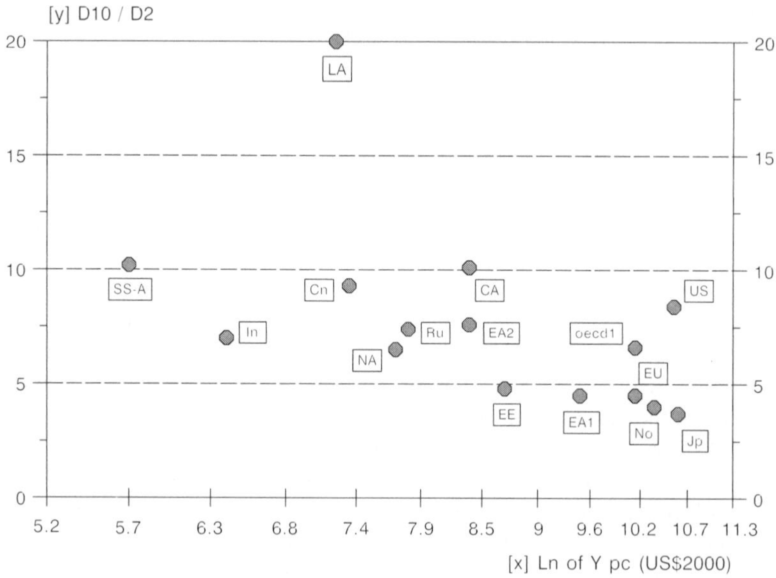

Note: [Y]=vertical axis; and [X]=horizontal axis. As Figure 7.7.

Figure 7.13 Income shares of D10 as a multiple of that of D2 and log of income per capita, c. 2005

paper on its own (Palma, 2010a). Basically, in this chapter I conclude that (except for South Africa and 'diamond-rich' Southern Africa – Angola, Botswana and Namibia), Latin America's distributional settlement is so unique that in Latin America the rich are not just (relatively) richer that those of other regions in the world, but that they do not seem to have proper counterparts elsewhere.

4 Income inequality and income per capita: testing for regional effects in a cross-section framework

The 'inverted U' framework is the most commonly used stylised fact for testing the relationship between income inequality and income per capita, both in a time series and in a cross-section framework. However, as mentioned above, in doing so, one has to distinguish crucially between two factors: first, whether there is a statistical relationship of this kind; and second, how to interpret this phenomenon *analytically* – that is, as it is often the case, when work of this nature produces statistically significant results, this '... involves the evolution of knowledge as well as ignorance' (Krugman, 2000).[21]

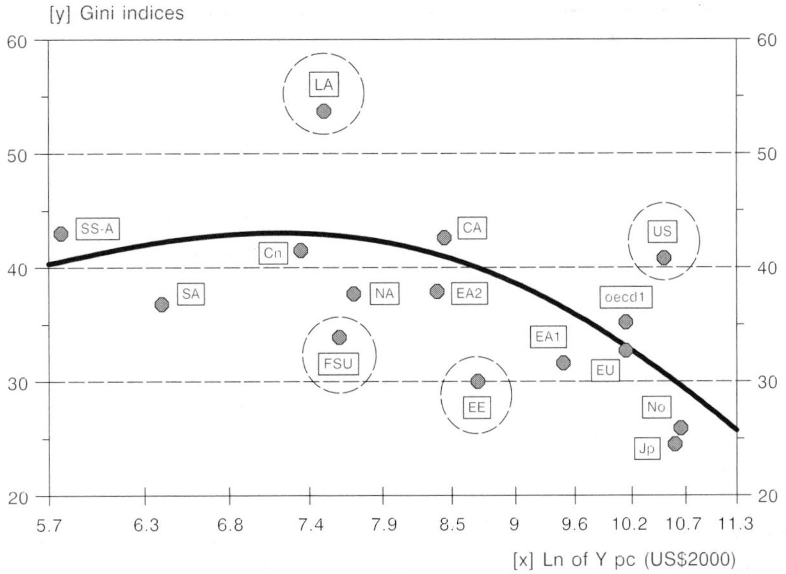

Notes: [Y]=vertical axis; and [X]=horizontal axis. As Figure 7.7.
For the summary statistics of the regressions, see Appendix 2 (Reg. 1).

Figure 7.14 The 'inverted U' relationship: Gini indices and log of income per capita, c. 2005

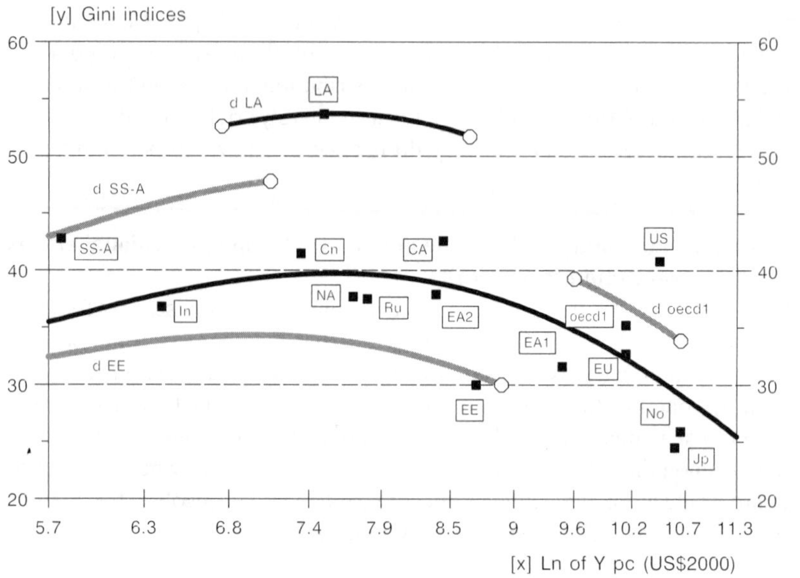

Notes: [Y]=vertical axis; and [X]=horizontal axis. As Figure 7.7. For the summary statistics of the regressions, see Appendix 2 (Reg. 2).
d LA=the regression with an intercept-dummy for Latin America; d SS-A=with an intercept-dummy for Sub-Saharan Africa; d OECD1=with a dummy in the square of income per capita variable for the Anglophone OECD; d EE=with a dummy in the square of income per capita variable for Eastern Europe.[24] In this and subsequent figure SA=India and FSU=Russia. There is also a significant intercept-dummy for 'mineral-rich' Southern Africa, not included in the figure.

Figure 7.15 The 'Inverted-U' relationship: Gini indices and log of income per capita including four regional dummies, c. 2005

In this chapter, I am going to use the traditional econometric specification to test for an 'inverted U' path. At the same time, following the findings above (homogeneous 'middle' versus heterogeneous 'poles'), after testing this relationship using the traditional Gini index as dependent inequality variable, the 'inverted U' path will be tested more accurately using the income shares of different income groups as dependent variables, with the right-hand side variables being an intercept, the log of income per capita, the square of the same variable and regional dummies.[22] Figures 7.15 and 7.16 shows the results of such tests for the Gini indices and the income share of the top decile.

In Figure 7.14, after correcting for heteroscedasticity, all parameters are significant at a 1 per cent level, and so is the F test for the whole regression.[23] The adjusted R^2 of the regression is 22 per cent.

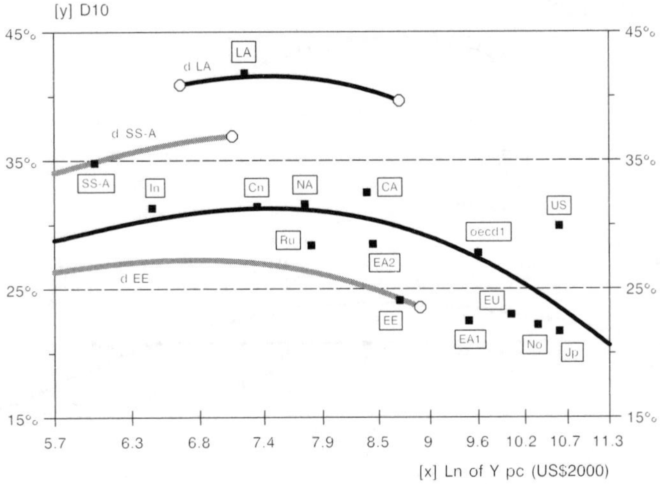

Note: [Y]=vertical axis; and [X]=horizontal axis. As Figure 7.7. For the summary statistics of the regressions, see Appendix 2 (Reg. 3).

Figure 7.16 Income share of D10 and log of income per capita including three regional dummies, c. 2005

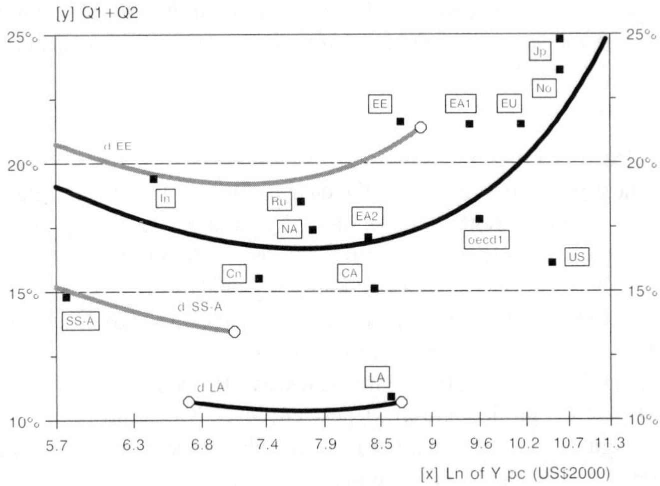

Note: [Y]=vertical axis; and [X]=horizontal axis. As Figure 7.7. For the summary statistics of the regressions, see Appendix 2 (Reg. 4).

Figure 7.17 Income shares of the bottom 40 per cent and log of income per capita including three regional dummies, c. 2005

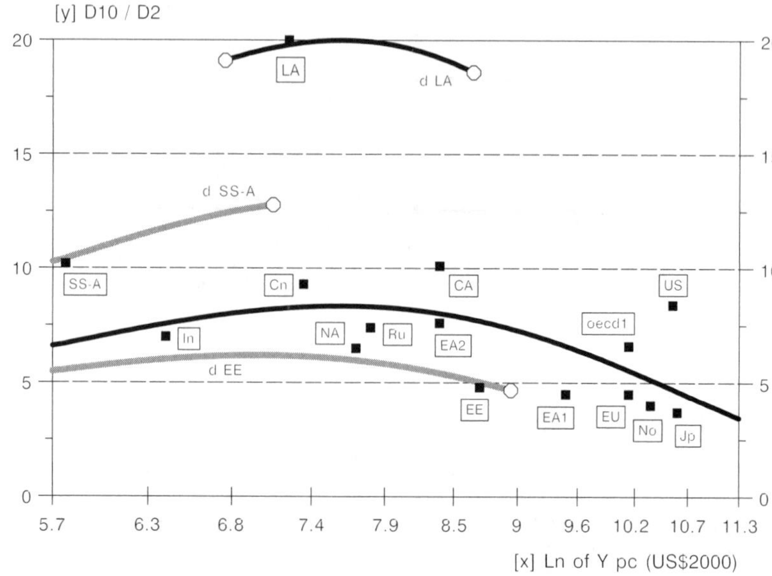

Note: [Y]=vertical axis; and [X]=horizontal axis. As Figure 7.7. For the summary statistics of the regressions, see Appendix 2 (Reg. 5).

Figure 7.18 Income shares of D10 as a multiple of that of D2 and log of income per capita including three regional dummies, c. 2005

As is clear from the graph, the regression line only fits the median-Gini of some of the regions, but that is not the case for others (those highlighted in the graph). Nevertheless, both from an analytical and a statistical point of view, when testing for the 'inverted U' path in a cross-sectional framework the more appropriate way of doing it is by including regional effects.

Figure 7.15 shows how widespread the regional effects are. In fact, there are no fewer than five highly statistically significant regional dummies (four are significant at the 1 per cent level, and the d OECD1 one at the 1.5 per cent), and the F test is also significant at the 1 per cent level. The adjusted R^2 is now 74 per cent. Figure 7.16 confirms the close correlation between the Gini and the top decile; the regression is also highly significant, with all parameters (except for the d OECD1, whose 'p-value' is 0.07), and the F test, significant at the 1 per cent level. The adjusted R^2 is 74 per cent.

Figure 7.17 in turn is another demonstration of the mirror relationship between the behaviour of the top decile and that of the bottom four deciles. Again the regression is highly significant, with all parameters and the F test significant

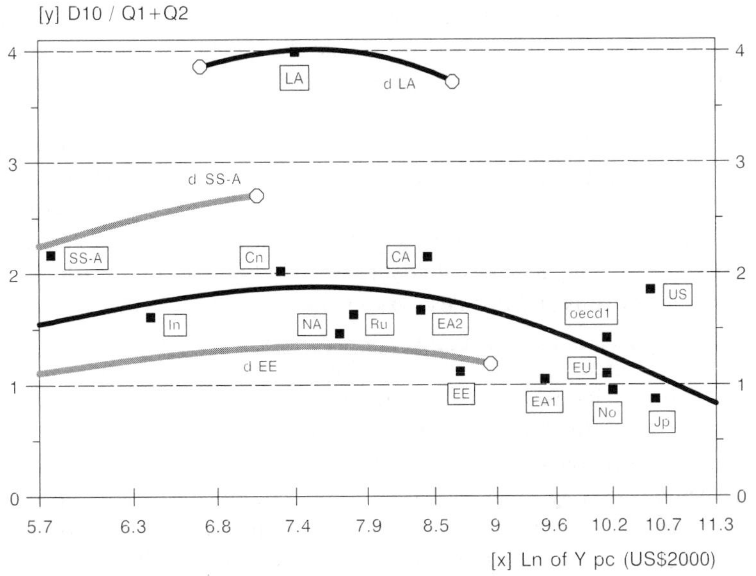

Note: [Y]=vertical axis; and [X]=horizontal axis. As Figure 7.7. For the summary statistics of the regressions, see Appendix 2 (Reg. 6).

Figure 7.19 Income shares of D10 as a multiple of that of the bottom 40 per cent and log of income per capita including three regional dummies, c. 2005

at the 1 per cent level (this time the d OECD1 has a 'p-value' of 0.012). The adjusted R^2 is 77 per cent

However, not surprisingly, the regionally homogeneous 'middle' (deciles 5 to 9) shows no significant regional effects for this half of the population. Finally, strong regional effects are again found when a 'inverted U' specification is tested with the ratio of deciles '10 to 2' and '10 to 1–4' as the dependent variables (see Figures 7.18 and 7.19).

In Figure 7.18, the regression is highly significant; all variables and dummies are significant at a 1 per cent level (with the d OECD1 dummy just above the 1 per cent level, with a 'p-value' of 0.017). The adjusted R^2 is 78 per cent. This is the specification of the regional distributional effects, in which the 'excess' Latin American degree of inequality is shown in a more extreme form – except, of course (with the problems mentioned above) for the D10/D1 regression.

In Figure 7.19, the regression is also highly significant; all variables and dummies are significant at a 1 per cent level, except for the OECD1 dummy that has a 'p-value' of 0.013. The adjusted R^2 is 77 per cent.

Finally, why is it that there is a statistically significant 'inverted-U'-type relationship between income inequality and the level of income per capita? That is, why is it that in the current cross-section setting income distribution still tends to get worse before getting better – even though the left-hand half of the 'inverted-U' seems to be much flatter now than in the past? This question has been central to the inequality debate ever since Kuznets developed his famous hypothesis on this subject in 1955. However, as mentioned above, this debate has often confused the significant statistical evidence for an 'inverted-U' path, with Kuznets' hypothesis regarding its nature. Although a proper answer to this question deserves a whole chapter on its own, the experience of many middle-income countries, particularly from Latin America, indicates that one economic and political issue central to this phenomenon is the changing relationship between productivity and wages. When countries move from a low-income to a middle-income level they tend to do so via an acceleration of productivity growth. However, when this happens, wages tend to lag behind, leading to an increase in profit margins. It is only much later when the process of 'catching-up' by wages begins to take place. Basically, countries tend to take a long time to commence developing the economic and political institutions that are necessary for this to happen. At the same time, the process of 'catching-up' by wages sets up another huge controversy in economics relating to the consequences of this increase in wages back on productivity growth.

A brief example from British economic history may help illustrate these two phenomena (why wages lag behind productivity growth and why they are able to begin their process of 'catching-up', and the effect that this could have on productivity). In Britain, wage-growth began the long process of 'catching-up' with productivity growth only towards the end of the 19th century, that is, well over a century after the beginning of the industrial revolution. When this began to happen, it was not due to some reduction in the supply of labour, or some progressive government in office, but to an increase in workers' militancy. One of the most important strikes of the time, a sign of things to come, was the now legendary 'London Dock Strike of 1889'. It was the first time that casual workers managed to organise themselves and take successful action. And it is important to note that they were not only fighting for higher wages; their first demand was a minimum daily pay (4 hours), regardless of whether there was work or not in the docks. When (to the surprise of many) they managed to win, the 'usual suspects' in the economics profession predicted the end of civilisation as they knew it – with forecasts of unemployment, the collapse of savings and investment, and so on and so forth. As it happens, what took place instead alongside the increases in wages was an acceleration of productivity growth, which led Marshall to write his famous 'efficiency wage' hypothesis in his *Principles*:

> But it was only in the last generation that a careful study was begun to be made of the effects that high wages have in increasing the efficiency not only of those who receive them, but also of their children and grandchildren. [...]. The application of the comparative method of study to the industrial problem of different countries of the old and new worlds is forcing constantly more and more attention to the fact that highly paid labour is generally efficient and therefore not dear labour; a fact which, though it is more full of hope for the future of the human race than any other that is known to us, will be found to exercise a very complicated influence on the theory of distribution. (1898).

Yes, a very complicated influence indeed! So much so, that most textbooks on macroeconomics today do not even mention the subject of efficiency wages to bypass these complications altogether. In Section 5, I will use the case of Mexico to illustrate briefly these issues. Mexico is a particularly interesting case of analysis because, in a way, it has followed the above process in reverse order. First, between the end of the war and the mid-1970s the PRI's (Partido Revolucionario Institucional) corporatist distributive policy led wages to grow at a pace similar to that of productivity growth. That is, the increased bargaining power of labour in a corporatist environment enabled it to gain the 'property right' to share in the benefits of economic growth – a right that most workers in other parts of Latin America did not have. However, one of the stated aims of neo-liberal reforms was to break this close connection between wages and productivity. They certainly succeeded in this; and (as Marshall would have probably predicted) productivity growth collapsed, leading Mexico to switch from a rank of 13 in the world in terms of GDP growth (1950–80), to one of 62 (1980–2009; see Palma, 2010b).

5 A brief case study of Mexico

A short analysis of Mexico could help us to understand why increased integration into the world economy, after economic reform in general and trade and financial liberalisation in particular, has had an increased inequalising effect at the top and bottom of the distribution (at least until 2000). Although political reform began in Mexico during the presidency of Lopez Portillo (1976–82), trade liberalisation began with President de la Madrid, who took office in the midst of the 1982 debt crisis. On the positive side, Mexico has never looked back in terms of growth of manufacturing exports – in constant US dollar terms, manufactured exports (including those of so-called 'maquila' activities – that is, those that consist mostly of assembly-type operations, which are highly intensive in the use of imported imputes) grew from US$8 billion in 1981 to nearly US$190 billion in 2008 (both figures in US$ of 2000 values). This 24-fold increase (equivalent to an annual average growth rate of 9 per cent) increased the share of manufactures in the country's total goods exports to 74 per cent from 10 per cent in 1981.[25]

Note: Intervals between circles correspond to presidential periods. 'Wages and salaries' include social security contributions and other similar payments made by employers.

Source: Palma (2005); this will also be the source of the following graphs on Mexico.[29]

Figure 7.20 Mexico: wages and salaries as a share of GDP, 1950–2000

Even though Mexican history shows that proximity to the US is *at best* a mixed blessing, as far as exports are concerned, no developing country has such a convenient geographical position, and has had such preferential access to the US market (via NAFTA).[26] Nevertheless, even bearing this fact in mind, as well as remembering the related flood of FDI,[27] the growth performance of Mexican manufactured exports in this period has been truly exceptional. Yet, this export expansion has had a complex – and much weaker – impact than expected on the Mexican economy as a whole, especially on growth, investment, productivity and wages. In particular, it has been associated with both a collapse of the export multiplier and the de-linking of the export sector from the rest of the economy. This has produced a situation in which increasing export competitiveness has had little effect on growth and living standards.[28]

Figure 7.20 shows the trademark of the 'liberalisation package' in Mexico (as in the rest of Latin America): a remarkable fall in the share of wages and salaries in GDP. In Mexico, over just two six-year presidential terms (1976–82 and 1982–88), and one economic crisis, the share of wages and salaries in GDP

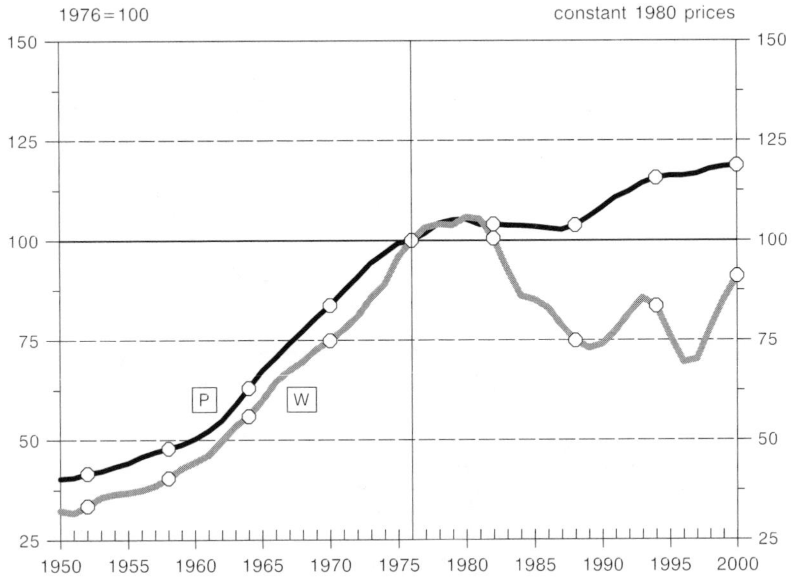

Note: [P]=average productivity and [W]=average real wage and salaries.

Figure 7.21 Mexico: average real wages and productivity, 1950–2000

fell by no fewer than 14 percentage points. In the last presidency of the 1990s (which saw yet another economic crisis), the overall share of wages in GDP fell by a further 8 percentage points. In all, the share of wages fell from 40 per cent of GDP in 1976 to just 18.9 per cent in 2000.

Figure 7.21 shows the root cause of this fall in the share of wages in GDP: the emergence of a new 'scissors' effect between wages and productivity after the neo-liberal political and economic reforms.

One can identify three distinct periods over the second half of the twentieth century. First, up to the Echeverría government (1970–76), one can see the essential characteristic of the traditional PRI distributive policy: wages were able to grow at a pace similar to that of productivity growth; that is, as mentioned above, increased bargaining power in a corporatist environment enabled labour to gain the 'property right' to share in the benefits of economic growth.

In the second period, during Lopez Portillo's term of office (1976–82), marking the beginning of politico-ideological and institutional change in Mexico, there was a progressive stagnation of wages (both in the manufacturing and non-manufacturing sectors), despite the vast new oil riches of the

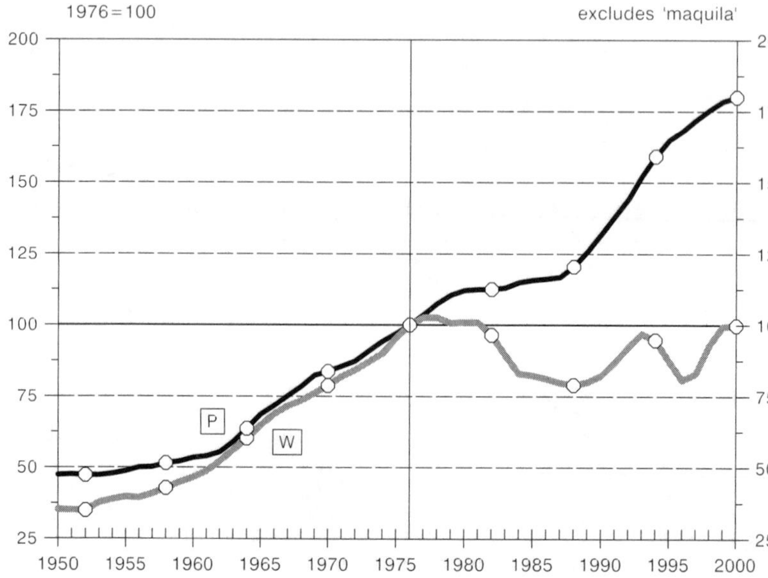

Note: [P]=average productivity; and [W]=average real wages and salaries.

Figure 7.22 Mexico: wages and productivity in the manufacturing sector, 1950–2000

country.[30] Then, when economic crisis struck Mexico in 1982, and with the ascendance to power of President de la Madrid and his neo-liberal economic reform team, a third period started that was characterised by a rapidly growing gap between productivity and wages. By 2000, two presidents and another economic crisis later, this gap had reached approximately 30 percentage points.

Figures 7.22 to 7.24 show that the gap between productivity and wages took a different form in manufacturing than in non-tradables.

Prior to 1976 there was a relatively stable relationship between productivity growth and wage growth in manufacturing; this pattern subsequently changed due to a sharp break in the trend of wage growth. In fact, by the end of the 1990s the average wage was only just recovering its 1976 level, while in the meantime productivity had increased by about 80 per cent: a clear case of a 'winner (capital) takes all' new pattern of distribution (by way of increased profit margins; see Figure 7.23 below).

As Kalecki would have predicted, the two crises (1982 and 1994) also contributed to the new distributional environment, by drastically weakening the

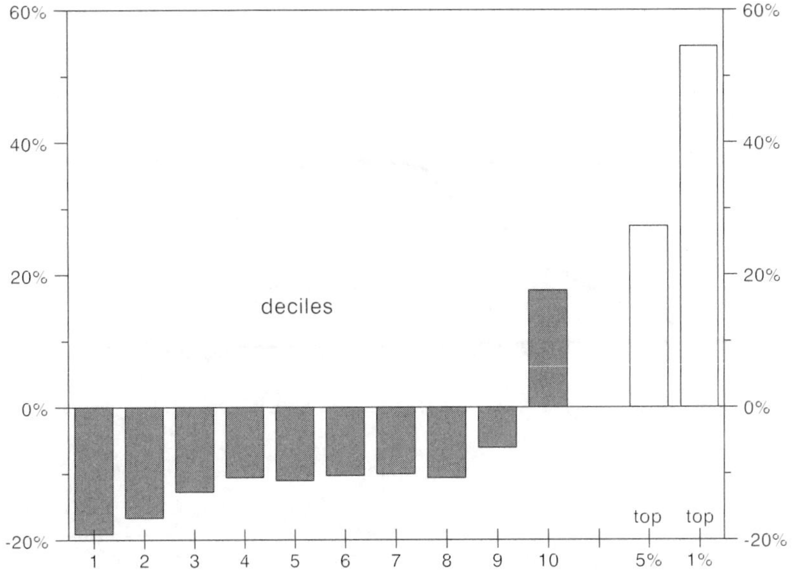

Source: Palma (1995) using data from household surveys.

Figure 7.23 Mexico: changes in income shares between 1984 and 1989

bargaining power of labour. So much so, that distributional changes in Mexico after the 1982 crisis (Figure 7.23) resemble what happened in Pinochet's Chile (see Figure 7.4 above). It is customary in Latin America to call the 1980s 'the lost decade'; well, it was not equally 'lost' for everybody!

Returning to Figure 7.22, the relationship between wages and productivity in the manufacturing sector, as Prebisch and Singer would have predicted, as soon as manufacturing became export-oriented (particularly with capital increasingly mobile) it began to behave as if it were a traditional primary commodity sector: wages immediately stagnated and all productivity growth was either captured by capital or transferred to consumers in the North (in this case in the US) via lower prices. In fact, wages were not able to grow in any significant way even in the motorcar industry – which during this period was the most dynamic activity within manufacturing – despite a 330 per cent productivity growth. Mexico's experience in this respect is certainly closer to the predictions of Prebisch and Singer than to those based on Samuelson's theorem of trade-related wage-equalisation across the world. In fact, as overall wages in Mexico declined in the post 'liberalisation' period (Figure 7.21), or at best they had returned by 2000 to their 1976 level (manufacturing, Figure 7.22), while in the

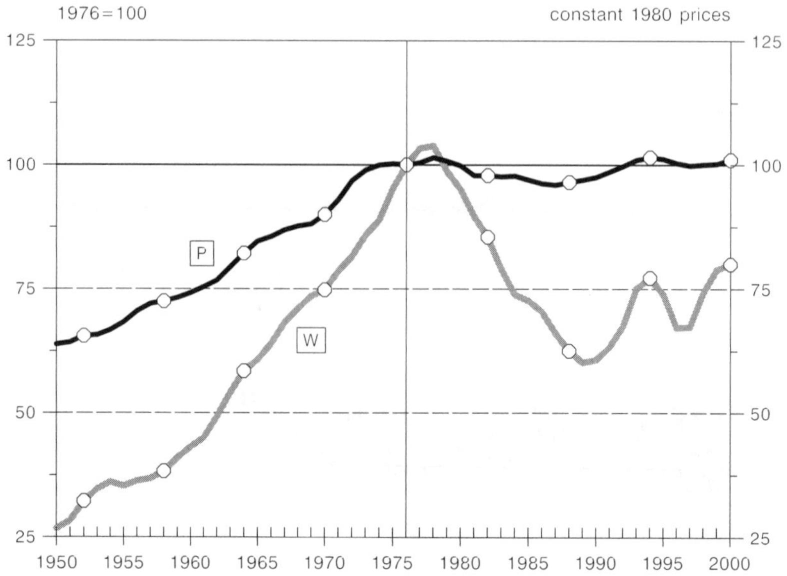

Note: [P]=average productivity and [W]=average real wage.

Figure 7.24 Mexico: wages and productivity in the non-tradable sector, 1950–2000

US they grew during the Clinton years (see Palma, 2009), Samuelson's trade-related wage equalisation theorem seems to have worked the other way round.

And what about the relationship between wages and productivity in a sector unable to deliver productivity growth?

Figure 7.24 indicates that non-tradables also find a way to generate a new gap between productivity growth and wage growth, but this time the move is in a different direction – that is, a similar 'scissors' pattern, but with a downward trend. Here, given the stagnation of productivity, for the gap to emerge (and profit margins to increase as in the rest of the economy), wages had to fall substantially.

This decline in wages in non-tradable sectors (mainly services and construction) contrasts sharply with the situation before 1976, when there was another gap (then in favour of labour), with wages growing *faster* than productivity. This was one of the characteristics of the previous 'corporatist' structure of property rights in the labour market: wages in manufacturing (which grew at a rate roughly similar to productivity growth in their sector) set the pace for wage growth in the whole economy – even in sectors (such as non-tradables) where productivity growth was much slower than in manufacturing.

In this way, a new pattern of accumulation emerged with neo-liberal economic reform in Mexico (as in the rest of Latin America). If there is productivity growth (manufacturing), 'winner takes all' (à-la-Prebisch–Singer). If there is none, capital benefits anyway via the contraction of wages (à-la-Lewis, because institutional changes in the labour market have allowed capital to shrink wages back towards their subsistence level). In fact, if the level of the minimum wage is set to 100 in (the peak year of) 1976, by 1994 it had fallen in real terms to just one-third of that value – and by 2000 to a remarkably low of one-fifth![31] In this way, even if productivity growth is disappointing, the stagnation of wages in some activities, and their decline in others, have proved to be an effective mechanism for capital to increase profit margins in this era of globalisation.

6 Conclusions

Although the Gini picture of the income distribution for different regions of the world clearly shows four 'layers' of income distribution across the world, this phenomenon only reflects what happens to half the world's population – those at the very top and those at the bottom of the distribution. The other half – in the middle and upper-middle deciles of the distribution – offers a rather different picture, and one of extraordinary homogeneity. This is a truly remarkable fact that has so far not been properly emphasised in the literature. Clearly more research needs to be done into the forces behind these opposite 'centrifugal' and 'centripetal' movements.

The similar income shares in the middle and upper-middle deciles across regions raise some doubts about distributional theories that give pride of place either to education or to ('augmented') trade-related wage differentials as the main determinants of income distribution. Groups with the highest degree of heterogeneity in distributional terms are more likely to have higher degrees of homogeneity in educational terms, and vice versa. Looking at trade-related wage differentials again, there does not seem to be much distributional variance in that part of the distribution where 'skilled' and 'unskilled' labour are most likely to be found. In general, political-institutional factors, and the nature of the political settlement, seem to have a far greater influence on the determination of income distribution than purely economic ones.[32]

The sample also shows a significant distributional difference between Anglophone and non-Anglophone OECD countries; a similar phenomenon is found within the ex-communist countries (the difference between those countries that used to belong to the Soviet Union and those in Eastern Europe).

Finally, in terms of the 'U' and 'inverted U' relationships between income distribution and income per capita in the era of globalisation – and taking into account all the necessary econometric caveats on cross-sectional regressions of this nature, the problems with the quality of the data, and the fact that in many countries (especially in Sub-Saharan Africa) the data refer to expenditure, not income – the relevant regressions seem to support several hypotheses. First, as the first half of the cross-section 'inverted U' is now nearly flat, the relationship between income distribution and income per capita only takes shape properly in the 'downwards' (or second half) side of the cross-section – which, in turn, is the one that makes analytical sense. Second (and in analytical terms far more importantly), within these relationships regional effects dominate. Third, Latin America and 'mineral-rich' Southern Africa has so far had the largest 'excess' inequality of any region in the world vis-à-vis their income per capita. In fact, Latin America may be characterised as 'middle-income', but while the top 10 per cent are able to live the equivalent of a modern European élite-lifestyle, the bottom 40 per cent are still living the equivalent of a medieval European lifestyle. In fact, the middle and upper-middle 50 per cent of the population are the only ones where the label 'middle-income' actually applies.

While political oligarchies all over the Third World would be very happy to appropriate such a high share of the national income, the question that still needs to be answered is why only those of middle-income Latin America and Southern Africa have managed to get away with it.

Notes

* Tony Atkinson, Stephanie Blankenburg, Jonathan DiJohn, Jayati Gosh, Andrew Glyn, Daniel Hahn, Pamela Jervis, Richard Kozul-Wright, Hugo Pagano, Guillermo Paraje, Hashem Pesaran, Guy Standing, and especially Bob Sutcliffe made very useful contributions. Participants at several conferences and seminars also made helpful suggestions. The usual caveats apply.

1. For a comprehensive analysis of this literature, see Kanbur (2000). See also Atkinson (1997), Aghion et al. (1999), IADB (1999) and UNCTAD (1996 and 2002).
2. At the time of the creation of NAFTA, there were already well over 10 million Mexicans living in the US.
3. For the Luxembourg Income Study (LIS), see http://www.lisproject/org. The WB basic information is published regularly in its World Development Indicators (WB, 2010). See also WIDER (2010).
4. In some Sub-Saharan countries, for example, surveys undertaken in the midst of civil wars, claim to have 'national' coverage. In the case of Latin America, a critical review of the quality of household surveys can be found in Székely and Hilgert (1999a).
5. See, for example, Székely and Hilgert (1999b).
6. See WIDER (2008).
7. Following advice from WB staff, data for eight countries are excluded from the sample due to inconsistencies.
8. See also UNCTAD (1996).
9. This is just one of the many instances of loss of information resulting from reporting the data only in terms of quintiles.
10. In fact, as discussed elsewhere, decile 10 also tended to have significant internal dispersion; and the real concentration of income is usually found within the first five percentiles of income recipients (see Palma, 2002a). This point is also clear in some country studies, see, for exam-

ple, Ferreira and Litchfield (2000) for Brazil, Panuco (1988) for Mexico, Paraje (2002) for Argentina; and Palma (2009) for the US. Consequently, one would really like to know the effects of globalisation on the income share of the top 5 per cent of the population; however, this is not possible with the available data.

11. Chile is only one of a few countries in the Third World for which there is relatively systematic income distribution data for any length of time. The calculations shown in Figure 7.3 are based on 'household per capita income', excluding from family incomes those of lodgers and domestic servants living in the house. We also exclude incomes when they are declared as 'zero', 'does not know', or 'does not answer'. The database corresponds to the 'Encuesta Trimestral de Ocupación y Desocupación en el Gran Santiago' carried out by Economics Department of the University of Chile since 1957. We used the household surveys done in June of each year, as these are the ones that carries a proper section on income.
12. Perhaps, it was the intuition of this type of situation that led a satirical magazine in Chile to characterise Chile's neo-liberal distributional outcome with a sort of 'post-modernist' Robin Hood metaphor: for them, this distributional outcome consisted of robbing the rich ... to give to the very rich!
13. The degree of polarisation found in D10/D1 is, of course, even more extreme; see Table 7.1.
14. See, for example, World Bank (1987) and Krueger (1983).
15. See, for example, Lall (1983).
16. See, for example, Juhn and Pierce (1993); Revenga (1995); Cline (1997; this book has a very useful survey of the literature); Haskel (1999); and Melendez (2001). For critiques of this literature, see Krugman and Lawrence (1993), Robinson (1996) and Atkinson (1997).
17. The exceptions that confirm the rule are the 'diamond-rich' Botswana and (especially) Namibia.
18. My friend Bob Sutcliffe suggested that I should graph in this way what he calls 'Palma's Law' of homogeneous middle vs. heterogeneous tails.
19. See, for example, Neal and Rosen (2000).
20. Wolfson (1997), for example, started the 'polarisation' literature by developing an index that cuts the Lorenz curve right in the middle! For a discussion of this point, see Palma (2002b).
21. Just to emphasise, even if the test shows a significant relationship of this kind, the Kuznets 'structural change' hypothesis is just one of many possible interpretations. In fact, there is already an extensive (and persuasive) literature arguing against the Kuznets hypothesis (see especially Kanbur, 2000). In Palma (2010a) I also conclude that this hypothesis is one of the least relevant for explaining Latin America's huge inequality.
22. For a discussion of the econometric issues raised by cross-section regressions like these, see Pesaran (2000); see also Palma (2002c). In particular, one has to understand that these regressions are simply a cross-sectional *description* of cross-country inequality differences, categorised by income per capita; that is, they should not be interpreted in a 'predicting' way, because there are a number of difficulties with a curve estimated from a single cross-section – especially regarding the homogeneity restrictions that are required to hold. This is one reason why the use of regional dummies is so important, as they can bring us closer to the required homogeneity restrictions. Nevertheless, there is no obvious way of knowing whether we are close enough to be able to predict with reasonable confidence. The jury is therefore still out regarding the predictive capacity of such regressions. Moreover, in any classification of this type there is a 'pre-testing' danger when determining regional dummies, as there is often more than one way to define a region.
23. All 't' statistics reported in this chapter are constructed using 'White heteroscedasticity-consistent standard errors'.
24. Dummies for each region were selected according to the Akaike Information Criterion.
25. Mexico's manufacturing exports reached a level 3.5 times greater than those of Brazil and Argentina taken together. In terms of overall merchandise exports, Mexico's share in the Latin American total doubled from just under one-quarter to about one-half.
26. As Mexicans like to say, their country may be far from God, but is certainly close to the US.

27. Between 1982 and 2010 Mexico received well over US$200 billion in net inflows of FDI.
28. For a detailed analysis of the Mexican economy after trade and financial liberalisation, see Palma (2005).
29. Unfortunately, a change in national accounts does not allow us to update the information after 2000 with compatible data. So, this graph and subsequent one will only cover the period 1950–2000. For a detailed analysis of neo-liberal economic reforms in Latin America, see Palma (2010b).
30. Wages stagnated at a time of economic euphoria in Mexico, with the new oil industry coming on stream at a time of particularly high oil prices. This mania reached such heights that the previous president had declared at the end of his term in office that from then on, 'economic policy was no longer an issue of allocation of scarce resources among multiple needs, but one of the distribution of abundance'. This 'abundance' clearly did not reach wages.
31. See http://www.inegi.org.mx. See also Palma (2005). Latin American neo-liberals have not paid much attention to Churchill's views that low wages only subsidise inefficient producers. For example, in his speech to the House of Commons proposing the legislation to create 'Trade Boards' to regulate workers' remuneration in industries with low wages (28 April 1909), he explained that the Boards were necessary in industries where the bargaining strength of employers greatly outweighed that of workers. According to Churchill, '... where you have what we call sweated trades, you have no organisation, no parity of bargaining, the good employer is undercut by the bad, and the bad employer is undercut by the worst.' For an analysis of the minimum wage in Britain, see http://www.iatge.de/aktuell/vero-eff/2005/gr2005-01.pdf.
32. This issue is discussed in more detail in the Latin American context in another two papers (Palma, 2002a, and 2010b). See also Krugman and Lawrence (1993).

Bibliography

Aghion, P., E. Caroli and C. Garcia-Peñaloza (1999), 'Inequality and economic growth: the perspective of the new growth theories', *Journal of Economic Literature*, **37**(4), 1615–60.

Atkinson, A.B. (1997), 'Bringing income distribution in from the cold', *The Economic Journal*, **107**(441), 297–321.

Atkinson, A.B. and F. Bourguignon (2000), *Handbook of Income Distribution*, Vol. 1, Amsterdam: North-Holland.

Cline, W. (1997), *Trade and Income Distribution*, Washington DC: Institute for International Economics.

FACEA (2010), 'Encuesta Trimestral de Ocupación y Desocupación en el Gran Santiago', available at http://www.empleo.microdatos.cl/encuesta_ocupacion/encuesta-ocupacion-basedatos.php?op=3; accessed 8 October 2010.

Ferreira, F. and J. Litchfield (2000), 'Desigualdade, Pobreza e Bem-Estar Social no Brasil: 1981/95', in R. Henriques (ed.), *Desigualdade e Pobreza no Brasil*, Rio de Janeiro: IPEA.

Haskel, J. (1999), 'The trade and labour approaches to wage inequality', Queen Mary and Westfield College, Working Paper No. 405.

IADB (Inter-American Development Bank) (1999), *Economic and Social Progress in Latin America*, available at http://www.iadb.org/res/ipes/2007/index.cfm?language=english; accessed 7 October 2010.

Juhn, C.K. and B. Pierce (1993), 'Wage inequality and the rise of returns to skill', *Journal of Political Economy*, **101**(3).

Kanbur, R. (2000), 'Income distribution and development', in Atkinson and Bourguignon (2000).

Krueger, A. (1983), *Trade and Employment in Developing Countries*, Vol. 3, *Synthesis and Conclusions*, NBER.

Krugman, P. (2000), 'The fall and rise of development economics', available at http://web.mit.edu/krugman/www/dishpan.html; accessed 8 October 2010.

Krugman, P. and R. Lawrence (1993), 'Trade, jobs and wages', NBER Working Paper No. 4478, September.

Kuznets, S. (1955), 'Economic growth and income inequality', *American Economic Review*, **45**(1), 1–28.
Lall, D. (1983), *The Poverty of 'Development Economics'*, Institute of Economic Affairs.
Marshall, A. (1898), *Principles of Economics*, 3rd edn, London: Macmillan and Co.
Melendez, J. (2001), 'The structure of wages under trade liberalisation: Mexico from 1984 to 1998', mimeo.
Neal, D. and S. Rosen (2000), 'Theories of the distribution of earnings', in Atkinson and Bourguignon (2000).
Palma, J.G. (1995), 'Income distribution in Latin America', mimeo, Cambridge.
Palma, J.G. (2002a), 'Property rights, institutional constraints and distributional outcomes: why does Latin America have the worst income distribution in the world?', mimeo, ILO.
Palma, J.G. (2002b), 'New indices of income polarisation: what do they tell us?', mimeo, Cambridge.
Palma, J.G. (2002c), 'The Kuznets Curve revisited: a neo-structuralist approach', *International Journal of Development Issues*, **1**(1).
Palma, J.G. (2003), 'National inequality in the era of globalisation: what do recent data tell us?', in *The Handbook of Globalisation*, First Edition, Cheltenham, UK and Northampton, MA, USA: Edward Elgar.
Palma, J.G. (2005), 'The seven main stylised facts of the Mexican economy since trade liberalisation and NAFTA', *Journal of Industrial and Corporate Change*, **14**(6), 941–91.
Palma, J.G. (2009), 'The revenge of the market on the rentiers: why neo-liberal reports of the end of history turned out to be premature', *CJE*, **33**(4); an extended version can be found in http://www.econ.cam.ac.uk/dae/repec/cam/pdf/cwpe0927.pdf; accessed 8 October 2010.
Palma, J.G. (2010a), 'Are the rich in Latin America (relatively) richer, or is there a group of rich people there simply not found elsewhere?' (Or how to rob the rich to give to the very rich), mimeo, Cambridge.
Palma, J.G. (2010b), 'Why has productivity growth stagnated in most Latin American countries since the neo-liberal reforms?', in J.A .Ocampo and J. Ros (eds), *The Handbook of Latin American Economics*, forthcoming, Oxford University Press. An extended version can be found at http://www.econ.cam.ac.uk/dae/repec/cam/pdf/cwpe1030.pdf; accessed 8 October 2010.
Panuco, H. (1988), 'Economic policy and the distribution of income in Mexico: 1984–1992', PhD thesis, London University.
Paraje, G. (2002), 'Inequality, welfare and polarisation in Great Buenos Aires, 1986–1999', PhD thesis, Cambridge University.
Pesaran, H., N.U. Haque and S. Sharma (2000), 'Neglected heterogeneity and dynamics in cross-country savings regressions', in J. Krishnakumar and E. Ronchetti (eds), *Panel Data Econometrics – Future Direction*, Amsterdam: Elsevier Science.
Revenga, A. (1995), 'Employment and wage effects of trade liberalization: the case of Mexican manufacturing', Policy Research Working Paper No. 1524, The World Bank.
Robinson, D.J. (1996), 'HOS hits facts: facts win. Evidence on trade and wages in the developing world', Development Discussion Paper No. 557, Harvard Institute for International Development.
Samuelson, P. (1948), 'International trade and the equalisation of factor prices', *Economic Journal*, **58**(230), 163–84.
Samuelson, P. (1949), 'International factor-price equalisation once again', *Economic Journal*, **59** (June), 181–97.
Székely, M. and M. Hilgert (1999a), 'What's behind the inequality we measure? An investigation using Latin American data', Inter-American Development Bank, Research Department, Working Paper No. 409.
Székely, M. and M. Hilgert (1999b), 'The 1990s in Latin America: another decade of persistent inequality', Inter-American Development Bank, Research Department, Working Paper No. 410.
UNCTAD (1996), *Trade and Development Report*.
UNCTAD (2002), *Trade and Development Report*.
WIDER (2008), World Income Inequality Database V2.0c May 2008, available at http://www.wider.unu.edu/research/Database/en_GB/database/; accessed 8 October 2010.

Wolfson, M. (1997), 'Divergent inequality: theory and empirical results', *Review of Income and Wealth*, **43**(3), 401–21.
World Bank (1987), *World Development Report.*
World Bank (2010), *World Development Indicators*.

Appendix 1

Latin America (LA) = Argentina, Bolivia, Brazil, Chile, Colombia, Costa Rica, Dominican Republic, Ecuador, El Salvador, Guatemala, Haiti, Honduras, Mexico, Nicaragua, Panama, Paraguay, Peru, Uruguay, and Venezuela.

Sub-Saharan Africa (SS-A; excludes Southern Africa) = Benin, Burkina Faso, Burundi, Cameroon, Cape Verde, Central African Republic, Chad, Congo, Rep., Cote d'Ivoire, Gabon, Gambia, The Ghana, Guinea, Guinea-Bissau, Kenya, Lesotho, Malawi, Mali, Mauritania, Mozambique, Niger, Nigeria, Papua New Guinea, Rwanda, Senegal, Sierra Leone, Swaziland, Tanzania, Togo, Uganda, Zambia, and Zimbabwe.

Southern Africa (SAf) = Angola, Botswana, Namibia, and South Africa.

North Africa (NA) = Algeria, Egypt, Morocco, and Tunisia.

East Asia-1 (EA1, or NICs-1) = Hong Kong, Korea, and Singapore.

East Asia-2 (EA2, or NICs-2) = Indonesia, Malaysia, and Thailand.

East Asia-3 (EA3, or NICs-3) = China, and Vietnam.

South Asia (SA) = Bangladesh, India, Pakistan, and Sri Lanka.

Former Soviet Union (FSU) = Armenia, Azerbaijan, Estonia, Georgia, Kazakhstan, Kyrgyz Republic, Latvia, Lithuania, Moldova, Mongolia, Tajikistan, Russian Federation, Ukraine, and Uzbekistan.

Eastern Europe (EE) = Albania, Belarus, Bosnia and Herzegovina, Bulgaria, Croatia, Czech Republic, Hungary, Macedonia, Poland, Romania, Slovak Republic, and Slovenia.

Non-Anglophone European Union (EU; includes Switzerland) = Austria, Belgium, France, Germany, Greece, Italy, Luxembourg, Netherlands, Portugal, Spain, and Switzerland.

Anglophone OECD (OECD-1) = Australia, Canada, Ireland, New Zealand, United Kingdom, and United States.

Nordic countries (No) = Denmark, Finland, Norway, and Sweden.

Caribbean (Ca) = Guyana, Jamaica, St. Lucia, and Trinidad and Tobago.

Not classified: Cambodia, Djibouti, Ethiopia, Iran, Israel, Jordan, Lao PDR, Philippines, Timor-Leste, Turkey, and Yemen.

Appendix 2

Table A.1 Parameters' point estimation

	Reg. 1	Reg. 2	Reg. 3	Reg. 4	Reg. 5	Reg. 6
Intercept	2.14	1.74	1.96	4.71	–1.61	–2.47
Ln GDP pc	0.45	0.515	0.40	–0.50	0.99	0.83
Ln GDP pc sq	–0.031	–0.034	–0.027	0.032	–0.065	–0.055
LA dummy	–	0.296	0.034	–0.057	0.854	0.751
SS-A dummy	–	0.179	0.148	–0.194	0.403	0.335
OECD1 dummy	–	0.001	–	–	–	–
EE dummy	–	–0.003	–0.003	0.003	–0.006	–0.309
SAf dummy	–	0.461	0.226	–0.051	1.467	1.356

Table A.2 't' values

	Reg. 1	Reg. 2	Reg. 3	Reg. 4	Reg. 5	Reg. 6
Intercept	5.3	5.9	6.6	11.9	–2.3	–3.9
Ln GDP pc	4.3	6.7	5.3	–4.9	5.5	5.1
Ln GDP pc sq	–4.7	–7.1	–5.8	5.1	–5.8	–5.4
LA dummy	–	9.1	8.4	–10.4	11.1	10.5
SS-A dummy	–	5.6	4.7	–4.6	5.3	4.6
OECD1 dummy	–	2.4	3.7	–	–	–
EE dummy	–	–5.7	–5.8	4.3	–5.0	–4.8
SAf dummy	–	7.7	3.7	–4.86	10.4	10.4

Table A.3 Regression statistics

	Reg. 1	Reg. 2	Reg. 3	Reg. 4	Reg. 5	Reg. 6
R^2	21.9	75.4	74.3	75.4	78.2	77.2
F	18.6	55.4	61.6	65.4	76.3	72.2

PART III

TRANSNATIONAL CORPORATIONS

8 The role of transnational corporations in the globalisation process

*Grazia Ietto-Gillies**

1 Introduction

Globalisation is a complex phenomenon that is more in the nature of a process than a state of affairs. There have been several attempts at definition (McGrew, 1992; Oman, 1996; Castells, 1996; Giddens, 1999; Held et al. 1999).[1] Most definitions boil down to the fact that globalisation is both a process of geographical/spatial outreach and of an increased degree of interconnectedness and interdependence between people, groups and institutions based in different countries of the world.

As a process of spatial outreach it is not new and has long historical antecedents (Held et al., 1999). Nonetheless, it is argued in this chapter that the current process is considerably different from any previous process of outreach. One of the major differences is seen in the role that transnational corporations (TNCs) play in the globalisation process.

The chapter proceeds in section 2 with an analysis of the salient characteristics of the globalisation process. The third section considers the role of TNCs in cross-border transactions. Section 4 develops the argument that the TNCs are a dominant cause of the globalisation process. Section 5 considers the wider policy implications of this perspective and the last section concludes.

2 Salient characteristics of globalisation

The current globalisation process is characterised by both qualitative and quantitative aspects and it differs from previous outreach processes in many of these aspects. The process is cumulative and thus the various aspects and mechanisms reinforce each other.

Among the qualitative aspects of globalisation the following play an important part:

- *Breadth of change*. The changes now involve a variety of fields or 'domains' (Held et al., 1999) ranging from the economy and society in general, to population movements, to the business sector, to politics, to the military, the environment and culture.
- *Political basis*. The process has been reinforced by the economic and social policies of deregulation and liberalisation now involving most countries in both the developed and developing regions.

- *Financial domination of the economy*. The dominance of finance capital is not new in capitalism. However, the last 20 years have seen such dominance reaching unprecedented levels both in terms of intensity of financial activities in relation to the size of economies, and in terms of the number of countries involved in financial transactions. On this issue Palma (2009, p. 834; italics original) writes: 'the four components of the stock of global financial assets (equity, public and private bonds and bank deposits) increased *9-fold* in real-terms between 1980 and 2007 … As a result, the multiple of the stock of financial assets to world output jumped from 1.2 to 4.4'.
- *Social and organisational changes*. The organisation of production and business in general has undergone considerable changes made possible and indeed necessary by the new technologies.
- *Transnational corporations*. The major changes are related to the organisation of production across countries due to the activities of TNCs, on which more in the rest of this chapter.
- *Technological basis of globalisation*. None of the above changes would have been possible on the scale in which we are witnessing them without the introduction and rapid spread of the information and communication technologies (ICTs). The ICTs affect every aspect of the globalisation process from the movement of people, products and resources, to the organisation of production. Considerable improvements have also occurred in the technology and costs of transportation.

As regards the quantitative aspects of the globalisation process, the following issues are relevant:

- There has been an increase in the *number of mechanisms* of interconnectedness across borders: from the traditional trade flows to foreign investment (direct and portfolio) and related incomes, to various types of collaborative business ventures.
- The *extensity* or geographical/spatial reach of interconnectedness has been increasing. Here, 'extensity' means the geographical scope and therefore the number of countries involved in cross-border operations within and between regions.
- The *intensity* of cross-border flows has also been increasing. By intensity I mean the ratio between cross-border transactions and the size of the domestic economy(ies). The latter can be represented by a variety of economic and social variables such as gross domestic product or domestic capital formation or population or labour force.

3 Cross-border transactions and the TNCs

The interconnectedness across countries manifests in a variety of transactions and flows, particularly in the following:

- international trade in goods and services;
- foreign direct investment;
- portfolio investment;
- profits, interests and dividends from the various types of foreign investment;
- inter-organisational collaborative partnerships;
- movements of people across borders for leisure or business activities or in search of jobs.

The institutions that participate and that are key to all the above activities are the TNCs, that is, those companies with *direct business activities* in at least two countries. These direct business activities involve the ownership of productive assets abroad in a percentage large enough to give control over the conduct of the business.[2]

The cross-border transactions that are most specific to – and indeed defining of – the TNC are those of foreign direct investment (FDI). From the 1970s onward there has been a steady and large increase in FDI, most of which originates in developed countries and is indeed directed to the same group of countries. In 2008, 84 per cent of the world stock of FDI originated from developed countries. The same group of countries received 68.5 per cent of the world stock (UNCTAD, 2009).

However, as well as being responsible for all or most FDI, the TNCs participate in all other cross-border business activities listed above. Over three-quarters of world trade originates with TNCs and indeed over a third of it is estimated to take place on an intra-firm basis (UNCTAD, 1996).[3]

Transnational corporations – including banks and other financial institutions – are responsible for large amounts of portfolio investment and cross-border loans. The incomes deriving from foreign investment – whether direct or portfolio or loans – will accrue to the institutions involved in such investment and therefore, largely, to the TNCs (Ietto-Gillies, 2000).

Most collaborative agreements are between firms, though there are many instances of collaboration between public and private institutions (Hladik, 1985; Contractor and Lorange, 1988; Hergert and Morris, 1988; Hagedoorn, 1996 and 2002).

The movement of people across frontiers may have the direct involvement of TNCs to a lesser extent than other cross-border movements. However, an increasing part of migration – that related to expatriate managers – is largely linked to activities of TNCs (Salt and Singleton, 1995; Salt, 1997).

In 2008 there were, worldwide, 82 053 TNCs operating with a network of 807 362 foreign affiliates (UNCTAD, 2009). Dunning (1981, ch. 1, p. 3) reports nearly 11 000 TNCs and 82 600 foreign affiliates in 1976. The huge growth between the mid-1970s and 2008 is the result of the following: a larger number of companies from developed countries operating abroad; the increasing involvement in foreign operations by both large and smaller companies; the transnationalisation of several state-owned companies; and the transnationalisation of many companies from developing countries and particularly from China.

4 TNCs as a dominant cause of globalisation

The analysis of globalisation in terms of causes, effects and policy implications has led Held et al. (1999) to summarise the positions into three approaches or theses. The hyperglobalist thesis – which has Kenichi Ohmae (1991, 1995a and 1995b) as its main exponent – sees the TNCs as the key agents of globalisation and the sources of efficiency and growth. The globalisation process itself is to be encouraged and any constraints to it removed. Traditional nation states with over-regulation and uneven regional development are among the obstacles to globalisation. Ohmae therefore advocates the demise of the nation state and the rise of smaller, more developmentally homogeneous region states.

An opposite point of view – the sceptic thesis – is taken by Carnoy et al. (1993), Hirst and Thompson (1996) and Kozul-Wright and Rowthorn (1998). These authors claim that the globalisation process has been exaggerated and that, in reality, most international activities by TNCs have a very strong home-country base. The nation state and its policies are seen as relevant as ever.

Held et al. (1999) see globalisation as a process of global transformations similar to other historical processes of global reach but far more advanced in geographical extensity and intensity.

Chesnais (1997) sees finance as the main basis of the globalisation process. In his view the deregulation and liberalisation policies of the 1980s have set in motion forces leading to a new regime of capitalist accumulation dominated by finance. He advocates the halting and reversing of this process by curbing the power of finance capital and its hold on industrial capital. Ietto-Gillies (2002, ch. 9) puts forward a different view on the causes of globalisation and this leads to specific policy implications. The analysis starts from the premise that the current economic and social developments are characterised by two specific types of innovation: (1) technological innovation in the field of communication and information; and (2) organisational innovation that allows a specific actor in the economic system – the transnational company – to use the ICTs to further the productive forces. Globalisation is indeed a new phase in capitalist development characterised by a tremendous increase in the potential – and, to a lesser extent, the actual – development of the productive forces.

Both the organisational and technological types of innovations have, so far, been exploited mainly by the transnational corporation. Though not all organisational innovations contribute to the development of the productive forces, many do. Indeed, the scope for further development and exploitation of innovation by the TNCs themselves and by other actors in the economic system is huge.

Starting from the above premises, let us turn to the causal analysis of globalisation. In this context it is useful to distinguish between the driving forces of globalisation and its dominant causes. The driving forces in the globalisation process are all those elements that contribute to the process and shape its pattern. In particular: the activities of TNCs and of financial institutions; the diffusion of the ICTs; the policies of governments, particularly those related to liberalisation and deregulation; the policies of international institutions such as the International Monetary Fund (IMF) and the World Trade Organization (WTO).

Not all these forces operate on an equal basis. Two in particular I consider to be the dominant causes, that is those at the root of the globalisation process and those that are largely irreversible. In trying to identify the dominant causes I apply the concept of *causa causans* developed by Keynes (1937).[4] He uses this concept in order to establish a basic, dominant cause of the level of output and employment in a complex system where many forces operate at once. This is indeed the situation as regards the globalisation process. In the identification of the dominant causes a litmus test will be used consisting of the following two conditions: (1) the dominant causes are a subset of the driving forces and they are identified as those that specifically contribute to the development of the productive forces at the basis of the globalisation process; (2) such a development of the productive forces and the dominant causes behind it are largely irreversible.

On the basis of these conditions the two dominant causes or *causae causantes* of globalisation can be identified in the following two areas of innovation, both of which contribute to the development of the productive forces: (1) technological innovation in the field of communication and information together with advances in the field of transportation; (2) organisational innovation and in particular the organisation of production across countries.

Technological and organisational innovations are strongly interlinked. The diffusion of ICTs makes possible the organisational innovation and the vast development of TNCs' activities we are witnessing. Conversely, the needs of TNCs are behind the rapid diffusion of ICTs. These two driving forces are largely irreversible and contribute to the development of the productive forces.

Other driving forces in the globalisation process – such as financial forces, or the liberalisation policies of national governments and international institutions – do not contribute to the development of the productive forces; moreover, they are indeed reversible. For these reasons they are here seen as different from the two dominant causes in the role they play in the globalisation process. Therefore, though I consider the impact of financial forces and deregulation/liberalisation as very important in the shaping of the current globalisation process, I do not see them as irreversible or as contributors to the development of the productive forces.

The main characteristic of the TNCs is their ability to plan, organise and control business activities across countries. It is a characteristic currently specific to them and one that, therefore, differentiates them from other actors in the economic system who cannot – or not yet – organise themselves internationally. Such actors include labour, the consumers, uninational companies and indeed local, regional and national governments.

The TNCs play a very important role in the globalisation process because: (1) they are key to organisational and technological innovations and therefore to the development of the productive forces; (2) they contribute to most flows of international transactions as listed in section 3 above; (3) they are, so far, the only actor that can truly plan, organise and control activities across borders; (4) they are in a position to take full advantage of the ICTs and indeed contribute to their diffusion and development; (5) they participate in the globalisation process as active rather than passive participants, unlike many other actors.[5]

5 Policy implications

There are specific long-term policy implications emerging from this analysis; most of them derive from the consideration that those driving forces of the globalisation process that are not dominant causes can be reversed. We shall deal with the relevant policy implications in three areas: the financial sector; the TNCs and the ICTs.

5.1 The financial sector

The analysis of the previous sections considers the growth of financial transactions to be a driving force, though not a dominant cause. Much financial activity, far from contributing to the development of the productive forces is a hindrance to it and has a purely distributive purpose. Moreover, the financial dominance of domestic and international economies is reversible if the political will is there.

The excessive growth of the financial sector worldwide has been at the root of the economic crisis of 2008 whose impact is still with us as this chapter is revised. The relationship between the crisis, the relative size of the financial sector and the lack of regulation has recently been the object of many works.[6]

The crisis has highlighted the following. (1) There has been excessive, unsustainable growth of the financial sector in the last 30 years. (2) This growth is connected with the liberal, market ideology in politics, business and much of the economics profession. (3) This growth together with a variety of government regulations ranging from taxation to liberalisation of the labour market have had a huge impact on the changes in the distribution of income and wealth in favour of the rich (Atkinson and Piketty, 2007; Lankester, 2009). (4) The growth of the financial sector has had a negative impact on the real sector of economies; it has also made the economic system as a whole more unstable. (5) The unregulated flows of finance across countries have made the world more interconnected and this has made the crisis more devastating for smaller and fragile economies such as Iceland, Ireland, Greece, the Eastern European and the developing countries (Wade, 2009).

As I write, the costs of the crisis are being met by taxpayers and so largely by the lower-income people in most countries including the UK. It is interesting to note that immediately after the crisis the liberal press and most of the economics profession have abandoned the 'market is best; no government intervention' stance and asked for the bailing out of the financial sector. Several banks have been taken into public ownership though the UK Labour government has stressed from the beginning its non-interference with the management of the nationalised banks.

There are policy implications from the role of the financial sector in globalisation, its growth and the current crisis. For years the public has been told that in order to get the full benefits of globalisation we must have an unregulated financial sector within and across borders. The approach adopted here claims the opposite. An unregulated financial sector has led to its excessive growth at the cost of the real sector and to the biggest economic crisis for 80 years. Regulation is possible and necessary in order to limit future instability and in order to achieve a globalisation process based more on the real sector and in favour of the many, not just the few.

Regulation should take account of both institutional and systemic risk and include the following. (1) Separation of financial institutions according to the type and level of institutional risk involved. Specifically: institutions dealing with commercial banking; with long-term borrowing and lending (i.e., housing mortgages) and with investment banking. Such separation would diminish future risks for the institutions as well as the system as a whole. It would also lead to smaller size for financial institutions, thus avoiding future situations in which an institution is deemed too big to fail; moreover, it would inject more competition into the system with benefits for the consumers. (2) The financial sector and those strata of society that most benefitted from deregulation should bear the cost of the crisis. (3) There should be a strong regulatory authority and framework at the national level. (4) At the international level, the crisis has highlighted the need for a new, regulatory institutional architecture dealing with cross-border flows, with tax revenues issues and with rescue packages. (5) A tax on cross-border financial transactions is long overdue.

5.2 *The transnational corporations*

Transnational activities can be part of the development of the productive forces and as such have the potential for vast contribution to the economy and society. However, there is a need to look again at the TNCs, their activities and power relationship with other actors and to develop a policy framework that increases the actual contribution to the economy in line with potential contribution.

In the last 30 years we have been bombarded with a rhetoric based on the assumption that globalisation equals liberalisation, unregulated markets and self-regulation by large businesses and particularly by the TNCs. This equation seems to have been accepted by many on both the right and the left: the former sees it as desirable, the latter as inevitable. It is neither, and we must reject the equation. We can have many positive aspects of globalisation without the – so far – associated deregulation binge of the 1980s and 1990s, with all the related problems it generated.

The TNCs play the key role in the development of organisational innovation within and across borders. In the previous sections their activities have been identified as one of the two dominant causes of the globalisation process. The other one being the ICTs. They are, at present, the only actor that can truly plan, coordinate and control activities across borders. This puts them in a position of considerable power vis-à-vis other actors and in particular labour, national governments, consumers and uninational companies.

The 1960s and 1970s were seen as decades of *confrontation* between TNCs and national governments, particularly but not exclusively those in developing countries. There were large numbers of nationalisations of foreign affiliates particularly in developing countries.

The wind changed in the political environment from the 1980s onward. These were seen as decades of *cooperation* between national governments and TNCs (Dunning, 1993, ch. 13). Far from threatening nationalisations, many governments in developing countries followed in the footsteps of some developed countries in engaging in large-scale privatisations. The privatised assets were often bought by foreign companies. UNCTAD (1993, fig. 1, p. 17) shows that the number of nationalisations peaked in the mid-1970s and became non-existent after the mid-1980s. Privatisations started in the mid-1970s and increased very rapidly in the 1980s and 1990s.

The cooperative stance went hand-in-hand with the establishment and diffusion of the liberal agenda. In this ideological framework, the cooperative stance has increasingly led to a stronger and stronger position for TNCs, leaving them free to follow their own strategies in an unfettered way. In effect we have seen cooperation turning into the TNCs' *domination* of other economic players including governments themselves.

Various groups in society saw their power waning while the distribution of income and wealth moved away from the poorest people, groups, communities, classes, countries, to the rich ones. This has led to a social and political environment characterised among other elements by the following. (1) Increasing discontent, which has taken the route of grassroots opposition to the visible face of global capitalism (such as high-profile TNCs and well-known brands). (2) Disillusion with the democratic process. Confrontation has come back on the world agenda but not as confrontation between governments and TNCs but rather between people – organised in various pressure groups – and TNCs as well as international institutions (such as the World Trade Organization) seen as the agents of TNCs and the midwives to the globalisation ills. Confrontation has often taken on the form of street protests. As governments followed strategies for the few, often in opposition to democratic principles, people have come to believe less and less in the democratic process as a way of changing the social and economic situation. The gradual fall in electoral participation in many developed countries – and most notably in the UK, and the US prior to the election of Obama – is a sad sign of this disillusionment with the democratic process.

The way out seems to be to channel this new style confrontation from street protests to politics. The democratic process must be made to work and this can only be achieved if we move from confrontation to regulation. National governments must regain the lead in developing appropriate policies to deal with the TNCs' powerful position. We need regulation to channel the many opportunities and cope with the many problems raised by the new technologies and by the TNCs' activities (in relation to the environment, safety, competition and labour standards). Many problems cannot be tackled without appropriate international institutions. Self-regulation is unlikely to work for most issues, including those related to the environmental and to labour standards; in the end these standards will always be in the way of profit-making. Moreover, self-regulation cannot secure the coordination within and between industries necessary for the long-term prosperity of companies and countries.

We need more coordination power within and across frontiers, by other actors. There is therefore a need to implement policies designed to develop countervailing transnational power in the other actors, be they labour, uninational companies, consumers or governments themselves. This will enable these actors to participate fully and actively in the globalisation process and will make the process more inclusive.

In a world in which much activity takes place across borders, there is an increased need for transnational governance as well as for the strengthening of national and regional governance. This can be achieved via the establishment of appropriate supranational institutions among whose aims should be the monitoring of transnational business activities.

Transnational companies have a positive role to play in the current phase of capitalist development. Many are involved in much-needed development and diffusion of innovation; many produce products that people genuinely want and need; many generate employment and develop skills. However, their activities must be regulated by a system of coherent governance within and between borders. The current pattern of social exclusion from the benefit of globalisation and of technological advances must be replaced by a more inclusive and participatory framework. Inclusiveness must also embrace present and future societies via a serious commitment to (and implementation of) a responsible strategy for the environment.

5.3 The technological basis of globalisation

The development of the ICTs and indeed of other technologies, particularly in the life sciences, are giving a tremendous boost to the productive forces. We are, in many ways, still at the beginning of the exploitation of productive potential of all the new technologies. There are some key questions arising from these developments and in particular the following. (1) Can knowledge and the results of research be kept private when its public character is so clear in terms of the scope for (and low marginal costs of) utilisation and diffusion? (2) For how much longer can the intellectual property laws protect the revenue of cultural industries in the context of technologies that allow free use of products?[7] (3) What is likely to happen to these industries long term (Knopper, 2009)? Can/should governments take them under their wings? (4) Can the social relations of production remain the same in the face of such sweeping changes in the productive forces?

6 Conclusions

This chapter starts with an analysis of the globalisation process in terms of its qualitative and quantitative characteristics. It then considers the main types of international transactions and the role played by transnational corporations in them.

A brief summary of various theoretical approaches to globalisation is followed by a specific approach that sees the TNCs and the ICTs as the dominant causes of globalisation. This conclusion is reached using Keynes's methodological use of the concept of *causa causans* and distinguishing between driving forces and dominant causes of globalisation.

Thus, the TNCs are here placed at the very centre of the globalisation process and in direct causal relationship with it. Their participation in it is seen as active and, indeed, causal. This contrasts with the passive role played by other actors such as labour, consumers and uninational companies.

There are specific policy implications arising from the approach presented here in relation to: the financial sector and the crisis of 2008; the role of TNCs in the economy and society; and the role of the new technologies. These implications are discussed in section 5.

Notes

* The views in this chapter are further developed in Ietto-Gillies (2002), particularly Chapters 1, 2, 9 and 10.

1. Details on definitions and on the theoretical positions of various authors are in Ietto-Gillies (2002, ch. 9).
2. The share of asset ownership that can secure control can be deemed to be as low as 10 per cent (IMF, 1977). Below it the equity investment is classified as portfolio. See Ietto-Gillies (2005, ch. 1) for more on control.
3. For the relationship between trade and international production cf. Cantwell (1994) and Ietto-Gillies (2005, ch. 19). These works discuss the theoretical underpinning of the relationship and give references to the relevant literature.
4. A fuller analysis of Keynes's position is in Gillies and Ietto-Gillies (2001) as well as in Ietto-Gillies (2002, ch. 9).
5. These points are developed at greater length in Ietto-Gillies (2005, ch. 15).
6. See in particular the special edition of the *Cambridge Journal of Economics* (2009).
7. The negative impact of the IPRs in both developing and developed countries is analysed in Pagano and Rossi (2009).

References

Atkinson, A.B. and Piketty T. (eds) (2007), *Top Income over the Twentieth Century: A Contrast Between European and English-speaking Countries*, Oxford: Oxford University Press.

Cambridge Journal of Economics (2009), **33**(4).

Cantwell, J. (1994), 'The relationship between international trade and international production', in D. Greenway and L.A. Winters (eds), *Surveys in International Trade*, Oxford: Blackwell, ch. 11, pp. 303–28.

Carnoy, M., M. Castells, S.S. Cohen and F.H. Cardoso (1993), *The New Global Economy in the Information Age. Reflections on our Changing World,* University Park, Pennsylvania: The Pennsylvania State University Press.

Castells, M. (1996), *The Information Age: Economy, Society and Culture, Vol. I, The Rise of the Network Society*, Oxford: Blackwell.

Chesnais, F. (1997), *La mondialisation du capital*, new edition, Paris: Syros.

Contractor, F.J. and P. Lorange (1988), 'Why should firms cooperate? The strategy and economic basis for cooperative ventures', in F.J. Contractor and P. Lorange (eds), *Cooperative Strategies in International Business: Joint Ventures and Technology Partnerships Between Firms*, Lexington, MA: Lexington Books, pp. 3–28.

Dunning, J.H. (1981), *International Production and the Multinational Enterprise*, London: George Allen and Unwin.

Dunning, J.H. (1993), *The Globalization of Business*, London: Routledge.

Dunning, J.H. and R. Pearce (1981), *The World's Largest Industrial Enterprises*, Farnborough: Gower Press.

Giddens, A. (1999), Reith Lectures (1999), 'Runaway world', Lecture 1: Globalisation, available at http://www.news.bbc.co.uk/radio4/reith1999/lecture1.shtml; accessed 11 October 2010.

Gillies, D.A. and G. Ietto-Gillies (2001), 'Keynes's notion of *causa causans* and its application to the globalisation process', in P. Arestis, S. Dow and M. Desai (eds), *Microeconomics, Methodology and Keynes. Essays in Honour of Victoria Chick*, London: Routledge.

Hagedoorn, J. (1996), 'Trends and patterns in strategic technology partnering since the early seventies', *Review of Industrial Organization*, **11**(5), 601–16.

Hagedoorn, J. (2002), 'Inter-firm R&D partnerships: an overview of major trends and patterns since 1960', *Research Policy*, **31**(4), 477–92.

Held, D., A. McGrew, D. Goldblatt and J. Perraton (1999), *Global Transformations*, Cambridge: Polity Press.

Hergert, M. and D. Morris (1988), 'Trends in international collaborative agreements', in F.J. Contractor and P. Lorange (eds), *Cooperative Strategies in International Business*, Lexington, MA: Lexington Books, pp. 99–109.

Hirst, P. and G. Thompson (1996), *Globalisation in Question*, Cambridge: Polity Press.

Hladik, K.J. (1985), *International Joint Ventures. An Economic Analysis of US Foreign Business Partnerships*, Cambridge, MA: Lexington Books.
Ietto-Gillies, G. (2000), 'Profits from foreign direct investment', in F. Chesnais, G. Ietto-Gillies and R. Simonetti (eds), *European Integration and Global Corporate Strategies*, London: Routledge, ch. 4, pp. 71–91.
Ietto-Gillies, G. (2002), *Transnational Corporations. Fragmentation amidst Integration*, London: Routledge.
Ietto-Gillies, G. (2005), *Transnational Corporations and International Production. Concepts, Theories and Effects*, Cheltenham, UK and Northampton, MA, USA, Edward Elgar.
International Monetary Fund (IMF) (1977), *Balance of Payments Manual*, 4th edn, Washington, DC: IMF.
Keynes, J.M. (1937), 'The general theory of employment', *The Collected Writings of John Maynard Keynes*, 1973, London: Macmillan Press.
Kozul-Wright, R. and R. Rowthorn (1998) 'Spoilt for choice? Multinational corporations and the geography of international production', *Oxford Review of Economic Policy*, **14**(2), 74–92.
Knopper S. (2009), *Appetite for Self-Destruction: The Spectacular Crash of the Record Industry in the Digital Age*, New York: Free Press.
Lankester, T. (2009), 'Commentary. The banking crisis and inequality', *World Economics*, **10**(1): January–March.
McGrew, A.G. (1992), 'Conceptualising global politics', in A.G. McGrew and P.G. Lewis (eds), *Global Politics: Globalisation and the Nation-State*, Cambridge: Polity Press, pp. 83–117.
Ohmae, K. (1991), *The Borderless World. Power and Strategy in the Interlinked Economy*, London: Fontana.
Ohmae, K. (1995a), 'Putting global logic first', *Harvard Business Review*, **73**(1), 119–25.
Ohmae, K. (1995b), *The End of the Nation State. The Rise of Regional Economics. How New Engines of Prosperity are Reshaping Global Markets*, London: The Free Press.
Oman, C. (1996), 'The policy challenges of globalisation and regionalisation', *Policy Brief* No. 11, OECD: OECD Development Centre.
Pagano, U. and M.A. Rossi (2009), 'The crush of the knowledge economy', *Cambridge Journal of Economics*, **33**(4): 665–83.
Palma, J.G. (2009), 'Why neo-liberal reports of the end of history turned out to be premature', *Cambridge Journal of Economics*, **33**(4): 829–69.
Salt, J. (1997), 'International movements of the highly skilled', *Directorate for Education, Employment, Labour and Social Affairs. International Migration Unit: Occasional Papers* no. 3, Paris: OECD/GD (97), 169.
Salt, J. and A. Singleton (1995), 'The international migration of expertise: the case of the United Kingdom', *Studi Emigrazione/Etudes Migration*, **XXII**(117), 12–30.
United Nations Conference on Trade and Development (UNCTAD) – Programme on Transnational Corporations (1993), *World Investment Report 1993, Transnational Corporations and Integrated International Production*, New York: United Nations.
United Nations Conference on Trade and Development (UNCTAD) (1996), *World Investment Report 1996. Investment, Trade and International Policy Arrangements*, Geneva: United Nations.
United Nations Conference on Trade and Development (UNCTAD) (2009), *World Investment Report. Transnational Corporations, Agricultural Production and Development*, Geneva: United Nations.
Wade, R. (2009), 'From global imbalances to global reorganization', *Cambridge Journal of Economics*, **33**(4): 539–62.

9 The role and control of multinational corporations in the world economy

*Gerald Epstein**

1 Introduction

Multinational corporations (MNCs) have become an increasingly important force in the dynamics of the global economy. For example, according to the United Nations, during the last 20 years, the gross product of the foreign affiliates of multinational corporations increased faster than global GDP while foreign affiliate sales increased faster than global exports. Taking into account both their international and national production, the United Nations Conference on Trade and Development (UNCTAD) estimates that multinational corporations produced about 10 per cent of the world's GDP in 1999 (UNCTAD, *World Investment Report*, 2000, p. xv).[1]

As one might expect, the impact of MNCs on developing and developed countries is hotly debated. At one extreme are the MNC boosters who argue that MNCs provide stable capital inflows, jobs, technology transfer and investment to 'host countries', while increasing growth and employment in the 'home' countries (Moran, 1998, 2002). On the other hand, critics contend that international capital mobility in general and MNCs in particular are creating a 'race to the bottom' around the globe, enhancing profits and political power for multinational corporations and local elites who benefit from their presence, while eroding wages, tax bases, social protections and the environment.

Importantly, different views on the impacts of MNCs not only characterise a divide between pro-labour forces on the one hand, and business boosters on the other; they also divide critics of globalisation, often along the lines of those from the 'North' vs. those from the 'South'. Northern labour's opposition to outward foreign direct investment (FDI) to the countries of the South is often seen by southern workers and NGOs as protectionist and harmful to workers in southern countries. At the same time, efforts by southern governments to attract foreign direct investment are sometimes seen by northern workers as an attempt to 'take good jobs' away from them.

Despite the fact that there has been a great deal of research during the last several decades on MNCs, there is no consensus on their effects. Still, the evidence that does exist suggests the following: though foreign direct investment can have positive impacts on home and host countries, the likelihood that these positive affects will materialise and be widely shared is greatly diminished by the 'neo-liberal' policy framework that is dominant in much of the world today. I conclude that what is needed, instead of more deregulation and 'free' capital mobility, is a more democratic framework of multinational investment regulation to help countries and their citizens reap the benefits that can be associated with international investment. If this was done properly, the tensions that arise between the interests of southern and northern workers might be significantly reduced.

2 Multinational corporations: some stylised facts[2]

Table 9.1 presents data on the rate of growth of several measures of MNC activity since the mid-1980s, as well as some measures of global economic activity as a basis for comparison. It indicates that with the exception of 2008, these estimates of MNC activities have been growing at a significantly faster rate in recent years than has world GNP, national gross fixed capital formation, or exports of non-factor goods and services.[3] The reversal in the growth rates of MNC activities in 2008 stem directly from the adverse conditions associated with the latest global financial crisis.

Taking a longer perspective, Table 9.2 presents data on the size of FDI stock and world exports relative to the size of the economy over the last century or

Table 9.1 The expansion of multinational corporations' international activities, 1986–2008 (annual rates of growth, per cent)

	1986–90	1991–95	1996–2000	2006	2007	2008
FDI inflows	23.6	22.1	39.4	50.1	35.4	−14.2
FDI outflows	25.9	16.5	35.6	58.9	53.7	−13.5
Cross border M&As	32.0	15.7	62.9	38.1	62.1	−34.7
Sales of foreign affiliates	19.7	8.8	8.1	18.9	23.6	−4.6
Gross product of foreign affiliates	17.4	6.8	6.9	21.6	20.1	−4.4
Exports of foreign affiliates	22.2	8.6	3.6	15.0	16.3	15.4
Employment of foreign affiliates	5.5	5.5	9.7	11.4	25.4	−3.7
Memorandum:						
GDP at factor cost	9.5	5.9	1.3	8.2	12.5	10.3
Gross fixed capital formation	10.0	5.4	1.1	10.9	13.8	11.5
Exports of goods and non-factor services	11.6	7.9	3.7	15.0	16.3	15.4

Source: UNCTAD, *World Investment Report (WIR)* (2009), Table I.6, p. 18.

Table 9.2 *World stock of FDI and exports relative to world GDP, 1913–2008 (per cent)*

	1913	1950	2008
FDI relative to GDP	9.0	4.0	24.5
World exports relative to GDP	8.7	7.0	32.9

Sources: FDI 1913, 1950: Burke and Epstein (2001); 2008: UNCTAD *World Investment Report* (2009), Table I.6. World exports 1913 and 1950: Angus Maddison, *Monitoring the World Economy, 1820–1992*, OECD (1995); 2008: UNCTAD *World Investment Report*, 2009, Table I.6.

so. The stock of foreign direct investment relative to GDP has grown six-fold since 1950 and almost tripled since 1913. The ratio of world exports to GDP has increased almost five-fold since 1950, and nearly quadrupled since 1913. The table suggests that, along with trade, MNCs have been a premier agent of globalisation in the last half-century.

Table 9.3 presents data on the regional distribution of the inward and outward stock of foreign direct investment and how it has evolved since 1980. The key point to notice is that stocks of both inward and outward FDI are highly concentrated in the developed economies; the overwhelming share of FDI flows is between the developed countries. In particular, in 2008, 68.5 per cent of the inward stock was in the developed economies; and almost 85 per cent of the outward stock was from the developed countries. Still, recently there has been an increase in the share of FDI going to the developing world, so that by 2008, almost one-third of the stock of inward investment was in the developing countries, compared with around 25 per cent in 1980.

Table 9.3 *The regional distribution of FDI inward and outward stock, 1980–2008 (percentage)*

	Inward Stock of FDI				Outward Stock of FDI			
	1980	1990	2000	2008	1980	1990	2000	2008
World	100	100	100	100	100	100	100	100
Developed	75.5	72.7	68.8	68.5	96.9	91.9	85.4	84.1
Developing	24.5	27.3	30.2	28.7	3.1	8.1	14.2	14.5
All developing minus China	23.2	26.2	26.8	26.1	3.1	7.9	13.7	13.6

Source: UNCTAD *World Investment Report* 1980, 1990, 2000, 2008 and 2009, authors' calculations from 2009, Table B2.

Within the developing countries themselves, however, these stocks are highly concentrated among a handful of countries. In the developing world, as is well known, China and other Asian countries, mostly Taiwan, Hong Kong, Thailand, Malaysia and Singapore, get a significant share of the developing world's FDI. As the fourth row of Table 9.3 shows, if China is excluded from the data, the share of inward stock held by the developing world has been more or less stagnant over the last 30 years, at a little more than a quarter. Among the developing countries, only ten developing countries received 64 per cent of total FDI flows to the developing world in 2008. More importantly, as the *World Investment Report* notes, there are no signs that the concentration of FDI across countries has been declining over time. Of course, if we had better data on other aspects of MNC activities, for example, sub-contracting, outsourcing and licensing, we might find evidence that MNC activities have become more dispersed in recent years, as the anecdotal evidence suggests.

Most authors agree on these basic stylised facts. What is in dispute, of course, is their implications. Has this tremendous increase in foreign direct investment and the role of MNCs been helpful or harmful to 'host' and 'home' countries? What policies and regulatory institutions are required to increase the size and widen the distribution of the benefits from foreign direct investment?

3 The impact of MNCs on 'host countries' in the developing world

Advocates for the contributions of MNCs to economic development cite several key channels through which FDI benefits developing host countries. In light of space limitations, I only briefly treat them below, and even then, can only consider the most important ones. I will suggest that, while there might be some truth to many of these claims, the evidence is far more mixed than advocates often claim. Moreover, because of space limitations, for the most part, I will not be able to discuss the impact on the developed countries (see Crotty et al., 1998 and Burke and Epstein, 2001 for more discussion of these issues).

3.1 Possible positive effects

3.1.1 'FDI is a stable source of finance' An increasingly common view in policy circles is that FDI is a better form of investment for developing countries because it is more 'stable' than portfolio investment (see, for example, Lipsey, 1999; UNCTAD, 1999). This view has gained adherents partly as a result of the recent Asian financial crisis when portfolio flows were highly unstable. For example, a number of papers have shown the coefficient of variation for FDI is smaller for most countries than for portfolio and other non-FDI flows. This contrasts with results from a study in the 1980s that showed no significant difference in the stability of the flows (Claessens and Gooptu, 1995).[4]

The implications of the claim that FDI is less volatile than portfolio investment, however, are not at all clear. For one thing, it may be a statistical artefact, due to the fact that most countries' FDI data do not include data on the reinvestment of retained earnings (the US is an exception). For example, it is possible that reinvestment of retained earnings is just as volatile as are portfolio investments, but does not show up as part of FDI. Moreover, the recent findings on the stability of FDI may be the result of special features of the Asian financial crisis itself. In particular, South Korea and other countries were forced to open up their firms to inward FDI or liberalise flows substantially, and therefore drew in a large amount of FDI. These one-time, special factors therefore may not be operative the next time there is a major outflow of portfolio investment.

Most important, however, is that these arguments do not take into account the overall costs and benefits of attracting FDI. Having a flow that is more stable, but that on balance does not yield net benefits, is not in itself beneficial.

3.1.2 Employment One of the most important reasons why developing countries want to attract FDI is to create more employment opportunities at home, and one of the biggest reasons why northern workers are suspicious of outward FDI is because they fear a loss of jobs. Of course, when a foreign company opens up a factory and hires workers, employment is generated. But a much more complicated question to ask is what is the impact on employment in the economy as a whole after all the other indirect effects are taken into account? For example, Braunstein and Epstein (2002) found that FDI had small or no net impacts on employment in China, once the impacts on domestic investment and other Chinese policy measures are taken into account. Lipsey (2002), on the other hand, finds that FDI does generate more employment, on balance, in many countries. Perhaps of equal if not more concern is the impact of FDI on wages and productivity associated with that employment.

3.1.3 Wages There are several arguments in the literature about the effects of FDI on wages: (1) that FDI leads to increases in the demand for labour, thereby raising wages; (2) with greater technological know-how, especially in developing countries, MNCs have higher productivity and can pay their workers more, an impact that could spill over into the rest of the economy and raise overall wages; and (3) because capital is internationally mobile and labour is not, FDI may enhance capital's bargaining power relative to labour, thereby lowering wages (Paus and Robinson, 1998). Some interesting but limited work has been done on these issues for developing countries. Using panel data that included both developing and developed countries, Paus and Robinson (ibid.) find that: FDI has a direct positive impact on real wages; that that impact is especially true in developing countries (but not in developed countries); and finally that this positive impact is true only for the period 1968–87, after which there is some evidence that the threat effect of relocating has had a negative effect on wage growth in industrialised countries. In a comparative study of Mexico, Venezuela and the US, Aitken et al. (1995) find that higher levels of FDI are associated with higher wages in all three countries, but in Mexico and Venezuela this association was limited to foreign-owned firms. This lack of evidence of wage spillovers to domestic firms is consistent with the large wage differentials between foreign and domestically owned firms in these countries.

Some interesting work has also been done on the impact of FDI on relative wages among workers in developing countries, based on the premise that FDI raises the relative demand for skilled labour. Hanson and Harrison (1995) and Feenstra and Hanson (1997), in separate studies of relative wages in Mexico, find that exporting firms and joint ventures pay higher wages to skilled workers and demand more skilled labour than other firms. Feenstra and Hanson (1997) use more specific measures, with the result that FDI growth is positively correlated with the relative demand for skilled labour in Mexico. In regions where FDI is concentrated, it accounts for over 50 per cent of the increase in the skilled labour wage share that occurred in this area in the late 1980s.

3.1.4 Investment: crowding in–crowding out One important factor that affects the degree to which a host country benefits from FDI is the degree to which inflows of FDI 'crowd in', that is, create more domestic investment rather than 'crowd out' domestic investment. Advocates often point to the crowding in effects, but recent evidence concerning developing countries suggest that crowding in cannot be taken for granted. Agosin and Mayer (2000) study the relation between inflows of FDI and domestic investment for the period 1970–96 in three regions: Africa, Asia and Latin America. Their basic finding is that crowding in occurred in Asia but crowding out occurred in Latin America. In Africa, the results were less clear. Moreover, recent research by Braunstein and Epstein (2002) indicates that even in China, there is no evidence of crowding in by FDI.

3.1.5 Technological development and spillover effects One of the claims most often repeated about the impact of FDI on developing country host countries is that it will lead to technology transfers, technological upgrading and productivity improvements. A number of papers, using country-level or industry-level data, have indicated a positive correlation between FDI and economic growth and FDI and productivity growth (see Hanson, 2001 and Braunstein and Epstein, 2002 for surveys). But, Gordon Hanson (2001), in an important UNCTAD study of the benefits of FDI for developing countries, is not very confident about the findings of these types of studies. He argues that although the early empirical literature was optimistic about the impact of MNCs on host-country productivity, its findings are open to several important problems. First, countries with higher growth attract more FDI so the direction of causality in the correlation between growth and FDI is unclear. Second, omitted variables, such as a good industrial policy, or better-educated workforce, for example, could explain both higher growth and more FDI. Hanson describes more recent and promising work done on the micro-level, where time series data of manufacturing plants provides solutions to these empirical problems by showing how the productivity of domestic plants changes over time in response to the presence of MNCs. Haddad and Harrison (1993), using data for Moroccan manufacturing plants in 1985–89, find a weak negative correlation between plant total factor productivity growth and the presence of MNCs in that sector. Aitken and Harrison (1999), using data on Venezuelan manufacturing plants for 1976–89, find that productivity growth in domestic plants is negatively correlated with foreign presence in that sector. Hanson concludes that micro-level data undermine empirical support for productivity spillovers from FDI, perhaps indicating that MNCs confine competing domestic firms to less profitable segments of industry.

3.2 Possible negative impacts

3.2.1 Asymmetries and threat effects As shown above, FDI is highly concentrated among countries. Nonetheless, FDI is still quantitatively quite important to many developing countries. Table 9.4 presents data of FDI inflows relative to gross domestic capital formation (GDCF) in all industries and in manufacturing, and private domestic capital formation (PDCF) in all industries, in the developed and developing world between 1980 and 1998 (with a separate section on Eastern Europe). Table 9.4 shows that FDI has become increasingly important in relation to capital formation between 1980 and 2007 especially in the developing world and especially in manufacturing. For the developing countries, the rates of growth of FDI as measured against GDCF have become quite high in all industries and for private investment. For example, by 1998, inward FDI flows into manufacturing comprised more than one-third of gross fixed capital formation in manufacturing for developing countries.

According to the *World Investment Report*, a large number of countries had FDI flows in excess of 20 per cent of GDCF (UNCTAD *World Investment Report*, 2008). Sixty-six out of 146 developing countries listed in the *World Investment Report*, or over 45 per cent of them, had FDI levels of 20 per cent of GDCF or greater. Thirty-two of these countries had FDI levels of 40 per cent or more of GDCF. This compares with 13 out of 38 developed countries with FDI levels in excess of 20 per cent of GDCF (or 34 per cent of them).[5]

Thus, many developing countries who get very little FDI from the point of view of the developed country investors nonetheless may be highly dependent on FDI in the sense that FDI inflows are large relative to the size of their econo-

Table 9.4 Ratios of FDI flows to gross domestic capital formation (GDCF) and private domestic capital formation (PDCF), by region and sector, 1980, 1990, 1998, 2007

Region/Country	FDI Inflows as a % of GDCF: All industries	FDI Inflows as a % of GDCF: Manufacturing	FDI Inflows as a % of PDCF: All industries
World			
1980	2.3	9.0	3.4
1990	4.1	14.0	5.4
1998	11.1	21.6	13.9
2007	16.0		
Developed countries			
1980	2.7	8.5	3.4
1990	4.9	11.9	5.2
1998	10.9	16.6	12.9
2007	17.1		
Developing countries			
1980	1.2	11.7	3.6
1990	4.0	22.3	6.7
1998	11.5	36.7	17.7
2007	13.1		

Source: UNCTAD *World Investment Report*, 2000, Table 1.2, p. 5.

mies. At the same time, FDI is also highly concentrated in the hands of a relatively small number of companies. For example, despite the fact that there were 82 000 parent firms with more than 810 000 foreign affiliates in 2008, only 100 firms, mainly from developed countries, account for approximately 9 per cent of the total assets of all foreign affiliates, 16 per cent of all foreign sales and 11 per cent of foreign employment among all MNCs (UNCTAD *World Investment Report*, 2008, p. xxi).[6]

These asymmetries lie at the heart of some of the most important dynamics between MNCs and developing countries. They are based on the fact that MNCs invest relatively little in most developing countries while, at the same time, even a little bit of investment for many developing countries constitutes a significant marginal contribution to those countries' investible resources. At the same time, there are a relatively large number of political jurisdictions in which MNCs can invest, and a relatively small number of MNCs who can make significant investments. The *World Investment Report* (1999, p. 154) estimates that perhaps as many as 6000 national, regional and local public sector entities compete for the various investment projects undertaken each year by MNCs.

Together, these asymmetries mean that, even though foreign investment *as a whole* is of enormous importance to MNCs, it is generally the case that any particular investment in a developing country, with one or two possible exceptions, is relatively unimportant to them. As a result, the bargaining power of political jurisdictions and workers relative to MNCs is often very low.

Certain aspects of the emerging global framework make this asymmetry worse: among these are the relative lack of foreign aid for the poorest countries; the erratic nature of portfolio flows, which makes FDI seem more attractive by comparison, even though FDI is fairly erratic itself; and the rules of the WTO and other trade/investment agreements, which make it difficult or impossible for countries to manage foreign investment in the interests of their citizens.[7]

These processes may generate negative impacts of MNCs on workers in many countries of the world, developed and developing alike. Here we only have space to discuss several characteristic problems: tax competition, policy competition and threat effects on wages.

3.2.2 Tax competition Economists and government officials have become increasingly concerned with the impact of international capital mobility on inter-jurisdictional tax competition.[8] Starting in the 1970s, Oates (1972) began the development of a canonical model of inter-jurisdictional tax competition. As Oates put it:

> The result of tax competition may well be a tendency toward less than efficient levels of output of local services. In an attempt to keep taxes low to attract business investment, local officials may hold spending below those levels for which marginal benefits equal marginal costs, particularly for those programs that do not offer direct benefits to local business. (Oates, 1972, p. 143, as quoted in Wilson, 1999)

While Oates focused on federalism, the same argument can be readily applied to issues of international taxation (Wilson, 1999).

There seems to be considerable evidence that international capital mobility is driving down taxes on a global basis. The OECD published a report in 1998 dealing with the increasingly common phenomenon of tax competition between states in order to attract MNCs (OECD, 1998). The study contends that the accelerating process of globalisation of trade and investment has fundamentally changed the relationship among domestic tax systems. In the OECD's words: 'Globalisation and the increased mobility of capital has also promoted the development of capital and financial markets and has encouraged countries to reduce tax barriers to capital flows' (ibid., p. 14). The study reviews empirical data to conclude that:

> harmful preferential tax regimes that drive the effective tax rate levied on income from the mobile activities significantly below rates in other countries have the potential to cause harm by: distorting financial and real investment flows, undermining the integrity and fairness of tax structures, discouraging compliance by all taxpayers, reshaping the desired level and mix of taxes and public spending, causing undesired shifts of part of the tax burden to less mobile tax bases such as labor, property and consumption and increasing the administrative costs and compliance burden on tax authorities and taxpayers. (Ibid., p. 16)

3.2.3 Policy competition Countries and other jurisdictions have other means of trying to attract investment: subsidies, infrastructure investment, the creation of a cooperative workforce are all examples of ways to create an 'investment-friendly' environment. While tax competition is beginning to be debated in developed countries, the other forms of competition being forced on developing countries attempting to integrate into the world market are less studied. It is clear from the few studies that have been done, however, that developing countries may be in a less advantageous position under the system of global competition for FDI. As Moran puts it:

> With the exception of some oil exporting states, the developing countries and economies in transition do not have the financial resources to offer grants along the lines of many OECD countries. Instead the most frequently used investment incentives are tax holidays … but the complexities of deploying these incentives and the administrative weakness in these countries themselves prevent these tools from being used effectively. (Moran, 1998, p. 101)

Nonetheless, bidding for foreign investment has become a major activity by both developed and developing countries.

The *World Investment Report* shows that many countries throughout the world have changed their tax and regulatory laws governing foreign direct investment in the last decade. Over the period 1992–2008, the overwhelming majority of national policy changes – 89.6 per cent of the 2650 changes – favoured foreign investors (UNCTAD *World Investment Report*, 2009, p. 31). In 2008 for example, these policies included more favourable entry (33 per cent of the changes), and improvement in the treatment or operational conditions (44 per cent of the changes).

These changes in national tax and regulatory policies are only part of the overall trend toward making the institutional environment more attractive for foreign investment in the past decade. Regional agreements have also been important, with NAFTA being the most famous but only one of several in recent years, including agreements between Chile and Mexico and between the members of the European Community and Mexico. More generally, investment liberalisation and protection has become an important issue in many international economic agreements, including many of the free trade and cooperation agreements signed between the European Community and third countries. Even the WTO Secretariat seems to agree that this may be a problem: 'as competition for FDI intensifies, potential host governments find it increasingly difficult to offer less favorable conditions for foreign investment than those offered by competing nations' (WTO, 1996).

Arguments in favour of incentives rely heavily on the assumption that governments have detailed knowledge of the value/size of the positive externalities associated with each FDI project. In practice, it would be an almost impossible task to calculate these effects with any accuracy, even with the aid of well-trained specialists. In reality, getting drawn into competitive bidding for an FDI project is like sending government officials to an auction to bid on an item whose actual value to the country is largely a mystery. Though the empirical evidence seems quite murky, the lessons we can draw from this discussion seem quite clear: incentives work often enough at the margin that they lead many policy-makers to believe that they must bid for investment; yet they work sufficiently infrequently that bidding is a high risk business. In the end, this suggests that dynamics of bidding is fraught with dangers for governments that engage in it, yet at the margin, under the current regime, there are strong pressures to continue playing the game.

3.3 Liberalisation vs. FDI control

The point above emphasises the question of whether liberalisation, even if it does bring in more FDI, allows a country to manage it sufficiently so that it benefits the domestic economy and its citizens. The most important conclusion of a good deal of literature is that for FDI to enhance economic development, it must fit within the overall development strategy (Dunning, 1994; Nembhard, 1996; UNCTAD *World Investment Report*, 1999; Amsden, 2001; Chang, 2002).

But liberalisation itself, and the investment treaties that are accompanying it, make it more difficult for economies to utilise FDI to its best advantage. While the extent of this liberalisation varies considerably by country, several policy changes prevail including reduction or elimination of screening and prior authorisation procedures, joint ownership requirements and restrictions on profit remittances. These changes along with the extension of national treatment to foreign firms, which prohibits discriminatory practices favouring domestic firms, are viewed by advocates of liberalisation as eliminating the principal policy obstacles that impeded foreign direct investment in the past.

The experiences of the East Asian NICs – the most successful developing nations over the past two decades – suggest the flaws in this approach. Education, infrastructure and other public services played a central role in their development strategies and contributed to their success by fostering environments favourable to both domestic and foreign investment. Moreover, this region attracted FDI despite the presence of some of the most restrictive investment regimes in the world. For example, China rigorously screens foreign investment, limits it to specific sectors and ties incentives to various export, foreign exchange, local content and other performance requirements while many other nations have been eliminating screening procedures, reducing sectoral restrictions and dismantling performance requirements. Similarly, Malaysia subjects projects (both foreign and domestic) to a demanding screening process that evaluates size, local involvement, labour and output market availability, and infrastructure and foreign exchange requirements or contributions (see Chang, 1998, for an important discussion of these issues).

In short, liberalisation, the rules in the WTO and other investment agreements may prohibit precisely those policies that in the past have contributed to the beneficial impacts of FDI, when and where they have been beneficial. As these tools for domestic management are taken away, it seems likely that many of the beneficial impacts may be reduced or eliminated as well (see Crotty et al., 1998 for an elaboration of these arguments).

4 Alternatives to the neo-liberal framework for MNCs

MNC boosters argue that the best way for developing countries to get more from MNCs is to liberalise and open their economies even more, not less (for example, Moran, 2002). According to them, misguided attempts to restrain or regulate MNCs will lead to less FDI, or to investment that is less integrated into MNCs' overall production networks and, so the argument goes, will be less beneficial to host countries.

Some important research has called into question the view that more regulation leads to less investment. Kucera (2001) for example, shows that higher levels of core labour standards are *not* associated with lower FDI, and might even be positively associated with it. He hypothesises that such labour standards might lead to greater political stability and therefore lead to more FDI. Similarly, studies have failed to find a consistent negative relation between higher environmental standards and foreign direct investment (see, for example, Oman, 2000).

Still, there is reason to be concerned that all is not well in the world of MNC regulation. There are strong theoretical reasons and anecdotal evidence to suspect that competition among jurisdictions for investment is fierce and that such competition makes it difficult for countries to implement and enforce socially desirable regulation; that empirical evidence is potentially flawed because FDI data reflect equity investments, not real capital investment data, and therefore have been skewed by high levels of mergers and acquisitions in recent years

(Fitzgerald, 2002); and, in any case, the empirical evidence on the 'race to the bottom' or 'social dumping' is mixed, rather than overwhelming.

Given the great empirical uncertainties involved and the potentially high costs of unfettered investment competition, it is encouraging that there are many initiatives, from many levels of society, to develop a regulatory framework to coordinate or reign in the intense competition for FDI that currently characterises the global economy (for example, Fitzgerald, 2002; Broad, 2002; Heintz, Chapter 13, this volume).

Surveying this large emerging literature is well beyond the scope of this chapter. But a few points are worth emphasising here. The first step forward is for governments to be sceptical about the benefits of FDI. As I have suggested, the evidence on the benefits is quite mixed and often may not be worth the intensive bidding associated with attempting to attract investment. Part of the problem here is surely the lack of transparency in the bidding process: government officials and associated business associates may well receive significant benefits, but these may not trickle down much. Second, there is no evidence that the push by international organisations such as the IMF, World Bank, OECD and WTO to promote more FDI liberalisation is well-founded theoretically or empirically. These organisations should desist in this promotion, unless and until there is stronger evidence that such investment is beneficial within the current regulatory environment. The implication of this moratorium on investment liberalisation would be a much greater tolerance by the international financial institutions of a variety of national regulatory regimes toward foreign investment, regimes that suit the particular circumstances of different countries. Finally, continued efforts by governments and international institutions should be undertaken to develop mechanisms to reduce 'prisoner's dilemma' outcomes, which are so likely in this current environment. Among the measures that should be considered are floors on taxation, subsidies and environmental regulations, and the increased commitment to the enforcement of core labour standards.[9]

Notes

* The author thanks without implicating his co-authors, Elissa Braunstein, James Burke, James Crotty and Patricia Kelly, for their contributions to joint work on multinational corporations on which this chapter has liberally drawn.

1. UNCTAD uses the term transnational corporation (TNC) rather than multinational corporation (MNC), which we use here. To a large extent, which term one uses is a matter of habit and preference.
2. This chapter partly draws on previous work: Crotty et al. (1998); Braunstein and Epstein (1999, 2002); Burke and Epstein (2001).
3. Foreign direct investment (FDI) is a financial measure of MNC behaviour, which refers to equity investments by a company or individual in a company in a foreign country, providing the investor has at least a 10 per cent ownership share. Two other variables – sales of foreign affiliates and gross product (or value-added) of foreign affiliates – quantify the real activity of foreign affiliates of MNCs. The advantage of these latter measures is that they measure international production itself, rather than simply financial investment. A disadvantage is that these data are not nearly as widely available as are data on FDI. Even these multiple measures miss

important aspects of MNC production, for example, increasingly important activities such as subcontracting.

4. Interestingly, the US is an important exception to these findings; its FDI inflows in the last several decades have been very volatile (Lipsey, 1999).
5. Of course, these data do not imply that all FDI inflows finance gross fixed investment. For example, mergers and acquisitions (M&As) generate inflows of FDI, but do not necessarily increase gross fixed capital formation (GFCF). Using the GFCF measure may therefore overstate the importance of FDI inflows for national investment and growth. They nonetheless do give a comparative sense of how large the flows are and suggest that these flows might be quite significant for many countries.
6. The *World Investment Report* (2000) warns us that these estimates are very rough and should be treated with caution (p. 93, fn. 2).
7. One could add to that the restrictive macroeconomic policy that, world-wide, has constrained economic growth for the last 20 years or so. See Crotty et al. (1998) for a similar argument, which also emphasises the aggregate demand context.
8. For an excellent recent survey of this literature, see Wilson (1999).
9. See Heintz, Chapter 13, this volume, and Braunstein and Epstein (1999) for more discussion of these issues.

References

Agosin, Manuel R. and Ricardo Mayer (2000), 'Foreign investment in developing countries: does it crowd in domestic investment?', UNCTAD Discussion Paper No. 146.

Aitken, Brian and Ann Harrison (1999), 'Do domestic firms benefit from foreign investment? Evidence from Venezuela', *American Economic Review*, **89**(3), 605–18.

Aitken, Brian, Ann Harrison and Robert E. Lipsey (1995), 'Wages and foreign ownership: a comparative study of Mexico, Venezuela, and the United States', NBER Working Paper No. 5102.

Amsden, Alice (2001), *The Rise of the Rest*, New York: Oxford University Press.

Braunstein, Elissa and Gerald Epstein (1999), 'Creating international credit rules and the multilateral agreement on investment: what are the alternatives?', in J. Michie and J. Grieve Smiths (eds), *Global Instability: The Political Economy of World Economic Governance*, London and New York: Routledge.

Braunstein, Elissa and Gerald Epstein (2002), 'Bargaining power and foreign direct investment in China: can 1.3 billion consumers tame the multinationals?', Political Economy Research Institute, Working Paper, available at http://scholarworks.umass.edu/peri_workingpapers/9/; accessed 11 October 2010.

Broad, Robin (ed.) (2002), *Global Backlash; Citizen Initiatives for a Just World Economy*, New York: Rowman and Littlefield.

Burke, James and Gerald Epstein (2001), 'Threat effects and the internationalization of production', available at http://www.umass.edu/236/hash/467d40595a/publication/59/; accessed 11 October 2010.

Chang, Ha-Joon (1998), 'Globalisation, transnational corporations, and economic development – can the developing countries pursue strategic industrial policy in a globalising world economy?', in D. Baker, G. Epstein and R. Pollin (eds), *Globalization and Progressive Economic Policy*, Cambridge: Cambridge University Press.

Chang, Ha-Joon (2002), *Kicking Away the Ladder*, London: Anthem Press.

Claessens, S. and S. Gooptu (1995), 'Can developing countries keep foreign capital flowing in?', *Finance and Development*, September, 62–5.

Crotty, James, Gerald Epstein and Patricia Kelly (1998), 'Multinational corporations in the neoliberal regime', in Dean Baker, G. Epstein and R. Pollin (eds), *Globalization and Progressive Economic Policy*, Cambridge: Cambridge University Press.

Dunning, John H. (1994), 'Re-evaluating the benefits of foreign direct investment', *Transnational Corporations*, **3**(1), February, 23–51.

Feenstra, Robert C. and Gordon H. Hanson (1997), 'Foreign direct investment in Mexico and relative wages: evidence from Mexico's maquiladoras', *Journal of International Economics*, **42**(3/4), 371–93.

Fitzgerald, Valpy (2002), 'Regulatory investment incentives', *QEH Working Paper Series*, February, QEHWPS80.
Haddad M. and A. Harrison (1993), 'Are there positive spillovers from direct foreign investment?', *Journal of Development Economics*, **42**(1), 51–74.
Hanson, Gordon H. (2001), 'Should countries promote foreign direct investment?', *UNCTAD G-24 Discussion Paper Series* No. 9.
Hanson, Gordon H. and Ann Harrison (1995), 'Trade, technology and wage inequality', NBER Working Paper No. 5110.
Kucera, David (2001), 'The effects of core worker rights on labour costs and foreign direct investment: evaluating the "conventional wisdom"', Working Paper, ILO, Decent Work Research Programme, DP/130/2001, http://earthmind.net/fdi/ilo/ilo-workers-rights-fdi.pdf; accessed 11 October 2010.
Lipsey, Robert E. (1999), 'The role of FDI in international capital flows', NBER Paper, No. 7094, April.
Lipsey, Robert E. (2002), 'Home and host country effects of FDI', National Bureau of Economic Research Working Paper No. 9293, October, available at http://www.nber.org/papers/w9293; accessed 11 October 2010.
Moran, Theodore H. (1998), *Foreign Direct Investment and Development*, Washington, DC: Institute for International Economics.
Moran, Theodore H. (2002), *Beyond Sweatshops; Foreign Direct Investment and Globalization in Developing Countries*, Washington, DC: Brookings Institution.
Nembhard, Jessica Gordon (1996), *Capital Control, Financial Regulation and Industrial Policy in South Korea and Brazil*, Westport, CT: Praeger Publishers.
Oates, Wallace (1972), *Fiscal Federalism*, New York: Harcourt Brace.
OECD (1998), *Harmful Tax Competition, An Emerging Global Issue*, Paris: OECD.
Oman, C.P. (2000), *Policy Competition for Foreign Direct Investment*, Paris: OECD.
Paus, Eva A. and Michael Robinson (1998), 'Globalization and labor: the impact of direct foreign investment on real wage developments, 1968–1993', paper prepared for the XXI International Congress of the Latin American Studies Association, Chicago, 24–26 September.
UNCTAD (1999), *Comprehensive Study of the Interrelationship Between Foreign Direct Investment (FDI) and Foreign Portfolio Investment (FPI)*, UNCTAD, 23 June, UNCTAD/GDS/DFSB/5.
UNCTAD (various years), *World Investment Report* (WIR), Geneva: UNCTAD.
Wilson, John D. (1999), 'Theories of tax competition', *National Tax Journal*, June, **LII**(2), 269–303.
World Trade Organization (1996), *Trade and Foreign Direct Investment Report*, available at http://www.wto.org/english/news_e/pres96_e/pr057_e.htm; accessed 27 October 2010, Geneva: WTO.

10 Foreign direct investment and development from a gender perspective

Elissa Braunstein

1 Introduction

While the wisdom of encouraging short-term capital flows is increasingly questioned, foreign direct investment (FDI) is still viewed as a central element of development strategy by international financial institutions. Many contentious issues remain in the literature about FDI. These pertain to both the growth and development effects of FDI as well as the appropriate kinds of regulatory frameworks that would render FDI flows more development oriented. However, while the development effects of FDI are debated, the literature on FDI and economic development has generally been gender blind. Nevertheless, a small but growing literature addresses the gender dimensions of FDI in the context of efforts to understand how neoliberal economic policies and globalization patterns have different impacts on women and men. Although the literature is relatively scant, there are some stylized facts and policy insights that can be drawn from this work.

2 Gender and FDI: the empirical research

Research on gender and FDI in developing countries has been confined, for the most part, to small-scale studies that take a case-study approach to women's employment by transnational corporations (TNCs). While this literature provides key insights into the specific contexts of its subjects, it is sometimes difficult to draw out stylized analyses that can be compared with the dynamics of FDI in other countries. For this reason, where appropriate, I also draw from the literature on gender and international trade.

2.1 Women's employment

In terms of employment, where FDI inflows have been sizeable – primarily in East and Southeast Asia and in parts of Latin America and the Caribbean – there is strong evidence that the share of female employees in the labour-intensive, export-oriented assembly and manufacturing sector is high (Joekes and Weston, 1994; Razavi, 2000; Pearson et al., 2004). With labour costs such a crucial part of international competitiveness, labour-intensive exporters prefer to hire women both because women's wages are typically lower than men's, and because employers perceive women as more productive in these types of jobs (Elson and

Pearson, 1981). Foreign investors looking for low-cost manufacturing platforms conform to the same pattern, at least on the lower rungs of the value-added ladder. At the same time, women may lose their comparative advantage in these job markets as industries upgrade, leading to a de-feminization of manufacturing employment as has happened in Mexico, India, Ireland and many parts of East Asia (Elson, 1996; Joekes, 1999; Fussell, 2000; Ghosh, 2007). One of the reasons the employment effects of FDI are difficult to gauge is the increasing prevalence of subcontracting and informalization, part of the trend toward creating more flexible structures of international production. These jobs are often directly connected to specific TNCs via local intermediaries, weakening the distinction between foreign and local ownership. Subcontracting also cuts off some of the pathways in which FDI may ultimately benefit women, as women are increasingly limited to jobs in the least valued part of the production chain, furthest removed from the potential benefits of formal employment.

2.2 Women's wages

In terms of the wages women earn from working for TNCs, there are good reasons to expect TNCs to pay wage premiums (and offer more job security) relative to locally owned firms: the greater resilience of TNCs better insulates employees from economic cycles; workers in larger enterprises tend to be better protected by labour legislation and are more likely to be unionized and receive benefits; and TNCs are concentrated in the relatively high-wage electronics sector (Lim, 1990; Joekes and Weston, 1994). This perspective is consistent with studies that contend that export-oriented employment offers women good options for work relative to their local alternatives (Kabeer, 2000, 2004; Davin, 2001).

In assessing the impact of TNCs on the level (and transformatory potential) of women's employment and wages, it is also essential to take into account the *dynamics* of women's employment in transnational sectors over the long term. In terms of wage levels, UN studies suggest a 'salary life cycle', where wages in newly established Enterprise Processing Zones tend to be higher than local wages, but over time these wage differentials decline (UNCTC/ILO, 1988).

A study of maquiladoras in Mexico, when the export industry was 25 years old, provides some support for this hypothesis (Fussell, 2000). Fussell compares women's wages in the maquiladora sector in Tijuana with those in traditional forms of female employment in urban Mexico, such as commerce and service employment as well as self-employment, and concludes that maquiladora wages are not higher than other types of work for women with comparable skills, though they are more stable. She also finds that women tend to sort into occupations along socio-demographic lines, with most service and commerce workers being young, single and childless, while the maquiladora workforce is more heterogeneous and includes higher proportions of older women, married women and women with young children. She concludes that maquiladoras are not offering higher wages than other employers in the local market but rather provide a stable alternative to self-employment, an option that is particularly attractive to workers with greater financial responsibilities. So while women workers in maquiladoras may be better off than they would be without these opportunities, that such a well-established export sector offered employment comparable to other types of domestic employment is consistent with life-cycle hypothesis predictions.

2.3 The gender-based wage gap

Studies of export-oriented trade have found that it does not systematically narrow the gender wage gap (Seguino, 2000a; Jomo, 2001; Berik et al., 2004; Cho et al., 2005). Looking at the effects of FDI only, Seguino (2000) considers the impact of capital mobility on gender wage differentials in the Republic of Korea and Taiwan. For Taiwan, measures of capital mobility that reflect (1) total inward and outward FDI as a share of GDP and (2) total inward and outward FDI as a share of gross fixed-capital formation indicate that high levels of both of these variables are associated with increases in the gender wage gap, as is a measure of crowding. Conversely, in Korea capital mobility did not negatively impact the gender wage gap. Seguino explains that this is partly due to differences in the type of FDI between the two countries, FDI in Korea being more capital intensive and in more male-dominated industries than those in Taiwan. She also notes that domestically owned Korean firms in female-dominated industries have faced strict controls on outward foreign investment as well as the control and rationing of subsidized credit to reward high-volume exporting firms. These firms have responded to increases in female wages by raising productivity and by moving into niche markets where quality matters.

Braunstein and Brenner (2007) test the impact of FDI on women's and men's wages in urban China at two different points in time, 1995 and 2002. After controlling for individual-, firm- and province-level factors, they find that both women and men received wage premiums for working in provinces with higher levels of FDI as a proportion of total investment. In 1995 women were found to experience larger gains from FDI than men, but those gender-based advantages reversed in 2002, with men experiencing larger wage gains from FDI than women. These gender differentials were even more pronounced after controlling for international trade, which is closely linked with FDI in China. They conclude that the results reflect the shift of foreign-invested enterprises in China to higher value-added, more domestically oriented production. Because women and men are segregated into different types of industries, with women more likely to be employed in lower-skilled, export-oriented production and men in higher value-added (and paid) industries, this changing composition of FDI is associated with an increase in the gender wage gap. In addition, FDI in male industries is likely to be less internationally mobile than FDI in women's industries because of the higher levels of capital involved in production. The result from a wage-bargaining perspective is that men may have more bargaining power vis-à-vis TNCs than women do, with the consequence that men get a higher relative wage.

On balance, then, the research on FDI is consistent with the findings on trade. The nature of gender-segregated employment by industry, whereby women are concentrated in highly competitive traded sectors, coupled with the macroeconomic policy environment that affects the mobility of transnational capital, are instrumental in determining the gender wage gap. While women's wages may undergo an absolute boost due to foreign investment, the findings on the effects of FDI on gender-based wage inequality are less sanguine.

3 Policies for managing FDI to promote growth and gender equality

Attracting foreign investment should not be regarded as an end in and of itself, either from a gender equality or development perspective. FDI must be managed in order to draw on its positive benefits. Here we review some of the specific policies that governments can use to manage FDI, drawing out the conditions and contexts under which FDI can improve gender equality (in terms of narrowing the gender wage gap), as well as the conditions under which it can prove beneficial for development and growth.

3.1 Giving advantages to domestically owned firms

Because foreign investors are seen as less closely allied with domestic economic interests, strengthening domestic economic capacities relative to foreign investors is sometimes preferred as a way to draw upon the benefits of global investment and trade competition – an improvement in absorptive capacity (Milberg, 1999). Giving targeted, sector-specific advantages to domestically owned firms as they collaborate and compete with TNCs may be beneficial from a development perspective because these policies build up domestic capacities. Examples include giving special loans or subsidies to domestic firms in ways that enhance their capacity to absorb technology, or restricting entry into certain segments of the economy to incubate domestic firms before exposing them to international competition.

A growing constraint on implementing these sorts of policies is the notion of 'national treatment', a central principle of current trade agreements, including the WTO's Trade-Related Investment Measures (TRIMs) and the General Agreement on Trade in Services (GATS). It means that host countries must treat foreign investors at least as well as domestic investors in 'like circumstances'. There are two points at which national treatment may come into play: in the pre-establishment phase and in the post-establishment phase. Despite the increase in liberalizing trade agreements, most developing countries still exercise control over market access, though there is variation by sector and industry

(UNCTAD, 2003b). National treatment in the post-establishment phase – a principle that is becoming increasingly common in international agreements – means that national regulations cannot discriminate based on the nationality of the investor and could limit the ability of developing-country governments to provide special assistance to domestic firms. However, the exception for 'like circumstances' leaves open the possibility that governments could successfully petition for special treatment in the short term.

In terms of the types of foreign-invested industries that employ women, the policy space for domestic-firm assistance is probably the narrowest of all industries. Manufacturing, the most likely sector for FDI in industries that traditionally employ women, is by far the most open to FDI (ibid.). Even in cases where strong regulation has been exercised regarding foreign investment, as in the East Asian cases, FDI in labour-intensive export industries has often enjoyed the most liberal of investment environments.

Furthermore, it is not clear that domestic exporters would be better employers for women. The rise of subcontracting by TNCs in labour-intensive export industries – such as garments, footwear, toys and consumer electronics – is instructive. These are buyer-driven supply chains in which large retailers, marketers and brands set up decentralized production networks in developing countries (Gereffi and Memedovic, 2003). This is partly the result of intense competition, which leads retailers to source from facilities in the lowest-cost countries. Women working in these industries find themselves at the least valued part of the production chain, where global competition often results in sudden closures and loss of employment and bars substantial improvements in wages and working conditions. One way that domestic subcontractors survive is by diversifying into higher value-added exports, where markets are less crowded and profits are greater. In many instances, the result has been a loss of employment for women, as the demand for higher-skilled (male) workers leads to defeminization (Carr and Chen, 2002). These trends indicate that in the current global economic context, domestic firms may in fact be a less desirable form of employment for women than working directly for TNCs. One way that domestic ownership may be a better option for women workers is if outward investment by domestic firms is less likely than the probability that foreign investors will leave. If this is the case, the lower mobility of domestically owned firms will mean more bargaining power for workers.

3.2 Performance requirements

Performance requirements are conditions applied to TNC operations, sometimes as a condition for market access or the granting of some kind of subsidy or tax break. Examples include local content laws or domestic equity rules. In the current global context of liberalization, there has been a decline in the use of mandatory performance requirements (those that are not linked to the take-up of a particular incentive or subsidy), as governments face mounting pressure to liberalize traded sectors. There are also direct prohibitions in the legally binding obligations of current trade agreements, like the WTO's TRIMs, which prohibit performance requirements that are considered trade distorting, like local content requirements and export controls. A range of other performance requirements that are not encompassed by TRIMs are also prohibited, made conditional or discouraged by investment agreements at the regional or bilateral level (UNCTAD, 2003a). Examples of the types of policy areas affected include employment, training, research and development, and technological transfer requirements. Growing constraints on performance requirements weaken the potential for government policy to ensure backward and forward economic linkages or spillovers, thereby decreasing the probability that FDI will encourage or 'crowd in' domestic investment, or result in improvements in domestic productivity.

Such measures pose an additional constraint on the potential for foreign investment in female-dominated industries to contribute to growth because this type of FDI is so closely linked with trade, and therefore highly restricted in terms of imposing performance requirements. These restrictions can act as obstacles to the sort of export upgrading that was successfully practised in East Asia in that they deter explicit government measures that guide TNC linkages with and spillovers into the domestic economy. That said, it is also true that TRIMs do not prohibit performance requirements that are not 'trade distorting', such as local hiring rules. A number of developing countries have called for amendments to TRIMs that would allow exceptions based on developmental grounds, but developed countries are very much opposed (ibid., p. 141).

If restrictions on performance requirements in traded sectors were eased under amendments to TRIMs, requirements on firms regarding employment and training, among other things, could be structured as a way to contribute to growth *and* gender equality. As a condition of market access, TNCs could be required to employ a certain number of women for pre-determined periods of time or in more skill-intensive and non-production jobs. They could be required to provide the types of training that women could transfer to other sectors of the labour market, especially in more skill-intensive and highly paid sectors and occupations. In other words, the types of performance requirements designed to improve the labour impact of TNC presence could be re-designed to become more gender aware.

3.3 Incentives

With the declining space for constraints on market entry and mandatory performance requirements, many developing countries have turned instead to using incentives as a way to influence the behaviour of foreign investors. Incentives designed to encourage technology transfers or specific activities – such as increasing training and assistance to local suppliers – have been successful in places like Hungary, Malaysia, the Republic of Korea, Singapore and South Africa (UNCTAD, 2003b). But the incentives most commonly used by developing countries are those targeted at merely attracting foreign investment, rather than guiding it once it has arrived. These sorts of incentives include fiscal incentives like tax holidays and regulatory concessions, such as freedom from environmental or labour laws.

Despite the increasing prevalence of these incentives, their success in attracting FDI, and ultimately contributing to growth and development, is doubtful. Most economists agree that foreign investors are primarily concerned with economic fundamentals when making their investment decisions (UNCTAD, 2004). The regulatory environment and the proffering of incentives are only a small part of a country's appeal. As a result, providing generous incentives for foreign investors sets up opportunities for wasteful giveaways, as foreign investors might have made the investment anyway. These giveaways can compromise the state's ability to finance development and provide social protection.

Still, incentives can matter in situations where countries are close substitutes, such as when countries are located in the same region and their economic fundamentals are similar. Recent econometric studies have shown that incentives have become a more significant determinant of FDI flows as more countries pursue export-led growth strategies (Clark, 2000; Taylor, 2000; Mutti, 2003). They are more likely to be important in female-dominated industries because export-oriented, low-wage production is a comparative advantage shared by many neighbouring countries (UNCTAD, 1996; Morisset and Prinia, 2001). Because of the concessionary nature of many of these incentives, incentive competition, especially for FDI in labour-intensive industries, may draw countries into a 'race to the bottom', whereby the goal of attracting FDI forces countries to maintain low wages, poor labour and environmental standards and weak tax structures.

The WTO's 1995 Agreement on Subsidies and Countervailing Measures does limit the use of incentives that constitute direct financial contributions to specific enterprises, industries or regions. Export subsidies and local content subsidies are the only types of subsidies that are expressly prohibited (those that are perceived as interfering with free trade). Other types of subsidies are 'actionable', meaning that they are subject to challenge by other WTO members if they can show such subsidies have direct adverse effects. Despite its prohibition of direct financial contributions, this Agreement is a double-edged sword because the trade subsidy prohibitions rule out import substitution and export promotion as development strategies. It seems important that the terms of the Agreement differentiate between beggar-thy-neighbour incentives and those that are developmentally defensible. In addition, by being limited to only financial incentives, the Agreement does not address the more pernicious problem of regulatory concessions.

Turning to the gendered aspects of incentives, regulating incentive competition could have a direct impact on gender equality for women working in TNCs, as their jobs would be protected from the cost-based pressure that such highly competitive industries carry with them. In addition, it could ease the pressure that incentive competition may have on public budgets, as when measures such as tax holidays or subsidized industrial sites result in less government revenue, lowering the government's ability to fund human development, an important aspect of advancing gender equality, and to conduct public investment, a key condition necessary for FDI to pay off in terms of growth. Indeed, trade and financial liberalization have been associated with increasing pressure on public budgets (Rao, 1999).

3.4 Global labour standards

One way to coordinate a decline in the use of regulatory concessions would be via adopting what have come to be known as global labour standards coordinated via international agreements. Global labour standards – including measures like minimum wages, health and safety regulations, and ensuring the right to organize – would not only serve as significant obstacles for incentive competition but also make countries less able to compete on the basis of low production costs and more likely to do so on the basis of the quality of their labour forces or products.

An immediate issue that arises when considering the cost-versus-quality competition is the relationship between wages and productivity. Certainly there are strong incentives to raise labour productivity, as the consequent decline in unit labour costs could allow for real wage increases, as has been the experience of the East Asian newly industrializing countries, such as Taiwan and the Republic of Korea (Singh and Zammit, 2000). But these results are more problematic in the current global context of labour-intensive export industries, where global labour surpluses and extreme competition make it difficult for workers to capture the benefits of productivity improvements in the form of higher wages (Heintz, 2003). In addition, as TNCs face a wide choice of low-cost production platforms and subcontractors, there is little incentive to introduce the sorts of productivity improvements that will result in higher wages, especially in cases where it is cheap and easy for capital to move. This is true in female-dominated industries, where women are crowded into export sectors, capital is highly mobile and countries can be close substitutes. With the option of moving to a cheaper production platform, firms can become 'lazy', responding to wage increases by moving rather than raising productivity (Seguino, 2007).

The question of how and where to enforce such standards is a contentious one. The global labour standards movement is sometimes identified as a thinly veiled attempt at trade protectionism in the North. Others have argued that externally imposed mandatory labour standards will ultimately hurt labour in the South, as the consequent increase in export costs is likely to lower employment, economic growth and/or result in more production shifting to the informal sector, presumably beyond the reach of such standards (Singh and Zammit, 2000, 2004; Kabeer, 2004). It is clear that this is an area requiring more research, especially from a gender-aware perspective, as relying on growth based on trade or financed by highly mobile foreign capital alone cannot be relied upon to bring about improvements in gender wage equality or women's working conditions in export sectors.

3.5 Regulating the mobility of capital

Another way to enhance the bargaining power of labour (and governments) relative to capital would be to regulate international capital flows through a combination of foreign exchange controls and the re-regulation of capital markets. Such regulations would enable governments to control the timing and amount of FDI, avoiding the financial fragility that can accompany unregulated foreign exchange inflows and outflows (Singh, 2001), as well as raise the cost of capital flight and reduce the conflict between the needs of host communities and the incentives facing TNCs. The trend, however, has been towards more liberalization. Resisting liberalization agreements is no small task for individual countries who want participate in the global economy. Moreover, the intellectual hegemony of freer capital flows is so widespread that there is little expressed desire to put up such resistance among national governments. Still, there are a number of examples of capital management techniques that are (or have been) successfully used by developing countries to manage the more volatile aspects of global financial integration (Epstein et al., 2003).

The impact of capital mobility on gender equality has been discussed in detail throughout this chapter. By raising the bargaining power of TNCs, greater mobility of capital limits the ability of governments to manage FDI for the good of development, as well as the capacity of women in particular industries to bargain for better wages relative to their male counterparts working in less mobile industries. The continuing liberalization of capital flows threatens to worsen these inequities, as it enables firms to more credibly threaten to leave. Because it is so cheap for labour-intensive producers to relocate or subcontract, women working in foreign-invested industries are highly exposed to the negative effects of capital mobility. Hence, managing this mobility is a key policy goal from a gender-aware perspective.

4 Concluding remarks

Looked at from a gender-aware perspective, foreign investment in labour-intensive industries has had a significant impact on women's work and development.

While there has been a positive relationship between women's employment and FDI in semi-industrialized countries, there is mounting evidence that women either lose these jobs to more qualified men as industries upgrade or get pushed down the production chain into subcontracted work, as competition forces firms to continually lower costs. There is likely to be some short-term improvement in women's incomes as FDI expands, but the longer-term trajectory of women's wages is less promising. These findings are consistent with those that indicate that trade and FDI have done little to narrow the gender wage gap. In terms of how to manage FDI for the good of gender equality and development, the main obstacles are the constraints posed by international competition in export markets and the neoliberal orientation of the global policy environment. Addressing these issues requires both international coordination and national industrial policies.

References

Berik, Günseli, Yana van der Meulen Rodgers and Joseph E. Zveglich Jr (2004), 'International trade and gender wage discrimination: evidence from East Asia', *Review of Development Economics*, **8**(2), 237–54.

Braunstein, Elissa and Mark Brenner (2007), 'Foreign direct investment and wages in urban China: the differences between women and men', *Feminist Economics*, **13**(3/4), 213–37.

Carr, Marilyn and Martha Alter Chen (2002), 'Globalization and the informal economy: how global trade and investment impact on the working poor', Working Paper on the Informal Economy No. 2002/1, Geneva: ILO Employment Sector.

Cho, Hyoung, Ann Zammit, Jinjoo Chung and In-Soon Kang (2005), 'Korea's miracle and crisis: what was in it for women?', in Ruth Pearson, Shahra Razavi and Caroline Danloy (eds), *Globalization, Export-Oriented Employment and Social Policy: Gendered Connections*, London: Palgrave Macmillan.

Clark, Steven W. (2000), 'Tax incentives for foreign direct investment: empirical evidence on effects and alternative policy options', *Canadian Tax Journal*, **48**(4), 1139–80.

Davin, Delia (2001), 'The impact of export-oriented manufacturing on Chinese women workers', paper prepared for the UNRISD project on Globalization, Export-Oriented Employment for Women and Social Policy, Geneva: UNRISD.

Elson, Diane (1996), 'Appraising recent developments in the world market for nimble fingers', in Amrita Chhachhi and Renée Pittin (eds), *Confronting State, Capital and Patriarchy: Women Organizing in the Process of Industrialization*, New York: St. Martin's Press.

Elson, Diane and Ruth Pearson (1981), '"Nimble fingers make cheap workers": an analysis of women's employment in Third World export manufacturing', *Feminist Review*, **7**, 87–107.

Epstein, Gerald, Ilene Grabel and K.S. Jomo (2003), 'Capital management techniques in developing countries: an assessment of experiences from the 1990s and lessons for the future', Working Paper No. 56, Amherst, MA: Political Economy Research Institute.

Fussell, Elizabeth (2000), 'Making labor flexible: the recomposition of Tijuana's maquiladora female labor force', *Feminist Economics*, **6**(3), 59–79.

Gereffi, Gary and Olga Memedovic (2003), 'The global apparel value chain: what prospects for upgrading by developing countries', paper prepared for UNIDO Sectoral Studies Series, Vienna: UNIDO.

Ghosh, Jayati (2007), 'Informalization, migration and women: recent trends in Asia', in Debdas Banerjee and Michael Goldfield (eds), *Labour, Globalization and the State: Workers, Women and Migrants Confront Neoliberalism*, London: Routledge.

Heintz, James (2003), 'The new face of unequal exchange: low-wage manufacturing, commodity chains, and global inequality', Working Paper No. 59, Amherst, MA: Political Economy Research Institute.

Joekes, Susan P. (1999), 'A gender-analytical perspective on trade and sustainable development', in UNCTAD (ed.), *Trade, Sustainable Development and Gender*, New York and Geneva: United Nations.
Joekes, Susan P. and Ann Weston (1994), *Women and the New Trade Agenda*, New York: UNIFEM.
Jomo, K.S. (2001), 'Globalization, export-oriented industrialization, female employment and equity in East Asia' (draft), paper prepared for UNRISD project on Globalization, Export-Oriented Employment for Women and Social Policy, Geneva: UNRISD.
Kabeer, Naila (2000), *The Power to Choose: Bangladeshi Women and Labour Market Decisions in London and Dhaka*, London: Verso Books.
Kabeer, Naila (2004), 'Globalization, labor standards, and women's rights: dilemmas of collective (in)action in an interdependent world', *Feminist Economics*, **10**(1), 3–35.
Lim, Linda C. (1990), 'Women's work in export factories: the politics of a cause', in Irene Tinker (ed.), *Persistent Inequalities: Women and World Development*, Oxford: Oxford University Press.
Milberg, William (1999), 'Foreign direct investment and development: balancing the costs and benefits', in *International Monetary and Financial Issues for the 1990s, Vol. XI*, Geneva: UNCTAD.
Morisset, Jacques and Neda Prinia (2001), 'How tax policy and incentives affect foreign direct investment: a review', in Louis T. Wells Jr., Nancy J. Allen, Jacques Morisset and Neda Prinia (eds), *Using Tax Incentives to Compete for Foreign Investment: Are They Worth the Costs?*, Foreign Investment Advisory Service (FIAS) Occasional Papers No. 15, Washington, DC: International Finance Corporation and World Bank.
Mutti, John (2003), *Foreign Direct Investment and Tax Competition*, Washington, DC: Institute for International Economics.
Pearson, Ruth, Shahra Razavi and Caroline Danloy (eds) (2004), *Globalization, Export-Oriented Employment and Social Policy: Gendered Connections*, New York: Palgrave Macmillan.
Rao, J. Mohan (1999), 'Globalization and the fiscal autonomy of the state', in UNDP (ed.), *Globalization with a Human Face: Human Development Report 1999 Background Papers*, Vol. 1, New York: UNDP.
Razavi, Shahra (2000), 'Export-oriented employment, poverty and gender: contested accounts', in Shahra Razavi (ed.), *Gendered Poverty and Well-being*, Oxford: Blackwell.
Seguino, Stephanie (2000), 'The effects of structural change and economic liberalization on gender wage differentials in South Korea and Taiwan', *Cambridge Journal of Economics*, **24**(4), 437–59.
Seguino, Stephanie (2007), 'Is more mobility good? Firm mobility and the low wage–low productivity trap', *Structural Change and Economic Dynamics*, **18**(1), 27–51.
Singh, Ajit (2001), 'Foreign direct investment and international agreements: a South perspective', Trade-Related Agenda, Development and Equity Occasional Paper, Geneva: South Centre.
Singh, Ajit and Ann Zammit (2000), *The Global Labour Standards Controversy. Critical Issues for Developing Countries*, Geneva: South Centre.
Singh, Ajit and Ann Zammit (2004), 'Labour standards and the "race to the bottom": rethinking globalization and workers' rights from developmental and solidaristic perspectives', *Oxford Review of Economic Policy*, **20**(1), 85–104.
Taylor, Christopher (2000), 'The impact of host country government policy on US multinational investment decisions', *World Economy*, **23**(5), 635–48.
United Nations Centre on Transnational Corporations and International Labour Organization (UNCTC/ILO) (1988), *Economic and Social Effects of Multinational Enterprises in Export Processing Zones*, Geneva: ILO.
United Nations Conference on Trade and Development (UNCTAD) (1996), *Incentives and Foreign Direct Investment*, New York and Geneva: United Nations.
United Nations Conference on Trade and Development (UNCTAD) (2003a), *Foreign Direct Investment and Performance Requirements: New Evidence from Selected Countries*, New York and Geneva: United Nations.
United Nations Conference on Trade and Development (UNCTAD) (2003b), *World Investment*

Report 2003: FDI Policies for Development – National and International Perspectives, New York and Geneva: United Nations.
United Nations Conference on Trade and Development (UNCTAD) (2004), *Incentives: UNCTAD Series on Issues in International Investment Agreements*, New York and Geneva: United Nations.

PART IV

LABOUR STANDARDS

11 The minimum wage in a global context

Peter Brosnan

A majority of countries have minimum wage laws. Convention 26, the principal ILO convention on minimum wages, has one of the highest ratifications by national governments. While it is easy to think of these minimum wage systems solely as arrangements for promoting some degree of fairness in national labour markets, the reality is much more complex. The ILO adopted Convention 26 in 1928, with two aims: on the one hand, to provide wages that were fair to the worker and reduced the risk of poverty, and on the other hand, to make international trade fair by preventing economic dumping whereby a country used low wages to gain a cost advantage in trade. Now minimum wage systems are used by governments for many purposes and their roles are challenged by globalisation in both developing countries and the advanced countries.

Today about 175 countries have some form of minimum wage. A minimum wage tends to be a correlate of economic development. Minimum wage systems are less common in very small countries such as the micro-states of Oceania and in less developed regions. Despite the truth of this generalisation, minimum wage legislation is most common in Africa where 48 out of the 57 countries have a minimum wage; on the other hand, the rates prescribed in Africa are generally very low. Europe also has a large proportion of countries with statutory minimum wages, but advanced countries such as Italy, Germany and Norway have no statutory minima. They have an extensive collective bargaining system and collective agreements are automatically extended to other firms in the same sector; thus, most European workers have a guaranteed legal minimum.

The objective of minimum wage systems

Today minimum wages play many and different roles in different countries. These different roles frequently conflict, and as we shall argue below, constitute one of the critical weaknesses of minimum wage systems. Minimum wage can be called upon to fill at least six different roles: (1) reduce poverty, (2) improve equity, (3) stimulate economic development, (4) set rates for social security benefits, (5) regulate wages in general, and (6) fight inflation.

Combating poverty

Many of the world's poorest are in paid employment. The ILO estimated for 2008 that 1.2 billion workers (40 per cent) earned wages that provided less than US$2 per family member per day in 2007. More than half these workers (633 million – 21 per cent) had less than US$1.25 per person per day (ILO, 2010). It is axiomatic that a higher minimum wage will mean less poverty.[1] Even a small increase in rates in countries with very low minimum wages would improve the position of millions of families.

Despite the unsurprising finding that that low pay is less common where there are minimum wage laws (Ioakimoglou and Soumeli, 2002), some argue that a minimum wage does little to relieve poverty since many of the poor are not in regular employment (e.g., Johnston and Stark, 1991; Standing, 1999), or that some of the lower paid belong to well-off households. This latter observation, however, is not a reason to permit low pay; it is a consequence of low pay. One of the main reasons the US minimum wage has been relatively ineffective in reducing US poverty is just that it is set so low (Pollin and Luce, 1998).

It is true, of course, that a decent minimum wage is not the only way alleviate poverty. The effectiveness of a minimum wage in alleviating poverty will depend on the tax system and the availability of additional social security benefits. This implies that a minimum wage is more important in developing countries where low-income families are less likely to have additional sources of income such as social security payments (Lustig and McLeod, 1997). Moreover, given the distribution of income, more workers are likely to benefit from an increase in the minimum wage in developing countries than in advanced countries (Saget, 2001).

Promoting justice

Low pay is a consequence of the way that labour markets are structured. Some jobs are socially constructed as deserving relatively low pay. At the same time, some categories of workers are less preferred by employers, or are in circumstances that prevent them applying for the better jobs. Thus, the preferred categories of worker get the better-paid jobs while the others have to compete for the jobs that are left – the poorer-paid jobs. Consequently 'workers with ... equal skills and abilities are available at widely different prices' (Wilkinson, 1984, p.422). The categories of worker who are less preferred tend to be women, racial or religious minorities, people with less education (even if education is irrelevant for the tasks to be performed) and other 'socially disadvantaged' groups. Foreign workers are particularly vulnerable; they are often driven to migrate on account of the low pay and high unemployment in their home country and are prepared to 'work cheap' in their new location. Their situation highlights the need for decent systems of minimum wages in all countries, so that people are not driven to migrate for economic reasons and, should they migrate, they receive an adequate wage in their new country.

These arrangements are clearly unjust in that many workers have to accept low wages. But the arrangements are unjust also in that the better paid within the same labour market benefit from the cheap labour of the low paid. They benefit from cheaper services where they employ the low paid directly. They also benefit if products or services they buy are 'subsidised' by low pay. Workers and other consumers in the advanced countries benefit too from the cheap labour of workers in the developing countries whose wages are much lower than theirs and whose products are priced correspondingly lower. Thus, minimum wages are essential to reducing inequities within and between countries.

It has been suggested (Brosnan and Wilkinson, 1989) that groups that are most likely to be low paid will be the principal beneficiaries of a minimum wage being introduced or of any increase in an established minimum. Therefore, improving minimum wages would assist in attaining equal pay for work of equal value. It changes the income of a substantial proportion of women each time the minimum wage is increased. A realistic minimum wage should therefore be an integral part of any campaign for equal pay.

Stimulating the economy

The advantages of a minimum wage system to the economy have been posited for at least a century (e.g., Webb and Webb, 1920). Wilkinson (1984) has argued that a realistic minimum wage alters the terms of trade between different productive systems, making it more difficult for disadvantaged firms to rely on disadvantaged labour, and thus forcing firms to become more efficient, by investing in better equipment, better methods and in the training of their workforces (Cahuc and Michel, 1996). At the international level, countries with higher minimum wages will have fewer inefficient firms and therefore be able to compete.

The other benefit is that the higher minimum boosts consumption spending. Workers on the minimum wage are likely to spend their entire wage (Borooah and Sharpe, 1986), and spend more of it on domestically produced products (Borooah, 1988). Thus, an increase in the minimum wage would add more to domestic demand than an increase in pay at other points in the income distribution.[2]

Setting social welfare levels

The minimum wage's role of providing an income that is both fair and sufficient to combat poverty leads to it being used as a basis for social welfare payments. Thus, in some countries the minimum wage is used as basis for setting pensions, unemployment benefits and dismissal compensation (Grimshaw and Miozzo, 2002).

Giving a lead to other wages

Because minimum wages are intended to provide a fair wage, employers can use them as a benchmark for fair remuneration. The US's minimum wage being increased so rarely, it provides an opportunity to see how other wages are affected by an increase in the minimum. In that country, a rise in the minimum wage is followed by further rises in wage rates above the minima as employers reinterpret what they consider a fair wage. This phenomenon is widely observed in Latin America too (Gutierrez et al., 2008). Maloney and Nuñez (2002) speak of a 'numeraire' effect in some Latin American countries where some well-paid workers receive an exact number of minimum wages as their salary. They further note that the effect of an increase in the official minimum wage translates into wage increases at higher levels – at levels up to four times the minimum wage. This is considerably higher than the US where the effect dies off more quickly.

Controlling wages and reducing inflation etc.
Where there are large numbers of workers paid the minimum wage, or where the minimum wage strongly influences other wages, the minimum wage becomes a useful tool for governments to control wages and prices. Direct state control of wage fixing has been a conspicuous policy in Latin America. Collective bargaining itself has been controlled and the growth in the minimum wage has been held back in an attempt to stabilise wages and prices. As a consequence, most Latin American countries experienced a decline in the real minimum wage over the 1980s and 1990s (Grimshaw and Miozzo, 2002). In the last decade however, most Latin American countries have been able to increase their minimum wages substantially (cf. Malinowski, 2008).

Globalisation and low pay

Of the many differences between developing and advanced countries, few are as spectacular as the differences in wages. The low wages in developing countries are cited as one of the reasons for MNEs moving production from the advanced to the developing countries.

Developing countries
The transfer of jobs from advanced to developing countries is mainly in manufacturing. This has followed the emergence of the NICs of East Asia where there are fewer labour standards and often no minimum wage. For example, Japan has been shifting its manufacturing to other countries since the late 1990s. Large and small firms are moving elsewhere, especially to China. Advances in communication technology have allowed services to be increasingly sourced from developing countries too. Many of the administrative functions of western corporations can be sourced from developing countries and call centres can be located away from the markets they service.

The garment industry provides an example of the changes in manufacturing. Starting in the 1960s and 1970s European and US companies outsourced to countries like Hong Kong, Singapore and South Korea. As wage levels and labour conditions improved in these countries, production moved to Indonesia, the Philippines, Thailand and Mexico. More recently, production has shifted to Bangladesh, Central America, Vietnam and increasingly China. The effects of competition and the complicated patterns of contracting and subcontracting mean that there is intense pressure on prices, and therefore on wages and hours, with the result that even in low-wage countries 'there is the constant threat of further relocation' (Hale, 2002, p. 194).

Globalisation has changed the direction of the production chain. Whereas previously the transition from raw materials to finished product was from developing countries to the advanced countries, now the geographic flow is much more complicated. Thus, formerly highly paid work is transferred to developing countries while some low paid work remains in the advanced countries. Hoogvelt (1997) has argued that because capital is mobile, but lower-ranked labour is not, low-paid workers are forced to compete with the low-paid workers in other countries so that the lowest common denominator prevails. Some would argue that the world 'has become a huge labour bazaar where states offer "their" labour forces at even lower rates' (Munck, 2002, p. 66).

Rather than impose labour standards – seen by many regimes as 'impediments to "progress"' – employers in export industries are freed from 'limits on working time, wages or benefits' (Standing, 1999, p. 64). Even where a developing country has a minimum wage, it may be ineffective in its application to the activities sourced by the MNEs. Many of these countries have large informal sectors where the minimum wage may not be enforced. Furthermore, many low-paid workers, particularly in developing countries, are homeworkers who may not be covered by minimum wage legislation, or even if they are, are unlikely to be able to enforce their rights.

The strength of this can be exaggerated. Only a small proportion of the labour force in developing countries is engaged in the production of tradeable goods. About '80 per cent of the fall in industrial employment in the advanced economies between 1964 and 1994 is able be explained by internal factors and only 20 per cent by competition from low wage economies' (British TUC, 2002). Automation has played a role. Nonetheless, at least 5 million manufacturing jobs have been lost in the last decade to low-wage economies (Rowthorn, 2005). Cheaper labour costs and a compliant workforce are important factors in the decision to relocate production to China or other developing countries. Consequently, China now has more manufacturing jobs than the rest of the world (Bannister, 2005).

These transfers occur despite the fact that the new arrangements are often less efficient. This phenomenon is illustrated by the example of an Australian clothing firm, Fletcher Jones. At one stage the company's Australian workers took 100 minutes to make a pair of trousers. With efficiency gains this was eventually reduced to 35 minutes. However, management decided to move production to China, where making the same trousers took 50 minutes (Smith, 2009). Despite the decrease in efficiency, the labour cost was reduced substantially. Depending on wage and exchange rates, the cost reduction was probably from about A$8.35 to A$1.35 per pair.[3]

The widespread availability of cheap Chinese manufactures makes it especially difficult for manufacturing firms in the rest of the world. Firms in the LDCs are unable to enter the market, despite their low wage rates, and firms in the advanced countries are unable to match the cheap labour costs. The losers in much of this are the LDCs in regions such as Africa who, despite having very low minimum wages, or none at all, are unable to gain access to this new globalised employment.

The behaviour of governments in developing countries is much more than a simple reaction to opportunity. The IMF and World Bank encourage governments to reduce labour costs with a view to increasing exports (Guille, 2007). Every country is asked to 'liberalise' their labour market. The result is that minimum wage laws become irrelevant. For example, when prices were 'liberalised' in the East European economies, the value of real wages fell and consequently the minimum wage regimes ceased to be effective (Ghellab, 1998, p. 34).

Advanced countries

While the experiences of workers in the advanced countries are vastly different from those of their counterparts in the developing countries, they too are subject to comparable pressure to work for low pay. The relocation of manufacturing to developing countries clearly affects labour markets in the advanced countries but the interrelated issue of global trends in employment forms are equally important in generating low pay in the advanced countries. The reduction in manufacturing employment sees a greater share of the labour force employed in the services sector. This has three main effects: the nature of employment is altered; trade unions are weakened; and pay declines for many workers.

The manufacturing jobs that have disappeared were nearly all full-time. However, a higher proportion of jobs in the service sector are part-time or temporary and in smaller workplaces. An additional feature is that many employees are being replaced with outside contractors, or becoming contractors themselves.

The service sector is therefore less conducive to traditional trade unionism, and the contingent labour force is hardly ever unionised. Thus, trade unions are undermined. These trends have helped ensure that union power has declined in virtually every country since the early 1980s – even in countries where membership levels have held up. A further related factor is that the decline of manufacturing reduces wages in manufacturing itself, and, by extension, the wages of comparable workers throughout the economy (Weisbrot, 2002). These factors all interact and the low-wage outcomes are one more factor making union membership unattractive for many workers.

The increasing globalisation of markets has promoted non-union competition and 'contributed to the elaboration of low-wage employment strategies' (Katz and Darbishire, 2000, p. 7). MNEs are able to use the threat of moving to developing countries to put pressure on trade unions and workers in advanced countries to concede wage levels and conditions. As unions have become generally weaker, and retreated to pockets of relative strength, bargaining has become increasingly decentralised with an emphasis on bargaining at company level, and the weakening of sectoral and national agreements. All these trends combined with persistent levels of unemployment have severely reduced the bargaining power and the income of vulnerable workers. Since the 1980s, the distribution of income has become more unequal in most advanced countries.

National governments in the advanced countries find themselves under similar pressure as the developing countries to constrain wages, or to implement policies that lower pay. Furthermore, the pressures of globalisation promote the proposition that wages in advanced countries need to match those in developing countries more closely. To the extent that other advanced countries follow this logic, it puts more pressure on those that might hold out. Thus, governments adopt similar policies and use international comparisons to justify change. Thus, the prevailing ideology becomes the need for workers to 'tighten their belts' for the common good.

Deficiencies of existing minimum wage systems

Introducing a minimum wage does not, of itself, ensure a fairer wage structure. The minimum wage must cover all the labour force. It must be set at a level that ensures that no one is low paid, and it must be adjusted regularly to take account of changing price levels and movements in other wages.

Coverage

A total of 103 countries have ratified ILO Convention 26, and about 70 countries have some form of minimum wage. The various ILO conventions concerned with minimum wages[4] allow for a wide variety of practices: some countries rely on collective bargaining but with extensions of collective agreements to other workers; in some a national minimum wage is negotiated through collective bargaining; in others the minimum wage is determined by government. However, the convention allows for a wide variety of practices and few countries have a minimum wage system that applies to every worker. The various arrangements can be grouped into nine categories:

1. a statutory national minimum wage with full application (e.g., New Zealand);
2. a system of statutory regional minimum wages with full application within each region (e.g., Canada, Thailand);

3. a statutory national minimum wage with exemption for certain industries or workers (e.g., South Korea, US);
4. a system of statutory regional minimum wages with exemption for certain industries or workers (e.g., Japan);
5. a national minimum wage negotiated through collective bargaining but with full, or near full, coverage (e.g., Greece, Belgium, Finland);
6. selective intervention with orders that provide for specific legal minima in certain industries or occupations (e.g., Australia);
7. reliance on collective bargaining but with extensions of collective agreements to other workers (e.g., Germany and Italy);
8. combinations of (1) to (7); for example, a statutory minimum wage with full application, which acts as a floor, but additional higher minima in certain industries or occupations (e.g., Mexico), or a national minimum with a higher minima in some regions (e.g., US);
9. no official wage but a strong tradition that establishes a going rate (e.g., Kiribati).

As can be seen, the arrangements vary substantially across nations. In some the minimum wage only applies to the private sector. Some have different rates for blue- and white-collar workers, for qualified and unqualified workers, or for different regions. Some countries have an experience requirement or different rates for trainees. Some countries exclude particular categories of worker or grant them a lower rate; for example, Portugal has a lower rate for domestics, while a number of countries, Kenya and Morocco being examples, have lower rates for agricultural workers. Many countries exclude part-time workers and young workers, or they provide lower rates for workers below certain ages.

Some countries also provide higher minima according to a worker's experience or qualifications. A substantial number of countries have lower rates for young workers (e.g., Papua-New Guinea, US), although these rates have become less common (New Zealand has recently[5] eliminated its lower rates for young workers). Few countries have a minimum wage system that applies to every worker.

Whatever the country, the majority of the labour force earns more than the minimum, but in general, the higher the level at which the minimum wage is set, the greater the proportion of the labour force that is affected. Thus, in Luxembourg, which has the highest minimum in Europe, the proportion is relatively high at around 16 per cent, while in Spain, where the minimum is very low, the proportion is only about 2 per cent.

In the developing countries, the group that is in most need of the protection of minimum wages comprises people employed in the informal sector. However, conditions in the informal sector are difficult to police. Furthermore, informal sector workers may work outside established legal frameworks and thus not be entitled to the minimum wage. While the informal sector in the advanced countries can be as low as 2 per cent (Standing, 1999), the share in developing countries can be as high as 80 per cent of the labour force.

Level

The ILO conventions on minimum wages offer little guide as to what is a reasonable level. The associated 'recommendations' do make reference to living standards, prevailing wages and so on, but are vague. The intention is that minimum wages must meet the cost of living, but it is often the case that the minimum wage comes nowhere close to that objective. Approximately 30 countries have set minimum wages that are less than US$1.25 per day (the defined level of extreme poverty for a family) and a further 50 or so have minimum levels higher than US$1.25 but less than US$8 per day (the level that defines poverty for a family of four persons).

Even the advanced countries often have minima set well below the level for a decent life. The Council of Europe (1977) suggested the minimum wage be set at 68 per cent of average full-time earnings; however, no European country has attained this level. Within the OECD, statutory minima range from 'roughly 25% of the average in Korea and Mexico to more than 45% in Australia, France, Ireland, the Netherlands and New Zealand' (OECD, 2007). Marlier and Ponthieux (2000) found that 77 per cent of the low paid in Europe were women.

The minimum wage is unstable in many countries, but particularly in the developing countries. Saget (2001) estimated that minimum wages in Latin American countries lost 30 per cent of their value between 1980 and 1990. There are only a few countries that adjust the minimum wage automatically with wage or price increases. Many do have regular review processes in place, but the effects on employment and on 'competitiveness' are often considerations. Consequently the value of the minimum wage can fall easily into the range where it fails to meet basic consumption needs.

Compliance and enforcement

Compliance is a serious problem in all countries. Possibly no country has a large enough inspectorate to enforce a minimum wage; and many countries have no inspectorate at all, merely relying on complaints from workers or trade unions. There are regimes that are unwilling to, or incapable of enforcing workers' rights, whatever the law may say. Many countries are unable to provide information about the minimum wage – the proportion of workers covered, the degree of compliance, or its impact on particular population sub-groups such as youth, women and so on. Saget (ibid.) quotes studies that indicate high levels of non-compliance in many developing countries: 54 per cent in Guatemala, 9 per cent in Chile and 15 per cent in Indonesia.

Government timidity

An effective minimum wage strategy is only possible if government supports it. Given the number of ratifications of the ILO conventions on minimum wages, it could appear that governments in general agree with the concept. However, the governments of many countries that have ratified the conventions have no minimum wage in place, have a defective minimum wage or have even abolished minimum wage systems that had been set up. For example, Zimbabwe increased its minimum wage during the 1980s but the economic reform of 1990 suppressed it except for gardeners and other domestic workers (ibid.).

There are several reasons why governments are reluctant to establish and maintain effective minimum wage systems: fear of inflation, concerns about the fiscal impact and unease over the possible employment effects.

Inflation

Policy-makers fear that higher minimum wage rates will cause a general upward movement in prices. This concern is especially important if trade partners or trade rivals have relatively stable prices. This consideration partly accounts for Portugal having a very low minimum wage compared with other European countries (€470 per month when most of the other West European countries have monthly minima well over €1000).

The probability of general inflation following a minimum wage increase is not high. Inflationary effects may be offset by increased productivity (Hughes, 1976) or a reduction in profits. An important factor will be the extent to which higher paid workers successfully restore differentials disturbed by the higher minimum wage. However, labour markets are segmented such that better paid workers are unlikely to be making comparisons with workers whose pay is so low to be on the minimum wage (Brosnan and Wilkinson, 1988). Perhaps most importantly, the globalisation processes described above have weakened the ability of trade unions to respond to changing differentials, should they wish to do so.

Fiscal effects

Governments are not unaware of the effects of the minimum wage on their fiscal position, particularly where government employees are on minimum wage rates, or where the government employs contractors who pay minimum wage rates. A further concern is where social security benefits or pensions are linked to minimum wages. This has been an obstacle for Brazilian governments wanting to improve the wages of the low paid. Concern with similar issues underlay the IMF's threat to Russia that it would block a scheduled loan if its (pathetically low) minimum wage were increased (Standing, 1999, p. 217).

Unemployment
A prevailing unease on the part of governments is the relation between the minimum wage and unemployment. The argument, derived from simplistic economic theories, is that fewer workers will be employed at higher minimum wage rates. Some of the arguments are summarised elsewhere (Brosnan, 2002). Although these propositions have been tested in various countries, the results are never conclusive. Econometric coefficients are frequently not significant or the predicted relationships are found not to exist. Where there does appear to be a relationship, other factors are usually responsible (Ghellab, 1998). Nonetheless, countries still hold down wages for fear of unemployment. This was a fundamental part of the Czech strategy for 'social peace' during the transition to a market economy (Orenstein and Hale, 2001).

The unemployment bogey is called upon by employers to dissuade governments from improving minimum wages. An amusing story from Papua-New Guinea had employers predicting an increase in crime if the minimum wage were increased, the alleged link being: increased minimum wage increases unemployment, unemployment increases crime (Marshall, 2009).

Why are governments reluctant to increase minimum wages despite there being only weak or non-existent effects on employment? In the context of a more globalised economy, one answer is pressure from international agencies such as the IMF (Schmidt, 2006; Guille, 2007). Another answer is that there may be concern that the higher minimum will increase the price of exports and render them uncompetitive. Given that low labour costs are one of the features that governments use when they hawk their country as a location for MNEs, this argument has to be taken seriously.

A number of factors reduce the force of the argument. In the first place, input–output tables show that, in general, export sectors have higher wages. This is not surprising. If exporting is based on efficient production, wages and profits are likely to be higher.

Second, many low-paid workers are in non-exporting sectors, such as personal services. Despite the fact that tourism (an export sector) draws on personal services, cheap services are rarely a key factor in determining preferred tourist destinations; the empirical evidence is that higher-wage countries are the most attractive destinations.

A third factor is that many developing countries export agricultural products that are sold at 'world prices' irrespective of the cost of production. They are usually produced in sectors with low wages or in the informal sector, which escapes regulation. For example, most of Chile's minimum wage earners are in the agricultural export sector. A higher minimum wage would not affect the price received – although a higher minimum would reduce profits!

Fourth, when we consider manufactures, we find that the developing and advanced countries do not compete strongly with each other. There is greater competition within these groupings (and sub-groupings). Even so, as noted above, a lot of manufacturing is for the local market, and in all cases wage levels do not affect price by much, for wage costs are usually a small proportion of value-added. As Roy has pointed out, a higher wage in the Indian carpet sector would not affect sales and employment because the mark-ups that determine the ultimate sale price occur elsewhere (quoted by Hensman, 2002, p. 360).

Fifth, we need to separate the rhetoric from the reality. While MNEs may say they want cheaper labour, it is only one of many factors in choosing a location. Stability, infrastructure, legal issues, supplies of raw material and access to markets may be more important. However, governments are keen to attract and retain new plants and will avoid increasing the minimum wage if they are told it is a deterrent. But once an MNE has located in a country, to move is expensive. Newer plants are usually high-tech and will not be moved because of a small increase in the minimum wage.

Thus, the argument that a higher minimum wage will damage exports does not have a strong basis. Nonetheless, it is a persuasive argument in policy circles and, if poverty is to be reduced and a more just economic system established, ways must be found to take minimum wages out of competition.

Conclusion

As the world economy becomes more globalised, stronger minimum wage laws are needed. On the positive side, a majority of countries have ratified the ILO conventions on minimum wages. On the negative side, there are many deficiencies in the various systems. They often do not cover all workers in the relevant country. They are invariably set at unrealistically low levels. Even countries with the better minimum wage systems fail to enforce them adequately. The most notable progress over the last decade has been the increased level of minimum wage rates in various countries and therefore a greater number of workers who have benefitted.

The financial crisis that began in 2008 has changed the framework in which minimum wages are set. Unemployment has increased, inflation has reduced and the long-term decline in working poverty may have ceased (ILO, 2010). In this context, one would expect that governments that hold back minimum wages for fear of inflation might see this as an opportunity to increase minima – they might even increase minimum wages as a stimulus to the economy. On the other hand, with policy advisors telling them that higher minimum wages will increase unemployment, this may not happen. The picture is mixed but it appears that minimum wages have increased in this period. In Europe the increases have been greater than the wage increases achieved by collective bargaining.

Using minimum wage rates to help manage the economy is aside from their primary purposes: to reduce poverty and inequality. Increasing inequality has been a correlate of globalisation (Goldberg and Pavcnik, 2007); the improvements in minimum wages in some countries will help constrain inequality by boosting the income of the lowest paid. However, other policies are required to constrain income at the other end of the distribution. As for those in the informal sector where minimum wages are irrelevant, they need other policies to improve their incomes such as fair prices for their products or access to formal sector employment (with an adequate minimum wage).

What of the idea that minimum wages can make trade fairer? The current levels of minimum wages differ enormously. France and Australia have hourly rates greater than US$12,[6] while Zambia's and Indonesia's rates are only about US$0.33. The countries of Central Asia have even lower rates. The issue of fair trade is not that these countries' low minimum wages are unfair to wealthier countries. The issues are much more complex and are about access to markets and fair prices for the products in which these countries have a comparative advantage. On the other hand, increasing minimum wages where they are very low is not going to disadvantage the countries concerned. The labour cost of a pair of shoes made in Indonesia is reported to be about US$2.75 when the shoes sell for about US$75. There is thus plenty of scope for increasing minima without adversely affecting trade or employment.

The ILO could go further than it has to promote better minimum wage legislation in member countries. It would be helpful if a convention required that *all* workers be entitled to a minimum wage and that it be backed up by some level of enforcement. These conventions could also be more adventurous in terms of level. The ILO has adopted conventions on hours and other matters where it does prescribe specific levels. It could adopt a similar approach with respect to minimum wages; for example, a convention could require countries to have minimum wages set at a specific level, which increases over time to allow the governments and employers in low-income countries to make the necessary adjustments. A suitable starting point might be a rate of US$1.00 an hour. This would be well below the existing minimum in many countries but would raise the minimum wage to meet basic consumption levels in a number of others. Over time, the minimum could grow to where it began to equalise minimum wages across a range of countries. The question is whether the government, trade union and employment representatives could agree on such a modest arrangement.

Stronger minimum wage systems are not a full solution to the problems of poverty, inequality or uneven economic development; nonetheless they are an essential component of any policy package for achieving these objectives, particularly if these problems are to be tackled in a global context.

Notes

1. This was the motivation behind the Indonesian government's decision to introduce a minimum wage in the 1970s. The government, employers and unions had agreed that a minimum wage

was needed to prevent a deterioration of the lowest wage level and to improve the standard of living (Ghellab, 1998).
2. These arguments are spelt out more fully in Brosnan (2002).
3. Lower productivity in exporting countries is not new. As Cohen (2006) has shown, India had lower productivity in textiles than the UK in the nineteenth century yet was a major exporter to the UK.
4. Also Convention 99 Concerning the Creation of Minimum Wage-fixing Machinery in Agriculture (1951), and Convention 135 Concerning Minimum Wage-fixing with Special Reference to Developing Countries (1970).
5. 2007.
6. Using current exchange rates (February 2010).

References

Bannister, J. (2005), 'Manufacturing employment in China', *Monthly Labour Review*, **128** (July).
Borooah, V.K. (1988), 'Income distribution, consumption patterns and economic outcomes in the United Kingdom', *Contributions to Political Economy*, **7**(1), 49–63.
Borooah, V.K. and D.R. Sharpe (1986), 'Aggregate consumption and the distribution of income in the United Kingdom: an econometric analysis', *Economic Journal*, **96**(382), 449–66.
British TUC (2002), *Globalisation: Myths and Realities*, London: TUC.
Broad, R. (ed.) (2002), *Global Backlash: Citizen Initiatives for a Just World Economy*, Lanham: Rowman and Littlefield.
Brosnan, P. (2002), 'The political economy of the minimum wage', in B. Burchell, S. Deakin, J. Michie and J. Rubery (eds), *Systems of Production: Markets, Organisations and Performance*, London: Routledge.
Brosnan, P. and F. Wilkinson (1988), 'A national statutory minimum wage and economic efficiency', *Contributions to Political Economy*, **7**(1), 1–48.
Brosnan, P. and F. Wilkinson (1989), *Low Pay and the Minimum Wage*, Wellington: New Zealand Institute of Industrial Relations Research.
Cahuc, P. and P. Michel (1996), 'Minimum wage unemployment and growth', *European Economic Review*, **40**(7), 1463–82.
Cohen, D. (2006), *Globalization and Its Enemies*, Cambridge, MA: MIT.
Council of Europe (1977), *Methods of Defining 'Decent' Remuneration*, Strasbourg: Council of Europe.
Ghellab, Y. (1998), *Minimum Wages and Youth Unemployment*, Geneva: ILO.
Goldberg, P.K. and N. Pavcnik (2007), 'Distributional effects of globalization in developing countries', *Journal of Economic Literature*, **XLV**(1), 39–82.
Grimshaw, D. and M. Miozzo (2002), *Minimum Wages in Latin America: Identifying the Employment and Pay Equity Effects*, Geneva: ILO.
Guille, H. (2007) 'Global pressure and minimum wages', in D. Banerjee and M. Goldfield (eds), *Labour, Globalization and the State: Workers, Women and Migrants Confront Neoliberalism,* Oxford: Routledge.
Gutierrez, C., P. Paci and M. Ranzani (2008), *Making Work Pay in Nicaragua: Employment Growth and Poverty Reduction*, Washington: World Bank.
Hale, A. (2002), 'What hope for "ethical" trade in the globalised garment industry?', in R. Broad (ed.), *Global Backlash: Citizen Initiatives for a Just World Economy*, Lanham: Rowman and Littlefield.
Hensman, R. (2002), 'How to support the rights of women workers in the context of trade liberalisation in India', in R. Broad (ed.), *Global Backlash: Citizen Initiatives for a Just World Economy*, Lanham: Rowman and Littlefield.
Hoogvelt, A.M.M. (1997), *Globalisation and the Postcolonial World*, Basingstoke: Macmillan.
Hughes, J. (1976), 'What part can a minimum wage play?', in F. Field (ed.), *Are Low Wages Inevitable?*, Nottingham: Spokesman.
ILO (2010), *Global Employment Trends: January 2010*, Geneva: ILO.
Ioakimoglou, E. and E. Soumeli (2002), 'Low-wage workers and the "working poor", available at www.eiro.eurofound.ie/2002/08/study/TN0208101s.html; accessed 20 October 2010.

Johnston, P. and G. Stark (1991), 'The effects of a minimum wage on family incomes', *Fiscal Studies*, **12**(3), 88–93.

Katz, H.C. and O. Darbishire (2000), *Converging Divergences: Worldwide Changes in Employment Systems*, Ithaca: ILR Press.

Lustig, N.C. and D. Mcleod (1997), 'Minimum wages and poverty in developing countries: some empirical evidence', in S. Edwards and N.C. Lustig (eds), *Labor Markets in Latin America*, Washington: Brookings Institution Press, pp. 62–103.

Malinowski, M. (2008), 'Minimum wage hike planned in Chile', *Patagonia Times*, 18 June.

Maloney, W.F. and J. Nuñez (2002), *Minimum Wages in Latin America*, Washington: World Bank.

Marlier, E. and S. Ponthieux (2000), *Low Wage Employees in EU Countries*, Luxembourg: Eurostat.

Marshall, S. (2009), 'PNG expects more crime if minimum wage increased', ABC news, available at http://www.abc.net.au/news/stories/2009/02/05/2483556.htm?section=world; accessed 11 October 2010.

Munck, R. (2002), *Globalisation and Labour: The New 'Great Transformation'*, London: Zed.

OECD (2007), *OECD Observer* No. 261 May.

Orenstein, M.A. and L.E. Hale (2001), 'Corporatist renaissance in post-communist Central Europe', in C. Candland and S. Rudra (eds), *The Politics of Labor in a Global Age: Continuity and Change in Late-industrializing and Post-socialist Economies*, Oxford: Oxford University Press.

Pollin. P. and S. Luce (1998), *The Living Wage: Building a Fair Economy*, New York: The New Press.

Rowthorn, B. (2005), 'The impact on advanced economies of north–south trade in manufacturing and services', *Revista de Economia Politica*, **25**(2), 60–73.

Saget, C. (2001), *Is the Minimum Wage an Effective Tool to Promote Decent Work and Reduce Poverty? The Experience of Developing Countries*, Geneva: ILO.

Schmidt, J.D. (2006), 'Flexicurity, casualization and informalization', in B.N. Ghosh and H.M. Guven (eds), *Globalization and the Third World*, Houndmills: Palgrave Macmillan.

Smith, D.K. (2009), *The Fabric of a Dream: The Fletcher Jones Story* (Film), Screen Australia.

Standing, G. (1999), *Global Labour Flexibility: Seeking Distributive Justice*, Basingstoke: Macmillan.

Webb, S. and B. Webb (1920), *Industrial Democracy*, London: Seaham Divisional Labour Party.

Weisbrot, M. (2002), 'Globalisation on the ropes', in R. Broad (ed.), *Global Backlash: Citizen Initiatives for a Just World Economy*, Lanham: Rowman and Littlefield.

Wilkinson, F. (1984), 'Productive systems', *Cambridge Journal of Economics*, **7**(3), 413–29.

12 Globalisation, labour standards and economic development

Ajit Singh and Ann Zammit

Preface

When this chapter was originally written for the first edition of *The Handbook of Globalisation* (Michie, 2003) the burning issue regarding labour standards was the attempt by advanced country governments and unions, particularly the US, to establish multilateral rules in the World Trade Organization (WTO) to enforce labour standards globally. This initiative did not succeed and the issues raised remain as relevant as ever, though they no longer command as much attention at the top of the international policy agenda. This slightly revised version therefore retains the basic structure of the arguments presented on labour standards in a developmental context. However, in view of the subsequent rise of China and India as major producers and exporters and the perception in the US that this presents a threat to its workers and industries alike, even the principal cause of its industrial and labour woes, this issue is briefly introduced at the end of the chapter in an Addendum.

1 Introduction

At the turn of the century the US and other advanced country governments, as well as their unions and some parts of the business sector, pressed proposals to establish multilateral rules through the WTO permitting punitive trade measures to be taken against countries deemed to be failing to uphold core labour standards. Their stated objective was to provide a 'social floor' to an integrating world economy. Developing countries, the supposed culprits, firmly rebutted these initiatives, which they maintained were thinly veiled protectionist devices. The initiative failed. Nevertheless, international controversy over labour standards continues.

This policy study seeks to shift the debate onto a more constructive plane. Whilst closely examining the economic arguments in this controversy, it is also concerned with the broader political and moral dimension. The authors suggest that developing countries are indeed committed to improving core and other labour standards; the reason why, in general, they are unable to implement many of these forthwith and much more widely is not because of the wickedness or perversity of their governments or employers but essentially because of their economic circumstances, the structure of their economies and the manner in which developing country producers are linked into the global production system through global production chains.[1] It is emphasised that developing countries should continue to adhere fully to these commitments both for intrinsic developmental reasons and also, importantly, so as not to lose the moral argument.

The topics examined below include the effect of developing country trade on labour market conditions in the North; the complex relationship between labour standards and economic development; the distinction between core and other labour standards and whether the core standards may be regarded as basic human rights; the evolution of labour standards in the South in response to development and structural changes in these economies; the sub-optimality for workers both in the North and South of the use of sanctions or other punitive measures to make labour standards compulsory in the South.[2]

It is important to appreciate that the following sections have not been thoroughly revised in the sense of updating the references. Rather, only those aspects that are new to the debate, including those that reflect changes in the nature of globalisation and policy implications, are taken further.

2 The North's case for a social clause

The pressure for adopting measures to compel developing countries to adhere to labour standards came in part from workers in the North, particularly those in the US, whose perceptions and fears inspired a powerful union campaign spearheaded internationally by various international trade union federations. They complain that competition from 'cheap labour', resulting from low labour standards in the South, is unfair. They also complain that, unless labour standards are observed in all nations, there will be a 'race to the bottom' with respect to the terms and conditions of work (ICFTU, 1999). Their perception is that the generally lower labour standards in the South pose direct threats to their own employment, wage levels and bargaining position.[3]

A more specific complaint is that:

> Unfair competition does not lie simply in the fact that labour costs (pay, health and safety requirements, social spending, etc.), are extremely low in the South compared with those prevailing in most of Europe; it is also that the state often acts to keep wages low by denying workers the rights necessary to improve their conditions and by failing to enforce even such legislation as may be on their statute books.[4] (Morris, 1994)

Particular targets for criticism have been those 'countries with development models based on manufacturing for export (and specifically Export Processing Zones) – underpinned by cheap labour, often comprising young female workers, and frequent lack of union rights' (ICFTU, 1996).

It is indeed true that during the 1980s and 1990s labour markets in advanced economies displayed unfavourable tendencies, especially compared with the previous two decades of the Golden Age (Singh, 1995a). These manifest themselves in three important areas: de-industrialisation; increased inequality of wages and incomes; and mass unemployment. The following examples suffice to indicate the nature of these deficits in the US and in European Union countries.

- During the 100 years before 1973, real average hourly earnings of US workers rose by nearly 2 per cent a year. At that rate real earnings doubled every 36 years. In other words, the standard of living of each generation of workers was double that of the previous one. This longstanding rise in the standard of living came to an abrupt end in 1973.[5] However, over the two decades between 1979 and 1998, instead of increasing, the average real wage fell.[6]
- At the same time, there was a reversal of the long-term trend towards reduced wage and income inequality that had been experienced in the couple of decades following World War II and some say goes back as far as the 1920s. To illustrate, in 1979 male workers who had received a college education earned on average 30 per cent more than those who only had high school education. By 1995, the college educated were earning 70 per cent more than those receiving only high school education. Considering only those with high school education, the top 10 per cent of these workers in terms of wages earned 60 per cent more than the average worker in 1979. By 1995, this wage gap had increased to 83 per cent (Slaughter, 1998).
- Rising inequality was also manifest not just in terms of education, but also in terms of experience and other indicators of skill, as indeed in the wage structure as a whole. As mentioned above, the real average hourly wage of the average US worker declined continuously between 1979 and 1998; that of those workers at the bottom of the wage distribution, that is, the lowest 10 per cent, declined over an even longer period, namely between 1973 and 1998. Real hourly wages stagnated for all other groups except those in the top 10 per cent of the distribution. Even for this top decile, real wages rose by a mere 6.6 per cent over the 25 years between 1973 and 1998 (McCall, 2000).
- Further, the erosion of trade union power represented another important deterioration of labour standards in the US in the 1980s and 1990s. While the US claims that its Constitutional guarantees of worker rights and freedoms absolves it from signing ILO Conventions, there was widespread failure to comply with some of the ILO's core labour standards.[7] Indeed, a number of independent studies and government reports indicate that US labour law no longer protected workers' fundamental right to join a union. Instead 'unions are involved in a battle in which workers risk losing their jobs to realize their rights' (Kochan, 2000). A number of states

passed anti-union legislation asserting the 'right to work', which has made it more difficult to organise a union and for unions to go on strike. In addition to this encouragement given to non-union plants, the right to organise continued to be denied in the agricultural sector, which is among the lowest paid. By the early 1990s, only 15 per cent of US workers were organised in unions, whose role in protecting and improving the terms and conditions of work through collective bargaining became much diminished.[8] While the tightening of the labour market in the latter few years of last century resulted in a halt to the decline in union membership, at the end of the century the US was still considered to have a relatively unregulated regime with regard to labour market issues and what was referred to as a 'union-avoidance culture' (Brown, 2000).

- European workers have had both similar and also different concerns compared with US labour. The European welfare state system, despite serious attempts by governments and employers to erode the scope of the benefits, still provides a floor for the lowest paid workers. However, unlike the US, in the 1990s leading West European countries were afflicted by mass unemployment. In the popular perception, this was attributed to outsourcing by multinationals and, among other important factors, to unfair competition from developing countries.
- Since the early 1970s, European countries have experienced a high rate of increase in unemployment, such that the average level of unemployment rose from an average of 2.7 per cent in the period 1964–73 to 10.3 per cent between 1990 and 1999.[9] In 1995, in France, Italy and the UK the rate was 10 per cent of the labour force, and in Spain and Finland over 15 per cent. Even in Sweden, which previously had maintained a high level of employment, the unemployment rate rose rapidly from 1.5 per cent in 1990 to over 10 per cent in 1995 (Singh and Zammit, 1995).[10]
- While the freedom to associate largely remained intact in Europe, the actual strength of trades unions in terms of membership diminished significantly and their role in collective bargaining became considerably eroded over the final two decades of the century. These changes were an integral part of the post-1980 economic order that was rooted in new social norms and that involved the unravelling of the social pact between government, employers and labour and a weakening of the welfare state (Singh, 1990).
- During the period 1980–88, trade union membership declined in all countries except Sweden and Finland. In France, trade union membership dropped from 19 to 12 per cent, in Italy from 50 to 39 per cent and in the Netherlands from 40 to 26 per cent. In the UK, trade union membership fell from over 50 per cent to about 33 per cent, covering only one in three employees (Milbank, 1993).

The above data regarding trends in the wages and employment of workers in the North over the four final decades of the twentieth century provide clear evidence that workers' concerns regarding their worsening position were genuine. A key issue here is whether these detrimental developments were due to competition from developing countries. As the analysis below suggests, this was not the case.

Between 2000 and 2007, however, the world economy (including that of the US) expanded rapidly, resulting in a fall in the US unemployment rate. In Europe too the unemployment rate fell. Subsequently there was a further significant change, this time for the worse, as a consequence of the onset of the acute financial and economic crisis in 2008 when all economic indicators moved in a negative direction. For reasons of space and time this chapter does not provide a detailed analysis of labour issues during the initial crisis years. Suffice it to say that unemployment levels rose appreciably in both the US and Europe.

3 Competition from developing countries and labour market outcomes in developed countries: an assessment

The labour market difficulties in the advanced countries outlined above are extremely important and deserve full consideration. If it were true that trade in manufactures with low-wage developing countries was the main cause of increasing inequality in the US or of mass unemployment in Europe, this would not bode at all well for constructive international cooperation particularly in the economic sphere. In the event, however, research, particularly the most recent contributions, indicated that this widespread perception had very little basis.[11] The important insights of this research may be summarised as follows:[12]

- An elementary but extremely important point is that most manufacturing trade of the advanced countries takes place between these countries themselves. Even at the end of the first decade of the twenty-first century only a small part is with developing countries. It is indeed true that, starting from a very low level, the volume of manufactured exports from developing countries to advanced countries expanded at a very fast rate of 12 per cent a year between 1970 and 1990. Similarly, their share of world exports of manufactures increased from just 12 per cent in 1980 to 25 per cent in 1996.[13] Nevertheless, despite this impressive increase in manufactured exports from developing countries, the total imports by advanced countries of manufactured goods from developing countries (excluding China) amounted to only about 1.5 per cent of the combined GDP of OECD countries. It will therefore be difficult to argue that the huge shifts in income inequality and phenomena such as mass unemployment in the North are being caused largely by this rather marginal amount of trade with the South.[14]

- Another simple but significant fact is that advanced countries, despite their increased manufactured imports from developing countries, have generally maintained a surplus in manufacturing trade with developing countries as a whole. UNCTAD (1995) carried out a comprehensive analysis of North–South trade over two decades – from the early 1970s to the early 1990s. This indicated that in 1993 the total OECD manufacturing imports from developing countries amounted to approximately US$150 billion (in 1985 prices). However, the corresponding exports from the OECD to developing countries totalled nearly US$250 billion, yielding a net OECD surplus of nearly US$100 billion. As a proportion of GDP, the OECD surplus was about 1 per cent, approximately the same as two decades earlier in 1974. Disaggregation of the OECD figures suggests important intercountry and interregional differences. The European Union's manufacturing trade balance with developing countries followed much the same pattern as that for the OECD as a whole. The situation, however, has been rather different with respect to the US and Japan: Japan's trade balance with developing countries increased appreciably between 1974 and 1993, while that for the US fell over this period, becoming negative by the mid-1980s.[15]
- The industrial countries' surplus in manufacturing trade with developing countries has fluctuated in response to world economic events: it rose in the 1970s as developing countries borrowed petro-dollars and greatly increased their imports of capital goods from advanced countries. With the debt crisis engulfing many developing countries in the 1980s, the surplus fell. Importantly, this was due to reduced exports to the developing countries rather than to increasing imports from them. In the first half of the 1990s, as economic growth in developing countries revived, the surplus again rose as a result of increased southern imports from the North.
- Research indicates that neither mass unemployment nor the extent of de-industrialisation, that is, the fall in employment in manufacturing in G7 advanced countries, are associated with fluctuations in this surplus but rather with cyclical and conjunctural movements in economic activity in these countries themselves.[16] Thus, for example, the US was among those G7 industrial countries losing the least number of manufacturing jobs during this period whilst experiencing a trade deficit with developing countries.
- The experience of the 1950s and 1960s on these issues is illuminating. Just as there had been a sharp increase in the import penetration of leading advanced country markets by manufactured imports from the South in the period 1974–93, there was a similar fast increase in imports in the 1950s and 1960s into the US and the original six EEC member states from Japan and Italy (which could be regarded as developing countries

in that period, much like the newly industrialising countries today).[17] However, this earlier acceleration in the North's imports did not lead to mass unemployment, reduced real wages, or increased income inequality. Rather, European countries had full employment and, in the US, real wages grew at a rate of nearly 2 per cent a year and inequality decreased. The main difference between then and the more recent period under discussion is that in the 1950s and 1960s advanced economies were growing at about 5 per cent a year compared with half that long-term rate since 1973.

- Most economists recognise that the unfavourable labour market characteristics in advanced countries detailed in the last section (de-industrialisation, mass unemployment and increased wage dispersion) are far-reaching economic and social phenomena that do not arise from a single cause. Although trade with developing countries may be one of the factors, there are additional interrelated factors that may be equally plausible and more important. These include trade imbalances between developed countries themselves, cyclical movements in economic activity and slow long-term growth in advanced countries, technical change and changes in economic and social policy in these countries. In practice it is difficult for economists to isolate and measure the influence of each of these possible causal factors and the considerable controversy over this matter is not surprising.[18]
- There is, however, agreement among mainstream economists that the proximate cause for these developments has been the diminished demand for unskilled labour. This is deemed to have caused increased wage inequality in the US because labour markets there are flexible, whilst in Europe, because of the welfare state and more rigid labour markets, the effect is in terms of increased unemployment. Incorporating the decline in the demand for unskilled labour, mass unemployment in Europe and the increased wage dispersion in the US into a unified explanatory framework is referred to as the 'transatlantic consensus' (Atkinson, 1999).
- The extent of the consensus is limited, however, to agreeing on the supposed fall in the demand for unskilled labour. As to what causes this fall in demand is subject to much debate. A large majority of mainstream specialists in this area attribute it mostly to technological progress that is biased in favour of those with more skills, rather than to trade with developing countries (see footnote 19).
- Some important research, however, criticizes the simple theoretical framework (the Heckscher-Ohlin two-factor, two-sector, two-country model) normally used in mainstream approaches as being too limited or unreal. This two-by-two-by-two model for North–South trade, with the North specialising in skill-intensive industries according to its comparative advantage and the South producing and exporting low-skill products,

predicts that there will be a fall in the demand for unskilled labour leading to increased wage dispersion in the US and unemployment in Europe. However, a somewhat more realistic formal model within the same paradigm involving trade between three groups of countries (the US, Europe and the NICs) does not yield such predictions at all.[19] Furthermore, other economists put greater emphasis on the lack of reality of the assumptions of the traditional trade models, namely the assumption of constant returns to scale, perfect competition and full employment, giving no consideration to demand-side factors or to the accumulation of capital and therefore to growth.

- Significantly, recent research also questions the underlying empirical generalisation on which the 'transatlantic consensus' is based, namely that there was a fall in the demand for unskilled labour in advanced economies in the 1980s and 1990s. The latter was inferred in the US, for example, from the fact that the relative wages of the unskilled workers fell relatively to those of skilled workers. The evidence for 1977 to 1987 is broadly compatible with this proposition: the earnings of the bottom decile (assuming these to be unskilled workers) fell with respect to the median. However, importantly, the corresponding data for the US economy for the period 1987 to 1997 suggests an opposite trend, that is, the ratio of the bottom decile rose in relation to the median. Similarly, wage differentials in the UK fell in the 1990s, in contrast to the 1980s when these rose substantially.

In short, research suggests that traditional trade models are not applicable and that the basic premise regarding a decline in the demand for unskilled labour cannot empirically be sustained for the 1990s. It also suggests that the principle explanations put forward for the ostensible fall in aggregate demand, namely technological change and trade, are not sufficient to account for the broader observed facts regarding increased inequality in incomes in general. Indeed, Atkinson (1999) pointed out that what was observed in many countries in the 1990s was not a decline in wages at the bottom end of the scale but rather a rise at the very top. This suggests the need to look to wider explanations. Indeed, the trend in the 1990s can be considered in part the result of new economic policies that reflected changing public perceptions of what is socially acceptable, rather than being entirely the result of economic factors, such as technological change or trade. In recent decades economists have tended to overlook the fact that labour markets are unlike product markets. In the real world, even the most flexible labour markets require social agreement on the fairness of wage and income differentials. How these norms are arrived at is a complex social and political process.

The limitations of the theoretical framework of mainstream models on the subject are further highlighted by considering the effects of the 1990s' Asian economic crisis on unemployment levels in advanced countries. In the late 1990s it was widely thought that the considerable fall in the price of manufactured exports from the Asian crisis countries consequent on devaluation would lead to a further net loss in US jobs. This, however, did not occur, as indicated by rising levels of employment, particularly among the unskilled. In fact it can be argued that these exports from crisis-affected Asian countries helped increase rather than decrease employment to the extent that they exerted downward pressure on wages and prices and hence lessened inflationary pressure. This enabled the Federal Reserve to allow the US economy to operate at a higher level of economic activity and employment than would otherwise have been possible. Thus, while the direct effect of reduced wages in the crisis-affected Asian countries on US employment may have been expected to be negative, once indirect effects are taken into account, the result was very different.

To sum up, analysis and evidence indicate that trade with developing countries does not necessarily lead either to unemployment or low real wages for workers in advanced countries. Between 1950 and 1970, despite the rapid increase in imports from the then NICs (newly industrialising countries), European countries enjoyed full employment and rising real wages. In the US, real wages grew rather than remaining stagnant as they were later. Income inequality and wage dispersion became less in both Europe and the US, unlike in the following period. Although there are many factors that could explain the differences, a very important cause was the much faster economic growth in northern economies in the earlier period. Even those economists who believe that there is a tendency for the trade between rich and poor countries to be detrimental to unskilled workers will recognise that this tendency can be overwhelmed by the 'lift all boats' effects of faster economic growth (Bhagwati, 1994).

Considered in these terms, even if there were some significant adverse labour market outcomes in the 1980s and 1990s of trade with the South, these could have been overridden by faster economic growth. However, the slower economic growth observed in advanced economies in these decades resulted from their own policy decisions and social and political dynamics (Glyn et al., 1990; Crafts and Toniolo, 1996). It did not result from manufacturing trade with developing countries.

Finally, it is important to reiterate that the empirical evidence for the 1990s, contradicts the key theoretical expectation of those mainstream economists who believe that trade with the South necessarily leads to a fall in the demand for unskilled labour.

4 Labour standards and economic development

The previous section considered the North's apprehensions that unemployment and increasing inequality in advanced countries were due to competition from developing country imports. The discussion concluded that this was neither a necessary outcome nor did the analysis of recent developments prove these apprehensions to be well founded.

This section considers the implications of imposing compulsory labour standards on developing countries. This is a complex question, with many layers of argument, which requires a careful and extensive analysis. However, the analysis of these issues here will be necessarily brief.

In advocating a social clause or other mechanisms to enforce labour standards, advanced countries suggest that they are only asking developing countries to adopt core labour standards, and not measures such as minimum wages. The former relate to the core conventions concerning freedom of association and collective bargaining, freedom from forced labour, non-discrimination and the abolition of child labour. This is justified on the grounds that they are basic human rights and hence no other considerations enter the picture. It is argued, further, that the enforcement of core labour standards will not, in any case, alter developing countries' comparative advantage in production and trade.[20] There are, of course, a whole host of 'other' labour standards, but in the context of fierce international competition and developing countries the most likely ones at issue would include minimum wages, employment guarantees and health and safety measures.

This perspective raises two issues that need to be addressed here in view of their importance for developing countries. The first concerns the suggestion that the implementation of core standards has no impact on wage levels and other labour costs. The second concerns the primacy of core labour standards, and whether their classification as human rights completely rules out any discussion of the best way to proceed to implement them.

4.1 Economic costs and benefits of core labour standards

While the implementation of core labour standards in developing countries will not necessarily affect the costs and pattern of production directly, a little reflection will show that the indirect effects may be quite important, and these could involve not just economic costs but also economic benefits. Further, the costs and benefits of implementing core labour standards are likely to be different for each of the various labour standards. It is also important to appreciate that the costs and benefits would be different if some or all of these core standards were to be implemented simultaneously. For example, the costs to producers of introducing equality of remuneration or non-discrimination in employment are likely to be higher if workers also have the right to organise and bargain collectively. To illustrate and clarify the main issues involved, the focus in the following discussion will first be on freedom of association and on free collective bargaining. Subsequently other labour standards, particularly that of the elimination of child labour, will be briefly considered.

The contention that the implementation of the two core standards under discussion here (freedom of association and the right to collective bargaining

– Convention Nos. 87 and 98) will have no economic consequences for producers or to the economy as a whole is not generally valid. At an elementary level, the mainstream textbook model of perfect competition would posit that the introduction of these standards would be distortionary as this will lead to monopsony in the labour market and thus to a misallocation of resources. This is, of course, a static analysis based on a rather restricted set of assumptions and one can envisage a dynamic model of the economy in which labour standards reduce conflict by providing an institutionalised way of minimising disruption, improving cooperation between the employees and employers and thereby encouraging the latter to invest more. This would generate greater growth in the national economy.[21]

While theoretically possible, such a model with positive effects on economic development does not correspond to the economic conditions of most developing countries. In the longer term, however, when a higher level of development and a more advanced economic and institutional structure has been attained, the economic impact of employers' and workers' associations is more likely to be favourable.

There are a number of reasons for expecting negative effects in the short to medium term for developing countries resulting from the compulsory introduction of freedom of association and collective bargaining, according to the terms of ILO Conventions Nos. 87 and 98. The most important of these are outlined below.

4.1.1 The structure of the economy Most developing countries are not only poor but have a sharply dualistic economic structure, extreme segmentation of the labour market and surplus labour. In the mid-1990s, on average, only a small proportion of developing countries' labour force (15 per cent) had employment in industry and services in which they had a formal wage contract. For this segment of the labour force it is feasible to consider applying core ILO labour standards. In contrast, however, 61 per cent of the labour force works in agriculture and another 22 per cent in rural non-farm and urban informal employment (World Bank, 1995). Even for the urban sector alone, UNDP (2000) reports that, in the 1990s, informal work accounted for 57 per cent of urban employment in Bolivia, 56 per cent in Tanzania and 48 per cent in Thailand.

In general, improvements in labour standards, core or otherwise, of this often considerable portion of the labour force in agriculture and the informal sector in developing countries depends on significant changes being made in economic structure. Labour standards improve as the proportion of the labour force in these two sectors declines while that in organised industry and the formal service sector, where labour standards are more likely to be observed or enforced, rise.[22] Fast economic growth may speed up the process of structural change but can also be associated with jobless growth in the industrial sector. (For a further discussion, see section 6 below.)

It is difficult to introduce and almost impossible to enforce ILO Conventions on this large part of the labour force. The vast majority of labour in these sectors gains a living in micro-enterprises including subsistence agriculture, which creates obvious problems of organising labour and monitoring standards. Further, in the more populous developing countries, there invariably exists a large reserve army of unskilled low-productivity labour that has to make ends meet by any means. In effect there is a large reserve of labour in search of work at any price. The possibilities for unionisation and collective bargaining of the sort traditionally associated with the advanced industrial economies are limited. With de-industrialisation and the rise of the service economy, even the advanced industrial countries are now confronted with this problem once again.[23]

4.1.2 Autocratic employers and immature trade unions As will be explained in the following section, freedom of association and collective bargaining in advanced countries has developed through an evolutionary process over a period of well over a century. In the course of this evolution the unions and employers developed responsible institutional mechanisms for conflict resolution. Employers themselves came to appreciate the advantages of trade unions and collective representation for the workers. On the union side wasteful and damaging inter-union rivalry and other dysfunctional features of early trade unions were curbed, and in many industrial countries centralised wage bargaining or other similar pay coordinating structures were put in place.

However, if in accordance with the advanced countries' proposals, the two labour conventions under discussion are imposed in a 'big bang' manner in a developing economy (through, for example, international trade sanctions), it is more than likely that this would lead not to conflict resolution, but rather to strikes and consequent economic disruption. Many developing country employers, including the largest ones, often have a feudal or paternalistic outlook and do not see any need for trade unions. It is not unusual for them to use violent methods to stop the formation of unions and their activities, much like the historical experience of advanced countries such as the US. On the side of the employees, in the early stages of unionisation there is also likely to be considerable inter-union competition for members, leading to populist positions being taken by union leaders. Further, attempts at violent suppression of trade union activity by employers invariably leads to counter-violence by unions. The consequent economic and social disruption discourages investment, both foreign and domestic, and therefore does not help the cause of economic development.

Moreover, free collective bargaining between employers and unions, if it takes place at all, will only be concerned with the wages and employment of those who are already working in the formal sector. The interests of the vast majority of workers in agriculture and in the informal sector who are not unionised would be ignored. Further, to the extent that formal sector unions succeed in getting higher wages and employment guarantees for their members, this is likely to reduce, other things being equal, the demand for labour in that sector, forcing the unemployed to seek work in the informal sector. So the paradoxical result of efforts to impose compulsory labour standards is that it would harm economic development, reduce structural change and thereby increase the numbers in the informal sector where labour standards hardly apply.

Thus, the compulsory introduction of free collective bargaining, if successfully implemented, is likely to widen the already considerable wage and income gap between workers in different parts of the economy. Instead of promoting equality and solidarity, the unintended result of unionisation of formal sector employees may well be the development of an aristocracy of labour based on extraction of rents by union members, particularly in more productive firms. In these circumstances a concern for broad social justice, especially with respect to the informal sector and small rural producers, may require government intervention and regulation of bargaining between unions and employers in the formal sector (see, for example, Stiglitz, 2000). Such intervention may also be necessary to cope with the adverse economic and social consequences of bargaining between autocratic management and immature unions as outlined above. However, many developed country governments lack the institutional and administrative capacity for adequate remedial intervention with unfavourable consequences for economic development.[24]

The paradoxical results of the enforcement of compulsory labour standards go further. Such enforcement would not only be counter-productive for developing countries, but is also unlikely to help the interests of those seeking protection in the advanced countries. To see this, assume that the imposition of labour standards leads, via trade union action, to higher wages and costs in the developing country's export sector – the most favourable assumption from the protectionist perspective in the advanced countries. Under this assumption, the competitiveness of developing country exports is likely to diminish, but this may provide only a brief respite for the advanced country producers.

In analysing this issue, it is useful to remember that most developing country exports to advanced countries are produced by a relatively small though growing number of NICs, whilst the vast majority of developing countries export only a very small fraction of the total. Although, in the short run, all countries are likely to be disadvantaged to a greater or lesser extent in terms of their competitiveness if core labour standards are made compulsory, the NICs are unlikely to be handicapped for long. As they have higher rates of investment, technological change and superior production and export dynamics, they will, in the medium term, be able to re-establish their competitiveness. The outstanding examples of this phenomenon are countries like Korea and indeed before then the example of Japan that started with Asian wage levels and has continued to be competitive in spite of continuing increases in real wages, as well as more and more stringent environmental standards imposed on its exports by importing countries. Higher labour costs in firms already competing in world markets are likely to stimulate investment in more productive techniques in order to maintain their competitive edge. China and India are current examples of this process.

However, turning from the NICs to the great majority of developing countries, although accounting for only a small proportion of total developing country manufactured exports to advanced countries, these exports are, nevertheless, crucial to their well-being. A rise in their export costs as a result of the compulsory introduction of labour standards would, under plausible assumptions, lead to a lower rate of economic growth of exports in both the short and medium term, worsening their balance of payments, such that the growth rate has to be lower to be compatible with current account equilibrium. This will reduce the pace of structural change and the improvement of labour standards.

It will be appreciated, however, that both for the NICs and other developing countries the costs of adjustment, whether in the short or long term will be lower, the faster the rate of economic growth of production and exports in the domestic and in the world economy.[25]

5 Labour standards: the experience of developing countries

It is interesting in this respect to reflect on the actual experience of East Asian and Latin American countries during the course of economic development. Taking East Asia first, notwithstanding the recent Asian crisis, these 'miracle' countries experienced very fast long-term growth (near double-digit rates for two decades or more). The result has been fast absorption of surplus labour, resulting in labour shortages; very high rates of growth of real wages by comparative international standards; and speedy structural change, resulting in the displacement of the informal sector activities by the formal sector. Real wages in the fast-growing East Asian and South East Asian economies rose at a rate of over 5 per cent a year between the mid-1980s and the mid-1990s.[26] In Taiwan, employment in the agricultural sector fell from 56.1 per cent in 1953 to 36.7 per cent in 1970 and was only 12.1 per cent in 1993. Industrial employment reached more than 40 per cent in 1990. In Korea in 1992, only about 15 per cent of the labour force were still in the agricultural sector and more than 25 per cent in the industrial sector (Lee and Park, 1995).

It is a matter of historical record that many of these countries repressed trade unions during the early phases of their developmental spurt. This was the case, for example, in Korea during the 1960s and 1970s. However, with the fast expansion of the formal economy and particularly the shrinking of the informal sector, not only labour standards in terms of employment and wages greatly improved; there was also a very considerable expansion of unionisation. By the end of the 1980s, 40 per cent of the labour force in Taiwan and 17.2 per cent in Korea were unionised, compared with only 15 per cent in the US (ibid.). These huge improvements in core as well as other labour standards took place in these countries through the process of economic development itself, without any international coercion.

A comparison of East Asian countries with those elsewhere (for example, in South Asia or Latin America) suggests that fast economic growth may not be a sufficient, but is certainly a necessary, condition for the speedy establishment and improvement of labour standards. To illustrate, a democratic country like India in the 1950s had much better core labour standards in the formal sector than say, Korea; but the situation is now quite the reverse. The proportion of the workforce in unions is much smaller than that in Korea, and workers' wages in India have grown much more slowly. Similarly, in Latin America, despite its long history of trade unionism compared with East Asia, its much slower long-term rate of economic growth in the 1980s and 1990s has contributed to further 'informalisation' of the economy.[27] Tokman (1997) reported that eight out of every ten new jobs in Latin America in the 1990s have been created in the informal sector with consequent unfavourable prospects for the workers involved to be able to exercise the rights given to them by the ILO Conventions. A small proportion of the increase in informal sector work could be due to labour-saving technical progress in the formal sector, rather than to slower growth. However, it is too early to tell whether the long-term relationship between economic growth and formal jobs has become worse over time.

There are a number of reasons why improved core and other labour standards are associated with structural change and particularly with industrialisation. In the first instance, in contrast with the small-scale agricultural sector and the informal sector, work in industry is usually organised in a way that facilitates trade union organisation and activities. The relatively higher rate of growth of productivity in industry also provides scope for improvements in substantive labour standards. Employers in the industrial sector who have invested substantial capital in the enterprise are also interested in promoting core and other labour standards such as health and safety standards since these tend to increase the level of commitment of the workforce and to increase the productivity of workers (see further Piore, 1990).

5.1 Core labour standards and human rights

The subsections above considered some of the most important costs and benefits of implementing the core labour standards relating to freedom of association and collective bargaining, and the appropriateness of such standards in the circumstances in which most developing countries find themselves. This subsection addresses the other central issue introduced at the beginning of the section, namely that concerning the primacy given to core labour standards, which have been accorded the status of human rights.

The unanimous adoption by ILO members in 1998 of the Declaration on Fundamental Principles and Rights at Work, embodying the seven core labour standards, is regarded as evidence of the widespread acceptance of the notion that certain labour standards have precedence. The rationale given for the primacy of the seven core standards is that they are universal human rights. Of these the freedom of association and trade union rights are given particular emphasis in that they give workers the freedom to pressure for improvements in other aspects of labour standards. Having the status of human rights purportedly pre-empts any economic cost–benefit analysis. These contentions are contested below.

5.1.1 Historical evolution of labour standards in advanced countries Historically, labour standards evolved in a rather different manner. In Europe, early efforts to improve labour standards focused on gaining legislation to eliminate the worst forms of child and female labour, and with initiatives to improve health and safety at work. It took many decades before workers' efforts to associate and bargain with their employers gained legal recognition. In many countries, it was only after many decades of struggle and political debate that trade unions were recognised and constituted a regulated institutional framework facilitating conflict resolution between employers and workers. Thus, broadly speaking, core and substantive labour standards evolved during the course of economic development, and legislation legitimising labour standards was introduced as a result of struggle by working people, and not through some *deus ex machina*. Labour standards have been both the cause and effect of democratisation in the advanced countries.[28] In the light of this evolution, the unions became increasingly responsible and both economic growth and labour standards improved.

5.1.2 A hierarchy of labour rights? Although these two core standards concerning the freedom of association and collective bargaining are indeed extremely important and should be given high status, the primacy of those over non-core standards needs to be questioned. For example, should health and safety at work be accorded lower priority than the right to free association and collective bargaining? It is indeed true that 'deficits' in the latter have often resulted in the imprisonment and even murder of trade unionists. On the other hand, the disregard for the health and lives of workers manifested by the widespread lack of health and safety regulations has resulted in appalling tragedies such as those in the Bangkok factory and the Bhopal chemicals plant in which fires and fumes cost the lives of thousands of workers. Less dramatically but more insidiously, tens of thousands of unprotected agricultural workers worldwide suffer slow poisoning by the chemicals used to produce agricultural exports.

Equally importantly, there is international recognition of the fact that absolute poverty blights the lives of over 1 billion people in developing countries. In 1995, 117 Heads of State or Government attending the Copenhagen Social Summit endorsed the Copenhagen Declaration, which put primary emphasis on the promotion of full employment and poverty reduction. Should not the right to a decent living also be regarded as a basic labour right?

5.2 Terms of Conventions 87 and 98 and the role of the government

There are also serious difficulties from the point of view of developing countries with the precise formulations of Conventions 87 and 98 concerning freedom of association, the right to organise and to engage in free collective bargaining. The texts of these conventions reflect the needs and institutions of advanced countries at a particular moment in time. The conventions do not take into account the fact that untrammelled collective bargaining may not only lead to social disruption as noted above, but also to serious macroeconomic disequilibria, all of which require government intervention in the bargaining process. Governments also need to intervene to ensure that the interests of the unemployed, low productivity sector workers or those in the informal sector or small-scale agriculture are taken into account. These concerns were recognised in European countries themselves during the so-called 'Golden Age' (1950–73) when many governments entered into social pacts with unions and employers to institutionalise the social market economy, which tried to achieve a broadly acceptable distribution of income and wealth (Glynn et al., 1990; Eichengreen, 1996; Flanagan, 1999).[29]

Moreover, the orthodox approach to trade unions implied in the terms of the two conventions is hardly relevant to peasant and small-scale farming in developing countries. These require different policies and institutions in which the government often plays a role, as for example, through price support programmes, technical assistance and promoting cooperatives. Some of these measures may be achieved through individual and collective initiatives and organisations, but in practice the government has to play a leading role. In developing country agriculture, one of the main issues is land reform, since the size of land-holding is a crucial factor in determining the capacity to earn a decent living and escape poverty.

It would appear that human rights defined and interpreted in terms of these two core conventions are destined only for a small part of the working population, benefiting mainly those who are already relatively privileged. Furthermore, the untrammelled exercise of these rights by the minority may well prejudice the chance for others to have a decent living or to be able to exercise their rights to freedom of association and to collective bargaining.

6 Should core conventions be made compulsory?

To sum up, from the perspective of developing countries, there are three significant policy conclusions with respect to the core conventions:

- The number of core conventions should be expanded to make them inclusive and relevant to the needs of the whole working population worldwide.
- Convention Nos. 87 and 98 require fundamental revision to make them relevant to the developing world.
- There are trade-offs between certain core conventions and therefore economic and social costs and benefits must be part of the moral equation.

These conclusions also have important implications for the question of whether core labour standards should be made mandatory by means of international trade sanctions or other punitive measures; these implications are examined below.

In the case of Conventions 87 and 98, the answer suggested by the above analysis is unambiguous. These conventions are deeply flawed, particularly from a developing country perspective, and it would be a mistake for developing countries to implement them in the fashion envisaged in the conventions. The argument here is not against workers' organisations as such, but the process of raising labour standards should ensure the inclusion of the mass of the working population. If these conventions were revised to make them more inclusive, developing countries would find them easier and more useful to implement. However, their mandatory application in developing countries under international coercion would still be unwise. This is because, although the acceptance of the role of the government in the collective bargaining process may help ameliorate some of the difficulties outlined earlier, there are still likely to be significant costs for the non-NIC majority of developing countries. Consequently, compulsory standards such as these will be resisted by these countries. However, encouragement to these countries through non-coercive means and technical assistance by agencies such as the ILO to implement the standards are more likely to lead to positive results (Bhagwati, 1994).

The arguments for compulsory implementation of labour standards in developing countries are sometimes based on advanced country allegations of the former's unfair advantages in trade that give rise to social dumping and race to the bottom. These issues will be examined in the concluding section where it will be seen that these considerations also do not in any way justify compulsion.

Although we argue here against compulsory imposition of Conventions 87 and 98, we do not take the same view for all other core conventions. For example, granting slave and bonded labour their freedom in recognition of their human rights should be implemented forthwith. In view of the limited numbers of people involved, compulsion cannot be rejected on grounds of costs to developing countries. However, in the case of the conventions on child labour, which we discuss briefly below, again compulsion will not be appropriate.

6.1 Child labour

Child labour (covered by a core ILO Convention [No. 138 on Minimum Age] and the Convention on the Elimination of the Worst Forms of Child Labour, which amplifies the former) raises other kinds of problems, which merit careful consideration.[30] The latter convention commits countries to working with the ILO to fix time-bound policies to eliminate the worst forms of child labour. As is increasingly recognised, the phenomenon of child labour is rooted in a number of fundamental factors, not least domestic and global policies that lead to income concentration, poverty, exclusion, under-employment and unemployment. The World Confederation of Labour (WCL) notes that, to abolish child labour, to prevent such situations arising, and to reintegrate children into society 'requires a broad-based strategy. ... Free compulsory and high-quality education is a pre-requisite for concrete results of such a strategy ... and has to include curricula for vocational training, which is now lacking in many countries' (WCL, 1997, pp. 6–7).

The essential point is that parents and governments in developing countries would like their children to be in school rather than at work, but in many poor countries they are unable to afford it. Detailed empirical studies from several countries confirm this view. (See, for example, Grootaert, 1998 and Addison et al., 1997. For a recent review of these and other studies see Basu, 1999.)

Empirical evidence further suggests that, where parents have been compensated for the loss of children's earnings, children do not work but go to school. A prominent and highly successful example is the government's massive Bolsa Familia programme in Brazil. However, without such compensations for the parents, the imposition of restrictions on child labour will simply lead to the children resorting to other often illegal or unsavoury activities, where they will be worse off than if they were working and earning some income for the family. Thus, without supporting measures, the enforcement of the child labour conventions in developing countries will hinder rather than help the realisation of the objective of promoting the welfare of children.[31]

7 Conclusion

An extremely important point that emerges from the discussion of core and other labour standards in this section is that substantial improvements in the achievement of these standards, as well as significant growth of real wages and other substantive standards, can be rapidly achieved voluntarily through the process of economic development itself. As indicated, the fast-growing East Asian countries were able to accomplish these objectives without any international enforcement measures.

Efforts to enforce core labour standards will not help to raise standards in much of the informal sector and could well lead to further informalisation. If punitive trade measures were used to enforce such standards, a reduction in trade through the application of trade sanctions could result in cuts in employment precisely in the industries where labour standards have generally been seen to grow fastest. This is likely to throw more workers into the informal sector, worsening the already low levels of remuneration and conditions of work. The net result will be the opposite of what is allegedly intended.

This is not to say that leaving it to the market or to the natural forces of economic development will always be adequate to improve labour standards at a fast enough rate. The promotion of labour standards on a voluntary basis, backed up with technical and financial assistance for both the monitoring and implementing of the standards by the countries themselves, will be helpful in hastening the process. As explained before, developing countries have continually demonstrated their commitment to raising their labour standards, as manifested by various national and multilateral actions, including their recent acceptance of the ILO Declaration on Fundamental Principles and Rights at Work and Their Follow-up (for the text, see ILO, 2000a, and for the Follow-up, see ILO, 2000b). In addition to the economic and practical arguments outlined above, they strongly object, however, on political grounds, to labour standards being made compulsory, whether the compulsion is enforced through the WTO or through joint ILO/WTO initiatives. Such measures would introduce yet a further layer of conditionalities to those already imposed on them by the international financial institutions and through the Uruguay Round trade and trade-related agreements in the WTO, all of which circumscribe developing countries' policy options in one way or another (South Centre, 1998a and 1998b).

The current ILO approach to labour standards seems to be more promising for the purpose of establishing a universal social floor for the globalising economy. It focuses on the notion of 'decent work' as a means of capturing and realising the aspirations of people throughout the world and seeking radically new solutions to the global problems of poverty and the working poor. At the opening session of the 88th ILO Conference in June 2000, ILO's Director General declared that decent work 'is not a straitjacket, a one-size-fits-all solution. On the contrary, it is a way of treating in a coherent and dynamic way the aspirations and goals of different individuals, different cultures, different societies. The question is how to make it real. We all understand that the possibilities for decent work evolve with social and economic progress, and goals can and should rise over time' (Somavia, 2000).

An important conclusion that can be drawn from the foregoing analysis is that the economic interests of informal sector low-productivity labour and those of the small-scale farming families must be promoted by other methods, including the development of popular organisations. The above analysis would also suggest that there is a clear need to redraft Conventions 87 and 98 so that they lead to more democratic outcomes in the sense of taking into account the conditions and economic structures of developing countries. The core standards could also be extended to include one focusing on the right to a decent living.

Addendum

Since the earlier version of this work was published the process of globalisation has advanced significantly and is acknowledged to be having both a positive and negative impact on most countries and regions. There are both winners and losers. Until the start of the current acute economic crisis that began with the demise of Lehman Brothers, the world economy was expanding rapidly: the rate of expansion was over 5 per cent per annum between 2003 and 2007. While the US among developed countries, and China and India among developing countries, were the most successful in terms of economic growth they were not so successful in improving income distribution. (However, there is no evidence that slower-growing economies were better in this respect.) In this brief Addendum we provide an overview of the evolution of labour markets and labour standards in these three countries and examine the implications of North–South interactions during this period of fast economic growth for workers in the North and South.

Taking first the case of the US, its economy enjoyed near full employment in the 2000s. The burst of the dot.com bubble at the beginning of 2000 was followed by fast economic recovery and with the achievement of near full employment. Public concern over labour standards in developing countries waned. It has, however, resurfaced with the current acute economic crisis and the resultant mass unemployment.[32] The Obama administration, to its credit, has not accepted labour unions' demands for protection but instead has outlined a positive programme of the doubling of US exports over the next five years. In the context of the current downturn in the world economy it remains to be seen how realistic this plan is likely to be.

Among developing countries, current fast growth of over 10 per cent in China and 9 per cent in India has led to considerable reductions in poverty in both countries and to substantial levels of employment and to improvements in labour standards in general, without coercive multilateral pressures. Nevertheless, the Obama administration is subject to pressure from trade unions to strengthen the labour standard dimensions of bilateral trade and development agreements between the US and developing countries.

Recent evidence suggests that labour standards in both China and India have improved as a result of local labour pressures, as well as the structural change brought about by government policies promoting fast economic growth. Hundreds of millions of rural workers in both countries have found work in the cities. Their labour standards may be expected to improve, as in the case of East Asian countries in the 1980s and 1990s, when labour standards improved rapidly in tandem with the increasing demand for non-agricultural labour. At the same time, economic growth in China and India has, inter alia, increased demand for imports from the US and elsewhere and hence reduced US financial deficits.

However, as Izurieta and Singh (2010) point out, fast growth in India and China is not an unalloyed good for the US economy and its workers. These countries' growth entails increased demand for imported energy and other raw materials, pushing world commodity prices sky high. Their simulation analysis based on an econometric model of the world economy suggests that fast Indian growth at 9 per cent per annum and Chinese growth at 10 per cent per annum is not compatible with a full employment level of growth of 3 per cent a year in the US. Were the US to have full employment growth, India and China could only grow at less than their desired rates of growth. The Izurieta and Singh analysis indicates that this conflict of interest can only be resolved by means of close cooperation between the three countries in energy conservation and environmental measures. Such a scenario will inevitably benefit labour markets and standards in both rich and poor countries particularly in the medium and long term. The full potential of globalisation in terms of improved labour standards and decent work can only be achieved if there is greater policy coordination between nation states. Globalisation left only to market forces cannot deliver worldwide full employment or decent livelihoods for the entire workforce.

Notes

1. The pressure on large northern companies at the top of value chains to keep their final prices low, and their substantial power to keep down the prices of their suppliers, makes them complicit in the continuation of low labour standards in developing countries (Zammit, 2010).
2. For a more extended discussion of these issues, see Singh and Zammit (2000).
3. A particular complaint is that the employment of forced labour and child labour facilitates the payment of extremely low wages, if any, thereby putting pressure on other segments of the labour market to accept low wages.
4 The necessary rights are those specified in ILO Conventions 87 and 98, granting workers the right to organise and to engage in free collective bargaining.
5. The basic source for the data in the following paragraphs is the US Council of Economic Advisers (1998) and Economic Policy Institute (1999).
6. For an analysis of the evolution of the world economy between 1973 and 1979 (the so-called 'inter-shock period', see Glyn et al. (1990).
7. On the issue of forced labour, the requirement that prisoners and youths in detention work for derisory pay is standard practice in the US and in Europe. In the US, the prison population numbers over 1 million while there are half a million in local county jails. There is a disproportionate number of black and Latino persons, often detained for minor offences and arguably as a form of social control (see, for example, Freeman, 1995). Prisoners are forced to work in factories, including clothing factories that have located their operations to prison sites, where they have a captive pool of cheap labour. It is estimated that in 1998 prison labour produced over 280 products worth over US$9 billion and replaced 400 000 jobs otherwise done by the normal workforce. Prison labour is paid the minimum wage but, after deductions for taxes, room and board, victims' compensation and so on, the pay may be only US$60 a month for nine-hour days. A number of harsh disciplinary measures and other penalties are

imposed if prisoners refuse to work. Federal law prohibits the domestic sale of prison-made goods unless prisoners are paid the going wage, so prison industries export the output, often to Asian countries (WINDS, 1996).

8. Unionisation becomes particularly difficult when a considerable part of the workforce consists of illegal migrant labour, as is the case in parts of the US. Employers are, of course, keen to employ such workers, since these are willing to work on almost any terms and in the worst of all possible jobs. However, the fear of being arraigned and deported as illegal migrants constrains them from joining efforts to unionise and improve their terms and conditions of work. Inflows of migrant labour, legal or otherwise, are unlikely to dry up until growth and development have improved the standard of living in the South.
9. The lower rate of unemployment in the US is partly explained by the fact that welfare provision for the unemployed is not as extensive as that in Europe, so that many people are obliged to seek work however unremunerative the wage. The higher level of unemployment in the EU compared with that in the US is the source of a vigorous academic and policy debate on labour market flexibility.
10. Since then unemployment levels have declined. The April 2000 figure for Sweden was 4.7 per cent and the average for the Euro-11, that is the members of the European single currency union, was 9.2 per cent (*The Economist*, 2000).
11. For research suggesting that trade with the South has a detrimental impact on employment and wages in the North, see in particular Wood (1994) and Wood (1995). However, Wood's estimates of the extent of the impact far exceed those of other economists.
12. The analysis in this section is based on Singh and Dhumale (2000). For detailed empirical evidence underlying the arguments in the first four paragraphs the reader is referred to UNCTAD (1995).
13. The bulk of developing country manufactured exports is accounted for by only 13 developing countries, mainly in Asia, the percentage reaching 87.9 in 1996 (Ghose, 2000).
14. Strictly speaking, under the rarified assumptions of general equilibrium trade models, it can be shown that small changes in quantities can cause large shifts in prices. For the intense academic controversy on this subject, see Krugman (2000) and Leamer (2000). For earlier contributions, see Bhagwati (1994).
15. It is also important to bear in mind a related point with respect to the effects of trade on jobs. Once a country starts trading there will normally be a gross loss of jobs, but not necessarily a net loss. Other things being equal, employment will contract in importing and expand in exporting industries. The magnitude of the net change in jobs will be determined by the relative growth rates of imports and exports, as well as by the capital intensity of production in the importing and exporting industries. For the individuals concerned, the gross loss of jobs is extremely important as many of them may not have the skills or the capacity to move to jobs created elsewhere in the economy. Thus, governments often need to provide special assistance to displaced workers. The US government, for example, provides trade adjustment grants to workers proven to have been displaced because of imports.
16. For a fuller discussion of de-industrialisation, see Rowthorn and Ramaswamy (1997), Singh (1989 and 1994) and Howes and Singh (2000).
17. Between 1958 and 1997, import penetration by Italy and Japan of the market for manufactures for the original six EEC countries, excluding Italy, rose from 0.5 per cent to 3.7 per cent of apparent consumption (gross output minus net exports); the corresponding figures for the US were 0.3 to 1.8. This acceleration in the North's imports is coincidentally similar to that experienced by these countries between 1975 and 1992. Over the latter period, the European Union's manufactured imports from developing countries rose from 0.9 to 2.8 per cent of apparent consumption. The analogous figures for the US for this later period were 0.8 and 4.3.
18. For recent reviews of this literature, see Burtless (1995), Gottschalk and Smeeding (1997), Slaughter and Swagel (1997). See also Krugman and Lawrence, (1994), Richardson (1995), Atkinson (1999), Singh and Dhumale (2000).
19. See Atkinson (1999, 2000) and Davis (1998a, 1998b).
20 See, for example, US Trade Representative Charlene Barshefsky's statement on this matter at the Singapore WTO Ministerial meeting in 1996.

21. The central question here is whether labour standards would help or hinder economic development, through their impact on the rate of growth of output, employment and labour costs. The general answer, as suggested by the analysis in the text, is that this depends on a number of complex factors and interrelationships, in particular the assumptions that are made with respect to 1) the range of labour standards being introduced and the speed with which they are implemented; 2) the level of development of the country and degree of export orientation; 3) the dynamics of the production structure and production and export capabilities, including the ability to absorb modern technology; 4) the rate of savings and investment among others. It may also be useful to note that this analysis of the relationship between labour standards and economic development is somewhat different from the examination of the effects of labour standards on economic welfare in terms of the conventional theories of welfare economics and international trade. For an example of the latter perspective see Brown et al. (1996).
22. Employment in the formal sector increases until a very high level of per capita income is reached. At that point, the share of employment in industry declines and that of services, particularly informal services (informal in the sense that many labour laws become difficult to apply due to the small size of the enterprise) begins to rise, as is indicated in the previous footnote.
23. The acquisition of labour rights and standards is not necessarily a permanent achievement. For example, the number of people employed in Indian restaurants in the UK now totals more than those in coal mining, steel making and shipbuilding put together. These once dominant industries were noted for their strong unions with substantial collective bargaining capacity, which brought continual improvements in substantive labour standards. In contrast, work in the restaurant business, which has low productivity, is typified by its informal, part-time nature, and the level of union organisation is low, as are labour standards. This needs to be distinguished from the growing phenomenon of 'informalisation' of the work contract, whereby the nature of the 'contract' is such as to turn the 'employee' into a virtually self-employed person, with few if any labour rights.
24. Contrary to popular prejudice in advanced countries, most developing country governments are neither perverse nor wicked or worse. Some in East and Southeast Asia have been recognised to be 'developmental states' with an outstandingly successful record of close government involvement in the economy (see, for example, Amsden, 1989; Wade, 1990; Singh, 1995b). Others, such as India, have been equally interventionist but have not been as successful. The large majority of Third World governments are less effective with considerably lower levels of institutional and administrative capacity. These governments may not always be multiparty democracies but it is important to recognise that they tend to be relatively 'inclusive', that is, they cannot simply be regarded as representing the interest of employers. There are, of course, a small number of southern countries that are totally corrupt, ineffective and non-inclusive, as was the case with Mobutu's Congo, for example. For such countries, neither compulsory nor voluntary labour standards would help.
25 For a fuller discussion of these issues see Singh (1990).
26. For further details, see Singh (2000).
27. The trend rate of growth of Latin American economies during the last 20 years has been only 3 per cent a year, compared with almost 6 per cent a year in the period 1950–80 (Singh, 2000).
28. In the words of E.P. Thompson, studying the making of the English working class, 'The working class did not rise like the sun at an appointed time. It was present at its own making'. See Thompson (1963, p. 9) and Hobsbawm (1964).
29. The European Common Agricultural Policy (CAP) was originally intended to improve the livelihoods of small-scale farmers and agricultural workers.
30. Due to the global campaign against child labour and to the ILO's special efforts in that direction, the 2010 Global Report (http://www.ilo.org/ipecinfo/product/viewProduct.do?productID=13853) suggests that the number continues to decline but only modestly, as 2015 million children are still affected. There are also fewer children in hazardous work but the number is still 115 million. Although child labour has declined in Latin America and Asia, it has increased in sub-Saharan Africa.

31. Recent theoretical research suggests that, under certain special circumstances, particularly where children constitute a significant proportion of the work force, the banning of child labour could lead to a rise in adult wages, enabling poor households to do without the income from child labour. The author of this theoretical result himself observes that 'This is unlikely to be true for very poor economies but maybe valid for better-off countries. Even so, one would need to do detailed empirical work to decide whether such a total ban is worthwhile. The interesting insight the theory gives us here is to tell us that it may be so and to give hints as to the type of economy where this is likely' (Basu, 1999, p. 62).
32. For an analysis of the causes of the current financial and economic crisis see Aiginger (2009), Solow (2009) and Singh and Zammit (2010).

References

Addison, T., Bhalotra, S., Coulter, F. and Heady, C. (1997), 'Child labour in Pakistan and Ghana. A comparative study', mimeo, University of Warwick, UK.

Aiginger, K. (2009), 'The current economic crisis: causes, cures and consequences', WIFO Working Papers No. 431, August, Osterreichisches Institut fur Wirtshaftschung.

Amsden, A. (1989), *Asia's Next Giant*, New York: Oxford University Press.

Atkinson, A. (1999), 'Is rising income inequality inevitable? A critique of the transatlantic consensus', 1999 WIDER Annual Lectures 3, Helsinki: UNU WIDER.

Atkinson, A. (2000), 'The changing distribution of income: evidence and explanations', *German Economic Review*, **1**(1), 3–18.

Basu, K. (1999), 'Child labour: cause, consequences, and cure, with remarks on international labour standards', *Journal of Economic Literature*, **XXXVII**(3).

Bhagwati, J. (1994), 'Free trade: old and new challenges', *Economic Journal*, **5**(423).

Brown, W. (2000), 'Protecting labour standards in a global economy', in *Proceedings of the 12th IIRA World Congress.*

Brown, D., Deardorff, A.V. and Stern, R.M. (1996), 'International labour standards and trade: a theoretical analysis', in J.N. Bhagwati and R.E. Hudec (eds) *Fair Trade and Harmonization. Prerequisites for Free Trade, Vol. II*, Cambridge, MA: MIT Press.

Burtless, G. (1995), 'International trade and the rise in earnings inequality', *Journal of Economic Literature*, **33**(2).

Crafts, N. and Toniolo, G. (eds) (1996), *Economic Growth in Europe Since 1945*, Cambridge: Centre of Economic Policy Research, Cambridge University Press.

Davis, D.R. (1998a), 'Does European unemployment prop up American wages? National labour markets and global trade', *American Economic Review*, **88**(3), 478–94.

Davis, D.R. (1998b), 'Technology, unemployment and relative wages in the global economy', *European Economic Review*, **42**(9), 1613–33.

Economist, The (2000), 'Economic indicators. Output, demand and jobs', 17–23 June.

Eichengreen, B. (1996), 'Institutions and economic growth: Europe after World War II', in N. Crafts and G. Toniolo (eds) *Economic Growth in Europe Since 1945*, Cambridge: Centre of Economic Policy Research and Cambridge University Press.

Economic Policy Institute (EPI) (1999), Online Data Series, Washington DC.

Flanagan, R.J. (1999), 'Macroeconomic performance and collective bargaining: an international perspective', *Journal of Economic Literature*, **XXXVII**(3).

Freeman, R.B. (1995), 'Are your wages set in Beijing?', *The Journal of Economic Perspectives*, **9**(3).

Ghose, Ajit (2000), 'Trade liberalization and manufacturing employment', Employment Paper No. 2000/3, Geneva: ILO.

Glyn, A., Hughes, A., Lipietz, A. and Singh, A. (1990), 'The rise and fall of the Golden Age', in S. Marglin and J. Schor (eds) *The Golden Age of Capitalism*, Oxford: Clarendon Press.

Gottschalk, P. and Smeeding, T. (1997), 'Cross-national comparisons of earnings and income inequality', *Journal of Economic Literature*, **35**(2), 633–87.

Grootaert, C. (1998), 'Child labour in Côte d'Ivoire: incidence and determinants', in C. Grootaert and H. Patrinos (eds) *The Policy Analysis of Child Labour: A Comparative Study*, mimeo, Washington DC: World Bank.

Hobsbawm, E.J. (1964), *Labouring Man. Studies in the History of Labour*, London: Weidenfeld and Nicolson.

Howes, C. and Singh, A. (2000), *Competitiveness Matters: Industry and Economic Performance in the U.S.*, Ann Arbor: University of Michigan Press.

ICFTU (International Confederation of Free Trade Unions) (1996), *Behind the Wire. Anti-Union Repression in the Export Processing Zones*, Brussels: ICFTU.

ICFTU (1999), *Building Worker's Human Rights into the Global Trading System*, Brussels: ICFTU.

ILO (2000a), *Your Voice at Work*, Geneva: ILO.

ILO (2000b), *Review of Annual Reports under the Follow-up to the ILO Declaration on Fundamental Principles and Rights at Work*, Geneva: ILO.

Izurieta, A. and Singh, A. (2010), 'Does fast growth in India and China help or harm US workers?', *Journal of Human Development and Capabilities*, **11**(1) February.

Kochan, T. (2000), 'A manifesto for America's workers', *Financial Times*, 28 August.

Krugman, P. (2000), 'Technology, trade and factor prices', *Journal of International Economics*, **50**(1), February.

Krugman, P. and Lawrence, R.Z. (1994), 'Trade, jobs and wages', *Scientific American*, **270**(4), 44–56.

Leamer, E.E. (2000), 'What's the use of factor content?', *Journal of International Economics*, **50**(1), 17–49.

Lee, J.S. and Park, Y. (1995), 'Employment, labour standards and economic development in Taiwan and Korea', *Review of Labour Economics and Industrial Relations*, Special Issue.

McCall, L. (2000), 'Increasing inequality in United States. Trends, problems, and prospects', *Economic and Political Weekly*, 27 May, 21–3.

Michie, J. (2003), *The Handbook of Globalisation*, 1st edn, Cheltenham, UK and Northampton, MA, USA: Edward Elgar.

Milbank, D. (1993), 'Unions lose ground as membership power declines across Europe', *The Wall Street Journal*, 8 December quoting OECD data.

Morris, W. (1994), 'Social clause in a trade pact to protect workers is not protectionist', *Financial Times*, 31 March.

Piore, M.J. (1990), 'Labor standards and business strategies', in *Labor Standards and Development in the Global Economy*, Washington DC: US Department of Labor.

Richardson, J. (1995), 'Income inequality and trade: How to think, what to conclude', *Journal of Economic Perspectives*, **9**(3), 33–55.

Rowthorn, R. and Ramaswamy, R. (1997), 'Growth, trade and deindustrialization', IMF Working Paper No. WP/97/42, Washington DC: IMF.

Singh, A. (1989), 'Third World competition and de-industrialization in advanced countries', *Cambridge Journal of Economics*, **13**(1), 103–20.

Singh, A. (1990), 'Southern competition, labour standards and industrial development in the North and the South', in S. Herzenberg and J.F. Perez-Lopez (eds) *Labour Standards and Development in the Global Economy*, Washington DC: US Department of Labour, pp. 1–16.

Singh, A. (1994), 'Industrial policy in Europe and industrial developments in the Third World', in F. Bianchi, K. Cowling and R. Sugden (eds) *Europe's Economic Challenge*, London: Routledge.

Singh, A. (1995a), 'Institutional requirements for full employment in advanced economies', *International Labour Review*, **134**(4/5), 471–96.

Singh, A. (1995b), 'The causes of fast economic growth in East Asia', in *UNCTAD Review*, Geneva: United Nations.

Singh, A. (2000), 'Global economic trends and social development', Occasional Paper No. 9, Geneva: UNRISD.

Singh, A. and Dhumale, R. (2000), 'Globalization, technology, institutions and income inequality: a critical analysis', WIDER Working Papers No. 201, December.

Singh, A. and Zammit, A. (1995), 'Unemployment, North and South', in J. Michie and J. Grieve Smith (eds) *Managing the Global Economy*, Oxford: Oxford University Press, pp. 11–134.

Singh, A. and Zammit A. (2000), *The Global Labour Standards Controversy. Critical Issues for Developing Countries*, Geneva: South Centre.

Singh, A. and Zammit, A. (2010), 'The global economic and financial crisis: which way forward?', paper presented at the European Corporate Governance Network Meeting, Brussels, May.
Slaughter, M.J. (1998), 'International trade and labour market outcomes: results, questions, and policy options', *The Economic Journal*, **108**(450).
Slaughter, M.J. and Swagel, P. (1997), 'Does globalization lower wages and export jobs?', *Economic Issues*, **11**, Washington DC: International Monetary Fund.
Solow, R. (2009), 'How to understand the disaster', *The New York Review of Books*, 14 May.
Somavia, J. (2000), 'Address by Juan Somavia, Secretary-General of the International Labour Conference, 88th Session', 5 June 2000, Geneva: ILO.
South Centre (1998a), *The WTO Multilateral Trade Agenda and the South*, Geneva: South Centre.
South Centre (1998b), *Towards an Economic Platform for the South*, Geneva: South Centre.
Stiglitz, J. (2000), 'Democratic development as the fruits of labour', Keynote Address at the Industrial Relations Research Association Meetings in Boston, 25 January.
Thompson, E.P. (1963), *The Making of the English Working Class*, London: Victor Gollancz.
Tokman, V.E. (1997), 'Jobs and solidarity: challenges for post-adjustment in Latin America', in Louis Emmerij (ed.) *Economic and Social Development into the Next Century*, Washington DC: Inter-American Development Bank, Johns Hopkins University Press.
UNCTAD (1995), *Trade and Development Report*, Geneva: United Nations.
UNDP (UN Development Programme) (2000), *The Human Development Report, 2000*, New York and Oxford: Oxford University Press.
US Council of Economic Advisors (1998), *1997 Economic Report of the President*, Washington DC: US Government Printing Office.
Wade, R. (1990), *Governing the Market*, Princeton, NJ: Princeton University Press.
WCL (1997), 'Stock-taking of the Conference of Amsterdam on Child Labour', *Labor,* May 1997-1, 6–7.
WINDS (1996), 'Slavery reinstituted in America', available at http://www.apfn.org/thewinds/1996/12/modern_slavery.html; accessed 11 October 2010.
Wood, A. (1994), *North–South Trade, Employment and Inequality: Changing Fortunes in a Skill-Driven World*, Oxford: Oxford University Press.
Wood, A. (1995), 'How trade hurt unskilled workers', *Journal of Economic Perspectives*, **9**(3), 57–80.
World Bank (1995), *World Development Report 1995: Workers in an Integrating World*, Oxford: Oxford University Press.
Zammit, Ann (2010), 'Value chains and decent work for women. What is to be done?', Working Paper No. 88, Geneva: Policy Integration Department, International Labour Organization.

13 Global labor standards: their impact and implementation

James Heintz

Estimates suggest that up to a fifth of all working individuals in developing countries live in households whose income per person falls below one dollar a day (Kaspos, 2004). The widespread incidence of poverty among working people is indicative of the general prevalence of indecent working conditions. Having a job is simply not enough – the quality of employment matters. Instituting a coordinated system of global labor standards represents one approach to creating a minimum floor of job quality. The following chapter takes a close look at the debates surrounding global labor standards. In particular, it summarizes the key arguments in support of global labor standards, evaluates the threat of negative consequences that could spring from such regulations and discusses current developments in implementation strategies.

The labor standards debate: what are the issues?

One of the most prevalent arguments as to why global labor standards are necessary is that they prevent a 'race to the bottom'. That is, upward harmonization of standards stops competitive pressures from reducing labor protections to their lowest common denominator. According to this logic, global integration creates a situation in which the deterioration of basic standards is rewarded by increased competitiveness and profitability. In the absence of international cooperation, individual countries cannot raise labor standards without jeopardizing their competitive advantage. The scenario represents the typical prisoner's dilemma problem – countries will adopt the same low standards, even if social welfare falls below its potential maximum. Because of this, competitive advantages derived from weak labor standards are frequently seen as 'unfair' competition, since international cooperation in the form of global standards could produce a better outcome (Sengenberger, 1994).

Others have extended this analysis, arguing that individuals and their labor are not commodities to be exchanged on unregulated markets.[1] The notion that labor should not be subjected to the unfettered machinations of a liberal market economy was given theoretical life by the Austrian economic thinker, Karl Polanyi. Polanyi argued that subjecting labor to unregulated market forces would generate external social costs – including health problems, a deterioration of family and community structures, an erosion of craft standards and a general degradation of many aspects of public and private life. According to Polanyi (1944, 1957), labor markets should be embedded in the larger society and must be governed by rules, norms and ethical standards that make allowance for the hidden costs of marketization.

Some proponents of labor standards have justified them in terms of their instrumental value in advancing economic efficiency (Buchele and Christensen 1995; Palley et al., 1999). According to this line of reasoning, labor standards support better labor relations, cooperation on the job and sharing of information, factors that would enhance productivity. In addition, better standards, including higher wages, could pay for themselves through efficiency wage effects that increase effort on the job (Shapiro and Stiglitz 1984; Levine 1992; Huang et al. 1998; Goldstein et al., 2000).

However, there is a theoretical problem with this argument: if higher standards are profitable, then why do employers fail to adopt them? One answer is that multiple equilibria exist and employers fall into low-wage, low-productivity traps. A policy intervention is necessary to move the labor market onto the high road of greater efficiency. Alternatively, substandard employment might arise from a focus on short-term gains while ignoring long-term dynamic efficiencies. For example, the use of child labor could maximize short-term profits despite the low productivity of the very young. However, keeping children out of school could be inefficient in the long run since it means forgoing the future benefits of a larger accumulation of human capital and higher productivity (Basu, 1999).

Labor standards could also produce faster growth due to their macroeconomic impact. Standards that increase labor's bargaining power will redistribute income towards workers. Higher labor incomes could raise global demand and yield faster growth (Marshall, 1994). Others have reversed the logic and argued that more expansionary macroeconomic policies will produce an environment conducive to improving international labor standards (Amsden, 1994; Singh and Zammit, 2000). In this case, faster growth raises labor standards, not vice versa.

The arguments in favor of a system of global standards must be evaluated against warnings as to the potential dangers. In general, most arguments against global labor standards claim they will trigger unintended consequences that will end up hurting the very people the policies aim to help. For example, eliminating child labor could encourage child prostitution. Raising wages could cost jobs. Stricter enforcement could cause firms to relocate. In short, global labor standards create market distortions that reduce economic well-being due to an inefficient allocation of resources.

The most common variant of this theme is the argument that global standards compromise the competitive position of those developing countries with an abundance of low-skill, low-wage labor (Bhagwati, 1995; Corden and Vousden,

2001). This loss of competitive advantage means fewer jobs and scarcer economic opportunities for poor workers with few skills. On the flip side, such protections shield workers in more affluent economies from global competition. In effect, there is a redistribution of wage income from developing to developed economies. Because of this, organizations advocating for better labor standards on a global scale have been accused of pushing an agenda of disguised protectionism (Bhagwati, 2002, pp. 47–90). Others have emphasized the relative importance of job opportunities over job quality for poor families in developing countries (Krugman, 1998; Kristof, 2002). They argue that, in the stark reality of the global economy, poverty-level wages and substandard employment represent an improvement over the next-best options in labor-surplus economies.

Still other analysts advance the position that, with complete markets, no externalities, and costlessly enforceable contracts, global labor standards will create a dead-weight welfare loss (Brown et al., 1996). However, this efficiency argument depends on perfect markets being able to seamlessly map shifts in relative factor prices onto the output prices of tradable goods and services in order to achieve Pareto optimal outcomes. As Tokman (2006) points out, there are many reasons why economic outcomes may deviate from the predictions of trade theory. Markets are rarely perfect and cross-border exchanges are subject to transactions costs. Standard trade theory relies on the existence of competitive markets, but the participants in cross-border transactions frequently have varying degrees of market power. If a firm has a sufficient degree of market power relative to its work force, firms may be able to secure a competitive advantage by using their market power to worsen working conditions, a kind of 'social dumping' (Granger and Siroën, 2006).

The idea that higher labor incomes support growth at the macroeconomic level has also been questioned. In the case of a small open economy, it is not always clear that a redistribution of income towards labor creates higher levels of aggregate demand (Bowles and Boyer, 1995). Wage income can be leaky in an economy with a strong propensity to import. Furthermore, insofar as investment responds positively to profitability, then standards that raise labor costs could have a dampening effect on investment, aggregate demand and ultimately growth. Of course, if standards were enforced internationally, then *global* aggregate demand would rise as standards improve. However, small, open economies that compete for external sources of aggregate demand might still be characterized as profit-led, since higher unit labor costs undermine their ability to sell on global markets (Amsden, 1997).

Finally, there are non-economic considerations that should be taken into account – in particular, the political process by which the standards are developed. If the movement for global standards is primarily an outcome of concerns raised only by advanced industrialized economies, then the justification for these standards to be foisted upon developing nations becomes questionable, particularly if such standards are not considered to be part of the body of commonly accepted international law. Under these conditions, charges of 'aggressive unilateralism' and 'disguised protectionism' carry additional weight (Alston, 1996). Similar concerns surface in proposals that delegate responsibility for labor standards to global governance institutions (e.g., the World Bank or the World Trade Organization) in which the balance of power tilts in favor of the world's rich countries.

Gender dynamics and informalization

With the new international division of labor, women frequently account for the majority of the labor in low-income sectors producing manufactured exports. Lower wages for women have supported demand for their labor in highly mobile, labor-intensive industries. These developments represent a more general trend towards increasing labor force participation by women and declining average job quality, which has been termed 'global feminization' (Standing, 1989). In addition, since labor markets around the globe remain segregated by gender, the growth in women's share of low-wage employment results from an expansion of jobs typically dominated by women, not simply an erosion of the quality of existing jobs as women enter the labor force (Elson, 1996). At first blush, the existence of a high proportion of women working in global manufacturing industries might imply that women would be the primary beneficiaries of improvements in labor standards. Such a cursory analysis, however, ignores the position women frequently occupy in both the household and in the paid labor market.

While the employment of women keeps labor costs low and enhances a firm's profitability, low-wage jobs also provide economic opportunities for women outside of the household and, in turn, can grant them a greater degree of choice in their lives (Kabeer, 2000). This enhanced freedom gives women the latitude to delay marriage and childbearing, gain labor market experience, protect their economic options outside of the household and increase their long-run earnings potential (Lim, 1983). Furthermore, access to money income improves women's bargaining position at home, thereby affecting gender dynamics and strengthening women's influence over the distribution of household resources (Joekes, 1987; Roldan, 1988; Sen, 1990; Heintz, 2006a). Insofar as better standards reduce employment, these job losses disproportionately affect women, directly through a loss of wage income, but also indirectly by exacerbating other gender-specific inequalities. Even if the number of jobs remains unchanged, better employment conditions can impact women's access to jobs. For example, there is evidence that as job quality improves, women's access to these opportunities declines relative to men's (Elson, 1996).

However, others have questioned the optimistic claim that low-wage employment provides an impetus for improvements in gender equality. Since women are often employed in globally mobile industries, an expansion of employment in these sectors may not raise women's bargaining power relative to men working in less footloose sectors, especially during periods of economic liberalization (Seguino, 2000). Along similar lines, a recent survey of women working in the maquiladoras of Tijuana found that the expansion of jobs had little impact on their ability to demand higher wages. The workers' income was not significantly higher than what they could earn elsewhere, although maquila earnings were more stable (Fussell, 2000). Survey work in Pakistan suggests that the availability of subcontracted work does not improve the autonomy of women workers when such work reinforces their marginal position in the economy. Furthermore, participation in the subcontracted labor market in Pakistan is often the result of the 'push' of poverty, rather than the 'pull' of securing an independent income (Khattak, 2002).

The question of global labor standards, worker welfare and gender dynamics becomes more complex when we consider the growing informalization of the low-wage labor market. Informalization refers to the process by which economic activities increasingly move into unregulated spheres. Informalization manifests itself in numerous ways: a growth of the informal economy relative to the formal sector; an expansion of temporary, contingent and marginal jobs; an increase in the incidence of outwork (e.g., home-based production); and a lack of adequate enforcement for existing regulations (Chen et al., 2005). In this respect, informalization reflects the erosion of job quality and the expansion of flexible employment practices that has become a defining feature of the current patterns of global integration (Standing, 1999).

Recent research has documented a world-wide resurgence of informalization beginning in the 1970s and continuing into the 1980s and 1990s (Portes et al., 1989; Charmes, 2000; Benería, 2001; ILO, 2002). The fact that many countries have seen informal employment expand during periods of relatively stable growth supports the argument that structural changes in the global economy are responsible for growing informalization. This stands in contrast to earlier counter-cyclical explanations that saw a rise in informal employment as being linked to poor economic performance in the formal sector.

Informalization impacts labor standards through two channels. By definition, informalization increases the share of workers who are not covered by existing regulations. More indirectly, an expansion of the informal sector can place downward pressure on standards in formal employment by weakening the bargaining power of formal sector workers. Since the supply price of labor for formal sector occupations depends, in part, on the income that could be earned elsewhere, patterns of informalization that reduce the average quality of economic alternatives will increase the vulnerability of employment conditions in many entry-level, formal sector jobs.

In most countries, women account for the majority of informal sector workers (Benería, 2001; Chen et al., 2005). Therefore, the process of informalization parallels the general expansion of low-wage employment for women. In addition, many informal sector workers face constraints that bar their participation in the formal labor market. For example, women engaged in childcare and other forms of unpaid household labor might be unable to participate in formal sector labor markets if the available jobs conflicted with patriarchal norms, the ability to perform unpaid work, or the quality of caring labor at home.[2] In such cases, informal employment offers greater flexibility. Furthermore, there is some evidence that more austere macroeconomic policies, such as those associated with structural adjustment programs, have squeezed household resources and reduced the number of formal sector jobs. These conditions create an incentive for greater participation in informal productive activities in order to maintain household incomes (Benería, 1991; Vandemoortele, 1991; ILO, 2002).

Informal employment poses important challenges for enforcing global labor standards. The unregulated nature of informal production reduces labor costs and gives the informal economy a competitive edge over formal employment arrangements. Raising standards in the formal sector, therefore, could displace economic activity into the informal sector. Indeed, the recent growth of the informal sector calls into question the effectiveness of a purely legislative approach towards improving employment conditions since existing labor protections are not enforced in the informal sector. A more effective strategy would improve employment conditions in the formal and informal sectors simultaneously. This would require a partial 'formalization' of informal sector activity.

Damned if you do: evaluating the risk of unintended consequences

Perhaps the strongest caution against global labor standards is the danger of job loss, particularly in developing countries with an abundance of low-wage labor and few alternative opportunities. This concern about jobs is not trivial. The International Labour Organization estimates that 212 million people were unemployed in 2009 (ILO, 2010, p. 9). The global recession triggered by the financial crisis that emerged in the second half of 2008 has adversely affected worldwide unemployment. Some may question a focus on labor standards as a luxury we cannot afford in the context of widespread joblessness.

Labor standards may reduce employment only when they raise the cost of labor. Obviously, new standards will have no impact on employment if current practices already fulfill all the regulatory stipulations. Nevertheless, improvements in standards are justified precisely because existing conditions generally fall below a perceived threshold of decency. Therefore, if global labor standards are designed to have a broad social impact, they will likely raise labor costs. Indeed, empirical studies have shown a correlation between better labor standards and higher labor costs (Rodrik, 1996). However, even when standards raise the cost of labor, these higher costs do not automatically translate into a substantial loss of jobs. The question of the connection between labor costs and jobs remains an empirical one.

In evaluating the possibility that better standards mean fewer jobs, we begin with a more focused question: have low-wage countries experienced faster rates of employment growth in labor-intensive manufacturing than high-wage countries? In answering this question, it is simplest to restrict attention to one sector: the manufacture of clothing and wearing apparel. Why clothing? First, clothing is a highly globalized, labor-intensive industry. Labor costs make up a large fraction of production costs and competitive pressures are fierce. Second, debates over global labor practices often center on clothing firms. For these reasons, clothing is a particularly relevant industry for this discussion.

Figure 13.1 plots the initial level of apparel wages, expressed in US dollars, against subsequent employment growth, expressed as the average annual growth rate, for 62 countries for which comparable data are available.[3] The initial wage level is measured as a three-year average, from 1980 to 1982, in order to smooth the distortions that could be introduced by exchange rate fluctuations in any given year. Employment growth reflects the 25-year period, 1982 to 2006.[4] The figure shows a clear negative relationship between initial wage levels and sub-

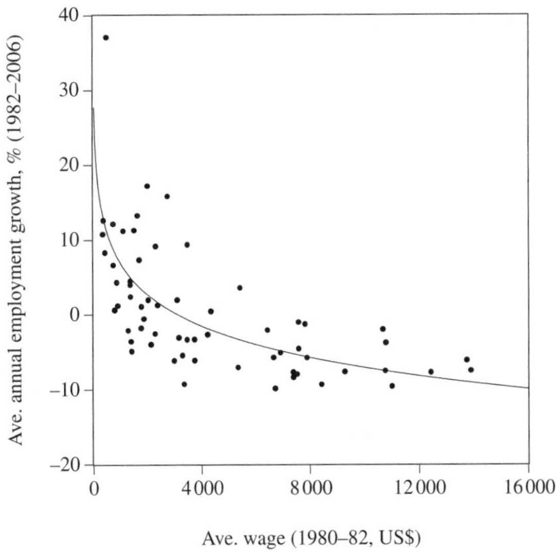

Source: Data from UNIDO Industrial Statistics Database

Figure 13.1 Initial wage levels against subsequent employment growth for clothing manufacture

sequent employment growth. The relationship is non-linear with the lowest wage countries having significantly faster rates of employment growth.[5]

The pattern of global clothing production appears to match the predictions of international trade theorists: countries with an abundance of low-wage labor have seen employment in their clothing sectors expand as markets have become more integrated. However, the relationships between initial wage rates and subsequent employment growth show a great deal of variation – countries with nearly identical initial wages demonstrate very different patterns of employment growth. More importantly, the relationships in Figure 13.1 do not tell us whether reasonable improvements in wages and working conditions in a particular country will always lead to job losses. For example, what would happen to employment if wages (and other components of labor costs) were to gradually improve in a low-wage country like Bangladesh?

Research into the impact that changes in real wages have on employment in the global apparel industry found no definitive relationship when other factors change along with wages (Pollin et al., 2004). If other factors – such as prices, productivity, or consumer demand – adjust appropriately when wages increase, space can be created to accommodate better standards without generating welfare-reducing job losses. An ILO (2000a, p. 43) study on the global garment and textile industries reaches similar conclusions: 'Labor costs remain an important cost factor, particularly in labor-intensive production such as footwear and clothing. Nevertheless … they are no longer a decisive factor in determining competitiveness on world markets.' Similarly, research into the impact of changes in the minimum wage on poverty rates in developing countries has shown that higher minimum wages reduce poverty, although the impact may not extend to very poor households that do not participate in the paid labor force (Lustig and McLeod, 1997; Saget, 2001). This evidence does not suggest that improvements in labor standards have no impact on employment, but it casts doubt on the argument that better standards leave workers worse off on average.

To sum up: the impact of labor costs on employment cannot simply be dismissed as unimportant or trivial. However, empirical research suggests that a carefully designed system for implementing global labor standards that allows for other adjustments when labor costs increase can reduce (or possibly eliminate) the risk of job loss and can be welfare-enhancing for those workers the policy aims to help.

Strategies for implementation: a brief history

Despite the potential a system of labor standards possesses for raising the well-being of wage earners around the world, designing and implementing an appropriate set of institutions to realize this goal remains a significant challenge. A review of the past strategies put forward by social reformers and the consequent institutional changes that have occurred helps set the stage for a discussion of current efforts to realize a coordinated approach to labor standards.

Early support for international labor standards first emerged in the nineteenth century. Advocates included Robert Owen, the Scottish industrialist and utopian thinker; Charles Hindley, a British Member of Parliament from 1835 to 1857; and Daniel Legrand, a prominent manufacturer from Alsace. As early as 1818, Owen was suggesting that the governments of continental Europe should implement a system of labor standards to improve conditions among Europe's working classes (Lorenz, 2001, p. 41). Foreshadowing today's 'race to the bottom' arguments, Hindley argued that international standards would prevent competitive pressures from eroding working conditions in Britain – in particular, lengthening the working day (Follows, 1951). In a similar vein, Legrand promoted international labor legislation for Europe in the mid-nineteenth century (ibid.). Legrand was strongly influenced by the Christian socialist tradition, which advocated reforming capitalism to produce humane social outcomes while condemning as heresies the demands of more radical socialist movements (Gide and Rist, 1948, pp. 514–44; Lorenz, 2001, pp. 41–4).

The work of these early proponents of international labor standards paved the way for the establishment of the International Labour Organization (ILO) in 1919 at the Versailles Peace Conference. After the turmoil of World War I, the creation of the ILO was seen as an important initiative to maintain peace, social stability and shared prosperity in the world.[6] In 1946, the ILO became the first specialized agency of the United Nations (UN) and represents the only institution created by the Treaty of Versailles to survive today. It is also the only UN agency in which non-government organizations play a large institutionalized role in formulating policy.

The ILO operates by creating conventions that address a range of labor market policies through a process of stakeholder negotiations (in general, business, labor and government). The ILO then attempts to persuade governments to ratify the conventions, with the understanding that ratification implies that domestic legislation will be adjusted, when necessary, to comply with the conventions. Of all the conventions developed by the ILO, eight are deemed 'core conventions' covering four key areas of basic human rights: freedom of association and collective bargaining, the abolition of forced labor, the elimination of child labor and non-discrimination.

While the ILO has had a significant impact on improving labor standards around the world, its approach has limitations. Ratification of an ILO convention does not guarantee enforcement of the standards in question. In many cases, the capacity to enforce labor laws is lacking and widespread abuses are common. In addition, membership in the ILO is not conditional on ratification of the core conventions. For example, the United States has ratified only two and China only four of the eight core conventions. Finally, with the growth of multinational production systems, a strategy aimed at influencing national policy on a case-by-case basis could be misdirected. Greater capital mobility and increased subcontracting mean that individual regulatory regimes are under pressure to relax controls or risk losing job-creating investments.

In reaction to the growing internationalization of economic activity, influential global organizations began to develop corporate codes of conduct in an effort to regulate the actions of multinationals. The UN took the lead and, in 1974, established the Centre on Transnational Corporations (UNCTC), which began developing a comprehensive code of conduct for multinational corporations covering many aspects of corporate behavior, including labor practices (United Nations, 1986). The OECD launched its own Declaration on International Investment and Multinational Enterprises in 1976, which also set up a framework for governing corporate actions (OECD, 2000). In 1977, the ILO followed suit, with its Tripartite Declaration of Principles Concerning Multinational Enterprises and Social Policy, which focused more directly on labor issues (ILO, 2000b).

These codes attempted to develop a universal set of standards that were to be sensitive to a country's level of development; they were meant to apply to all multinationals; and they were developed by prominent international organizations. However, not one has been implemented in a meaningful way. Despite several drafts, the UN code was never ratified and the Centre on Transnational Corporations disappeared completely in 1993, having been incorporated into the United Nations Conference on Trade and Development, or UNCTAD (Jenkins, 2001). While the OECD and ILO codes achieved a higher level of consensus, there was no comprehensive plan for implementation, monitoring, or enforcement. Compliance was voluntary, but the codes contained few, if any, incentives to encourage firms to change their practices.

Moreover, in the 1980s the global policy climate began to shift. Instead of questioning the behavior of multinationals, many developing nations emphasized the need to attract a growing share of foreign investment. In this context of a new neoliberal, market-oriented ideology, the ILO has had trouble expanding its base of national governments that have ratified its conventions, let alone influencing the behavior of multinationals (Pearson and Seyfang, 2001). The ultimate outcome was that these early efforts to regulate global corporate behavior failed to deliver (Tsogas, 2001, pp. 61–2).

As these first codes of conduct faded into obscurity, there was little to replace them until the 1990s. However, growing public awareness over sweatshop practices and human rights violations among the suppliers to brand-name manufacturers prompted the development of a new type of corporate code of conduct. These new codes were created by the multinationals themselves in response to the increasingly public accusations of profit-hungry corporations turning a blind eye to labor abuses. In 1991, Levi-Strauss & Co. became the first brand-name corporation in this new wave of social responsibility to adopt a code of conduct. Many other US and European companies followed suit. Literally hundreds of different codes currently exist. Because these codes were developed with little coordination, there is an enormous amount of variation from one code to the next (Kolk et al., 1999).

These corporate codes of conduct have numerous shortcomings. First, they suffer from the 'fox in the chicken coop' problem – corporations have an incentive to minimize the damage of a negative report by limiting the number of monitored suppliers or by restricting what information is made public. Second, they frequently pay scant attention to issues of implementation. Developing a code of conduct for public relations purposes receives much more attention than insuring that the standards are actually implemented. Third, because of the variation in the content of the codes, consumers find it difficult to determine what compliance with a code of conduct really means. For the producers of the goods, the existence of multiple codes increases the difficulty of compliance. Many subcontractors accept jobs from different multinationals, each with a different code of conduct (Kemp, 2001). Often producers opt for the lowest common denominator and follow the codes that are easiest to implement.

In recent years, an alternative approach to implementing global labor standards links labor practices to the rules governing international trade. The idea of a 'social clause' would allow trade sanctions to be directed at countries in which substandard labor practices exist (Caire, 1994). Theoretically, a social clause would prevent 'social dumping' – for example, securing a competitive advantage from labor abuses or lax environmental protections. While the social clause was first framed within the context of the General Agreement on Tariffs and Trade (GATT), today's debate focuses on the World Trade Organization (WTO), GATT's successor. Some have argued that the social clause should be a joint project of the ILO and the WTO (Ehrenberg, 1996).

The idea of a social clause has frequently been criticized for its potential to be used as a tool for disguised protectionism. Since it imposes trade sanctions on the offending country, the penalties could harm export workers in developing countries, making them worse off than they would have been without a social clause. Others have questioned whether the WTO is the appropriate institution for addressing labor standards. In particular, some have argued that introducing a social clause into the WTO would lead to inefficient negotiations, since it requires the simultaneous determination of domestic and international policies (Brown, 2001). In addition, the social clause sanctions a particular state for abuses found in a transnational production chain. It is unclear whether punishments directed at national governments are always the most appropriate measures for enforcing labor standards in the context of global production.

In terms of the binding provisions of trade agreements, there are two broad approaches to enforcement: those that employ negative incentives (fines or sanctions) and those that use positive incentives (rewards for progress in achieving labor standards). This creates a fundamental challenge associated with the design of incentives in trade agreements to enforce labor standards. Trade agreements, by their nature, represent agreements between sovereign states. However, violations of labor standards often happen at the level of the firm (Tokman, 2006). Therefore, incentives to support labor standards in trade agreements may not always be well targeted, if the incidence of the penalties, for example, falls on the state and not on the firms in which the violations are occurring.

Fines for violations represent one negative incentive that has been incorporated into US bilateral trade agreements that contain provisions for labor (Polaski and Vyborny, 2006). Imposing fines on countries may represent a poorly targeted enforcement mechanism, for the reasons noted above: the incidence of the fines falls on the government and not the firm in which the violations take place. Alternatively, negative incentives may take the form of a withdrawal of benefits inferred under the trade agreement. The withdrawal of trade benefits can be better targeted than the imposition of fines, since the offending firms have a stake in maintaining market access (ibid.). However, a reduction in market access will also punish firms that have not violated labor standards.

Commodity chains and global standards

The concept of a global commodity chain has been used to analyze the relationships that exist in a globalized production system. The global commodity chain refers to the way in which the production, distribution and sales of goods are organized across national borders. Global commodity chain analysis has been developed in the work of Gary Gereffi (1994) and others as a means of understanding the organization and influence of different players in global production systems. For example, a commodity chain for the production of a pair of sports shoes includes the subcontractor that actually assembles the shoes, the intermediary (or 'jobber') that coordinates production among a network of subcontractors, the brand-name multinational that designs the shoe and builds the brand image, and the retailer that ultimately sells the shoe to the consumer.

The labor-intensive production of many consumer goods (e.g., clothing, electronics, or footwear) is often characterized by buyer-driven commodity chains in which large retailers or brand-name corporations set up and influence a decentralized system of production and distribution.[7] Market power differs dramatically among the different players along the chain. The actual production is subcontracted out to small firms that generally face extremely competitive conditions (Gereffi, 1994; Bonacich and Appelbaum, 2000). Therefore, subcontractors cannot easily raise the price of their output without risking a loss of business. On the other hand, retailers and brand-name multinationals enjoy some degree of market power that they can use to keep prices low for the goods they purchase or to earn rents through the development of monopolistic brand identities (Heintz, 2006b).

Since subcontractors face intense competition, focusing adjustment strategies on these firms is likely either to fail completely or to produce the type of unintended consequences previously discussed. However, brand-name manufacturers and large retailers could use their market power to implement improvements in labor standards at the level of production by compensating subcontractors for the cost increases. For example, they could raise retail prices modestly and pass these revenues back to finance the improvements in employment conditions. Unintended job losses would be avoided since subcontractors who complied with the standards would receive the resources necessary to implement the improvements.

A study of the possibility of financing workplace improvements through such a scheme found that a 2–6 percent increase in the final retail price could finance a 100 percent increase in production worker wages for a variety of different garments (Pollin et al., 2004). The magnitude of this price increase falls well below the amount that consumers have said they would be willing to pay to insure that their clothes are not produced under sweatshop conditions (see, for example, Elliot and Freeman, 2000). Therefore, by making adjustments in the upper segments of a global commodity chain, resources can be generated for financing substantial changes in working conditions at the point of production. Furthermore, since profits of large retailers and brand-name producers depend on the careful cultivation of their brand images and corporate reputations, an association with substandard labor practices could damage profitability. Similarly, a good reputation with respect to labor standards would enhance a company's competitive position.

Standardized codes of conduct for multinational commodity chains

In a departure from other approaches to global labor standards, there has been a movement towards establishing a standardized code of conduct, with independent monitoring and enforcement, to implement labor standards across entire commodity chains. Examples of organizations embracing this approach include the Fair Labor Association (US), the Ethical Trading Initiative (UK), the Clean Clothes Campaign (Europe) and Social Accountability International (US). With these approaches, multinational firms insure that labor practices meet a common set of standards across all their suppliers. These standards include issues of health and safety, hours of work, human rights, freedom of association, wages and discrimination. A process of independent verification through factory inspections and visits to production sites – including informal sector producers – insures that the code has been implemented. Firms that meet the basic standards can use this seal of approval in marketing and promotion. Substandard labor practices that are not corrected are publicized with the result that the reputation and brand-image of the company in question suffers.

While these independent monitoring and certification organizations avoid many of the problems associated with corporate codes of conduct, certain constraints remain. Many limit themselves to one particular market or one particular industry. There is no universal code of conduct and substantial variations among the established codes persist. Furthermore, many rely on professional auditors with little or no experience with the countries and communities involved. Finally, participation is voluntary. Therefore, compliance depends to a large extent on the strength of the incentives created.

However, these limitations can be addressed in a number of ways. Borrowing from the earliest codes of conduct, a single enforcement agency to monitor multinational behavior could be housed in a well-established international organization, such as the ILO. Of course, additional resources would need to be channeled to the agency for operational support – through fees paid by member corporations, an expanded budget for the international institution, or a combination of sources. Furthermore, the enforcement agency could establish a network of NGOs, trade unions and informal sector organizations to develop a mechanism of lodging complaints and grievances. A subset of the local non-governmental and labor organizations could also be encouraged to undergo training to serve as external auditors in the certification program. Such an arrangement would take into account relationships across the global commodity chain while providing space for input from more domestic organizations.

Limitations of global labor standards

Regardless of the implementation strategy, the limitations of any scheme along these lines to introduce global labor standards should be explicitly recognized. Most significantly, only a subset of the world's workforce would receive any benefits, since the standards are aimed at workers who produce goods for export. Workers producing non-traded goods and services would not be directly affected by interventions such as a standardized code of conduct or a social clause. In these cases, the ongoing mission of the ILO to encourage states to implement and enforce better domestic standards remains invaluable. Furthermore, adopting expansionary macroeconomic policies could be more strategic for improving the well-being of all workers than a targeted set of labor standards. A coordinated approach involving a range of interventions – both macroeconomic and in terms of international regulation – would also reduce the tensions between better standards and job creation.

Despite the limitations of global labor standards, the potential that such interventions have for improving the working lives of a significant number of people should not be underestimated. Furthermore, the possible impact of such a system extends well beyond the benefits generated by its core policies. The development of an appropriate regulatory scheme for enforcing basic standards of decency could serve as a model for governing multinational economic activities more generally. Because of these possible contributions, striving to create an effective framework for global labor standards represents an important policy goal in this era of the new international division of labor.

Notes

1. The International Labour Organization (ILO) adopted this stance in its 1946 Declaration of Philadelphia. The Declaration was attached as an appendix to the ILO Constitution.
2. For example, Sathar and Kazi (1989) found that Pakistani households in which women worked in more formal factory settings had a higher incidence of child mortality than households in which women were engaged in paid home-base production.
3. Data are taken from the United National Industrial Development Organization (UNIDO), Industrial Statistics Database INDSTATZ ISIC REV. 3, 2009.
4. The final year for which data are available varies from country to country. For this reason, changes in employment are expressed as average annual growth rates.
5. The curved line in Figure 13.1 represents a simple bivariate regression in which the initial wage has been converted to natural logarithms in order to fit the curve to the data.
6. See the 1919 Constitution of the ILO, especially the Preamble, for an eloquent justification for the founding of the organization.
7. Buyer-driven commodity chains can be contrasted with producer-driven commodity chains in which large industrial enterprises set up the system of global production. The relatively capital-intensive manufacture of automobiles, aircraft and electrical machinery can be thought of as examples of producer-driven commodity chains.

References

Alston, Philip (1996), 'Labor rights provisions in U.S. trade law: "aggressive unilateralism"?', in L. Compa and S. Diamond (eds) *Human Rights, Labor Rights, and International Trade*, Philadelphia: University of Pennsylvania Press, pp. 71–95.

Amsden, Alice (1994), 'Macro-sweating policies and labour standards', in W. Sengenberger and D. Campbell (eds) *International Labour Standards and Economic Interdependence*, Geneva: International Institute for Labour Studies (ILO), pp. 185–93.

Amsden, Alice (1997), 'International labor standards: hype or help?', *The Boston Review*, **20**(6).

Basu, Kaushik (1999), 'Child labor: cause, consequence, and cure, with remarks on international labor standards', *Journal of Economic Literature*, **37**(September), 1083–119.

Benería, Lourdes (1991), 'Structural adjustment, the labour market, and the household: the case of Mexico', in G. Standing and V. Tokman (eds) *Towards Social Adjustment: Labour Market Issues in Structural Adjustment*, Geneva: ILO, pp. 161–83.

Benería, Lourdes (2001), 'Shifting the risk: new employment patterns, informalization, and women's work', *International Journal of Politics, Culture, and Society*, **15**(1), 27–53.

Bhagwati, Jagdish (1995), 'Trade liberalization and "fair trade" demands: addressing the environmental and labour standards issues', *World Economy*, **18**(6), 745–59.

Bhagwati, Jagdish (2002), *Free Trade Today*, Princeton, NJ: Princeton University Press.

Bonacich, Edna and Richard Appelbaum (2000), *Behind the Label: Inequality in the Los Angeles Apparel Industry*, Berkeley, CA: University of California Press.

Bowles, Samuel and Robert Boyer (1995), 'Wages, aggregate demand, and employment in an open economy: an empirical investigation', in G. Epstein and H. Gintis (eds) *Macroeconomic Policy After the Conservative Era*, Cambridge, UK: Cambridge University Press, pp. 143–71.

Brown, Drusilla (2001), 'Labor standards: where do they belong on the international trade agenda?', *Journal of Economic Perspectives*, **15**(3), 89–112.

Brown, Drusilla, Alan Deardorff and Robert Stern (1997), 'International labor standards and trade: a theoretical analysis', in J. Bhagwati and R. Hudec (eds) *Fair Trade and Harmonization: Prerequisites for Free Trade?* Vol. 1, Cambridge, MA: The MIT Press, pp. 227–80.

Buchele, Robert and Jens Christensen (1995), 'Productivity, real wages, and workers' rights: a cross-national comparison', *Labour*, **9**(3), 405–22.
Caire, Guy (1994), 'Labour standards and international trade', in W. Sengenberger and D. Campbell (eds) *International Labour Standards and Economic Interdependence*, Geneva: International Institute for Labour Studies (ILO), pp. 297–317.
Charmes, Jacques (2000), 'Informal sector, poverty, and gender: a review of empirical evidence', background paper prepared for the World Development Report 2001, World Bank.
Chen, M., J. Vanek, F. Lund, J. Heintz, R. Jhabvala and C. Bonner (2005), *Progress of the World's Women 2005: Women, Work, and Poverty*, New York: UNIFEM.
Corden, W. Max and Neil Vousden (2001), 'Paved with good intentions: social dumping and raising labour standards in developing countries', in Z. Drabek (ed.) *Globalization Under Threat: The Stability of Trade Policy and Multilateral Agreements*, Cheltenham, UK and Northampton, MA, USA: Edward Elgar, pp. 124–43.
Ehrenberg, Daniel (1996), 'From intention to action: an ILO-GATT/WTO enforcement regime for international labor rights', in L. Compa and S. Diamond (eds) *Human Rights, Labor Rights, and International Trade*, Philadelphia: University of Pennsylvania Press, pp. 163–80.
Elliott, Kimberly and Richard Freeman (2000), 'White hats or Don Quixotes? Human rights vigilantes in the global economy', National Bureau of Economic Research Conference on Emerging Labor Market Institutions, August.
Elson, Diane (1996), 'Appraising recent developments in the world market for nimble fingers', in A. Chhachhi and R. Pittin (eds) *Confronting State, Capital, and Patriarchy: Women Organizing in the Process of Industrialization*, New York: St. Martin's Press, pp. 35–55.
Follows, John W. (1951), *Antecedents of the International Labour Organization*, Oxford: Clarendon Press.
Fussell, Elisabeth (2000), 'Making labor flexible: the recomposition of Tijuana's maquiladora female labor force', *Feminist Economics*, **6**(3), 59–80.
Gereffi, Gary (1994), 'The organization of buyer-driven global commodity chains: how U.S. retailers shape overseas production networks', in G. Gereffi and M. Korzeniewicz (eds) *Commodity Chains and Global Capitalism*, Westport, CT: Greenwood Press, pp. 95–122.
Gide, Charles and Charles Rist (1948), *A History of Economic Doctrines From the Time of the Physiocrats to the Present Day*, 2nd edn, trans. R. Richards, Boston: D.C. Heath and Co.
Goldstein, Arthur, Jonathan Veum and William Darity (2000), 'Working hard for the money? Efficiency wages and worker effort', *Journal of Economic Psychology*, **21**(4), 351–85.
Granger, Clotilde and Jean-Marc Siroën. (2006), 'Core labour standards in trade agreements: from multilateralism to bilateralism', *Journal of World Trade*, **40**(5), 813–36.
Heintz, James (2006a), 'Globalization, economic policy, and employment: poverty and gender implications', Employment Strategy Papers, No. 2006/3, Employment Strategy Department, Geneva: ILO.
Heintz, James (2006b), 'Low-wage manufacturing and global commodity chains: a model in the unequal exchange tradition', *Cambridge Journal of Economics*, **30**(4), 507–20.
Huang, Tzu-Ling, Arne Hallam, Peter Orazem and Elizabeth Paterno (1998), 'Empirical tests of efficiency wage models', *Economica*, **64**, 125–43.
ILO (2000a), *Labour Practices in the Footwear, Leather, Textile, and Clothing Industries*, Geneva: International Labour Organization.
ILO (2000b), 'Tripartite Declaration of Principles Concerning Multinational Enterprises and Social Policy', Document: OB Vol. LXXXIII, 2000, Series A, No. 3.
ILO (2002), *Decent Work and the Informal Economy*, Report VI presented at the 90th session of the International Labour Conference, Geneva: ILO.
ILO (2010), *Global Employment Trends January 2010*, Geneva: ILO.
Jenkins, Rhys (2001), 'Corporate codes of conduct: self-regulation in a global economy', *Technology, Business, and Society Programme Paper*, No. 2, United Nations Research Institute for Social Development (UNRISD).
Joekes, Susan (1987), *Women in the World Economy*, Oxford, UK: Oxford University Press.
Kabeer, Naila (2000), *The Power to Choose: Bangladeshi Women and Labour Market Decisions in London and Dhaka*, London, New York: Verso.
Kaspos, Steven (2004), 'Estimating growth requirements for reducing working poverty: can the

world halve working poverty by 2015?', Employment Strategy Papers, No. 2004/14, Employment Strategy Department, Geneva: ILO.

Kemp, Melody (2001), 'Corporate social responsibility in Indonesia. Quixotic dream or confident expectation?', *Technology, Business, and Society Programme Paper* No. 6, United Nations Research Institute for Social Development (UNRISD).

Khattak, Saba Gul (2002), 'Subcontracted work and gender relations: the case of Pakistan', in R. Balakrishnan (ed.) *The Hidden Assembly Line: Gender Dynamics of Subcontracted Work in a Global Economy*, Bloomfield, CT: Kumarian Press, pp. 35–61.

Kolk, Ans, Rob van Tulder and Carlijn Welters (1999), 'International codes of conduct and corporate social responsibility: can transnational corporations regulate themselves?', *Transnational Corporations*, **8**(1), 143–80.

Kristof, Nicholas (2002), 'Let them sweat', *New York Times* (25 June).

Krugman, Paul (1998), *The Accidental Theorist*, New York: Norton.

Levine, David (1992), 'Can wage increases pay for themselves? Tests with a production function', *Economic Journal*, **102**(414), 1102–15.

Lim, Linda (1983), 'Capitalism, imperialism, and patriarchy: the dilemma of third-world women workers in multinational factories', in J. Nash and M. Fernández-Kelly (eds) *Women, Men, and the International Division of Labor*, Albany, NY: SUNY Press, pp. 70–91.

Lorenz, Edward (2001), *Defining Global Justice: The History of U.S. International Labor Standards Policy*, Notre Dame, IN: Notre Dame University Press.

Lustig, Nora and Darryl McLeod (1997), 'Minimum wages and poverty in developing countries: some empirical evidence', in S. Edwards and N. Lustig (eds) *Labor Markets in Latin America: Combining Social Protection with Market Flexibility*, Washington, DC: Brookings Institution Press, pp. 62–103.

Marshall, Ray (1994), 'The importance of international labour standards in a more competitive global economy', in W. Sengenberger and D. Campbell (eds) *International Labour Standards and Economic Interdependence*, Geneva: International Institute for Labour Studies (ILO), pp. 65–78.

OECD (2000), 'The OECD declaration and decisions on international investment and multinational enterprises: basic texts', DAFFE/IME(2000)20.

Palley, Thomas, Elizabeth Drake and Thea Lee (1999), 'The case for core labor standards in the international economy: theory, evidence, and a blueprint for implementation', AFL-CIO Economic Policy Papers, No. E041.

Pearson, Ruth and Gill Seyfang (2001), 'New hope or false dawn? Voluntary codes of conduct, labor regulation, and social policy in a globalizing world', *Global Social Policy*, **1**(1), 49–78.

Polanyi, Karl (1944), *The Great Transformation: The Political and Economic Origins of Our Time*, Boston: Beacon Press.

Polanyi, Karl (1957), 'Aristotle discovers the economy', in K. Polanyi, C. Arensberg and H. Pearson (eds) *Trade and Market in the Early Empires*, New York: The Free Press, pp. 64–94.

Polaski, Sandra and Katherine Vyborny (2006), 'Labor clauses in trade agreements: policy and practice', *Integration and Trade*, **10**(25), 95–124.

Pollin, Robert, Justine Burns and James Heintz (2004), 'Global apparel production and sweatshop labor: can raising retail prices finance living wages?', *Cambridge Journal of Economics*, **28**(2), 153–71.

Portes, Alejandro, Manuel Castells and Lauren A. Benton (eds) (1989), *The Informal Economy: Studies in Advanced and Less Developed Countries*, Baltimore: Johns Hopkins University Press.

Rodrik, Dani (1996), 'Labor standards in international trade: do they matter and what do we do about them?', in R. Lawrence, D. Rodrik and J. Walley, *Emerging Agenda For Global Trade: High Stakes for Developing Countries*, Washington, DC: Overseas Development Council, pp. 35–79.

Roldan, Martha (1988), 'Renegotiating the marital contract: intrahousehold patterns of money allocation and women's subordination among domestic outworkers in Mexico City', in D. Dwyer and J. Bruce (eds) *A House Divided: Women and Income in the Third World*, Stanford, CA: Stanford University Press, pp. 229–47.

Saget, Catherine (2001), 'Poverty reduction and decent work in developing countries: do minimum wages help?', *International Labour Review*, **140**(3), 237–69.

Sathar, Zeba and Shahnaz Kazi (1989), 'Female employment and fertility: further investigation of an ambivalent association', *The Pakistan Development Review*, **28**(3), 175–94.
Seguino, Stephanie (2000), 'The effects of structural change and economic liberalization on gender wage differentials in South Korea and Taiwan', *Cambridge Journal of Economics*, **24**(4), 437–59.
Sen, Amartya (1990), 'Gender and cooperative conflicts', in I. Tinker (ed.) *Persistent Inequalities: Women and World Development*, Oxford, UK: Oxford University Press, pp. 123–49.
Sengenberger, Werner (1994), 'International labour standards in a globalized economy: the issues', in W. Sengenberger and D. Campbell (eds) *International Labour Standards and Economic Interdependence*, Geneva: International Institute for Labour Studies (ILO), pp. 3–15.
Shapiro, Carl and Joseph Stiglitz (1984), 'Equilibrium unemployment as a worker discipline device', *American Economic Review*, **74**(3), 433–44.
Singh, Ajit and Ann Zammit (2000), *The Global Labour Standards Controversy: Critical Issues for Developing Countries*, Geneva: The South Centre.
Standing, Guy (1989), 'Global feminization through flexible labor', *World Development*, **17**(7), 1077–95.
Standing, Guy (1999), *Global Labour Flexibility: Seeking Distributive Justice*, New York: St. Martin's Press.
Tokman, Victor (2006), 'Free trade and labor standards: a developing relationship', *Integration and Trade*, **10**(25), 53–93.
Tsogas, George (2001), *Labor Regulation in a Global Economy*, Armonk, NY: M.E. Sharpe, pp. 61–2.
United Nations (1986), 'The United Nations code of conduct on transnational corporations', UNCTC Current Studies, Series A, No. 4, September.
Vandemoortele, Jan (1991), 'Labour market informalization in sub-Saharan Africa', in G. Standing and V. Tokman (eds) *Towards Social Adjustment: Labour Market Issues in Structural Adjustment*, Geneva: ILO, pp. 81–113.

PART V

EUROPE AND NORTH AMERICA

14 Productivity and competition from a global point of view*

Joseph Plasmans

1 Introduction

This chapter essentially deals with the interplay of productivity and competition. The productivity of a production unit[1] is defined as the ratio of a measure of output produced by this production unit over a measure of input used during the same time period. If the input measure is comprehensive, then the productivity concept is called Total Factor Productivity (TFP) or Multifactor Productivity (MFP). We use TFP and MFP interchangeably, even if there is a slight difference between what they may include.[2] If the input measure is (the number of) labour hours, then the productivity concept is called Labour Productivity (LP). Diewert (2006, p. 1) states that:

> A problem with the Total Factor Productivity concept is that it depends on the units of measurement for outputs and inputs. Hence TFP can only be compared across production units if the production units are basically in the same line of business so that they are producing the same (or closely similar) outputs and using the same inputs.

Therefore, we concentrate in this chapter on firms as production units operating in the manufacturing market. Usually TFP growth (TFPG) or MFP Growth (MFPG) can be decomposed into factors such as technical change, technical efficiency (efficient allocation of inputs to outputs), scale effects, input- and output-mix effects (deviations of perfect competition, higher production capabilities), and other components that may be related to productivity changes (uncertainty) (see e.g., Morrison, 1999; Balk, 2008). Therefore, TFPG equals technical change when all the other TFPG decomposition elements are not present as in the neoclassical case.

Neoclassical assumptions, such as constant returns to scale and perfect competition, make it relatively easy to calculate estimates of technological change. However, there is enough empirical evidence that shows that such assumptions are not adequate for all markets (see e.g., Basu and Fernald, 2007). Therefore, it would be discomforting to have such assumptions built into the methodological foundations of productivity and growth accounting statistics.

TFPG can be calculated by different approaches, that is, by the growth accounting approach, the index number approach, the distance function approach, and the econometric approach (see e.g., Feng and Serletis, 2008 for a recent overview).

Growth accounting was suggested by Solow (1957) as a method of estimating TFPG. Growth accounting calculation of TFPG requires the explicit specification of a neo-classical production function and identifies TFPG as the output change that cannot be accounted for by the growth in inputs according to a specific production function. Under perfect competition and usually under a Cobb-Douglas production technology, TFPG is commonly called the Solow residual since 1957. In a review of the New Zealand economy, Bates (2001) explains that the main determinants of output growth are the input growth and TFPG. TFPG is output growth that cannot be directly explained by input growth.[3]

The index number approach is an extension of (and complement to) growth accounting. It involves dividing a (real) output quantity index, or the ratio between two outputs at two different time periods in case of one single output, by an input quantity index to obtain a measure of TFPG.[4] However, as Feng and Serletis (2008, p. 283) assert:

> one critical issue regarding this approach is the selection of the appropriate indexes. In fact, statistical indexes are mainly characterized by their statistical properties. These properties were examined in great detail by Fisher (1922) and serve as tests in assessing the quality of a particular statistical index.

And

> The index that Fisher (1922) found to be the best, in the sense of possessing the largest number of desirable statistical properties, has now become known as the 'Fisher ideal' index. Another index found to possess a very large number of such properties is the discrete time approximation to the continuous Divisia index, usually called the Törnquist index or just the Divisia index (in discrete time). In fact, the primary advantage of the Fisher ideal index over the Divisia index is that the Fisher ideal index satisfies Fisher's 'factor reversal test' – which requires that the product of the price and quantity indexes for an aggregated good should equal actual expenditures on the component goods – while the discrete time approximation of the Divisia index fails that test. However, the magnitude of the error is very small – third order in the changes.

Notice that the index number approach does not require an aggregate production function.[5]

The distance function approach to measuring TFPG separates TFPG into two components: changes resulting from a movement toward the production frontier (technical efficiency change) and shifts of this frontier (technical change). The distance function was first introduced separately by Shephard (1953) in the context of production function analysis and by Malmquist (1953) in the context of consumption function analysis. But it was introduced as a theoretical TFPG index by Caves et al. (1982), and then popularized as an empirical TFPG index by Färe et al. (1994). Although the latter empirical TFPG index has several advantages (e.g., neither a specific functional form, nor information on prices are required and it does not assume that firms are operating at their efficient level), it requires full information about the state of technology at every point in time and all production units should have identical production functions, which is not realistic.

Finally, the econometric approach to TFPG measurement involves estimating the parameters of an aggregator function, being a flexible cost, profit, or production function as the locally flexible generalized Leontief, the translog, and the normalized quadratic specifications. TFPG can then be expressed in terms of the estimated parameters. The advantage of this econometric approach is that we can now identify the various components of TFPG so that this method is more adequate for our purposes (e.g., imperfect competition and scale effects).

In this chapter we follow the econometric approach to TFPG. We develop a framework within which we can analyse the link between competitive behaviour, economies of scale and TFPG. Such a framework allows us to take into account the positive contribution of scale economies and market power. Furthermore, for a relatively small open economy such as the Netherlands, scale economies, competition, capital and labour growth are all interrelated. This is important for a society because it is only on the basis of a consistent measure of productivity growth and competition that policy-makers can make the right decisions in order to improve or maintain the same level of welfare at all levels of the economy.

The analysis and measurement of productivity performance has attracted a great deal of attention ever since Solow (1957) decomposed the growth in output into the growth of inputs and a residual-based productivity term. In a series of papers Hall (1986, 1988 and 1990) stresses that the Solow residual is no longer equal to the rate of technical change when there is imperfect competition in product markets, but that the two are related by an equation that includes a component involving the *markup* of a price over marginal cost. Hall's approach has the advantage that it does not require measuring the user cost of capital. Hall (1990) even demonstrates that if one relaxes the assumption of constant returns to scale, the above-mentioned equation also includes another additional term that can be used to estimate jointly the average markup and the elasticity of scale (see also Klette, 1999; Ohinata and Plasmans, 2002).

Crépon et al. (1999, 2002 and 2007), Dobbelaere (2004) and Dobbelaere and Mairesse (2009) also introduce imperfect competition in labour markets in Hall's (1990) model. This is argued from the observation that numerous studies have documented large wage differentials across firms or industries for apparently homogeneous types of workers and occupations. Such wage differentials indicate that labour markets are far from being competitive. They discuss a generalization of Hall's (1990) approach to allow for the possibility that wages are contractually determined between employers (firms) and employees (workers) according to an efficient bargaining model, where similarly schooled and experienced employees in some high-profit firms can get higher wages than in low-profit firms. We introduce their extension in our model setting. The aim of the strand of literature up to now was to examine the discrepancies between factor elasticities in the production function and their corresponding shares in revenue due to both imperfections in the product and labour markets. The novelty in our model consists in embedding such a framework to determine changes in productivity growth.

Using Dutch firm-level data over 22 industries and for the period 1989–2005, we find that firms set their prices above their marginal costs and workers are bargaining over their salaries. At the manufacturing level, our results, compared with Dobbelaere and Mairesse's (2009) analysis on French manufacturing enterprises, indicate less imperfect competition on the output market (the price–cost markup is found to be 1.06 versus 1.17 for French firms) and more imperfect competition in the labour market (workers' bargaining power is 0.61 versus 0.44 for French data). Moreover, we find that deviating from the assumption of perfect markets implies a possible heterogeneity in production technologies and varying returns to scale within the 22 industries. We also find that, for many of these industries, firms' pricing behaviour tends to be directly associated with the characteristics of their production technology, including changes in efficiency that translate into productivity growth. Our finding is in line with well-known models of endogenous growth (e.g., Romer, 1990; Grossman and Helpman, 1991; Aghion and Howitt, 1992). As a matter of fact, a decrease of the level of product market competition has a positive effect on productivity growth, by augmenting the monopoly rents that reward new innovation. Furthermore, connected to the innovation process and labour market imperfections, as in Aghion and Howitt (1994), we find that labour market imperfection yields a lower productivity growth rate. Firms are subject to idiosyncratic shocks due to product innovations calling for labour force reallocations. As rigidity of the labour market does not allow firms from adjusting their labour factor, labour market imperfection then causes a lower innovation rate. These findings bring together existing branches of literature to provide a unique global understanding of the impact of market behaviour on productivity change.

The chapter is organized as follows. In section 2, we formulate a TFPG measure that allows for market power and time-varying economies of scale, and use the traditional markup as measure for competition, but corrected for imperfect competition in the labour market. Section 3 describes the data and reports results on market imperfection parameters. In section 4 we report and concisely discuss results for the TFPG measure discussed in section 2. In the final section we conclude with some policy implications.

2 TFPG based on the markup as a measure of competition

We propose a measure for TFPG that allows for both monopoly power and scale economies and is directly related to the markup. The markup is a measure of market power based on price–cost margins that is often applied in the literature. In fact, research has indicated that the markup is to be preferred over the other often employed measure of competition, the Herfindahl index. We derive the estimating equation for a setting of three inputs (capital, labour and intermediate goods) under imperfect competition in the goods and labour markets. In Appendix 1 we analyse the imperfectly competitive set-up in the goods market based on time-varying markups and returns to scale in a setting with an arbitrary number of perfectly competitive inputs.

Here, we use gross output, Y_{it}, as a measure of output and relate it to three specific inputs:

$$Y_{it} = A_{it}F_i(K_{it}, L_{it}, M_{it}) \quad i = 1, 2, \ldots N; t = 1, \ldots, T, \tag{14.1}$$

where capital, labour and intermediate goods, the latter consisting of materials and energy, are denoted for firm i at period t as K_{it}, L_{it} and M_{it}, respectively. A_{it} is defined as TFP and $F_i(\cdot)$ is assumed to be homogeneous of degree θ_{it}, so that growth in output can be decomposed into growth in technology and inputs by logarithmic differentiation of the production function (14.1) (see also Eq. (14A.2) in Appendix 1)

$$\frac{dY_{it}}{Y_{it}} = \frac{dA_{it}}{A_{it}} + \frac{K_{it}}{F(\cdot)}\frac{\partial F_i(\cdot)}{\partial K_{it}}\frac{dK_{it}}{K_{it}} + \frac{L_{it}}{F_i(\cdot)}\frac{\partial F_i(\cdot)}{\partial L_{it}}\frac{dL_{it}}{L_{it}} + \frac{M_{it}}{F_i(\cdot)}\frac{\partial F_i(\cdot)}{\partial M_{it}}\frac{dM_{it}}{M_{it}} \tag{14.2}$$

We now relax the conventional assumption of perfect competition in the labour market, allowing both firms and workers' unions to have some market power. Many authors have studied the influence of the market power of unions, by introducing wage rigidities through efficiency wages. For instance, Hall's model (1990) assumes that the firm wages and level of employment are jointly determined according to an efficient bargaining scheme between the firm and its workers. Interestingly to note now is that, following MacDonald and Solow's (1981) efficient bargaining model, in which both wage and employment are bargained between firms and their workers, it can be shown that the wage of workers is determined at a level that is higher than the firm's marginal revenue of labour, that is, $\frac{\partial \ln Y_{it}}{\partial \ln L_{ikt}} = \frac{1}{(1-\ell_{it})}\frac{W_{ikt}L_{ikt}}{Y_{it}P_{it}(Y_t)}$ (W_{it} is the negotiated wage, $P_{it}(Y_t)$ is the market price as a function of aggregate output, and ℓ_{it} is the Lerner index; see Eq.

(14A.10) in Appendix 1). Hence, workers in firms with market power on the output market can earn wages that are much higher than the competitive industry wage level.

Introducing the nominal input prices R_{it}, W_{it} and Z_{it} as firm i's rental price of capital, wage rate and unit price for intermediate goods, respectively, the efficient bargaining model can be summarized as follows.

The workers in the firm bargain with the firm over both the level of employment L_{it} and of the wage W_{it}. According to MacDonald and Solow (ibid.) the workers' objective in their efficient bargaining model can be specified in two alternative ways, that is, either as the workers' (or union membership) aggregate gain from employment, $L_{it}(W_{it} - \overline{W}_{it})$, or, taking account of the unemployment benefits, as $L_{it}W_{it} + \overline{W}_{it}(N_{it} - L_{it})$, where $\overline{W}_{it}$ is the reservation wage, W_{it} the negotiated wage and N_{it} is the labour supply. MacDonald and Solow (ibid.) judge the first specification as the most appropriate one for real life. As a matter of fact, the unemployment benefits may vary in magnitude, duration and eligibility (Bean, 1994), therefore, similarly to Dobbelaere and Mairesse (2009),[6] we advocate MacDonald and Solow's (1981) suggestion.

The firm's objective is to maximize its short-run profit given by the difference between the total revenue and the total costs, that is, as $P_{it}(Y_t)Y_{it} - W_{it}L_{it} - R_{it}K_{it} - Z_{it}M_{it}$.

The solution to the Nash bargaining problem results in the maximization of a (multiplicative) weighted average of the workers' aggregate gain from employment and the firm's short-run profit:

$$\max_{W_{it}, L_{it}, K_{it}, M_{it}} [L_{it}(W_{it} - \overline{W}_{it})]^{\phi_{it}} [P_{it}(Y_t)Y_{it} - W_{it}L_{it} - R_{it}K_{it} - Z_{it}M_{it}]^{1-\phi_{it}}$$

where $\phi_{it} \in [0, 1]$ is the degree of workers' bargaining power.

Maximizing with respect to employment and to wage, yields the reservation wage:[7]

$$\overline{W}_{it} = \frac{P_{it}(Y_t)}{\mu_{it}} \frac{\partial Y_{it}}{\partial L_{it}},$$

which is the solution of the Nash bargaining model. Hence, the reservation wage is the theoretical wage valid on an imperfectly competitive output market and a perfectly competitive labour market.

Given the equilibrium reservation wage, we can express the elasticity of labour θ_{iLt} as (for complete derivations, see Appendix 2):

$$\theta_{iLt} = \mu_{it} s_{iLt} - \phi_{it}\mu_{it} + \phi_{it}\theta_{it} \tag{14.3}$$

s_{ikt} denotes the share of the cost of input k in the total production value of firm i, s_{iLt} is therefore the share of the cost of labour, and θ_{it} is the returns to scale parameter.

Firm i's elasticities of output with respect to capital, labour and intermediate goods (θ_{iKt}, θ_{iLt}, θ_{iMt}, respectively) at period t can then be expressed as:

$$A_{it}\frac{\partial F_i(\cdot)}{\partial K_{it}}\frac{K_{it}}{Y_{it}} = \theta_{iKt} = \mu_{it}s_{iKt}, \tag{14.4}$$

$$A_{it}\frac{\partial F_i(\cdot)}{\partial L_{it}}\frac{L_{it}}{Y_{it}} = \theta_{iLt} = \mu_{it}s_{iLt} - \phi_{it}\mu_{it} + \phi_{it}\theta_{it}, \text{ and} \tag{14.5}$$

$$A_{it}\frac{\partial F_i(\cdot)}{\partial M_{it}}\frac{M_{it}}{Y_{it}} = \theta_{iMt} = \mu_{it}s_{iMt}. \tag{14.6}$$

Only when the technology is constant returns to scale and the output and labour markets are perfectly competitive will the elasticities be equal to the observed input shares. Due to the imperfect competition on the labour market, establishing the relationship $\theta_{it} = \sum_{k=1}^{J_i}\theta_{ikt} = \mu_{it}\sum_{k=1}^{J_i}s_{ikt} = \mu_{it}s_{it}$ is no longer valid. Indeed, adding the right-hand sides of (14.4)–(14.6), the correct relationship between θ_{it} and $\mu_{it}s_{it}$ is found as:

$$\theta_{it} = \frac{\mu_{it}}{(1-\phi_{it})}(s_{it} - \phi_{it}), \tag{14.7}$$

where the labour market bargaining elasticity, ϕ_{it}, is now involved. Note that if $\phi_{it} = 0$, expression (14.7) can be reduced to the time-varying markup derived in Appendix 1 (Eq. (14A.15)).

Following the standard convention, we will use the differences of the logarithms to approximate the logarithmic growth rates; logarithms of variables will be denoted as lower case letters. Substituting the output elasticities (14.4)–(14.6) into (14.2) and taking account of production function (14.1) and the corrected scale elasticity (14.7), we solve for the TFPG rates Δa_{it} from the resulting output growth equation:

$$\begin{aligned}\Delta y_{it} &= \mu_{it}s_{iKt}\Delta k_{it} + (\mu_{it}s_{iLt} - \phi_{it}\mu_{it} + \phi_{it}\theta_{it})\Delta l_{it} + \mu_{it}s_{iMt}\Delta m_{it} + \Delta a_{it} \\ &= \mu_{it}(s_{iKt}\Delta k_{it} + s_{iLt}\Delta l_{it} + s_{iMt}\Delta m_{it}) + \mu_{it}\frac{\phi_{it}}{(1-\phi_{it})}(s_{it}-1)\Delta l_{it} + \Delta a_{it}\end{aligned} \tag{14.8}$$

This equation is general in the sense that it is derived without assuming a constant returns to scale technology or perfect competition in the output market.

Defining $\Delta x_{it} \equiv s_{iKt}\Delta k_{it} + s_{iLt}\Delta l_{it} + s_{iMt}\Delta m_{it}$ and $\mu_{it}\frac{\phi_{it}}{(1-\phi_{it})} \equiv \gamma_{it}$, we can rewrite our estimating equation in a compact form:

$$\Delta y_{it} = \mu_{it}\Delta x_{it} + \gamma_{it}(s_{it} - 1)\Delta l_{it} + \Delta a_{it} \quad (14.9)$$

where the bargaining elasticity ϕ_{it} equals $\gamma_{it}/(\gamma_{it} + \mu_{it})$.[8]

We assume that the Hicks neutral technological progress is a random variable such that the growth rate of firm i in period t consists of a firm-specific growth rate, a_i, and a period specific growth rate, δ_t, which captures the macroeconomic shock that is common across industries in the same period, plus a white noise, u_{it}. Therefore TFPG $\equiv \Delta a_{it} = a_i + \delta_t + u_{it}$.

Under the profit-maximizing approach, provided that the firm's perceptions of the elasticities of demand remain unchanged, the markup would remain constant over time (μ_i). Once a firm has discovered a markup of price over marginal costs that serves its purposes, then it is quite likely that it will maintain that markup (Coutts et al., 1978; Basu and Fernald, 1997).[9] The constancy over time does not rule out the possibility for the structural parameters μ_{it} and ϕ_{it} to vary across firms.[10]

In this chapter, we are going to apply model (14.9) on yearly firm-level data.

3 Data and results

We extract data from Statistics Netherlands for the years 1989–2005. The output and the input variables are defined as follows. As an output measure, we use the value of gross output ($P_{it}Y_{it}$) of each firm i. Labour (L_{it}) refers to the number of employees in each firm for each year, collected in September of that year. The corresponding wages (W_{it}) include the total labour costs (gross wages plus salaries and social contributions) before taxes. The costs of intermediate inputs ($Z_{it}M_{it}$) include costs of energy, intermediate materials and services. The user costs of capital stock ($W_{it}K_{it}$) are calculated as the sum of the depreciation of fixed assets and the interest charges.

We use a two-digit NACE deflator of fixed tangible assets calculated by Statistics Netherlands in order to compute the volume index of capital stock (Δk_{it}). The nominal gross output and intermediate inputs are deflated with the appropriate price indices from the input–output tables available at the NACE Rev. 1 two-digits sector classification.[11]

The data extracted from the Production Statistics (PS) constitutes a highly unbalanced panel (with a minimum of 1259 firms in 1994 and a maximum of 6277 enterprises in 1997) of 73 427 observations spanning over 16 years and over 22 industries. Furthermore, for some firms, we observed negative correlation between capital growth rate and output growth. As a matter of fact, if the firm produces non-tangible goods, even if capital asset is growing, the output is decreasing as it acquires more technology, which allows the enterprise to reduce the output volume. Since our specification of a production function is meant to represent manufacturing firms only, we exclude this type of firms. For the estimates, we only include firms for which we have at least two consecutive observations for all variables, ending up with 7161 firms. Throughout our sample period, the PS surveys included some changes in their population designs, resulting in an unbalanced panel of the entire population. As a result, we can not distinguish whether the entry or exit rates of firms resulted from survey response behaviour or real economic structural behaviour. The number of firms (*N*) for each NACE Rev. 1 industry are calculated by Statistics Netherlands. Table A.1 in Appendix 3 reports the sectors that were chosen with a corresponding NACE two-digit code and the corresponding number of firms.

3.1 Empirical results for the complete sample of Dutch firms

Table 14.1 reports the means, medians, standard deviations and first and third quartiles of the included data for our main variables. A summary of the aggregate annual growth of all inputs and output along with inputs' shares in revenue is presented. During 1989–2005, the gross output and the material input grew at a rate of about 1.87 and 1.9 per cent annually, respectively. Annual capital growth rate is dramatically higher than labour growth rate, implying increased capital intensity over time. However, the capital input constitutes only 4.9 per cent of gross output, while the share of labour is almost 28 per cent, and intermediate inputs constitute more than half of gross output (60.65 per cent). Further consideration concerns the dispersion of all these variables that, as expected for firm-level data, is considerably large.

Table 14.1 Summary statistics

Var.	Δy_{it}	Δm_{it}	Δk_{it}	Δl_{it}	s_{iMt}	s_{iKt}	s_{iLt}	Δx_{it}	s_{it}	*T*/Firm
Mean	0.017	0.019	0.076	0.000	0.606	0.049	0.278	0.019	0.935	4.3
St.dv.	0.174	0.229	0.087	0.128	0.148	0.042	0.131	0.153	0.096	–
P25	–0.060	–0.080	0.001	–0.046	0.511	0.023	0.185	–0.050	0.890	2
Median	0.015	0.015	0.066	0.000	0.609	0.040	0.267	0.014	0.942	4
P75	0.098	0.124	0.144	0.047	0.705	0.064	0.356	0.086	0.983	6

Notes:

a. $\Delta x_{it} \equiv s_{iKt}\Delta k_{it} + s_{iLt}\Delta l_{it} + s_{iMt}\Delta m_{it}$.

b. The number of time observations per firm (*T*/firm) varies between two and 16 years (30 660 obs. for 7161 firms).

c. P25 and P75 are, respectively, the 25th and the 75th percentile.

Source: Source for all tables and figures in this chapter is the author's own calculations.

Productivity shocks u_{it}, such as positive technology shocks, might affect the level of factor inputs. It is indeed a plausible assumption that the composite error Δa_{it} includes an unobservable component that is taken into account in the firm's information set before input choices are made. The existence of such components raises the possibility that the input choices are correlated with u_{it}. Hence, we treat all firm-specific variables as potentially endogenous. In such a case, Ordinary Least Squares (OLS) estimates would be inconsistent and biased.

The estimation of a panel data model with predetermined variables is typically done by means of Generalized Method of Moments (GMM) estimators applied to the first differences transformation of the equation of interest, where all the available lags of the predetermined variables are used as instruments. The purpose of this approach is to remove time-invariant unobserved individual heterogeneity. Therefore, under the assumption that current random shocks are serially uncorrelated[12] and defining $w_{it} \equiv (\Delta x_{it}, (s_{it} - 1)\,\Delta\, l_{it})'$, the orthogonality conditions can be written as $E(w_{it-j}u_{is}) = 0$, for $j = 2, 3\ldots,T$. The instruments we use are therefore lagged values of Δx_{it} and $(s_{it} - 1)\,\Delta l_{it}$ from $(t - 2)$ and before. The exogeneity of the instruments with respect to the error term is tested by the Hansen's J test statistic. In addition, we also include time dummies to capture possible unobservable shocks common to all firms.

However, this approach yields inaccurate estimates in the case of a panel with a small number of time periods with highly persistent data. In this context, as it has been stressed in Hall and Mairesse (2002), the application of first-differences GMM estimators with lagged levels of the series as instruments has produced unsatisfactory results. More specifically, the coefficient of the capital stock is generally low and statistically insignificant, and returns to scale appear to be unreasonably low. Blundell and Bond (1998) suggest that the problem of 'weak instruments' is behind the poor performance of standard GMM estimators in this context. This problem of weak instruments can be overcome by applying an extended GMM estimator proposed by Arellano and Bover (1995). This estimator, labelled as 'system GMM', is based on an augmented system that includes level equations with lagged differences as instruments in addition to the differenced equations with lagged levels as instruments.

First, we focus on the manufacturing industry as a whole over the period 1989–2005, without looking at the potential heterogeneity in the markup and the bargaining power parameters among sectors. Estimation results for the entire manufacturing market are reported in Table 14.2 and are organized in two parts. The first three columns display the estimated structural parameters of our estimating equation (14.9) for a range of estimators (levels OLS, first-differenced OLS, first-differenced GMM). The last two columns report the results of estimating a dynamic specification of Eq. (14.9), allowing for an autoregressive component in the productivity shocks.

The first section of each part of the table gives the estimated price–cost markup $\hat{\mu}$, the corresponding rent-sharing $\hat{\theta}$ and the estimated scale elasticity $\hat{\theta}$. The second and the third sections present production function coefficient estimates assuming perfect competition in the output market ($\mu_{it} = 0$) and in the labour market ($\phi_{it} = 0$), respectively. In the first two columns of Table 14.2 (OLS and OLS diff) we observe that the derived price–cost markups are not significantly different from 1 and the corresponding extent of rent-sharing is quite small (respectively 0.268 and 0.278). Furthermore, both OLS and first-difference (FD) OLS[13] suggest decreasing returns to scale. The main drawbacks to these estimators are that part of the information in the data is left unused. A fixed-effect estimator uses only the across time variation, which tends to be much lower than the cross-section one for not particularly persistent data. Second, the assumption that the firm's specific attributes are fixed over time may not always be reasonable. Although biased, OLS estimators of the Hall (1988) approach, which assumes allocative wage ($\phi_{it} = 0$), generates a downward bias of price–cost markups (from 0.994 to 0.991 for the OLS level and from 0.988 to 0.985 for the FD OLS) and an upward bias of returns to scale parameters (from 0.905 to 0.926 and from 0.884 to 0.921 for OLS level and FD OLS, respectively). Intuitively, the underestimation of the markups, ignoring imperfect competition in the labour market, corresponds to the omission of the part of product rents captured by the workers, which are hidden in a larger-scale parameter. On the other hand, when holding the markups fixed at 1, the rent-sharing parameter slightly increases.

As stressed above, OLS methods tend to underestimate the structural coefficients when the error term of the production function is expected to influence the choice of factor inputs and when the data is not particularly persistent (i.e., the across-time variation is much lower than the cross-section one). Despite the signal of non-persistency, we estimate a dynamic panel data model by considering an AR(1) extension of (14.9) and report the estimated coefficients in the second part of Table 14.2 (columns 4 and 5). We report results for the two-step GMM estimator for both the first-differenced equations (FD GMM) and the system (SYS GMM).

We take as instruments the lagged levels dated $(t - 2)$ and $(t - 3)$ in the first-differenced equations. As additional instruments in the system GMM estimation, we take the lagged differences dated $(t - 1)$. Year dummies have been included in both models. At a first glance, it is clear that the AR(1) structure that we assume for the idiosyncratic error term is not needed, as the coefficient ρ of the lagged dependent variable is statistically not significant for the system GMM, and statistically significant for the FD GMM, but approximately equal to zero. Moreover, the validity of the instruments is rejected by the Sargan (1958) test[14] of overidentifying restrictions in both the first-differenced GMM and the system GMM estimator. Nevertheless, the gains of the system GMM estimation,

Table 14.2 General results for all 22 industries

	Static Specification			Dynamic Specification	
	OLS LEVEL	FD OLS	FD GMM	FD GMM	SYS GMM
$\hat{\phi}$	0.268	0.278	0.614	0.434	0.319
	(0.044)	(0.058)	(0.054)	(0.024)	(0.035)
$\hat{\mu}$	0.994	0.988	1.063	1.010	1.026
	(0.006)	(0.008)	(0.026)	(0.013)	(0.012)
$\hat{\theta}$	0.905	0.884	0.993	0.894	0.906
	(0.006)	(0.026)	(0.025)	(0.012)	(0.008)
$\hat{\rho}$				–0.018(0.009)	–0.013(0.009)
$\hat{\phi}(\hat{\mu} = 1)$	0.269	0.278	0.621	0.4202	0.453
	(0.044)	(0.057)	(0.056)	(0.024)	0.057
$\hat{\theta}(\hat{\mu} = 1)$	0.910	0.909	0.910	0.887	0.880
	(0.002)	(0.001)	(0.040)	(0.002)	(0.004)
$\hat{\rho}(\hat{\mu} = 1)$				–0.132(0.014)	–0.141(0.019)
$\hat{\mu}(\hat{\phi} = 0)$	0.991	0.985	1.044	0.988	1.034
	(0.006)	(0.008)	(0.027)	(0.008)	(0.059)
$\hat{\theta}(\hat{\phi} = 0)$	0.926	0.921	0.976	0.924	0.952
	(0.006)	(0.008)	(0.025)	(0.007)	(0.012)
$\hat{\rho}(\hat{\phi} = 0)$				–0.021(0.008)	–0.005(0.008)
Hansen's J χ^2_{df}			1.719 $df = 4$ pval(0.423)		
Sargan test χ^2_{df}				348.624 $df = 26$ pval(0.000)	64.661 $df = 40$ pval(0.008)
Time dummies	Yes	Yes	Yes	Yes	Yes
No. of firms	7161			7161	7161

Notes:
a. Sample period 1989–2005.
b. Dependent variable: output growth Δy_{it}.
c. Hansen J/Sargan test: test of the overidentifying restrictions.
d. Standard error in parentheses.

claimed to be a more robust estimator (Arellano and Bover, 1995; Blundell and Bond, 1998), compared with the first-differenced GMM estimates, are not very apparent in terms of economically meaningful interpretation. All structural parameters behave similarly to the OLS estimators.[15] The markups equal to 1 and the corresponding bargaining power parameters are slightly larger (0.434 and 0.319, respectively for first-differenced and system GMM). Accounting for imperfect competition on the labour market yields to larger returns to scale than assuming perfect competition.

On the other hand, the Hansen's (1982) J test[16] of overidentifying restrictions is not rejected for our last estimator, the first-differenced GMM applied to the static model. Results are displayed in the third column of Table 14.2. The parameter of bargaining power $\hat{\phi}$ is very high (0.614), reflecting the influence of labour behaviour on output growth. Nevertheless, taking into account the existence of rent-sharing translates in a rise in the estimated markup $\hat{\mu}$ (from 1.04 to 1.06) and a rise in the estimated elasticity of scale $\hat{\theta}$ (from 0.976 to 0.993). Our last estimation technique allows us to draw some conclusions for the Dutch manufacturing industries. In particular, we find some evidence of imperfect competition on the output market and strong unions' power on the labour market. Markups are significantly and fairly larger than one and returns to scale are constant or moderately decreasing, in the range of 0.9 to 1.0.

3.2 Across-industry estimates

Since firms' production behaviour is very likely to vary even across industries, we also investigate across-industry firm heterogeneity in estimated markup and rent-sharing parameters.

For 22 industries, we estimate Eq. (14.9) with and without the extension to labour imperfections, by relying on our trusted first-differenced GMM estimator. As instruments we take an appropriate number of lagged levels. Year dummies are always included. The estimated parameters are reported in Table 14.3.

Results show that for all industries, the magnitude of the estimated markup, elasticity of scale and bargaining power are likely to vary among industries. The price–cost margin μ is estimated to be lower than 1.01 for the first quartile of industries and higher than 1.16 for the top quartile. However, almost all industries reveal constant or increasing returns to scale (that is likely to be the case for manufacturing industries).

Within-industry imperfect competition on the labour market is present in 14 sectors. Then we reshape our results, by considering two subsamples. The first subsample (Table 14.3a) includes the estimates showing evidence of perfect competition on the output market (price–cost markup less than or equal to 1).[17] The second subsample (Table 14.3b) contains the estimates of those sectors for which the price–cost markup exceeds 1.[18] Moreover, each table has two extra columns where we consider sub-subsamples of sectors. The first extra column displays results for industries (29, 33 and 35) where the extent of rent-sharing is found to be significant and bounded between 0 and 1 ($\mu > 1$ and $\phi \neq 0$). The second sub-subsample includes the estimates for those sectors (30, 32 and 34) showing no evidence of rent-sharing ($\mu > 1$ and $\phi = 0$).

Table 14.3 Estimates for 22 industries

Industry	GMM DIFF						
	ϕ	μ	θ	$\Delta\bar{a}(\%)$	μ only	$\theta(\phi = 0)$	N(obs/firm)
15	1.305(0.891)	1.031(0.042)	1.251(0.847)	0.02	1.018(0.042)	0.951(0.039)	1168(3.8)
16	0.143(0.089)	1.107(0.168)	1.019(0.156)	0.47	1.119(0.205)	1.047(0.192)	16(3.8)
17	0.288(0.185)	1(0.044)	0.887(0.103)	1.51	1.042(0.108)	0.974(0.101)	286(3.6)
18	0.693(0.092)	0.977(0.035)	0.780(0.067)	5.53	0.853(0.064)	0.825(0.152)	142(2.8)
19	0.307(0.033)	0.958(0.152)	0.961(0.924)	7.02	1.014(0.130)	0.948(0.122)	83(3.4)
20	–0.495(7.333)	0.982(0.098)	0.933(0.190)	0.49	0.984(0.089)	0.920(0.083)	262(3.7)
21	0.647(0.135)	1.118(0.162)	1.187(0.204)	1.46	1.035(0.091)	0.967(0.085)	289(4.0)
22	0.825(0.045)	1.330(0.213)	1.346(0.211)	–0.87	1.073(0.213)	1.003(0.199)	840(3.5)
23	–	–	–		–	–	15(2.6)
24	0.761(0.068)	1.025(0.094)	1.054(0.100)	1.49	0.994(0.092)	0.929(0.086)	508(3.9)
25	0.708(0.113)	1.182(0.119)	1.223(0.117)	0.72	1.023(0.049)	0.956(0.046)	540(3.3)
26	0.579(0.083)	1.169(0.112)	1.294(0.196)	1.42	1.077(0.088)	1.007(0.082)	428(4.2)
27	1.207(0.741)	0.946(0.086)	0.936(0.077)	2.46	0.975(0.052)	0.912(0.048)	146(4.6)
28	0.697(0.073)	1.020(0.040)	1.070(0.059)	–0.30	1.013(0.040)	0.947(0.038)	1391(3.6)
29	0.789(0.128)	1.238(0.086)	1.339(0.094)	–0.68	1.229(0.065)	1.148(0.061)	1047(3.1)
30	0.903(0.019)	1.720(0.166)	1.727(0.165)	8.77	1.341(0.152)	1.254(0.142)	36(2.4)
31	–1.275(3.457)	1.009(0.071)	0.967(0.072)	0.88	1.004(0.072)	0.967(0.072)	265(3.4)
32	1.468(0.929)	1.047(0.189)	1.031(0.173)	5.94	1.196(0.057)	1.118(0.053)	69(2.4)
33	0 .906(0.034)	1.130(0.065)	1.137(0.065)	–0.50	1.035(0.080)	0.967(0.075)	250(3.2)
34	0.798(0.450)	1.324(0.087)	1.344(0.141)	3.02	1.369(0.096)	1.279(0.090)	210(3.6)
35	0.666(0.146)	1.151(0.047)	1.208(0.092)	–2.98	1.102(0.039)	1.031(0.036)	217(3.2)
36	0.602(0.079)	1.045(0.077)	1.161(0.163)	–0.10	1.046(0.077)	0.978(0.072)	454(3.4)

Notes:

a. Std. err. in parentheses.

b. Sample period 1989–2005.

c. Dependent variable: output growth Δy_{it}.

Table 14.3a 16 sectors where $\hat{\mu} \leq 1$

	Sectors where $\hat{\mu} \leq 1$	$\hat{\mu} \leq 1 \wedge \hat{\phi} \neq 0$	$\hat{\mu} \leq 1 \wedge \hat{\phi} = 0$
$\hat{\hat{\phi}}$	0.611	0.533	
	(0.059)	(0.061)	
$\hat{\hat{\mu}}$	1.022	1.033	
	(0.027)	(0.034)	
$\hat{\hat{\theta}}$	0.847	0.874	
	(0.022)	(0.029)	
$\hat{\hat{\mu}}(\phi = 0)$	1.018		1.010
	(0.027)		(0.045)
$\hat{\hat{\theta}}(\phi = 0)$	0.844		0.953
	(0.022)		(0.042)
No. of firms	6010	3903	2107
No. of obs	24929	16771	8158

Notes:
a. Std. err. in parentheses.
b. Sample period 1989–2005.
c. Dependent variable: output growth Δy_{it}.

Table 14.3b Six sectors where $\hat{\mu} > 1$

	Sectors where $\hat{\mu} > 1$	$\hat{\mu} > 1 \wedge \hat{\phi} \neq 0$	$\hat{\mu} > 1 \wedge \hat{\phi} = 0$
$\hat{\hat{\phi}}$	0.260	0.562	
	(0.110)	(0.116)	
$\hat{\hat{\mu}}$	1.149	1.095	
	(0.036)	(0.033)	
$\hat{\hat{\theta}}$	1.058	0.924	
	(0.033)	(0.041)	
$\hat{\hat{\mu}}(\phi = 0)$	1.204		1.256
	(0.026)		(0.061)
$\hat{\hat{\theta}}(\phi = 0)$	1.101		1.186
	(0.058)		(0.058)
No. of firms	1734	302	1326
No. of obs	5731	1575	4156

Notes:
a. Std. err. in parentheses.
b. Sample period 1989–2005.
c. Dependent variable: output growth Δy_{it}.

Estimates of Table 14.3a are in line with what we found up to now. Taking into account the existence of rent-sharing increases the estimated markup $\hat{\mu}$. This result is further confirmed by the subsample of 3903 firms for which the bargaining power was found to be significantly different from zero. The consequent decrease in the estimated elasticity of scale θ due to a reallocation of resources is more apparent in the second part of Table 14.3a (i.e., the two extra columns), where from a decreasing return to scale (0.87) we move to a constant elasticity of 1.01. Furthermore, we find relatively large unions' power estimates (0.61 and 0.53).

However, the six sectors, for which estimates are reported in Table 14.3b, behave differently. Including the rent-sharing actually reduces the level of imperfect competition from 1.20 to 1.14. This result is in contrast with some empirical findings (Krueger and Summers, 1987; Katz and Summers, 1989), yet we try to justify it. Workers will tend to gain higher wage rents in those sectors where there is less competition, which in turn generates a surplus, to which workers have a claim of a share. In other words, workers' unions' power, and in general rigidities of the labour market, will affect firms' marginal cost, and, consequently, the markups.

Therefore, rigidities and frictions in the labour market might be crucial for understanding firms' behaviour. To the extent that wages are allocative, we find that labour market frictions are the key factor. However, the exact form that these frictions take still remains ambiguous and will be a stimulus to carry on further research.

4 Impact on TFPG

Introducing imperfect competition on both output and labour markets, we see that changes in the level of competition vary by industry. This section incorporates these findings to analyse the relationship between imperfect competition, varying returns to scale and productivity growth.

The effect of markups on TFPG, measured in a growth accounting framework, has been addressed in a number of related papers.[19] Azzam et al. (2004) decompose sources of TFPG by economies of scale, markups and demand growth. Using US food industry data for 1973–92, these authors find that, on average, productivity grew by 0.22 per cent due to markups and 0.10 per cent due to increases in economies of scale. Morrison (1992) finds that the TFPG adjusted for markups in total manufacturing has increased during 1960–81 for Japan, the US and Canada. It is also noted that variable returns to scale tend to neutralize the implications of the markup adaptation. Harrison (1994) measures changing markups and productivity of manufacturing firms in the Côte d'Ivoire. Annual TFPG measured as the Törnquist index number formula, (1) rises from 0.4 per cent to 1.4 per cent under the assumption of perfect competition and constant returns to scale, (2) rises from 0.5 per cent to 1.4 per cent if the assumption of perfect competition is relaxed, and (3) if both assumptions are relaxed, productivity growth rises from 0.6 per cent to 1.8 per cent. Kee (2004) finds that the average annual growth rate of the productivity of Singapore's manufacturing sector from1974 to 1992 is 7 per cent while the TFP index takes imperfect competition and non-constant returns to scale into account, whereas the TFPG is less than 3 per cent by conventional measurement.

Note that van Leeuwen and van der Wiel (2003) find evidence of an opposite effect in the (market) service sector when the TFP is adjusted by a markup ignoring economies of scale. Based on firm-level data between 1994 and 1999, their study finds that the modified TFPG is 0.2 per cent higher than the traditional TFPG.

Table 14.4 Averages of multifactor productivity (%)

GMM FD				
MFPG	$\phi \in (0, 1]$	$\phi = 0$	$\phi = 0, \mu = 1$	$\phi = 0, \theta = \mu = 1$
Mean	0.95	1.00	–0.20	–0.73
Median	0.93	1.00	–0.10	0.61
Sectors where $\hat{\mu} > 1$				
Mean	2.30	2.60	0.02	–0.47
Median	1.50	2.40	0.23	–0.27
Sectors where $\hat{\mu} \leq 1$				
Mean	0.94	1.03	–0.26	–0.78
Median	0.91	1.04	–0.16	–0.66

In Table 14.4, we summarize our estimation results. In particular, when adopting the conventional framework of perfect competition and constant returns to scale, the residually estimated productivity growth is –0.73 per cent. When relaxing the assumption of constant returns to scale, the average (across years) TFP growth rate for all industries rises to –0.20. Moreover, introducing imperfect competition on the output market dramatically increases the productivity growth (1 per cent). This finding is in line with the majority of models of endogenous growth (e.g., Romer, 1990; Grossman and Helpman, 1991; Aghion and Howitt, 1992). Indeed, a decrease of the level of product market competition has a positive effect on productivity growth, by augmenting the monopoly rents that reward innovations.

Furthermore, connected to the innovation process and labour market imperfections, as in Aghion and Howitt (1994), we find that labour market imperfection results in a lower productivity growth rate (TFPG slightly decreases to 0.95 per cent). As a matter of fact, firms are subject to idiosyncratic shocks due to innovations that are implicitly asking for labour force reallocations. Labour reallocation influences the productivity growth rate, as it determines the speed with which resources are moved around to the most profitable firms. As rigidity of the labour market does not allow firms from adjusting their labour factor, labour market imperfection then causes a lower innovation rate.

As in the previous section, we reshape our results by considering two subsamples. One sample contains the estimates of those sectors for which the price–cost markup exceeds 1 and the other subsample considers the sectors showing evidence of perfect competition on the output market (price–cost markup less than or equal to 1). As expected, the average TFPG is remarkably higher for the first subsample of sectors (2.3 per cent) than for the second one, where the mean TFPG is approximately the same of the whole sample (0.94 per cent). We also find that this downward effect on TFPG is particularly remarkable for those firms exhibiting higher markups. As a further analysis, we take into account the possibility of correlation between class size (number of employees) and productivity growth. Figure A.2 in Appendix 3 shows no evidence of a distinct relationship between class size and TFPG. The same Appendix reports LOWESS[20] estimates of TFP growth rates for all sectors are graphed, aiming at discerning a distinct pattern over time. Some industries clearly show a positive trend in the productivity growth; therefore, a nonparametric test[21] to detect a significant trend over time is carried out. According to the results of Table A.5 in Appendix 3, only four out of 22 sectors have a significant trend. Food, beverages and tobacco, leather products and motor vehicles exhibit a positive trend, while paper products, publishing and printing show a decrease in TFPG.

5 Conclusion

In this chapter, we explore both theoretically and empirically a framework where we integrate possible labour market rigidities and output market behaviour in the total factor productivity growth (TFPG) measure. We consider market power measured by the traditional markup, and we propose an alternative markup proxy, which should capture possible effects of inefficiencies in production.

Embedding Hall's (1990) efficient bargaining model, which introduces a substantial degree of labour market imperfections, we show that rigidities and frictions in the labour market might be crucial for understanding the firms' marginal costs and their price-setting behaviour. We apply this analysis to 22 industries in Dutch manufacturing for the period 1989–2005.

By comparing a range of econometric estimators (level OLS, first-differenced OLS, first-differenced GMM, Arellano and Bover, 1995, and Blundell and Bond,

1998), we estimate a standard production function, allowing for an autoregressive component in the productivity shocks.

We show some evidence of imperfect competition on the output market and strong unions' power on the labour market. Markups are significantly and fairly larger than 1.0 and returns to scale are constant or moderately decreasing, in the range of 0.9 to 1.0. On the other hand, our data do not support the AR(1) structure that we assume for the idiosyncratic error term.

The variation of imperfect competition across sectors is large. The price–cost margin is lower than 1.01 for the first quartile of industries and higher than 1.16 for the top quartile. Workers' union power also takes values that range from 0.143 to 0.903, while returns to scale are likely to be homogeneously constant across sectors.

To the extent that wages are allocative, we find that labour market imperfections play a main role in either determining the market behaviour and in assessing the correct TFPG.

When adopting the conventional framework of perfect competition and constant returns to scale, the estimated productivity growth is –0.7 per cent, while when relaxing it, the average TFPG for all industries rises to –0.02 per cent. Then, introducing imperfect competition on the output market dramatically increases the productivity growth (to 1 per cent). Hence, a decrease of the level of product market competition has a positive effect on productivity growth. Furthermore, we find that labour market imperfection leads to a lower productivity growth rate (TFPG decreases to 0.95 per cent).

Notes

* This chapter is a result of a Dutch National Science Foundation (NWO) project under the author's supervision (Dynamism of Innovation research project 472-04-019). The author recognizes this financial support, together with the research support of his colleagues Sara Amoroso, Peter Kort and Bertrand Melenberg of Tilburg University and Mark Vancauteren of Hasselt University, and the editing assistance of Jonathan Michie, Sandra Gee and the publisher.

1. A production unit could be an establishment, a firm, an industry, or an entire economy.
2. Taking into account all the factors influencing output levels can be unrealistic, therefore MFP may be a more appropriate term to use.
3. According to Diewert (2006), factors that will tend to augment TFPG are: rapid investment growth (in reproducible or physical capital); rapid growth in investments in education, training and human capital; rapid growth in primary inputs will tend to lead to an even more rapid growth of output due to increasing returns to scale in production; increases in TFP are associated with increased specialization, which in turn is driven by growth in the size of the market; improvements in the functioning of markets, 'which could occur in a variety of ways, including: (i) improvements in personal security; (ii) improvements in property rights; (iii) reductions in trade barriers; (iv) improvements in telecommunications (in particular, the growth of internet driven markets) and (v) improvements in transportation and infrastructure' (p. 29); access to new knowledge about the development of new commodities and processes.
4. Under perfect competition on the input markets, the input quantity index is a function of the input prices and quantities for the two periods under consideration (Laspeyres [1871], Paasche [1874], Fisher's [1922] ideal quantity index being the square root of the product of the Laspeyres and Paasche quantity indexes, and Törnquist's [1936] quantity index).

5. Diewert (1976) showed that the Divisia index is 'exact' for the linearly homogeneous translog production function and is, therefore, superlative (since the translog is a flexible functional form).
6. Dobbelaere and Mairesse (2009) (also) end up with an expression adding a term with composite parameter $\phi_{it}/(1 - \phi_{it})$ to Hall's (1990) original decomposition of the Solow residual (and of TFPG).
7. The complete derivation of the efficient bargaining model is provided in Appendix 2.
8. Without having reliable data on the share of capital, s_{iKt}, model (14.9) can be rewritten using Hall's (1990) original decomposition of the Solow residual. Defining the Solow residual for three inputs, denoted by q_{it}, as the difference between the output growth rate and the input share weighted average of the input growth rates:

$$q_{it} \equiv \Delta y_{it} - s_{iLt}\Delta l_{it} - s_{iMt}\Delta m_{it} - (1 - s_{iLt} - s_{iMt})\,\Delta k_{it}, \tag{14.10}$$

we can substitute the (first) output growth equation in (14.8) with the elasticity of capital $\theta_{iKt} = \mu_{it}s_{iKt}$ replaced by $\theta_{it} - \theta_{iLt} - \theta_{iMt} = \theta_{it} - (\mu_{it}s_{iLt} - \phi_{it}\mu_{it} + \phi_{it}\theta_{it}) - \mu_{it}s_{iMt}$ herein, so that for $\Delta x_{it} \equiv (\Delta l_{it} - \Delta k_{it})s_{iLt} + (\Delta m_{it} - \Delta k_{it})s_{iMt}$, the Solow residual (14.10) can be rewritten as:

$$q_{it} = \Delta a_{it} + (\mu_{it} - 1)\,\Delta x_{it} + (\theta_{it} - 1)\,\Delta k_{it} - \phi_{it}(\mu_{it} - \theta_{it})(\,\Delta l_{it} - \Delta k_{it}), \tag{14.11}$$

so that the often very volatile firm-level output growth should no longer be explained according to (14.8) but the much smoother Solow residual could be explained according to (14.11), again with TFPG decomposed as $\Delta a_{it} = a_i + \delta_t + u_{it}$.
9. A supplementary estimation has been carried out for the time-varying markups μ_{it} and the bargaining power parameters ϕ_{it}, by introducing a general third-order polynomial in time:

$$\mu_{it} \equiv \beta^{\mu}_{i0} + \beta^{\mu}_{i1}t + \beta^{\mu}_{i2}t^2 + \beta^{\mu}_{i3}t^3$$
$$\phi_{it} \equiv \beta^{\phi}_{i0} + \beta^{\phi}_{i1}t + \beta^{\phi}_{i2}t^2 + \beta^{\phi}_{i3}t^3$$

Parameter heterogeneity across industries is modelled as stochastic variation by performing Swamy's (1970) random-coefficients linear regression model. A comparison between constant and time-varying markups shows that variation over time does not affect the size or the pattern of TFPG. Results are not reported, but available upon request.
10. Due to the scarce number of time observations per firm, we will estimate the parameters μ_{it} and ϕ_{it} as if they were constant over time and across firms. The effects of such aggregation may result in a misspecification of the firm-specific growth rate, a_i. Therefore, in subsection 3.2 we will consider a more appropriate level of aggregation (industry-level).
11. NACE Rev. 1 is a two-digit activity classification that was drawn up in 1990. It is a revision of the General Industrial Classification of Economic Activities within the European Communities, known by the acronym NACE and originally published by Eurostat in 1970.
12. When a variable is predetermined (not completely exogenous), the current period error term u_{it} is uncorrelated with current and lagged values of the predetermined variable but may be correlated with future values. An unpredictable technology shock will be uncorrelated with past (and potentially current) production settings, but will surely be correlated with future ones.
13. The two estimators give us more or less the same results as a consequence of estimating a static model. However, the FD estimator has the weaker exogeneity assumption that permits future values of production factors to be correlated with the error. This results in a light downwards bias of the markup and elasticity of scale.
14. The Sargan/Hansen tests should not be relied on too devotedly, as this type of test grows weaker the more moment conditions there are (Roodman, 2009).
15. To show the inapplicability of a dynamic panel data model to our data, we estimated the parameters of interest in the steady-state equilibrium. Results displayed in Table A.2 in Appendix 3 corroborate our propensity for a static model. Indeed, the steady-state markup μ^* is smaller both in the GMM FD and the system GMM (0.976 and 1.012, respectively).

16. The simplest case in which errors are believed to be homoskedastic, the Hansen J test coincides with the Sargan test. But if correlation is suspected in the errors, the Sargan test is inconsistent and the Hansen J test is used instead.
17. According to Table 14.3, the selected sectors that exhibit $\mu \leq 1$ are 15–28, 31, 36.
18. According to Table 14.3, the selected sectors that exhibit $\mu > 1$ are 29, 30, 32, 33, 34, 35.
19. We note that there is also another strand of literature that (usually through regressions) looks immediately at the effect of competition and broader definitions of economic performance (including productivity). For a comprehensive survey of empirical studies, see Nickell (1996). The author concludes that the empirical evidence for the relation is not convincing.
20. LOWESS smooth technique carries out locally weighted time series smoothing for both equispaced and non-equispaced data. LOWESS stands for 'locally weighted scatterplot smoothing' (Cleveland, 1979).
21. Cuzick's (1985) trend test is an extension to the Wilcoxon-type test for trend across a group of three or more independent random samples.

References

Aghion, P., M. Braun and J. Fedderke (2006), 'Competition and Productivity Growth in South Africa', CID Working Paper No. 132, Boston: Harvard University.

Aghion, P. and P. Howitt (1992), 'A Model of Growth through Creative Destruction', *Econometrica*, **60**(2), 323–51.

Aghion, P. and P. Howitt (1994), 'Growth and Unemployment', *Review of Economic Studies*, **61**(3), 477–94.

Arellano, M. and O. Bover (1995), 'Another Look at the Instrumental Variable Estimation of Error Component Models', *Journal of Econometrics*, **68**(1), 29–51.

Azzam, A., E. Lopez and R.A. Lopez (2004), 'Imperfect Competition and Total Factor Productivity Growth', *Journal of Productivity Analysis*, **22**, 173–84.

Balk, B.M. (2008), 'Measuring Productivity Change without Neoclassical Assumptions: A Conceptual Analysis', Working Paper No. ERS-2008-077-MKT, Erasmus Research Institute of Management (ERIM), Rotterdam: Erasmus University.

Basu, S. and J.G. Fernald (1997), 'Returns to Scale in US Production: Estimates and Implications', *Journal of Political Economy*, **105**(2), 249–83.

Bates, W. (2001), *How Much Government? The Effects of High Government Spending on Economic Performance*, Wellington: New Zealand Business Roundtable.

Bean C.R. (1994), 'European Unemployment: A Survey', *Journal of Economic Literature*, **32**(2).

Blundell, R. and S. Bond (1998), 'Initial Conditions and Moment Restrictions in Dynamic Panel Data Models', *Journal of Econometrics*, **87**(1), 115–43.

Bloch, H. and M. Olive (2001), 'Pricing Over the Cycle', *Review of Industrial Organization*, **19**(1), 99–108.

Bresnahan, T.F. (1988), 'Empirical Studies of Industries with Market Power', in R. Schmalensee and R. Willig (eds), *Handbook of Industrial Organization, Vol. II*, Amsterdam: North-Holland, pp. 1011–57.

Caves, D.W., L.R. Christensen and W.E. Diewert (1982), 'The Economic Theory of Index Numbers and the Measurement of Input, Output, and Productivity', *Econometrica*, **50**(6), 1393–414.

Chambers, R.G. (1988), *Applied Production Analysis: A Dual Approach*, Cambridge: Cambridge University Press.

Chirinko, R.S. and S.M. Fazzari (1994), 'Economic Fluctuations, Market Power, and Returns to Scale: Evidence from Firm-level Data', *Journal of Applied Econometrics*, **9**(1), 47–69.

Cleveland,W.S. (1979), 'Robust LocallyWeighted Regression and Smoothing Scatterplots', *Journal of the American Statistical Association*, **74**(368), 829–36.

Coutts, K., W. Godley and W. Nordhaus (1978), 'Industrial Pricing in the United Kingdom', Cambridge: Cambridge University Press.

Crépon, B., R. Desplatz and J. Mairesse (1999), 'Estimating Price–Cost Margins, Scale Economies and Workers' Bargaining Power at the Firm Level', CREST Working Paper No. G9917, Paris: CREST (ENSAE).

Crépon, B., R. Desplatz and J. Mairesse (2002), 'Price–Cost Margins and Rent Sharing: Evidence from a Panel of French Manufacturing Firms', revised version of CREST Working Paper No. G9917, Paris.

Crépon, B., R. Desplatz and J. Mairesse (2007), 'Price–Cost Margins and Rent Sharing: Evidence from a Panel of French Manufacturing Firms', mimeo.

Cuzick, J. (1985), 'A Wilcoxon-type Test for Trend', *Statistics in Medicine*, **4**(1), 87–90.

Diewert, W.E. (1976), 'Exact and Superlative Index Numbers', *Journal of Econometrics*, **4**(2), 114–45.

Diewert, W.E. (1993), 'Duality Approaches to Microeconomic Theory', Chapter 6 in W.E. Diewert and A.O. Nakamura (eds), *Essays in Index Number Theory, Volume I*, Amsterdam: Elsevier, 105–89.

Diewert, W.E. (2006), 'The Measurement of Productivity', Chapter 6 in W.E. Diewert, *Applied Economics*, Vancouver: University of British Columbia.

Diewert, W.E. and K.J. Fox (2004), 'On the Estimation of Returns to Scale, Technical Progress and Monopolistic Markups', Working Paper, Vancouver: University of British Columbia.

Dobbelaere, S. (2004), 'Estimation of Price–Cost Margins and Union Bargaining Power for Belgian Manufacturing', *International Journal of Industrial Organization*, **22**(10), 1381–98.

Dobbelaere, S. and J. Mairesse (2009), 'Panel Data Estimates of the Production Function and Product and Labour Market Imperfections', Working Paper No. 2009/586, Ghent University.

Domowitz, I., R.G. Hubbard and B.C. Petersen (1988), 'Market Structure and Cyclical Fluctuations in U.S. Manufacturing', *Review of Economics and Statistics*, **70**(1), 55–66.

Färe, R., S. Grosskopf, M. Norris and Z. Zhang (1994), 'Productivity Growth, Technical Progress, and Efficiency Change in Industrialized Countries', *American Economic Review*, **84**(1), 66–83.

Feng, G. and A. Serletis (2008), 'Productivity Trends in U.S. Manufacturing: Evidence from the NQ and AIM Cost Functions', *Journal of Econometrics*, **142**(1), 281–311.

Fisher, I. (1922), *The Making of Index Numbers*, Boston: Houghton-Mifflin.

Grossman, G. and E. Helpman (1991), 'Innovation and Growth in the Global Economy', Cambridge MA: MIT Press.

Hall, R.E. (1986), 'Market Structure and Macroeconomic Fluctuations', *Brookings Papers on Economic Activity*, **2**, 285–322.

Hall, R.E. (1988), 'The Relationship Between Price and Marginal Cost in U.S. Industry', *Journal of Political Economy*, **96**(5), 921–47.

Hall, R.E. (1990), 'Invariance Properties of Solow's Productivity Residual', in P. Diamond (ed.), *Growth, Productivity, Unemployment*, Cambridge MA: MIT Press, pp. 71–112.

Hall, B.H. and J. Mairesse (2002), 'Testing for Unit Roots in Panel Data: An Exploration for Econometric Models', in D. Andrews and J.H. Stock (eds), *Identification and Inference for Econometric Models: A Festschrift in Honor of Thomas Rothenburg*, New York: CUP.

Hansen, L.P. (1982), 'Large Sample Properties of Generalized Methods of Moments Estimators', *Econometrica*, **50**, 1029–54.

Harrison, A. (1994), 'Productivity, Imperfect Competition and Trade Reform: Theory and Evidence', *Journal of International Economics*, **36**(1/2), 53–73.

Hylleberg, S. and R.W. Jorgenson (1998), 'A Note on the Estimation of Markup Pricing in Manufacturing', CNLME Working Paper, No. 1998-6, University of Aarhus.

Johnson, W.E. (1913), 'The Pure Theory of Utility Curves', *Economic Journal*, **23**, 483–513.

Katz, L.F. and L.H. Summers (1989), 'Industry Rents: Evidence and Implications', *Brookings Papers on Economic Activity, Microeconomics*, **1989**(1), 209–75.

Kee, K. (2004), 'Estimating Productivity when Primal and Dual TFP Accounting Fail: An Illustration Using Singapore's Industries', *Topics in Economic Analysis & Policy*, Vol. 4, Article 26.

Klette, T.J. (1999), 'Market Power, Scale Economies and Productivity: Estimates from a Panel of Establishment Data', *The Journal of Industrial Economics*, **47**(4), 451–76.

Krueger, A.B. and L.H. Summers (1987), 'Reflections on Inter-Industry Wage Structure', in K. Lang and J. Leonard (eds), *Unemployment and the Structure of Labour Markets*, Oxford: Basil Blackwell.

Laspeyres, E. (1871), 'Die Berechnung einer mittleren Waarenpreissteigerun', *Jahrbücher für Nationalökonomie und Statistik*, **16**, 292–314.

Leeuwen, G. van and H. van der Wiel (2003), 'Do ICT spillovers matter: Evidence from Dutch firm-level data', CPB Discussion Paper 26, The Hague.

MacDonald I.M. and R.M. Solow (1981), 'Wage Bargaining and Employment', *The American Economic Review*, **71**(5), 896–908.
Malmquist, S. (1953), 'Index Numbers and Indifference Surfaces', *Trabajos de Estadistica*, **4**(1), 209–42.
Martins, J.O. and S. Scarpetta (1999), 'The Levels and Cyclical Behaviour of Markups across Countries and Market Structures', Working Paper No. 213, OECD Economic Department, Paris: OECD.
Morrison, C.J. (1992), 'Unravelling the Productivity Growth Slowdown in the United States, Canada and Japan: The Effects of Subequilibrium, Scale Economies and Markups', *The Review of Economics and Statistics*, **74**(3), 381–93.
Morrison, C.J. (1994), 'The Cyclical Nature of Markups in Canadian Manufacturing: A Production Theory Approach', *Journal of Applied Econometrics*, **9**(3), 269–82.
Morrison, C.J. (1999), *Cost Structure and the Measurement of Economic Performance*, Massachusetts: Kluwer Academic Press.
Nickell, S. (1996), 'Competition and Corporate Performance', *Journal of Political Economy*, **104**(41), 724–46.
Ohinata, S. and J. Plasmans (2002), 'Markups and International Competition with an Application to the Benelux Countries', Working Paper, University of Antwerp.
Paasche, H. (1874), 'Uber die Preisentwicklung der letzen Jahre nach den Hamburger Börsennotirunger', *Jahrbücher für Nationalökonomie und Statistik*, **23**, 168–78.
Romer, P. (1990), 'Endogenous Technological Change', *Journal of Political Economy*, **98**(5), 1002–37.
Roodman, D. (2009), 'How to do xtabond2: An Introduction to Difference and System GMM in Stata', *Stata Journal*, StataCorp LP, **9**(1), 86–136.
Sargan, J.D. (1958), 'The Estimation of Economic Relationships using Instrumental Variables', *Econometrica*, **26**(3), 393–415.
Shapiro, M. (1988), 'Measuring Market Power in U.S. Industry', NBER Working Paper No. 2212, Cambridge, MA.
Shephard, R.W. (1953), *Cost and Production Functions*, Princeton, NJ: Princeton University Press.
Solow, R.M. (1957), 'Technical Change and the Aggregate Production Function', *Review of Economics and Statistics*, **39**(3), 312–20.
Swamy, P.A.V. (1970), 'Efficient Inference in a Random Coefficient Regression Model', *Econometrica*, **38**(2), 311–23.
Törnquist, L. (1936), 'The Bank of Finland's Consumption Price Index', *Bank of Finland Monthly Bulletin*, **10**, 1–8.
Wu, Y. and J. Zhang (2000), 'Endogenous Markups and the Effects of Income Taxation: Theory and Evidence from OECD Countries', *Journal of Public Economics*, **77**, 383–406.

Appendix 1 Varying markups and returns to scale in a general setting

This Appendix presents a detailed analysis of the production function and the TFPG set-up allowing for market imperfections and scale economies. The derivation of markups, scale elasticities and TFPG is based on a single-output production technology for an arbitrary number of inputs.

In particular, we let each firm $i \in \{1,\ldots N)$ face the following production function for period t:

$$Y_{it} = A_{it}F_i(\mathbf{X_{it}}) \quad i = 1, 2,\ldots N; \quad t = 1,\ldots, T, \tag{14A.1}$$

where Y_{it} measures firm i's gross output, $\mathbf{X_{it}} \equiv (X_{i1t}, X_{i2t},\ldots, X_{iJ_it})'$ denotes the vector of J_i non-negative factor inputs, $F_i(.)$ is the core of the (differentiable) production function and A_{it} is TFP measured as the rate of a Hicks-neutral disembodied technology. Logarithmic differentiation of production function (14A.1) yields:

$$\frac{dY_{it}}{Y_{it}} = \frac{dA_{it}}{A_{it}} + \sum_{j=1}^{J_i} \frac{X_{ijt}}{F_i(\cdot)} \frac{\partial F_i(\cdot)}{\partial X_{ijt}} \frac{dX_{ijt}}{X_{ijt}}, \tag{14A.2}$$

with $\frac{dY_{it}}{Y_{it}}$ (logarithmic) output growth and $\frac{\partial \log Y_{it}}{\partial t} = \frac{dA_{it}}{A_{it}}$ (logarithmic) TFPG.

How does imperfect competition enter (14A.2)? Firms with market power do not set their value of the marginal product, $P_{it}A_{it}\frac{\partial F_i(\cdot)}{\partial X_{ijt}}$, equal to their corresponding factor price. It is assumed that each firm i faces an inverse demand function, $P_{it}(Y_t)$, which represents the market price as a function of aggregate (industry) output $Y_t \equiv \sum_{i=1}^{N} Y_{it}$, that is, by specifying firm i's (output) price as an arbitrary function of aggregate output we allow for various potential degrees of firm i's market power on its output market.

Firm i's optimization problem can be written as:

$$\max_{Y_{it},\mathbf{X}_{it}} \{P_{it}(Y_t)Y_{it} - \mathbf{V}_{it}'\mathbf{X}_{it} \mid Y_{it} = A_{it}F_i(\mathbf{X}_{it})\}, \tag{14A.3}$$

where $\mathbf{V}_{it} \equiv (V_{i1t}; V_{i2t},\ldots, X_{iJ_it})'$ is firm i's vector of J_i input prices. Assuming, in the first instance, that there is imperfect competition on the output market and perfect competition on the input markets (a monopolistic firm acting as a price-setter on its output market and a price-taker on its input markets), the first-order conditions (FOCs) implied by the solution of (14A.3) yield the following equations for the Lagrange multiplier and the nominal input prices:

$$P_{it}(Y_t) + \frac{\partial P_{it}(Y_t)}{\partial Yt}\frac{\partial Y_t}{\partial Yit}Y_{it} = P^*_{it} \text{ and} \tag{14A.4}$$
$$\left[P_{it}(Y_t) + Y_{it}\frac{\partial P_{it}(Y_t)}{\partial Y_t}\frac{\partial Y_t}{\partial Y_{it}}\right]\frac{\partial Y_{it}}{\partial \mathbf{X}_{it}} = \mathbf{V}_{it},$$

where, according to Diewert (1993) and Diewert and Fox (2004), the Lagrange multiplier P^*_{it} is firm *i*'s shadow or marginal price of output under profit maximization and market power enables firm *i* to set each input's marginal product, $\frac{\partial Y_{it}}{\partial X_{ikt}}$, above the respective factor cost, or:

$$\frac{\partial Y_{it}}{\partial X_{ikt}} = \left[\frac{1}{1 + \frac{\partial P_{it}(Y_t)}{\partial Y_t}\frac{Y_{it}}{P_{it}(Y_t)}}\right]\frac{V_{ikt}}{P_{it}(Y_t)} \quad \text{for } k = 1,\ldots,J_i, \tag{14A.5}$$

where the term between square brackets is firm *i*'s markup. Note that in case of perfect competition $\frac{\partial P_{it}(Y_t)}{\partial Y_t}$ goes to zero, implying that prices are set at marginal cost since marginal revenue (MR_{it}) is (always) equal to marginal cost (MC_{it}) (or $MR_{it} = P^*_{it} = MC_{it}$) and inputs are paid their marginal products (markup equal to 1) then.

For firm *i*, the first-order condition with respect to output in (14A.4) can be rewritten as:

$$\frac{P_{it}(Y_t) - MC_{it}}{P_{it}(Y_t)} = \frac{\partial P_{it}(Y_t)}{\partial Y_t}\frac{Y_{it}}{Y_t}\frac{Y_t}{P_{it}(Y_t)} \tag{14A.6}$$

or the Lerner index as a measure of a monopolist's market power is inversely related to the price elasticity of market demand:[1]

$$\ell_{it} = \frac{ms_{it}}{\varepsilon_{it}} \tag{14A.7}$$

where $\ell_{it} \equiv \frac{P_{it}(Y_t) - MC_{it}}{P_{it}(Y_t)}$ is firms *i*'s Lerner index or (relative) price–cost margin, $\varepsilon_{it} \equiv -\frac{\partial Y_t}{\partial P_{it}(Y_t)}\frac{P_{it}(Y_t)}{Y_t}$ is firm *i*'s elasticity of demand with respect to price and $ms_{it} = \frac{Y_{it}}{Y_t}$ is its market share. The Lerner index (14A.7) is defined in the range of $0 \leq \ell_{it} < 1$. Note that the markup (ratio) μ_{it}, which we define as the ratio of output price over marginal (production) cost, can easily be related to the Lerner index:

$$\mu_{it} \equiv P_{it}/MC_{it} = 1/(1 - \ell_{it}) \geq 1, \tag{14A.8}$$

so that it becomes clear that, if firm *i* is not perfectly competitive, then the value of its marginal product exceeds its factor cost by some markup μ_{it} in (14A.5), that is:

$$\mu_{it} = \left[\frac{1}{1 + \frac{\partial P_{it}(Y_t)}{\partial Y_t} \frac{Y_{it}}{P_{it}(Y_t)}} \right]. \tag{14A.9}$$

From (14A.6) we obtain that the second FOC in (14A.4) can be rewritten as:

$$\mathbf{V}_{it} = P_{it}(Y_t)(1 - \ell_{it}) \frac{\partial Y_{it}}{\partial \mathbf{X}_{it}}$$

or for any individual input factor $k \in J_i$:

$$P_{it}(Y_t)(1 - \ell_{it}) \frac{\partial \ln Y_{it}}{\partial \ln X_{ikt}} \frac{Y_{it}}{X_{ikt}} = V_{ikt} : k = 1, 2, \ldots, J_i; t = 1, \ldots, T \tag{14A.10}$$

$$\frac{\partial \ln Y_{it}}{\partial \ln X_{ikt}} = \frac{1}{(1 - \ell_{it})} \frac{V_{ikt} X_{ikt}}{Y_{it} P_{it}(Y_t)} = \mu_{it} s_{ikt},$$

where s_{ikt} denotes the share of the cost of input k in the total production value of firm i, or $s_{ikt} \equiv V_{ikt} X_{ikt} / [Y_{it} P_{it}(Y_t)]$, so that firm i's total (factor) input share can be written as:

$$s_{it} = \sum_{k=1}^{J_i} s_{ikt} = \frac{\mathbf{V}'_{it} \mathbf{X}_{it}}{Y_{it} P_{it}(Y_t)}. \tag{14A.11}$$

Hence, following Ohinata and Plasmans (2002), firm i's total input share is found to be equal to the inverse of its average markup at period t, since the latter can be defined as the profit ratio or the ratio of firm i's output price over its average (production) cost at that period, or:

$$\mu_{it}^{a} \equiv \frac{P_{it}(Y_t)}{AC_{it}} \tag{14A.12}$$

with the average cost being defined as $AC_{it} \equiv \frac{TC_{it}}{Y_{it}} = \frac{\mathbf{V}'_{it}\mathbf{X}_{it}}{Y_{it}}$. Eq. (14A.10) says that the output elasticity of any individual input k equals the markup times the share of input k in the total production value of firm i.

The returns to scale parameter θ_{it} measures the responsiveness of output to an increase in all firm i's inputs by a scalar factor λ at period t. Under the homogeneity assumption of production function (14A.1) we have that $F(\lambda \mathbf{X}_{it}) = \lambda^{\theta_{it}} F(\mathbf{X}_{it})$ with $0 < \theta_{it} < \infty$, where $\theta_{it} = 1$ denotes constant returns to scale, $\theta_{it} > 1$ increasing returns to scale and $\theta_{it} < 1$ decreasing returns to scale. The time-varying, input-dependent returns to scale parameter, expressed as an elasticity of scale, θ_{it}, is defined as follows (see, e.g., Chambers, 1988):

$$\theta_{it} \equiv \frac{\partial \ln F(\lambda \mathbf{X}_{it})}{\partial \ln \lambda}\Big|_{\lambda=1} = \frac{\partial F(\lambda \mathbf{X}_{it})}{\partial \lambda} \cdot \frac{\lambda}{F(\lambda \mathbf{X}_{it})}\Big|_{\lambda=1}. \qquad (14A.13)$$

Hence, under constant returns to scale, $\frac{\partial F(\lambda \mathbf{X}_{it})}{\partial \lambda} = F(\mathbf{X}_{it})$ and $\frac{\lambda}{F(\lambda \mathbf{X}_{it})} = \frac{1}{F(\lambda \mathbf{X}_{it})}$, or (14A.13) implies $\theta_{it} = 1$. By analogous reasoning, we find variable returns to scale implying $\theta_{it} \neq 1$. Since the elasticity of scale θ_{it} is equal to the sum of all output elasticities with respect to inputs given by the sum of equation (14A.10) over all inputs (Johnson, 1913), we can directly express this time-varying, input-dependent elasticity of scale θ_{it} in (14A.13) as the sum over all partial elasticities of scale θ_{ikt}:

$$\theta_{it} \equiv \frac{\partial \ln F(\lambda \mathbf{X}_{it})}{\partial \ln \lambda}\Big|_{\lambda=1} = \sum_{k=1}^{J_i} \frac{\partial Y_{it}}{\partial X_{ikt}} \frac{X_{ikt}}{Y_{it}} = \sum_{k=1}^{J_i} \theta_{ikt}, \qquad (14A.14)$$

so that, using the first part of the last equality in (14A.10) and taking account of (14A.3), (14A.11), and (14A.12), the time-varying markup in (14A.8) can be rewritten as the ratio between the time-varying, input-dependent elasticity of scale and the total input share (the inverse average markup):

$$\mu_{it} = \frac{Y_{it} P_{it}(Y_t)}{\mathbf{V}_{it}' \mathbf{X}_{it}} \theta_{it} = \frac{\theta_{it}}{s_{it}} = \mu_{it}^{a} \theta_{it}. \qquad (14A.15)$$

There are two important features of the markup involved in (14A.15). First, it allows for time-varying returns to scale. Under constant returns to scale and constant markups, equation (14A.15) is equivalent to the measure proposed by Hall (1988). However, the assumption of the constant (or non-variable) returns to scale restriction is a strong one that has received criticism from many authors (e.g., Bresnahan, 1988; Chirinko and Fazzari, 1994; Hylleberg and Jorgenson, 1998; Klette, 1999; Martins and Scarpetta, 1999 and Aghion et al., 2006). Second, the markup measure in equation (14A.15) is allowed to vary over time. There are several possible factors that may cause cyclical behaviour of markups. Hall (1986) originally suggested that capacity utilization fluctuations are closely linked to markup levels. Domowitz et al. (1988) found that markups are more pro-cyclical in concentrated than in less concentrated US industries. Shapiro (1988) notes that demand elasticities might affect markups. Morrison (1994) takes into account a number of factors (economies of scale, utilization, unemployment, import prices) and finds that estimated markups tend to increase over time and appear to be cyclical. In addition, Chirinko and Fazzari (1994) find a strong correlation between economies of scale and markups, which is obviously also implied by (14A.15). Several studies also relate markups to business cycles (e.g., Wu and Zhang, 2000 and Bloch and Olive, 2001).

Note

1. The larger the elasticity of demand in absolute terms, the smaller the monopolistic firm's market power.

Appendix 2 Bargaining model

This Appendix provides the solution of the Nash bargaining model and the derivation of the labour elasticity.

The solution to the bargaining problem:

$$\max_{W_{it},L_{it},K_{it},M_{it}} \left[L_{it}(W_{it}-\overline{W}_{it})\right]^{\phi_{it}}\left[P_{it}(Y_t)Y_{it}-W_{it}L_{it}-R_{it}K_{it}-Z_{it}M_{it}\right]^{1-\phi_{it}}$$

is obtained by maximizing with respect to employment and to wage, and then combining the two FOCs. The FOC for employment gives the following results:

$$\frac{\partial\left[L_{it}(W_{it}-\overline{W}_{it})\right]^{\phi_{it}}(P_{it}(Y_t)Y_{it}-W_{it}L_{it}-R_{it}K_{it}-Z_{it}M_{it})^{1-\phi_{it}}}{\partial L_{it}}=0 \quad (14A.16)$$

$$\phi_{it}L_{it}^{\phi_{it}-1}(W_{it}-\overline{W}_{it})^{\phi_{it}}(P_{it}(Y_t)Y_{it}-W_{it}L_{it}-R_{it}K_{it}-Z_{it}M_{it})^{1-\phi_{it}}=$$
$$(1-\phi_{it})(P_{it}(Y_t)Y_{it}-W_{it}L_{it}-R_{it}K_{it}-Z_{it}M_{it})^{-\phi_{it}}[L_{it}(W_{it}-\overline{W}_{it})]^{\phi_{it}}\left(W_{it}-\frac{\partial P_{it}(Y_t)Y_{it}}{\partial L_{it}}\right)$$

or

$$\phi_{it}L_{it}^{\phi_{it}-1}(P_{it}(Y_t)Y_{it}-W_{it}L_{it}-R_{it}K_{it}-Z_{it}M_{it})=(1-\phi_{it})[L_{it}]^{\phi_{it}}\left(W_{it}-\frac{\partial P_{it}(Y_t)Y_{it}}{\partial L_{it}}\right)$$
$$\frac{\phi_{it}}{L_{it}}(P_{it}(Y_t)Y_{it}-W_{it}L_{it}-R_{it}K_{it}-Z_{it}M_{it})=(1-\phi_{it})\left(W_{it}-\frac{\partial P_{it}(Y_t)Y_{it}}{\partial L_{it}}\right)$$
$$-\phi_{it}W_{it}+\frac{\phi_{it}}{L_{it}}(P_{it}(Y_t)Y_{it}-R_{it}K_{it}-Z_{it}M_{it})=W_{it}-\phi_{it}W_{it}-(1-\phi_{it})\frac{\partial P_{it}(Y_t)Y_{it}}{\partial L_{it}}$$
$$W_{it}=(1-\phi_{it})\frac{\partial P_{it}(Y_t)Y_{it}}{\partial L_{it}}+\frac{\phi_{it}}{L_{it}}(P_{it}(Y_t)Y_{it}-R_{it}K_{it}-Z_{it}M_{it})$$
$$W_{it}=\frac{\partial P_{it}(Y_t)Y_{it}}{\partial L_{it}}-\phi_{it}\frac{\partial P_{it}(Y_t)Y_{it}}{\partial L_{it}}\cdot\frac{L_{it}}{L_{it}}+\frac{\phi_{it}}{L_{it}}P_{it}(Y_t)Y_{it}-\frac{\phi_{it}}{L_{it}}R_{it}K_{it}-\frac{\phi_{it}}{L_{it}}Z_{it}M_{it}$$
$$W_{it}=\frac{\partial P_{it}(Y_t)Y_{it}}{\partial L_{it}}+\frac{\phi_{it}}{L_{it}}\left(P_{it}(Y_t)Y_{it}-R_{it}K_{it}-Z_{it}M_{it}-\frac{\partial P_{it}(Y_t)Y_{it}}{\partial L_{it}}\cdot L_{it}\right) \quad (14A.17)$$

Defining $\frac{\partial P_{it}(Y_t)Y_{it}}{\partial L_{it}}\equiv r_{iLt}$, we can rewrite equation (14A.17) as:

$$W_{it}=r_{iLt}+\frac{\phi_{it}}{L_{it}}(P_{it}(Y_t)Y_{it}-R_{it}K_{it}-Z_{it}M_{it}-r_{iLt}\cdot L_{it}) \quad (14A.18)$$

Maximizing with respect to wage leads to:

$$\frac{\partial [L_{it}(W_{it}-\overline{W}_{it})]^{\phi_{it}}(P_{it}(Y_t)Y_{it}-W_{it}L_{it}-R_{it}K_{it}-Z_{it}M_{it})^{1-\phi_{it}}}{\partial W_{it}}=0 \quad (14A.19)$$

$$L_{it}^{\phi_{it}}\phi_{it}(W_{it}-\overline{W}_{it})^{\phi_{it}-1}(P_{it}(Y_t)Y_{it}-W_{it}L_{it}-R_{it}K_{it}-Z_{it}M_{it})^{1-\phi_{it}}+$$
$$+L_{it}^{\phi_{it}}(W_{it}-\overline{W}_{it})^{\phi_{it}}(1-\phi_{it})(P_{it}(Y_t)Y_{it}-W_{it}L_{it}-R_{it}K_{it}-Z_{it}M_{it})^{-\phi_{it}}\cdot(-L_{it})=0$$

$$L_{it}^{\phi_{it}}\phi_{it}(W_{it}-\overline{W}_{it})^{\phi_{it}-1}(P_{it}(Y_t)Y_{it}-W_{it}L_{it}-R_{it}K_{it}-Z_{it}M_{it})^{1-\phi_{it}}=$$
$$=L_{it}^{\phi_{it}}(W_{it}-\overline{W}_{it})^{\phi_{it}}(1-\phi_{it})(P_{it}(Y_t)Y_{it}-W_{it}L_{it}-R_{it}K_{it}-Z_{it}M_{it})^{-\phi_{it}}\cdot L_{it}$$

$$\phi_{it}(W_{it}-\overline{W}_{it})^{-1}(P_{it}(Y_t)Y_{it}-W_{it}L_{it}-R_{it}K_{it}-Z_{it}M_{it})=(1-\phi_{it})L_{it}$$

$$\frac{\phi_{it}(P_{it}(Y_t)Y_{it}-W_{it}L_{it}-R_{it}K_{it}-Z_{it}M_{it})}{L_{it}}=(1-\phi_{it})(W_{it}-\overline{W}_{it})$$

$$-\phi_{it}W_{it}+\frac{\phi_{it}(P_{it}(Y_t)Y_{it}-R_{it}K_{it}-Z_{it}M_{it})}{L_{it}}=W_{it}-\overline{W}_{it}-\phi_{it}W_{it}+\phi_{it}\overline{W}_{it}$$

$$W_{it}=(1-\phi_{it})\overline{W}_{it}+\frac{\phi_{it}}{L_{it}}(P_{it}(Y_t)Y_{it}-R_{it}K_{it}-Z_{it}M_{it}) \quad (14A.20)$$

Combining the two FOCs (Eq. (14A.16) and Eq. (14A.19)), taking account of the markup (14A.9) in Appendix 1, leads to the reservation wage $\overline{W}_{it}$:

$$\overline{W}_{it}=r_{iLt}\equiv\frac{\partial P_{it}(Y_t)Y_{it}}{\partial L_{it}}=\left[P_{it}(Y_t)+Y_{it}\frac{\partial P_{it}(Y_t)}{\partial Y_t}\frac{\partial Y_t}{\partial Y_{it}}\right]\frac{\partial Y_{it}}{\partial L_{it}},$$
$$=P_{it}(Y_t)\left[1+\frac{\partial P_{it}(Y_t)}{\partial Y_t}\frac{Y_{it}}{P_{it}(Y_t)}\right]\frac{\partial Y_{it}}{\partial L_{it}}=$$
$$\overline{W}_{it}=\frac{P_{it}(Y_t)}{\mu_{it}}\frac{\partial Y_{it}}{\partial L_{it}} \quad (14A.21)$$

Once we have achieved the optimal reservation wage, we plug expression (14A.21) in expression (14A.19), obtaining:

$$s_{iLt}=(1-\phi_{it})\theta_{iLt}\frac{1}{\mu_{it}}+\phi_{it}(1-s_{iKt}-s_{iMt}) \quad (14A.22)$$

where s_{iLt}, s_{iKt} and s_{iMt} denote the shares of labour cost in revenue, $\frac{W_{it}L_{it}}{P_{it}(Y_t)Y_{it}}$, capital cost in revenue, $\frac{R_{it}K_{it}}{P_{it}(Y_t)Y_{it}}$, and intermediate goods cost in revenue, $\frac{Z_{it}M_{it}}{P_{it}(Y_t)Y_{it}}$, respectively. From Eq. (14A.22) we can express the elasticity of labour as:

$$\theta_{iLt} = \frac{\mu_{it}s_{iLt}}{(1-\phi_{it})} - \frac{\mu_{it}\phi_{it}(1-s_{iKt}-s_{iMt})}{(1-\phi_{it})}. \tag{14A.23}$$

Eq. (14A.22) is derived by plugging expression (14A.21) into expression (14A.20).

Multiplying both sides of Eq. (14A.20) by $\frac{L_{it}}{Y_{it}}$, we have:

$$\begin{aligned}
\frac{W_{it}L_{it}}{Y_{it}} &= (1-\phi_{it})\frac{P_{it}(Y_t)\partial Y_{it}}{\mu_{it}}\frac{\partial Y_{it}}{\partial L_{it}}\frac{L_{it}}{Y_{it}} + \frac{\phi_{it}}{L_{it}}P_{it}(Y_t)Y_{it}\frac{L_{it}}{Y_{it}} - \frac{\phi_{it}}{L_{it}}R_{it}K_{it}\frac{L_{it}}{Y_{it}} - \frac{\phi_{it}}{L_{it}} \\
&\quad Z_{it}M_{it}\frac{L_{it}}{Y_{it}} \\
&= (1-\phi_{it})\frac{P_{it}(Y_t)}{\mu_{it}}\theta_{iLt} + \phi_{it}P_{it}(Y_t) - \frac{\phi_{it}}{L_{it}}R_{it}K_{it}\frac{L_{it}}{Y_{it}} - \frac{\phi_{it}}{L_{it}}Z_{it}M_{it}\frac{L_{it}}{Y_{it}} \\
&= (1-\phi_{it}\frac{P_{it}(Y_t)}{\mu_{it}}\theta_{iLt} + \phi_{it}P_{it}(Y_t)\left[1 - \frac{R_{it}K_{it}}{P_{it}(Y_t)Y_{it}} - \frac{Z_{it}M_{it}}{P_{it}(Y_t)Y_{it}}\right] \\
\frac{W_{it}L_{it}}{P_{it}(Y_t)Y_{it}} &= (1-\phi_{it})\frac{1}{\mu_{it}}\theta_{iLt} + \phi_{it}\left[1 - \frac{R_{it}K_{it}}{P_{it}(Y_t)Y_{it}} - \frac{Z_{it}M_{it}}{P_{it}(Y_t)Y_{it}}\right] \\
s_{iLt} &= (1-\phi_{it})\theta_{iLt}\frac{1}{\mu_{it}} + \phi_{it}(1-s_{iKt}-s_{iMt})
\end{aligned}$$

from which we obtain:

$$\theta_{iLt} = \frac{\mu_{it}s_{iLt}}{(1-\phi_{it})} - \frac{\mu_{it}\phi_{it}(1-s_{iKt}-s_{iMt})}{(1-\phi_{it})}.$$

Substituting $s_{iKt} = \frac{\theta_{it}-\theta_{iLt}-\theta_{iMt}}{\mu_{it}}$ in the last equation, we get:

$$\begin{aligned}
\theta_{iLt} &= \frac{\mu_{it}s_{iLt}}{(1-\phi_{it})} - \frac{\mu_{it}\phi_{it}\left(1-\left[\frac{\theta_{it}-\theta_{iLt}-\theta_{iMt}}{\mu_{it}}\right]-s_{iMt}\right)}{(1-\phi_{it})} \\
&= \frac{\mu_{it}s_{iLt}}{(1-\phi_{it})} - \frac{\phi_{it}(\mu_{it}-\theta_{it}+\theta_{iLt})}{(1-\phi_{it})} \\
&= \frac{\mu_{it}s_{iLt}}{(1-\phi_{it})} - \left[\frac{\phi_{it}}{(1-\phi_{it})}\mu_{it} - \frac{\phi_{it}}{(1-\phi_{it})}\theta_{it} + \frac{\phi_{it}}{(1-\phi_{it})}\theta_{iLt}\right] \\
\frac{\theta_{iLt}}{(1-\phi_{it})} &= \frac{\mu_{it}s_{iLt}}{(1-\phi_{it})} - \frac{\phi_{it}}{(1-\phi_{it})}\mu_{it} + \frac{\phi_{it}}{(1-\phi_{it})}\theta_{it}
\end{aligned}$$

Then, rearranging terms, the elasticity of labour can be expressed in terms of the markup, μ_{it}, the elasticity of scale, θ_{it}, and the degree of workers' bargaining power ϕ_{it},

$$\theta_{iLt} = \mu_{it} s_{iLt} - \phi_{it}\mu_{it} + \phi_{it}\theta_{it}.$$

Appendix 3 Tables and figures

Table A.1 NACE two-digit code and number of firms

Code	Sector	*N*
15–16	Food, beverages, tobacco	2342
17	Textiles	584
18	Wearing apparel	518
19	Leather	235
20	Wood	666
21	Paper products, publishing, printing	436
22	Publishing, printing and reproduction of recorded media	2095
23	Coke, refined petroleum products and nuclear fuel	56
24	Chemicals and chemical products	902
25	Rubber and plastic products	942
26	Other non-metallic mineral products	793
27	Basic metals, Fabricated metal products	256
28	Fabricated metal products, except machinery and equipment	3093
29	Machinery and equipment	2362
30	Electrical and optical equipment	99
31	Electrical machinery and apparatus	617
32	Radio, television and communication equipment and apparatus	224
33	Medical, precision and optical instruments, watches and clocks	690
34	Transport equipment	407
35	Motor vehicles and other	515
36	Other	1106
	Total	15976

Table A.2 Steady-state equilibrium

	Equilibrium Spec	
	GMM DIFF	GMM SYS
ϕ_{it}	0.445	0.869
	(0.023)	(0.180)
μ_{it}	0.976	1.012
	(0.013)	(0.016)
θ_{it}	0.861	0.506
	(0.011)	(0.011)
$\mu_{it}(\theta_{it} = 0)$	0.967	1.006
	(0.013)	(0.014)
$\theta_{it}(\phi_{it} = 0)$	0.904	0.940
	(0.012)	(0.013)
No. of firms	7161	7161

Notes:
a. Std. err. in parentheses.
b. Sample period 1989–2005.
c. Dependent variable: output growth Δy_{it}.

Table A.3 MFPG(%) per estimation method

MFPG	$\phi \in (0, 1]$	$\phi = 0$	$\mu = 1$
OLS level			
Mean	0.00	0.00	0.00
Median	0.07	0.08	0.07
OLS FD			
Mean	0.00	0.00	0.00
Median	0.00	0.00	0.00
GMM FD			
Mean	0.95	1.00	0.83
Median	0.93	1.00	0.85

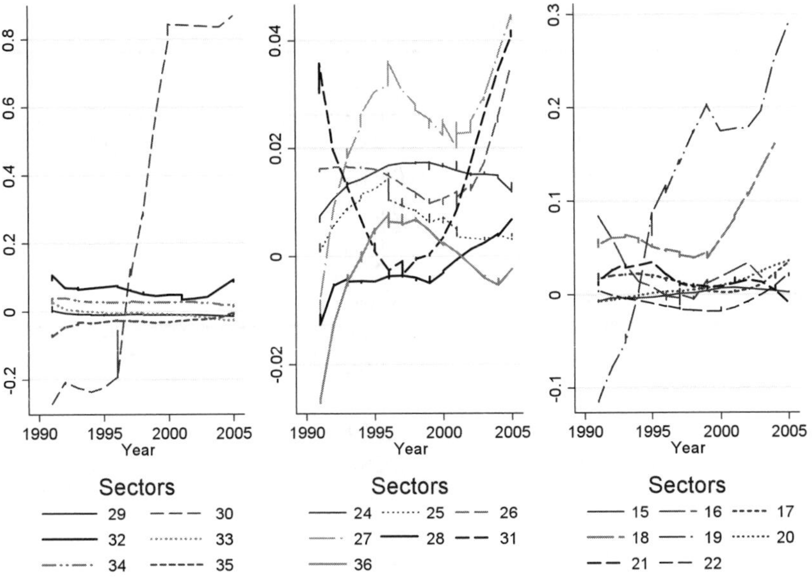

Figure A.1 *TFPG per sector*

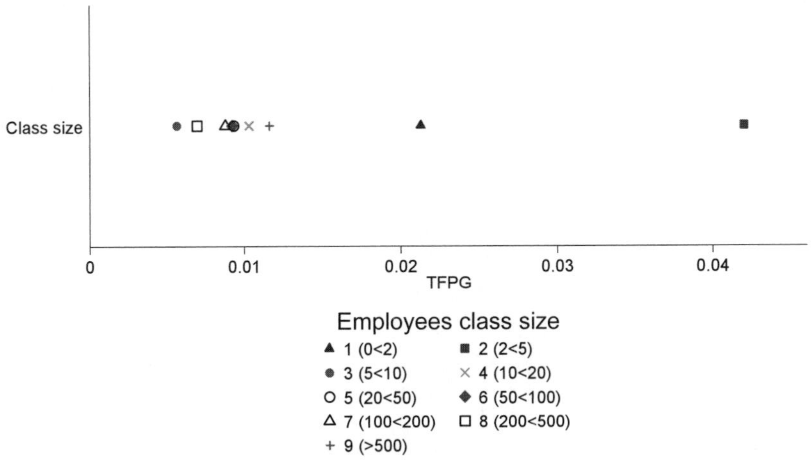

Figure A.2 *TFPG per class size*

Table A.5 Time trend test per sector

Industry	*z*	p-value
15	1.96	0.050
17	–0.82	0.413
18	–2.07	0.038
19	6.10	0.000
20	1.23	0.219
21	–2.74	0.006
22	–1.22	0.221
24	–0.17	0.865
25	–0.25	0.799
26	–0.23	0.819
27	–0.28	0.780
28	0.58	0.564
29	–1.03	0.304
30	0.85	0.396
31	0.82	0.413
32	–0.59	0.556
33	–0.71	0.476
34	–1.03	0.304
35	1.65	0.098
36	1.44	0.150

15 European integration and the 'euro project'

Philip Arestis and Malcolm Sawyer

Introduction

The euro was introduced as a 'virtual' currency in January 1999, and then as a 'real' currency in January 2002. There were 12 EU member countries adopting the euro in 2002, since joined by a further five other countries,[1] and subsequently, but prior to the financial crisis of 2007–09, a number of other countries were on the road to joining. The creation of a single currency covering a substantial number of countries has been a significant step in the integration of the economies of those countries, which form the European Union (EU), and more notably for those who are part of the Economic and Monetary Union (EMU). The adoption of the euro is not just a matter of a single currency now prevailing across the eurozone with reduced transactions costs for trade between member countries. It is more notable that the euro is embedded in a particular set of institutional and policy arrangements, which can tell us much about the nature of the economic integration processes in the EU. In this chapter, we examine the neo-liberal nature of the ideas, which are associated with the euro, and in light of the experiences of economic performance over the first decade or so of the euro, not forgetting the financial crisis of 2008–09, which has exposed the problematic nature of the policy structures of EMU.

The adoption of the euro was a further step in a process of economic integration, which began with the signing of the Treaty of Rome by the six founder member countries (see Arestis et al., 2001, especially Chapter 2, for discussion). Proposals for a single currency began in earnest with the Werner Report in 1970, which advocated the movement toward economic and monetary union by 1980. The European Monetary System (EMS) was launched in March 1979 seeking to establish monetary and exchange rate stability, based around the introduction of the Exchange Rate Mechanism (ERM) and centred on the European Currency Unit (ECU). In 1986 the EU amended the Treaty of Rome with the Single European Act, and set the end of 1992 as a target date for the removal of all remaining barriers to the free flow of goods, services and resources.

The countdown to the single currency can be seen to have started with the signing of the Maastricht Treaty (or Treaty on European Union to give its full title). The so-called convergence criteria, which were to determine whether a national currency would join the single currency, provide some insights into the nature of the euro project and are discussed in the next section. The introduction of the euro was also accompanied by the adoption of the Stability and Growth

Pact (SGP) with its constraints on fiscal policy; this is taken up in the section that follows that of the Maastricht Treaty discussion. The neo-liberal nature of the EMU and its policy framework are then discussed, followed by some reflections on the impact of the framework on inflation and unemployment. The last main section outlines the relatively poor economic performance under the euro and the major issues that are now emerging.

The Maastricht Treaty and all that

The convergence criteria under the Maastricht Treaty for a country's membership of the single currency and, by implication, membership of the independent European System of Central Banks (ESCB), comprising the European Central Bank (ECB) and national central banks of those countries that belong to the EMU, are: (1) a high degree of price stability, with an inflation rate within 1.5 per cent of the average inflation rate of the three-best performing member states; (2) 'healthy' government finance, defined as a maximum ratio of 3 per cent government deficit to GDP at market prices, and a maximum ratio of 60 per cent of government debt to GDP at market prices; (3) observance of the normal ERM fluctuation margins for at least two years without any devaluation with respect to the member state currencies; and (4) long-term interest rate levels that do not deviate by two percentage points from the nominal long-term government bond rates of the average of the three best-performing member states in terms of price stability.[2] Countries are also required to enact legislation for their central banks to become 'independent'. The convergence criteria could be viewed as of mainly historic interest, though they remain relevant for countries seeking to join the EMU. But the criteria are of significance for what was viewed as important for the formation of the euro, and by omission what was viewed as unimportant.

These convergence criteria related to what may be called nominal variables – inflation rates, interest rates and budget deficits. There is some rationale for concerns over convergence of inflation and interest rates for the formation of a single currency, since a single currency area will have a single monetary policy and hence a single central bank interest rate. Similarity of inflation rates across countries would seem a requirement for a single currency area to be sustained. But the requirement related to the rate of inflation at a point in time, and did not pay any attention to the inflationary processes in different countries, and, as will be seen below, differential inflation rates have been a continuing problem.

But any rationale for the inclusion of the convergence of budget deficits to less than 3 per cent of GDP and for government debt to be less than 60 per cent of GDP has been generally lacking. The numbers appear plucked out of the air. The adoption of these criteria not only brought in a deflationary element to the Maastricht Treaty, but also reflected the general rejection of Keynesian economics and the potential use of fiscal policy to stimulate employment.

It is also evident that there was no reference to real convergence, that is, the convergence of economic growth, unemployment levels, level of national income per head, the business cycles and the like. Indeed, there remain massive differences in living standards and unemployment rates across the EU. The single currency is much more likely to operate effectively if there is some real convergence between participating economies; yet those concerns were dismissed (Arestis et al., 2001). The omission of reference to countries' trade accounts is particularly significant: for a country with a large trade deficit this may be evidence of an over-valued exchange rate (at least relative to that which would generate trade balance) and covering the deficit requires borrowing from outside the country. A continuing deficit leads to rising debt levels, and places a country at the mercy of the international financial markets. In a currency union there is clearly no possibility for a country to address a trade deficit through devaluation.

The institutional macroeconomic policy framework of the EMU has three key elements. First, the ECB is the only effective federal economic institution. The ECB has the one policy instrument of the rate of interest to pursue the main objective of low inflation. The single monetary policy has a euro-area-wide perspective. A quantitative definition of price stability has been adopted in the form of, initially, a 0–2 per cent target for the annual increase in the Harmonised Index of Consumer Prices (HICP) for the euro area; it was later changed, in May 2003, to 'below but near to 2 per cent' target. The ECB has adopted a 'two-pillar' monetary strategy to achieve this target through the policy instrument of interest rate. The 'first pillar' is a commitment to analyse monetary developments for the information they contain about future price developments. This is the quantitative reference value for monetary growth, where a target of 4.5 per cent of M3 has been imposed. The 'second pillar' is a broadly based assessment of the outlook of price developments and the risks to price stability. This broad range of indicators includes: the euro exchange rate; labour market indicators, such as wages and unit labour costs; fiscal policy indicators; financial market indicators, such as asset prices. The order of the significance of the two 'pillars' was reversed in May 2003.

Second, the ECB and the national central banks are linked into the ESCB with a division of responsibility between them. The ECB has the responsibility for setting interest rates in pursuit of the inflation objective and the national central banks have responsibility for regulatory matters.

Third, the ECB is structured to be independent of the EU Council and Parliament and of its member governments. Thus, there is a complete separation between the monetary authorities, in the form of the ESCB, and the fiscal authorities, in the shape of the national governments comprising the EMU. There can then be little effective coordination of monetary and fiscal policy. For apart from the separation of the monetary and fiscal authorities, there is also the requirement that national governments (and hence the fiscal authorities) should not exert any influence on the ECB (and hence the monetary authorities). Any strict interpretation of that edict would rule out any attempt at coordination of monetary and fiscal policies. Since the ECB is instructed to focus on inflation while the fiscal authorities will have a broader range of concerns, there are considerable grounds for potential conflict. This suggests a need for the evolution of a body that would be charged with the coordination of EMU monetary and fiscal policies. In the absence of such a body, tensions will emerge in the real sector when monetary policy and fiscal policy pull in different directions. But so far these issues have in effect been resolved by establishing the dominance of the monetary authorities (ECB) over the fiscal authorities (national governments).

The Stability and Growth Pact (SGP)

The SGP created four rules for economic policy: the ECB was given independence from political influence; the rule of no-bailout of national government deficits; the monetary financing of government deficits was prohibited; and member states must avoid 'excessive' deficits (defined as more than 3 per cent of GDP).

The core elements of the SGP with respect to fiscal policy are: (1) to pursue the medium-term objectives of budgetary positions close to balance or in surplus; (2) the submission of annual stability and convergence programmes by the member states; and (3) the monitoring of the implementation of the stability and convergence programmes. The main feature of the core elements is the requirement that the national budget deficit does not exceed 3 per cent of GDP. Failure to meet that requirement could lead to a series of fines depending on the degree to which the deficit exceeds 3 per cent. It is also necessary for national budgetary policies to:

> support stability oriented monetary policies. Adherence to the objective of sound budgetary positions close to balance or in surplus will allow all Member States to deal with normal cyclical fluctuations while keeping the government deficit within the reference value of 3% of GDP.

Furthermore:

> Member States commit themselves to respect the medium-term budgetary objective of positions close to balance or in surplus set out in their stability of convergence programmes and to take the corrective budgetary action they deem necessary to meet the objectives of their stability or convergence programmes, whenever they have information indicating actual or expected significant divergence from those objectives. (Resolution of the European Council on the Stability and Growth Pact, Amsterdam 17 June 1997)

Each year a country has to submit a stability programme to the Commission for scrutiny, containing, inter alia, information about the paths of the ratios of budget deficit to GDP and national debt to GDP. If the stability programme reveals that a country is significantly diverging from its medium-term budgetary objective, then the Council will recommend that the stability programme is 'strengthened' – that is, cuts in public expenditure and increases in taxation imposed. If the situation persists then the member state will have been judged to have breached the reference values. The Pact details 'escape' clauses, which allow a member state that has an excessive deficit to avoid sanctions.

Neo-liberalism and the euro

The policy framework governing the euro can be aligned with a more general theoretical framework, which finds its expression in the 'new consensus in macroeconomics'.[3] The essential features of that theoretical framework are as follows (see also Arestis and Sawyer, 2003, 2006):

- Politicians in particular, and the democratic process in general, cannot be trusted with economic policy formulation with a tendency to make decisions, which have stimulating short-term effects (reducing unemployment) but which are detrimental in the longer term (notably a rise in inflation). In contrast, experts in the form of central bankers are not subject to political pressures to court short-term popularity, and can take a longer-term perspective where it is assumed that there is a conflict between the short term and the long term. Policy-makers' scope for using discretion should be curtailed and the possibility of negative spillovers from irresponsible fiscal policy must be reduced.
- Inflation is a monetary phenomenon and can be controlled through monetary policy. The money supply is difficult (if not impossible) to control directly, and the demand for money is thought to be highly unstable. However, the central bank can set the key policy interest rate to influence monetary conditions, which in turn influence the future rate of inflation. Central banks have no discernible effects on the level or growth rate of output in the long run, but do determine the rate of inflation in the long run. Thus, inflation is still a monetary phenomenon and ultimately it is central banks that determine the inflation rate.
- The level of unemployment fluctuates around a supply-side-determined equilibrium rate of unemployment, generally labelled the NAIRU (Non-accelerating Inflation Rate of Unemployment). The level of the NAIRU may be favourably affected by a 'flexible' labour market, but is unaffected by the level of aggregate demand or by productive capacity.
- Fiscal policy is impotent in terms of its impact on real variables (essentially because of beliefs in crowding out and that fiscal policy is

inflationary), and as such it should be subordinate to monetary policy in controlling inflation. It is recognised, though, that the government budget position will fluctuate during the course of the business cycle but in the context of an essentially passive fiscal policy.

The structure of the ECB clearly conforms to the first point. The sole objective of the ECB is price stability, and decisions are made by a governing body composed of bankers and financial experts. There are, and can be, no involvement by any other interest groups or any democratic bodies. The only EU-level policy from controlling inflation is monetary (interest rate) policy, which presumes that monetary policy is a relevant and effective instrument for the control of inflation.

The second point is an interesting one in terms of the ECB approach in that although it is accepted, the ECB still adopts the 4.5 reference value for the money supply. The third point is fully accepted and adopted by the ECB. This can clearly be confirmed by the monthly statements of the Governor of the ECB at his press conferences after the announcement of the decisions on the level of the rate of interest.

The implementation of what is in effect a balanced budget requirement at the national level under the SGP and the absence of fiscal policy at the eurozone level has eliminated the use of fiscal policy as an effective instrument for the reduction of unemployment (or indeed of inflation). This approach to fiscal policy fits in very well with our fourth point listed.

Inflation, unemployment and inequality

The ECB is the only EU-level economic institution and it operates with the objective of attaining low inflation. There are three points of note here. First, this key institution is undemocratic in nature (indeed, it is barred from taking instructions from democratic organisation) and operates in a secretive and non-transparent way. The ECB decision-makers are central bankers, and there is no representation of other interests (e.g., industry, trade unions) in the decision-making process. It is only the interests of bankers and the financial sector, that are represented.

Second, the only objective addressed through macroeconomic policy (and then that is monetary policy) at the EU level is price stability (with inflation of just less than 2 per cent, a target that has been generally missed over the years). Employment targets have been set by the EU:

> Policies should contribute to achieving an average employment rate for the European Union (EU) of 70% overall, of at least 60% for women and of 50% for older workers (55 to 64) by 2010, and to reduce unemployment and inactivity. Member States should consider setting national employment rate targets. (European Commission, 2008)

These objectives are part of the European Employment Strategy, and are to be achieved through measures such as increased labour market flexibility, life-long learning and so on, and more generally adoption of 'flexicurity' (European Commission, 2007). There is no macroeconomic policy, based on fiscal or monetary policy, designed to create high levels of employment. Indeed, the general tenor of macroeconomic policy runs counter to the creation of high levels of employment.

Third, this policy operates according to the notion that monetary policy is the relevant policy for the control of inflation. Yet, monetary policy has become interest rate policy, and the linkages between changes in interest rates and changes in inflation are at best weak, and at worst obscure (see, for example, Arestis and Sawyer, 2004, 2008). Any significant upswing in inflation would reveal that the ECB is unable to control inflation or even possess policy instruments which can effectively tackle inflation. The eurozone would be revealed to be bereft of any counter-inflation policy. The emperor would be revealed to have no clothes!

The countries of the EMU are heavily constrained in their ability to use fiscal policy to combat economic slowdown and recession. There is no fiscal policy operated at the European level. The size of the European budget is relatively small at around 1.1 per cent of combined EU members' GDP in 2010, and is still dominated by the needs of the Common Agricultural Policy (about 40 per cent).[4] Yet, the European Commission MacDougall Report (1977) suggested that monetary union would not be viable without a sufficiently large community budget for fiscal policy (7.5 per cent of members' GDP). A group of independent experts (Commission of the European Communities, 1993) recommended a rather smaller budget of around 2 per cent of GDP with a much smaller role for agriculture policy, but a budget still around double the present size. The EU budget is clearly too small to operate as an effective stabiliser or to redistribute funds from richer regions to poorer ones in any significant manner.

The national fiscal policies are, in principle, constrained by the maximum of 3 per cent of GDP deficit and balance or small surplus over the cycle. There have been many occasions on which countries have exceeded the 3 per cent limit, the most dramatic being during the 'great recession' of 2008–09. The response of the EU authorities has varied from mild censure to insisting on plans for deficit reduction and to court action to enforce the SGP (see Arestis and Sawyer, 2006, for a summary). During the 'great recession' it is fortunate that the rules of the SGP were put to one side as budget deficits soared with the sharp decline in tax revenues. But the pressures on national governments to resort to 'fiscal consolidation', to bring deficits down through tax rises, and to cuts in public expenditure, did not take long to resume.

The sole focus for fiscal policy in the SGP is on a form of balanced budget, rather than on addressing issues of inadequate aggregate demand. The SGP imposes in effect a 'one size fits all' policy on all countries in the sense of seeking for all to have a balanced budget, whether or not that is appropriate to its circumstances. It is also a stringent target, which has rarely been achieved by countries. For example, the German historic experience is of an average budget deficit of 2 per cent of GDP over the period 1970 to 1991.[5] It is also inconsistent with a 60 per cent debt/GDP ratio.[6] Although, as illustrated by the budget deficits during 2009–10, the 3 per cent limit has not been enforced, it is still putting pressures on reductions of budget deficits and a general thrust in the deflationary direction.

One other feature of these monetary and fiscal policies is that they, and the corresponding institutional arrangements, are embedded in the Treaty of Lisbon (and are exact continuations of the policies and arrangements in the Treaties that preceded Lisbon). The Treaty can only be changed with the unanimous agreement of the 27 EU member states, which means that change is almost impossible. In effect, the EMU is locked into the present set of monetary and fiscal policies with little possibility of escape.

In 2005, there was some 'softening' in the agreed interpretation of the SGP. The main points of the agreement were more budgetary consolidation in good times; more flexibility in reducing deficits in bad times; more focus on cutting the debt to GDP ratio; more room for manoeuvre for countries carrying out structural reforms; countries with sound finances allowed to run small deficits to invest. The ECB argued:

> It is essential that, in applying the new framework, the right precedents are established from the outset. A rigorous and consistent implementation of the revised rules would be conducive to fiscal discipline and would help to restore the credibility of the EU fiscal framework as well as confidence in prudent fiscal policies. (ECB, 2005, p. 59)

The achievement of full employment does require an appropriate high level of aggregate demand, and that does require some combination of increased demand for exports, for consumption, for investment and for public expenditure. Whether such a level of aggregate demand would require a substantial budget deficit inevitably depends on what happens to the other sources of demand. But a high level of aggregate demand is only one, albeit rather important, condition for the achievement of full employment. In the context of the eurozone, there are two rather obvious and significant obstacles to the achievement of full employment. The first is the lack of productive capacity in many regions to provide high levels of employment. Estimates by the OECD of the 'output gap' suggest that even prior to the financial crisis actual output is about equal to potential output – over the period 2002 to 2008 actual output was within 0.1 per cent of potential output; yet this is combined with around 8 per cent unemployment. In a similar vein, the OECD's estimates of the NAIRU averaged 8 per cent for the eurozone over the period 2002 to 2008 close to the actual experience.[7] Interpreting the NAIRU as an indicator of a capacity constraint suggests capacity problems. In this context, higher levels of aggregate demand would place pressure on capacity and could well have some inflationary consequences. The second obstacle is the disparity of unemployment – a general increase in demand would push some regions to or even above full employment.

A major weakness of the present institutional arrangements is the separation between monetary policy conducted by the ECB and the constrained fiscal policy operated by national governments. There is clearly a requirement for the coordination of economic policy across the member countries of the EU, and for the emergence of appropriate institutional arrangements and policies at the European level. Economic policy at the EU level faces the additional issue of the disparities of economic performance in terms of employment and unemployment rates and of the level of GDP per capita across the regions and countries of the EU.

Some experiences of the euro

In the first eight years of the euro as 'real' currency (and after three years as a virtual currency) the targets set by the SGP have often been missed. Even over the relatively good years of 2002 to 2007 the average budget deficit was 2.2 per cent of GDP (which rises to 2.7 per cent if 2008 and 2009 are included) (calculated from OECD *Economic Outlook*); four countries had a budget in surplus on average (Finland, Luxembourg, Ireland and Spain), but when the period is extended to 2009 the latter two countries average a deficit. The public debt ratio targets were generally missed, and even before the onset of the recession only the four countries named above plus the Netherlands had a debt ratio below 60 per cent of GDP. The euro area inflation rate was outside the 'below but near to 2 per cent' range deemed to constitute price stability, albeit by only a small margin, with the inflation rate lying between 2 per cent and 2.5 per cent in every year of the new decade until 3.3 per cent in 2008. These outcomes did little to bolster the credibility of the EMU, which had been the basic plank on which the SGP was based.

The growth performance of the eurozone could be described as lacklustre after the formation of the euro. In the ten years 1985 to 1995, the now eurozone member countries grew at an average of 2.5 per cent, compared with an OECD average of 2.9 per cent; in the years 1999 to 2007 (using that end date before the onset of the financial crisis) the comparable figures were 2.2 per cent and 2.7 per cent.[8] Unemployment rates were somewhat better as compared with the second half of the 1990s when unemployment averaged over 10 per cent in the eurozone, but remained around 8 per cent for most of the decade of the euro (even before the financial crisis).

It is significant to note that current account deficits have persisted for Greece, Ireland, Italy, Portugal and Spain throughout the 2000s. In the euro area there has been a tendency for its overall current account to be broadly in balance, and for some countries, notably Germany, to have current account surpluses. This implies that other countries have to have current account deficits. The three key issues are some long-standing ones. First, a continuing current account deficit will leave a country vulnerable to problems of funding the deficit and attracting the corresponding capital inflow. Second, the deficit continues to rise as the interest and related payments on the cumulative debt increases (unless imports fall relative to exports). Third, particularly in a fixed exchange rate regime, the deficit countries will be under pressure to 'balance the books' unless the surplus countries are willing themselves to expand.

For the Mediterranean countries there has generally been a gradual loss of competitiveness arising from differences in price and wage inflation. The differences in inflation have not been very large in any single year, but the cumulative effect has been that, based on the retail price index, whereas prices in Germany were 14 per cent higher in 2009 as compared with 2001, the figures for Italy and Portugal were 20 per cent, Spain 25 per cent and Greece 28 per cent. Unit labour costs (figures from OECD *Economic Outlook* database) in the countries listed above rose by nearly 10 per cent relative to the euro area average (figures for Portugal are not available) over the period 2002–09. By contrast, (with the exception of Luxembourg) unit costs for other countries either fell (notably in Germany where there was a 10 per cent fall) or changed in line with the average.

Concluding remarks

The establishment of the euro and the European Monetary Union has been undertaken within a specific institutional and policy framework. The institutional framework gives prominence in policy formulation to an undemocratic and unaccountable European Central Bank. It is a policy framework that emphasises the control of inflation over the reduction of unemployment, although it provides a weak instrument (monetary policy) for the control of inflation and generates macroeconomic policies. The latter tend to increase rather than diminish the level and disparity of unemployment. Economic performance with the euro has been disappointing, and the eurozone is facing very considerable pressures, which puts its future in doubt.

Notes

1. Eleven countries (Austria, Belgium, Finland, France, Germany, Ireland, Italy, Luxembourg, Netherlands, Portugal, Spain) were the founding members in 1999, joined by Greece in 2001. They, thus, formed the 12 EU countries using the euro as a 'real' currency from 2002. The five countries joining subsequently are Cyprus, Malta, Slovenia and Slovakia, and at beginning of 2011 Estonia).
2. These convergence criteria were to be applied to countries entering the euro at its creation, though in the event many of the criteria were fudged (see Arestis et al., 2001). These criteria now apply to countries seeking to join the euro.

3. See, for example, Arestis (2007), Arestis and Sawyer (2008) for discussion and critique of that framework.
4. See http://ec.europa.eu/budget/budget_detail/next_year_en.htm; accessed 15 October 2010.
5. Calculated from OECD *Economic Outlook* database, using various issues.
6. A budget deficit (relative to GDP) of d is consistent over the long haul with a debt ratio of $b = d/g$ where g is the nominal rate of growth: with a nominal rate of growth of 5 per cent per annum, a debt ratio of 60 per cent would be consistent with a deficit of 3 per cent of GDP.
7. Figures in this paragraph calculated from OECD *Economic Outlook* database, various issues.
8. Calculated from OECD *Economic Outlook*, December 2009; the figures for 2002 to 2007 were 1.9 per cent and 2.6 per cent respectively. As the OECD area includes the eurozone, clearly these figures imply that the differences between eurozone countries and other industrial countries were even wider.

References

Arestis, P. (ed.) (2007), *Is There a New Consensus in Macroeconomics?*, Basingstoke: Palgrave, Macmillan.

Arestis, P. and Sawyer, M. (2003), 'Macroeconomic Policies of the Economic and Monetary Union: Theoretical Underpinnings and Challenges', *International Papers in Political Economy*, **10**(1), pp. 1–54, reprinted in P. Arestis and M. Sawyer (eds) (2004) *Neo-Liberal Economic Policy: Critical Essays*, Cheltenham, UK and Northampton, MA, USA: Edward Elgar, pp. 194–231.

Arestis, P. and Sawyer, M. (2004), 'Can Monetary Policy Affect the Real Economy?', *European Review of Economics and Finance*, **3**(2), 9–32.

Arestis, P. and Sawyer, M. (2006), "Macroeconomic Policy and the European Constitution", in P. Arestis and M. Sawyer (eds), *Alternative Perspectives on Economic Policies in the European Union*, Basingstoke: Palgrave Macmillan.

Arestis, P. and Sawyer, M. (2008), 'A Critical Reconsideration of the Foundations of Monetary Policy in the New Consensus Macroeconomics Framework', *Cambridge Journal of Economics*, **32**(5), 761–79.

Arestis, P., Brown, A. and Sawyer, M. (2001), *The Euro: Evolution and Prospects*, Cheltenham, UK and Northampton, MA, USA: Edward Elgar.

Commission of the European Communities (1993), 'Stable Money – Sound Finances: Community Public Finance in the Perspective of EMU', *European Economy* No. 53.

European Central Bank (ECB) (2005), 'The Reform of the Stability and Growth Pact', *Monthly Bulletin*, August, 59–74.

European Commission (2007), *Towards Common Principles of Flexicurity: More and Better Jobs Through Flexibility and Security*, Communication from the Commission to the European Parliament, the Council, the European Economic and Social Committee and the Committee of the Regions, adopted on 27 June 2007.

European Commission (2008), *Guidelines for Growth and Jobs (2008–2010)*, Brussels: European Commission.

European Commission (MacDougall Report) (1977), *Report of the Study Group on the Role of Public Finance in European Integration*, Brussels: European Commission.

16 The North American Free Trade Agreement: context, structure and performance

Jim Stanford

1 Introduction and overview

The North American Free Trade Agreement (NAFTA) came into effect on 1 January 1994, creating a continental free trade zone incorporating Canada, the US and Mexico. The NAFTA was constructed on the framework of an earlier bilateral agreement between the US and Canada, implemented five years earlier on 1 January 1989.

The NAFTA zone rivals the European Union in terms of total population and total GDP (see Table 16.1). However, the intensity of integration is much deeper

Table 16.1 Comparing NAFTA and the EU (2009 data)

	NAFTA	EU
Member countries	3	27
Population	440 million	500 million
GDP (US$)	17 trillion	17 trillion
Initial formation and membership	1989; 2 members	1957; 6 members
Number of times expanded	1	9
Forms of integration	Tariff-free internal trade; dispute settlement; investment rights; symbolic labour and environmental institutions	Tariff-free internal trade; removal of internal borders; internal labour mobility; common external tariff and foreign policy; monetary and currency union (for most members); supranational political institutions; harmonized regulatory structures; continental social and labour standards

in Europe than in North America, and the NAFTA to date does not envision any further processes of monetary, labour market, political and institutional integration akin to the EU's. Within NAFTA, each member nation continues to independently set its own external tariffs and trade policies (that is, the NAFTA is not a customs union); border controls remain in place between the three member countries; no form of monetary union is presently considered; the NAFTA includes only minimal provisions for mobility of particular kinds of specialized labour between NAFTA countries; and there have been virtually no supranational political or democratic institutions established as part of the NAFTA.[1] In contrast to the EU then, the NAFTA represents a far less ambitious effort to establish a common continental market for goods and services, and common protections for private investors and businesses, with little attention or interest devoted to developing a deeper continental political or institutional dimension.

This overview of the context, structure and performance of the NAFTA is presented in the following sections. First, an overview of the historical and political context in which the NAFTA was negotiated is provided. Then the NAFTA's specific provisions are described, followed by a summary of the agreement's apparent economic effects. Finally, the discussion concludes with consideration of the problems and prospects facing the integrated North American market.

2 Historical and political context

The NAFTA is dominated both economically and politically by the US, which accounts for about two-thirds of its population, and 85 per cent of its economic output. Consequently, the negotiation and implementation of the NAFTA were much more important events in Canada and Mexico, than in the US itself. For both of those countries, the implementation of free trade with their much larger neighbour was an event of decisive historical importance, culminating a longer-term evolution in their respective bilateral relationships with the US. A former Prime Minister of Canada, Pierre Trudeau, once described Canada's relationship with the US as being akin to 'a mouse in bed with an elephant'. Similarly, a popular Mexican parable asks for pity because Mexico is 'so far from heaven, and so close to the United States'. In both countries, choices regarding how to manage the dominant and complex relationship with the US are of immense political and economic importance. And for both countries, the decision to embark on a course of tighter continental economic integration marked a defining moment in their national histories. For the US, on the other hand, the implementation of a North American free trade zone represented an important but hardly epochal development, one that mostly served to reinforce its already existing economic and strategic dominance on the continent.

Despite their increasingly tight economic relationships, great economic, political and social differences continue to exist between the three NAFTA

Table 16.2 *Characteristics of NAFTA member countries (2008 data unless otherwise noted)*

	Canada	Mexico	US
Population (million)	33.1	106.7	303.6
Population growth rate (% per year, 1998–2008 avg.)	0.9	1.1	1.0
GDP (US$ trillion)	1.5	1.1	14.4
GDP per capita (US$ PPP, 2007)	38 500	14 004	45 489
Foreign trade (% GDP)[a]	68.7	58.8	30.3
Current account balance (% GDP)	0.5	–1.5	–4.9
Manufacturing (value-added as % GDP)	18.4	17.1	17.7
Labour force participation (% working age population, OECD standardized)	80.1	65.0	75.6
Labour cost (hourly compensation, manufacturing, US$/hour, 2007)	31.91	3.91	30.56
Labour productivity growth (% per year, 1998–2008 avg.)	0.9	1.1	1.9
Inflation (avg. % change CPI per year, 1998–2008)	2.3	6.3	2.8
Life expectancy (years at birth, 2005)	80.4	75.5	77.8
Infant mortality (per 1000 live births, 2005)	5.4	18.8	6.9
Inequality (inter-decile ratio, P90/P10, mid-2000s)	4.12	8.53	5.91

Note: a. Sum of exports and imports of goods and services as share of GDP.

Source: Author's calculations from OECD (2008, 2009a, 2009b), Council of Economic Advisers (2010), Bureau of Labor Statistics (2009), Bureau of Economic Analysis (2010), Statistics Canada CANSIM Table 379-0027, Instituto Nacional de Estadistica Geografia e Informatica (2009).

members (see Table 16.2). The US economy is the richest of the three, measured in per capita incomes, and its political economy reflects an extreme of deregulation and market orientation that is unique in the industrialized world. Canada's economy is somewhat less productive than that of the US (although it still ranks in the top tier of nations according to per capita income), and has traditionally exhibited a more mixed pattern of development – with a larger economic role for the state, and a range of social programmes and protections similar in spirit (if not in extent) to the social-democratic traditions of Europe. Mexico is a middle-income, industrializing economy. Its average per capita real income is less than one-third that of the US (even after adjusting for purchasing power parity exchange rates).[2] Hourly wages in Mexico are about one-tenth the levels in the US and Canada.[3] Income inequality (measured, for example, by the ratios of income received by the 90th percentile to the 10th percentile of population) is much more severe in Mexico than in the US, which in turn is a far more unequal society than Canada. Both Mexico and Canada continue to rely on the production and export of a range of natural resource staples (especially energy, and especially to the US market) as an important economic activity. In contrast, the US economy demonstrates a more mature industrial structure, with a greater reliance on high-technology and high-value service industries as the leading drivers of economic growth. On the other hand, the traditional US manufacturing base has declined in relative and absolute terms during recent decades, producing a consequent polarization in the economy and labour market between high-wage and low-wage service industries, and contributing to the uniquely severe and chronic balance of payments problems experienced by the US. These important structural and institutional differences among the NAFTA partners help to explain why the NAFTA has limited its scope to the deregulation of trade and investment flows within the NAFTA zone, rather than attempting a deeper, European-style political and regulatory harmonization.

The NAFTA was created in the wake of the 1989 Canada–US Free Trade Agreement (FTA). The initial push for that bilateral treaty reflected a historic shift in the thinking of Canadian business and political elites. Through much of the postwar era, Canada had pursued a relatively interventionist and nationalist development strategy, relying on a range of regulatory measures to promote a pattern of industrial development oriented around the country's small domestic market. This general strategy had both successes and failures, but through most of the postwar period Canada's economy grew significantly faster than its southern neighbour, and its living standards (especially considering the more generous provision of social benefits in Canada) increased rapidly. At the same time, however, Canada's economy remained structurally underdeveloped, both more dependent on resource extraction, and more reliant on incoming foreign direct investment, than any other major industrialized economy.

After negative experiences with inflation, fiscal imbalances and unsettled labour relations, which Canada (like most other industrialized countries) endured in the 1970s and early 1980s, Canada's business and political elites began to cast about for a new economic and social direction. A defining point in this process was the so-called Macdonald Commission on Canada's economic future (Royal Commission on the Economic Union and Development Prospects for Canada, 1985). Chaired by a former finance minister of the Liberal-nationalist government of Pierre Trudeau, the commission issued a surprising call for the negotiation of a general free trade agreement with the US. The proposal was taken up enthusiastically by the newly elected Conservative federal government of Brian Mulroney, who agreed with then US President Ronald Reagan to negotiate a comprehensive bilateral free trade deal. The proposal was strongly supported by Canadian business, indicating their rejection of the former domestically oriented development strategies and their embrace of the US – both the US market for Canadian exports, and the US model for domestic economic and social policy. A draft agreement was reached in late 1987, and put to the test in Canada in a uniquely contested national election in November 1988. The majority of Canadians voted for parties opposed to free trade (the Liberals and New Democrats). However, as a result of vote-splitting in Canada's first-past-the-post electoral system, the pro-FTA Conservatives won a majority of seats, and the FTA was implemented on 1 January 1989. In the US, in contrast, the FTA was not controversial, and was endorsed overwhelmingly by the US Congress with little public debate.

In Canada, implementation of the FTA coincided with other far-reaching neoliberal policy initiatives, including: a uniquely strict monetary policy regime (Canada was one of the first industrial nations to adopt formal inflation targeting in 1991, and has recorded the lowest inflation among the three NAFTA member countries since then); significant deregulation of labour markets (including dramatic reductions in unemployment benefits and steady de-unionization); and widespread privatization and deregulation. The period since the FTA has therefore seen a clear pattern of policy convergence in Canada toward the US model – although important economic and social differences remain between the two neighbours. How much of this convergence reflects the (direct and indirect) influence of the FTA remains a subject for debate (Clarkson, 2002).

In the wake of the successful passage of the FTA, the new US government of George Herbert Walker Bush initiated negotiations to expand the free trade area to include Mexico. In Mexico, too, the decision to embrace free trade was the culmination of a historic evolution in the economic and political thinking of that nation's business and political elite. Mexico had been governed since the 1920s by the Partido Revolucionario Institucional (PRI). During the postwar decades, the PRI had followed a heavily interventionist strategy. This development strategy relied on widespread state ownership of industry, an alliance with a powerful class of domestic industrialists, tariffs and other trade policies to promote manufacturing development (on the import-substitution model), and the widespread communal ownership of land in agricultural regions. This statist development strategy demonstrated a strong initial vitality, generating annual average expansion in real GDP of over 6 per cent between 1950 and 1980, and substantial increases in real per capita incomes. By the late 1970s, however, the strains of this inward-focused strategy became more apparent, manifested in the form of growing external imbalances, growing public sector deficits and rising inflation. Weakening world prices for oil (a major Mexican export) and rising global interest rates triggered a major financial crisis culminating in August 1982, when Mexico announced its inability to service its large sovereign debt. The regime of Miguel de la Madrid, which took power in the wake of this crisis, began to move the economy in a more market-oriented direction, implementing drastic reductions in public spending, weakening labour market regulations and opening the economy increasingly to foreign investment and competition.

This broadly neoliberal direction in economic and social policy was put to the test in the 1988 Mexican federal election, which was even more historic and bitterly contested than the Canadian election of the same year. The austere policies of the PRI were challenged by an insurgent electoral campaign led by former PRI minister Cuauhtemoc Cardenas, heading a coalition of left opposition forces called the Frente Democrático Nacional. The PRI was declared elected, amidst allegations of widespread electoral fraud and corruption, and the election ushered in a new and even more market-oriented administration under Carlos Salinas de Gortari, confirming the general direction of Mexican policy. The Salinas government went on to negotiate the NAFTA and implement other business-oriented structural reforms in the economy (Lustig, 1998).

A draft NAFTA was signed by Salinas, Bush and Mulroney on 17 December 1992. The ratification of this treaty was much more controversial in the US than had been the FTA, because of widespread opposition from union members and others concerned with the potential flight of investment and employment to low-wage Mexico. Independent candidate Ross Perot made opposition to the NAFTA a major theme of his upstart campaign in the 1992 US presidential election. After the election, incoming Democratic President Bill Clinton abruptly softened his initial scepticism regarding the NAFTA and began to work energetically for its passage. To this end, the US insisted on negotiating two largely symbolic 'side-agreements' to the NAFTA: one concerning the regulation of labour standards within the NAFTA free trade zone, and one concerning environmental standards. These side-agreements contain no legislative force, and have been dismissed by most labour and environmental advocates as transparently symbolic. At the time, though, they were important in helping Clinton to justify the shift in his position on NAFTA, and subsequently lobby Congress (together with US business interests) for its ratification. Ironically, then, while the NAFTA was negotiated (from the US side) by a business-friendly Republican administration, it eventually required a Democratic administration (with its ability to discipline traditional Democratic constituencies) to ensure its ultimate passage.

In Canada, meanwhile, the NAFTA was less controversial than was the initial FTA. The incremental effects of adding Mexico to the continental free trade zone were clearly less important (though still potentially negative) than was the initial bilateral deal with the US. Advocates of Canada's participation in a trilateral NAFTA argued that a unified continental deal was better for Canada than a 'hub-and-spoke' structure centred on the US. Labour movement and social constituencies opposed the NAFTA on grounds it would exacerbate the 'race to the bottom' already unleashed by the FTA. Mirroring the experience with President Clinton in the US, Canada's Liberal Party, which had (in opposition) opposed the FTA and demanded important changes to the draft NAFTA, won power in October 1993 and subsequently implemented the NAFTA without any of the changes it had called for.[4]

Meanwhile, in Mexico the Salinas government assembled a diverse but fragile coalition in support of NAFTA implementation (Poitras and Robinson, 1994), including business groups, PRI-affiliated labour unions and the right-wing opposition party Partido Acción Nacional (PAN). The left opposition party, the Partido de la Revolución Democrática (PRD – an outgrowth of the left coalition from the 1988 elections) called for revisions to the initial treaty to better protect Mexican farmers, public ownership of energy and other concerns, but did not fundamentally oppose the core idea of continental economic integration. The NAFTA came into force on 1 January 1994 (the last year of Salinas's term in office).

However, the hope that NAFTA membership would usher in a new era of investor-friendly stability in Mexico was abruptly crushed, on the very day of the NAFTA's formal implementation; 1 January 1994 signified not only Mexico's accession to the free trade zone, but also the spectacular onset of an armed leftist insurrection, centred in the far south of the country, led by the Ejército Zapatista de Liberación Nacional (EZLN, known as the 'Zapatistas'). This event shocked financial investors, and exposed the fragility resulting from the extremely large financial inflows (mostly of short-term financial capital) that had anticipated Mexico's accession to NAFTA (Ros and Lustig, 2000; Blecker, 2008). Self-fulfilling fears of depreciation sparked a financial flight out of Mexico, resulting in a two-year currency and financial crisis (known as the 'tequila crisis'), and a deep Mexican recession. This was hardly an auspicious beginning for Mexico's membership in the continental market. Nevertheless, in the presidential elections held in August of 1994, the PRI candidate, Ernest Zedillo Ponce de León,[5] won by a convincing margin, seemingly validating the support of most Mexicans for the NAFTA (and for the PRI's strategy for addressing the financial crisis). Economic and financial conditions eventually recovered, and after some years the Zapatista insurrection receded into the political background (although the EZLN still exists as a non-violent political movement). Nevertheless, the notion that accession to a free trade agreement could single-handedly produce a sea change in investor attitudes and economic and financial stability[6] was dashed from the very day of NAFTA's birth.

To sum up, the decisions by the Canadian and Mexican governments to enter into a free trade agreement with the US signalled an important change of course on the part of business and political leadership in both countries. A postwar tradition of more interventionist economic and social policy was largely abandoned, in favour of an outward-oriented and business-led development strategy, based on the perceived benefits from closer integration with the largest (and most laissez faire) country in the capitalist world. For both Canada and Mexico, therefore, the advent of continental free trade marked a decisive turning point in their historical evolution. Continental free trade, in essence, *became* the major economic development strategy for both countries, coincident with the abandonment of earlier efforts to proactively shape a more nationalist model of development. In the US, on the other hand, the advent of the NAFTA represented no such dramatic change in the domestic political economy. The decision to forge a bilateral free trade agreement with Canada, and then to expand that agreement to include Mexico, was for US elites a non-controversial forward step in both economic and foreign policy. The NAFTA would draw both neighbours more closely into the US sphere of influence, reducing the perceived geopolitical risk to US interests that had been posed by occasional outbreaks of nationalist and/or interventionist sentiment in those two neighbours. The freedoms and protections accorded to US business throughout the continent would also be enhanced (although, as discussed below, these benefits for US-based businesses are quite distinct from whether or not the NAFTA was good for the US economy, or for Americans in general).

3 Provisions of the NAFTA

The NAFTA contains 22 chapters, several appendices and two 'side-agreements'.[7] The effect of these provisions is summarized under the following sub-headings:

3.1 Tariff elimination

The tariff reduction schedule provided for under the NAFTA is fully described in just one section of NAFTA's Chapter 3. Tariffs on bilateral trade between Canada and the US were already being phased out under the ten-year timetable prescribed by the 1989 Canada–US FTA; the NAFTA confirmed the continuing elimination of those residual tariffs. The NAFTA then set a similar ten-year timetable for the gradual elimination of tariffs on merchandise trade between Mexico and the US, and between Mexico and Canada.[8] Almost all tariffs on intra-North American trade, therefore, were fully eliminated by 2003. To qualify for tariff-free status within North America, a product must comply with North American rules of origin that are specified on a sector-by-sector basis. The small amount of text required to describe this relatively straightforward process of tariff elimination seems to verify that the NAFTA in its entirety represents far more than just the liberalization of continental merchandise trade. It is the other, lengthier sections of the agreement that describe a more far-reaching process of integration and deregulation, including some very novel features intended to enhance the security and primacy of private investment in the continental economy.

3.2 Reduction of non-tariff barriers

The NAFTA prescribes the easing of a wide range of non-tariff barriers to trade in goods and services within the NAFTA zone. These non-tariff liberalization initiatives include strong statements regarding national treatment and market access in all sectors (including services); the specification of acceptable customs and clearing procedures; limits on the application of food inspection and health standards that may inhibit trade; limits on the application of other technical standards that may limit trade; and restrictions on government procurement practices (requiring federal-level, and some lower-level, governments and agencies to competitively tender their purchases without regard to the intra-NAFTA origin of competing providers).

3.3 Deregulation of key industries

For the most part, specified government regulations governing output, investment and pricing in particular industries could be grandfathered under the NAFTA.[9] The agreement did, however, restrict the incremental policy-making leeway of national governments by prohibiting or limiting the further expansion of regulations (especially those specifying domestic content, domestic ownership, or other trade-restricting outcomes). And in some cases, the NAFTA itself required the proactive elimination of government regulations and restrictions on private business. Most notable in this case were commitments that the Mexican government made under the NAFTA to privatize and/or deregulate sections of its energy, banking, insurance, advertising, communications and trucking industries. These measures indicate again that the main goal of the NAFTA, from the perspective of both the Mexican government and of foreign companies operating in Mexico, was to facilitate and solidify the broader deregulation of the Mexican economy – not just to facilitate greater two-way trade in goods and services between Mexico and its northern neighbours.

3.4 Enshrinement of investment rights

The NAFTA contains provisions to protect the economic interests and legal status of foreign investors that were unique at the time in international trade agreements, and that prefigured similar provisions subsequently enshrined in other multilateral trade agreements. The path-breaking Chapter 11 of the NAFTA guarantees a wide range of protections for intra-NAFTA foreign investments, including: specified national treatment rights for investors (supplementing the broad national treatment provisions that apply to other provisions of the NAFTA); the prohibition of performance requirements on foreign investors (including those defined with respect to trade balances and other foreign trade variables); the prohibition of restrictions on transfers of ownership, financial transfers and capital flows; and the prohibition of restrictions on the nationality of investors and corporate directors. Other sections of the NAFTA (in particular,

Chapter 12, which deals with intellectual property issues) further reinforce the cross-national rights of investors and private corporations operating in the continental free trade zone.

3.5 Dispute settlement

The Canada–US FTA had introduced a unique new form of dispute settlement, in the form of special tribunals empowered to rule on the acceptable use by a member country of countervailing measures and other trade remedies.[10] These tribunals were maintained and expanded under the NAFTA. Even more innovative was NAFTA's creation of a special dispute settlement procedure to enforce the investor rights provisions contained in Chapter 11 of the agreement. Under this process, which has been one of the most controversial aspects of the NAFTA, private corporations are given the power to file complaints against NAFTA-member governments for alleged violations of the investment protections of the agreement. These complaints are then reviewed and decided upon by quasi-judicial tribunals, acting independently of standard legal channels in the member countries. In other words, the NAFTA established a parallel quasi-judicial system, accessible only to corporations and investors, for pursuing business claims against NAFTA-member governments (including subnational levels of government). The implications of this parallel, 'members only' court system for the democratic rule of law have sparked widespread criticism. By 2008, almost 50 business complaints had been filed under the NAFTA Chapter 11 provisions, involving total claims for damages from member governments exceeding US$30 billion (see Table 16.3). Most cases involve corporate objections to government rules and regulations concerning a range of important public policy issues, including environmental protection and public health. Confirmed tribunal judgments against the governments of Canada and Mexico (with corresponding payment of damages by these governments) demonstrate that the Chapter 11 tribunals are willing to interpret NAFTA commitments in a broad manner, and equally willing to impose significant monetary penalties on governments that are held to violate the business protections provided by the agreement. While some of the filed complaints have little merit (even within the skewed criteria of Chapter 11), there is little doubt that the system has exerted a chilling effect on governments in any areas in which policy changes could create financial losses for private companies. The operation of this unique investor–state dispute settlement mechanism, on top of the generally far-reaching investor protections contained in the NAFTA, has fuelled the argument of NAFTA critics that the agreement in fact constitutes a new 'corporate constitution' for the continent – much more than simply an agreement to promote continental trade in goods and services.

Table 16.3 Summary of cases filed under NAFTA Chapter 11 provisions (to January 2008)

Respondent Country	Number of Cases Filed	Damages Claimed (US$)	Offending Measures	Disposition
Canada	18	12.2 billion	6 environmental 5 natural resources 2 postal services 1 cultural policy 1 agriculture 3 other	2 decided against Canada (with damages) 2 settled out of court 1 dismissed 9 in process 3 withdrawn
US	14	17.2 billion	4 softwood lumber 3 environmental 3 state court decisions 1 procurement 3 health or food	4 dismissed 9 in process 1 withdrawn
Mexico	17	1.7 billion	5 manufacturing 4 environmental 4 real estate & development 1 financial services 1 gambling 1 tobacco 1 other	3 decided against Mexico (with damages) 6 dismissed 8 in process

Note: 'In process' includes cases in tribunal process, pending further actions, or 'on hold' awaiting further decision.

Source: Compiled from Sinclair (2008).

3.6 Energy

The original Canada–US FTA featured a novel provision cementing US security of access to Canadian energy supplies; this provision was carried forward in Chapter 6 of the NAFTA. Even prior to the FTA, Canada had been an important source of petroleum, natural gas and other energy sources to its southern neighbour. Cementing US access to Canadian reserves was an important strategic goal for the US – a quid pro quo, in the mind of US negotiators, for the security of US market access that the FTA supposedly granted to Canadian exporters. The FTA specified a complex proportional sharing formula, whereby Canadian energy supplies would have to keep flowing to the US market even in event of a supply disruption or other emergency; the guaranteed US supply in those circumstances would have to match or exceed the proportion of total Canadian supply of each energy commodity that the US purchased in the three years prior to the emergency. This unprecedented provision is still unique in international trade law (Laxer and Dillon, 2008). Mexican negotiators refused to accept similar terms in its accession to the NAFTA; indeed, the NAFTA explicitly grandfathers Mexico's right to manage energy resources, and to maintain the public ownership of PEMEX (the dominant petroleum firm in Mexico).[11] The unique Canada–US energy security deal has helped spark a significant shift in the structure and importance of energy trade between the two countries. Most Canadian energy production is now exported to the US, and energy has become Canada's largest export (replacing automotive products in the mid-2000s); some analysts link this boom in energy exports to the corresponding de-industrialization of Canada's industrial base (Stanford, 2008). Meanwhile, US energy planners appreciate the unique security of access to Canada's massive tar sands resources (which contain more oil than Saudi Arabia) resulting from this unique trade provision.

3.7 Mobility for specialized forms of labour

In general the NAFTA does not address issues of migration or freedom of movement of persons between the member countries, with one exception. Chapter 16 of the agreement provides for temporary entry of certain classifications of business persons and professionals. Beyond this exception, each country's existing immigration laws and procedures continue to apply, and immigration has continued to be an important and controversial matter in relations between the three countries (especially between Mexico and the US).

3.8 Side-agreements on labour and the environment

As discussed, to support the ratification of the NAFTA, US President Clinton negotiated two side-agreements to the NAFTA regarding the protection of labour and environmental standards (Compa, 1997; Kirton and de Castro, 1997; Koehl, 2004). These side-agreements contain no measures with legislative force. Rather, they simply commit each government to greater transparency in reporting on labour and environmental conditions, and to the enforcement of existing national labour and environmental laws. The agreements also created small tri-national institutions to oversee their operation and effect. In general, these symbolic bodies are not viewed as a meaningful or important features of the NAFTA.

4 Economic effects of the NAFTA

4.1 Predictions and reality

The predictions of economists regarding the likely effects of the NAFTA (and the earlier Canada–US FTA) played an important role in the political debates that accompanied the free trade negotiations in all three countries. Conventional neoclassical thinkers emphasized the mutual and automatic gains expected to result from increased specialization on comparative advantage grounds. They also predicted significant benefits resulting from the impact of tariff reduction on firm behaviour (since less tariff protection would force domestic firms to be more productive and competitive). Their predictions of mutual but modest economic gains were seemingly verified by the output of numerous quantitatively calibrated economic models (most of which utilized the methodology of 'computable general equilibrium' systems). However, other analysts suggested that the main effects of the NAFTA would be felt through other structural channels – such as the impact of the agreement on investment decisions (capital mobility was not modelled in most of the neoclassical simulations), and the impact of neoliberal policy reforms within Mexico. Some analysts have criticized the accuracy and relevance of the modelling predictions (Stanford, 2003), while others argue those predictions were largely correct (Burfisher et al., 2001). Post hoc, numerous additional studies have attempted to identify and report the incremental economic impacts of the NAFTA (see, for example, Congressional Budget Office, 2003; US International Trade Commission, 2003; and Lederman et al., 2003) although this task is inherently uncertain due to the difficulty of defining the 'counterfactual', and separating out the impacts of the NAFTA from the effects of other global, regional and domestic factors. In general, most studies have found that the direct incremental impacts of the NAFTA on trade, growth, productivity and income distribution have been small (Hornbeck, 2004).

The following sub-sections will briefly consider the apparent impact of the NAFTA on a range of economic indicators in all three countries:

4.2 Expansion of trade

Intra-NAFTA trade expanded notably in each of the three member countries following the transition to free trade on the continent. Increased trade within North America reflects a range of motives, including improved market access, the development of more intensive cross-border supply chains, and even trade diversion from other trading partners.[12] Not surprisingly, the expansion of intra-NAFTA trade was most dramatic for Canada and Mexico, given the greater relative importance of their trade links with the US. In Canada's case (Figure 16.1), intra-NAFTA trade flows initially doubled as a share of GDP, equivalent to a full one-third of GDP by 2000. However, much of that initial growth has

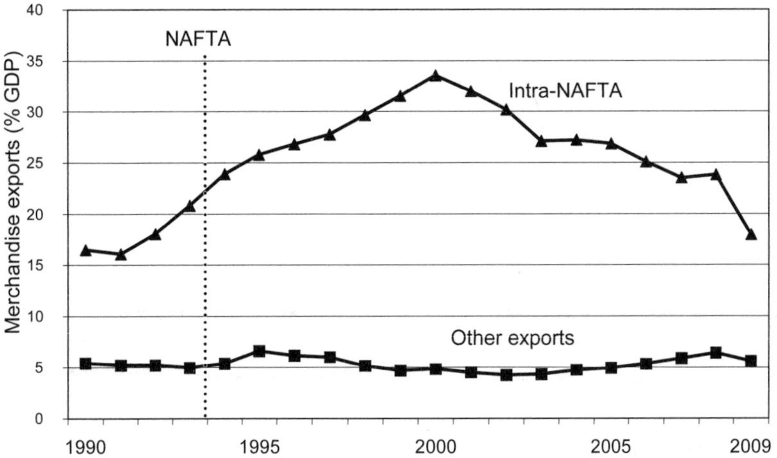

Source: Author's calculations from Industry Canada (2010) and Statistics Canada (2010) Table 3800017.

Figure 16.1 Export intensity: Canada 1990–2009

subsequently been unwound: intra-NAFTA exports have declined notably as a share of Canadian GDP since then, falling back to pre-NAFTA levels by 2009. This surprising result probably reflects the impact of booming energy exports on Canada's overall trade portfolio; while energy exports have grown, manufacturing exports (squeezed by an appreciating currency) have fallen significantly more, and overall economic activity has shifted notably into non-tradable sectors (Stanford, 2008). Also, Canada's once-leading import position in the US market (which pre-dated the FTA) has been eroded by the spectacular growth of US imports from China and other emerging economies. Canada's foreign trade flows with the rest of the world did not increase following the NAFTA.

Mexico experienced an even more dramatic, and more permanent, expansion in the importance of intra-NAFTA trade following NAFTA's implementation (see Figure 16.2). Exports to the US and Canada doubled as a share of GDP in the first years of the NAFTA. This was complemented by a more modest but significant expansion in trade with non-NAFTA partners, which increased by half (as a share of GDP) in the years following NAFTA's implementation; this, again, is consistent with the conclusion that for Mexico the NAFTA represents part of a broader package of deregulatory initiatives, which served to open Mexican markets in a broader sense. The increased economic reliance by Mexico on intra-NAFTA exports (mostly to the US) has remained a continuing feature of that country's economic structure.

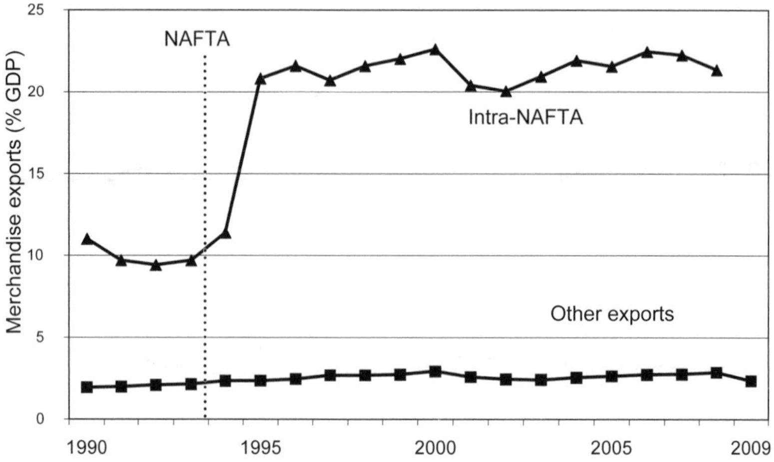

Source: Author's calculations from United Nations (2010), Industry Canada (2010), US Census Bureau (2010), OECD (2009c).

Figure 16.2 Export intensity: Mexico (1990–2009)

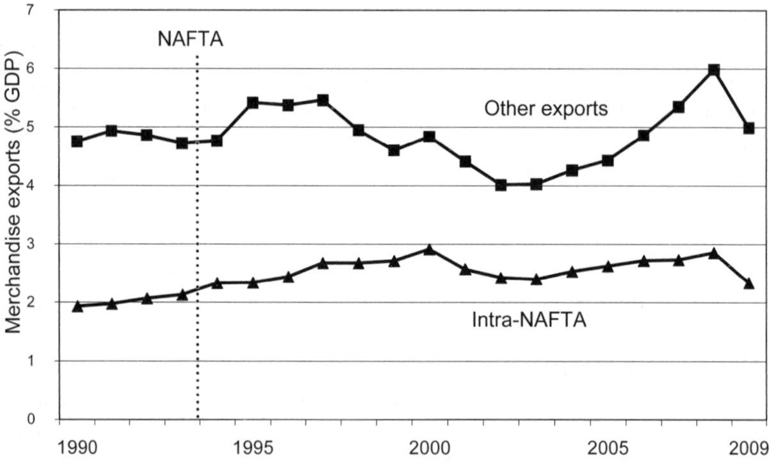

Source: Author's calculations from US Census Bureau (2010), Council of Economic Advisors (2010).

Figure 16.3 Export intensity: US (1990–2009)

Finally, in the US case (Figure 16.3), the discrete impacts of the NAFTA are barely perceptible in the aggregate trade data. NAFTA-bound exports grew by about half, from 2 to 3 per cent of US GDP, alongside a more gradual long-term expansion in the relative importance of foreign trade with non-NAFTA partners. On the whole, US trade developments post-NAFTA have been dominated by more volatile developments in other areas – such as its enormous trade deficit with China (which surpassed Canada in 2007 to become the largest single source of US imports) and dramatic swings in international financial flows.

4.3 Structure of NAFTA trade

Trade patterns within the NAFTA conform largely to a 'hub-and-spoke' structure, with the US located at both the geographical and the economic centre of the continent. Bilateral trade flows are largest between the US and Canada, and are also large between the US and Mexico. Bilateral flows are small between Canada and Mexico (see Table 16.4). Canada and Mexico are the second and fourth largest trading partners of the US, respectively – and, of course, the US is the largest trade partner for each of Canada and Mexico.[13] Canada and Mexico both rely upon the US market for about 80 per cent of their total exports; both are thus directly impacted when US market conditions turn down (as they did, spectacularly, during the financial crisis and subsequent recession of 2008–09). In contrast, intra-NAFTA exports account for just one-third of the US's total foreign exports. This reinforces the conclusion that the implementation of the NAFTA was a much more significant event in Canada and Mexico than it was in the US. Despite the elimination of tariffs and the expansion of intra-NAFTA trade, research indicates the continuing importance of border effects limiting goods and services trade between the NAFTA partners (McCallum, 1995); due to a range of remaining frictions (including borders,

Table 16.4 Merchandise trade flows within NAFTA, 2008 (US$ billion, and as share of exporter's total exports)

	Importer		
Exporter	Canada	US	Mexico
Canada		339.5 (78%)	5.5 (1%)
US	261.1 (21%)		151.2 (12%)
Mexico	16.8 (2%)	215.9 (80%)	

Source: Author's calculations from Industry Canada (2010), US Census Bureau (2010), United Nations (2010).

national currencies and others), the NAFTA is still far from constituting a true 'single market'.

4.4 Trade imbalances

Merchandise trade flows within North America are characterized by significant long-term bilateral imbalances. These imbalances have fuelled arguments, especially in the US, that the NAFTA has undermined domestic employment and output levels (Scott, 2001). The US experiences large merchandise trade deficits with both of its NAFTA partners: almost $80 billion (US) with Canada in 2008, and almost $65 billion with Mexico (see Table 16.5). Relative to the total bilateral flow, the US–Mexico trade flow is more unbalanced than the US–Canada trade flow, with the US deficit with Mexico equalling some 18 per cent of the total bilateral flow. Proportionately, the bilateral flow between Canada and Mexico is the most unbalanced of all, with Canada's merchandise trade deficit equivalent to a full 50 per cent of the value of total bilateral trade (so that, in effect, Canada imports $3 from Mexico for every dollar it exports there). The US merchandise trade deficits are partially offset by patterns of service trade and investment income flows. Since the US typically maintains a surplus in the services trade and investment income accounts with its North American neighbours, its final bilateral current account deficits with Canada and Mexico are smaller than its merchandise trade deficits. Both Canada and Mexico rely on an ongoing trade surplus with the US to offset trade deficits with the rest of the world; they are both vulnerable, therefore, to any downturn in US economic performance. Similarly, a significant share of Canadian and Mexican exports are produced by the domestic affiliates of US-based multinational firms. In this regard, too, the Canadian and Mexican economies remain firmly dependent on the longer-run success of US companies, and the US economy.

Table 16.5 Merchandise trade imbalances, NAFTA, 2008

Surplus Partner	Deficit Partner	Imbalance (US$ billion)	Imbalance as % Bilateral Trade
Canada	US	78.4	13.1
Mexico	US	64.7	17.6
Mexico	Canada	11.3	50.7

Source: Derived from Table 16.4.

4.5 Foreign direct investment

A major motivation for the NAFTA, from the Mexican perspective, was to signal to foreign corporations and investors Mexico's permanent commitment to a

Table 16.6 Foreign direct investment in North America

Net Inward Stock of FDI	Canada		US		Mexico	
	US$ billion	% GDP	US$ billion	% GDP	US$ billion	% GDP
1987	24.0	5.7	–143.5	–3.0	14.3[a]	6.6[a]
1993	14.8	2.6	–130.2	–2.0	41.9	9.5
2008	–124.1	–8.3	–1051.9	–7.3	249.3	22.9
Change 1987–1993	–9.2	–3.1	13.3	1.1	27.6	2.9
Change 1993–2008	–138.9	–10.9	–921.7	–5.3	207.4	13.4
Change 1987–2008	–148.1	–14.0	–908.4	–4.3	235.0	16.2

Note: a. 1985 data.

Source: Author's calculations from UNCTAD (1995, 2009), Nguyen (2009), Statistics Canada (2010) Table 3760037, OECD (2009c).

business-friendly model of development. In this understanding, a major effect of the NAFTA would be to motivate an increasing inward flow of direct investment to Mexico – not just from the US and Canada, but from investors in other jurisdictions pleased with the cementing of Mexico's neoliberal policy stance. Foreign capital did indeed flow rapidly into Mexico – both in anticipation of the NAFTA, and then in its wake (once the country recovered from the 1994–95 financial crisis, which was itself arguably exacerbated by the pre-NAFTA capital inflow). The stock of net foreign direct investment in Mexico grew almost 20-fold between 1985 and 2008 (Table 16.6), reaching $250 billion (US) by 2008.[14] As a share of Mexican GDP, the net stock of inbound FDI almost quadrupled during this period, reaching nearly one-quarter of Mexico's GDP by 2008. There's little doubt that incoming direct investment has contributed positively to Mexico's growth, productivity and export performance. However, the volatility of capital flows into and out of Mexico, their concentration in newly deregulated and privatized sectors (such as banking and telecommunications) and the failure of incoming FDI to leverage corresponding increases in total domestic investment in Mexico (Zepeda et al., 2009) have served to limit the benefits of this inward FDI flow to the overall Mexican economy. Research has also indicated that export-oriented FDI in Mexico has not had positive spin-off effects on other Mexican production (Weeks, 2007). So while the NAFTA seems to have contributed to a major direct investment inflow to Mexico, as predicted, the overall economic benefits of that inflow may not have been as large as expected.

In Canada, in contrast, continental integration has been accompanied by a large outflow of net direct investment. This is surprising, since a major argument of Canadian FTA advocates was that free trade would enhance Canada's appeal to foreign investors, by creating a tariff-free export platform located adjacent to the large US market. Bedevilling these predictions, Canada's net FDI position began to deteriorate substantially following the FTA. Canada shifted from being a net receiver to a net source of FDI, with the balance shifting from a positive 6 per cent of GDP in 1987 (before the FTA was implemented) to an outbound stock equal to 8 per cent of GDP by 2008 (Table 16.6). The cumulative decline in Canada's net FDI position since 1987 (−14 per cent of GDP) is almost as large as the improvement in Mexico's position (+16 per cent of GDP) in the same period. For the US, a continuing (but proportionately smaller) net outward migration of FDI has been experienced throughout the period of North American economic integration.[15] US net FDI assets abroad equalled $144 billion, equal to 3 per cent of US GDP; by 2008 that outward flow had grown to over $1 trillion (equal to over 7 per cent of the US GDP).

The contrast between the significant inflow of direct investment to Mexico, combined with ongoing outflows of real capital from the US and Canada, is especially interesting in light of the predictions of the computerized economic models that were built to simulate the economic effects of the NAFTA. Some of those models attempted to capture the NAFTA's impacts on international capital mobility – but generally in a very one-sided manner. The models allowed for large capital inflows to Mexico (with consequent spin-off benefits on growth and productivity there), yet they allowed for no capital *outflows* from the other two countries![16] By ignoring the potential economic losses associated with capital mobility, and considering only the benefits, these simulations clearly mischaracterized the net impacts of the agreement. The experience since the NAFTA was implemented verifies that capital can both enter and exit a country, with consequent costs as well as benefits.

4.6 Employment

There was much debate in all three NAFTA countries regarding the aggregate employment impacts of continental free trade. Within Canada, the Canada–US FTA was widely blamed for a precipitous decline in manufacturing employment during the first years of that agreement; Canada lost nearly 20 per cent of its manufacturing employment during the first four years of the FTA, through a painful wave of plant closures and industrial restructuring. The FTA sparked a one-time process of adjustment in Canadian industry (which was forced to evolve away from its previous reliance on the domestic market). In retrospect, however, this employment decline was also the result of a very aggressive anti-inflation monetary policy that was implemented in Canada during the same period (Gaston and Trefler, 1997). Canadian manufacturing recovered later in the 1990s (helped by the depreciation of the Canadian currency), but then entered a more sustained and long-term decline after the turn of the century. A large expansion of resource exports (especially synthetic crude oil extracted from the Alberta tar sands) produced an appreciating currency and the displacement of manufacturing exports and jobs (in classic 'Dutch disease' fashion).

In the US, labour advocates point to large trade deficits with Canada and Mexico to suggest that NAFTA trade flows have undermined domestic employment levels, especially in manufacturing. Between 1995 and 2009, US manufacturing employment declined by over 5 million positions (or over 30 per cent). This reflected many factors, of course, including the impact of the 2008–09 recession, the generalized pressures of globalization and faster-than-average productivity growth in this sector. Nevertheless, the conclusion that the NAFTA has contributed to the enormous dislocation experienced in US manufacturing regions is widespread.

Even in Mexico, meanwhile, the promise that the NAFTA would spark a wave of job creation in export-oriented industries has been largely unfulfilled. Export-oriented employment did expand in the late 1990s, especially in the northern border zone of maquiladora export production facilities;[17] but the number of new jobs created in those industries remained small relative to the overall size of Mexico's labour market. Then, after 2000, manufacturing employment in Mexico began to decline (in both maquiladora and non-maquiladora regions), reflecting weakness in the US market, and the displacement of Mexican exports by cheaper products from China and other low-cost producers. Meanwhile, the liberalization of agricultural trade (and the consequent inflow of agricultural imports from mechanized, and subsidized, US farms) has displaced as many as 2 million Mexican workers from the agricultural sector since NAFTA (Zepeda et al., 2009). That displacement from rural industries far outstrips any job creation in other export-oriented sectors. In none of the three countries, therefore, can a convincing argument be made that continental economic integration has had a positive impact on labour markets (Campbell et al., 1999; Scott et al., 2006). Of course, overall labour market conditions in each country reflect a wide range of determinants, including demographic trends, monetary policy and labour market structures; in that context, it is impossible to specify the NAFTA's incremental impact on labour market outcomes. Real wages have stagnated, at best, in Mexico since the NAFTA was implemented, and there has been no harmonization of wages between Mexico and the rest of the continent (as many economic models of the NAFTA had predicted).

4.7 Economic growth, innovation and productivity

It is hard to argue that continental free trade has had any perceptible impact on real economic growth rates on the continent, which also continue to reflect primarily domestic factors (such as the stance of monetary policy and the gen-

Table 16.7 Real growth rates, NAFTA countries, 1970–2007 (average annual growth rate, real GDP, %)

	1970–89 (pre-FTA)	1989–94 (FTA)	1994–2007 (NAFTA)
Canada	3.6	1.2	3.2
United States	3.3	2.3	3.0
Mexico	4.1	3.9	2.9

Source: Author's calculations from Organisation for Economic Co-operation and Development (2009c).

eral vitality of business investment). None of the NAFTA member countries have exhibited stronger economic growth in the wake of continental free trade, than before it (Table 16.7). This finding seems particularly damaging to the claim of NAFTA proponents that pro-competitive structural changes in the Mexican economy, implemented in conjunction with the NAFTA, would significantly enhance economic growth there (Fernandez-Arias and Montiel, 2001). In fact, Mexico's growth under the NAFTA has been notably slower than in previous periods (and significantly slower than during the golden years of import-substitution industrialization from the 1950s through the 1970s). Indeed, Mexican growth under NAFTA has lagged other emerging Latin American countries (notably Brazil), casting great doubt on the special benefits that Mexico was assumed to derive from NAFTA membership. Productivity growth in both Canada and Mexico has been sluggish over the past decade (Table 16.2), and has badly lagged both US productivity growth and average OECD rates. In Canada's case, this reflects the negative productivity impacts of that country's emerging specialization in resource extraction (which is subject, especially in non-renewable energy sectors, to diminishing returns). In Mexico's case it reflects the weaker than expected growth in high-productivity export sectors following the NAFTA, the mass displacement of labour from other sectors, and the growth of non-traded service industries as a 'fallback' source of employment. For both countries, this poor productivity performance belies predictions (once again, buttressed by quantitative economic models) that continental integration would spark continental harmonization of productivity; to the contrary, productivity differentials between the US on one hand, and Canada and Mexico on the other, have widened since the NAFTA was implemented.

4.8 Conclusions

In summary, the NAFTA has certainly had some visible and important economic effects on the continental economy. In Mexico's case, the NAFTA has clearly been associated with a substantial inflow of foreign direct investment, and an increase in manufactured and other exports. The spin-off impacts of those developments on overall Mexican economic performance, however, have been disappointing: overall Mexican investment, economic growth and incomes have not improved under the NAFTA, and in some cases have deteriorated (Gallagher et al., 2009). In Canada's case, the most lasting impact of the NAFTA seems to have been a reorientation of its exports away from industrial products, and toward natural resources. The impact of continental integration on Canadian productivity has similarly disappointed optimistic predictions of an upward harmonization with US levels. US economic developments, meanwhile, have been dominated (for better or worse) by other domestic and global factors, including monetary policy, the rise of China, and the 2008–09 financial crisis and recession. It is very difficult, therefore, to identify any lasting and substantial shift in the economic trajectory of any of the NAFTA countries that could credibly be attributed to the process of continental integration.

5 NAFTA's problems and prospects

The NAFTA has become a central structural feature of the North American economy. Its overall economic effects, however, have not matched the optimistic projections made by neoclassical economists in the political debates that led to its implementation. More recently, of course, the North American economic trajectory has been battered by the financial crisis and subsequent recession of 2008–09, which originated in the US financial and real estate sectors. And from a deeper, longer-term perspective, the NAFTA's future seems to be tied to the uncertain economic and political prospects facing its dominant member. The loss of US economic leadership (in contrast to European and especially Asian development), and consequent erosion of global political and strategic hegemony, would seem to suggest that the NAFTA is also destined to experience a long, slow loss of importance. Canada and Mexico were expected (in the economic models) to be the major 'winners' from the NAFTA; but in retrospect, have both countries only succeeded in tying themselves more tightly to a sinking ship?

This section will consider some of the specific issues that cast further questions on the continuing relevance and vitality of the NAFTA:

5.1 Expansion of the NAFTA

In the years after the initial implementation of the NAFTA, political leaders in several Western Hemisphere countries initiated negotiations to create a hemisphere-wide Free Trade Area of the Americas (FTAA), building on the framework of the NAFTA (Lee, 2001). The plan received initial tentative approval at hemispheric political summits, Miami in 1994, Santiago in 1998 and Quebec City in 2001, and working groups were established to identify key issues and begin negotiating draft text. The Quebec City summit (marked by large anti-globalization and human rights protests) adopted an 'action plan' in which the progress of free trade negotiations would supposedly be linked to the maintenance of democratic rights through the continent. Subsequent political events, however, have undermined the prospects for the FTAA. Following the Argentine debt and political crisis of 2001–02, public sentiment across Latin America swung definitively against the firmly neoliberal precepts that are embedded in the NAFTA; left-wing governments came to power in most Latin American countries, more critical of the business-friendly features of the NAFTA. The emergence of Brazil as the leading economic force in Latin America, on the basis of a development strategy that in many respects differs from the standard neoliberal model, has had an especially important impact on the political and economic balance of influence. Brazil strongly opposed many of the NAFTA-like features that were being advanced by US and Canadian negotiators. The FTAA process ground to a halt; no negotiations have been held since 2003, and none are likely to occur in the near future without a fundamental realignment of hemispheric politics. Meanwhile, the countries of Latin America and the Caribbean, exuding a more confident and independent stance in the wake of the US financial meltdown, in 2010 proposed the creation of a new hemispheric organization that would exclude the US and Canada. This organization would be a rival to the Organization of American States (founded in 1949, and traditionally displaying an anti-Communist, US-dominated outlook). In sum, if there is to be any expansion of free trade within the Western Hemisphere, it is likely to deviate fundamentally from the template that was provided by the NAFTA.

5.2 Dilution of the NAFTA

In the wake of the failure of the FTAA, and the deadlocked state of multilateral liberalization talks at the WTO, some governments have placed more emphasis on the negotiation of additional bilateral FTAs. Mexico has been a leader in this regard. Since the implementation of the NAFTA, it has negotiated nine other FTAs involving a total of 42 countries (Table 16.8). Most important was an FTA implemented between Mexico and the EU in 2000; among other effects, this deal provided European-based firms with a tariff-free low-wage export platform from which to service the entire North American market.[18] Those new Mexican FTAs cover about one-tenth of Mexico's total exports (in addition to the 80 per cent of exports covered by the NAFTA itself). US trade negotiators have also energetically pursued other FTAs, settling ten in total (beyond the NAFTA) by 2009, covering a combined 8.5 per cent of US exports. Canada has been the laggard among the three countries in negotiating additional FTAs (in part because of continuing political opposition to free trade agreements in Canada). These extra-NAFTA FTAs are likely to further dilute the economic effect and

Table 16.8 Dilution of the NAFTA: other free trade agreements signed by NAFTA partners (and year of implementation)

	Canada	Mexico	US
FTAs with non-NAFTA countries	Israel (1997) Chile (1997) Costa Rica (2002) EFTA[a] (2009) Peru (2009)	G-3 (Colombia, Bolivia, Costa Rica, 1995) Chile (1999) Nicaragua (1999) European Union (2000) Israel (2000) Northern Triangle (El Salvador, Guatemala, Honduras, 2001) EFTA[a] (2001) Uruguay (2004) Japan (2005)	Israel (1985) Jordan (2001) Chile (2004) Singapore (2004) CAFTA-DR (Costa Rica, El Salvador, Guatemala, Honduras, Nicaragua, Dominican Republic, 2004) Australia (2005) Bahrain (2006) Morocco (2006) Oman (2009) Peru (2009)
Total agreements	5	9	10
Total countries	8	42	15
Covered exports as share total exports (2009)	1.3%	9.8%[b]	8.5%

Notes:
a. European Free Trade Association (Iceland, Norway, Switzerland and Liechtenstein).
b. 2008 data.

Source: Author's compilation from Office of the United States Trade Representative (2010), Foreign Affairs and International Trade Canada (2010), Organization of American States (2010), Industry Canada (2010), United Nations (2010), US Census Bureau (2010).

political importance of the NAFTA itself. This is certainly clear in Mexico's case, where the government has indicated its goal of lessening dependence on its northern neighbour through the negotiation of new deals with Europe and South America (including talks with Brazil). Similarly, in 2009 the Canadian government launched free trade discussions with the EU, with a similar goal of lessening dependence on the faltering US market.

5.3 Exchange rate volatility

Unlike the EU, the NAFTA contains no provisions for harmonization in monetary or exchange rate policy. Each member country sets its own monetary policy (through its own central bank), and each country's currency trades flexibly on international markets. Indeed, intra-North American exchange rates have fluctuated dramatically under the NAFTA (Figure 16.4), imposing major uncertainty on trade and investment decisions. The Canadian dollar has varied wildly against its US counterpart, swinging between periods of depreciation and appreciation that have altered the Canadian dollar's value against the greenback by as much as 50 per cent (with consequent dramatic effect on competitiveness, trade flows and real incomes). Meanwhile, Mexico's currency has experienced periods of nominal stability (1990–95, 1998–2001 and 2004–08), interspersed with stepwise depreciation episodes usually associated with broader financial crises (such as the tequila crisis of 1994–95, the Argentine debt crisis of 2001–02, and the global financial crisis of 2008–09). Even when nominal rates were stable, however, the Mexican real exchange rate was appreciating (since Mexican inflation remained higher than in the US); this undermined the already disappointing performance of Mexican export industries (Galindo and Ros, 2008).

The introduction of the euro in 1999 sparked some discussion in North America regarding the idea of a continental currency (perhaps to be called the

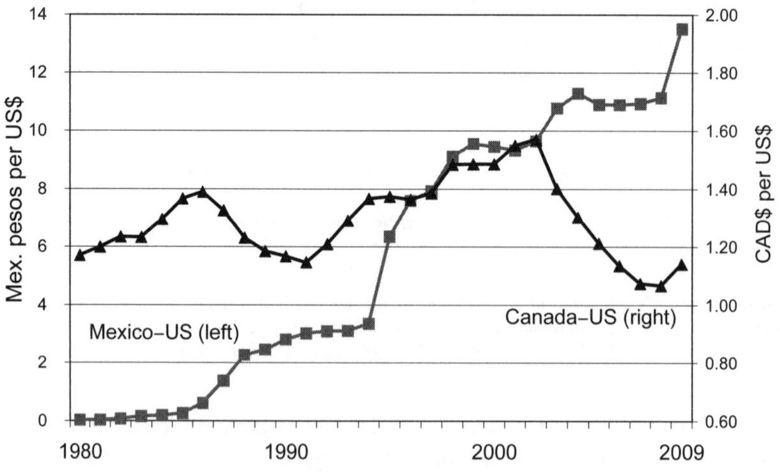

Note: Mexico exchange rate pre-1992 adjusted for new peso conversion.

Source: Statistics Canada (2010) Table 1760064, Officer (2009).

Figure 16.4 North American exchange rates 1980–2009

'amero'). Some analysts have suggested that a unified currency would protect Mexico and/or Canada against the effects of these fluctuations (Courchene and Harris, 1999), while others argue that a unified currency would merely suppress and relocate adjustment pressures onto other, less flexible variables (like prices and wages; Blecker and Seccareccia, 2008). The great asymmetry in size between the US and its two NAFTA partners implies that a unified North American currency would, in practice, be dominated by US policy priorities; this is another barrier to acceptance of the idea in Canada and Mexico (which would have to, in essence, unilaterally cede sovereignty over monetary policy as a consequence). The prospects for monetary union in the North American setting, therefore, seem highly remote, and hence trade and investment flows within the continent will continue to be subject to the volatility of the current exchange rate regime.

5.4 Migration

Mexico has long been the largest source of immigrant labour to the US. Official census data (US Census Bureau, 2009) indicated 12 million Mexican-born immigrants living in the US in 2007 (equivalent to over one-tenth of all Mexicans); this understates the true Mexican presence in the US, which includes several million undocumented migrants. Most economists predicted that NAFTA would reduce migration flows, thanks to the expected trade-induced reduction of the wage gap between the two countries; neither result has been obtained in practice. Legal and illegal immigration continues to be a very volatile political subject in the US; conservatives agitate for a clampdown on border security, the cancellation of health insurance for undocumented migrants and other punitive measures. In Mexico, too, the subject is controversial, with many Mexicans bemoaning the often-harsh experiences of Mexicans living north of the border. Some Mexican policy-makers have called for provisions within the NAFTA for greater mobility by persons within North America, and to protect the interests and standing of Mexican migrant workers in the US (Castañeda, 2008). Progress on this front seems unlikely, however, given the polarized nature of the debate in the US, where there is little political support for measures allowing freer cross-border flows of people within North America. For the foreseeable future, it seems, North American economic integration will continue to allow for free flows of commodities and capital, but not of human beings.

5.5 Borders

An important consequence of the September 11, 2001 terrorist attacks in the US was the exacerbation of congestion and traffic delay at Canada–US and Mexico–US border crossings. An immediate US security crackdown in the wake of the attacks produced unprecedented backlogs in cross-border traffic; while those disruptions were temporary they did highlight the extent to which North

American businesses have been dependent on cross-border flows of inputs – and hence vulnerable to disruptions and delays in those flows. High-level initiatives have since been taken to enhance traffic flows at both borders, including the expansion of physical infrastructure and the introduction of new high-speed screening measures for regular pre-screened shipments. As yet, there is no significant discussion in North America about European-style efforts to eliminate border crossings within the free trade zone; this approach would require a prior harmonization of immigration, customs and security policies, which is not considered feasible in any of the NAFTA countries. Among US policy-makers, ensuring border security is now considered a priority; the elimination of intra-NAFTA border controls would imply the partnering of perimeter security functions with Canadian and Mexican border agencies, a move that is not considered politically feasible in the US.

5.6 *Stability and democracy in Mexico*

After seven uninterrupted decades of rule, the PRI was defeated in the 2000 presidential election by the right-wing PAN, led by Vicente Fox Quesada. The largely peaceful transition to a new administration was a hopeful sign, interpreted by many as proof that Mexico's membership in NAFTA was sparking improvements in the transparency and functioning of Mexican political and legal institutions. The Mexican trade union movement has also made some uneven progress in freeing itself from decades of state-sponsored oversight, and forming itself into a more authentic and independent social force (perhaps out of necessity, with its traditional patron, the PRI, now in opposition). It would be very premature, however, to conclude that Mexico has become uniformly more democratic under the NAFTA. The troubled 2006 presidential election was reminiscent of the bitterly contested 1988 election. A resurgent left campaign by the PRD (under Andrés Manuel López Obrador) captured as many votes as the incumbent PAN (now led by Felipe Calderón Hinojosa); amidst accusations of fraud, another democratic crisis ensued (PRD supporters, initially, even attempted to form an alternative government). Following several recounts, and with strong support from business and US diplomats, the PAN consolidated its governing power. Mexico continues to be bedevilled by political violence, intensifying criminal activity and violence (much of it associated with illegal drug exports to the US), corruption and the questionable democratic credibility of many public institutions.

5.7 *North America's fading competitiveness*

The financial crisis and recession that began in 2008 in the US exposed the financial fragility of the over-leveraged US economy. But it also exposed the underlying industrial malaise of the continental economy. Several major North American industrial corporations (most notably in the automotive industry) were driven to the brink of collapse by the impacts of the crisis (including falling sales and dramatically tightened credit conditions). North American industrial firms have lost market share at home, and globally, to those based in Europe and Asia, on the basis of cost, innovation, quality and design. North America as a whole endures a very large trade deficit in manufactured products (worth over US$500 billion in 2008). Tightening the internal links within North America has not altered the failure of North American value-added producers in general to innovate, win markets and attain sustainable profitability. This failure of global competitiveness can be compensated, for a while, by large net exports of resource-based commodities (in the Canadian and Mexican cases), and/or by financial inflows and net global borrowing (in the US case). But in the longer run, neither of these options can compensate for the generally disappointing performance of North American industry under the NAFTA.

6 Conclusion

The implementation in 1994 of the NAFTA, building on the earlier framework of the 1989 Canada–US FTA, marked a watershed in the historical political-economic evolution of Canada and Mexico. Political and business elites in both countries abandoned earlier attempts to forge more nationalist, proactive development strategies, and instead embarked on a course of closer integration with the US market, and the US model of political-economy. The NAFTA had less dramatic, though still important, effects in the US. The relatively simple task of eliminating tariffs on intra-NAFTA merchandise trade constitutes a modest portion of the overall NAFTA package. More important has been the NAFTA's attempt to establish a continent-wide regime of deregulated, market-oriented economic development. Indeed, the Mexican government's primary interest in the NAFTA may have been precisely to commit itself publicly and permanently to a broadly neoliberal development strategy, thus winning the confidence and approval of both international investors and domestic wealth-holders. The NAFTA has had a significant impact on trade and direct investment flows within North America, but the overall impact of NAFTA on aggregate economic variables (such as investment, growth, productivity and incomes) has been disappointing, including for Mexico (which was expected by economists to benefit dramatically from its integration within the continental market). The prospects for the expansion of NAFTA (to include other countries in the Western Hemisphere), or for its deepening (to address topics such as monetary integration or migration) seem dim. Meanwhile, the broader relative decline of the US economy (most dramatically visible in the financial crisis and recession of 2009) has imposed spillover consequences on its NAFTA partners, and on the long-run vitality of the continental market generally. Without a substantial revitalization of both North American economic leadership, and initiatives to further intensify and deepen economic links between the three NAFTA partners, it would seem that NAFTA's long-run economic and political importance is likely to fade.

Notes

1. The only exception was the creation of largely symbolic tri-national commissions to monitor labour and environmental policy developments in the three countries, discussed below.
2. The cross-national gap in living standards within the NAFTA zone is significantly wider than the corresponding gap within the EU. The NAFTA zone therefore incorporates a much wider range of living standards and income levels than does the EU.
3. The gap between Mexican wages and those in Canada and the US is larger than the gap in per capita real GDP. This is partly because the latter is adjusted for PPP comparisons, and partly because the wage share of GDP is significantly smaller in Mexico than in the other two countries.
4. The Liberals then became staunch supporters of the NAFTA and its proposed expansion throughout the Western Hemisphere – completing a full-circle transformation from their initial strident opposition to the FTA in the pivotal 1988 election.
5. Zedillo replaced the first PRI candidate, Luis Donaldo Colosio, who was assassinated in March of 1994.
6. In those quantitative economic models that attempted to estimate the economic impacts of the NAFTA on Mexico, this effect was proxied by an exogenous reduction in a perceived risk premium on investment in Mexico, thus resulting in a large inflow of capital to reduce the differential in profit rates between Mexico and other countries; see Stanford (2003).
7. A searchable text of the entire NAFTA can be viewed at the website of the NAFTA Secretariat, www.nafta-sec-alena.org; accessed 15 October 2010.
8. A longer tariff elimination schedule was permitted for a small range of sensitive agricultural products.
9. These exemptions were most important in the cases of Canada and Mexico, whose economies continued to reflect the legacy of more interventionist economic policy approaches adopted in earlier times. But important US measures, such as the Buy America Act (requiring US content in federally funded public developments) and the Jones Act (requiring US content in inshore shipping and shipbuilding), were also protected under this approach.
10. These FTA tribunals represented an attempt by US negotiators to mollify their Canadian counterparts, who had entered negotiations demanding full exemption for Canadian products from US trade remedies. The US was unwilling to grant this exemption, so instead agreed to the creation of special tribunals that would determine whether existing trade remedies in a country had been reasonably and legitimately applied (according to the criteria of that country's domestic trade remedy law). The operation of these panels since 1989 is widely viewed to have been unsatisfactory; a particularly discouraging indication has been the failure of the panels, despite repeated rulings against the US, to eliminate punitive US countervailing duties applied to Canadian exports of softwood lumber.
11. Annex 605 of the NAFTA exempts Mexico from the proportional sharing rule and other restrictions on energy exports.
12. Several studies have estimated modest trade diversion effects from the NAFTA, especially in labour-intensive commodities such as textiles; see Fukao et al. (2003).
13. Mexico ranks as Canada's fourth-largest bilateral trade partner, while Canada is Mexico's third largest trade partner.
14. The net FDI stock positions described in Table 16.6 include flows to and from all nations (not just NAFTA members), and hence reflect the impacts of broader economic and global changes (not just North American integration).
15. At the same time, of course, the US has experienced a large financial inflow of capital, offsetting its large and chronic current account deficits.
16. See Stanford (2003, pp. 33–4).
17. Maquiladora export-processing rules were implemented in the 1960s to stimulate labour-intensive manufacturing activity along Mexico's northern border; they allowed for the tariff-free

import of manufactured inputs to Mexico, which were then transformed by Mexican workers and then re-exported back across the border to the US. Employment in these maquiladora facilities peaked at just over 1 million workers in 2001.

18. So long as their Mexican output satisfies the NAFTA's rules of origin.

References

Blecker, Robert A. (2008), 'External Shocks, Structural Change, and Economic Growth in Mexico 1979–2006', Working Paper No. 2008-04, American University, Department of Economics.

Blecker, Robert A. and Mario Seccareccia (2008), 'Would a North American Monetary Union Protect Canada and Mexico Against the Ravages of "Dutch Disease?"', Working Paper No. 2008-07, American University, Department of Economics.

Bureau of Economic Analysis, US Department of Commerce (2010), 'National Income and Product Accounts,' online database, available at www.economicindicators.gov; accessed 15 October 2010.

Bureau of Labor Statistics (2009), *Hourly Compensation Costs for Production Workers in Manufacturing, 34 Countries or Areas, 22 Manufacturing Industries, 1992–2007*, Washington: US Department of Labor.

Burfisher, Mary E., Sherman Robinson and Karen Thierfelder (2001), 'The Impact of NAFTA on the United States', *Journal of Economic Perspectives*, **15**(1), 125–44.

Campbell, Bruce, Maria Teresa Gutierrez Haces, Andrew Jackson and Mehrene Larudee (1999), *Pulling Apart: The Deterioration of Employment and Income in North America Under Free Trade*, Ottawa: Canadian Centre for Policy Alternatives.

Castañeda, Jorge G. (2008), *Ex Mex: From Migrants to Immigrants*, New York: New Press.

Clarkson, Stephen (2002), *Uncle Sam and Us: Globalization, Neoconservatism and the Canadian State*, Toronto: University of Toronto Press.

Compa, Lance (1997), 'NAFTA's Labor Side Accord: A Three-year Accounting', *NAFTA: Law and Business Review of the Americas*, **3**(3), 6–23, Summer.

Congressional Budget Office (2003), *The Effects of NAFTA on US–Mexican Trade and GDP*, Washington: Congressional Budget Office.

Council of Economic Advisors (2010), *Economic Report of the President*, Washington: US Government Printing Office.

Courchene, Thomas and Richard Harris (1999), 'From Fixing to Monetary Union: Options for North American Currency Integration', Commentary No. 127, Toronto: C.D. Howe Institute.

Fernandez-Arias, Eduardo and Peter Montiel (2001), 'Reform and Growth in Latin America: All Pain, No Gain?', *IMF Staff Papers*, **48**(3), 522–46, September.

Foreign Affairs and International Trade Canada (2010), *Trade Negotiations and Agreements*, Ottawa: Department of Foreign Affairs and International Trade, available at www.international.gc.ca/trade-agreements-accords-commerciaux; accessed 15 October 2010.

Fukao, Kyoji, Toshihiro Okubo and Robert M. Stern (2003), 'An Econometric Analysis of Trade Diversion Under NAFTA', *North American Journal of Economics and Finance*, **14**(1), 3–24.

Galindo, Luis and Jaime Ros (2008), 'Alternatives to Inflation Targeting in Mexico', *International Review of Applied Economics*, **22**(2), 201–14.

Gallagher, Kevin P. et al. (2009), *The Future of North American Trade Policy: Lessons from NAFTA*, Boston: Frederick S. Pardee Center.

Gaston, Noel and Daniel Trefler (1997), 'The Labour Market Consequences of the Canada–US Free Trade Agreement', *Canadian Journal of Economics*, **30**(1), 18–41, February.

Hornbeck, J.F. (2004), *NAFTA at Ten: Lessons from Recent Studies*, Washington: Congressional Research Service, February.

Industry Canada (2010), Strategis Trade Data Online, Canada: Industry Canada, www.ic.gc.ca/eic/site/tdo-dcd.nsf/eng/Home; accessed 15 October 2010.

Instituto Nacional de Estadistica Geografia e Informatica (2009), *Sistema de Cuentas Nacionales de México*, Mexico: INEGI.

Kirton, John and Rafael Fernandez de Castro (1997), *NAFTA's Institutions: The Environmental Potential and Performance of the NAFTA Free Trade Commission and Related Bodies*, Montreal: Commission for Environmental Cooperation.

Koehl, Albert (2004), 'The Commission for Environmental Cooperation: NAFTA's Environmental Watchdog Might Actually Work, If Given the Chance', *CCPA Monitor*, May.

Laxer, Gordon and John Dillion (2008), *Over a Barrel: Existing from NAFTA's Proportionality Clause*, Edmonton: Parkland Institute.

Lederman, Daniel, William F. Maloney and Luis Serven (2003), *Lessons From NAFTA for Latin America and the Caribbean Countries: A Summary of Research Findings*, Washington: World Bank.

Lee, Marc (2001), *Inside the Fortress: What's Going on at the FTAA Negotiations*, Ottawa: Canadian Centre for Policy Alternatives.

Lustig, Nora (1998), *Mexico: The Remaking of an Economy*, Washington: Brookings Institution.

McCallum, John (1995), 'National Borders Matter: Canada–US Regional Trade Patterns', *American Economic Review*, **85**(3), 615–23.

Office of the US Trade Representative (2010), *Trade Agreements*, Washington: USTR, available at www.ustr.gov/trade-agreements; accessed 15 October 2010.

Officer, Lawrence H. (2009), 'Exchange Rates Between the United States Dollar and Forty-one Currencies', Measuring Worth, available at www.measuringworth.org/exchangeglobal; accessed 16 October 2010.

Organisation for Economic Co-operation and Development (2008), *OECD Annual National Accounts, Volume 2*, Paris: Organisation for Economic Co-operation and Development.

Organisation for Economic Co-operation and Development (2009a), *OECD Factbook 2009: Economic, Environmental and Social Statistics*, Paris: Organisation for Economic Co-operation and Development.

Organisation for Economic Co-operation and Development (2009b), *OECD Economic Outlook, 2009:2*, Paris: Organisation for Economic Co-operation and Development.

Organisation for Economic Co-operation and Development (2009c), *SourceOECD National Accounts Database*, Paris: Organisation for Economic Co-operation and Development.

Organization of American States (2010), Foreign Trade Information System, Washington: Organization of American States available at www.sice.oas.org; accessed 15 October 2010.

Poitras, Guy and Raymond Robinson (1994), 'The Politics of NAFTA in Mexico', *Journal of Interamerican Studies and World Affairs*, **36**(1), 1–35.

Ros, Jaime and Nora Claudia Lustig (2000), 'Trade and Financial Liberalization with Volatile Capital Inflows: Macroeconomic Consequences and Social Impacts in Mexico During the 1990s', Working Paper No. 18, New York: Center for Economic Policy Analysis, New School University, February.

Royal Commission on the Economic Union and Development Prospects for Canada (1985), *Report of the Royal Commission on the Economic Union and Development Prospects for Canada*, Ottawa: Minister of Supply and Services.

Scott, Robert E. (2001), *Fast Track to Lost Jobs: Trade Deficits and Manufacturing Decline are the Legacies of NAFTA and the WTO*, Washington: Economic Policy Institute.

Scott, Robert E., Carlos Salas and Bruce Campbell (2006), *Revisiting NAFTA: Still Not Working for North America's Workers*, Washington: Economic Policy Institute.

Sinclair, Scott (2008), *NAFTA Chapter 11 Investor–State Disputes*, Ottawa: Canadian Centre for Policy Alternatives.

Stanford, Jim (2003), 'Economic Models and Economic Reality: North American Free Trade and the Predictions of Economists', *International Journal of Political Economy*, **33**(3), 28–49.

Stanford, Jim (2008), 'Staples, Deindustrialization, and Foreign Investment: Canada's Economic Journey Back to the Future', *Studies in Political Economy*, **82**, 7–34.

Statistics Canada (2010), *CANSIM Multidimensional Matrix*, Ottawa: Statistics Canada, available at http://cansim2.statcan.gc.ca; accessed 15 October 2010.

United Nations (2010), *Commodity Trade Statistics Database*, New York: United Nations, http://comtrade.un.org; accessed 15 October 2010.

United Nations Conference on Trade and Development (UNCTAD) (1995), *World Investment Report*, Geneva: United Nations Conference on Trade and Development.

United Nations Conference on Trade and Development (UNCTAD) (2009), *World Investment Report*, Geneva: United Nations Conference on Trade and Development.

United Nations Development Programme (2009), *Human Development Report*, New York: United Nations Development Programme.

US Census Bureau (2009), *Characteristics of the US Foreign-born Population*, Washington: Census Bureau, February.

US Census Bureau (2010), Country and Product Trade Data, Washington: Census Bureau. www.census.gov/foreign-trade/statistics/country.

US International Trade Commission (2003), *The Impact of Trade Agreements: Effect of the Tokyo Round, US–Israel FTA, US–Canada FTA, NAFTA, and the Uruguay Round on the US Economy*, Washington: International Trade Commission, Publication 3621, August.

Weeks, John (2007), 'Exports, Foreign Investment and Growth in Latin America: Scepticism by Way of Simulation', in Anwar Sheikh (ed.), *Globalization and the Myths of Free Trade*, New York: Routledge.

Zepeda, Eduardo, Timothy A. Wise and Kevin P. Gallagher (2009), *Rethinking Trade Policy for Development: Lessons From Mexico Under NAFTA*, Washington: Carnegie Endowment for International Peace Policy Outlook, December.

17 The low road to competitive failure: immigrant labour and emigrant jobs in the US

Charles Craypo and Frank Wilkinson

Introduction

The dominant system of ideas structuring the US productive system has been described as *corporate liberalism.* Corporate liberalism is a reworking of the core beliefs of liberal economics to accommodate large corporations, and is given effect by legislation and judicial ruling (Berk, 1994). Liberal economics is rooted in a utopian vision of self-regulating markets that transform the inherent selfishness of individuals into general good. The market is seen as providing the opportunity and incentives for individuals to exploit to the full their property (labour in the case of workers) but prevents them from exploiting any advantage they might have by throwing them into competition with others. For liberal economists, market forces deliver distributional justice and optimal economic welfare and this gives them supremacy over man-made laws and institutions. Unless these conform to the laws of the market they risk being in *restraint of trade* and economically damaging.

The charge of restraint of trade is particularly targeted at worker organisation and protective labour laws because they are interpreted as hindering market forces. By contrast, market dominance by large firms is tolerated on the grounds that, as the products of successful competition from efficient and innovating entrepreneurs, they are the consequences of the effective working of market forces. In a similar way, the stock exchange has come to be theorised as efficient markets for corporate control, the means by which shareholders can punish inefficient and malfeasant managers and reward successful and reliable ones by selling them their shares. By these means, the consolidation of market power by hostile takeovers is justified by the working of the market, which by definition serves the general interest (Deakin and Slinger, 1997). Thus the corporate liberal position is that although the market concentrates economic power, it also yields important benefits for society in the form of technical progress and economic growth. What is good for business is also good for society, and although the excesses of dominant firms need checking, it would check progress if their market opportunities were unduly restricted.

The reality is that the imbalance of power between labour and capital that exists in unrestricted markets guarantees workers little more than the freedom to be exploited. The recognition of this, together with the failure of corporate America to deliver full employment, led to a dilution of corporate liberalism to encompass state intervention to secure full employment, establish a safety net of basic employment and social rights, and legitimise trade unions and collective bargaining. The validity of these reforms was increasingly questioned, however, as US competitiveness faltered and with the growing inflationary crises in the 1970s. This led to a corporate liberal revival resulting in the strengthening of the rights of business and a weakening of the economic and social rights of workers and communities.

Deregulated markets, short-term corporate performance objectives and overriding shareholder and executive claims on resources now dominate the US productive system. These, together with the increasing globalisation of this system, encourage corporations to cut pay and worsen conditions of work – moves that workers are increasingly powerless to resist. When dominant firms drive down labour costs in this way, others are forced to follow suit or risk operating at considerable disadvantage. This builds on a long historical tradition of wage cost competition based on cutting the pay of existing workforces, recruiting other workers who will work for less, or by simply relocating production to more employer-friendly sites. Within the global productive system, US employers increasingly resort to importing low-wage labour and exporting production processes to low-wage countries. Immigrant labour and emigrant jobs have thus become the hallmark of US labour relations and production strategies.

The impact on US employment structures and standards has been dramatic. Deindustrialisation has been progressive. In 1957, goods-producing and support industries together accounted for 48 per cent of all jobs, service-providing industries for 38 per cent and government for the remaining 14 per cent. By 1998 the ratios had shifted to 25 per cent in goods-producing and support industries, a drop of nearly half; 59 per cent in services, an increase of more than half; and 16 per cent in government. Under the impact of these profound structural shifts and worsened job opportunities for blue-collar – and many white-collar – workers, wages and benefits have progressively worsened, and work intensity has increased, despite brief periods of respite, as in 1996–2000 (Mishel et al., 2001, Chapter 2). For the first time in the US there is a widespread feeling amongst the younger generation that they will be worse off than their parents.

Globalisation thus coincides and interacts with other adverse trends to reduce the ratio of good jobs and lower overall labour standards in America. Either cheaper labour is brought into the US or contested jobs are moved out of the US as part of larger corporate labour and product market strategies. It is, therefore, a matter of either immigrant labour or emigrant jobs, or some combination of the two.

Immigrant labour

In a geographically large and populous country like the US, relocating production from the more progressive and unionised northern and coastal states to the conservative, non-union south and south-west provided an opportunity to cut labour costs. Thus textile, garment and other light manufacturers moved wholesale to the south before and after World War II, and electrical components, car parts, fabricated steel, tyre and other metal and durable goods producers followed in the final decades of the twentieth century. Then, with the revival of conservative political forces and the consequent decline of 1930s New Deal and 1960s Great Society programmes and regulations, with the advent of enabling technological advances in communications and transportation, and with the emergence of new business norms, goals and methods, the US search for cheap labour became global.

As a result, the US is now experiencing the greatest influx of immigrant labour in nearly a century. 'In terms of sheer numbers, the 1980s witnessed the largest infusion of foreign-born persons for permanent settlement in the history of the United States'. Without much debate or analysis, says Vernon Briggs (1992, p. 1), 'the level of immigration slowly began to rise during the mid-1960s; it accelerated in the 1970s; it soared in the 1980s; and, as a consequence of the significant statutory, judicial, and administrative actions taken during that decade, the phenomenon [became] institutionalized as a fact of life for the 1990s'. Why the 1980s? Simply put, the federal government, led by the Reagan White House, acceded to business demands for low-wage immigrant labour. Unfortunately for blue-collar workers, this coincided with a rapid decline in employment in the goods-producing and support industries when the children of high-wage industrial workers were being forced into rapidly expanding but low-paying service and retail jobs. Large supplies of immigrant labour put a lid on already low wage levels, and made unionisation even more difficult than it had become in the face of increasing employer, judicial and administration hostility.

The composition of the current immigrant labour force, including both legal and illegal entrants, is so varied that they are employable at every level of the occupational hierarchy. Those who lack occupational credentials and job experiences have to work in low-wage, dead-end occupations: 'backroom' jobs in restaurants; domestic cleaning and care-giving in the personal service sector; office cleaning in the business service sector; field work in agriculture; labourer jobs in construction; hourly production jobs in garment, food processing and other light manufacturing industries. For a few, at most, low-level employment in these industries can, with time and appropriate effort and attitude, progress to middle-level positions. At the high end of the job ladder, by contrast, employment often starts at or near the top, as in the case of immigrant physicians, engineers and electronic information specialists. This chapter focuses on the impact of low, middle and high-level immigrant labour on US workers and unions in the global setting.

Low-end immigrant occupations

Low-end immigrant labour is increasingly indispensable to the comfortable living standards enjoyed by middle and upper class Americans. Women and men from Mexico, Central America, the Philippines, the Caribbean and elsewhere perform home and landscape tasks making life easier for their employers. It is now estimated that one-half of all American households employ directly or indirectly one or more immigrant workers as nannies, gardeners, house cleaners and other domestic service providers. (National Public Radio, 'Marketplace', 6 September 2002.) As more and more mothers and wives become permanent members of the workforce, the need for domestic help arises even among those families that send two or more wage earners into the labour market, increasingly of necessity, and that would not and could not have afforded this luxury in the past. Cheap labour for domestic work also enables employers to pay less for the labour of working mothers (Johnson, 2002).

These immigrants are an exploitable labour force at a time when US employers are under increasing incentive – or, pressure as the case may be – to hold down labour costs. Increased labour demand in the non-durable goods-producing and service sectors of the economy might have exerted upward pressure on wage levels, but this has been more than offset by increased supplies of immigrant workers. Immigrant labour simply adds to the already large pool of disadvantaged workers created by the need for households to put additional members into the labour market to maintain living standards after nearly three decades of falling real wage levels, by the large numbers of displaced factory and support workers and of their children who are now joining the labour force, and by other disadvantaged workers having few if any resources with which to compete (Cormier and Craypo, 2000).

Meatpacking illustrates the undermining effect of the use of immigrant labour on labour standards. The job and labour force stability that characterised beef and pork packing plants and communities in the decades following World War II has given way to low-wage, transient, dangerous work in the huge, state-of-the-art slaughtering and processing factories of the high plains states including Kansas, Nebraska and Texas. Until the late-1960s, hourly wages in beef and pork packing plants were much above the average for manufacturing and only 10 to 15 per cent below those in car assembly plants and basic steel mills. Two meatpacking unions together represented nearly the entire production workforce and coordinated rather than competed in negotiating strong pattern settlements on a company-wide basis. In the early 1960s, however, aggressive new entrants broke the old oligopoly that had dominated meatpacking since the turn of the last century and took over the industry, in part by keeping unions out and refusing to accept industry pattern settlements where they inherited unions in acquired plants. Before long, meatpacking became synonymous with low wages, unsafe jobs, transient labour and community discord (Craypo, 1994).

Unable to hire and retain local residents at the wages and working conditions they offered, the new breed of packers brought in immigrant labour to break the union and drive down labour standards. They have recruited refugees who are desperate for work and therefore willing to tolerate the low standards and harsh conditions which have come to characterise the industry. At first Asian boat people were employed, then Hispanic workers escaping high unemployment levels and subsistence incomes at home. More recently, recruitment efforts have involved Bosnians and other refugees from the Balkan wars.

Much the same has happened in the poultry processing plants in the South and Mid-Atlantic states, except here labour standards have never been high and mainly Central American immigrants have displaced African Americans. Also unlike beef and pork, poultry plants are located mainly in the eastern half of the country. When native workers began unionising in the 1980s, the major employers brought in immigrants. But, in a repeat of earlier immigrant history, they too have begun to fight back. Some of the poultry processors have been forced to recognise and bargain with the union (Craypo, 1994, pp. 87–8).

Finally, recent and shocking discoveries of boatloads of undocumented Chinese males stranded in US waters and hundreds of Asian women being held as captive workers in garment shops in New York, Los Angeles and other major American cities have unveiled well organised networks of illegal Chinese immigration, much of it coming from the southern province of Fuzhou, China's most impoverished region. Such networks, operated by the notorious 'snakeheads', funnel low-wage, vulnerable workers into US labour markets. The full extent of these networks is not known, although overall Chinese emigration has reached 180 000 a year.

Middle and high-end level immigrant occupations

Among those at the middle and high end of the immigrant labour force are registered nurses, physicians and other health care professionals; computer specialists and other technical workers in the information industries; advanced degree holders in maths, science and engineering; and, from Latin America, baseball players. In order to import foreign workers having the necessary credentials to take high-paying jobs, employers have to obtain H-1B visas from the US Labor Department. These allow US employers to hire foreign workers to fill specific job vacancies on the grounds that they cannot find US workers.

Acting at the request of employers for more H-1B visas – based on a 1980s report by the National Science Foundation predicting a shortfall of at least

675 000 scientists and engineers in America by the end of the century – Congress enacted the Immigration Act of 1990, more than quadrupling the number of skilled immigrant workers allowed into the country. The Labor Department also cooperated. More legal immigrants entered the US the following year than ever before in American history. Altogether during the 1990s, hundreds of thousands of high tech workers received H-1B visas. But then in 1990–93, contrary to the expectations of the NSF report, US universities saw the graduation of twice as many highly skilled technical workers as there were job vacancies. So great was the combined effect of the number of new graduates and the influx of foreign workers that professional occupational groups, unions and academic analysts warned that the current oversupply threatened the future labour supply by discouraging Americans from entering these occupations. This time Congress responded by providing funds for increased domestic training and education, but at the same time increasing yet again the number of job visas. In 2000 it passed legislation providing nearly 600 000 more such visas although it did double the fee employers had to pay for each immigrant visa from $500 to $1000, with the proviso that the money collected be used to finance training and education for US workers (*Washington Post*, 7 October 2000, p. A-8).

One of the most visible and publicised examples of immigrant labour in middle- and high-range employment today involves computer technicians. The US industry is said to confront a serious shortage of skilled workers in this fast-growing sector and therefore needs to import more foreign labour to fill the gap and in the process keep America globally competitive. A major recruiting ground is India, where well-educated and trained individuals are in abundance, including Cambridge and Oxford graduates.

By the beginning of the new century, however, Indian software programmers in turn were being under-priced by equally capable programmers from even lower-wage countries. Notable was the progress made by Vietnam. By 2002 Ho Chi Minh City-based Quantic Software was filling work orders from North America, Europe and Asia, including computer giants such as Nortel, Japan's NTT and Cisco Systems. But Quantic was not alone. The industry had expanded from a handful of software companies two years earlier to more than 250 domestic and foreign-owned companies. So rapid was its growth that industry analysts agreed that it was only a matter of time before Vietnam became a world-class player. And what was Vietnam's competitive advantage? Low wages. Independent analyst Research Vietnam estimated that corporations pay about $20 000 a year per Vietnamese programmer compared to $30 000 in Russia and Romania, and $40 000 in India. 'If you want fast turnaround, go somewhere established like India', said Research Vietnam's director, 'But if you're looking for a long-term, cost-effective partner, Vietnam has the potential to be that' (Tran, 2002). Of course the same thing could have been said about India a decade earlier, that is, before India's labour costs were undercut by Vietnam.

Another example involves registered nurses (RNs) from the Philippines. For years Philippine development policy has involved exporting labour, including nannies, housekeepers, sailing crews and trained nurses. Again, US hospitals and other health care institutions claim they cannot recruit enough RNs and constantly petition government for more foreign workers, in this case often from the Philippines. Permission is usually granted but on condition they pay wages comparable to those in the region, which the employers dutifully promise. Government agencies seldom check to see whether in fact they do pay the advertised wage, but in the few instances where they did it was discovered that many imported nurses were paid below area standards.

Thus in both low- and high-end labour markets, in both traditional and newer industries, immigrant workers increasingly satisfy the growing employer demand for cheap labour. Briggs (1992, p. 227) estimates that at the end of the 1980s immigrant labour accounted for 30–40 per cent of the annual increase in the US labour force. Employers justify recruiting so many immigrants on grounds that not enough domestic workers want to do this work and therefore they have no choice. Critics counter that no domestic workers will or can afford to work at the terms and conditions being offered.

Emigrant jobs

If an immigrant worker is one that has arrived and is employed, an emigrant job is one that has left the country, either through imports of foreign-made goods and services or through actual relocation overseas by domestic producers. Notable examples of emigrant jobs as a result of imports are the US auto and steel industries. The loss of these jobs, the highest paying mass manufacturing employment in the country, has been stupendous. In 1999 the Auto Workers union, historically one of the most powerful in the US, bargained for 44 per cent fewer car workers than it had in 1978, 379 000 as opposed to the earlier 675 000. In 2003 they will bargain for 269 000 at most (*Monthly Labor Review*, various years; Hudson, 2002, p. A9). In steel the cuts have been even more severe and the outlook is more dim.

The stories of steel and auto decline and the impact on unions, workers and communities are generally known and well documented (for example, Hoerr, 1988; Mangum and McNabb, 1997; Serrin, 1993; Lichtenstein, 1997; Green and Yanarella, 1998; Katz, 1985). More germane to this discussion, however, is the impact of globalisation on the high-tech glamour industries that were supposed to replace the electro-mechanical dinosaurs of the last century as the source of good manufacturing and service jobs. Two key high-tech sectors in this regard are the electronic communication and information processing industries and commercial aircraft parts and assembly. What we find upon investigation is that both immigrant labour and emigrant jobs, particularly the latter, have destroyed hundreds of thousands of jobs and eroded labour standards in these sectors.

Household appliances and audio/visual systems

Post-World War II analysts predicted that America's seemingly insurmountable technology lead and production know-how in consumer electronics guaranteed a future of good jobs and strong exports. Within a few decades, however, it had become clear that this was not to be. Experiences in the important household appliances and audio/visual equipment industries illustrate the overall story. Firms making these products employed well over a million workers in the 1950s and 1960s and were still contributing to positive US trade balances. By the end of the century they employed little more than a quarter of that number.

Take the case of TV sets. Bad business decisions by RCA, GE and other electronic oligopolists in the post-World War II decades decimated an important basic industry. Television technology and manufacturing had developed mainly in the US. But by the mid-1960s technological know-how was universal and both domestic and foreign manufacturers were taking advantage of labour cost differentials to make black-and-white receivers in developing countries. More important, large US producers were licensing fast-growing Japanese electronics manufacturers like Sony and Mitsubishi to make and sell colour sets. The latter had nothing to do with wage differentials but with short-term profit maximisation at the expense of long-term market position. The number of domestic production workers consequently fell from roughly 130 000 in 1966 to fewer than 60 000 by the late 1970s and then to barely 20 000 in the early 1990s (Cowie, 1999, pp. 93–6, 127–30).

Having done this, domestic manufacturers then accused the same Japanese companies of illegal export dumping (that is, pricing below cost) and the Japanese government of having strategically targeted the US electronics market. Although US courts dismissed the charges, it was later made clear that the Japanese had in fact targeted the industry as part of its larger industrial growth strategy, which included an array of TV export subsidies to the US and TV import barriers into Japan (Magaziner and Reich, 1983, p. 177).

The final chance for American workers to make TV sets of any kind came and went with high-definition television (HDTV). Again the promise was that US electronic manufacturers would use their technological edge to develop a superior product, one that would stimulate domestic sales, just as colour TV had in the 1970s and large screen sets had in the 1980s and 1990s, only this time they would be made in the US. Again, it was not to be. After considerable delay and much confusion, global industry leaders and government officials in North America, Europe and Japan agreed on a production and distribution network that kept financial and technological control of HDTV in the advanced industrial nations under the leadership of Phillips, the largest European consumer electronics producer, and located manufacturing of HDTV receivers mainly in low-wage countries.

Between 1980 and 2000, therefore, the number of production workers in household appliances, by far the most highly unionised segment of the electronic and electrical equipment group, declined by a quarter. Figures are not available on changes in overall hourly employment for this sector but total employment fell slightly during 1980–2000, from 1.77 to 1.70 million. Electronic components and accessories, the only segment in which hourly jobs grew, remains largely non-union (*Statistical Abstract of the United States, 2001*, Table 609; Hirsch and MacPherson, 1997, Table 7a).

In numerous small and large cuts under CEO Jack Welch, General Electric, the largest US producer of such equipment, slashed its workforce by nearly half during these years. Fearing competition from Japanese producers, he concedes, he transformed the company by divesting the household appliance, electronics and military hardware divisions, and instead moved into broadcasting, medical equipment, and telecommunications (Welch, 2001). At the end of the 1960s, the International Union of Electrical workers (IUE) represented some 150000 GE workers. (Ten other unions divided the remaining roughly 35000.) In 2002 the IUE, still the major organisation, represents about one-tenth as many GE workers, if that. Moreover, although GE made many acquisitions and started many new businesses after Welch took over, no union has organised a GE plant in the US during his chairmanship, indeed not since the mid-1980s (Wypijewski, 2001).

Communications and information industries

By the 1980s there was no more talk of consumer and industrial electronics replacing auto and steel as a source of good jobs. Now it was computers and information processes. But events involving relationships among US firms and those in developing countries would soon frustrate these hopes.

In 1986 the Indian government decided that the country's comparative advantage in the global economy was in the English-speaking, highly educated segment of its labour force. The logical target was the information industry. Modern technology made it possible. 'Even if the client is situated 10000 miles away from the software company in Asia, the client is still able to monitor the software development on a minute-by-minute basis, ensure quality checks, communicate with the programmers as if they were just next door and get efficient software developed', observed the New Delhi trade association.

The Indian government therefore set about establishing a Department of Electronics of India, whose task it was to develop the necessary physical infrastructure and provide a package of industry incentives and subsidies for the purpose of exporting computer software services. This was largely accomplished by 1990, with a number of computer parks complete with state-funded office space, electricity, and satellite hook-ups to the West.

The programme was an immediate success. 'Why pay a domestic computer specialist $50 000 to $70 000 a year plus benefits when you can indirectly hire someone in India with a master's degree from Cambridge or Oxford for less than $10 000?', American businesspeople asked themselves. By the mid-1990s, Hewlitt-Packard, Digital Equipment, Motorola, Novell, Texas Instruments, Oracle, IBM, Zenith, Microsoft and Apple, among others, were outsourcing computer programming and related work in India. Bangalore was becoming the Silicon Valley of Southern Asia.

After a trip to India in 1989, GE's Jack Welch decided to outsource the company's entire information system. 'The cost-of-living in India, about one-sixth that of the United States, provides capability for extremely cost-effective solutions', he explained to his employees back home, some of whom certainly had reason to fear the outcome, considering how many of the company's employees he had shed in his rise to the top and after. Welch began with a pilot of five outsourcing contracts but when the experiment proved even more productive than anticipated he signed 37 more involving projects in eight GE divisions. Even though 30 per cent of the work was still done in the States, project savings were said to total 60 per cent on each year of work effort (Barlett and Steele, 1996, pp. 97–9).

Finally, there is the matter of computer manufacturing. Americans probably buy and use more computers than any other people. Making computers is a major industry, but it is done largely by contractors rather than computer companies and outside the US except for final assembly, the way it was with TV sets before production left the States altogether. Household names like Dell, Compaq, Sony and HP sell them but little-known contractors like Flextronics, Jabil Circuit and Solectron make them, or at least the parts that go into them. This is because the leading computer sellers want to focus on product design and marketing rather than on making the sizeable (and often risky) investments of time and money that are involved in parts manufacturing when the consumer neither knows nor cares where they come from or who makes them.

The preferred location for parts production is Mexico. Labour is cheaper there, which of course is important in this price-competitive business. But perhaps more important, Mexico is closer to the US market than are the Asian countries that make many of the electronic components sold in the US. The sooner a product that has such a short life cycle as computers have can be produced and put on the retail shelf the sooner it can be sold. Seven of the ten largest computer parts contractors thus have chosen to manufacture in Mexico.

Within Mexico, the preferred location to date is Guadalahara, an interior city of 3.2 million inhabitants. This is not the result of random selection. Guadalahara was Mexico's shoe manufacturing centre before cheap Asian imports wiped it out. With generous business tax breaks, lots of golf courses and an ideal climate, the city set out to attract high-tech US manufacturers when the North American Free Trade Agreement took effect in 1994. But the determining factor, officials say, were Guadalahara's seven universities and dozens of technical schools, assuring contractors a trained labour force. 'Here, we get the best and the brightest', commented one of the major contractors. The strategy worked. In 1995 the electronics industry employed 5000 Guadalaharans; in 2000 it employed 60 000. 'As darkness falls each day, planes owned by cargo handlers Federal Express and United Parcel Service take off from the airport here for a short hop to US cities, their bellies full of modems, routers and other essential paraphernalia of the Information Age' (Friedland and McWilliams, 2000, p. A1).

Boeing Company commercial aircraft

'We're not talking about shirts or shoes moving to low-wage countries', complained the US machinists' union official. 'We're talking about the most advanced manufacturing technologies in the world. These are the high-tech skilled jobs, remember, that were going to be our future, that were supposed to save us in the global economy' (Greider, 1997, p. 127). He was commenting on the loss of hundreds of thousands of high-paying jobs at the world's largest commercial aircraft manufacturer, an ominous trend since aircraft and aerospace is the largest US manufacturing exporter and the nation's second largest manufacturing employer.

Boeing Company is still the world's biggest aircraft company and the largest US manufacturing exporter. The latter may be changing, however, as the European consortium Airbus Industrie, the only other major producer, gains global market shares at Boeing's expense and as developing economies, especially China, pursue infant industry strategies in developing capability in aircraft production (Bloomberg, 2000). Jobs at Boeing's main plant in Seattle and smaller ones in Kansas and Philadelphia have plummeted. In 1990, Boeing employed 156 000 high-paid hourly and salaried workers. It began cutting jobs dramatically during the early 1990s, however – 50 000 in Seattle alone. By 2002, Boeing employed about 30 000, some 26 000 of them represented by the blue-collar International Association of Machinists (IAM) and most of the remainder by the white-collar Society of Professional Engineering Employees in Aerospace (SPEEA). In 2002, hourly production workers at Boeing earned an average of \$52 000 a year and salaried technical and professional employees \$72 000.[1]

The problem for them is not wages but outsourcing, which often takes the form of offset production agreements between Boeing and foreign governments. To Boeing workers the problem is endemic. Outsourcing involves domestic and foreign contracts, usually the latter, in which parts-manufacturing – work traditionally done by union members in Boeing's US plants – is transferred overseas. Offset production agreements occur when Boeing agrees to manufacture assembly parts in, transfer technology to, and even build and equip plants in other countries – in exchange for sales contracts to those countries.

Boeing's Moscow Design Center, for example, uses 500 engineers (averaging $10 000 a year) and technicians designing parts for Boeing's 777 and others jetliners – work previously performed by SPEEA members. Chinese parts vendor Xian Aircraft was making wing components for the Boeing 747 and complete tail sections for the Boeing 737. Polish vendor WZK-Mielec was turning out doors for the Boeing 757. And Mexican vender Mexmil produce fuselage-insulation blankets for all of Boeing's jetliners. In Japan, Mitsubishi, Kawasaki and Fuji are all offset partners with Boeing in its 777 production, so much so that 500 Japanese workstations are connected to Boeing Seattle on Seattle time. At one time there was talk of developing an Asian aircraft consortium involving Boeing, China and Japan, the object being to design and produce a 100-seat regional jet, mainly in China. Boeing's long-term objective doubtless was to keep out Airbus.

As a result of myriad offset production arrangements, it is estimated that half or more of Boeing's latest model aircraft components are being made overseas. This has been a progressive phenomenon. None of Boeing's commercial lead carrier of the 1950s, the 707, was ever outsourced; no more than 2 per cent of its 1960s 727; less than 10 per cent of its 1970s 737; 15 per cent of its 1980s 767; and 30 per cent of its 1990s 777. What explains this increase? Outsourcing contracts usually came about when foreign governments (or airlines) agreed to purchase Boeing planes in return for vendor rights. The Chinese, for example, insisted that in exchange for signing a $5 billion order for 737s Boeing would contract parts production there, but also give to Chinese engineers access to the company's basic aircraft production and, more important for the long term, help China develop its own aircraft industry. Accordingly, Boeing supplied the necessary tooling technology, flight and maintenance training and safety instruction. Boeing also opened a support office in Beijing.

Outsourcing is transforming Boeing from being a vertically integrated producer that made its own parts for assembly, to a final assembly producer increasingly dependent on foreign suppliers. CEO Philip M. Condit acknowledged the transition: 'We are an assembler, an integrator', he told reporters at a July 2002, British air show. 'We will probably [make fewer] parts, which are most efficiently made by people who focus on doing that.' Condit could hardly deny the trend. He had himself just appointed former US foreign ambassador Thomas Pickering as Boeing senior vice-president in charge of finding additional 'strategic partners' with which to negotiate new outsourcing agreements. In defence of the practice Boeing argued that it had to outsource in order to be competitive.

Such agreements nevertheless enable Boeing to cut labour costs significantly as part of the deal by giving it access to cheap labour. The wage differentials are enormous. As a result of all the job cuts in the US, Boeing's hourly labour force averages 46 years of age and $54 000 a year in earnings. In addition, according to investigative reporters Donald Barlett and James Steele (1996, pp. 51–2), the Boeing-China deal 'was also made at the expense of the American taxpayer – on two counts'. First, the US government's Export–Import Bank guaranteed $1.4 billion in loans for the Chinese to purchase Boeing aircraft.

Second, Boeing and the rest of the civilian aviation industry, perhaps more than any other industry, owe their technology leadership to the tens of billions of taxpayer dollars spent on research and development of military aircraft. Now some of Boeing's technology is being given away to China.

Boeing's outsourcing strategy was short-term and self-destructive, the trade unions charged. Giving too much work to parts suppliers and sub-assemblers erodes both worker skills and company control over critical design and production processes. This has already happened, claims the IAM's chief negotiator. Between 1997 and 2002, he points out, Boeing executives spent $10 billion buying back Boeing stock in order to raise share prices. This is about how much money it takes a major aircraft manufacturer to develop a new model jetliner, he says, leaving Boeing with nothing more to show during these years than a 777 upgrade, as Airbus meanwhile introduced three new models. 'So while Boeing is giving money back to investors, Airbus is ensuring that it will dominate [product] market share in years to come.'

In addition, union officials say, Boeing should compete by producing more efficiently at home. 'We're looking at being partners at creating value – or adversaries who will be fighting over an ever-shrinking pie', explained IAM strategic-resources director. Several Boeing technical professionals reportedly support the union's position. A senior Boeing engineer, for example, reminded top managers that McDonnell Douglas outsourced to the point that it diverted so much revenue and profit to suppliers that it went into the long-term decline that led to Boeing's takeover of commercial aircraft and eventually of McDonnell itself. In any event, it appears the union is right, for while Boeing officers busied themselves buying back shares, Airbus was proceeding with plans to develop the 500-seat A380, the world's largest passenger jet, at an estimated cost of $11 billion. It already had at least one firm airline order in hand. Then, in late 2002, Easy-Jet, Europe's largest discount airline, announced a $6 billion order for 120 new jets from Airbus after having purchased exclusively from Boeing. The effect was to cut Boeing's expected deliveries of commercial jets to little more than half its 2001 output. Boeing officials blamed the loss on cut-rate Airbus prices (Allison, 2002)!

About this time a previously undisclosed Federal Aviation Administration special audit of Boeing was obtained and reported by a Seattle newspaper. The

FAA found no fewer than 107 production and quality control failings in the past year, 87 of them in Boeing's production system – many its outsourced parts – and 20 in its engineering design system. It attributed these and other assembly problems to a 'systemic breakdown' of operations. The audit produced an unprecedented five areas of further investigation based on the agency's concerns about the scope of the difficulties. Ten separate teams would have to conduct thorough checks and data collections for all of Boeing's commercial jet models aimed at future 'systemic process improvements'. This revelation came on the heels of an unrelated FAA announcement of a record $1.24 million in penalties against Boeing for poor supervision of parts suppliers and failure to report cracked parts promptly (Wallace, 2002).

For years both unions have been, understandably, in conflict with Boeing management over job preservation and related issues. The parties have never engaged in worker participation programmes and never negotiated profit sharing, productivity gains or any of the other jointly beneficial systems found in other basic industries (Erickson, 1994). A 69-day strike by the Machinists in 1995 was settled only after Boeing agreed to give the union a chance to match the costs of job bids by offshore vendors. When this failed to stem the flow of work overseas, another stoppage in 1999 was avoided when Boeing accepted limited guarantees against further outsourcing. These too failed. Following the attacks of September 11, Boeing laid off nearly 30 000 employees in response to subsequent airline cancellations of and reductions in aircraft orders. But Boeing also continued outsourcing despite union protests. Both unions made outsourcing overseas the major bargaining item. 'They have to stop boxing up our work and sending it to Moscow', SPEEA's executive director complained.

Union concern over outsourcing and the impact of job losses on an ageing workforce shaped its demands in bargaining a new contract in 2002. The already deteriorating relationship between the parties had only worsened following Boeing's announcement that it was relocating company headquarters from the West Coast to Chicago. The union interpreted the move as another signal that Boeing had no long-term commitment to domestic production or, for that matter, to production of any kind. Lately, company officials had taken to saying that Boeing is in the 'aerospace solutions' business, one more indication of a diminishing interest in the production end.

Union negotiators proposed a formula to preserve the jobs it still had. Under it, Boeing would guarantee a minimum number of jobs that would rise or fall with the company's total revenue or number of planes on order. 'If your revenues are up, if your orders are up, you hire more workers, you don't ship work overseas. But we understand that if your revenues are down, then you may lay people off', explained the union's chief negotiator. Boeing rejected the proposal: 'The market realities are such that even with our efficiencies, even with our abilities to squeeze cost out of our product, we're still not cost effective', countered the company negotiator. 'We've got to become more competitive.'

The parties were so far apart that government mediators were called in to assist in the talks. The contract had expired, Boeing refused to compromise on anything and the members were free to strike if they chose, but they did not. They rejected the company final offer by a wide margin but, fearing a lengthy walkout at a time when Boeing production was down by half, they failed to provide the two-thirds majority necessary for the union to call a strike, which under its constitution meant Boeing's final offer was accepted. The agreement gives workers modest wage and pension improvements but allows Boeing to continue contracting and adds an estimated $2000 a year to the amount that each employee must pay for health care coverage. Boeing's president was elated: 'We're looking forward to getting back to the business of building airplanes', he said, without specifying where.

Finally, it is worth noting in all of this that shortly before its demise as a major commercial aircraft producer McDonnell Douglas had also struck up a sales deal with the Chinese requiring it to produce in that country the MD-180s it was under contract to sell there. McDonnell Douglas also justified the arrangement on grounds of its dwindling market share – 10 per cent of the commercial market: 'We're in the business of making money for our shareholders', explained the company president, 'If we have to put jobs and technology in other countries, then we go ahead and do it' (Greider, 1997, p. 126). All for naught, as Boeing promptly drove McDonnell Douglas out of commercial aircraft and eventually acquired it for its military know-how and Pentagon contracts – what would turn out to be valued properties for Boeing when the civilian market later collapsed.

Aircraft engines

Boeing is not the only aircraft manufacturer shedding domestic jobs in order to meet short-term performance goals and long-term structural objectives. In this instance the transfer of domestic union jobs overseas is less a matter of substituting low-wage for high-wage labour than of forming strategic corporate alliances. Pratt & Whitney (United Technologies) and GE are the world leaders in manufacturing large turbo-jet engines, together having accounted for 85–90 per cent of the market over the past three decades. Both are profitable businesses. Yet during the 1990s they cut domestic hourly and salary jobs altogether by about 35 per cent while succeeding in keeping union wages flat at their major plants. At the same time, US imports of turbine engine parts increased from less than 5 per cent to roughly 30 per cent, all from advanced industrial economies – France, the UK, Germany, Canada and Japan, in order of importance.

Both GE and Pratt & Whitney are in fact getting out of the business of manufacturing jet engine parts and assembling the final product. Like Boeing, they see themselves as aerospace conceptualists engaged in designing, marketing and servicing jet engines for the global market rather than in making them. Both have acquired corporate partners who are more than happy to join in developing new commercial engine designs and more than willing to assume the high-end production and processing function. Simply stated, GE and Pratt & Whitney are abandoning the kinds of investments that increase or even sustain high-wage jobs domestically. 'Under the banner of focusing on their "core competencies", the leading [US] producers have been gradually getting out of the business of building equipment in favor of designing, marketing, and servicing aircraft engines', says IAM researcher Beth Almeida.

> At this time [2000], there is not a single large commercial turbofan engine in production at GE or Pratt & Whitney that was not developed and is not being produced without some involvement of overseas partners. Foreign firms have in many cases moved on from simple 'build to spec' arrangements to key roles in prototyping and design work (Almeida, 2000, p. 180).

Conclusions

The founding principle of the US was individual freedom. This found expression in the US productive system in the Adam Smithian notion of benefits of unrestricted markets. With the increasing concentration of economic power in larger and larger corporations the unrestricted rights of the individuals in markets was extended to corporations on the pretext that markets work to select and foster those forms of power that benefit economic performance. On the other hand, any suggestion that such benefits can arise from collective action was denied on the grounds that they restrain the market forces generating efficient economic outcomes. Corporate liberalism therefore served to legitimise the power of large corporations whilst illegitimatising the power that workers and small organisations can mobilise by working together. The incorporation of corporate liberalism into the law and policy in the US productive system means there are few legal constraints on big business and that there are few inter-mediating institutions and organisations between large corporations and individuals. Consequently, the US productive system evolved arm's length non-cooperative relations between firms, low commitment employment relations and antagonistic work organisation.

The freedom of US corporations to single-mindedly pursue their own interests allowed them in the past to rapidly develop new products, processes and organisational forms so that the US productive system became highly dynamic. However, whilst the US productive system is highly creative it is also highly destructive. The paucity of the rights of workers and communities allows corporations to engage in unrestricted competition and single-mindedly to pursue their controllers' interests in the knowledge that they can cover their downstream risks by firing workers, decimating communities and reneging on commitments to their customers, suppliers and creditors. The lack of corporate accountability puts a premium on innovation in opportunism which extends from new ways of breaking faith with employees, trading partners, host communities and creditors to major corporate frauds of which Enron, WorldCom and Global Crossing are only the latest examples to come to light. As with its counterpart in primitive agriculture, this slash and burn approach to economic activity is destructive of the long-term viability of the US productive system by progressively eroding its skill and technology base and the probity of its labour, product and financial markets, and denying labour market resources to large segments of its production labour force.

This reality has become increasingly clear over the past 40 years. Until the 1960s, technological leadership, large-scale mass production and a freewheeling market system appeared to give the US productive system competitive supremacy. But the market success of US corporations was also based on the almost complete closure of the US market to foreign competition. Furthermore, the high demand for products based on rapidly growing real incomes in the early post-war period created a seller's market. In these benign conditions oligopolistic producers could impose upon their customers the variety and quality of goods dictated by their production priorities and the price and non-price consequences of their conflictual relations of production. From the early 1960s, however, the US markets were progressively opened up to foreign competition to which US producers increasingly succumbed. Big Three cars, for example, were mechanically unreliable, functionally obsolete and operationally inefficient compared to European and Japanese models. Big Steel was handicapped by structurally obsolete plant and equipment, price inflexibility, poor product quality and managerial desire to divest operations into unrelated businesses. Big Four tyre makers adamantly refused to phase out cross-ply tyres in favour of radials until it was too late. As performance continued to worsen in these domestic industries, they have either closed or relocated production facilities rather than contest lost markets or, in the case of tyres, they have been acquired by foreign producers.

This 'new competition' (Best, 1990) came from productive systems that gave the quality of productive relations much higher priority than did US corporations. It originated with Japanese and European producers who had evolved high degrees of cooperation with their workers and suppliers. Within these productive systems, employment relations tend to be non-hierarchical and overtly cooperative and inter-firm links are relational rather than hands-off. Priority is also given to good faith in contractual relations, and the state, trade associations, trade unions and other organisations and institutions intervene separately and in collaboration to set norms, rules and standards for the regulating of labour, product and financial markets. The consequence has been the more effective mobilisation of the skills and knowledge of workers, higher rates of product and process innovation, improved design, greater variety and higher quality, as well as keener prices than could be achieved in the US.

The demonstration effect of foreign competition was not the only pressure for a change to more cooperative forms of productive relations; management theory also moved in that direction. With the evolution of the theory and practice of work organisation from Taylorism to human resource management the role of management has been recast from that of an authoritarian initiator, organiser and director of work to that of a democratic 'facilitator' of a participatory, co-operative and self-regulating system (Wilkinson, 2002). In this process, workers have been recast from factors of production to full partners in cooperative production. There can be little disagreement regarding the benefits to be derived from close cooperation in production. Not only does it allow for the close working together needed to raise and maintain productivity, but it also fuels learning within organisations by which new information is generated, new knowledge is created and diffused, and product, process and organisational innovations are encouraged. The resulting operational and dynamic efficiencies are crucial determinants of competitive success, as are the ability to create new opportunities and to respond quickly and flexibly to changing circumstances.

Close cooperation between workers and management is therefore a potent force for improving industrial performance. Effective cooperation requires workers to accept high levels of responsibility for operating, coordinating and developing production to high levels of quality and efficiency and to be completely open with any knowledge and suggestions they might have to improve production. To be successful, this requires goodwill, trust and long-term commitment. But the commitments made by corporations are highly conditional when they are pursuing short-term competitive strategies and prioritising shareholder demands for short-term gain. The unconditional demands made by management require workers to be totally committed to organisational objectives and to collectivise their effort, while conditional promises managers make mean that risk is individualised and that workers are readily disposable. Considering the illustrative nature of managerial priorities in electronics and aircraft, it is not surprising that high performance work systems have proved difficult to implement and sustain in the US (Appelbaum and Batt, 1994; Konzelmann and Forrant, 2002).

The need for high levels of cooperation extends to technical change. As competition has intensified, innovation has become more and more important and this has been shown to require close collaboration within and between firms, and between business and research institutions (Keeble and Wilkinson, 1999 and 2000). Innovation can best be understood as a process, the beginning stage of which is the development of radical new ideas from the science and technology base and the end stage of which is the wide diffusion of new products and processes. For any productive system, acquiring the full value from technical advance requires a balance between a high quality scientific and technology base, a high-technology sector for developing the commercial capabilities of new research findings, and an industry tradition in which innovations are embodied into new products and processes. The process of developing and using new technology also requires an institutional framework that supports technological diffusion and the necessary learning processes within and between these sectors (Wilkinson and Moore, 2000).

During the process of innovation, new technology passes from the 'newly emerging' and 'widely diffusing' technologies (McArthur, 1990). The US played a leading role in the 'newly emerging' phases of most recent new technologies. However, the lead in the wide diffusion of these generic changes has usually passed to other productive systems. This relative failure by American business can be accounted for by the lack of success in fostering cooperative learning processes in the workplace, in supply chains, and with the science and technology base because of extreme individualism and antagonistic inter- and intra-firm relationships. It can also be explained by the prevalence of adversarial work relations and the idea that skilled work can be readily replaced by technology. The corollary of this supposed deskilling effect of technology is a concentration of education and training at higher scientific, technological and managerial levels and a neglect of the middle range technical skill base – the low levels of which place limitations on organisational learning (Lazonick, 1997). This absence of effective collaboration within the technology development chain and the weakness of the skill base explain why, for example, America lost to Japan the world lead in the development and sale of machine tools, a primary route for the diffusion of electronics and computing into manufacturing (Forrant, 1997). Finally, the US failure to capitalise on its technological lead is explained by the speed with which US corporations internationally outsource the production of new products and services and in the process externalise knowledge transfer, learning processes and expertise and skill development necessary to deepen the technological base.

Thus, America's relative failure at the 'widely diffusing stage' can be explained by a failure to make radical innovations in work and industrial organisation and related policies to support its lead in radical new science and technology, and the speed by which these processes are outsourced abroad. This conclusion reinforces the argument that the lack of organisational flexibility will lessen the ability to meet the challenge of radical change. The locking-in of American business into a mode of rationality (Pratt, 1996) typified by extreme individualism, cut-throat competition, and adversarial employment and business relationships inhibited learning capabilities (Lazonick, 1991) and serves as a barrier to the full exploitation of radically new knowledge from its scientific base.

The twin strategies of sucking in cheap immigrant labour and expelling jobs to low-wage areas is a witness to the locking in of the US productive system into low road competition at the expense of the high road, and evidence of its long-run competitive decline. In the process of switching from US to global sourcing, and in moving from concentrating on producing goods and services to concentrating on maximising shareholder value – or, more recently, CEO compensation – American corporations have effectively hollowed out the technical capabilities of the US productive system and reduced its capacity to innovate and compete. The resulting collapse in productive sector jobs precipitated a fall in real wages, which was exacerbated by an increase in household labour market activity to stave off a fall in the standard of life, and by the rising tide of cheap immigrant labour. This was to the advantage of what Galbraith (1992) described as the contented classes whose real income, linked to corporate financial success, has been further enhanced by the declining cost of personal and other services provided by the low paid. However, many of these became less contented as the inward migration of highly skilled workers and the outward migration of highly skilled jobs eroded their earning and job opportunities.

It is also argued that the relocation of production out of the US merely reflects the comparative advantage of developing countries in the price of low-skilled labour (Wood, 1994). But as was shown above, the labour migration and job emigration now affects all grades of workers and the driving force of labour immigration and job emigration is tapping sources of low pay whatever the level of skill. Moreover, it is not altogether clear how the immiseration of a large proportion of the US population benefits world development even if jobs are created elsewhere. And, there must be a question of the overall effect on jobs as the lowering of pay relative to productivity to enhance profits reduces the capability of the world's workers to consume what they produce and therefore the overall level of effective demand. There can be no doubt that the transfer of technological enterprise accompanying the global activity of US corporations has advantages for other countries but this is offset by its destructive capabilities. But the greater threat to the world economic order is the globalisation of corporate liberalism, the dominant ideology of the US productive system, with its insistence on low-wage and *flexible* labour markets, reduced levels of welfare provision and of unrestricted corporate activity, however exploitative and destructive that might be. As a consequence, despite the superior economic performance of the productive systems that lead in establishing the comparative advantages of high road competitive strategies, they are currently being pressed to move to the low road by deregulating their labour, product and financial markets to free-up their corporate sectors. How this propels them down the route pioneered by the US will determine the extent to which they replicate that productive system's poverty, inequality and operational and dynamic inefficiencies.

Note

1. Unless otherwise noted, the Boeing discussion is based on Greenhouse (2002a and 2002b); and Lunsford (2002a and 2002b).

References

Allison, Melissa (2002), 'Airbus tops Boeing for sale; European maker closing gap on jets', *Chicago Tribune*, 15 October, sec 3, pp. 1,4.

Almeida, B. (2000), 'Linking institutions of governance and industrial outcomes: the case of global aircraft engine manufacturing', *Proceedings of the 52nd Annual Meeting*, Madison, WI: Industrial Relations Research Association, pp. 174–83.

American Social History Project (1989), *Who Built America? Working People & the Nation's Economy, Politics, Culture and Society*, Volume One, *From Conquest & Colonization Through Construction & the Great Upheaval of 1877*, New York: Pantheon Books.

Appelbaum E. and R. Batt (1994), *The New American Workplace: Transforming Work Systems in the United States*, New York: ILR Press.

Barlett, D.L. and J.B. Steele (1996), *America: Who Stole the Dream?*, Kansas City, MO: Andrews and McMeel.

Berk, G. (1994), *Alternative Tracks: The Constitution of American Industrial Order*, 1865–1917, Baltimore, The Johns Hopkins University Press.

Best, M. (1990), *The New Competition: Institutions of Industrial Restructuring*, Cambridge, MA: Harvard University Press.

Bloomberg News (2000), 'Airbus to make huge jet to challenge Boeing', *Washington Post*, 20 December, p. E3.

Bouchard, P. (2002), 'Non-majority union finds ways to make gains organizing: union takes the long, bottom-up route at GE', International Union of Electrical Workers–Communications Workers of America, Local 201, July.

Briggs, V.M., Jr. (1992), *Mass Immigration and the National Interest*, Armonk, NY: A.E. Sharpe.

Byerly, V. (1986), *Hard Times Cotton Mill Girls: Personal Histories of Womanhood and Poverty in the South*, Ithaca, NY: Cornell ILR Press.

Commons, J.R. (1956), *Institutional Economics: Its Place in Political Economy*, Madison, WI: University of Wisconsin Press.

Cormier, D. and C. Craypo (2000), 'The working poor and the working of American labour markets', *Cambridge Journal of Economics*, **24**, November, pp. 691–708.

Cowie, J. (1999), *Capital Moves: RCA's Seventy-Year Quest for Cheap Labor*, Ithaca, NY: Cornell University Press.

Craypo, C. (1994), 'Meatpacking: industry restructuring and union decline', in Paula Voos (ed.), *Contemporary Collective Bargaining in the Private Sector*, Madison, WI: Industrial Relations Research Association, pp. 63–96.

Deakin, S and G. Slinger (1997), *Hostile Takeovers, Corporate Law and the Theory of the Firm,* ESRC Centre for Business Research, Working Papers No. 56.

Erickson, C. (ed.) (1994), *Contemporary Collective Bargaining in the Private Sector*, Madison, WI: Industrial Relations Research Association, pp. 97–133.

Forrant, R. (1997), 'The cutting-edge dulled: The post-second world war decline of the United States machine tool industry', *International Contributions to Labor Studies*, **7**, 37–58.

Friedland, J. and G. McWilliams (2000), 'How a need for speed turned Guadalahara into a high-tech hub', *The Wall Street Journal*, 2 March, pp. A1, A8.

Galbraith, J.K. (1992), *The Culture of Contentment*, New York: Houghton Mifflin Company.

Green, W. and E. Yanarella (eds) (1998), *North American Auto Unions in Crisis: Lean Production as Contested Terrain*, Albany, NY: SUNY Press.

Greenhouse, S. (2002a), 'Mediator joins stalled talks by Boeing and its unions', *New York Times*, 17 August.

Greenhouse, S. (2002b), 'Boeing strike vote fails: Company offer is in effect', *New York Times*, 15 September.

Greider, W. (1997), *One World, Ready or Not*, New York: Simon and Schuster.

Hirsch, B.T. and D.A. MacPherson (1997), *Union Membership and Earnings Data Book: Compilations from the Current Population Survey*, Washington DC: Bureau of National Affairs.

Hoerr, J. (1988), *And the Wolf Finally Came: The Decline of the American Steel Industry*, Pittsburgh: University of Pittsburgh Press.

Hudson, M. (2002), 'UAW braces for '03 talks', *Detroit Free Press*, 20 October, pp. A1, A9.

Johnson, J. (2002), *Getting By On the Minimum: The Lives of Working-Class Women*, New York: Routledge.

Katz, H. (1985), *Shifting Gears: Changing Labor Relations in the US Automobile Industry*, Cambridge, MA: MIT Press.

Keeble, D. and F. Wilkinson (eds) (1999), *Regional Studies:* Special Issue on Collective Learning and the Evolution of Regional Clusters of High Technology SMEs in Europe, **34** (4).

Keeble, D. and F. Wilkinson (eds) (2000), *High Technology Clusters, Networking and Collective Learning in Europe*, Aldershot: Ashgate.

Konzelmann, S. and R. Forrant (2002), 'Creative work systems and destructive markets', in B. Burchell, S. Deakin, J. Michie and J. Rubery (eds), *Systems of Production: Markets, Organizations and Performance*, London: Routledge.

Lazonick, W. (1991), *Business Organisation and the Myth of the Market*, Cambridge: Cambridge University Press.

Lazonick, W. (1997), 'Organisation learning and international competition: the skill base hypothesis', *The Jerome Levy Economics Institute Working Paper* No. 201, Annadale-on-Hudson, New York State.

Lichtenstein, N. (1997), *Walter Reutner: The Most Dangerous Man in Detroit*, Champaign, IL: University of Illinois Press.

Lunsford, J. (2002a), 'Boeing and Machinists union heading for contract showdown', *The Wall Street Journal*, 27 August, p. A1.

Lunsford, J. (2002b), 'Boeing union fails in strike vote', *The Wall Street Journal*, 16 September, p. A11.

Magaziner, I.C. and R.B. Reich (1983), *Minding America's Business: The Decline and Rise of the American Economy*, New York: Vintage Books.

Mangum, G. and S. McNabb (1997), *The Rise, Fall and Replacement of Industrywide Bargaining in the Basic Steel Industry*, Armonk, NY: M.E. Sharpe.

McArthur, R. (1990), 'Replacing the concept of high technology: towards a diffusion-based approach', *Environment and Planning A*, **22**, 811–28.

Mishel, L., J. Bernstein and J. Schmitt (2001), *The State of Working America: 2000/2001*, Ithaca, NY: Cornell ILR Press.

Pratt, A. (1996), 'The emerging shape and form of innovation networks and institutions', in J. Simmie (ed.), *Innovations, Networks and Learning Regions*, London: Jessica Kingsley, pp. 124–36.

Serrin, W. (1993), *Homestead: The Glory and Tragedy of an American Steel Town*, New York: Vintage.

Tran, T. (2002), 'Vietnam's high-tech industry growing', *South Bend (IN) Tribune*, 13 May, p. B8.

Wallace, J. (2002), 'FAA audit rips Boeing', *Seattle Post-Intelligencer*, 11 August.

Ware, N. (1964), *The Industrial Worker, 1840–1860: The Reaction of American Society to the Advance of the Industrial Revolution*, (originally published in 1924), Chicago: Quadrangle Books.

Welch, J. (with J. Byrne) (2001), *Jack: Straight From the Gut*, New York: Warner Business Books.

Wilkinson, F. (2002), 'Productive systems and the structuring role of economic and social theories', in B. Burchell, S. Deakin, J. Michie and J. Rubery (eds), *Systems of Production: Markets, Organizations and Performance*, London: Routledge.

Wilkinson, F. and B. Moore (2000), 'Concluding remarks: some policy implications', in D. Keeble and F. Wilkinson (eds), *High Technology Clusters, Networking and Collective Learning in Europe*, Aldershot: Ashgate.

Wood, A. (1994), *North–South Trade, Employment and Inequality, Changing Fortunes in a Skill Driven World*, Oxford: Oxford University Press.

Wypijewski, J. (2001), 'GE brings bad things to life', *The Nation*, 12 February, pp. 18–23.

PART VI

GOVERNANCE

18 Governance in a globalised world

Richard Woodward

Throughout the twentieth century, mainstream social sciences proceeded from the premise that human activities corresponded with the territorial boundaries of sovereign states. The privileging of sovereign territoriality by sociologists, economists and political scientists did not reflect a poverty of scholarly thinking but was a by-product of the social world they inhabited (Taylor, 1996). From the seventeenth century onwards the state's role steadily outgrew the domain of security to encompass commercial, cultural and social responsibilities. By the middle of the twentieth century, in advanced industrialised countries at least, state power had infiltrated the everyday lives of citizens to an unprecedented degree. Meanwhile, at the international level, the Cold War backcloth of two nuclear-armed superpowers poised on the brink of mutual annihilation underscored the view that states constituted the most powerful actors on the world stage. Paradoxically it was the development of nuclear weapons, perhaps the most potent symbol of the state's power, that instigated a debate about its possible obsolescence. Intercontinental ballistic missile technology enabled states to obliterate each other from a distance. The absence of effective devices to intercept them meant states could not fulfil their elementary mission of guaranteeing the security of their citizens through maintaining their territorial integrity (Herz, 1957). In the following decade, Charles Kindleberger's (1969, p. 207) remark that 'the state is just about over as an economic unit' was another foretaste of transformations afoot in the social world. The amplified intensity, extensity and velocity of cross-border movements of trade, capital, production, people, pollution, violence and culture (Held et al., 1999), encapsulated by the portmanteau term 'globalisation', seemed to dispute the state-centred social ontology of the social sciences.

Nowhere did globalisation challenge the 'methodological territorialism' (Scholte, 2005) of the social sciences more than in the discipline of international relations (IR), which, as the 'international' prefix connotes, presupposes nation states to be the locus of the world's power and authority. This chapter's cardinal contention is that the novelty of globalisation derives from its designation as an '*ation*' not a '*nation*'. Whereas 'national' perspectives are suffused with the assumption that governance is the exclusive province of the nation state, globalisation as an 'ation' makes no prior hypotheses about the main actors or the dominant patterns of power and authority in global politics. For this reason some are ditching 'international relations' for more neutral terms as regards the actors wielding power and authority. For instance, the editors of one bestselling introductory text testify that their decision to favour 'world politics' over 'international relations' as the title of their volume was 'to denote the fact that our interest is in the politics and political patterns in the world, and not only those between nation-states' (Baylis et al., 2008, p. 3).

Governance in international relations theory: governance by governments

Over the last two decades much ink has been spilt on the concept of governance. Although the definition is controversial many coalesce around the idea that governance refers to the totality of institutions, mechanisms and processes imbued with political power and authority that permit humankind to manage their collective affairs (Commission on Global Governance, 1995; Malpas and Wickham, 1995; see Rosenau, 1997). IR's dominant theoretical approaches champion the idea that the world is organised around the system of states first formalised by the Treaty of Westphalia in 1648. Embedded into these paradigms is a political geography that partitions the globe into discrete parcels of land, each governed by a sovereign body wielding absolute and exclusive authority. Political space is equated with conceptions of place, and conceptions of place are dictated by state territoriality. As Walker (1995, p. 29) observes, 'because states are, other forms of politics cannot be'. From this it follows that the study of states and relations between states is a necessary and sufficient basis for understanding and explaining the governance of global affairs. In short, international relations scholars held that gover*nance* was synonymous with govern*ments*. Indeed because states were alleged to be the solitary repository of power and authority, governance was absent from the IR lexicon (Rosenau, 2000).

Throughout the 1970s and 1980s the sentiment that governance was tantamount to government was already at odds with a world undergoing 'a technological revolution in information and communications … diffusing power away from governments and empowering individuals and groups to play roles in world politics – including wreaking massive destruction – that were once reserved for governments of states' (Nye, 2002, p. x). Apprehension about the shortcomings of analysis that overlooked or marginalised non-state actors stimulated a series of analytical innovations in IR. Work on transnational relations (Keohane and Nye, 1972), interdependence (Keohane and Nye, 1977) and international regimes (Krasner, 1983) each assigned a more prominent role to non-state actors. These frameworks appeared to convey a more intricate image of world politics where outcomes were mediated by a variety of actors. Ultimately, however, these frameworks were still tethered to IR's state-centred moorings believing that the behaviour of non-state actors were determined by the overarching framework of inter-state relations and denying them the possibility of possessing or exercising authority in their own right. Rather than seriously challenging the epistemological and ontological foundations of IR these accounts basically tinkered with the orthodox narrative retaining states as the sole cache of power, authority and governance.

Governance in a globalised world

Despite the deluge of literature on globalisation commentators are no nearer an agreement on precisely what the phenomenon entails. The intention here is to conjecture about what, if any, implications globalisation has for our understanding of governance, and whether it obliges social scientists to discard the spatial blinkers of methodological territorialism.

Conventional wisdom espoused by the 'hyperglobalist' thesis (Held et al., 1999, p. 3) asserts that we dwell in a 'borderless world' (Ohmae, 1990) where sovereign boundaries are rendered irrelevant by the torrential flows ricocheting over their borders. Bled of their power and authority, states are unable to define and deliver the public goods upon which their legitimacy depends and become marginal players in global governance. The hyperglobalist thesis sees political, social and economic processes being organised on a regional or global scale or by private actors, generating alternative forms of social organisation and governance that have displaced the state. The hyperglobalist outlook is now generally derided as empirically and epistemologically suspect. From an empirical standpoint the hyperglobalists ignore that sovereign states have flourished in tandem with intensified globalisation. In excess of half of today's sovereign states did not exist in 1945 and, moreover, their portfolio of responsibilities has mushroomed. As tourists, immigrants, students, entrepreneurs, criminals and aspiring terrorists can attest, state borders are hardly porous and for all the wherewithal attributed to regional, global and private actors, states retain unique capabilities, as the bailouts following the 2007–08 financial crisis vividly demonstrated. Those adopting a more sceptical stance insist that the state's power remains intact because globalisation has been wildly exaggerated. They argue that the evidence points only to intensified internationalisation (Hirst et al., 2009), that is to say most of the world's connections are amongst creatures rooted in specific national contexts. The snag is that the sceptics share the hyperglobalisers' methodological shortcomings. Both present the state and globalisation as competing forms of social organisation engaged in a zero-sum battle for power and authority (Clark, 1999). While the hyperglobalisers assume that any advance for the forces of globalisation automatically drains the power of the state, the sceptics seize upon instances of states wielding their power as evidence that globalisation is illusory.

The sceptics and the hyperglobalisers go some way toward illuminating globalisation and the patterns of power and authority escorting it. While overblown, the hyperglobalists alert us to the state not being an eternal feature of our physical and imagined geography and that frequently the activities social science sought to investigate had global dimension. Indeed, in the 1990s, it became commonplace for finance, trade, pollution, society and a host of other social science concerns to acquire a 'global' prefix. Conversely, the sceptical thesis highlights the vitality of state power as a fulcrum of global governance. Defining globalisation in such absolute terms, however, precludes the likelihood of strong states being compatible with globalisation and has served to deflect attention from the more convoluted transformations of power and authority accompanying it. Globalisation's significance for social world and the configurations of power and authority within it lies in its specification as an 'ation' not a 'nation'. Inter*national* and the related levels of analysis to which it has given rise (sub*national*, trans*national*, supra*national*) infer that states are the singular reference points for conceiving political space and exercising power and authority. Globalis*ation*, in contrast, is a less loaded expression. Most writing on globalisation now concludes that states endure as significant containers of power, authority and governance. Equally, however, the 'ation' suffix suggests that states have no monopoly on political power and authority and cannot be deemed necessary and sufficient conditions for governance. The straightforward and parsimonious vision of a planet governed by states clashes with visions of a 'turbulent' world (Rosenau, 1997) governed by 'a complex cast of ceaselessly changing performers' (Woodward, 2005, p. 57) that embraces but is not reducible to the state.

No serious analyst writes states out of the global governance equation. Their bilateral and multilateral interactions and the treaties, institutions and organisations that arise are the skeleton upon which the broader anatomy of global governance is draped. If anything, states have stepped up the incidence and intimacy of their contacts as they grapple with the problems of the globalised world. In 1909, there were 37 active intergovernmental organizations but by 1981 there were over a thousand. By the turn of the century there were 2545 (Boli, 2006) with concomitant growth in multilateral treaties and conferences. In many arenas the power and authority of states is paramount. The embers of IR's traditional political geography burn most brightly in the realm of security, where non-state actors are more peripheral (Kaplan, 2009). The world's flashpoints from Afghanistan to Iraq, worries about Iran's nuclear ambitions, and quandaries anticipated from the rise of the 'BRICs' (Brazil, Russia, India and China) are normally the result of, and resolved by, state mediation. Counterinsurgents and terrorist groups notwithstanding, non-state actors are no match for states in their ability to sustain violent conflict. The power and authority of these actors are apt to be transient, drifting in and out of global governance rather than amounting to an overarching set of political relationships.

Elsewhere the state's grip over the trajectory of world politics is more tenuous and it is recognized that states and inter-state relationships are only one thread of power and authority woven into the fabric of global governance. As the twentieth century wore on, private and non-state structures of power and authority (re)emerged, becoming more numerous and more important to global governance. Between 1909 and 1981, the number of international non-governmental organisations (INGOs) vaulted from 374 to 4265 (Boli, 2006). Over the next quarter century, the INGOs expanded by a further 70 per cent reaching 7306 by 2006 (Kaldor et al., 2007, p. 315). Multinational corporations (MNCs) have likewise blossomed. In 1973 the planet hosted 9482 MNCs (Hood and Young, 1979), a figure spiking to 30000 by 1990 and 82000 by 2008 (UNCTAD, 2009, p. 17). Moreover, non-state actors were no longer seen as mere pawns on a state-dominated chessboard but to be the possessors of political power and authority that supplement and occasionally supplant the state. This prompted some to muse over 'governance without government' (Rosenau and Czempiel, 1992) by mechanisms whose authority neither springs from, nor is exercised over, territorial space. Private and non-state structures of authority, long eclipsed by social science's infatuation with the state, were resurrected as pertinent avenues of enquiry (see Hall and Biersteker, 2002; Hansen and Salskov-Iversen, 2007; Graz and Nolke, 2008). These surveys conclude that non-state sources of power and authority were always salient to global governance but report the extraordinary breadth and depth of their influence in the current epoch.

There are few fields of global governance that private authority has failed to penetrate. Private structures of authority govern significant portions of global affairs from the Internet and telecommunications through to insurance, shipping, pharmaceutical and chemical safety standards. These actors have thrived in part because issues have materialised that states and their various collaborative institutions have proved unwilling or ill-suited to deal with. The esoteric and arcane world of finance has, for instance, provided a fertile soil for the cultivation of private authority (see Porter, 2005). The International Accounting Standards Board (IASB), an independent cadre of 15 experts from the academic, regulatory and accountancy profession, spearheads the quest for globally harmonised standards for accounting and auditing while in the 1990s the Derivatives Policy Group (DPG), consisting of six weighty US securities dealers, was the crucible for voluntary standards and disclosure in derivatives markets. Credit ratings agencies are private companies that pass judgement on the creditworthiness of debtors and the instruments they issue. Their widespread use by investors, debt issuers, regulators and governments in determining financial policies means they exert powerful pressure on rated agents to pursue strategies the ratings agencies feel acceptable. Failure to do so could lead to debt being downgraded, raising the cost of tapping, or even denying access to, international capital markets (Sinclair, 2005). Think-tanks such as the Group of 30 (G30), an accumulation of senior figures from the public and private sectors, have contributed reforms in a range of areas including clearing and settlements of securities and the international financial architecture. Norms and standards also emanate from professional bodies whose licensing and accreditation requirements compel members of their communities to conform to expected standards of behaviour. The orthodoxy propagated by the professional economists populating the world's central banks, finance ministries, regulatory agencies and the plethora of private institutions previously portrayed has tapered the options available in global financial governance (Baker, 2006). To re-emphasise, this does not mean the state is irrelevant. The state and state-based networks and organisations still provide the scaffolding of global financial governance (see Davies and Green, 2008). Nonetheless, there is clear evidence of private or hybrid public and private actors formulating and monitoring their own rules or being employed to strengthen compliance with state regulation.

Frameworks of global governance

Endeavours to impose blueprints on the morass of structures of authority carry with it the dangers of distortion and oversimplification. Nevertheless, several analytical frameworks have been developed over the past two decades that seek to provide mental maps to try to make sense of governance in a globalised world. The final section of the chapter briefly considers the merits and demerits of three such frameworks: (1) multilevel governance; (2) transgovernmental networks; and (3) neo-medievalism.

Multilevel governance

Multilevel governance began life as a way of interrogating the dispersal of decision-making competencies across different tiers of government in the European Union (EU) (see Marks et al., 1996) but has since been invoked more widely to describe, explain and understand governance in a globalised world (see Bache and Flinders, 2004; Baker et al., 2005; Hirst et al., 2009). Multilevel governance pertains to the 'simultaneous mobilization of public authorities at different jurisdictional levels' (Piattoni, 2010). Typically models of multilevel governance envisage public authorities stacked in the 'club-sandwich'-style arrangement outlined in Figure 18.1 with the bottom tiers comprising subnational and national actors while the upper echelons contain regional, international and global actors.

As a prototype for visualising the dizzying array of power and authority structures multilevel governance has much to commend it. First, multilevel governance chimes with the everyday experiences of citizens. Those inhabiting federal political systems are familiar with multilevel politics and in most other polities, no matter how centralised, states devolve power down to regional and local government and up to regional and international organisations. Second, while it maintains a pivotal role for states and public authorities multilevel governance is sensitive to the ongoing metamorphoses of the state's duties and

Group of 3 (European Union, North America, Japan)

International Regulatory Agencies (WTO, IMF, World Bank etc.)

Regional Governance (EU, APEC etc.)

National-level Governance

Subnational Governance

Source: Adapted from Hirst et al. (2009).

Figure 18.1 Multilevel governance

the way in which its enmeshment in a labyrinth of wider assemblage of governance structures constrains and enables its sphere of autonomy. Last, multilevel governance encourages us to think about the interdependence of governance structures and how (or not) they blend to provide for effective control of global problems. Nevertheless, multilevel governance has its drawbacks. The model tends to conflate governance with government and struggles to cope with private actors whose authority is not obtained from control over a sovereign territorial space nor circumscribed by its boundaries. The reimposition of customary spatial scales predicated on territoriality (subnational, international) in models of multilevel governance suggests that it is 'a means for preserving a statist agenda with its conventional geographical mosaic of territories' (Taylor, 2000, p. 1105). Some theoretical and practical points are also underdeveloped. There are questions about how levels are fabricated and the acquaintances within and between those levels. For instance, models of multilevel governance seem to declare that levels are cohesive entities constructed of homogeneous actors. If the state level is selected as an example such certainties swiftly evaporate. The theory and practice of international relations demonstrates that cooperation amongst states is a variable and fractures between them are commonplace. Furthermore, there is a mass of scholarly literature detailing the spectrum of state structures and the impact this has on their engagement with globalisation and governance (see Weiss, 2003). Ambiguities also surround whether actors can concurrently belong to different layers, plausibly playing different roles and taking different forms in the process. States might perform as monolithic actors in the state level but take on a more disjointed form at the international level with representatives of particular state institutions operating with a degree of autonomy from the parent state in their dealings with colleagues in international organisations.

Transgovernmental networks

In the aftermath of the 9/11 terrorist attacks the foremost attention was reserved for the recruitment of states to a coalition prepared to prosecute the idiosyncratic 'war on terror'. Just as vital, if less acknowledged, were the networks of police, border and intelligence agencies and financial regulators that scrambled to exchange information on and detain suspects and to freeze and sequestrate their assets. While the former stressed states operating as unitary bodies the latter hinted that states were 'disaggregating into [their] functionally distinct parts'. In turn these separate parts are 'networking with their counterparts abroad, creating a dense web of relations that constitutes a new, transgovernmental order' (Slaughter, 1997, p. 184). From this vantage point the building blocks of global governance are not states but the ministries, regulatory agencies, executives and legislatures of which they are composed and the political and bureaucratic linkages they are fomenting within and across sovereign borders. Transgovernmental ties are not a novelty but the magnitude, span and levels of institutionalisation are (Slaughter, 2004). Networks discharge an assortment of functions from fostering trust and reciprocity amongst national officials, erecting, policing and implementing internationally agreed best practices, promoting convergence of national practices and providing technical assistance to developing states.

Slaughter (2004, p. 132) propounds that the newfound density and coverage of networks makes them the 'foundation of a full-scale disaggregated world order'. Likewise, the Commission on Global Governance (1995, p. 184) suggests that in global finance 'it is probable, but not certain, that these networks are the best defence against system failure'. As a framework, the sketch of a transgovernmental order has the advantage of conserving the state as a key, albeit transformed, strand of power and authority. Transgovernmental networks surmount the dilemma of attaining global rules in the absence of global authority, an arch dilemma of global governance. Moreover, transgovernmental rules are devised and enforced by national-level organisations that are domestically accountable. Transgovernmentalism, which involves state actors operating at national, regional and international levels, may offer insights into how the levels in multilevel governance models consort. Again, however, transgovernmentalism offers only a partial account of *global* governance. First, while it is acknowledged that transgovernmental networks operate in conjunction with existing international organisations they underplay private actors. Some transgovernmental networks are hybrids containing governmental and private participants that represent different constituents and interests. Second, many states are only tangential members of transgovernmental networks. The thickness of transgovernmental relationships withers outside the hallowed clubs of the advanced industrialised states. The OECD, 'the quintessential host of transgovernmental regulatory networks' (Slaughter 2004, p. 46), has just 31 members. The OECD's 69 non-member observers are very much second class citizens that, with a few exceptions, attend rather than actively participate in the organisation's work.

Neo-medievalism

Neo-medievalism surmises that the world is going 'back to the future' (Kobrin, 1998) because rather than the orderly agglomeration of collective interests suggested by Westphalian geography today's world again resembles the crisscrossing and competing fiefdoms emblematic of the period of medieval Christendom (Ruggie, 1993). Jumbled boundaries and fissured loyalties are thought to jeopardize sovereignty, reducing the state to just one actor amongst many. Today, billions of people live in blissful ignorance of who their sovereign rulers are with many answering to tribal elders, feudal landlords, mercenary commanders, religious leaders, or corporate executives (Khanna, 2009).

The benefit of this perspective is that it conveys the fluidity and messiness of the prevailing landscape with many things subject synchronously to several authority structures. Furthermore, by suggesting that territory is no longer the sole organising principle for governance, neo-medievalism is better able to account for the private 'sovereignty-free' (Rosenau, 1990) sources of power and authority. The neo-medieval slant is not free of difficulty, however. First, it overstates the changes in a manner analogous to the hyperglobalisers with all the attendant dangers. Despite the state's many vulnerabilities there are few areas where its power and authority do not operate. In areas where private actors appear to vie for superiority with states this often reflects a mix of ideology and goodwill on behalf of the latter. States also have the ascendancy in where situations involve high risks, enforcement, or the application of legitimate coercion. Second, neo-medievalism does not offer an alternative map. It presents governance structures as an undifferentiated mass offering few clues as to how this messy world can be understood, where power lies or how the system of global governance works. Like many general definitions of governance, neo-medievalism 'tends to mix together all those involved on the international scene, without ranking their functions, the lines of authority and force that connect them, their political influence, or the nature of their specific contribution to regulatory structures' (de Senarclens, 1998, p. 98). Finally, neo-medievalism reimposes the Eurocentrism of much social science theorising, taking European politics before the confinement of the modern nation state as its inspiration. Unfortunately, this has been the norm for a large part of the globe. By taking Europe as its starting point the neo-medievalists might be overstating past changes and thus overstating changes in the present.

Conclusion

Many leading pundits judge that state-centred notions of politics 'appear to account for less and less of contemporary patterns of power and authority in an era of globalization' (Pierre, 2000, p. 5). This chapter has argued that globalis'ation' confronts directly the 'national', state-centred script dramatised by the twentieth century's political scientists. Whereas 'national' approaches to politics believe that the mysteries of governance can be deciphered by probing states and their interactions, globalis'ation' notifies us of the multitude of other structures and actors that, alongside states, possess the power and authority to contribute to management of our collective affairs. There are many aspects of world politics, particularly in the ambit of security and military affairs, where the power and authority of states reigns supreme and where inter-state relations do largely explain outcomes. Equally, there are provinces where the authority of the state is contested, compromised or delegated and where the slack is picked up by structures of authority from beyond the state system. The recognition that global governance is more complicated than state-centred analyses insinuate is only the first step; the next is to evolve analytical and theoretical models capable of depicting and understanding the puzzles of governance in a global age. The models outlined in this chapter encapsulate only parts of the emergent tangle of power and authority in the global political system. Nonetheless, cartographers charting the changing contours of global governance increasingly agree that while the power and authority of states provide prominent coordinates they should not define the map.

References

Bache, Ian and Matthew Flinders (eds) (2004), *Multi-level Governance*, Oxford: Oxford University Press.

Baker, Andrew (2006), *The Group of Seven: Finance Ministries, Central Banks and Global Financial Governance*, London: Routledge.

Baker, Andrew, David Hudson and Richard Woodward (eds) (2005), *Governing Financial Globalization: International Political Economy and Multi-level Governance*, London: Routledge.

Baylis, John, Steve Smith and Patricia Owens (2008), 'Introduction', in John Baylis, Steve Smith, and Patricia Owens (eds), *The Globalization of World Politics: An Introduction to International Relations* (4th edition), Oxford: Oxford University Press, pp. 1–13.

Boli, John (2006), 'International nongovernmental organizations', in Walter W. Powell and Richard Steinberg (eds), *The Non-Profit Sector: A Research Handbook* (2nd edition), New Haven: Yale University Press, pp. 333–53.

Clark, Ian (1999), *Globalisation and International Relations Theory*, Oxford: Oxford University Press.

Commission on Global Governance (1995), *Our Global Neighbourhood: The Report of the Commission on Global Governance*, Oxford: Oxford University Press.

Davies, Howard and David Green (2008), *Global Financial Regulation: The Essential Guide*, Cambridge: Polity.

de Senarclens, Pierre (1998), 'Governance and the crisis in the international mechanisms of regulation', *International Social Science Journal*, **50**(155), 91–104.

Graz, Jean-Christophe and Andreas Nolke (2008), *Transnational Private Governance and its Limits*, Abingdon: Routledge.

Hall, Rodney B. and Thomas J. Biersteker (eds) (2002), *The Emergence of Private Authority in Global Governance*, Cambridge: Cambridge University Press.
Hansen, Hans K. and Dorte Salskov-Iversen (eds) (2007), *Critical Perspectives on Private Authority in Global Governance*, Basingstoke: Palgrave.
Held, David, Anthony McGrew, David Goldblatt and Jonathan Perraton (1999), *Global Transformations: Politics, Economic and Culture*, Cambridge: Polity Press.
Herz, John H. (1957), 'Rise and demise of the territorial state', *World Politics*, **9**(4), 473–93.
Hirst, Paul, Grahame Thompson and Simon Bromley (2009), *Globalization in Question* (3rd edition), Cambridge: Polity.
Hood, Neil and Stephen Young (1979), *The Economics of Multinational Enterprise*, London: Longman.
Kaldor, Mary, Martin Albrow, Helmut Anheier and Marlies Glasius (eds) (2007), *Global Civil Society 2006/7*, Oxford: Oxford University Press.
Kaplan, Robert D. (2009), 'The revenge of geography', *Foreign Policy*, **172**, 96–105.
Keohane, Robert O. and Joseph S. Nye (1972), *Transnational Relations and World Politics*, Cambridge, MA: Harvard University Press.
Keohane, Robert O. and Joseph S. Nye (1977), *Power and Interdependence: World Politics in Transition*, Boston: Little, Brown and Company.
Khanna, Parag (2009), 'The next big thing: neomedievalism', available at http://www.foreignpolicy.com/articles/2009/04/15/the_next_big_thing_neomedievalism; accessed 17 October 2010.
Kindleberger, Charles P. (1969), *American Business Abroad: Six Lectures on Direct Investment*, Cambridge, MA: MIT Press.
Kobrin, Stephen J. (1998), 'Back to the future: neomedievalism and the postmodern digital world economy', *Journal of International Affairs*, **51**(2), 361–86.
Krasner, Stephen D. (1983), *International Regimes*, Ithaca: Cornell University Press.
Malpas, Jeff and Gary Wickham (1995), 'Governance and failure: on the limits of sociology', *The Australian and New Zealand Journal of Sociology*, **31**(3), 37–50.
Marks, Gary, Liesbet Hooghe and Kermit Blank (1996), 'European integration from the 1980s: state-centric v. multi-level governance', *Journal of Common Market Studies*, **34**(3), 341–78.
Nye, Joseph S. (2002), *The Paradox of American Power: Why the World's Only Superpower Can't Go It Alone*, Oxford: Oxford University Press.
Ohmae, Kenichi (1990), *The Borderless World: Power and Strategy in the Interlinked Economy*, London: Collins.
Piattoni, Simona (2010), *The Theory of Multi-level Governance: Conceptual, Empirical, and Normative Challenges*, Oxford: Oxford University Press.
Pierre, Jon (2000), 'Introduction: understanding governance', in Jon Pierre (ed.), *Debating Governance: Authority, Steering and Democracy*, Oxford: Oxford University Press, pp. 1–10.
Porter, Tony (2005), *Globalization and Finance*, Cambridge: Polity.
Rosenau, James N. (1990), *Turbulence in World Politics: A Theory of Change and Continuity*, Princeton: Princeton University Press.
Rosenau, James N. (1997), *Along the Domestic–Foreign Frontier: Exploring Governance in a Turbulent World*, Cambridge: Cambridge University Press.
Rosenau, James N. (2000), 'Change, complexity and governance in a globalising space', in Jon Pierre (ed.), *Debating Governance: Authority, Steering and Democracy*, Oxford: Oxford University Press, pp. 167–200.
Rosenau, James N. and Ernst-Otto Czempiel (eds) (1992), *Governance Without Government: Order and Change in World Politics*, Cambridge: Cambridge University Press.
Ruggie, John G. (1993), 'Territoriality and beyond: problematizing modernity in international relations', *International Organization*, **47**(1), 139–74.
Scholte, Jan A. (2005), *Globalization: A Critical Introduction* (2nd edition), Basingstoke: Palgrave.
Sinclair, Tim (2005), *The New Masters of Capital: American Bond Rating Agencies and the Politics of Creditworthiness*, Ithaca: Cornell University Press.
Slaughter, Anne-Marie (1997), 'The real new world order', *Foreign Affairs*, **76**(5), 183–97.
Slaughter, Anne-Marie (2004), *A New World Order*, Princeton: Princeton University Press.
Taylor, Peter J. (1996), 'On the nation-state, the global, and social science', *Environment and Planning A*, **28**(11), 1917–28.

Taylor, Peter J. (2000), 'Embedded statism and the social sciences 2: geographies (and metageographies) in globalization', *Environment and Planning A*, **32**(6), 1105–14.
UNCTAD (2009), *World Investment Report 2009: Transnational Corporations, Agricultural Production and Development*, New York: United Nations.
Walker, Robert B.J. (1995), 'From international relations to world politics', in Joseph A. Camilleri, Anthony P. Jarvis and Albert J. Paolini (eds), *The State in Transition: Reimaging Political Space*, Boulder: Lynne Rienner, pp. 21–38.
Weiss, Linda (ed.) (2003), *States in the Global Economy: Bringing Domestic Institutions Back In*, Cambridge: Cambridge University Press.
Woodward, Richard (2005), 'Money and the spatial challenge: multi-level governance and the "territorial trap"', in Andrew Baker, David Hudson and Richard Woodward (eds), *Governing Financial Globalization: International Political Economy and Multi-level Governance*, London: Routledge, pp. 49–61.

19 Global governance

Mathias Koenig-Archibugi

Globalisation represents a major challenge to governance. Indeed, for many the concept of globalisation itself is inextricably linked to the idea of *ungovernability*. This association is comprehensible, since the classic locus of governance is the state, and the debate on globalisation concerns mainly the allegedly declining capacity of states to regulate what happens within their territories as a result of their growing enmeshment in cross-border flows and networks.[1]

This chapter does not address to what extent the governance capacity of states has been curtailed by global forces: other chapters in this volume assess the extensive literature on this question. Its aim is rather to review a substantial body of research that shows that the performance of governance functions is not limited to the actions of governments exercising sovereign powers over their jurisdictions, but occurs also at supranational and transnational levels. Governance – understood as the establishment and operation of rule systems facilitating the coordination and cooperation of social actors – is conceptually distinct from government – understood as an organisation in charge of administering and enforcing those rules (Young, 1999). The literature discussed in this chapter (originating mostly from political scientists and international relations scholars) maintains that governance is not co-extensive with government, and that government should not be seen as a necessary condition of governance. More specifically, it shows that the absence of a world government does not mean that governance is impossible beyond the level of individual states. Global issues such as ozone depletion, the spread of financial crises and the prohibition of certain kinds of weapons are managed by governance structures that do not conform to the hierarchical model of rule-setting and enforcement that is typical of states. The combination of these structures can be said to form a system of global governance.

What is global governance?

During the 1990s, 'global governance' emerged as the key term of a political programme for international reform[2] as well as a conceptual tool in political research.[3] Disparate issues have been examined through the lens of global governance, such as the role of business in environmental policy[4] the negotiation and implementation of public health policies,[5] peace-keeping,[6] gender policies,[7] weapons bans,[8] the regulation of world trade[9] and the reform of the United Nations system.[10]

Lawrence S. Finkelstein (1995, pp. 370–1) probably provided the most comprehensive description of what global governance is about:

> Governance should be considered to cover the overlapping categories of functions performed internationally, among them: information creation and exchange; formulation and promulgation of principles and promotion of consensual knowledge affecting the general international order, regional orders, particular issues on the international agenda, and efforts to influence the domestic rules and behavior of states; good offices, conciliation, mediation, and compulsory resolution of disputes; regime formation, tending and execution; adoption of rules, codes, and regulations; allocation of material and program resources; provision of technical assistance and development programs; relief, humanitarian, emergency, and disaster activities; and maintenance of peace and order.

The complexity of this description reflects the problem of conceptualising governance with precision. The term 'governance' itself has been used in a variety of contexts.[11] What is common to most uses of the term 'governance' is that it denotes a form of social steering that does not necessarily rely on hierarchy and command, as the concept of government implies, but also on processes of self-organisation and horizontal negotiation. In systems of governance, problem-solving is not the preserve of a central authority able to impose solutions on subordinate agencies and individuals, but the result of the interaction of a plurality of actors, who often have different interests, values, cognitive orientations and power resources.[12]

Sceptical views on global governance

To the extent that governance implies the possibility of 'order without hierarchy', it is especially relevant to the discussions about the management of problems in the global arena, where no supreme political authority exists. But to conceive the international or global system as orderly does not necessarily imply the recognition that a form of global governance has been established. Order is not ipso facto governance. According to the so-called 'realist' tradition of international studies, the main feature of the international system is anarchy – that is, the absence of a world sovereign. The international system can nonetheless be orderly, but realists hold a restrictive view of the conditions leading to international order. Order is said to be possible only through two mechanisms (stressed by two different strands within the realist tradition): the balance of power or the hegemony by one state over the rest. In the first case, order emerges as a by-product of alignment decisions made by states seeking survival.[13] In the second case it results from some degree of 'steering' by the most powerful actor in the system.[14] In both cases, order is unstable as inter-state rivalry always threatens to disrupt economic relations and generate armed conflicts for supremacy.

Other components of the realists' conception of international order contribute to their scepticism towards the idea that global governance exists or is a concrete possibility.[15] First, this tradition is interested in *international* order, understood as *inter-state* order. States are considered by far the most important actors in world affairs. To the extent that other actors have an impact on global political and economic conditions, this happens within a framework constituted and governed by states.[16] Second, in the realist conception of international order there is little room for international institutions. International institutions are either irrelevant or epiphenomenal, that is, devoid of autonomous causal power.[17]

Institutionalist perspectives on international governance

To date the most elaborate response to this restrictive conception of order comes from the so-called 'institutionalist' approach to international relations. Institutionalist scholars generally retain realism's emphasis on the centrality of states, but deny that institutions have no real role in creating and preserving orderly and cooperative relations between states. On the contrary, international institutions can affect deeply how states behave towards each other, and enable them to cooperate in matters where otherwise conflictual relationships would have prevailed.[18]

The institutional form that has attracted more attention and study is international regimes, that is, 'sets of principles, norms, rules, and decision-making procedures around which actor expectations converge in a given issue area of international relations' (Krasner, 1983, p. 2). It is the pervasive presence of regimes that enabled several scholars to conclude that 'governance without government' is a real feature of the global system (Rosenau and Czempiel, 1992).

While all institutionalists agree that international regimes *do* matter in international politics, they disagree on the best way to characterise their impact. This disagreement reflects a more general divide between rationalist ('thin') and sociological ('thick') institutionalism in political science.[19] According to the former, institutional rules operate as external constraints, providing incentives and information to rational actors whose preferences are exogenously determined (or assumed for heuristic purposes). According to sociological institutionalists, on the other hand, institutions affect actors' choices in a broader range of ways: by defining standards of culturally and normatively appropriate behaviour and common world views, they structure not only external incentives but also the basic goals and identities of actors. Institutions affect not only what actors can do, but also what they want to do and even who they are.

These differences are reflected in the study of international regimes (Young, 1999). Rational-choice institutionalists in international relations theory often draw on transaction cost economics and other economic approaches, but the most developed theoretical framework for studying 'cooperation under anarchy' (Oye, 1986) derives from game theory. Non-cooperative game theory examines social situations in which rational actors cannot enter binding agreements and identifies the conditions under which cooperation is nonetheless possible (Axelrod, 1984). These results have been applied to the study of international regimes, originating a flow of theoretical and empirical work that shows how states – conceived as rational egoists – can benefit from an institutionalised environment when interacting with each other.[20]

For sociologically minded regime theorists, on the other hand, the institutional environment in which states interact does not simply affect their strategies, but participates in shaping their identity and goals.[21] Cooperation under anarchy is possible because states' actions are not oriented only to 'logics of consequences' (rational behaviour designed to maximise exogenous utility) but also to 'logics of appropriateness' (rules, roles and identities that stipulate appropriate behaviour in given situations).[22] Norms have an independent causal impact on the behaviour of actors, which have been socialised through domestic and international learning processes. The recent wave of constructivist theorising presents in a different form some of the insights of the English school, which depicted the international system as an 'anarchical society' (Bull, 1977) where order is assured by a mix of power politics and common values. Insights from constructivism and English school theory have been recently been synthesised in a theory of the social structure of globalisation (Buzan, 2004)

The effects of international institutions in general and of regimes and organisations in particular on the behaviour of states are summarised in Box 19.1.

From international regimes to global governance

Regime theory has produced an impressive amount of theoretical and empirical knowledge on various aspects of international affairs. This body of knowledge is an indispensable foundation for the study of global governance. Conventional regime theory, however, tends to ignore the contribution of non-state actors to the management of cross-border issues. The concept of governance, on the contrary, is frequently used to convey the idea that public actors have no monopoly over the resolution of public problems and that they increasingly collaborate with other actors in various stages of the policy-making process (Koenig-Archibugi, 2002). This section provides an overview of the literature on the contribution of non-state actors to global governance, and focuses on three types of non-state actors: not-for-profit non-governmental organisations (NGOs), business entities and the staff of intergovernmental organisations (IGOs).

Over the last decade there has been a proliferation of studies on NGO participation in global public policy, which have examined several issue areas: human rights,[23] rules of war,[24] humanitarian emergencies,[25]gender issues,[26] economic development,[27] demography,[28] health policy,[29] business regulation[30] and environmental protection.[31] Several studies provide comparisons across issue areas or general reflections on public–private cooperation.[32]

BOX 19.1 FUNCTIONS OF INTERNATIONAL INSTITUTIONS AND ORGANISATIONS ACCORDING TO INSTITUTIONALIST APPROACHES TO WORLD POLITICS

	INTERNATIONAL INSTITUTIONS AND ORGANISATIONS
Rationalist institutionalism ⇓	provide information about common problems provide information about preferences facilitate the signalling of intentions constrain bargaining strategies provide focal points in negotiations facilitate tactical issue linkage increase the credibility of promises multiply interactions disseminate information about past behaviour define obligations and cheating define appropriate sanctions for non-compliance improve the monitoring of compliance coordinate decentralised sanctioning
	....
⇑ *Sociological institutionalism*	define standard operating procedures stabilise routines generate cognitive models define rules of appropriate behaviour consolidate normative world views shape the formation of identities

According to Thomas Risse (2001), it is no longer disputed that NGOs and other 'not-for-profit' transnational actors make a difference in world politics: now the interesting question is: why, and under what conditions? Some go as far as claiming that, in the steering of global affairs, states have been joined by other actors that are 'equally important' (Rosenau, 2000, p. 187).

The available evidence does not support the 'equal importance' thesis: global public policy-making is characterised by conspicuous asymmetries in power and tasks, and the current balance of power (still) favours states. Having said that, it seems indeed indisputable that NGOs are nearly ubiquitous, having established their presence in virtually all international policy domains. They are well entrenched in traditional areas such as development policy, humanitarian assistance and environmental protection, but their presence is increasing also on previously less accessible issues like finance (debt cancellation) and arms control (land mines). Wolfgang Reinicke and his associates (2000) showed that a number of important global problems are dealt with by tripartite networks, bringing together public agencies, business actors and advocacy groups on an informal basis. It has even been argued that 'human rights NGOs are the engine for virtually every advance made by the United Nations in the field of human rights since its founding' (Gaer, 1996, p. 51).

On the other hand, presence is not necessarily influence. For instance, the authors of a comprehensive study of the relationship between three global social movements (environmental, labour and women's movements) and three multilateral economic institutions (the IMF, World Bank and WTO) conclude that some change in the way the institutions make policy has occurred as a result of this relationship, but they add: 'While signalling an alteration to the method of governance, it is less clear that there is a change either in the content of governing policies or in the broad interests they represent' (O'Brien et al., 2000, p. 206). Another study, comparing NGO 'participation' in the UN World Conferences on the environment, human rights and women held during the 1990s, shows that NGOs were granted high visibility and access to many official fora, but there is little evidence that the states accepted the NGOs' perspective on the problems debated. Considering moreover that access itself was conditional, the authors conclude: 'state sovereignty sets the limits of global civil society' (Clark et al., 1998, p. 35). In sum, the existing empirical literature on the contribution of NGOs to global governance does not seem to allow general conclusions yet.

With regard to the role of the business actors in the management of cross-border activities and exchanges, several recent studies demonstrate that this is significant. Some sceptics hold that 'International firms create the need for improved international governance, but they do not and cannot provide it' (Grant, 1997, p. 319), but other researchers have shown that, in many areas, business actors have established transnational regimes that give order and predictability to the massive flow of transactions that takes place across state borders. A major study on global business regulation finds that in all the sectors considered 'state regulation follows industry self-regulatory practice more than the reverse, though the reverse is also very important' (Braithwaite and Drahos, 2000, p. 481). Other researchers have highlighted several regimes whose members are mainly or exclusively private actors.[33] These transnational regimes overlap with and sometimes are functional equivalents of the international regimes established by governments. In addition, business actors – that is, interest associations or powerful corporations – participate regularly in the international policy-making process, and in many cases have a decisive influence on the outcomes.[34]

Conventional regime analysis tends to neglect not only non-state actors such as NGOs and companies, but also international organisations *as organisations*. Most institutionalist analyses focus on the operation and effectiveness of regimes, which are not actors in their own right and affect outcomes only by influencing the behaviour of members and others subject to their provisions. In comparison, less attention has been paid to intergovernmental organisations, which are often at the centre of a regime and which in principle *are* capable of agency.

Research on IGOs as autonomous policy-making actors has been quite scarce.[35] However, in the past few years a number of studies have advanced interesting hypotheses about the goals, functions and power of IGOs, which can provide a theoretical foundation for further empirical research.[36] Case studies of multilateral negotiations have already highlighted the active role of the bureaucrats who staff international organisations, showing that they are able to exercise influence by forging strategic alliances, sponsoring research, mobilising technical expertise, raising public awareness and playing a leadership role in negotiations.[37] This involves a certain degree of operational autonomy, that is, the officials' capacity to act independently of their 'principals' – namely, the governments that have collectively delegated functions to them.

In sum, the management of global affairs is not the preserve of governments, but involves a broad range of actors, at the domestic and transnational levels. Specifically, global governance implies that firms and NGOs are not simply the passive recipients of the rules negotiated by governments above their heads, but participate in various ways in the formulation of those rules through public–private partnerships, or even by establishing purely private regimes to regulate certain domains in their common interest. Therefore, *actor pluralism* should be added to the *possibility of non-hierarchical order* and the *role of institutions* as a defining characteristic of global governance.

Normative perspectives on global governance

This chapter had focused on analytical and empirical work on global governance, but normative approaches to the problem deserve at least a brief mention. The legitimacy of global governance can be assessed from a variety of perspectives, most of which are based on the commitment to democracy as an essential condition for the legitimisation of political orders.[38] Roughly two main positions can be distinguished: democratic inter-governmentalism and democratic cosmopolitanism.

According to democratic inter-governmentalism, global governance cannot receive direct democratic legitimisation, but must obtain its legitimacy indirectly through the participation of democratically elected governments in global policy-making.[39] In this view, democracy requires a public sphere, and no transnational public sphere exists now or is in sight. There are at least two formidable obstacles to the formation of a public sphere beyond the nation state, one cognitive and one affective. On the one hand, democratic deliberation is impossible when de facto the majority of people are excluded from global networks of political communication, notably because of insufficient foreign language skills. Deliberation in supranational fora would be monopolised by educated elites and therefore remain undemocratic. On the other hand, the acceptance of the results of collective and possibly majoritarian decisions requires a degree of solidarity and sense of common belonging that is extremely weak beyond the national level.

According to democratic cosmopolitanism, democratic legitimacy can and should be conferred through multiple channels, in a pattern that corresponds to the pluralistic character of global governance. Moreover, the democratisation of international institutions itself can extend the focus of concern and loyalty of individuals and groups beyond the national dimension, and for this reason democratic restructuring should be conceived as a dialectical process of mutual reinforcement. Cosmopolitan institutions (such as a global assembly of peoples and forceful international tribunals) will enhance the effectiveness of global public policy-making by increasing its legitimacy and at the same time they will promote domestic democracy.[40]

Debating the normative strengths and benefits of different models of global governance is important because, while the establishment of a genuinely democratic system of global governance may be unlikely in the near future, there is little reason to believe that it is impossible.[41]

Notes

1. Held et al. (1999); Hirst and Thompson (1999); Koenig-Archibugi (2003).
2. Commission on Global Governance (1995).
3. Rosenau (1997); Held and McGrew (2002).
4. Levy and Newell (2005); Falkner (2008).
5. Söderholm (1997); Lee (2003); Hein et al. (2007).
6. Cunliffe (2009).
7. Meyer and Prügl (1999); Hafner-Burton and Pollack (2002).
8. Price (1999).
9. Shaffer (2005).
10. Knight (1995); Weiss (2008).
11. See the overview in Hirst (2000).
12. Rosenau (1997); Pierre (2000).
13. Waltz (1979).
14. Gilpin (2001).
15. Gilpin (2002).
16. Waltz (1979); Krasner (1995).
17. Strange (1983); Mearsheimer (1994/95).
18. Hansenclever et al. (1997); Martin and Simmons (1998).
19. Hall and Taylor (1996); Scharpf (2000).
20. Keohane (1984); Oye (1986); Martin (1999); Haftendorn et al. (1999); Boehmer et al. (2004); Fortna (2008).
21. Kratochwil (1989); Katzenstein (1996); Finnemore (1996); Ruggie (1998); Wendt (1999); Risse (2000); Johnston (2008).
22. This distinction stems from March and Olsen (1989).

23. Cohen (1990); Gaer (1996); Korey (1998); Schmitz (2006).
24. Finnemore (1999); Price (1999).
25. Natsios (1996); Mills (2005).
26. Berkovitch (1999); Joachim (2007).
27. Nelson (1995); Fox and Brown (1998); Wenar (2006).
28. Barrett and Frank (1999); Eager (2004).
29. Jönsson and Söderholm (1996); McCoy et al. (2009).
30. Braithwaite and Drahos (2000); Kantz (2007).
31. Lipschutz and Mayer (1996); Raustiala (1997); Arts (1998); Betsill and Corell (2008).
32. Gordenker and Weiss (1996); Willetts (1996); Charnovitz (1997); Clark et al. (1998); Keck and Sikkink (1998); Boli and Thomas (1999); Higgott et al. (2000); O'Brien et al. (2000); Benner et al. (2004); Börzel and Risse (2005); Koenig-Archibugi and Zürn (2006); Steffek et al. (2007).
33. Spar (1999); Ronit and Schneider (2000); Haufler (2001); Buse and Harmer (2004); Bartley (2007); Pattberg (2007); Macdonald (2007); Dingwerth (2008).
34. Braithwaite and Drahos (2000); Sell (2000); Collin et al. (2002); Ruggie (2003); Levy and Newell (2005); Falkner (2008).
35. Verbeek (1998).
36. Abbott and Snidal (1998); Barnett and Finnemore (2004); Hawkins et al. (2006); Thompson (2009).
37. Hampson (1995). See also Cox et al. (1974); Reinalda and Verbeek (1998).
38. McGrew (2000, 2002).
39. Grimm (1995); Dahl (1999); Scharpf (1999); Hirst and Thompson (1999); Kymlicka (1999).
40. Falk (1995); Held (2003); Archibugi (2008); Marchetti (2008).
41. Koenig-Archibugi (2011).

References

Abbott, Kenneth W. and Duncan Snidal (1998), 'Why states act through formal international organizations', *Journal of Conflict Resolution*, **42**(1), 3–32.

Archibugi, Daniele (2008), *The Global Commonwealth of Citizens: Toward Cosmopolitan Democracy*, Princeton, NJ: Princeton University Press.

Arts, Bas (1998), *The Political Influence of Global NGOs: Case Studies on the Climate and Biodiversity Conventions*, Utrecht: International Books.

Axelrod, Robert (1984), *The Evolution of Cooperation*, New York: Basic Books.

Barnett, Michael N. and Martha Finnemore (2004), *Rules for the World: International Organizations in Global Politics*, Ithaca, NY: Cornell University Press.

Barrett, Deborah and David John Frank (1999), 'Population control for national development: from world discourse to national policies', in J. Boli and G.M. Thomas (eds), *Constructing World Culture: International Nongovernmental Organizations Since 1875*, Stanford: Stanford University Press, pp. 198–221.

Bartley, Tim (2007), 'Institutional emergence in an era of globalization: the rise of transnational private regulation of labor and environmental conditions', *American Journal of Sociology*, **113**(2), 297–351.

Benner, Thorsten, Wolfgang H. Reinicke and Jan Martin Witte (2004), 'Multisectoral networks in global governance: towards a pluralistic system of accountability', *Government and Opposition*, **39**(2), 191–210.

Berkovitch, Nitza (1999), 'The emergence and transformation of the international women's movement', in J. Boli and G.M. Thomas (eds), *Constructing World Culture: International Nongovernmental Organizations Since 1875*, Stanford: Stanford University Press, pp. 100–26.

Betsill, Michele and Elisabeth Corell (eds) (2008), *NGO Diplomacy: The Influence of Nongovernmental Organizations in International Environmental Negotiations*, Cambridge, MA: MIT Press.

Boehmer, Charles, Erik Gartzke and Timothy W. Nordstrom (2004), 'Do intergovernmental organizations promote peace?', *World Politics*, **57**(1), 1–38.

Boli, John and George M. Thomas (1999), 'INGOs and the organization of world culture', in J. Boli and G.M. Thomas (eds), *Constructing World Culture: International Nongovernmental Organizations Since 1875*, Stanford: Stanford University Press, pp. 13–49.

Börzel, Tanja A. and Thomas Risse (2005), 'Public–private partnerships: effective and legitimate tools of international governance?', in Edgar Grande and Louis W. Pauly (eds), *Complex Sovereignty. Reconstituting Political Authority in the Twenty-first Century*, Toronto: University of Toronto Press.

Braithwaite, John and Peter Drahos (2000), *Global Business Regulation*, Cambridge: Cambridge University Press.

Bull, Hedley (1977), *The Anarchical Society: A Study of Order in World Politics*, New York: Columbia University Press.

Buse, Kent and Andrew Harmer (2004), 'Power to the partners? The politics of public–private health partnerships', *Development*, **47**(2), 43–8.

Buzan, Barry (2004), *From International to World Society? English School Theory and the Social Structure of Globalization*. Cambridge: Cambridge University Press.

Charnovitz, Steve (1997), 'Two centuries of participation: NGOs and international governance', *Michigan Journal of International Law*, **7**(1), 183–286.

Clark, Ann Marie, Elisabeth J. Friedman and Kathryn Hochstetler (1998), 'The sovereign limits to global civil society: a comparison of NGO participation in UN world conferences on the environment, human rights, and women', *World Politics*, **51**(1), 1–35.

Cohen, Cynthia Price (1990), 'The role of nongovernmental organizations in the drafting of the Convention on the Rights of the Child', *Human Rights Quarterly*, **12**(1), 137–47.

Collin, Jeff, Kelley Lee and Karen Bissell (2002), 'The framework convention on tobacco control: the politics of global health governance', *Third World Quarterly*, **23**(2), 265–82.

Commission on Global Governance (1995), *Our Global Neighbourhood*, Oxford: Oxford University Press.

Cox, Robert, Harold Jacobson, Gerald Curzon, Victoria Curzon, Joseph Nye, Lawrence Scheinman, James Sewell and Susan Strange (1974), *The Anatomy of Influence: Decision Making in International Organization*, New Haven: Princeton University Press.

Cunliffe, Philip (2009), 'The politics of global governance in UN peacekeeping', *International Peacekeeping*, **16**(3), 329–36.

Dahl, Robert A. (1999), 'Can international organizations be democratic? A skeptic's view', in I. Shapiro and C. Hacker-Cordon (eds), *Democracy's Edges*, Cambridge: Cambridge University Press, pp. 19–36.

Dingwerth, Klaus (2008), 'Private transnational governance and the developing world: a comparative perspective', *International Studies Quarterly* **52**(3), 607–34.

Eager, Paige Whaley (2004), *Global Population Policy: from Population Control to Reproductive Rights*, Aldershot, UK: Ashgate.

Falk, Richard (1995), *On Humane Governance: Towards a New World Politics*, Cambridge: Polity.

Falkner, Robert (2008), *Business Power and Conflict in International Environmental Politics*, Basingstoke: Palgrave Macmillan.

Finkelstein, Lawrence S. (1995), 'What is global governance?', *Global Governance*, **1**(3), 367–72.

Finnemore, Martha (1996), *National Interests in International Society*, Ithaca: Cornell University Press.

Finnemore, Martha (1999), 'Rules of war and wars of rules: the international Red Cross and the restraint of state violence', in J. Boli and G.M. Thomas (eds), *Constructing World Culture: International Nongovernmental Organizations Since 1875*, Stanford: Stanford University Press, pp. 149–65.

Fortna, Virginia Page (2008), *Does Peacekeeping Work? Shaping Belligerents' Choices After Civil War*, Princeton, NJ: Princeton University Press.

Fox, Jonathan A. and David L. Brown (eds) (1998), *The Struggle for Accountability: The World Bank, NGOs and Grassroot Movements*, Cambridge, MA: MIT Press.

Gaer, Felice D. (1996), 'Reality check: human rights NGOs confront governments at the UN', in T.G. Weiss and L. Gordenker (eds), *NGOs, the UN, and Global Governance*, Boulder: Lynne Rienner, pp. 51–66.

Gilpin, Robert (2001), *Global Political Economy*, Princeton, NJ: Princeton University Press.
Gilpin, Robert (2002), 'A realist perspective on international governance', in D. Held and A. McGrew (eds), *Governing Globalization*, Cambridge: Polity.
Gordenker, Leon and Thomas G. Weiss (1996), 'NGO participation in the international policy process', in T.G. Weiss and L. Gordenker (eds), *NGOs, the UN, and Global Governance*, Boulder: Lynne Rienner, pp. 209–21.
Grant, Wyn (1997), 'Perspective on globalization and economic coordination', in J.R. Hollingsworth and R. Boyer (eds), *Contemporary Capitalism: The Embeddedness of Institutions*, Cambridge: Cambridge University Press, pp. 319–36.
Grimm, Dieter (1995), 'Does Europe need a constitution?', *European Law Journal*, **1**(3), 282–302.
Hafner-Burton, Emilie and Mark A. Pollack (2002), 'Mainstreaming gender in global governance', *European Journal of International Relations*, **8**(3), 339–73.
Haftendorn, Helga, Robert O. Keohane and Celeste A. Wallander (eds) (1999), *Imperfect Unions: Security Institutions over Time and Space*, Oxford: Oxford University Press.
Hall, Peter A. and Rosemary C.R. Taylor (1996), 'Political science and the three new institutionalisms', *Political Studies*, **44**(5), 936–57.
Hampson, Fen Osler (1995), *Multilateral Negotiations: Lessons from Arms Control, Trade, and the Environment*, Baltimore: Johns Hopkins University Press.
Hasenclever, Andreas, Peter Mayer and Volker Rittberger (1997), *Theories of International Regimes*, Cambridge: Cambridge University Press.
Haufler, Virginia (2001), *A Public Role for the Private Sector: Industry Self-regulation in a Global Economy*, Washington, DC: Carnegie Endowment for International Peace.
Hawkins, Darren G., David A. Lake, Daniel L. Nielson and Michael J. Tierney (eds) (2006), *Delegation and Agency in International Organizations*, Cambridge: Cambridge University Press.
Hein, Wolfgang, Sonja Bartsch and Lars Kohlmorgen (eds) (2007), *Global Health Governance and the Fight Against HIV/AIDS*, Basingstoke: Palgrave Macmillan.
Held, David (2003), 'From executive to cosmopolitan multilateralism', in D. Held and M. Koenig-Archibugi (eds), *Taming Globalization: Frontiers of Governance*, Cambridge: Polity.
Held, David and Anthony McGrew (eds) (2002), *Governing Globalization: Power, Authority, and Global Governance*, Cambridge: Polity.
Held, David, Anthony McGrew, David Goldblatt and Jonathan Perraton (1999), *Global Transformations: Politics, Economics and Culture*, Cambridge: Polity.
Higgott, Richard A., Geoffrey R.D. Underhill and Andreas Bieler (2000), 'Introduction: globalisation and non-state actors', in R.A. Higgott, G.R.D. Underhill and A. Bieler (eds), *Non-state Actors and Authority in the Global System*, London and New York: Routledge, pp. 1–12.
Hirst, Paul (2000), 'Democracy and governance', in J. Pierre (ed.), *Debating Governance: Authority, Steering, and Democracy*, Oxford: Oxford University Press, pp. 13–35.
Hirst, Paul and Grahame Thompson (1999), *Globalization in Question*, 2nd edn, Cambridge: Polity.
Joachim, Jutta M. (2007), *Agenda Setting, the UN, and NGOs: Gender Violence and Reproductive Rights*, Washington, DC: Georgetown University Press.
Johnston, Alastair Iain (2008), *Social States: China in International Institutions, 1980–2000*, Princeton, NJ: Princeton University Press.
Jönsson, Christer and Peter Söderholm (1996), 'IGO–NGO relations and HIV/AIDS: innovation or stalemate?', in T.G. Weiss and L. Gordenker (eds), *NGOs, the UN, and Global Governance*, Boulder: Lynne Rienner, pp. 121–38.
Kantz, Carola. (2007), 'The power of socialization: engaging the diamond industry in the Kimberley process', *Business and Politics*, **9**(3).
Katzenstein, Peter J. (ed.) (1996), *The Culture of National Security: Norms and Identity in World Politics*, New York: Columbia University Press.
Keck, Margaret E. and Kathryn Sikkink (1998), *Activists Beyond Borders: Advocacy Networks in International Politics*, Ithaca: Cornell University Press.
Keohane, Robert O. (1984), *After Hegemony: Cooperation and Discord in the World Political Economy*, Princeton: Princeton University Press.
Knight, W. Andy (1995), 'Beyond the UN system? Critical perspectives on global governance and multinational evolution', *Global Governance*, **1**(2), 229–53.

Koenig-Archibugi, Mathias (2002), 'Mapping global governance', in D. Held and A. McGrew (eds), *Governing Globalization*, Cambridge: Polity.
Koenig-Archibugi, Mathias (2003), 'Introduction: globalization and the challenge to governance', in D. Held and M. Koenig-Archibugi (eds), *Taming Globalization: Frontiers of Governance*, Cambridge: Polity.
Koenig-Archibugi, Mathias (2011), 'Is global democracy possible?, *European Journal of International Relations*, forthcoming.
Koenig-Archibugi, Mathias and Michael Zürn (eds) (2006), *New Modes of Governance in the Global System*, Basingstoke: Palgrave Macmillan.
Korey, William (1998), *NGOs and the Universal Declaration of Human Rights: 'A Curious Grapewine'*, New York: St Martin's Press.
Krasner, Stephen D. (1983), 'Introduction', in S.D. Krasner (ed.), *International Regimes*, Ithaca: Cornell University Press.
Krasner, Stephen D. (1995), 'Power politics, institutions, and transnational relations', in T. Risse-Kappen (ed.), *Bringing Transnational Relations Back In: Non-State Actors, Domestic Structures and International Relations*, Cambridge: Cambridge University Press, pp. 257–79.
Kratochwil, Friedrich (1989), *Rules, Norms and Decisions: On the Conditions of Practical and Legal Reasoning in International Relations and Domestic Affairs*, Cambridge: Cambridge University Press.
Kymlicka, Will (1999), 'Citizenship in an era of globalization: commentary on Held', in I. Shapiro and C. Hacker-Cordon (eds), *Democracy's Edges*, Cambridge: Cambridge University Press, pp. 112–26.
Lee, Kelley (ed.) (2003), *Health Impacts of Globalization: Towards Global Governance*, Basingstoke: Palgrave Macmillan.
Levy, David L. and Peter J. Newell (eds) (2005), *The Business of Global Environmental Governance*, Cambridge, MA: MIT Press.
Lipschutz, Ronnie D. and Judith Mayer (1996), *Global Civil Society and Global Environmental Governance: The Politics of Nature from Place to Planet*, Albany: State University of New York.
Macdonald, Kate (2007), 'Globalising justice within coffee supply chains? Fair Trade, Starbucks and the transformation of supply chain governance', *Third World Quarterly*, **25**(7), 793–812.
March, James G. and Johan P. Olsen (1989), *Rediscovering Institutions: The Organizational Basis of Politics*, New York: Free Press.
Marchetti, Raffaele (2008), *Global Democracy: For and Against*, London: Routledge.
Martin, Lisa L. (1999), 'The political economy of international cooperation', in I. Kaul, I. Grunberg and M.A. Stern (eds), *Global Public Goods: International Cooperation in the 21st Century*, New York and Oxford: Oxford University Press, pp. 51–64.
Martin, Lisa L. and Beth A. Simmons (1998), 'Theories and empirical studies of international institutions', *International Organization*, **52**(4), 729–57.
McCoy, David, Gayatri Kembhavi, Jinesh Patel and Akish Luintel (2009), 'The Bill & Melinda Gates Foundation's grant-making programme for global health', *The Lancet*, **373**(9675), 1645–53.
McGrew, Anthony (2000), 'Democracy beyond borders?', in D. Held and A. McGrew (eds), *The Global Transformations Reader*, Cambridge: Polity.
McGrew, Anthony (2002), 'Liberal internationalism: between realism and cosmopolitanism', in D. Held and A. McGrew (eds), *Governing Globalization*, Cambridge: Polity.
Mearsheimer, John J. (1994/95), 'The false promise of international institutions', *International Security*, **19**(3), 5–49.
Meyer, Mary K. and Elisabeth Prügl (eds) (1999), *Gender Politics in Global Governance*, Lanham, MD: Rowman & Littlefield.
Mills, Kurt (2005), 'Neo-humanitarianism: the role of international humanitarian norms and organizations in contemporary conflict', *Global Governance*, **11**, 161–83.
Natsios, Andrew S. (1996), 'NGOs and the UN system in complex humanitarian emergencies: conflict or cooperation?', in T.G. Weiss and L. Gordenker (eds), *NGOs, the UN, and Global Governance*, Boulder: Lynne Rienner, pp. 67–81.
Nelson, Paul (1995), *The World Bank and Non-Governmental Organizations*, London: Macmillan.

O'Brien, Robert, Anne Marie Goetz, Jan Aart Scholte and Marc Williams (2000), *Contesting Global Governance: Multilateral Economic Institutions and Global Social Movements*, Cambridge: Cambridge University Press.
Oye, Kenneth (ed.) (1986), *Cooperation Under Anarchy*, Princeton, NJ: Princeton University Press.
Pattberg, Philipp (2007), *Private Institutions and Global Governance: The New Politics of Environmental Sustainability*, Cheltenham, UK and Northampton, MA, USA: Edward Elgar.
Pierre, Jon (2000), 'Introduction: understanding governance', in Jon Pierre (ed.), *Debating Governance: Authority, Steering, and Democracy*, Oxford: Oxford University Press, pp. 1–10.
Price, Richard (1999), 'Weapons bans: norms and mechanisms of global governance', in Raimo Väyrynen (ed.), *Globalization and Global Governance*, Lanham, MD: Rowman & Littlefield, pp. 223–44.
Raustiala, Kal (1997), 'States, NGOs, and international environmental institutions', *International Studies Quarterly*, **41**(4), 719–40.
Reinalda, Bob and Bertjan Verbeek (eds) (1998), *Autonomous Policymaking by International Organizations*, London: Routledge.
Reinicke, Wolfgang H. et al. (2000), *Critical Choices: The United Nations, Networks, and the Future of Global Governance*, Ottawa: International Development Research Centre.
Risse, Thomas (2000), '"Let's Argue!": communicative action in world politics', *International Organization*, **54**(1), 1–39.
Risse, Thomas (2001), 'Transnational actors and world politics', in W. Carlsnaes, T. Risse and B. Simmons (eds), *Handbook of International Relations*, London: Sage.
Ronit, Karsten and Volker Schneider (eds) (2000), *Private Organisations in Global Politics*, London: Routledge.
Rosenau, James N. (1997), *Along the Domestic–Foreign Frontier: Exploring Governance in a Turbulent World*, Cambridge: Cambridge University Press.
Rosenau, James N. (2000), 'Change, complexity, and governance in globalizing space', in J. Pierre (ed.), *Debating Governance: Authority, Steering, and Democracy*, Oxford: Oxford University Press, pp. 167–200.
Rosenau, James N. and E.O. Czempiel (eds) (1992), *Governance without Government: Order and Change in World Politics*, Cambridge: Cambridge University Press.
Ruggie, John Gerard (1998), *Constructing the World Polity*, London: Routledge.
Ruggie, John Gerard (2003), 'Taking embedded liberalism global: the corporate connection', in D. Held and M. Koenig-Archibugi (eds), *Taming Globalization: Frontiers of Governance*, Cambridge: Polity.
Scharpf, Fritz W. (1999), *Governing in Europe: Effective and Democratic?*, Oxford: Oxford University Press.
Scharpf, Fritz W. (2000), 'Institutions in comparative policy research', Working Paper No. 00/3, Köln: Max-Planck-Institut für Gesellschaftsforschung.
Schmitz, Hans Peter (2006), *Transnational Mobilization and Domestic Regime Change: Africa in Comparative Perspective*, Basingstoke: Palgrave Macmillan.
Sell, Susan K. (2000), 'Structures, agents and institutions: private corporate power and the globalisation of intellectual property rights', in R.A. Higgott, G.R.D. Underhill and A. Bieler (eds), *Non-state Actors and Authority in the Global System*, London and New York: Routledge, pp. 91–106.
Shaffer, Gregory (2005), 'Power, global governance and the WTO', in Michael Barnett and Raymond Duvall (eds), *Power and Global Governance*, Cambridge: Cambridge University Press, pp. 130–60.
Smith, Jackie, Ron Pagnucco and George A. Lopez (1998), 'Globalizing human rights: the work of transnational human rights NGOs in the 1990s', *Human Rights Quarterly*, **20**(2), 379–412.
Söderholm, Peter (1997), *Global Governance of AIDS*, Bromley: Lund University Press.
Spar, Debora L. (1999), 'Lost in (cyber)space: the private rules of online commerce', in A.C. Cutler, V. Haufler and T. Porter (eds), *Private Authority and International Affairs*, Albany: State University of New York Press, pp. 31–51.
Steffek, Jens, Claudia Kissling and Patrizia Nanz (eds) (2007), *Civil Society Participation in Eu-*

ropean and Global Governance: A Cure for the Democratic Deficit?, Basingstoke: Palgrave Macmillan.

Strange, Susan (1983), '*Cave! Hic dragones*: a critique of regime analysis', in S.D. Krasner (ed.), *International Regimes*, Ithaca: Cornell University Press, pp. 337–54.

Thompson, Alexander (2009), *Channels of Power: The UN Security Council and U.S. Statecraft in Iraq*, Ithaca, NY: Cornell University Press.

Verbeek, Bertjan (1998), 'International organizations: the ugly duckling of international relations theory?', in B. Reinalda and B. Verbeek (eds), *Autonomous Policy Making by International Organizations*, London and New York: Routledge, pp. 11–26.

Waltz, Kenneth N. (1979), *Theory of International Politics*, Reading, MA: Addison-Wesley.

Weiss, Thomas (2008), *What's Wrong with the United Nations and How to Fix It*, Cambridge: Polity Press.

Wenar, Leif (2006), 'Accountability in international development aid', *Ethics and International Affairs*, **20**(1), 1–24.

Wendt, Alexander (1999), *Social Theory of International Politics*, Cambridge: Cambridge University Press.

Willetts, Peter (ed.) (1996), *'The Conscience of the World': The Influence of Non-governmental Organisations in the UN System*, London: Hurst & Co.

Young, Oran R. (1999), *Governance in World Affairs*, Ithaca and London: Cornell University Press.

20 The political economy of the third way: the relationship between globalisation and national economic policy

Simon Lee

Introduction

There have been few more important debates in the discipline of political economy in the modern era than those relating to the relationship between globalisation and national economic policy. Three principal perspectives have been advanced (Held et al., 2000). First, the 'hyperglobalisers' who have contended that globalisation has rendered national economic policy largely redundant (Ohmae, 1995). Second, the 'sceptics' for whom the notion of the powerless state has been exaggerated to the point of mythology (Hirst et al., 2009). Third, the 'transformationalists' for whom globalisation has unleashed an unprecedented period of social change upon states and societies (Blair, 1996; Giddens, 1998). These perspectives have been accompanied by a parallel discourse concerning the transition from government to governance in the relationship between the public and private, and the state and market, in the conduct of economic policy-making at all levels from the local to the global (Rodrik, 2007). The ideological context of these discourses has been a vigorous argument concerning the viability and legitimacy of the economic policy prescriptions of the neoliberal orthodoxy of the 'Washington Consensus' (Williamson, 1993; Serra and Stiglitz, 2009). On the one hand, the market fundamentalism of the 'Washington Consensus' has had its vigorous advocates, notably the former Chairman of the US Federal Reserve Board (Greenspan, 2007). On the other hand, the likely dividend both for global growth and national economic development has been contested by academics (Hutton, 2002; Gamble, 2009), market economists and traders (Soros, 2008; Bootle, 2009), Nobel Prize winning economists (Sen, 1999; Stiglitz, 2009) and the anti-capitalist movement (Callinicos, 2003).

This chapter analyses the relationship between national economic policy and globalisation by focusing upon the political economy of the third way as implemented by the Blair governments in the United Kingdom (UK) from May 1997 until June 2007, and the Brown government thereafter. The UK provides a particularly important case study for analysing the impact of globalisation upon national economic policy choices for three reasons. First, the era of globalisation has been much longer and more pronounced for the UK economy than for most of its major competitors (Hirst et al., 2009). Second, the presence of the volatile markets of the City of London since long before the UK became the world's first industrialised economy has confronted successive UK governments with the challenge of attempting to implement and reconcile expansionist domestic modernisation strategies, designed to arrest the UK's longstanding relative economic decline, with the more orthodox and prudential economic policies required to maintain sufficient confidence among the City's investors to avoid undermining the value of the pound sterling. Third, the economic policies implemented by the Blair and Brown governments have assumed that there is no insurmountable conflict between New Labour's domestic modernisation agenda and the exigencies of globalisation. Indeed, New Labour has been almost messianic in its advocacy of the opportunities provided by liberalised markets and globalisation not only to remedy national decline but also to both improve the performance of the European Union's economies (Brown, 2005a) and eliminate world poverty (HMT/DFID, 2005). However, the chapter concludes that the onset of the severest global recession since the Great Depression has shown how the third way overestimated the capacity of national governments to manage the economic, political and social consequences of the risk, volatility and contagion that is characteristic of liberalised global markets.

'One size fits all': the rise of the 'Washington Consensus'

The global environment for national economic policy-making has changed dramatically since the early 1970s. Liberalisation of markets for capital, goods and services, the spectacular growth of Foreign Direct Investment (FDI), the volatility of financial markets allied to the increasing incidence of financial crises and the huge political and economic power exercised by transnational corporations (Reich, 2009) have all served to constrain the autonomy of national monetary, fiscal and competitiveness policies. For example, FDI inflows in global markets in 2008 reached $1.7 trillion, propelled by the more than 82000 transnational corporations and their 810000 overseas affiliates (UNCTAD, 2009: 4, 8). At the same time, national governments now confront a context for economic policy-making in which their policies and performance are regularly audited and benchmarked in a series of monitoring reports and scoreboards produced by public institutions, notably the regular economic outlooks and national surveys produced by IMF and Organisation for Economic Co-operation and Development (OECD), and private market institutions, notably the annual *World Competitiveness Scoreboard* and *Yearbook* produced by the Institute for Management Development.

Given this challenging global context for economic policy-making, national governments have continued to search for the optimum model among rival national capitalisms. Following the collapse of communism, it was suggested that the 'Rhine model' (characteristic most notably of Germany and Japan) would triumph over the 'neo-american' model (characteristic of the US and UK) because of its economic and social superiority resulting from an interpenetration rather than a separation (as in the US and UK) of finance and industry (Albert, 1993). In the event, the *World Competitiveness Scoreboard 2009* has ranked the US as the world's most competitive economy for the second consecutive year. By contrast, Japan has been ranked only 17th out of 57 major industrialised economies (IMD, 2009). Indeed, where once Japan's developmental state had been identified as the model for rival economies to emulate, including the US (Vogel, 1979), by the early 1990s Japan's status had changed to that of an economy facing imminent collapse (Reading, 1992; Wood, 1992). The growth of Japan's real GDP has declined from an annual average of 4.5 per cent from 1971 to 1980 to 4.0 per cent from 1981 to 1990 and only 1.4 per cent from 1991 to 2000 (World Bank, 2001: 234). This decline has eminent commentators to question whether the Japanese economy can still compete in international markets and to advocate the competitive strategies of both the Japanese government and Japan's private corporations moving closer to the Anglo-American model of competitiveness (Porter et al., 2000).

In a departure from the capital controls and managed exchange rate regime of the postwar Bretton Woods international economic order, national governments have increasingly adopted the economic policy prescriptions of the dominant neoliberal orthodoxy of the 'Washington Consensus' (Williamson, 1993). This American model for reconciling national economic policy choices with globalisation has prescribed the pursuit of monetary stability and fiscal prudence, with budget deficits small enough to be financed without extra taxation; the establishment of priorities in public expenditure through a transfer of resources from politically sensitive areas, such as welfare payments, towards neglected fields with high economic returns, such as investment in tangible and intangible infrastructure; and tax reforms to broaden the tax base and cut marginal tax rates to provide incentives. Despite the repeated promise of a dividend of macroeconomic stability and higher rates of economic growth, the 'Washington Consensus' has actually delivered slower growth. During the inflationary and recession-ridden 1970s, annual world output growth had increased by 4.4 per cent, but this duly declined to only 3.4 per cent during the 1980s in the era of Thatcherism and Reaganomics. Following the collapse of communism and the further rolling forward of the frontiers of the market, during the 1990s, world output growth had barely averaged 3.0 per cent (IMF, 1999: 2, 27).

Even before the onset of the global financial crisis in 2007, as the IMF's own data have demonstrated, far from delivering increased stability, the 'Washington Consensus' has fostered greater volatility in global markets and an increasing incidence of recessions. Most of the Bretton Woods era (1950–72) was characterised by recessions that averaged 1.1 years and led to an average 2.1 per cent decline in output. A total of 94.4 per cent of these recessions were only one year in length. In overall terms, only 5.6 per cent of the Bretton Woods era was spent in recession. By comparison, the IMF has shown that the post-Bretton Woods era (1973–2000) has witnessed recessions averaging 1.5 years and leading to a 2.5 per cent average decline in output. While 60 per cent of these recessions were one year in length, no fewer than 32.5 per cent were two years in length and the remainder three years or longer. There were no recessions of more than three years in length during the Bretton Woods era. In terms of expansions, Bretton Woods was characterised by a 102.9 per cent average increase in output compared with an average of only 26.9 per cent since 1973. Moreover, Bretton Woods saw an average 5.3 per cent annual growth rate, arising from expansions averaging 10.3 years in length, which occupied no fewer than 94.8 per cent of the years from 1950 to 1972. In sharp contrast, the post-Bretton Woods era has seen an average annual growth rate of only 2.6 per cent and expansions that have averaged only 6.9 per cent and occupied only 86.6 per cent of the period from 1973 to 2000 (IMF, 2002: 45).

The political economy of the third way

Confronted by a global context for national economic policy-making characterised by increasing volatility, slower rates of economic growth and greater external scrutiny of policy, some national governments chose to pursue a third way, claimed to lie beyond the postwar social democratic Keynesian consensus and the more recent neoliberal political economy of the New Right. This third way was defined by its leading academic proponent, Anthony Giddens, as 'the renewal of social democracy in contemporary social conditions'. Globalisation, the emergence of the knowledge economy, and the rise of individualism were held to have transformed the landscape of politics. In response to this challenging context, Giddens claimed that the third way was able to deliver a politics capable of reconstructing the public realm, renewing public institutions and offering an integrated and robust political programme based upon the key insight that 'a strong civil society is necessary both for effective democratic government and for a well-functioning market system' (Giddens, 2000: 2–3, 29). Although not exclusively an Anglo-American project, the ideology and policies of the third way were most widely promulgated in the US by the Clinton administration and in the UK by the Blair governments. Thus, it was Bill Clinton who proclaimed in his 1998 State of the Union Address that 'We have moved past the sterile debate between those who say government is the enemy and those who say government is the answer. My fellow Americans, we have a found a third way' (Clinton, 1998: 1). For his part, Tony Blair followed Giddens in defining the third way as a 'modernised social democracy', one that understood that 'Effective markets are a pre-condition for a successful modern economy' (Blair, 1998: 1).

Prior to any evaluation of its economic policies, it is important to acknowledge the strength of the critique of the broader ideology of the third way, especially from those on the left of the political spectrum. Giddens himself acknowledged the criticism that the third way was 'an amorphous political project, difficult to pin down and lacking direction', which had failed 'to sustain the proper outlook of the left and hence, whether deliberately or not, lapses into a form of conservatism' (Giddens, 2000: 22). The assertion that it was fundamentally a market-driven Anglo-American project, which had accepted the basic tenets of neoliberalism, particularly with regard to global markets, led some of the third way's most vehement critics to suggest that third way governments had merely 'embraced and in certain respects radicalised the neo-liberal policies of their predecessors' (Callinicos, 2001: 107). Moreover, the third way was portrayed as 'the best ideological shell of neo-liberalism today' (Anderson, 2000: 11). Despite this critique, because it claimed to be able to reconcile globalisation with national economic development, the third way assumed particular importance in the political economy of the UK. Successive British governments had found the implementation of their respective state-led modernisation programmes undermined by repeated currency crises and a loss of investor confidence in the City of London's financial markets. While raising interest rates and cutting public expenditure had enabled past UK governments to restore confidence and stabilise the value of the pound, such short-term austerity measures had been at the expense of long-term investment in the modernisation of Britain's infrastructure, frequently resulting in damaging strikes as public sector unions sought to defend their members' pay and employment.

The third way of economic policy implemented by the New Labour governments led by Tony Blair therefore constituted both a reaction to and a critique of the perceived failure of the postwar economic policies of the first and second ways. For New Labour, the first way denoted the social democratic Keynesian welfare state political settlement implemented by Labour and Conservative governments between 1945 and 1979. The economic policies of this era had been criticised for both their 'exaggerated belief in demand management' and their failure to provide macroeconomic stability 'Even in the most successful years of the postwar period' (Blair, 1996: 77, 79). For New Labour, the election of the first Thatcher government in 1979 marked the beginning of the second way or 'British Experiment', which lasted until the defeat of the Major government at the 1997 General Election (ibid.: 82). Blair criticised the macroeconomic policy regime of the Thatcher and Major governments for changing 'whenever it seemed convenient' and failing 'to respond to excessive imbalances in the economy even if they are produced by the private sector' (ibid.: 82–3). As a consequence, the absence of a tough, credible and transparent macroeconomic framework, allied to a failure to see macroeconomic and microeconomic policy as inseparable and complementary had destabilised domestic policy. This was especially so given the UK's location 'in the middle of an active global market for capital – a market which is less subject to regulation today than it has been for several decades'. Given this context, controlling public expenditure would be a long and gruelling slog for New Labour and the third way (ibid.: 84–6).

A rhetoric of stability and prudence, a record of boom and bust

To surmount the errors of the first and second ways, for the Blair governments the implementation of national economic policy in an era of globalisation and open-deregulated markets meant a fixation, at least rhetorically, with stability and prudence in monetary and fiscal policy. The Blair government's primary monetary policy objective for the Bank of England was the maintenance of price stability. Indeed, the Bank should only support the government's growth and employment objectives, subject to the maintenance of price stability. To demonstrate New Labour's commitment to low inflation and stability in monetary policy, one of Gordon Brown's first acts as Chancellor of the Exchequer in May 1997 was to grant the Monetary Policy Committee (MPC) of the Bank of England full operational independence over the implementation of the government's inflation target.

To achieve price stability, the MPC was charged with setting interest rates to an inflation target (the Retail Prices Index excluding mortgage interest payments) of 2.5 per cent. Like many elements of New Labour's economic policy, this constituted a refinement of the policies first adopted by the Major government. In October 1992, the Conservative Chancellor Norman Lamont had set an explicit inflation target of 1–4 per cent, a target whose range was narrowed to 2.5 per cent by his successor, Kenneth Clarke. Inflation had averaged 2.8 per cent from 1993 to 1997 under the Conservatives' monetary policy framework. The accomplishment of an average inflation rate of 2.4 per cent during the Blair government's first term of office, with inflation moving within the range of 1.8–3.2 per cent, appeared to have vindicated the third way's framework for monetary policy. The spectre of currency instability, devaluation crises and rising inflation, which had haunted the previous 'Old Labour' Callaghan government and seen inflation above 10 per cent in every year between 1974 and 1981, resulting in a tripling of prices (Richards, 2002: 9), appeared to have been banished for good.

As Chancellor of the Exchequer, Gordon Brown proclaimed that the UK was 'no longer the boom–bust economy' and that there would be 'No return to boom and bust' (Brown, 2004, 2005b, 2006). During his tenure at the Treasury, the UK economy delivered 40 consecutive quarters of economic growth, a better sustained performance than under any of his predecessors, Labour or Conservative. Brown claimed that New Labour's monetary and fiscal policy regime had been founded upon 'stability first, foremost and always, stability yesterday, today and tomorrow'. In reality, economic policy had been based upon the inherently unstable and volatile risk-based 'light touch system' of financial regulation (Brown, 2006). As he prepared to succeed Tony Blair as Prime Minister, Brown confidently forecast 'an era that history will record as the beginning of a new golden age for the City of London' (Brown, 2007). In practice, the City was soon to face its biggest financial crisis since the Great Crash of 1929, and the UK economy would face the deepest recession since the Great Depression of the 1930s.

This achievement of price stability came at a very high price for the UK's manufacturing sector, which in turn made the UK's overall economy performance overly dependent upon consumer borrowing and spending, itself contingent upon inflationary property prices and spiralling personal indebtedness. By the end of November 2009, total UK personal debt stood at £1459 billion, including £227 billion of consumer credit lending. This meant that every adult in the UK owed £30 226 (including mortgages) or 133 per cent of average earnings (Creditaction, 2010: 1). While the MPC's interest rate setting neither damaged the growth of the UK's services sector nor dampened the rampant property market in London and the South East of England, one of the biggest shortcomings of New Labour's monetary policy was its failure to create the conditions to redress the process of deindustrialisation.

Under both the Blair and Brown governments, the UK's annual balances on its current account and overall balance of payments continued to deteriorate, accentuating the trend established by the economic policies of the second way. During the 1990s, UK manufacturing had grown at annual rate of only 0.5 per cent. Having recorded a surplus of £2.7 billion in 1980, the UK's trade balance in manufactured goods had fallen into deficit in 1984, a trend sustained throughout the remaining tenure of the Thatcher and Major governments. Under New Labour, there were few signs of a reversal of deindustrialisation.

From negotiated discretion to centralised prescription

In the field of fiscal policy, the Blair government's inheritance was an increase in taxation by the Major government equivalent to around 1 per cent of GDP in 1994–95 and more than twice that in 1995–96 and 1996–97. Despite this fiscal conservatism, Gordon Brown signalled New Labour's own commitment to fiscal prudence and his own status as the 'Iron Chancellor' by adhering to the Major government's very tight spending plans for 1997–98 and 1998–99, which meant that public expenditure would be £4 billion or 1.2 per cent lower in real terms (at 1999–2000 prices) in 1998–99 than in 1996–97. Indeed, public expenditure would fall from 41.2 per cent of GDP in 1996–97, the final year of the second way's economic policies, to 37.8 per cent of GDP in 1999–2000, a real terms decline in spending of £1.4 billion or 0.4 per cent (Dilnot et al., 2001: 11–12). In this way, New Labour had chosen to 'lock in' fiscal prudence and stability through a rules-based approach to fiscal policy. A 1997 General Election manifesto pledge 'not to raise the basic or top rates of income tax throughout the next Parliament' was reinforced by the implementation of two further fiscal policy rules. First, the 'golden rule' of public expenditure, that is, 'over the economic cycle, we will only borrow to invest and not to fund current expenditure'. Second, the 'sustainable investment rule', that is, 'over the economic cycle public debt as a proportion of national income is a stable and prudent level' (Labour Party, 1997: 11–12). These rules were subsequently given greater coherence by their incorporation in March 1998 into the Code for Fiscal Stability, a measure that enshrined the Blair government's five principles of fiscal management, that is, transparency, stability, responsibility, fairness and efficiency.

Since most of the policies and principles incorporated in the Code for Fiscal Stability had already been put into practice by Gordon Brown, the Code constituted little more than a retrospective device for codifying and justifying fiscal policy choices to investors in the City of London's financial markets. Moreover, the 'golden rule' and 'sustainable investment rule' were damned with faint praise by leading commentators who have depicted them as 'sensible rules of thumb, but they are no more than that'. Moreover, it was asserted that 'There is nothing sacrosanct about these two rules, nor are they necessarily optimal' since, while adherence to these rules might maintain fiscal discipline, it might not necessarily meet New Labour's goal of spreading the burden of public expenditure across present and future generations. Indeed, 'slavish adherence to the golden rule may also be suboptimal' (Emmerson and Frayne, 2001: 2). In the event, both the golden rule and the sustainable investment rule were abandoned in 2008 by Alistair Darling, Brown's successor as Chancellor. Rather than delivering fiscal prudence, the third way had ushered in an era of increasing fiscal imprudence. It was projected that public sector net borrowing would rise to 12.6 per cent of GDP or £177.6 billion during 2009–10 and that public sector net debt would soar from 44.0 per cent of GDP in 2008–09 to 77.7 per cent of GDP by 2014–15 (HMT, 2009: 28).

For the conduct of government and New Labour's statecraft, by far the most important fiscal policy innovation introduced by New Labour was the implementation of biennial spending reviews in 1998, 2000 and 2002 because these gave the Treasury an unprecedented degree of control over the domestic policy agenda. However, this role was consistent with Brown's own redefinition of the mission for the Treasury to act as 'the guardian of the public finances and the guarantor of monetary stability', so as to be 'not just a Ministry of Finance, but also a Ministry working with other departments to deliver long-term economic and social renewal' (Brown, 1999: 11). Under previous governments, the Treasury's capacity to control public expenditure and to intervene in domestic policy choices had been based upon 'the exercise of discretionary authority constrained by the exercise of countervailing discretionary power by each autonomous spending department in the particular circumstances of an expenditure proposal' (Thain and Wright, 1995: 537). New Labour's spending reviews, commencing with the year-long Comprehensive Spending Review (CSR), published in July

1998, helped to accomplish a 'paradigm shift' in expenditure planning and control that threatened 'the permanent abandonment (not merely temporary relaxation) of the pre-existing paradigm of negotiated discretion' (ibid.: 543) in favour of a Treasury-driven system of central prescription over expenditure and policy choices.

The Treasury's increasing control over domestic policy choices, especially in the English regions beyond London that lacked the counterbalance of elected, devolved governments similar to those operating in the other constituent nations of the UK, was entrenched further by the principle of 'money for modernisation'. Whitehall departments and other public spending bodies have been allocated additional resources by the Treasury, but only in accordance with Public Service Agreements (PSAs) and Service Delivery Agreements (SDAs), which incorporated new objectives, defined by central government, and measurable efficiency targets, including measures of policy outputs, inputs and processes. The creation of the spending reviews, the PSAs and SDAs, and the role this has accorded the Treasury, attracted a withering critique from the House of Commons' Treasury Select Committee (TSC). It took a malign view of the Treasury's greatly increased power over 'the strategic direction of the Government', claiming that 'The Treasury as an institution has recently begun to exert too much influence over policy areas which are properly the business of other departments and that it is not necessarily in the best interests of the Treasury or the Government as a whole' (TSC, 2000: paras 19, 21). Moreover, in exercising this undue influence, rather than practising transparency the Treasury's role was portrayed as being 'opaque, hidden behind a curtain of Whitehall secrecy' (TSC, 2001: para 48).

The failure of the UK competition state

If its monetary and especially its fiscal policies were to prove controversial, the third pillar of the Blair government's third way approach to economic policy was much more aligned with developments in policy elsewhere. Globalisation of markets had inspired a transformation in the role of the advanced industrialised state away from its previous incarnations as a social democratic welfare state or industrialisation-driven developmental state towards a competition state. Having previously served as a decommodifying hierarchy, attempting to withdraw certain economic activities from the realm of the market, the contemporary competition state had acted increasingly as 'a collective commodifying agent – i.e., putting activities *into* the market) – and even as *a market actor itself*' (Cerny, 1997: 267; italics original). This transformation had in turn been marked by a movement from industrial policy through competitiveness policy to enterprise policy, that is, a shift in public policy 'away from policies that constrain the freedom of firms to contract and towards policies enabling the start-up and viability of knowledge-based entrepreneurial firms', not least because 'the comparative advantage of the high-cost countries in the OECD is increasingly based on knowledge-driven innovative activity' (Audretsch and Thurik, 2001: 5, 29).

One of the most conspicuous trends in competitiveness policy has been the emphasis, both rhetorically and in the substance of policy, placed upon the importance of the quality of the institutional and policy environment for fostering an entrepreneur-driven enterprise culture capable of generating new sources of innovation, employment and prosperity. The Blair government was at the forefront of these trends in economic policy. Drawing upon the insight that 'The only meaningful concept of competitiveness at the national level is national productivity', and that certain characteristics of a nation can create and sustain competitive advantage through a highly localised process (Porter, 1990: 6–13), Gordon Brown defined the objective for the UK economy for the forthcoming decade as achievement of 'the fastest rise in productivity of competitor economies' so as to create 'a wider and deeper enterprise culture that promotes investment and entrepreneurship and rewards success' (Brown, 2001: 2–3). However, despite its attempts to bridge the productivity gap, following its first term in office, the Blair government's evaluation of the UK's competitiveness concluded that the UK's 'overall performance in terms of GDP per head and productivity is disappointing' (DTI, 2001: 80). While the UK's GDP per head remained near to the EU average, it was nevertheless 21 per cent below the G7 average. More importantly, whether in terms of output per worker or output per hour worked, the UK remained far behind the United States, France and Germany, with the gap widening (in terms of output per worker) between the UK and the US during the first three years of the Blair government. This poor performance was attributed by New Labour to some of the poorest levels of basic literacy and numeracy in the OECD countries, an R&D performance that was falling further behind the UK's principal competitors, a failure to develop attitudes to risk-taking characteristic of a genuine enterprise society, and 'decades of underinvestment, both public and private' (DTI, 2001: 80). None of these weaknesses were redressed by the economic policies of the Blair and Brown governments (Lee, 2009). By 2008, despite the fact that UK GDP per worker had grown by 39 per cent since 1991, and in terms of GDP per hour worked UK productivity had increased by 49 per cent between 1991 and 2007, UK productivity remained lower than that of the United States, Italy and France, and lower than the average of the G7 countries (excluding the UK) (ONS, 2009: 1).

Conclusion

In implementing its third way of economic policy-making, in an attempt to reconcile domestic policy choices in the UK with globalisation, New Labour claimed not only to have stabilised both monetary and fiscal policy but also to have broken 'decisively with the short-termist secretive and unstable record of macroeconomic policy-making of the past two decades' (Brown, 1999: 10). Indeed, in his final Pre-Budget Report as Chancellor, Brown boasted that the UK was experiencing an economic expansion 'not only without precedent in the post-war history of the UK, but also the longest on post-war record for any G7 economy and the longest expansion of any OECD country' (HMT, 2006: 14). However, just as the third way Clinton administration in the US had misinterpreted the speculation- and consumer-led boom of the 'dotcom bubble' as the onset of 'a New Economy', characterised by '*extraordinary gains in performance – including rapid productivity growth, rising incomes, low unemployment, and moderate inflation*' (United States Government, 2001: 23; italics original), so too the transition from boom to bust, with the onset of a major financial crisis and the deepest recession since 1929, exposed New Labour's risk-based model of political economy as one founded upon unsustainable debt and imprudence in public and private finances (Lee, 2009).

The third way has not reconciled UK domestic economic policy choices with globalisation in a manner that has been able to insulate domestic modernisation from the consequences of increasing volatility and contagion in global financial markets. Following the global financial crisis, during 2009 the UK has experienced a fall in GDP of 4.8 per cent, a bigger fall than any year of the Great Depression and the UK's biggest contraction since 1921 (NIESR, 2010: 1). The demise of the political economy of the third way has demonstrated that long-term stability in monetary and fiscal policy cannot be guaranteed in a world of liberalised financial markets and volatile short-term capital flows, without effective regulation (United Nations, 2009). Under the political economy of the third way, the sources of imprudence, debt, risk and instability emanated from the private sector and liberalised markets overseas rather than solely from the public sector. The provision of an initially prudent (and latterly imprudent) framework for national macroeconomic policy was not sufficient to guarantee economic stability in the face of a 'risk-based' approach to the governance of financial markets, which empowered speculation and irresponsible risk-taking, at the expense of the taxpayer and manufacturing industry (Lee, 2009).

References

Albert, Michel (1993), *Capitalism Against Capitalism*, London: Whurr.

Anderson, P. (2000), 'Renewals', *New Left Review*, **2**(1), 5–24.

Audretsch, David and Roy Thurik (2001), 'Linking entrepreneurship to growth', Paris: Organisation for Economic Co-operation and Development STI Working Paper No. 2001/2.

Blair, Tony (1996), *New Britain: My Vision of a Young Country*, London: Fourth Estate.

Blair, Tony (1998), *The Third Way: New Politics for the New Century*, London: The Fabian Society Pamphlet No. 588.

Bootle, Roger (2009), *The Trouble with Markets: Saving Capitalism from Itself*, London: Nicholas Brealey.

Brown, Gordon (1999), 'Modernising the British economy – the new mission for the Treasury', HMT Press Release 86/99, London: Her Majesty's Treasury.

Brown, Gordon (2001), 'Speech by the Chancellor of the Exchequer to the Institute of Directors', HM Treasury News Release, 15 November, London Her Majesty's Treasury.
Brown, Gordon (2004), Speech to the Labour Party Conference, Brighton, 27 September.
Brown, Gordon (2005a), *Global Europe: Full-employment Europe*, London: Her Majesty's Treasury.
Brown, Gordon (2005b), Speech to the Labour Party Conference, Brighton, 26 September.
Brown, Gordon (2006), Budget Statement, 22 March.
Brown, Gordon (2007), Speech at the Lord Mayor's Banquet, Mansion House, London, 20 June.
Callinicos, Alex (2001), *Against the Third Way: An Anti-Capitalist Critique*, Cambridge: Polity.
Callinicos, Alex (2003), *An Anti-Capitalist Manifesto*, Cambridge: Polity.
Cerny, P. (1997), 'Paradoxes of the competition state: the dynamics of political globalisation', *Government and Opposition*, **22**(2), 251–74.
Clinton, William J. (1998), *State of the Union Address January 27*, Washington DC: United States Historical Documents Archive.
Creditaction (2010), *Debt Facts and Figures: Compiled January 2010*, London: Creditaction.
Dilnot, Andrew, Carl Emmerson and Helen Simpson (2001), *The IFS Green Budget: January 2001*, London: Institute for Fiscal Studies.
DTI (2001), *UK Competitiveness Indicators: Second Edition*, London: Department of Trade and Industry.
Emmerson, Carl and Chris Frayne (2001), *Overall Tax and Spending*, London: Institute for Fiscal Studies Election Briefing Note Number 2.
Gamble, Andrew (2009), *The Spectre at the Feast: Capitalist Crisis and the Politics of Recession*, London: Palgrave Macmillan.
Giddens, Anthony (1998), *The Third Way: The Renewal of Social Democracy*, Cambridge: Polity Press.
Giddens, Anthony (2000), *The Third Way and its Critics*, Cambridge: Polity.
Greenspan, Alan (2007), *The Age of Turbulence: Adventures in a New World*, London: Allen Lane.
Held, David and Anthony McGrew, David Goldblatt and Jonathan Perraton (2000), *Global Transformations: Politics, Economics and Culture*, Cambridge: Polity Press.
Hirst, P., G. Thompson and S. Bromley (2009), *Globalization in Question*, Cambridge: Polity.
HMT (2006), *Investing in Britain's Potential: Building our Long-term Future. Pre-Budget Report 2006, Cm.6984*, London: The Stationery Office.
HMT (2009), *Securing the Recovery: Growth and Opportunity: Pre-Budget Report 2009, Cm.7747*, London: The Stationery Office.
Hutton, Will (2002), *The World We're In*, London: Little, Brown.
IMD (2009), *The World Competitiveness Yearbook 2009*, Lausanne: Institute for Management Development.
IMF (1999), *World Economic Outlook. International Financial Contagion: May*, Washington DC: International Monetary Fund.
IMF (2002), *World Economic Outlook. Recessions and Recoveries: April*, Washington DC: International Monetary Fund.
Labour Party (1997), *New Labour: Because Britain Deserves Better*, London: The Labour Party.
Lee, Simon (2009), *Boom to Bust: The Politics and Legacy of Gordon Brown*, Oxford: Oneworld.
NIESR (2010), 'Biggest Contraction since 1921', *NIESR Monthly Estimates of GDP*, 13 January.
Ohmae, Kenichi (1995), *The End of the Nation State*, New York: Free Press.
ONS (2009), *International Comparisons of Productivity: New Estimates for 2008*, Newport: Office for National Statistics.
Porter, Michael (1990), *The Competitive Advantage of Nations*, London: Macmillan.
Porter, Michael, Hirotaka Takeuchi and Mariko Sakakibara (2000), *Can Japan Compete?*, London: Macmillan.
Reading, Brian (1992), *Japan: The Coming Collapse*, London: Orion.
Reich, Robert (2009), *Supercapitalism: The Battle for Democracy in an Age of Big Business*, London: Icon Books.
Richards, Patsy (2002), 'Inflation: the value of the pound 1750–2001', London: House of Commons Library Research Paper No. 02/44.

Rodrik, Dani (2007), *One Economics, Many Recipes: Globalization, Institutions, and Economic Growth*, Princeton: Princeton University Press.
Sen, Amartya (1999), *Development as Freedom*, Oxford: Oxford University Press.
Serra, Narcis and Joseph Stiglitz (ed.), *The Washington Consensus Reconsidered: Towards a New Global Governance*, Oxford: Oxford University Press.
Soros, George (2008), *The New Paradigm for Financial Markets: The Credit Crisis of 2008 and What it Means*, New York: PublicAffairs.
Stiglitz, Joseph (2009), 'Is there a post-Washington Consensus consensus?', in Narcis Serra and Joseph Stiglitz (eds), *The Washington Consensus Reconsidered: Towards a New Global Governance*, Oxford: Oxford University Press.
Thain, Colin and Maurice Wright (1995), *The Treasury and Whitehall: The Planning and Control of Public Expenditure, 1976–1993*, Oxford: Clarendon Press.
TSC (2000), *Spending Review 2000. Ninth Report from the House of Commons Treasury Select Committee, Session 1999–2000, HC 485*, London: The Stationery Office.
TSC (2001), *HM Treasury. Third Report from the House of Commons Treasury Select Committee, Session 2000–2001, HC 73-I*, London: The Stationery Office.
UNCTAD (2009), *World Investment Report 2009: Transnational Corporations, Agricultural Production and Development*, New York: United Nations Conference on Trade and Development.
United Nations (2009), *Report of the Commission of Experts of the President of the United Nations General Assembly on Reforms of the International Monetary and Financial System*, New York: United Nations.
United States Government (2001), *Economic Report of the President 2001*, Washington DC: United States Government.
Vogel, Ezra (1979), *Japan as Number One: Lessons for America*, Cambridge, MA: Harvard University Press.
Williamson, J. (1993), 'Democracy and the "Washington Consensus"', *World Development*, **21**(8), 1329–36.
Wood, C. (1992), *The Bubble Economy: The Japanese Economic Collapse*, London: Sidgwick and Jackson.
World Bank (2001), *Building Institutions for Markets: World Development Report 2002*, Washington DC: The World Bank.

PART VII

INTERNATIONAL ECONOMIC INSTITUTIONS

21 The WTO and its GATS

Scott Sinclair

Introduction

The General Agreement on Trade in Services (GATS) has been described as 'perhaps the most important single development in the multilateral trading system since the GATT itself came into effect in 1948'.[1] Despite its importance, the GATS was hardly known when the Uruguay Round of international trade negotiations concluded in 1994. It has only recently begun to attract deserved public scrutiny. This broadly worded treaty to enhance the rights of international commercial service providers has potentially far-reaching public policy impacts that merit serious attention and debate.

From the GATT to the WTO

The GATS came into being when the World Trade Organization (WTO) was created on 1 January 1995, after eight years of complex and difficult negotiations. The WTO Agreements subsumed and ranged far beyond the General Agreement on Tariffs and Trade (GATT), which had regulated international trade since 1948. While the GATT system had gradually been amended and elaborated throughout the post-war period, the advent of the WTO suddenly and profoundly transformed the multilateral trading regime in several fundamental respects.

Some of the most important of these fundamental changes include the following:

- While the GATT was simply an international agreement among 'contracting parties', the WTO is a fully-fledged multilateral institution with 'member governments'. It now takes a place alongside the International Monetary Fund, the World Bank and other elite international economic institutions.
- While GATT rules primarily covered tariffs and trade in goods, the WTO rules cover not only trade in goods, but also agriculture, standards-setting, intellectual property and services.
- While the GATT focused primarily on reducing tariffs and other 'at-the-border' trade restrictions, the far broader scope of the WTO means that it intrudes into many 'behind-the-border' regulatory matters.
- While the GATT was concerned primarily with challenging discriminatory policies, many of the new WTO agreements (SPS, TRIPS, TBT

and the GATS) aim to discipline explicitly non-discriminatory measures, either by stipulating substantive norms,[2] procedural norms,[3] or by putting the WTO dispute settlement machinery in a position to impugn explicitly non-discriminatory public standards or measures if they are deemed to be more burdensome than necessary on foreign commercial interests.[4]

- While the GATT agreements had gradually expanded to cover new matters such as procurement or standards-setting, adhering to such 'side codes' was optional. By contrast, the WTO agreements are a 'single undertaking', meaning that member governments have no choice but to be bound by all WTO agreements.
- Perhaps most significantly, while the GATT dispute settlement system was essentially 'diplomatic' (panel rulings had to be adopted by consensus, including the agreement of the defendant government), the WTO dispute system is 'legally binding' (the adoption of panel rulings can only be blocked by consensus, including the agreement of the complaining government).

These changes qualitatively transformed not only the GATT regime, but the entire multilateral system. Taken together, they amount to a constitutional shift: a fundamental reworking of the basic legal precepts of the multilateral trading regime and of its role in the international system. There is now a huge asymmetry between multilateral rules – and particularly enforcement – to protect broadly defined commercial trading interests and multilateral rule-making and enforcement in vital areas such as environmental protection, human rights, public health and cultural diversity. These changes, relatively unnoticed and undebated at the conclusion of the Uruguay Round, are now proving both controversial and destabilising.

This constitutional shift has resulted in serious tension and instability in the multilateral system. These strains are evident along at least three axes. There has been north–south conflict over the development impacts of the Uruguay Round agreements. Developing countries charge that implementing the WTO agreements has been arduous and costly and that the promised development benefits have generally not materialised. Meanwhile, there have been serious East–West disputes between the major trading powers. The US and the EU, for example, have clashed over approaches to regulating food safety and environmental protection (especially regarding the role of the precaution).[5] Finally, there has been a growing critique of the WTO's 'democratic deficit' and commercial biases from within civil society. Non-governmental organisations (NGOs) have criticised the WTO rules on an array of important issues ranging from decreased access to essential medicines, increased food insecurity and the institution's closed decision-making and dispute settlement processes. Increasingly, NGOs have begun to direct attention to the GATS and its far-reaching policy implications.

The GATS debate

There is now a lively – and sometimes caustic – international public debate on the GATS.[6] The main protagonists have been a range of non-governmental analysts and activists on the one side, whose GATS critiques have provoked an angry and defensive backlash from Quad (US/Japan/Canada/EU) trade negotiators, and the WTO secretariat and OECD trade officials on the other. More recently, certain developing country representatives have articulated some similar concerns to those raised by NGOs and other distinct, offensive negotiating interests with respect to the GATS.[7]

The GATS imposes, for the first time, multilateral trade law restrictions on trade and investment in the vast services sector. It has become a political flashpoint because it intensifies already existing pressures to commercialise and commodify services that have traditionally been provided through non-market means – including social services such as health and education and basic services such as water, electricity and postal services. It is doubly controversial because, as we will see, it also aims to restrict public interest regulation in the universally acknowledged 'regulation-intensive' service sectors (OECD, 2001). It is an imperfect, but potentially powerful, tool for transnational services corporations to 'break out of the boundaries that close non-market spheres to commodification and profit-making' (Leys, 2001, p. 4).

Fathoming the GATS legal complexities is challenging. The best place to turn for enlightenment is to the GATS text itself, but this is unusually complicated – even for a trade treaty. The purpose of this chapter is to assist the discerning reader to understand the legal text of GATS itself and the emerging debate about its role and significance. It argues that the GATS seriously overreaches, intruding into vital areas of public policy-making that are only indirectly related to conventional international trade matters. It contends that the GATS unacceptably restricts democratic policy-making, by privileging international commercial interests over other legitimate societal interests. And it asserts that, contrary to the sometimes strident denials of many proponents, the GATS does, in fact, threaten serious harm to public services and public interest regulation.[8]

The scope of the GATS

First, a few basic facts. As previously noted, the GATS was concluded in 1994 as part of the Uruguay Round. It took effect on 1 January 1995. It is part of the WTO's single undertaking and therefore binds all WTO member governments. It is subject to a legally binding dispute settlement. The GATS consists of a 'top-down' framework of rules that cover all services, measures and ways (or 'modes') of supplying services internationally. This framework is combined with more intrusive rules that apply only to services that governments explicitly agree to cover. Further negotiations to expand GATS rules and to increase its coverage are built into the agreement. The first of these successive rounds to broaden and deepen the GATS is currently underway in Geneva.

GATS critics and proponents agree on at least one critical point. The scope of the GATS is very broad: far broader than traditional rules governing trade in goods. Indeed, the subject matter of the GATS – services – is immense. These range from birth (midwifery) to death (burial); the trivial (shoe-shining) to the critical (heart surgery); the personal (haircutting) to the social (primary education); low-tech (household help) to high-tech (satellite communications); and from our wants (retail sales of toys) to our needs (water distribution).

Moreover, the GATS applies to all measures affecting services taken by any level of government, including central, regional and local governments. Therefore, no government action, whatever its purpose, is, in principle, beyond GATS scrutiny and potential challenge. As noted, all service sectors are also on the table in ongoing, continuous negotiations.

For the critics, this breadth and the GATS' novel restrictions set off alarms. As a former director general of the WTO has admitted, the GATS extends 'into areas never before recognized as trade policy'.[9] Not limited to cross-border trade, it extends to every possible means of providing a service internationally, including investment. While this broad application does not, of course, mean that all services-related measures violate the treaty, it does mean that any regulatory or legislative initiative in any WTO member country must now be vetted for GATS consistency, or risk possible challenge.

How flexible is the GATS?

The proponents, however, while acknowledging the treaty's universal scope, stress its 'remarkable flexibility'.[10] They also point to its controversial exclusion for governmental services and the range of exceptions available to protect otherwise non-conforming measures from successful challenge.

Proponents sometimes refer to the GATS as a 'bottom-up' agreement. This refers to a treaty that applies only to those specific government measures and sectors that individual governments explicitly agree to cover. By contrast, 'top-down' treaties automatically apply to all measures and sectors unless governments explicitly exclude them by negotiating them off the table. The GATS, however, is not a purely bottom-up agreement. It is, in fact, a hybrid agreement that combines both bottom-up and top-down approaches.

Certain GATS obligations, notably the most-favoured-nation treatment (MFN) rule, already apply unconditionally across all service sectors. And while it is true that the most forceful GATS obligations only apply to sectors that governments explicitly agree to cover, there are serious limits to this flexibility:

- Most governments have already given up much flexibility by not making full use of their one-time chance to specify limitations to their initial GATS commitments.
- Members remain under intense pressure to cede flexibility in successive rounds of negotiations to expand GATS coverage.
- The GATS requires governments that withdraw previously made commitments to compensate other governments whose service suppliers are allegedly adversely affected.
- Protective country-specific limitations will endure only if all future governments are committed to maintaining them.

The GATS' vaunted flexibility is therefore considerably less than is often claimed by its proponents. Indeed, much of what passes for flexibility in the GATS is temporary and deliberately designed to disappear over time.[11]

The GATS governmental services exclusion

The GATS covers all services, except those 'supplied in the exercise of governmental authority'. At first glance, this controversial exclusion is a potentially broad one. But it is highly qualified. GATS Article I:3 excludes services provided 'in the exercise of governmental authority', but it goes on to define these as services provided neither on commercial nor a competitive basis. These terms are not further defined and, if left to the dispute settlement process, will most likely be, according to the rules of treaty interpretation, interpreted narrowly.

'Public services' are rarely delivered exclusively by government. They are complex, mixed systems that combine a continually shifting mix of public and private funding, and public, private not-for-profit and private for-profit delivery. A truly effective exclusion for public services should safeguard governments' ability to shift this mix and to regulate all aspects of these mixed systems. When the GATS exclusion is most needed – when governments want to expand or restore the public, not-for-profit character of the system – it is least effective. This controversial exclusion is therefore ambiguous at best and ineffective at worst.

The GATS preamble and the 'right to regulate'

A common refrain in every official rejoinder to GATS critics is that the GATS specifically recognises governments' right to regulate. Regrettably, it is terribly misleading to suggest that the mere affirmation of the right to regulate, contained in the treaty preamble, fully protects the right to regulate. It does not. While the preamble does contain a clause that 'recognises the right of Members to regulate', this language has strictly limited legal effect. It would have some interpretive value in a dispute but should not be construed as providing legal cover for regulations that would otherwise be inconsistent with the substantive provisions of the treaty. In short, governments retain their freedom to regulate only to the extent that the regulations they adopt are compatible with the GATS.

The MFN rule

The GATS most-favoured-nation treatment rule, which applies to all service sectors, has proven to be a surprisingly powerful obligation in two recent GATS-related disputes.[12] This rule (GATS Article II) is best understood as a most-favoured-foreign *company* rule, as it requires that any regulatory or funding advantage gained by a single foreign commercial provider must be extended, immediately and unconditionally, to all. The MFN obligation has the practical effect of consolidating commercialisation wherever it occurs. While not legally precluding a new policy direction, this rule makes it far more difficult for governments to reverse failed privatisation and commercialisation.

The national treatment and market access rules

The hard core of the GATS comprises restrictions that apply only to the sectors, or sub-sectors, where governments have made specific commitments. These commitments, together with any country-specific limitations, are listed in each government's GATS schedule.

The GATS national treatment rule (GATS Article XVII) requires governments to extend the best treatment given to domestic services (or service providers) to like foreign services (or service providers). In the GATS, this rule is quite intrusive, as it explicitly requires government measures to pass a very tough test of de facto non-discrimination. That is, measures that at face value are impartial can still be found inconsistent if they modify the conditions of competition in favour of domestic services or service providers. This gives dispute panels wide latitude to find measures 'GATS-illegal' even when they seem to be non-discriminatory or when such measures alter the conditions of competition merely as an unintended consequence in the legitimate pursuit of other vital policy goals. The GATS' stiff national treatment requirement thus opens the doors for non-discriminatory public policy to be frustrated for reasons that are unrelated to international trade.

The GATS Market Access rule (GATS Article XVI) is one of the treaty's most novel, and troublesome, provisions. There is nothing quite like this rule in other international commercial treaties. Framed in absolute rather than relative terms, it precludes certain types of policies whether they are discriminatory or not. A government intent on maintaining otherwise inconsistent measures is forced to inscribe them in its country schedules when it makes its specific commitments. This rule prohibits governments from placing restrictions on: the number of service suppliers or operations; the value of service transactions; the number of persons that may be employed in a sector; and, significantly, the types of legal entities through which suppliers may supply a service.

Such prohibitions call into question, for example, the GATS-consistency of government-set limits to conserve resources or protect the environment. To take another example, many governments restrict the private delivery of certain social services such as childcare to legally constituted non-profit agencies. Many also confine certain basic services such as rail transportation, water distribution, or energy transmission to private, not-for-profit providers. Such public policies certainly restrict the market access of commercial providers, whether domestic or foreign. But they have never before been subject to binding international treaty obligations. Now, these vital policies are exposed to the GATS challenge.

GATS restrictions on monopolies and exclusive service suppliers

The GATS restrictions on monopolies and exclusive service suppliers (GATS Article VIII) impose new restrictions on monopolies and exclusive service supplier arrangements. In fact, monopolies and exclusive service suppliers are GATS-inconsistent and must be listed as country-specific exceptions in committed sectors. Any government wishing to designate a new monopoly in a listed sector is required to negotiate compensation with other member governments or face retaliation.

Monopolies, while not as prevalent as formerly, are still relied upon to provide basic services in many countries. Postal services, the distribution and sale of alcoholic beverages, electrical generation and transmission, rail transportation, health insurance, water distribution and waste disposal are just some of the more widespread examples. Exclusive supplier arrangements are commonplace in post-secondary education, health care and other social services. The consequences of these GATS rules, which so far have gone largely unexamined, are likely to be significant in all of these important areas.

GATS restrictions on domestic regulation

If proposed GATS restrictions on domestic regulation (GATS Article VI:4), now being negotiated in Geneva, were ever agreed to, they would constitute an extraordinary intrusion into democratic policy-making. At issue is the development of 'disciplines' on a member country's domestic regulation – explicitly non-discriminatory regulations that treat local and foreign services and service providers evenhandedly. The subject matter of these proposed restrictions is very broad, covering measures relating to qualification requirements and procedures, technical standards and licensing procedures – a wide swathe of vital government regulatory measures.

Critically, these proposed restrictions are intended to apply some form of 'necessity test', that is, that regulations must not be more trade restrictive than necessary and that measures must be necessary to achieve a specified legitimate objective. Perversely, the proposed GATS restrictions would turn the logic of the long-established GATT necessity test on its head. They would transform it from a shield to save clearly discriminatory measures from challenge into a sword to attack clearly non-discriminatory measures.[13] The proposed GATS restrictions on domestic regulation are a recipe for regulatory chill; they are among the most excessive restrictions ever contemplated in a binding international commercial treaty. This excess is concrete evidence of the hazards of leaving the ambitions of commercial ministries, and the corporate lobbyists driving them on, unchecked by broader public scrutiny and debate.

Conclusion

The GATS is a deservedly controversial agreement. Its broadly worded provisions give too much weight to commercial interests, constraining legitimate public interest regulation and democratic decision-making.

As GATS proponents frequently insist, the treaty does not *force* governments to privatise public services. But, nevertheless, as previously discussed:

- through continuous negotiations it exerts constant pressure to open services to foreign commercial providers;
- the GATS MFN rule helps consolidate commercialisation;
- the GATS monopoly provisions make it more difficult for governments to maintain public services by hamstringing their ability to compete;
- where GATS commitments are made, the GATS restricts the ability of governments to restore, revitalise or expand public services; and
- in such cases, compensation must be negotiated or retaliatory sanctions faced.

Similarly, the GATS does not *eliminate* governments' ability to regulate, but:

- the recognition of the right to regulate in the preamble has little legal effect;
- the GATS clearly applies to government regulatory measures, whatever their form or purpose;
- the GATS applies a very tough test of non-discrimination when considering the possible adverse effects of domestic governmental measures on foreigners;
- the GATS prohibits certain types of measures, whether they are discriminatory or not; and
- negotiations to apply a necessity test to non-discriminatory domestic regulation pose a very serious threat to crucial regulatory instruments.

The GATS strictly limits the pursuit of more progressive and egalitarian forms of social reproduction while privileging the interests of private capital, chiefly transnational service corporations, and their goal of accumulation. Although multilateral negotiations to broaden and deepen the GATS, launched in 2001 in Doha,[14] have faltered, the legal framework pioneered by the GATS continues to expand through the proliferation of bilateral trade and investment agreements. Ironically, the high levels of public debt incurred to stabilise financial capital during the recent crisis will likely be used to justify a new wave of global restructuring of public services characterised by privatisation, outsourcing and increased corporate provision of publicly funded basic services. The constitutional role of the GATS in shaping this restructuring to serve global corporate interests raises such serious challenges to democratic governance and social cohesion that it is certain to stimulate further public interest and controversy.

List of Acronyms

EU	European Union
GATT	General Agreement on Tariffs and Trade
GATS	General Agreement on Trade in Services
MFN	Most favoured nation
NGOs	Non-governmental organisations
OECD	Organisation for Economic Co-operation and Development
SPS	Agreement on the Application of Sanitary and Phytosanitary Measures
TBT	Agreement on Technical Barriers to Trade
TRIPS	Agreement on Trade-Related Aspects of Intellectual Property Rights
WTO	World Trade Organization

Notes

1. World Trade Organization (1999) p. 1.
2. Such as the minimum 20-year term of patent protection in TRIPS.
3. Such as risk assessment in the SPS Agreement.
4. For example, under Article VI of the GATS.
5. The successful North American challenge of the European ban on hormone-treated beef may foreshadow an even more contentious WTO dispute over Europe's approach to regulating genetically modified foods.
6. A valuable collection of NGO critiques of the GATS can be found on the GATS Watch website at http://www.gatswatch/factfict.html. Both the WTO and the OECD have responded directly to GATS critics; World Trade Organization (2001a), available on the WTO website at www.wto.org; OECD (2001).
7. Communication from Cuba, Senegal, Tanzania, Uganda, Zimbabwe and Zambia, 'Assessment of Trade in Services', 6 December, 2001, S/CSS/W/132, para. 8.
8. These themes are developed more fully in Sinclair and Grieshaber-Otto (2002).
9. Renato Ruggiero, former WTO Director, 2 June 1998.
10. See WTO (2001a), p. 6 and OECD (2001), p. 10 para. 12.
11. The public policy and development impacts of an international treaty should not be judged against the ability of the countries to opt out of particular GATS provisions or to limit their application. It is fair rather, to judge its impacts assuming, as is intended over time, that its provisions are fully applicable (cf. Luff, 2002).
12. The two cases are: 'Canada: certain measures affecting the automotive industry', WTO (2000) and 'European communities – regime for the importation, sale and distribution of bananas', WTO (1997). For summaries and analysis of these cases see Sinclair (2000), chapter 3.
13. Under GATT Article XX, a government can, as a last resort, try to save an otherwise GATT-inconsistent measure from successful challenge by arguing that it is necessary to achieve a GATT-sanctioned legitimate objective. But this general exception has been interpreted very

restrictively. Indeed, under GATT jurisprudence, 'a measure cannot be deemed necessary if satisfactory and effective alternative means to achieve the same objective are reasonably available to the Member enacting it'. World Trade Organization, Council for Trade in Services, 'Article VI.4 of the GATS: Disciplines on Domestic Regulation Applicable to all Services', Note by the Secretariat, 1 March 1999, para. 27 (S/C/W/96).

14. WTO (2001b).

References

Leys, Colin (2001), *Market-driven Politics: Neo-liberal Democracy and the Public Interest*, London: Verso.

Luff, David (2002), *Regulation of Health Services and International Trade Law*, Study prepared for OECD–World Bank Services Experts Meeting, OECD Paris, 4–5 March.

Organisation for Economic Co-operation and Development (2001), Working Party of the Trade Committee, *Open Services Markets Matter*, Paris: Organisation for Economic Co-operation and Development. TD/TC/WP(2001)24/PART1/REV1.

Sinclair, Scott (2000), *GATS: How the World Trade Organization's New 'Services' Negotiations Threaten Democracy*, Ottawa: Canadian Centre for Policy Alternatives.

Sinclair, Scott and Jim Grieshaber-Otto (2002), *Facing the Facts: A Critical Guide to WTO and OECD Claims about the GATS*, Ottawa: Canadian Centre for Policy Alternatives.

World Trade Organization (1997), 'European communities – regime for the importation, sale and distribution of bananas', Appellate Body, 9 September.

World Trade Organization (1999), Trade in Services Division, *An Introduction to the GATS*, Geneva: World Trade Organization.

World Trade Organization (2000), 'Canada: certain measures affecting the automotive industry', Appellate Body, 31 May.

World Trade Organization (2001a), Trade in Services Secretariat, *GATS: Fact and Fiction*, Geneva: World Trade Organization.

World Trade Organization (2001b), Ministerial Declaration, Ministerial Conference Fourth Session Doha, 9–14 November, WT/MIN(01)/DEC/1 20.

22 The International Monetary Fund and the World Bank

John Toye

The IMF

The Fund's original aims and its modalities

The IMF was established in 1947, as an international institution to manage international payments, in the chaotic economic conditions that obtained at the end of World War II. The Fund's objectives were stated in its Charter. It aimed to restore a system of multilateral payments for current transactions between its members; to reduce the duration and intensity of disequilibrium in member states' balances of payments; and to promote exchange rate stability. The final (and most usually forgotten) aim was 'to facilitate the expansion and balanced growth of international trade, and to contribute thereby to the promotion and maintenance of high levels of employment and real income' (Articles of Agreement of the IMF, Article 1, item (ii)).

In promoting all of these objectives, the Fund operated a set of rules of international monetary behaviour. It managed a system of fixed, but adjustable, exchange rates against the US dollar, which itself was anchored to a unit of gold at a fixed price. To keep exchange rate fluctuations within narrow limits, each member country paid into the Fund a capital sum, determined by a complex formula supposed to measure the country's global economic importance, and was given a borrowing 'quota' related to its capital. Voting power in the organisation is also related to the size of this capital.

Under the IMF rules, the onus of adjustment fell on those countries with balance of payments deficits, not those with balance of payments surpluses. If a balance of payments deficit began to threaten the stability of its exchange rate, a member country was permitted to borrow from the Fund and repay over the following two or three years. In facilitating deficit country borrowing and repayment, the Fund acted as a bank, but the scale of the 'banking' operation was initially small. Between 1947 and 1955, 14 out of 59 members made drawings, at an annual rate of $46m. This equalled 0.06 of world imports. In 1990–98, when 78 out of 182 members made drawings, the rate was $13.4bn, or 0.29 of world imports.

The gold exchange standard devised at Bretton Woods succeeded in re-establishing current account convertibility in the industrialised nations, while permitting countries to maintain capital account controls. Controversy related to the IMF's role as a banker, particularly about its success in shortening and reducing the severity of balance of payments disequilibria (Killick, 1985). Nevertheless, under this system, international trade did grow rapidly, and employment and real income also grew at faster rates than subsequently, so that the period 1946–71 has been called 'the Golden Age'.

The anchor of the whole system was the fixed parity between gold and the US dollar, at the official price of $35 per ounce of gold. In 1968, this price became unsustainable, as confidence in the dollar–gold convertibility guarantee began to evaporate. It was partly to forestall this outcome that Special Drawing Rights (SDRs) in the IMF were created in 1967: this was the First Amendment of the Fund's Articles of Agreement, but it was already too late. The ratio of US gold reserves to its liquid liabilities had fallen from 2.73 in 1950 to 0.41 by 1968. Once the private market gold price rose above the official gold price, dollar–gold convertibility was suspended de facto. Revaluation of gold to $38 an ounce was no lasting solution, as it simply strengthened the forces of speculation against the dollar, and the US commitment to buy and sell gold at a fixed dollar price was officially abandoned in 1971. The collapse of the gold exchange system resulted from an inherent design flaw, not from any particular failures of its umpire and manager, the IMF.

The IMF in the post-Bretton Woods world

The end of the system of fixed parities was also the end of the Fund's role as banker to the OECD countries, apart from its loans to Italy and the UK in 1976 (for the UK, see Wass, 2008). This was important for two reasons. The Fund began to cast around to find a new role for itself, and it looked increasingly towards clients in the developing countries. However, as this happened, a divorce occurred between the industrial countries, whose entrenched voting power still directed the Fund, and the users of the Fund, the developing countries. The latter now maintained substantial net debtor positions with the Fund, while the former remained in net credit (Boughton, 2009, pp.65–7). The Fund thus changed from being an institution of collective self-help for industrial countries into an instrument by which the G7 countries could discipline the economies of the developing world.

At first, the move towards floating exchange rates was thought to be temporary, but none of the various grand designs for a new international monetary system commanded general agreement (Williamson, 1977). Instead, the industrial countries learned to live with a non-system based de facto on a strong US dollar. The Second Amendment to the IMF Articles in 1978 allowed all forms of national exchange rate mechanism, except pegging to gold, which was demonetised. Many of the larger economies chose to float their currency, for example, the US, UK, Japan and those in the European Union (which latter adopted the euro). Many of the smaller economies chose to peg their exchange rates to other currencies or baskets of currencies. The role of the IMF was thus reduced to surveillance and reporting on the exchange rate arrangements chosen by members, plus advocating 'principles of guidance' that it had no power to enforce.

Freely floating exchange rates produced rate fluctuations among major currencies greatly in excess of changes in macroeconomic fundamentals of the real economies, measured in terms of departures from purchasing power parity. The first half of the 1980s saw a 40 per cent real appreciation of the dollar, followed by an equal depreciation in the second half. The uncertainties created by currency speculation have acted to magnify the exchange rate effects on real income and employment. Yet international economic coordination shrivelled to periodic communiqués from G7 meetings that tried to 'talk down' or 'talk up' particular key currencies. Innovation was left to the private banking sector, which responded with the invention of 'credit derivatives' to mitigate currency risk (Tett, 2009).

Many developing countries had never properly integrated into the gold exchange system at all, apart from certain Latin American countries (Peru, Paraguay) where the Fund pioneered the use of policy conditionality in its lending. From the early 1960s onwards, largely under pressure from the United Nations, the Fund did develop additional 'banking' facilities relevant to the needs of developing countries, characterised by interest rates below those of commercial sources of finance. The Compensatory Financing Facility, established in 1963, made limited credit available to countries experiencing a temporary fall in their trend export revenues. More significant was the Extended Fund Facility (EFF) of 1974, which provided medium-term finance, beyond the limits of normal lending, to support agreed stabilisation programmes requiring structural adjustments.

The Fund and the debt crisis of the 1980s

In the wake of the oil price rises of the 1970s, private commercial banks were left to undertake the task of recycling the savings of the oil-producing countries to the non-oil-producing developing countries. The election of Reagan, Thatcher and Kohl around 1980 soon produced policies of severe disinflation in the industrialised world, which sparked off a deep debt crisis in Latin America. The Mexican debt crisis (1982) was a turning point in the history of the Fund and the World Bank. Following the Baker Plan of 1985, the US Administration recruited the Fund, along with the Bank, to be its managers at one remove of the prolonged debt crisis that for several years threatened the survival of major Western banks. The capital available to both institutions was increased. Building on the EFF, new longer-term lending facilities were created to channel credit to indebted developing countries. The Structural Adjustment Facility (SAF) was set up in 1986, followed by the Extended Structural Adjustment Facility (ESAF) in 1987.

SAF/ESAF resources are provided as loans to low-income countries suffering protracted balance of payments problems. Interest was very low at 0.5 per cent and repayment was deferred to between five-and-a-half and ten years. Policy conditionality was strong under ESAF loans, specified in the annual Policy Framework Papers (PFPs) (from 1999 Poverty Reduction Strategy Papers) drawn up jointly with the World Bank. SAF and ESAF allowed the Fund to adopt a mediating role between debtors and creditors. IMF stabilisation programmes were intended to restore macroeconomic balance in the countries that adopted them, so that they would be able to pay their debt service obligations (rescheduled if necessary) to their creditors in an orderly manner. Participation in an IMF programme was therefore expected to be a 'seal of approval' that would encourage private creditors to roll over existing loans and supply new loans to the debtors. Thus, IMF money was expected to 'leverage' or 'catalyse' private flows.

In the event, matters did not work out quite so well. On the one hand, the stabilisation programmes did not always have the intended effect of rendering the borrowing country creditworthy. They frequently broke down before completion. Between 1979 and 1993, 53 per cent of 305 Fund programmes were uncompleted. This was for a variety of different reasons, but was often connected with inadequate financing (Killick, 1995, pp. 58–65). Estimates of the impact of IMF programmes showed that they improved the current account and the overall balance of payments, and slowed inflation. On the other hand, there was also a short-term reduction in the growth rate and the IMF seal of approval rarely acted as a catalyst for new private lending. The overall balance of payments rarely improved by more than the improvement on the current account, as would have happened had the catalytic effect been positive. Although private markets (and certainly aid donors) valued a government's commitment to sound economic policies, they might doubt also that Fund conditionality would ensure that correct policies were designed and pursued, or worry that the amount of IMF financing was inadequate (Bird and Rowlands, 2000).

After the fall of the Berlin Wall and the collapse of the Soviet Union, the IMF, along with the World Bank, found a second new area of influence. Both had to absorb many new members and to attempt to provide them with appropriate financial assistance, to help them to undergo the transition from socialist to proto-capitalist economies. The Fund established a Systemic Transformation Facility under pressure from OECD countries in 1993. Nevertheless, the transition countries did not displace developing countries as the main users of IMF funds. Over the period 1988–93, developing countries borrowed four times as much as transition countries. Lending in transition countries was highly political, and heavily influenced by the policies of the US Treasury. The Fund policies of liberalisation, stabilisation and privatisation were controversial. Whether the economic failures that followed in Russia should be attributed to the Fund's choice of policies, or the way they were implemented continues to be debated. Reform in Russia was made even more difficult by the outbreak of the Asian financial crisis (1997–99).

The Asian financial crisis and criticism of the Fund

The outbreak of the Asian financial crisis, in Thailand in July 1997, took the Fund unawares, and led to dramatic falls in the exchange rates of Asian countries, losses of income and employment and rises in poverty. There was a knock-on effect in Africa, as the pre-existing recovery of primary commodity prices was reversed. At the time, this was the worst global recession since 1945, although it hardly touched the US or European economies. As a result, there was strong criticism of the Fund. Critics claimed variously that the Fund should have been aware of the fragility of the economies of East Asia; should have been able to prevent the crisis from happening; and should not have pushed remedies, especially higher interest rates, that were counter-productive (Stiglitz, 2002). Finally, critics saw moral hazard in the fact that the costs of the crisis were borne wholly by the public taxpayer, while Western bankers who had made unwise loans were repaid in full.

An effective early warning system for financial crises is probably utopian. Financial crises are products of complex non-linear causes. Government policy preferences, investors' expectations and herd behaviour all enter the equation, as well as measurable economic quantities such as the assets and liabilities of the banking system, the balance of payments deficit and the size of the foreign exchange reserves. This makes forecasting crises extremely difficult. Moreover, the Fund's surveillance faces problems to the extent that countries avoid publication of information that might reveal signs of their financial fragility. Limited disclosure is not the whole story, however. Much vital macroeconomic and financial information was in the public domain in July 1997. What was lacking was its adequate evaluation both by the Fund and the Bank, and by the markets.

The Fund published a Special Data Dissemination Standard (SDDS) for macroeconomic variables in April 1996. This was broadened in 1998 to include net reserves and private debt. The Fund encourages the definition and promulgation of appropriate accounting standards for firms and banks, insisting that its members adopt such standards for the information provided to the Fund. In 1999 new transparency guidelines were agreed for authorities conducting monetary policy, financial regulation and oversight of payments systems. The Fund, previously the most secretive of public organisations, became more transparent, putting the onus on a member government to veto the disclosure of any information that they supply to the Fund.

The fundamental defect of floating exchange rates is the large and frequent misalignment of the key world currencies – the dollar, the euro, the yen and the renminbi. The solution would be to specify exchange rate targets for these currencies, and find instruments to move them towards the specified targets. The US and other G20 member countries are unwilling to contemplate this. The financial systems of developing countries are relatively small, and often fragile. Poor credit evaluation and poor control of banks' foreign currency exposure are typical aspects of fragility. These weaknesses become much more dangerous after liberalisation of the capital account. A crisis develops when foreign transactions, induced by interest rates in combination with investors' expectations of exchange rate movements, are large in relation to the system, though small in relation to the foreign investor's portfolio. Moreover, the quality of bank assets changes with changes in economic conditions, and no amount of Fund surveillance can prevent this kind of 'contagion'. This is a new danger that developing countries face in a more financially integrated world.

When the Fund suspects that a crisis is about to happen, it has a problem. By giving a public warning, or giving exceptional assistance to a country, it may provoke an earlier or worse crisis than would otherwise have occurred. It may not be able to provide sufficient help to prevent a crisis, without at the same time signalling that a crisis is imminent. Similarly, while better domestic banking supervision would clearly help to prevent crises, it is doubtful whether the time to begin to improve standards is in a period of banking fragility. Such a move could trigger the collapse of already weakened banks. The problems are illustrated by the fate of the 1999 Contingency Credit Line. A large proportion of the funding would be made available immediately on demand, at a low interest rate and without prior policy conditions. Few countries have drawn on this facility, presumably because its use would be read as a sign of distress.

The Fund's defence against the accusation that the conditions of its lending to the Asian crisis countries were misconceived was that, in a short-term crisis, the resources at its disposal are fixed, and they cannot fully substitute for the private outflow (and indeed should not, given the moral hazard). Thus, private capital outflow has to be balanced by loss of foreign exchange reserves, by a depreciation of the exchange rate or, failing these, interest rate rises to make the adjustment via loss of output, and/or to reverse the outflow of private capital. Practically, it appeals to the outcome from the IMF conditions, pointing to the speed of recovery of the countries, like Korea, that complied with them most fully, compared with the slowness of recovery of those, like Indonesia, that resisted most. Critics maintain that looser monetary and fiscal policy, combined with rapid corporate restructuring, would have restored confidence and reversed the capital outflow with less damage to the real economy.

More radical ideas for Fund reform

In recent decades, the IMF has been hobbled by a series of interlinked problems. They include:

- its out-of-date quota system, which, after several minor small revisions, still does not reflect the true relative economic strength of its developing country members;
- the resulting veto on major changes to the institution that can be exercised by the US;
- the European–US informal agreement on the appointment of the Managing Director and the Deputy Managing Director;
- the restriction of its resources to the point where it can influence only small poor countries, making it virtually helpless in the face of the 2007–08 Wall Street collapse;
- the resulting lack of legitimacy of its decisions; and
- the fragmentation of its responsibilities for ensuring global financial instability.

However, for all its past failings, the IMF is a near-universal institution and could become, if radically reformed, a more effective body for the purposes of multilateral financial coordination. To regain its legitimacy in this role, it will need to accelerate the changes in its quota system to reflect current economic realities, shrinking the inflated quotas of the US and smaller European countries, and depriving the US of its veto power. Once this is done, the institution could be given a transparent multilateral political directorate. Indeed, with very little change the loosely institutionalised G20 could be formalised as a new Council of the IMF to give it strategic direction. The governance structures of the Executive Board and management also need to be reshaped to improve their accountability, along the lines proposed by the Committee on IMF governance reform in March 2009.

These far-reaching governance reforms are necessary, but not sufficient to restore the IMF's legitimacy. The Fund needs additional resources to provide adequate international liquidity on appropriate conditions to support macroeconomic and exchange rate adjustment. The issue of new allocations of SDRs is a costless and efficient method to create extra liquidity, and the G20's agreement to its use in April 2009 was a hopeful indication that the Fund can be allowed to adopt a less restrictive stance on this matter.

Finally, there is the question of the extension of the IMF mandate to include the capital as well as the current account. At present, the sole formal jurisdiction that the IMF has over members' capital accounts is the right to require members to impose capital controls in certain circumstances. In the late 1990s, the Interim Committee of the IMF recommended that the Fund's Articles of Agreement be changed so that the liberalisation of international capital movements became a central purpose of the Fund, and its jurisdiction be extended to capital movements (Fischer, 1997). These recommendations were put on hold after the Asian crisis, but are being revived as part of current IMF reform plans. This poses a dilemma. The push for the liberalisation of capital accounts is seen by many as the high point of neo-liberal hubris, and is resisted for that reason. (The Fund denies this, claiming that it was aiming at the orderly liberalisation of capital movements.) On the other hand, leaving the capital account outside the multilateral framework would make it impossible to deal with the volatile capital movements that are so damaging to developing economies. A more representative political Council for the IMF would help to ease the fears of the sceptics, but this would have to be accompanied by a thorough overhaul of the technical expertise of the Fund staff to improve its ability to detect systemic risk arising from international capital movements.

The World Bank (WB)

The Bank's original mandate and its early years

The International Bank for Reconstruction and Development (IBRD) was established in 1946 in order to provide medium-term, lower than commercial interest rate loans to governments for (post-war) reconstruction and for the development of capital-poor areas. Since then other parts of what is now called the World Bank Group have been added. There are three organisations that deal with the private sector, the International Finance Corporation (IFC) set up for lending to the private sector in 1956, the International Centre for Settlement of Investment Disputes (ICSID) of 1966 and the Multilateral Investment Guarantee Agency (MIGA) of 1988. However, the most significant addition was the International Development Agency (IDA), which was added in 1960 to provide long-term, highly concessional loans to the poorest countries. This was a response to a long campaign in the UN to establish a new source of development capital for poor countries. Initially, the Bank opposed the idea, but was finally persuaded by the US government to agree to it, as a way of preventing this facility being set up under UN auspices.

The IBRD played a minimal role in the reconstruction of Europe, because the US decided not to channel their Marshall Aid through the Bank. Marshall Plan aid amounted to $12.7bn in 1948–51, while IBRD loans to Europe were less than $1bn during this period. Having largely missed out on reconstruction lending, the Bank began to focus on project lending for economic development. The procedure chosen was to borrow on the developed country capital markets and re-lend (plus a small margin) for specific investment projects in developing countries. In the early years, this was a slow process, explained by Bank officials in terms of the low absorptive capacity of developing countries, and their failure to prepare a sufficient number of sound projects.

The initial mode of operation, as a public sector development bank, was justified on the grounds of private capital market imperfections. Engineers and engineering dominated the early operations. The project portfolio of the Bank was originally concerned with large physical infrastructure schemes, such as dams and electricity generation. After IDA added to the Bank the function of a development agency in 1960s, the composition of Bank investments began to change, gradually including agricultural and urban redevelopment projects. The lending vehicle remained the project, however. The evaluation of project success was with reference to calculations of the ex post rate of return on each project. A semi-independent Operations Evaluation Department was established for this purpose.

In its first 30 years, the Bank provided both project finance and technical assistance in formulating and executing projects, and in developing associated pricing and maintenance policies. The Bank's participation in these projects almost certainly produced a better quality of project than would have occurred in its absence. However, the force of the argument of the fungibility of funds was increasingly recognised. In the presence of fungibility, the economic effect of the investment cannot be measured by its ex post rate of return. If the government would have undertaken the project that the Bank financed even in the absence of the loan, then the loan actually financed some other project – the one that would not otherwise have been undertaken. In that case, the economic effect of the loan was to fund the (unidentified) marginal investment project, whose rate of return might be much less satisfactory than that of the Bank-financed project. Although fungibility need not disturb a development bank, whose chief aim is to recover its loans, it should worry a multilateral aid agency funded by public capital, whose main objective is to promote the sound development of the borrower's economy. To be sure of doing that, projects need to be part of a comprehensive development plan, precisely in order to avoid the fungibility problem.

The move to policy-based lending after 1979

In the 1970s, the economies of developing countries experienced substantial economic shocks, favourable and unfavourable, arising from oil price increases, and the recycling of petro-dollars by commercial banks. The World Bank judged that the success of its individual loan projects, as measured by their ex post rates of return, was being affected negatively by the broader economic environment in which they had to operate (rising oil price, high inflation, fixed nominal exchange rates, import restrictions, and so on). In 1979, after a number of previously unsuccessful forays, the Bank initiated a new type of lending, called programme lending. This had previously been regarded as unsound banking, but the need for additional balance of payment finance was very pressing, and programme loans could be justified on the grounds that if successful they would render themselves redundant in future. The new types of loans, structural (SAL) and sectoral (SECAL) adjustment lending, provided rapidly disbursing foreign exchange on condition that the borrowing government undertook economic policy changes, either economy-wide or sectorally. This form of lending rose to be one-third of new lending, the other two-thirds remaining as project finance.

Programme lending with policy conditions attached provided the instrument that the Bank could bring to the task of co-managing the 1980s debt crisis with the Fund. At the same time it blurred the previous functional boundaries of the two organisations. The Bank took up economy-wide policy issues just as, through SAF and ESAF, the Fund moved into adjustment lending. This brought them into potential conflict. Various coordination problems arose from their overlap of functions, notably the incident in 1988 when the Bank (under US pressure) made a loan to Argentina, while the Fund refused its support. A Fund–Bank 'concordat' (1989) established effective (though not formal) cross-conditionality of Fund and Bank loans. Bank adjustment lending became conditional on a pre-existing Fund programme, and a statement of economic policy for the borrowing country had to be agreed by both institutions. In usual practice, they jointly drafted the Policy Framework Paper, and the country government agreed to it.

Evaluation of bank lending

The Bank, through its Operations Evaluation Department, evaluates the outcome of its projects. This is done on the simplifying assumption of ceteris paribus – nothing changes outside the project. Overall, the ex post rate of return on Bank projects has been 10 per cent, although this has been lower in recent years (despite the Bank's efforts to reform the overall economic environment!). This was certainly a good performance, given that developing countries provide a relatively risky environment for most forms of investment. Nevertheless, the need to continue Bank lending of the IBRD type has been questioned, both by appeal to the fungibility argument, and on the grounds that private flows to developing countries can do the job instead (Krueger, 1998). In 1970, IBRD net lending was about 10 per cent of net private flows. In 1996, this share had fallen to 0.7 per cent. In 25 years, private flows had increased 40-fold, while IBRD flows had increased three-fold in nominal terms. The original justification of IBRD loans in terms of imperfect private capital markets seems weak in the light of these figures, although private finance is very concentrated geographically and the Asian crisis showed how short term and volatile private money can be.

The evaluation of the effects of programme lending is more difficult and controversial. Governments of developing countries have been reluctant to comply with some of the conditions for policy change laid down in the loan agreements. This is often described as a result of their lack of ownership of the economic reform process. The Bank itself had to contend with internal incentives that made it unlikely that it would react to non-compliance consistently with a discontinuation of funding (Mosley et al., 1995). Thus, the evidence suggests that the Bank's loan conditionality, at least in its early forms, was a weak instrument for inducing policy change (Ferreira and Keely, 2000). More recently, the Bank has favoured a lending strategy of selectivity, in which loans are directed increasingly to countries that have already demonstrated their zeal for reform.

The Bank's contribution to the development dialogue

Apart from project and programme lending, the Bank undertakes many other activities. It conducts what is probably the largest single publication programme on development issues in the world. This includes its own research across the field of development problems, published in two house journals, flagship reports like the annual *World Development Report* and *Global Economic Prospects*, a host of monographs and a multitude of Working Papers. The Bank has also become a major provider of statistical data, including regular published series and data from household and firm surveys.

Complementing its publications are its other methods of disseminating its views on development. At the Economic Development Institute, the Bank maintains an in-house training facility for developing country economics professionals, many of whom return to work at the Bank. Policy advice is also provided separately from loan operations, something that the strategy of more selective lending is likely to increase

The Bank's justification for undertaking research and its dissemination in-house is that this gives it better control over the topics of research, and makes it more likely that the results will be used in its operations. Critics note that in-house research is less independent of management's desire to promulgate a particular perspective, which became compelling in the early 1980s, and that top-level editorial control will have the inevitable effect of dampening in-house intellectual creativity. Attempts to evaluate the quality of the Bank's research and publication activities have noted that their extensive influence on policy-makers and educators has not been matched by the extent of their intellectual comprehensiveness or innovation. One critic who previously worked at the Bank has criticised the series of *World Development Reports* for 'frequent changes in messages [and] the sloppy vagueness of [the] explanatory factors' cited for short- and medium-term economic growth (Easterly, 2009, p. 128).

What should be done to reform the World Bank?

The World Bank also began to get into political difficulties in the mid-1980s. US environmental NGOs attacked Bank-financed projects in Brazil for damaging the environment. They claimed the Bank's procedures for making environmental impact assessments of its projects were inadequate. The Bank gave in under pressure from the US Congress and Treasury and set up an Environment Department in 1987. Then in 1992, an independent review charged that the Bank had breached its own guidelines with respect to the resettlement of people displaced by the Narmada dams in India. During these controversies, US NGOs demonstrated their ability to harass the Bank by means of well-organised lobbying of the US Congress (Wade, 1997). The Bank put in place new measures of accountability, including an independent inspection panel to make public reports on contentious cases. The irony of this was that the NGOs themselves are, for the most part, not publicly accountable; and that the Bank became more accountable to US politicians, rather than to the politicians of its client countries (Woods, 2003, pp. 100–102).

Under the presidency of James Wolfensohn (1996–2004), the Bank proactively reached out to its NGO critics, shaping its policies to reflect their concerns. Wolfensohn pursued this political approach both in his public rhetoric and in a managerial style that placed him at odds with the bureaucratic culture of the institution. The invention of the Comprehensive Development Framework (CDF), a matrix for coordinating all the development activities of a country, led the Bank to adopt a central position in the development process. Through the CDF the Bank provides a diverse range of services (loans, technical assistance, advice) to the entire development community, branding itself as a development partner and facilitator, instead of as the home of arrogant bankers. At the same time, Bank lending has been increasingly diversified to support a new development agenda that would find favour with the US NGOs – gender equality, participation, civil society and good governance, in addition to environmental conservation (Miller-Adams, 1999).

The Bank has long suffered from multiple conflicting objectives – sound banking, promoting development and neo-liberal policy advocacy are just three of them. In this context, a populist approach of co-opting potential NGO critics of the Bank has its own dangers. Despite the declaration that poverty reduction is the Bank's paramount goal, overall focus on strategic priorities is blurred. The Bank is also failing to exploit fully the functions in which it has a genuine comparative advantage, and, by extending the responsibilities of its staff members into areas where they have relatively little competence, it is confusing and demoralising them. The Bank may well also be alienating the governments of developing countries, on whom it relies as customers for its loans.

The past trends stem from the dominance of the US in the political direction of the Bank. The need of the hour is for a broadening of the political leadership of the Bank to regain legitimacy and strategic focus. It happens that there is an almost perfect symmetry in the composition and status of the decision-making bodies of the Bank and the IMF. (This is because the Bretton Woods conference ended up adopting the respective IMF quotas to determine the subscriptions for members of the Bank.) It follows that certain reforms of the IMF (advocated above) are inextricably linked with counterpart reforms at the Bank. A realistic quota system at the Fund would have to be matched by an equally realistic subscription and voting system at the Bank. A more transparent political directorate at the Fund would have to be matched at the Bank. A merit-based appointment procedure for the top managers of the Fund would have to be matched by a similar procedure at the Bank. It is virtually inconceivable that one of the Bretton Woods twins could be radically reformed in these ways while the other remains as it is.

One further way to bring the Fund and the Bank together around a new agenda of catch-up growth is to revive the proposal of an organic aid–SDR link. The idea of the link fell into abeyance in the 1980s because of US reluctance to move forward with further creation of SDRs. It was argued for two decades that the development of private capital markets and the accumulation of reserves in emerging market economies provided sufficient liquidity. Financial crises provoked two further distributions of SDRs in 1997 and 2009, but both of these were on a universalistic basis. They were not directed to the funding of multilateral aid agencies, although they remain strapped for cash to pursue internationally agreed development assistance targets. Apart from the provision of necessary additional resources, funding of the World Bank and other multilateral development banks by this route would do much to counteract the current tendency to make them a hostage of NGO fashions and the wishes of the US Congress and Treasury Department.

A direct link between SDR creation and aid would be simple to operate. The Bank and other multilateral development agencies would have accounts with the IMF, into which the newly created SDRs would be paid. They would lend in the normal way, and when the loan recipient made purchases with the loan, the exporters from whom they purchased would be paid in SDRs out of the loan agency's IMF account. No doubt the old argument that this would be inflationary would then be heard again, but the scale of SDR creation remains very small relative to the GDP of the developed countries, and their anti-inflation policies are unlikely to be changed because of anything on this scale.

This new source of funding should be negotiated in return for a number of changes in the Bank's lending practices. The need for the Bank to continue project lending to middle-income developing countries (on IBRD terms) has been doubted, given the increased availability of private capital flows. Between 1970 and 1995, private flows to developing countries increased 40-fold, while IBRD flows increased three-fold in nominal terms, so the original post-1945 justification of this type of lending, in terms of the need for intermediation in imperfect private capital markets, became much weaker (Krueger, 1998). However, private finance flows are quite concentrated geographically on about a dozen countries and they also tend to flow in procyclically, so that they are there when they are least needed and absent when they would be most useful. Other justifications are that private flows do not reach the 'pockets of poverty' in middle-income countries; and that Bank intermediation has desirable risk-reduction benefits. Nevertheless, it would make sense to let the regional development banks complement private flows to the middle-income developing countries, and to focus World Bank loans and grants on low-income developing countries. Even in this niche, however, the Bank must refine its role further in relation to two striking twenty-first-century developments: the move to using grants rather than low-interest loans and the explosive growth of private philanthropy. In middle-income countries, the Bank could explore the option of floating bonds in local currencies to help to develop a market in long-term bonds, especially for financing infrastructure.

It has been suggested that the Bank could also play a role in relation to any new climate change agreement that involves financing new low carbon technology transfer to developing countries. The Bank could certainly take on some new responsibilities in this area – whether technical, administrative or fiduciary, but they would need to be carefully selected to avoid creating further conflicting objectives and internal conflicts of interest in the absence of adequate checks and balances.

Another proposal has also been discussed – the transformation of the Bank into a 'university of development', specialising in non-lending educational activities that can be justified as public goods, and subsidising their provision with income from the Bank's subscribed capital and accumulated reserves. Lending would continue in a selective mode to safe borrowers, but would cease to be the Bank's major function. The prospects for reinventing itself as a 'knowledge bank' depend on the extent to which its research and publication activities could continue in the same way if its lending were scaled down, and on the feasibility of introducing greater selectivity in lending, which as yet remains underexplored. In any case, such a transformation would require improved intellectual standards in its publications, if the Bank's critics are anywhere near right.

References

Bird, G. and D. Rowlands (2000), 'The catalyzing role of policy-based lending by the IMF and the World Bank: fact or fiction?', *Journal of International Development*, **12**(7), 951–74.

Boughton, J. (2009), 'The case for a universal financial institution', in J. Boughton and D. Lombardi (eds), *Finance, Development and the IMF*, Oxford: Oxford University Press, pp. 65–80.

Easterly, W. (2009), 'The indomitable in pursuit of the inexplicable', in S. Yusuf (ed.), *Development Economics through the Decades: A Critical Look at 30 Years of the World Development Report*, Washington DC, The World Bank, pp. 121–30.

Ferreira F. and L.C. Keely (2000), 'The World Bank and structural adjustment: lessons from the 1980s', in D. Vines and C. Gilbert (eds), *The World Bank: Structure and Policies*, Cambridge, CUP, pp. 159–95.

Fischer, S. (1997), *Capital Account Liberalization and the Role of the Fund*, Washington DC: International Monetary Fund.

Killick, T. (1985), *The Quest for Economic Stabilization: The IMF and the Third World*, Aldershot: Gower.

Killick, T. (1995), *IMF Programmes in Developing Countries: Design and Impact*, London: Routledge.

Krueger, A.O. (1998), 'Whither the World Bank and the IMF?', *Journal of Economic Literature*, **XXXVI**(4), 1983–2020.

Miller-Adams, M. (1999), *The World Bank: New Agendas in a Changing World*, London: Routledge.

Mosley, P., J. Harrigan and J. Toye (1995), *Aid and Power: the World Bank and Policy-based Lending Vol.1*, 2nd edition, London: Routledge.

Stiglitz, J. (2002), *Globalization and Its Discontents*, London: Allen Lane/Penguin Press.

Tett, G. (2009), *Fool's Gold*, London, Little, Brown Book Group.

Wade, R. (1997), 'The greening of the Bank: the struggle over the environment 1970–95', in D. Kapur, J. Lewis and R. Webb (eds), *The World Bank: Its First Half Century, Vol. II*, Washington DC: Brookings Institution, pp. 611–734.

Wass, D. (2008), *Decline to Fall: The Making of British Macro-economic Policy and the 1976 IMF Crisis*, Oxford: Oxford University Press.

Williamson, J. (1977), *The Failure of World Monetary Reform, 1971–74*, Sunbury-on-Thames: Thomas Nelson and Sons Ltd.

Woods, N. (2003), 'Order, justice, the IMF and the World Bank', in R. Foot, J. Gaddis and A. Hurrell (eds), *Order and Justice in International Relations*, Oxford: Oxford University Press, pp. 80–102.

23 A new 'Bretton Woods' system?

Mića Panić

Introduction

Every international financial and economic crisis since the 1970s has, sooner or later, led to calls for another 'Bretton Woods' Conference to create a global institutional framework that would prevent similar systemic failures in future. The present and, by far, the most serious of these crises has been no exception.

This immediately raises now, as in the past, three important questions. Are *new* global economic institutions really necessary? What would be their objectives? And how would they be achieved?

The first question is relatively easy to answer. The world has changed almost beyond recognition since that famous Conference at Bretton Woods, New Hampshire in July 1944. The need for the international community to observe certain rules of behaviour, essential if economically interdependent countries are to achieve their domestic policy objectives, has become even greater as a result of the profound changes that have taken place since World War II – many of them as a result of decisions made in 1944. That, in turn, has increased the need for supranational organisations that would promote international harmony of interests and cooperation by acting for the benefit of *all* their members.

These changes mean that, for reasons explored briefly in the next two sections, a new framework of global economic institutions would have to differ, both in its concept and practice, significantly from the one created at Bretton Woods.

The spirit of 'Bretton Woods'

It is impossible even to think of a comprehensive reappraisal of the 1944 initiatives without a clear notion of what the concept 'Bretton Woods' stands for. This is essential because, as I show elsewhere (Panić, 2003, Chapter 10), there was a significant difference between the Bretton Woods System as conceived by its architects and the way that it actually operated. This section highlights some of the key concerns and aims that inspired what is still the only successful attempt by a large number of countries to construct a new global economic order.

The process of industrialisation involves continuous specialisation – national and international – and, consequently, a progressive reduction in national economic self-sufficiency. This is true of all countries, though the reduction is normally more extensive in small than in large economies. As a result, the higher the level of industrialisation the greater is the dependence of national economies on the performance and policies of other nations, especially those with which they have close economic ties. The willingness of the international community to pursue compatible economic and social objectives and to collaborate in achieving them is, therefore, of critical importance.

This was demonstrated globally in the 1930s and 1940s at an exceptionally high human and social cost. It was that experience that led to the 1944 Conference and shaped the blueprint for a new world economic order that is associated with 'Bretton Woods'.

There was a significant increase between 1870 and 1913 in the proportion of exports in GDP in virtually all the countries for which we have relevant data. (cf. Maddison, 2001; Panić and Vacić, 1995). Increases in international capital flows were even greater (Bloomfield, 1963 and 1968).

The growth of the international economy and optimism about the existing economic order that it generated were reversed dramatically during the Great Depression in the 1930s, as all countries resorted to a variety of protective measures in order to minimise the economic and social cost of the Depression. That, as they were to discover, made it even more difficult to stage the strong, sustainable economic recovery required to lift them out of the slump.

Between 1929 and 1932 the volume of world exports declined by 27 per cent (Maddison, 1995, pp. 238–9). To make matters worse, the flow of international capital dried up in the 1930s and international immigration was reduced to less than 20 per cent of the average annual level between 1911 and 1930 (Panić, 1988, p. 172). In many industrial countries GDP did not recover to the level reached in 1929 until after World War II; and it was only in the early 1950s that peacetime unemployment in most industrialised countries fell back to the 1929 level (Maddison, 1991).

Those who lived through these events were convinced that the economic failure, social divisions and the rise of political extremism that led eventually to World War II were avoidable. What the world needed was a combination of national policies that would achieve and maintain satisfactory levels of economic security and social well-being, and an effective international institutional framework for dealing collectively with economic problems that affected all countries.

The result was a unique consensus that included countries at different levels of development and with different economic and political systems (see US Department of State 1948a, and 1948b). A radically new global economic order had to be created after the war to preserve world peace by preventing unemployment and poverty, social friction and political instability within countries; and that was possible only through active international cooperation spearheaded and supervised by supranational organisations. The cooperation was essential because 'world prosperity, like world peace, is indivisible' (US Department of State, 1948b, p. 1600).

It is this recognition by governments as diverse as those represented at the 1944 Conference that, in the words of the US Secretary of the Treasury Morgenthau, 'the wisest and the most effective way to protect our national interests is through international co-operation' (ibid., p. 1226) that has come to symbolise 'Bretton Woods'. Even more remarkably, they translated their conversion to internationalism into something that the world has failed to achieve before or since: an agreement in principle concerning the ends, the means, the policy instruments and the institutional framework that the new global economic order would require.

The ends were defined in strictly national terms. Those attending the Bretton Woods Conference never pretended that they were doing anything other than, as Morgenthau told them approvingly, acting 'in the particular national interests' that they were 'sent … to represent' (ibid., p. 1225). The 'interests' are reflected in the national objectives that they set out to achieve: a high level of employment and income, balanced economic development and sustainable balance on external trade. Together with price stability and an equitable distribution of income, they became the social welfare goals pursued by many governments, especially in industrial countries, after World War II (see Panić, 2011; Goodin et al,. 1999).

However, the interwar period had taught them an important lesson: to realise these goals they had to re-establish the old trading links. The main task of the two institutions set up at Bretton Woods was, therefore, to help restore *multilateral* international trade so that individual countries could achieve their national objectives (cf. US Department of State, 1948a, pp. 942 and 1016).

At the same time, it was recognised that there was a great difference in the ability of countries to reconcile their internal and external economic objectives. The degree of trade liberalisation and the period over which it was to be achieved would have to vary, therefore, if all of them were to benefit significantly from a more open international economic system. Consequently, there was no attempt at Bretton Woods, in the General Agreement on Tariffs and Trade (GATT) or in the policies pursued by the United States after 1948 to impose uniform institutional arrangements and an identical package of policies on all countries.

The IMF Articles of Agreement permitted countries to introduce 'restrictions on payments and transfers for current international transactions' if they could not balance their external account without such restrictions (Article XIV). For the same reason, GATT allowed member states to resort to restrictions on imports (General Agreement, Article XII). It also recognised the importance of 'infant industries' and gave a wide measure of discretion to developing countries to employ tariffs and quantitative controls: (a) to make it possible for them to establish such industries and (b) to enable them to have adequate foreign currency reserves to finance their trade in goods and services (Article XVIII). The United States adopted a similar attitude when providing external assistance to Western Europe in the early postwar period (Panić, 1992a).

There was, however, one 'impediment to trade' that they agreed to remove as soon as possible: exchange rate protection through the competitive currency devaluation. All the countries that signed the IMF Articles of Agreement undertook to adhere strictly to a regime of fixed exchange rates. But, as in the case of trade policy, this arrangement contained an important element of discretion: the rates were to be fixed but adjustable (see IMF Articles of Agreement in US Department of State, 1948a, pp. 942–84). A country experiencing 'fundamental disequilibrium' was permitted to devalue its currency. The concept was never defined officially though, given the primacy of the domestic policy goals that they had adopted, this could mean only one thing: that the country was incapable of balancing its external trade account 'in the long term at socially acceptable levels of unemployment and inflation' (Panić, 1988, p. 66). Countries that were able to reconcile internal and external balances risked provoking costly retaliation if they devalued their currency.

The advantage of a regime of fixed parities was that it would facilitate the revival of multilateral trade by removing exchange rate protection as well as exchange rate risks. That could be achieved only, experience had taught them, by maintaining exchange controls, because a regime of fixed exchange rates was incompatible with free flows of capital between countries. IMF Article VI.3 stated, therefore, that: 'Members may exercise such controls as are necessary to regulate international capital movements'. In other words, it was left to individual countries to decide whether the need to achieve and maintain important domestic objectives made it essential for them to maintain/impose controls on capital flows.

The necessity to continue with exchange controls (on capital movements other than those connected with current account transactions) meant that they had to find an alternative way of ensuring adequate provisions of short-term finance to enable individual countries to deal with temporary, unforeseen external deficits *without* resorting to deflationary policies and/or devaluation. This was essential if they were to avoid a return to the economic stagnation and 'beggar-my-neighbour' policies of the 1930s, destroying the new global order and spirit of internationalism that the Bretton Woods Conference was trying to create.

The same reasoning made it also essential to secure adequate international provisions of long-term capital to finance the reconstruction of advanced economies and the development of low-income countries. That would make it unnecessary for them to impose restrictions on trade in order to economise on their limited holdings of foreign exchange needed to finance domestic investment and development (see Panić, 1988, Part II).

The result was that most visible and enduring of Bretton Woods initiatives: the creation of supranational financial institutions to manage the new international order instead of relying, as in the past, on capital markets of the dominant economy to perform this role. There were important reasons for this, all based on what actually happened towards the end of the Classical Gold Standard and, even more so, during the 1930s and 1940s (cf. Kindleberger, 1973 and Panić, 1992b).

First, a dominant economy will pursue policies that are in *its* interest. There is no guarantee that the same policies will be in the interest of other countries. Second, the proportion of external trade in its total output may be so small that it will lack financial institutions with the experience to perform a global role. Third, even if this is not the case, the country's authorities may not be willing, unlike the British government and the Bank of England in the interwar period, to sacrifice the country's economic security and social well-being in the hope of sustaining the existing international financial system and the role of its powerful financial institutions within it. Finally, in a dynamic world economy no country is likely to retain its economic dominance for more than a relatively short period. Hence, the creation of a viable, lasting international trading and financial system requires a different, supranational solution.

The proposals tabled at the Bretton Woods Conference dealt, therefore, specifically with the establishment of supranational financial institutions (see US Department of State 1948a and 1948b). The International Monetary Fund was created to provide short-term finance and supervise the maintenance of fixed exchange rates. The International Bank for Reconstruction and Development (World Bank) was given the responsibility of providing the long-term capital that could not be raised from other sources.

There were also plans to set up a third supranational institution, the International Trade Organization (ITO), to facilitate and supervise extensive trade liberalisation. However, national concerns about its responsibilities and potential power ensured that the plans were soon abandoned (see MacBean and Snowden, 1981). Instead, the General Agreement on Trade and Tariffs (GATT) was created in 1948. Although it was given much more limited responsibilities than those planned for the ITO, it provided a useful forum for tariff bargaining and negotiations on trade liberalisation. It was superseded in 1995 by the World Trade Organization (WTO).

The old spirit in a new century

The Bretton Woods System may never have operated as planned, but the spirit that made it possible had a lasting influence on the institutions created and the policies pursued by national governments after World War II. Hence, it is the spirit – and US adherence to it while it managed the System – rather than the supranational institutional blueprint that made it possible to realise many of its objectives to an extent that its architects, like Keynes, could never have expected. In the process, new conditions have been created and new problems have emerged. Is the spirit still strong enough for the international community to translate it into the institutions and policies appropriate to the international environment at the beginning of the twenty-first century?

To answer this question, even in a brief and sketchy form, it is necessary to take into account the extent to which the Bretton Woods aims have been realised, whether they are still relevant, and how the existing framework of international organisations might be reformed to reflect the far-reaching changes that have taken place since the 1940s.

The starting point now, as in 1944, would have to be the ends – 'the primary objectives' of national economic policy. They determine the nature of economic institutions, national and international, and the policies that individual organisations pursue. Furthermore, the capacity of individual countries to implement successfully the policies needed to achieve their desired ends will influence the nature and extent of international cooperation.

The improvements in material standard of living achieved over the last 50 years in many countries are without historical parallel (cf. Maddison, 2001). But the progress has been unequal, increasingly so since the 1980s (Milanović, 2002). Poverty, homelessness and deprivation have not been eliminated even in the most advanced economies. They are widespread in large parts of the developing world, where over a billion people live in conditions of extreme poverty (cf. Collier, 2007). Moreover, there is a high level of dissatisfaction with their economic performance even in countries with the most advanced economies (see, for instance, Panić, 2011, Chapter 7). Persistently high unemployment, job insecurity and growing inequalities are among the main reasons for this. In addition, aspirations tend to grow with income, for reasons that I discuss elsewhere (Panić, 2003, Chapter 7).

Not surprisingly, surveys of global public opinion show with remarkable consistency the extent to which people everywhere support the Bretton Woods economic objectives of high levels of employment, economic development and a satisfactory level of income equitably shared (Taylor-Gooby, 1993; Goodin et al., 1999; Panić, 2011).

To help satisfy these aspirations a new Bretton Woods would have to solve two difficult, interrelated *political* problems.

First, the prevalence of autarky and extensive wartime controls and cooperation within countries made it possible in 1944 to assume that governments would be able to apply successfully whatever policies were needed to achieve national economic objectives. The unprecedented increase in international interdependence over the last 40 years has diminished national economic sovereignty even of the largest economies to such an extent that it would be impossible to build a new global order starting from the premise that national economies are largely insulated from external influence. The change requires, therefore, a completely new, much more complex approach to international economic cooperation (see Panić, 2011).

The second problem stems directly from the first and raises questions of fundamental importance for the optimum level of economic openness and interdependence. As recognised explicitly at the 1944 Conference, countries at different levels of development, or with different institutions, can realise the same objectives only if they follow *different*, but compatible, policies – appropriate to their particular circumstances, problems and priorities. To impose the same policy package on *all* of them in these conditions – rather than to let them develop their own programme of action – is to condemn, as the African experience shows (Devarajan et al., 2001), a large proportion of the world's population to poverty, social frictions and armed conflicts (see also Panić, 2011, Chapter 9). The twentieth century demonstrated more than once that an integrated international system was unsustainable under these conditions.

Trade liberalisation since the 1970s illustrates the danger inherent in such a system. Restoration of multilateral international trade, intended by the Bretton Woods blueprint to be one of the means to a general improvement in social welfare of *all* nations, has become a major obstacle to economic progress in many developing countries.

GATT negotiations over the years have reduced tariffs and quotas to, probably, their lowest level since the beginning of the Industrial Revolution. The task of the WTO is to oversee and accelerate this process further (see Hoekman and Kostecki, 1995, 2001; Krueger, 1998). The extent of trade liberalisation achieved so far might have been a remarkable realisation of one of the key Bretton Woods intentions. However, contrary to the intention, the quest for *freer* trade has degenerated over the last three decades in particular into a rapid, indiscriminate, across-the-board pursuit of 'free trade' in those industries in which OECD countries, especially the United States, dominate.

Even the classical economists warned of economic and social costs that could result from premature trade liberalisation (Panić, 1988, Chapter 7). The pace of liberalisation, both Adam Smith and Ricardo cautioned, should reflect the ability of a country to adjust. Ceteris paribus, this depends, for reasons given by John Stuart Mill, on its relative level of development – which is particularly relevant now. Oligopolistic competition, economies of scale, capital intensity of production, unequal endowment in human capital and capacity for technical change give the established firms in advanced economies an advantage that few developing countries can challenge without protecting their 'infant' industries (Panić, 2011; Krugman, 1986). Nevertheless, although it has been recognised since the beginning of the Industrial Revolution that a country's trade policy should reflect its level of development – as a result of policies pursued by major industrial countries and international trade and financial organisation – many developing countries have been forced to liberalise their trade and capital flows to an extent that prevents rather than assists their attempts to escape from the underdevelopment/poverty trap (cf. Thirlwall and Pacheco-Lopez, 2008).

One of the consequences of what is, effectively, unequal 'reciprocity' in trade agreements is that they make it difficult for developing countries to pursue an 'outward-looking growth strategy' (as urged by international donors) based on exports of primary commodities and labour-intensive manufactures in which they have comparative advantage. The reason is that agriculture and labour-intensive products, such as textiles and clothing, are precisely the sectors that industrial countries have been able to protect under the various international trade agreements. In addition, they have often used anti-dumping rules to make it difficult for developing countries to exploit the one advantage that they have in trade in manufactures: low costs and prices.

A new system of global economic institutions would, clearly, have to be based on a fundamental reform of the existing international trade rules and policies. That would require the constitution, modus operandi and governance of the WTO to be changed radically. Trade policies and 'transition periods' would differ according to a country's level of development and capacity for adjustment. Equally important, trade agreements would require all the participating countries to observe at least the minimum internationally agreed labour (health, safety, working conditions, hours of work, retirement provisions, membership of unions, use of child labour) and environmental (exploitation of all natural resources – especially land and drinking water, pollution and climate stability) standards.

In the absence of clearly defined standards, supervision and sanctions, trade liberalisation is synonymous with 'fair trade', beneficial to all those who participate in it, only in economics textbooks. Unequal labour and environmental standards and practices give unscrupulous producers an important competitive advantage by allowing them to pass important and, often irreversible, social costs to the communities in which they operate. To survive, the competitors have no alternative but to do the same – making the whole system unsustainable.

Hence, to ensure that the new trading agreements are fully observed, the WTO would have to monitor the actions not only of governments but also of transnational enterprises, the driving force behind the process of globalisation (see Panić, 2011). The monitoring would also have to include their small and medium-size suppliers, as this is where some of the worst violations of the basic labour and environmental standards are to be found.

Widespread disregard of these standards and basic human rights explains why, as Samuelson (1939, p. 203; italics in original) concluded after examining possible gains from trade: 'If self-sufficiency is not an end in itself … trade is always preferable to no trade, although it is not necessarily true that *free* trade is the best policy'. Despite claims to the contrary, it cannot be demonstrated 'rigorously that *free* trade is better (in some sense) for a country than *all* other kinds of trade' (ibid., p. 195; italics in original).

For all these reasons, a new and more equitable approach to international trade would also make it necessary to revise, even alter completely, many of the existing agreements. Whether a particular trade regime is superior or inferior to all possible alternatives depends on the socioeconomic conditions under which it operates.

Compared with trade, the architects of a new global financial system would have to adopt a completely different approach to exchange rate protection and international capital movements from the one adopted in 1944.

A regime of fixed exchange rates is impossible to resurrect in the conditions of massive capital flows common since the 1980s; and a return to extensive controls on cross-border capital flows would be difficult to enforce effectively. The choice is, therefore, between managed flexibility of currencies and the creation of a global monetary union with a single currency. As the latter belongs to a distant future, a continuation of the regime of managed floating is unavoidable. Moreover, it is also less of a threat to multilateral trade now than in the 1940s. One of the lessons of the 1970s and 1980s is that competitive devaluations or depreciations are ineffective, even counterproductive, in conditions of economic interdependence (IMF, 1984; Goldstein and Kahn, 1985; Panić, 2011, Chapter 5). This means that, unlike in 1944, it is now the scale of global capital movements and the crises that they generate that require special attention. Strict capital controls cannot be implemented effectively for long in dynamic capitalist economies, especially when they are dominated by *transnational* enterprises. The result is financial crises (Kindleberger, 1978; Reinhart and Rogoff, 2008) – too serious to be prevented by measures like the Tobin tax on cross-border capital flows (Tobin, 1982).

An effective system of regulation and supervision becomes, therefore, essential (Panić, 2011, Chapter 7). As no regulatory framework can eliminate the crises completely, the main purpose of such a system is to reduce their scale and frequency. However, even this more modest aim can succeed only if there is active control and cooperation at the three levels: within financial institutions, national and international.

The main concern of a new international financial framework would be the last of these. There would have to be an international organisation within which the international community would set the standards for dealing with common problems, monitor that all its members observe them, and organise technical assistance to enable developing countries to implement effective regulatory frameworks. Equally important, the institution would not be allowed to pursue a dogmatic policy towards financial deregulation and liberalisation. The sterling crisis in 1947 and the Asian crisis in 1997 demonstrated how highly destabilising the two could be if a country is forced to adopt them before it is ready. Hence, as under the original Bretton Woods agreement, no country would be required to introduce such policy changes if they threatened its social welfare. Given its experience in this field (cf. Basle Committee on Banking Supervision 1997, 1999), a reconstituted Bank for International Settlements (BIS) would be the obvious institution to coordinate international regulation and supervision of financial institutions.

However, it is those two flagships of the 1944 System, the IMF and the World Bank, that would present reformers of the international financial system with their greatest challenge.

The role of the two institutions has changed in many ways since the 1940s (James, 1996; Nayyar, 2002). The problem is that these changes are widely seen as betraying the principles of 'Bretton Woods'. Both have been accused for some time now of acting in the interest of powerful financial and commercial interests in industrial countries by promoting dogmatically the ideology of neoliberalism to the detriment of economic progress in developing countries (Payer, 1974; Korten, 1996; Chwieroth, 2009). The high economic and social cost of the policies imposed by the two organisations on many developing and transition economies – notably on those at the centre of the Asian financial crisis in the 1990s – has also raised serious doubts about their ability to contribute to global public goods (Lavigne, 1999; Nayyar, 2002; Stiglitz, 2002).

The letter written at the beginning of July 2002 by 100 members of the Indonesian Parliament to the Heads of the IMF and World Bank is a devastating criticism of their contribution to the collapse of the country's economy and its social consequences. It also adds a question of fundamental importance to those already raised: are these organisations intended to be the servants of the international community or its masters? (The letter is reported in *Bretton Woods Update* July/August, 2002.) This has inevitably created a good deal of hostility towards both these two and other international organisations without which a highly integrated global economic system cannot function for long.

The need for international economic institutions to help achieve global public goods is as great now as it was 70 years ago (see Kaul et al., 1999 for a discussion of global public goods). The growth of transnationals and the liberalisation of international capital flows have reduced the risk, which concerned Keynes and his contemporaries, that a shortage of international liquidity could plunge the world into another round of protectionism, depression and war. The problem is that all countries do not have equal access to the private funds available on international financial markets. Most developing countries still rely heavily on the kind of assistance that the IMF and World Bank were created to provide. A reformed international economic order would have to ensure that they receive it on conditions consistent with the original Bretton Woods intentions.

This would require specific measures to prevent the potential misuse of authority and resources at the disposal of the two organisations. These could range from avoiding overlap in their responsibilities to changes in their accountability, governance and restrictions on 'conditionality' that they impose on the borrowers, to ensure that it is not a threat to global economic and social progress. Each would be required to establish branches in different parts of the world, making it better informed about local conditions, needs and resources. Neither would be allowed to impose the neoliberal or any other ideology on the borrowing countries. Given that resources are limited, strict auditing would be needed to prevent them from lending, as they have done in the past, to corrupt governments as an inducement to support the policies of the United States or other major industrial countries (See Alesina and Dollar, 1998; Devarajan *et al.* 2001; Barro and Lee, 2002).

Finally, it is clear even from the sketchy analysis in this section that a new Bretton Woods would have to broaden the original institutional framework. Bringing the BIS within it would help the stabilisation effort. Involving more closely the International Labour Organization (ILO) – with its long experience in the promotion and supervision, on a tripartite basis, of international labour standards (cf. ILO 2004a, 2004b and 2010) – would help achieve a more equitable distribution of global wealth, the most important precondition for global cooperation and sustainability of globalisation.

Equally essential is the need for a global environmental agency – something along the lines of the World Environment Organisation suggested by Simonis (2002). Given the effect of industrialisation on the environment so far, a long-term global strategy for economic and social progress that does not take into account its impact on the environment is unlikely to be sustainable for long in the twenty-first century (cf. Stern, 2006; UNEP, 2007).

To avoid costly duplications of effort or conflicts of interest, the international community would have to define clearly the interrelationship between the six core economic organisations considered briefly in this section, and their relations with other important international institutions (especially the United Nations) whose responsibilities tend to overlap in many areas with theirs.

Conclusion

Whatever the original intentions, the performance of supranational or any other institutions depends on those who exercise effective control over them. Hence, in the absence of a global government, the failure of the Bretton Woods institutions to act in accordance with the principles that led to their creation stems not so much from the institutions themselves as from the attitude and policies of the governments of their dominant members. Members of the Indonesian Parliament should, therefore, have addressed their letter to the heads of these governments rather than to those of the IMF and World Bank!

Given the extent of global economic interdependence at the beginning of the twenty-first century, it is increasingly apparent that the world urgently needs a new international institutional framework capable of helping individual countries solve their most pressing economic problems under these conditions. The objective of achieving global public goods through improvements in national economic security and social well-being is as relevant now as it was in the 1940s. However, without the spirit of 'Bretton Woods' – the absence of which is equally obvious at present – it would be virtually impossible to convene another 'Bretton Woods' Conference, let alone to agree on a common course of action and implement it. Much more likely, the realities of interdependence may force an increasing number of countries to organise regional 'Bretton Woods' systems or, following the example of Western Europe, create economic and monetary unions.

Globally, however, the most that one can hope for at present is an improvement in the work of the existing institutions along at least *some* of the lines suggested in this chapter. Unfortunately, the attitude and actions of the world's largest economies in particular, especially since the 1980s, make even the objective of such modest improvements look positively utopian.

References

Alesina, A. and Dollar, D. (1998), 'Who gives foreign aid to whom and why?', *NBER Working Paper No. 6612*, Cambridge, MA: NBER.

Barro, R.J. and Lee, J.W. (2002), 'IMF programs: who is chosen and what are the effects?', *NBER Working Paper*, Cambridge, MA: NBER.

Basle Committee on Banking Supervision (1997), *Core Principles for Effective Banking Supervision*, Basle: Bank for International Settlements.

Basle Committee on Banking Supervision (1999), *A New Capital Adequacy Framework – Consultative Paper*, Basle: Bank for International Settlements.

Bloomfield, A.I. (1963), 'Short-term capital movements under the pre-1914 gold standard', *Princeton Studies in International Finance*, Princeton: Princeton University Press.

Bloomfield, A.I. (1968), 'Patterns of fluctuations in international investment before 1914', *Princeton Studies in International Finance*, Princeton: Princeton University.

Bretton Woods Update (2002), No. 29, July/August, available at http://www.brettonwoodsproject.org/art-15979; accessed 20 October 2010.

Chwieroth, J.M. (2009), *Capital Ideas: The IMF and the Rise of Financial Liberalisation*, Princeton: Princeton University Press.

Collier, P. (2007), *The Bottom Billion*, Oxford: Oxford University Press.

Devarajan, S., Dollar, D.R. and Holmgren, T. (eds) (2001), *Aid and Reform in Africa*, Washington, DC: The World Bank.

Goldstein, M. and Kahn, M.S. (1985), 'Income and price effects in foreign trade', in R.W. Jones and P.B. Kenen (eds), *Handbook of International Economics*, vol. II, Amsterdam: Elsevier.

Goodin, R.E., Heady, B., Muffels, R. and Dirven, H.J. (1999), *The Real Worlds of Welfare Capitalism*, Cambridge: Cambridge University Press.

Hoekman, B.M. and Kostecki, M.M. (1995), *The Political Economy of the World Trading System – From GATT to WTO*, Oxford and New York: Oxford University Press.

Hoekman, B.M. and Kostecki, M.M. (2001), *The Political Economy of the World Trading System – The WTO and Beyond*, Oxford and New York: Oxford University Press.

ILO (2004a), *Economic Security for a Better World*, Geneva: ILO.

ILO (2004b), *Fair Globalisation: Creating Opportunities for All*, Geneva: ILO.

ILO (2010), *Labour Law and Workers' Protection in Developing Countries*, Geneva: ILO.

IMF (1984), 'Exchange rate volatility and world trade', *Occasional Paper No. 28*, Washington, DC.

James, H. (1996), *International Monetary Cooperation since Bretton Woods*, Washington, DC: International Monetary Fund.

Kaul, I., Grunberg, I. and Stern, M.A. (1999), *Global Public Goods – International Cooperation in the 21st Century*, Oxford and New York: Oxford University Press.
Kindleberger, C.P. (1973), *The World in Depression, 1929–1939*, London: Allan Lane.
Kindleberger, C.P. (1978), *Manias, Panics and Crashes: A History of Financial Crises*, New York: Basic Books.
Korten, D.C. (1996), *When Corporations Rule the World*, London: Earthscan Publications.
Krueger, A.O. (ed.) (1998), *The WTO as an International Organization*, Chicago: Chicago University Press.
Krugman, P.R. (ed.) (1986), *Strategic Trade Policy and the New International Economics*, Cambridge, MA: MIT Press.
Lavigne M. (1999), *The Economics of Transition – From Socialist to Market Economy*, London: Macmillan.
MacBean, A.I. and Snowden, P.N. (1981), *International Institutions in Trade and Finance*, London: George Allen & Unwin.
Maddison, A. (1991), *Dynamic Forces in Capitalist Development – A Long-run Comparative View*, Oxford and New York: Oxford University Press.
Maddison, A. (1995), *Monitoring the World Economy 1820–1992*, Paris: OECD.
Maddison, A. (2001), *The World Economy – A Millennial Perspective*, Paris: OECD.
Milanović, B. (2002), 'True world income distribution, 1988 and 1993: first calculations based on household surveys alone', *Economic Journal*, **112**(476).
Nayyar, D. (ed.) (2002), *Governing Globalization – Issues and Institutions*, Oxford: Oxford University Press.
Panić, M. (1988), *National Management of the International Economy*, London and New York: Macmillan/St. Martin's Press.
Panić, M. (1992a), 'Managing reforms in the East European countries: lessons from the postwar experience of Western Europe', *UN/ECE Discussion Paper No. 3*, New York: United Nations.
Panić, M. (1992b), *European Monetary Union – Lessons from the Classical Gold Standard*, London and New York: Macmillan/St. Martin's Press.
Panić, M. (2003), *Globalization and National Economic Welfare*, London and New York: Palgrave Macmillan.
Panić, M. (2011), *Globalisation: A Threat to International Cooperation and Peace?*, London and New York: Palgrave Macmillan.
Panić, M. and Vacić, A. (1995), 'International economic integration and disintegration: an overview', in M. Panić and A. Vacić (eds), *Economic Integration in Europe and North America*, Geneva and New York: United Nations.
Payer, C. (1974), *The Debt Trap – The International Monetary Fund and the Third World*, New York: Monthly Review Press.
Reinhart, C. and Rogoff, K. (2008), 'This time is different: a panoramic view of eight centuries of financial crises', *NBER Paper No. 13882*, March.
Samuelson, P.A. (1939), 'The gains from international trade', *Canadian Journal of Economics and Political Science*, **29**(2) May.
Simonis, U.E. (2002), 'Advancing the debate on a World Environment Organisation', *The Environmentalist*, **22**(1).
Stern, N. (2006), *Stern Review on the Economics of Climate Change*, Cambridge: Cambridge University Press.
Stiglitz, J.E. (2002), *Globalization and Its Discontents*, New York and London: Norton.
Taylor-Gooby, P. (1993), 'What citizens want from the state', *International Social Attitudes – the Tenth BSA Report*, Aldershot, UK: Dartmouth Publishing Co.
Thirlwall, A.P. and Pacheco-Lopez, P. (2008), *Trade Liberalisation and the Poverty of Nations*, Cheltenham, UK and Northampton, USA: Edward Elgar.
Tobin, J. (1982), 'A proposal for international monetary reform', in his *Essays in Economic Theory and Policy*, Cambridge, MA: MIT Press.
UNEP (2007), *Global Environmental Outlook 4*, New York: United Nations.
US Department of State (1948a), *Proceedings and Documents of United Nations Monetary and Financial Conference – Bretton Woods, New Hampshire July 1–22, 1944*, vol. I, Washington, DC: US Government Printing Office.

US Department of State (1948b), *Proceedings and Documents of United Nations Monetary and Financial Conference – Bretton Woods, New Hampshire July 1–22, 1944*, vol. II, Washington, DC: US Government Printing Office.

PART VIII

POLICY IMPLICATIONS AND RESPONSES

24 Kicking away the ladder – globalisation and economic development in historical perspective*

Ha-Joon Chang

1 Introduction

To most of those who govern the global economy today – the developed country policy-makers, international business leaders, and the international economic organisations (the IMF, the World Bank, and the WTO) – the solution to the problem of economic development is obvious. What the developing countries need, they argue, is the 'good' economic policies and institutions that the developed countries themselves used in order to develop – such as liberalisation of trade and investment and strong patent law. Their belief in their own recommendation is so absolute that in their view it has to be imposed on the developing countries at all costs, through strong bilateral and multilateral external pressures.

As is well known, there have been heated debates on whether these policies and institutions are suitable to the developing countries. However, the curious thing is that even those who are sceptical of their suitability rarely question whether these are the policies and the institutions that the developed countries actually used in order to become rich.

The historical fact is, though, that the rich countries did not develop on the basis of the policies and the institutions that they now recommend to, and often force upon, the developing countries. In this chapter, I will establish this fact and draw from it some implications for today's debates on globalisation and economic development. But before doing so, let me first critically examine what I call the 'official history of capitalism' which informs these debates.

2 The official history of capitalism

According to the 'official history of capitalism', the world economy has developed in the following way over the last few centuries.

From the eighteenth century, Britain proved the superiority of free-market and free-trade policies by beating interventionist France, its main competitor at the time, and establishing itself as the supreme world economic power. In particular, once it had abandoned its deplorable agricultural protection (the Corn Law) and other remnants of old mercantilist protectionist measures in 1846, it was able to play the role of the architect and the hegemon of a new 'liberal' world economic order. This liberal world order, perfected around 1870, was based on: *laissez faire* industrial policies at home; low barriers to the international flows of goods, capital and labour; and macroeconomic stability, both nationally and internationally, guaranteed by the Gold Standard and the principle of balanced budgets. A period of unprecedented prosperity followed.

Unfortunately, according to this story, things started to go wrong with World War I. In response to the ensuing instability of the world economic and political system, countries started to erect trade barriers again. In 1930, the USA abandoned free trade and raised tariffs with the infamous Smoot–Hawley tariff, which the famous free-trade economist Jagdish Bhagwati called 'the most visible and dramatic act of anti-trade folly' (Bhagwati, 1985, p. 22, fn. 10). The world free trade system finally ended in 1932, when Britain, hitherto the champion of free trade, succumbed to the temptation and re-introduced tariffs. The resulting contraction and instability in the world economy and then finally World War II destroyed the last remnants of the first liberal world order.

After World War II, so the story goes, some significant progress was made in trade liberalisation through the early GATT (General Agreement on Trade and Tariffs) talks. However, unfortunately, *dirigiste* approaches to economic management dominated the policy-making scene until the 1970s in the developed world, and until the early 1980s in the developing world (and the Communist world until its collapse in 1989).

Fortunately, it is said, interventionist policies have been largely abandoned across the world since the 1980s with the rise of neo-liberalism, which emphasises the virtues of small government, *laissez faire* policies, and international openness. Especially in the developing world, by the late 1970s economic growth had begun to falter in most countries outside East and South-east Asia, which were already pursuing 'good' policies (of free market and free trade). This growth failure, which often manifested itself in economic crises of the early 1980s, exposed the limitations of old-style interventionism and protectionism. As a result, most developing countries have come to embrace 'policy reform' in a neo-liberal direction.

When combined with the establishment of new global governance institutions represented by the WTO, these policy changes at the national level have created a new global economic system, comparable in its (at least potential) prosperity only to the earlier 'golden age' of liberalism (1870–1914).

As we shall see later, this story paints a fundamentally misleading picture, but a no less powerful one for it. And it should be accepted that there are also some senses in which the late nineteenth century can indeed be described as an era of *laissez faire*.

To begin with, there was a period in the late-nineteenth century, albeit a brief one, when liberal trade regimes prevailed in large parts of the world economy. Between 1860 and 1880, many European countries reduced tariff protection substantially. At the same time, most of the rest of the world was forced to practise free trade through colonialism and through unequal treaties in the cases of a few nominally 'independent' countries – such as the Latin American countries, China, Thailand (then Siam), Iran (then Persia), and Turkey (then the Ottoman Empire), and even Japan (until 1911). Of course, the obvious exception to this was the USA, which maintained a very high tariff barrier even during this period (see below). However, given that the USA was still a relatively small part of the world economy, it may not be totally unreasonable to say that this is as close to free trade as the world has ever got (or probably ever will).

More importantly, the scope of state intervention before World War II (or at least before World War I) was quite limited by modern standards mainly for institutional reasons – such as the absence of income tax, the absence of the central bank, and the Gold Standard.

Despite these limitations, as we shall see in the next section, virtually all now-developed countries (NDCs) actively used interventionist industrial, trade and technology (ITT) policies which are aimed at promoting infant industries during their catch-up periods.

3 History of industrial, trade and technology policies: widespread use of tariffs and subsidies

Almost all of today's rich countries used tariffs and subsidies to develop their industries in the earlier stage of their development. It is particularly important to note that Britain and the USA, the two countries that are supposed to have reached the summit of the world economy through free-market, free-trade policy, are actually the ones that most aggressively used protection and subsidies.

Contrary to the popular myth, Britain was an aggressive user, and in certain areas a pioneer, of activist policies intended to promote its industries. Such policies, although limited in scope, date back from the fourteenth century (Edward III) and the fifteenth century (Henry VII) in relation to woollen manufacturing, the leading industry of the time. At the time, England was an exporter of raw wool to the Low Countries, and various English monarchs tried to change this by protecting domestic woollen textile producers, taxing raw wool exports, and poaching skilled workers from the Low Countries.

Particularly between the trade policy reform of its first Prime Minister Robert Walpole in 1721 and its adoption of free trade around 1860, Britain used very *dirigiste* trade and industrial policies, involving measures very similar to those that countries like Japan and Korea later used in order to develop their economies. During this period, it protected its industries a lot more heavily than did France, the supposed *dirigiste* counterpoint to its free-trade, free-market system (Nye, 1991). Germany, another country frequently associated with state interventionism, had much lower tariffs than Britain during this period, although the German states tended to use other means of economic intervention more actively.

Given this history, argued Friedrich List, the leading German economist of the mid-nineteenth century, Britain preaching free trade to less advanced countries like Germany and the USA was like someone trying to 'kick away the ladder' with which he had climbed to the top. He is worth quoting at length on this point.

> It is a very common clever device that when anyone has attained the summit of greatness, he *kicks away the ladder* by which he has climbed up, in order to deprive others of the means of climbing up after him. In this lies the secret of the cosmopolitical doctrine of Adam Smith, and of the cosmopolitical tendencies of his great contemporary William Pitt, and of all his successors in the British Government administrations.
>
> Any nation which by means of protective duties and restrictions on navigation has raised her manufacturing power and her navigation to such a degree of development that no other nation can sustain free competition with her, can do nothing wiser than *to throw away these ladders* of her greatness, to preach to other nations the benefits of free trade, and to declare in penitent tones that she has hitherto wandered in the paths of error, and has now for the first time succeeded in discovering the truth (List, 1885, pp. 295–6, italics added).

The USA, today's supposed champion of free trade, was even more protectionist than Britain throughout most of its history before World War II. According to the authoritative study by Paul Bairoch (1993), between the Civil War and World War II, it was literally the most heavily protected economy in the world. Indeed, even the Smoot–Hawley Tariff of 1930, which Bhagwati in the above quote portrays as a radical departure from its free-trade tradition, only marginally (if at all) increased the degree of protectionism in the US economy. The average tariff rate for manufactured goods that resulted from this bill was 48 per cent, and it still falls within the range of the average rates that had prevailed in the USA since the Civil War (40–50 per cent), albeit in the upper region of this range.

In this context, it is also important to note that the American Civil War was fought on the issue of tariffs as much as, if not more than, on the issue of slavery. Of the two major issues that divided the North and the South, the South had actually more to fear on the tariff front than on the slavery front. Abraham Lincoln was a well-known protectionist who had cut his political teeth under the charismatic politician Henry Clay in the Whig Party, which advocated the 'American System' based on infrastructural development and protectionism (thus named on recognition that free trade was in 'British' interests). On the other hand, Lincoln thought the blacks were racially inferior and slave emancipation was an idealistic proposal with no prospect of immediate implementation – he is said to have emancipated the slaves in 1862 as a strategic move to win the War rather than out of some moral conviction.

The USA was also the intellectual home of protectionism throughout the nineteenth century. It was in fact American thinkers like Alexander Hamilton, the first Treasury Secretary of the USA, and the now-forgotten economist Daniel Raymond, who first systematically developed the so-called 'infant industry' argument which justifies the protection of manufacturing industries in the less developed economies. Indeed, List, who is commonly known as the father of the infant industry argument, started out as a free-trader and learnt about the Hamiltonian infant industry argument during his exile in the USA during the 1820s.

In heavily protecting their industries, the Americans were going directly against the advice of such prominent economists as Adam Smith and Jean Baptiste Say, who saw their country's future in agriculture. However, they knew exactly what the game was. They knew that Britain had reached the top through protection and subsidies and therefore that they needed to do the same if they were going to get anywhere. Criticising the British preaching of free trade to his country, Ulysses Grant, the Civil War hero and the US President between 1868–1876, retorted that 'within 200 years, when America has gotten out of protection all that it can offer, it too will adopt free trade'. When his country later reached the top after World War II, it too started 'kicking away the ladder' by preaching and forcing free trade on the less-developed countries.

The UK and the USA may be the more extreme examples, but almost all the rest of today's developed countries used tariffs, subsidies and other means to promote their industries in the earlier stages of their development. Cases like Germany, Japan and Korea are well known in this respect. But even countries like Sweden, which later came to represent the 'small open economy' to many economists, also strategically used tariffs, subsidies, cartels and state support for R&D to develop key industries, especially textile, steel and engineering.

There were some exceptions like the Netherlands and Switzerland that have maintained free trade since the late eighteenth century. However, these were countries that were already on the frontier of technological development by the eighteenth century and therefore did not need much protection. Also, it should be noted that the Netherlands had deployed an impressive range of interventionist measures up till the seventeenth century in order to build up its maritime and commercial supremacy. Moreover, Switzerland did not have a patent law until 1907. More interestingly, the Netherlands abolished its 1817 patent law in 1869 on the grounds that patents were politically created monopolies inconsistent with its free-market principles – a position that seems to elude most of today's free-market economists – and did not introduce a patent law again until 1912.

4 History of institutional development: the long and winding road

The story is similar in relation to institutional development. Contrary to what is assumed by today's development orthodoxy, most of the institutions that are regarded as prerequisites for economic development emerged after, and not before, a significant degree of economic development in the now-developed countries. Without claiming to be exhaustive, let us examine the six categories of institutions that are widely believed to be prerequisites of development: democracy, bureaucracy, intellectual property rights, institutions of corporate governance, financial institutions (including public finance institutions), and welfare and labour institutions.

Whatever one's position is on the relationship between democracy and economic growth in today's world, it is indisputable that today's developed countries did not develop under democracy. Until the 1920s even universal male suffrage was a rarity. It was not until the late twentieth century that all developed countries became truly democratic. Spain and Portugal were dictatorships until the 1970s, votes were given to all ethnic minorities in Australia and the USA only in 1962 and 1965 respectively, and women in many countries were given the suffrage only after World War II, and in Switzerland as late as 1971. Until World War II, even when democracy formally existed, its quality was extremely poor. Secret balloting was introduced only in the early twentieth century even in France and Germany, and corrupt electoral practices, such as vote buying, electoral fraud and legislative corruption, lasted in most of today's developed countries well into the twentieth century.

In terms of bureaucracy, sales of offices, spoils system and nepotism abounded in most countries until the early twentieth century. Modern professional bureaucracy first emerged in Prussia in the early nineteenth century, but much later in other countries – even Britain got a modern bureaucracy only in the mid-nineteenth century. Until the Pendleton Act in 1883, none of the US federal bureaucrats were competitively recruited, and even at the end of the nineteenth century, less than half of them were competitively recruited.

A similar story emerges in terms of intellectual property rights institutions, which have become a key issue following the recent controversy surrounding the TRIPS (trade-related aspects of intellectual property rights) agreement in the WTO. Until the late nineteenth century, many countries allowed patenting of imported inventions. As mentioned earlier, Switzerland and the Netherlands refused to protect patents until the early twentieth century. The US did not recognise foreign citizens' copyrights until 1891. And throughout the nineteenth century, there was a widespread violation of British trademark laws by the German firms producing fake 'Made in England' goods.

Even in the most developed countries (the UK and the USA), many key institutions of what is these days regarded as a 'modern corporate governance' system emerged after, rather than before, their industrial development. Until the

1870s, in most countries limited liability, without which there would be no modern corporations based on joint stock ownership, was something that was granted as a privilege to high-risk projects with good government connections (for example, the British East India Company), and not as a standard provision. Until the 1930s, there was virtually no regulation on company audit and information disclosure. Until the late nineteenth century, bankruptcy laws were geared towards punishing the bankrupt businessmen (with debtors' prison being a key element in this) rather than giving them a second chance. Competition law did not really exist in any country until the 1914 Clayton Act in the USA.

As for financial institutions, it would be fair to say that modern financial systems with widespread and well-supervised banking, a central bank, and a well-regulated securities market did not come into being even in the most developed countries until the mid-twentieth century (Kindleberger, 1984). In particular, until the early twentieth century, countries such as Sweden, Germany, Italy, Switzerland and the US lacked a central bank.

A similar story applies to public finance. The fiscal capacity of the state remained highly inadequate in most now-developed countries until the mid-twentieth century, when most of them did not have income tax. Even in Britain, which introduced the first permanent income tax in 1842, William Gladstone was fighting his 1874 election campaign with a pledge to abolish income tax. With limited taxation capability, local government finance in particular was in a mess. A most telling example is an episode documented in Cochran and Miller (1942, p. 48), where the British financiers put pressure in vain on the US federal government to assume the liabilities of a number of US state governments after their defaults on British loans in 1842 – a story that reminds us of the events in Brazil following the default of the state of Minas Gerais in 1999.

Social welfare institutions (for example, industrial accident insurance, health insurance, state pensions, unemployment insurance) did not emerge until the last few decades of the nineteenth century, although once introduced they diffused quite quickly. Germany was a pioneer in this respect. Child labour regulations started emerging in the late eighteenth century, but until the early twentieth century, most of these regulations were extremely mild and poorly enforced. Until the early twentieth century, in most countries regulation of working hours or working conditions for adult male workers was considered unthinkable. For example, in 1905 the US Supreme Court declared in a famous case that an Act introduced by the New York state restricting bakers to a 10-hour working day was unconstitutional because 'it deprived the baker of the liberty of working as long as he wished' (Garraty and Carnes, 2000, p. 607).

One important conclusion that emerges from historical examination is that it took the developed countries a long time to construct institutions in the earlier days of their development. Institutions typically took decades, and sometimes generations, to develop. Just to give one example, the need for central banking was perceived, at least in some circles, from as long ago as the seventeenth century, but the first 'real' central bank, the Bank of England (founded in 1694), was instituted only by the Bank Charter Act of 1844, some two centuries later.

Another important point emerges from historical comparison of the levels of institutional sophistication in today's developed countries in the earlier period with those in today's developing countries.

For example, measured by the (admittedly highly imperfect) per capita national income level, in 1820, the UK was at a somewhat higher level of development than that of India today, but it did not even have many of the most 'basic' institutions that India has today. It did not have universal suffrage (it did not even have universal *male* suffrage), a central bank, income tax, generalised limited liability, a generalised bankruptcy law, a professional bureaucracy, meaningful securities regulations, and even basic labour regulations (except for a couple of minimal and hardly enforced regulations on child labour).

This kind of comparison can go on, but the point is that the developed countries in earlier times were institutionally *less* advanced compared to today's developing countries at similar stages of development. Needless to say, the quality of their institutions fell well short of the 'global standards' institutions that today's developing countries are expected to install.

5 Concluding remarks

If the policies and institutions that the rich countries are recommending to the poor countries are not the ones that they themselves used when they were developing, what is going on? We can only conclude that, whether intentionally or not, the rich countries are effectively 'kicking away the ladder' that allowed them to climb to where they are now.

It is no coincidence that economic development has become more difficult during the last two decades, when the developed countries have been turning up the pressure on the developing countries to adopt the so-called 'good' policies and institutions. Their average annual per capita income growth rate has been halved (from 3 per cent to 1.5 per cent) between the 1960–80 period and the 1980–2000 period. And even this disappointing growth rate would not have been achieved except for rapid growths in large countries like China and India, which have not followed the orthodox strategy but have reformed and opened up their economies at their own pace. During this period, Latin America has virtually stopped growing, while sub-Saharan Africa and most ex-Communist countries have experienced a fall in absolute income. Economic instability has increased markedly, as manifested in the dozens of financial crises we have witnessed over the last decade alone. Income inequality has been growing in many developing countries and poverty has increased, rather than decreased, in a significant number of them.

What can be done to change this situation?

First, the facts about the historical experiences of the developed countries should be more widely publicised. This is not just a matter of 'getting history right', but also of allowing the developing countries to make more informed choices about their strategies of economic development and global integration.

Second, the conditions attached to bilateral and multilateral financial assistance to developing countries should be radically changed. It should be accepted that the orthodox recipe is not working, and also that there can be no single 'best practice' policies that everyone should use. More specifically, the 'bad policies' that most of today's developed countries used with so much effectiveness when they were developing countries themselves should be at least allowed, if not actively encouraged, by the developed countries and the international financial institutions that they control. While it is true that activist trade and industrial policies can sometimes degenerate into a web of red tape and corruption, this should not mean that these policies should never be used.

Third, the WTO rules should be re-written so that the developing countries can more actively use tariffs and subsidies for industrial development. They should also be allowed to have less stringent patent laws and other intellectual property rights laws.

Fourth, improvements in institutions should be encouraged, but this should not be equated with imposing a fixed set of (in practice, today's – not even yesterday's – Anglo-American) institutions on all countries. There need to be more serious attempts, both at the academic and the practical levels, to explore exactly which institutions are necessary, or at least beneficial, for what types of countries, given their stages of development and their economic, political, social and even cultural conditions. Special care has to be taken in order not to demand excessively rapid upgrading of institutions by the developing countries, especially given that they already have quite sophisticated institutions when compared to today's developed countries at comparable stages of development, and given that establishing and running new institutions is costly.

By having the freedom to choose policies and institutions that are more suitable to their conditions, the developing countries will be able to develop faster. This will also benefit the developed countries in the long run, as it will increase their trade and investment opportunities. That the developed countries cannot see this is the tragedy of our time.

Note

* This chapter summarises the arguments presented in Ha-Joon Chang (2002), *Kicking Away the Ladder – Development Strategy in Historical Perspective*, London: Anthem Press. References and notes have been kept to a minimum in this chapter; further references can be found in the book.

References

Bairoch, P. (1993), *Economics and World History – Myths and Paradoxes*, Brighton: Wheatsheaf.
Bhagwati, J. (1985), *Protectionism*, Cambridge, MA: The MIT Press.
Cochran, T. and W. Miller (1942), *The Age of Enterprise: A Social History of Industrial America*, New York: The Macmillan Company.
Garraty, J. and M. Carnes (2000), *The American Nation – A History of the United States*, 10th edn, New York: Addison Wesley Longman.
Kindleberger, C. (1984), *A Financial History of Western Europe*, Oxford: Oxford University Press.
List, F. (1885), *The National System of Political Economy*, translated from the original German edition published in 1841 by Sampson Lloyd, London: Longmans, Green, and Company.
Nye, J. (1991), 'The myth of free-trade Britain and fortress France: tariffs and trade in the nineteenth century', *Journal of Economic History*, **51**(1), 23–46.

25 Time to replace globalisation with localisation

Colin Hines

The P word

Protectionism is a dirty word among economists, but, if managed properly, offers a solution to the problems of rich and poor countries alike, argues Colin Hines (2009).

Put a leading trade unionist, the head of a development charity, a Conservative MP, the Prime Minister, a chief banker and the boss of a large multinational in one room and there is probably only one thing they will all huff and puff about in unison: the need at all costs to prevent the spread of protectionism. All will agree that the despised P word either caused or made worse the Great Depression, and that the logical next step is the idea that all nations, rich and poor, are better off with open markets and more international trade.

Learning from history

Let's start with the usual cliché of the lessons of the 1930s. The first thing to make clear is that the post-crash efforts to protect national economies did not cause the Great Depression. That, like the global recession we face today, had its beginning in feckless, greedy financiers profiting hugely from the vulnerable. The latter were assured that their investments could defy the laws of economic gravity and that the market could only go up. In the 1920s the investing frenzy centred on shares, in the Noughties on property.

The collapse of the banking system in the 1930s led to huge increases in unemployment. Governments reacted to electorates' fears about more job losses caused by foreign imports by trying one-sided protectionism, putting up barriers whilst hoping that others would keep theirs low. Not surprisingly this made an already bad situation worse.

In the post-war era, big business and neoliberal economists called for all countries to open their markets. But the power realities meant that the global South was forced to open more rapidly and extensively than the North. For poor countries, traditionally reliant on notoriously fickle commodity markets, this exacerbated already serious problems.

Take coffee, the world's most valuable export after oil. With the aid of World Bank loans, Vietnam invested heavily in this crop and tripled its coffee output between 1995 and 2000, becoming the second largest coffee producer after

Brazil. This increased the vulnerability of more than 20 million farmers in the 49 other coffee growing countries.

More recently, Chinese exports of clothing and cheap electronics have gutted domestic production in other Third World competitors. A new carve up of Africa has begun, led by China looking for oil and other raw materials and India seeking to dominate parts of the continent's hi-tech industries.

But the boom in Asia's powerhouse economies was largely built on the precarious sands of consumer debt in the advanced industrial countries. Three decades of deregulated open markets allowed bankers to slip the national leash and spread debt globally, generating an artificial life support system for massive consumer spending on globally traded goods. This, in turn, has depended on huge increases in fossil fuel use and natural resource extraction.

A brave new world

That was then. The global credit crisis has brought that process to a juddering halt, and has coincided with a growing sense of urgency about the need to tackle climate change by moving to a low carbon society.

Corporate globalisation vs. internationalism

It is crucial to make a clear distinction between, for example, a global flow of technology, ideas and information to rebuild sustainable local communities – that is, a supportive 'internationalism' – and the process of globalisation. In essence, the latter is the systematic reduction of protective barriers to the flow of goods and money by international trade rules shaped by and for big business. It pits country against country, community against community and workers against workers. That is the point of it, because such a structure and process is the route to maximising profits. Internationalism can be thought of as the flow of ideas, technologies, information, culture, money and goods with the end goal of protecting and rebuilding local economies worldwide. Its emphasis is not on competition for the cheapest, but on cooperation for the best.

Linguistic clarity is vital since the advocates and beneficiaries of globalisation misuse the indisputable benefits that can accrue from such constructive international flows to justify the destructive process of globalisation. In tandem with this misleading approach is invariably a promise that some day the growth resulting from globalisation will somehow trickle down to benefit the majority.

Corporate globalisation

Corporate globalisation: the ever-increasing integration of national economies into the global economy through trade and investment rules and privatisation, aided by technological advances. These reduce barriers to trade and investment and in the process reduce democratic controls by nation states and their communities over their economic affairs. The process is driven by the widespread lobbying of large corporations who use the theory of comparative advantage, the goal of international competitiveness and the growth model to achieve the maximisation of their profits. It is occurring increasingly at the expense of social, environmental and labour improvements and rising inequality for most of the world.

Or more bluntly, globalisation: (1) the process by which governments sign away the rights of their citizens in favour of speculative investors and transnational corporations; (2) the erosion of wages, social welfare standards and environmental regulations for the sake of international trade; (3) the imposition worldwide of a consumer monoculture. Widely but falsely believed to be irreversible. See also financial meltdown, casino economy, Third World debt and race to the bottom (sixteenth century: from colonialism, via development).[1]

An alternative: localisation

Localisation: a process that reverses the trend of globalisation by discriminating in favour of the local. Depending on the context, the 'local' is predominantly defined as part of the nation state, although it can on occasions be the nation state itself or even occasionally a regional grouping of nation states. The policies bringing about localisation are ones that increase control of the economy by communities and nation states. The result should be an increase in community cohesion, a reduction in poverty and inequality and an improvement in livelihoods, social infrastructure and environmental protection, and hence an increase in the all-important sense of security.

Localisation is not about restricting the flow of information, technology, trade and investment, management and legal structures – which further localisation; indeed these are encouraged by the new localist emphasis in global aid and trade rules. Such transfers also play a crucial role in the successful transition from globalisation to localisation. It is not a return to overpowering state control, merely governments' provision of a policy and economic framework that allows people, community groups and businesses to rediversify their own local economies.

The route to localisation consists of seven interrelated and self-reinforcing policy areas. The basic steps are:

1. reintroduction of protective safeguards for domestic economies;
2. a site-here-to-sell-here policy for manufacturing and services domestically or regionally;
3. localising money such that the majority stays within its place of origin;
4. local competition policy to eliminate monopolies from the more protected economies;

5. introduction of resource taxes to increase environmental improvements and help fund the transition to the 'Protect the Local, Globally' approach;
6. increased democratic involvement both politically and economically to ensure the effectiveness and equity of the movement to more diverse local economies;
7. reorientation of the end goals of aid and trade rules such that they contribute to the rebuilding of local economies and local control.

Under these circumstances, beggar-your-neighbour globalisation gives way to the potentially more cooperative better-your-neighbour localisation.

A wake-up call for the politically active – globalisation can't be tinkered with

What we have at present is an array of largely futile efforts by political activists from trades unionists to development NGOs, to tame globalisation. Campaigns for 'labour standards' or 'fair trade' or 'voluntary ethical codes' fundamentally mistake the nature of the trade liberalisation beast. These attempts are like trying to lasso a tiger with cotton. It is now time to return this tiger to its original habitat. Trade was initially a search for the novel; Europeans went to India for spices and other exotics, not coal. That is precisely the 'localisation' approach, but without the former's disastrous social effects. Long-distance trade is only for acquiring what cannot be provided within the region where people live. The rules for this diminished international sector then become those of the 'fair trade' movement, where preference is given to goods supplied in a way that benefits workers, the local community and the environment.

The politically active need to demand a new direction and end goal for trade rules. The latter must contribute to the rebuilding and protection of local sustainable economies. In the process, the myriad goals of movements for social and animal welfare, development, human and labour rights and environmental protection have much more potential to be met.

Bringing about the change in direction

To bring about this change it is crucial to play the globalisers at their own game. They have a clear end goal: maximum trade and money flows for maximum profit. From this end goal comes a clear set of policies and trade rules supporting this approach. Those seeking a more just, secure, environmentally sustainable future need to have their own clear end goal and policies for achieving it. This will require the 'mind-wrench' mentioned above, away from mostly concentrating on opposing globalisation towards considering the detailed policy route to its alternative – localisation.

A programme for localisation

To achieve such a dramatic turnaround I have drawn from many people's ideas and detailed in my book (Hines, 2002)[2] a 'Protect the Local, Globally' set of interactive and self-reinforcing policies that can bring about localisation.

Protecting the local economy

The first step must be a 'mind-wrench' away from the passive acceptance that globalisation is as inevitable as gravity and towards support for a set of self-reinforcing measures that will bring about a 'Protect the Local, Globally' end goal internationally. Protective safeguards, such as import and export controls, quotas, subsidies and so on, will need to be introduced over a clearly agreed transition period to all continents. This will not be old-style protectionism that seeks to protect a home market whilst expecting others to remain open. The emphasis will be on local trade. Any residual long-distance trade will be geared to funding the diversification of local economies. Such a dramatic, radical change will need to overcome TNC opposition and so will need to take place at the level of regional groupings of countries, especially the most powerful – in Europe and North America.

Localising production and controlling TNCs

Industry and services will be localised by site-here-to-sell-here policies to ensure localised production. Threats by TNCs to relocate thus become less plausible, as the market is lost to existing, or government encouraged, new local competitors. Once TNCs are thus grounded, then their domestic activities and the levels of taxation paid are back under democratic control. Campaigners' demands for social, labour and environmental standards also become feasible. Adequate company taxation can help compensate the poor for any increases in prices.

Localising money

The disastrous effects of the unfettered international flow of money have led to global calls for some controls to be reintroduced. What is required is a regrounding of money to remain predominantly in the locality or country of origin to fund the rebuilding of diverse, sustainable local economies. Measures include controls on capital flows, Tobin-type taxes, control of tax evasion, including off-shore banking centres, the floating of civic bonds and the rejuvenation of locally orientated banks, credit unions, Local Exchange and Trading Schemes (LETS) and so on. Public and private flows of money to other countries must also be directed to strengthen the local economies of the countries concerned.

A localist competition policy

Local competition policies will ensure that high-quality goods and services are provided by ensuring a more level, but more local, playing field. Free of the 'race to the bottom' competitive pressures from foreign competition, business can be carried out within the framework of ever-improving labour, social and environmental regulations, enhanced by the best ideas and technologies from around the world. Government competition policy will cover the structure and market share of businesses, plus regulate the behaviour of firms.

Taxes for localisation

To pay for the transition to localisation and to improve the environment the majority of taxation will come from gradually increasing resource taxes, such as on non-renewable energy use and pollution. To promote a more equitable society, the removal of the option of relocation or the availability of foreign tax havens will make it possible to tax companies and individuals according to their wealth, their income, their spending through value-added tax and their land. Part of this taxation will be used to compensate the poorer sections of society for any price rises and by shifting taxes away from employment to encourage more jobs.

Democratic localism

A diverse local economy requires the active democracy of everyday involvement in producing the maximum range of goods and services close to the point of consumption. To ensure the broadest distribution of the ensuing benefits will simultaneously require wider, political, democratic and economic control at a local level. A Citizen's Income will allow involvement in the economy as a matter of right. Political funding will be strictly constrained and power will pass from the corporations to the citizens. This will involve the encouragement of maximum participation in defining priorities and planning local economic, social and environmental initiatives. This will require a balance of involvement of the state, community networks and organisations and citizen's movements.

Trade and aid for localisation

The GATT rules at present administered by the WTO should be revised fundamentally to become a General Agreement for Sustainable Trade (GAST), administered by a democratic World Localisation Organisation (WLO). Their remit would be to ensure that regional trade and international aid policies and flows, information and technological transfer, as well as the residual international investment and trade, should incorporate rules geared to the building up of sustainable local economies. The goal should be to foster maximum employment through a substantial increase in sustainable, regional self-reliance.

Localising food security

Globalisation is increasing control of the world's food system by transnational companies (TNCs) and big farmers. There is a backlash from both consumers and farmers to this process that provides less safe food, environmental threats and rural impoverishment. Localisation can reverse this trend. Food security both for rich and poor countries requires an increase in the level of self-sufficiency. Also needed is a dramatic reduction in international trade in foodstuffs until the commerce left becomes a useful adjunct to increased self-reliance. This should be governed by fair trade rules benefiting small farmers and food producers, animal welfare and the environment. Land reform and the rebuilding of rural economies is an integral part of such food localisation.

Finally, 'localisation' is not about trying to put the clock back. Globalisation is doing that as it reduces the security, basic needs provision and employment prospects for billions for whom things had been improving since World War II. The 'Protect the Local, Globally' policies of 'localisation' could return us to a path that advances the majority and doesn't mire them in cruel insecurity. It is not against trade; it just wants trade, where possible, to be local. The shorter the gap between producer and consumer, the better the chance for the latter to control the former. Adverse environmental effects are more likely to be experienced through long-distance trade and lack of consumer control over distant producers. Local trade should significantly lessen these problems and make possible the tighter regulation required.

Why should this radical change come about?

The global credit crisis has brought that process of thinking that globalisation is both inevitable and good to a juddering halt. The resulting growing resistance to the idea that economies must bow the knee to the dictates of the financial wing of economic globalisation can be built upon to help fashion a viable localist alternative. For years there have already existed countless people and groups strengthening their local economies from the grassroots up. The latest form of this has been calls for a Green New Deal whereby tackling the triple crisis of the credit crunch, climate change and energy security has taken the form of demands for large-scale financing of local energy efficiency and renewables.[3] A continuous spur to consideration of such radical local alternatives at the governmental level will be the need to respond to global economic upheavals and the deflation, the job losses and inadequate consumer demand that will come in its wake. Equally crucial in shaping a different localist imperative amongst politicians will be the pressure that the politically active can bring to bear. This must shift from just fighting separate issue-specific aspects of globalisation to realising that their individual successes can only be secured as part of an overarching change to localisation, but in an internationally supportive manner.

Development professionals' calls for a 'fairer' liberalised trading system ignore the reality of what the rules of trade liberalisation have done to the poor in the South. Development NGOs also adhere to the flawed paradigm that exports from the South to the North are a major route for the poor's development.

Southern critics of this approach point to the inevitability of adverse competition between poor exporting countries, its hijacking of national priorities to the provision of the cheapest exports, the adverse working conditions and country-hopping demanded by the companies involved and instead propose the alternative of a localist development policy.

Development NGOs must recognise these facts and make their campaigns more effective by putting them within an overarching and internationalist 'localisation' context. Thus, campaigns against the World Bank, IMF, Debt, WTO and so on must recognise that it is not the actual institutions or the people working in them that are the problem. Rather it is the end goal of their activities and policies. What must be challenged up-front is the fact that they are geared to the continued contortion and distortion of every country's economy in order to prioritise international competitiveness and obey the diktats of globalisation.

Were trade and aid rules and debt forgiveness geared to the radically different end goal of protecting and rebuilding local communities globally then such dramatically altered institutions could play a useful part in the necessary transition of saving the world from globalisation by shifting it to localisation.

Just as the last century saw the battle between the left and the right, what needs to become the big battle of this century must be an alliance of localists, red-greens and small 'c' conservatives pushing a localist agenda, defeating the doomed globalists of the political centre. So, with apologies to Karl Marx and Margaret Thatcher, the rallying cry should be: 'Localists of the World Unite – There is an Alternative'.

Notes

1. International Society for Ecology and Culture (1999), *From Global to Local – Resisting Monoculture, Rebuilding Community*, Devon: ISEC.
2. Hines, Colin (2002), *Localization – A Global Manifesto*, London: Earthscan.
3. See http://www.greennewdealgroup.org/; accessed 21 October 2010.

26 Free trade or social tariffs?

George DeMartino

Introduction

The last quarter of the twentieth century was marked by dramatic steps toward the achievement of global neo-liberalism. This is a policy regime that in principle features largely unregulated market forces that override the state in directing international trade and investment flows. It therefore comprises 'free' trade, the liberalisation of international financial markets, the global protection of property rights, and so forth. The neo-liberal project has been advanced through a series of important international agreements, including notably the North American Free Trade Agreement (NAFTA), the GATT agreement that established the World Trade Organization, and through other explicit policy choices taken at the national and multilateral levels.

Things have changed since then. As Polanyi (1944) understood but we have had to relearn, global neo-liberalism is an unachievable utopia, the pursuit of which can be harmful and even dangerous. As in the past, the severe dislocations and instability that are associated with today's increasingly market-driven international trade and financial flows are instigating political reaction in the form of demands on national governments for economic protection and security. But global neo-liberalism has made it difficult for national governments to provide these protections, not least since this regime creates ample opportunity for private investors and firms to escape taxation by relocating their assets internationally. At just the time that workers and other vulnerable groups need greater state assistance, then, the burden of taxation required to fund social programmes has shifted onto the shoulders of these very same groups. While free trade promises economic growth that might be expected to offset the effects of growing instability, estimates find that trade has a larger effect on inequality than it does on growth (Rodrik, 1997). Equally important, recent evidence indicates that unskilled workers in the developing world have largely failed to benefit in the ways predicted by mainstream trade theory (Goldberg and Pavcnik, 2007).

Facing these difficulties, states are being pressed once again by diverse constituencies to establish protective barriers to insulate their domestic economies from global economic forces. Not least, they are being pressed to renege on their commitment to free trade. The important question that arises in this context is what will come next, after the current experiment with free trade has been abandoned?

During the 1990s, heterodox economists and social movements across the globe advocated what came to be called 'fair trade', or new trade and investment regimes that could reap the potential benefits of international economic integration, while protecting vulnerable groups from the most damaging tendencies of neo-liberalism. Many argued that if the campaign for a new, just trade and investment regime failed, we risked the prospect of a return to antagonistic, nativist and neo-mercantilist trade policies of the past that have proven so destructive. In response to the fair traders, neoclassical trade theorists reasserted their commitment to free trade throughout the 1990s and beyond, and indeed advocated further liberalisation. Unfortunately, they were just as hostile to progressive, egalitarian trade initiatives – initiatives that sought to retain an open international regime – as they were to patently nationalist, reactionary measures.

Paul Krugman was particularly outspoken in making the case against fair trade. He argued consistently from the early 1990s until recently that fair traders were either ignorant of economic theory, or simply closet protectionists who exploited fair trade rhetoric for nationalist purposes. For example, in a 1997 article entitled 'In praise of cheap labor' Krugman argued that the fair trade position was nonsensical, grounded as it was in an unethical 'fastidiousness' of US consumers:

> Unlike the starving subsistence farmer, the women and children in the sneaker factory are working at slave wages *for our benefit* – and this makes us feel unclean. And so there are self-righteous demands for international labor standards: We should not, the opponents of globalization insist, be willing to buy those sneakers and shirts unless the people who make them receive decent wages and work under decent conditions. (Italics original)

But not buying these goods, Krugman continued, would hurt those whom the fair traders purported to want to help:

> A policy of good jobs in principle, but no jobs in practice, might assuage our consciences, but it is no favor to its alleged beneficiaries … In short, [fair traders] are not entitled to their self-righteousness. They have not thought the matter through. And when the hopes of hundreds of millions are at stake, thinking things through is not just good intellectual practice. It is a moral duty. (Krugman, 1997)

Krugman maintained this stance toward fair traders at least through 2001 when he published biting critiques of those who demonstrated against the WTO in Seattle in 1999 and elsewhere. Yes, he says, the fact the poor people including children work in sweatshops under horrible conditions is regrettable. But the efforts of the protestors to end the practice through fair trade initiatives would only make matters worse:

> [Fair trade is] not a serious position. Third-world countries desperately need their export industries... They can't have those export industries unless they are allowed to sell goods produced under conditions that Westerners find appalling, by workers who receive very low wages. And that's a fact the anti-globalization activists refuse to accept. (Krugman, 2001)

In the event the orthodox trade economists won this debate. NAFTA was passed despite substantial opposition in the US and Canada with only a gesture toward labour rights and environmental protection. The Uruguay Round of GATT was completed successfully with even less regard for these concerns. Since then there has been a steady parade of new bilateral trade agreements across the globe, most all of which enshrine free as opposed to fair trade. So we might expect that trade economists today would be self-satisfied that they had saved the world from the misguided and even dishonest fair traders.

But today we find little gloating, and a good bit of concern. There is growing anxiety today among prominent economists about the flows and outcomes that have emerged under the emerging neo-liberalism. Over the past several years economists of the stature of centrist Paul Samuelson, conservative Paul Craig Roberts and liberals Alan Blinder and Paul Krugman have taken the unprecedented step of worrying out loud, within earshot of the public, about the damaging effects of free trade. This shift has been associated with the beginnings of a new approach to trade policy in Washington, DC. In 2007 the Democratic Congressional leadership reached an agreement with United States Trade Representative Susan C. Schwab, 'A New Trade Policy for America'. This pact committed the Bush Administration to include in pending free trade agreements (with Peru and Panama) provisions that require the parties 'to adopt, maintain and enforce in their own laws and in practice the five basic internationally-recognized labor standards, as stated in the 1998 ILO Declaration'. In response, Krugman (2007a) had this to say:

> Even trade skeptics tend to shy away from a return to outright protectionism, and to look for softer measures, which mainly come down to trying to push up foreign wages. The key element of the new trade deal is its inclusion of 'labor standards': countries that sign free trade agreements with the United States will have to allow union organizing, while abolishing child and slave labor ... So the inclusion of these standards in the deal *represents a real victory for workers.* Realistically, however, labor standards won't do all that much for American workers. No matter how free third-world workers are to organize, they're still going to be paid very little, and trade will continue to place pressure on U.S. wages ... *By all means, let's have strong labor standards in our pending trade agreements, and let's approach proposals for new agreements with an appropriate degree of skepticism.* But if Democrats really want to help American workers, they'll have to do it with a pro-labor policy that relies on better tools than trade policy. Universal health care, paid for by taxing the economy's winners, would be a good place to start. (Emphasis added)

Elsewhere Krugman adds that 'those who are worried about trade have a point, and deserve some respect' (Krugman, 2007b).

This shift in position may signal a more general openness to the case for fair trade. But an important and difficult question arises in this context. What kind of fair trade regime might achieve the purpose of ensuring that the benefits of international economic integration are fairly shared? This chapter explores one important aspect of the trade controversy – it concerns the proposal by labour and human rights advocates to incorporate labour standards into trade agreements. Neoclassical economists have until now argued that such measures would subvert the project to establish free trade. Making this argument has required them to re-theorise the concept of comparative advantage that is at the heart of trade theory. Many critics object to this re-theorisation. In what follows, I will examine this theoretical innovation, argue that it is flawed, and then conclude with a very brief survey of new trade (and investment) proposals that seek genuine global equality and economic security.

Rescuing free trade

The neoclassical case for free trade based on the existence of comparative advantages is intuitively appealing. Since countries differ amongst themselves in critical ways, they will exhibit different levels of competence in the various industries in which they engage. A country that is relatively well endowed with fertile soil is likely to be relatively efficient (and therefore have a comparative advantage) in agricultural production, while a country that enjoys a relatively large supply of skilled workers will have a comparative advantage in manufacturing. Given these differences, each country can improve its situation by specialising in what it does best (relative to other countries), and then trading with other nations to secure those goods for which it is not so well suited. It can be shown that with each country specialising in this way, even those countries that are deficient relative to their neighbours in all industries can gain through trade.

This account begs an important question: just why do nations differ among themselves in industrial performance? Why might one country be better suited to agriculture, and another to industry? The example given above suggests one part of the answer: countries enjoy different resource endowments, such as fertile soil or supply of skilled labour. Countries also exhibit different levels of technology; moreover, their inhabitants might hold distinct preferences. For instance, workers in one country might prefer agriculture to manufacturing, while workers in another might prefer the opposite. These three categories of differences – in *endowments, technology and preferences* – will yield different levels of economic efficiency and costs of production. It must be emphasised that these differences, which give rise to distinct comparative advantages, are taken to be entirely natural and, partly on that account, unobjectionable. The determinants of comparative advantage are not right or wrong in this account, they just *are*. A country should not complain about the endowments or technology of its neighbour – it should instead trade freely to reap the benefits of its neighbour's greater competencies.

So far, this account of comparative advantage has ignored the matter of labour standards, which are now at the heart of the controversy over free trade. Critics of neo-liberalism have begun to demand that trade and investment agreements include labour standards that will ensure basic worker rights across trading partners. They claim that without such protections, free trade will put undue pressure on workers to accept deficient working conditions in order to save their jobs in the face of foreign competition and threats of capital flight.

Re-theorising comparative advantage

Neoclassical defenders of free trade have resisted the momentum building for labour standards in trade agreements by extending the concept of comparative advantage. As the demand for labour standards strengthened during the 1990s, they began to argue that cross-national differences in labour standards simply represent another *natural* and therefore *legitimate* determinant of comparative advantage. This argument is crucially important: it places governments' policy choices on an equal normative footing with nations' natural resources in driving trade flows. It therefore inoculates a nation's labour standards from outside inspection or complaint by those who seek to establish global economic policies that will ensure equality and justice.

How do neoclassical theorists sustain this claim? Consistent with the thorough reductionism of neoclassical thought,[1] these economists now claim that a nation's labour standards are the direct result of its endowments, technology and preferences. One country may be wealthy enough (owing to favourable endowments and technology) to be able to afford strong labour standards. Moreover, its citizens might prefer to allocate substantial funds to ensure such labour protections. In such a nation, strong standards are perfectly natural and legitimate since they reflect its particular endowments, technology and preferences. But another country, with fewer resources and relatively impoverished workers who are willing to sacrifice safety in order to find employment, is warranted in establishing much weaker standards – in keeping with its particular endowments, technology and preferences. The key point is this: when we encounter differences between countries in labour standards, we should treat them as entirely natural and legitimate determinants of comparative advantage since they result from natural differences between countries. Rather than complain about lower standards abroad, then, we should recognise that everyone benefits when a higher-standard country imports goods now produced more cheaply in a low-standard country. The importing country gains access to inexpensive goods, while workers in the low-standard country get jobs and income that would otherwise be unavailable to them. To complain about the weaker labour standards abroad that generate this mutually beneficial trade would be as nonsensical as complaining about the fertility of its soil or the quality of its other natural resources. From the neoclassical perspective, far better that we should all enjoy the growth and prosperity that trade allows, irrespective of the basis of the comparative advantages that induce this trade.

The campaign to write labour standards into trade agreements is therefore unwise, since it will necessarily undermine economic welfare (Krugman, 1997). But it is also unfair. Neoclassical theory treats a nation's labour standards (and other policies) as a consequence of the preferences of its citizens in the context of the endowments and technology they face, as we have just seen. Since these agents are assumed to be rational, they are taken to know what is in their own best interests. Hence, it is inappropriate for the economist (and by extension, people in other countries) to assess their choices. This refusal to judge agents' preferences stems equally from the neoclassical pursuit of objective science. Assessing agents' choices would require the economist to impose an explicit set of value judgements – something that would disqualify neoclassical thought as an objective account of social affairs.

The treatment of national policy as the outcome of simple choice, combined with an antipathy to judging the preferences that induce those choices, generates in neoclassical thought a strident commitment to what is called cultural relativism. This is the idea that each society should be allowed to choose for itself how to live, in accordance with its own cultural norms (or preferences), free of unwarranted intervention by outsiders. Given this commitment, neoclassical theorists argue that it is unfair for activists in one country to try to impose their own preferences and ensuing policies on those in other countries with different preferences and policy choices. In this view, the campaign to write labour standards into trade agreements amounts to cultural imperialism, even when those advocating universal labour standards claim that they are advancing the interests of workers worldwide.

To sum up: neoclassical theorists have corralled and domesticated the new challenge to free trade emanating from labour rights activists by expanding the concept of comparative advantage to comprise international differences in labour standards. Just as countries exhibit different bundles of endowments, technology and preferences, so do they exhibit different levels of labour standards. Indeed, since the latter is a direct consequence of the former, we must take differences in standards to be entirely natural and legitimate determinants of comparative advantage. Rather than complain about weak standards abroad, we should celebrate the difference – not just because it is right to do so, but because it will also make us rich!

Contesting free trade

Labour rights advocates object to the extension of comparative advantage to include countries' labour standards (and other policies) on multiple grounds. In what follows, I will examine several of their most important arguments.

First, labour rights advocates view the neoclassical claim that a country's labour standards reflect a simple national choice as an extraordinarily naive and, indeed, dangerous fiction. On important policy matters, members of a society typically differ among themselves about the right course of action. This implies that any policy will reflect the views of some groups and conflict with the views of others. But this also implies that when evaluating the legitimacy of nations' standards we must always attend to the matter of power – to the institutional arrangements under which policies are devised and enacted, and ultimately to the ability of the relatively powerless to achieve political voice and effective representation.

This simple insight leads us to what ought to be a rather obvious point, but which eludes most free traders: citizens in countries lacking basic worker protections and rights do not typically choose weak standards. Instead, oppressive standards are imposed on them by autocratic regimes. Weak standards are routinely enforced across the globe through the liberal use of the military to break strikes, through harassment, imprisonment and even execution of labour activists, and through the concerted denial of basic political rights (cf. Dorman, 1988). Given the obvious record of coercion across the globe, the economist's claim that weak standards represent a simple national choice, based on aggregated preferences, strikes labour advocates as not just wrong but disingenuous.

A focus on political arrangements and power leads to the view that a country's labour standards at any given moment are an indicator of the balance of political forces in that country. In the view of its critics, global neo-liberalism is now weakening labour's power, certainly in the US where the labour movement has withered over the past 40 years but even in those countries that have historically featured stronger labour movements. Labour advocates contend that it is far more accurate to interpret this trend toward weaker labour standards as an effect of the coercive force of global neo-liberalism, than as an unproblematic choice reflecting national preferences.

It must be said that neoclassical economists typically reject the argument that neo-liberalism has in fact undermined labour standards. They claim that the evidence on this point is at best inconclusive, not least since too few firms migrate to low-standard countries to affect workers' bargaining power (Bhagwati and Srinivasan, 1996). But in researching this matter they have missed the mark on two counts: they have focused on explicit revisions to standards, when the more prevalent danger is *lax enforcement* of existing standards; and they have focused narrowly on actual corporate relocations, when the broader danger lies in *threats* of relocation. These two matters are related. The effective enforcement of labour standards depends on labour's political and economic power. When labour's power is eroded, existing standards provide weaker protection. And under neo-liberalism, the mere threat of corporate relocation often succeeds in undermining workers' power and rights.

The situation facing labour in the United States today exemplifies the connections between neo-liberalism, the erosion of labour's effective power and the diminution of labour rights. In the United States, workers seeking unionisation must petition the National Labor Relations Board (NLRB) to secure a government-supervised election. Under NLRB rules, the union must secure a majority of the vote in order to secure bargaining rights. In the months leading up to the election, employers do whatever they can to dissuade their workers from voting for the union.

In the 1950s, about one-third of all eligible workers in the US were represented by unions. Today, about 12 per cent enjoy union representation. To what degree is global neo-liberalism culpable in this trend? The evidence on this is instructive. A series of recent studies by Bronfenbrenner (1996, 2000) found that during the late 1990s, following the passage of the NAFTA, 70 per cent of firms in mobile industries such as manufacturing threatened to relocate abroad when facing unionisation drives. These threats were found to be effective in dissuading workers from voting for unions. In firms in which workers actually voted to unionise despite these threats, the rate at which firms made good on their threats and actually relocated abroad tripled as compared with the 1980s. In short, US workers are effectively losing their ability to form unions, in part as a consequence of global neo-liberalism. But because there has been no formal change in US labour law – indeed, on paper US workers enjoy the same rights to unionise today that they have for decades – this erosion has occurred below the radar screen of those economists who refute the connection between neo-liberalism and worker rights. They infer from union defeats a *preference* on the part of workers to remain union-free. In this way, they shield neo-liberalism from any culpability for de-unionisation in the US.

In short, the idea that a nation's standards simply reflect the preferences of its citizens is naive, dangerous and even disingenuous. It overlooks the obvious ways in which weak standards are imposed on relatively powerless members of society; and it also overlooks the more subtle ways in which neo-liberalism undermines the efforts of workers to secure basic rights. In the view of labour rights advocates, weak labour standards therefore distort the trade patterns that would otherwise occur, and disrupt the benefits from trade that would otherwise flow to vulnerable workers.

Labour advocates also reject the cultural relativism that underlies the neoclassical antipathy to universal labour standards. I pursue this matter at length elsewhere (DeMartino, 2000); here, I want to make just one argument against neoclassical theory's romantic view of culture. As many theorists have by now argued, culture is never unequivocally benign. All cultures affect the rights and freedoms of societies' members. People contest culture all the time, precisely because there is so much at stake in this domain. We rightly contest our own; and for those of us who are concerned about global justice, we must also contest cultures abroad. But we must also be prepared to welcome the complaints voiced abroad against our own, especially when it can be shown that the way we live undermines the well-being of those who are worse off in other societies.

The main problem with neoclassical theory's refusal to judge culture is this: in any society in which oppression is rife, we can be certain that its culture will obscure and/or defend the legitimacy of that oppression. In very few societies do oppressors rely merely on the threat of force. Even slave societies typically produce elaborate accounts of the justness of that kind of social order. Justifications for slavery typically draw in equal measure on biology and religion for sustenance; they posit the slaves as biologically and morally deficient, and in need of the kinds of control and spiritual enhancement that slavery affords them.

For better or worse, it appears that those who are oppressed often come to accept their situation; Jon Elster (1982) calls this a case of 'adaptive preferences'. The idea is that those who are denied vital rights and freedoms may lose the aspiration to achieve them as a way of coping with their predicament. Some may even come to embrace the very cultural norms that oppress them. In the words of Amartya Sen, 'acute inequalities often survive precisely by making allies out of the deprived. The underdog comes to accept the legitimacy of the unequal order and becomes an implicit accomplice' (Sen, 1990, cited in Crocker, 1992). But this suggests that the stronger is the regime that secures the oppression, the more likely it is that those who are oppressed will resign themselves to their plight. Hence, we may find less rather than more cultural contest in those societies where oppression is most egregious.

The problem with the stridency of the neoclassical embrace of cultural relativism, then, is that it strips from us any normative foundation to indict practices beyond our own borders that perpetuate even egregious exploitation. It romanticises culture, treating it as the natural compilation of a society's preferences, rather than seeing it as the outcome of a struggle among different groups in society to order their lives and their communities. It fails to appreciate that preferences are shaped (for better or worse) by the social circumstances in which people find themselves. It then validates whatever labour standards emerge as simple national choices that can and should form the basis of beneficial trade.

After free trade: in pursuit of international egalitarianism

The controversy over free trade runs even deeper than all this, however. It derives from a fundamental conflict between normative perspectives. Neoclassical theory is rooted in a normative commitment to what is called 'welfarism', a perspective that judges social arrangements by exclusive reference to the preferences of the people affected by those arrangements, whatever those preferences might be (or how they were formed). This perspective yields the famous Kaldor–Hicks 'compensation' criterion, under which one social outcome is deemed better than another if the winners under the former can fully compensate the losers and still enjoy net benefit.

Labour rights advocates, along with political theorists and philosophers and most heterodox economists, typically reject this normative perspective. In the first place, as Elster's emphasis on adaptive preferences reminds us, preferences are an inadequate indicator of people's well-being. Second, welfarism pays scant attention to the matter of inequality, and so has little to say about the legitimacy of measures that would redistribute from the wealthy to the poor.[2] It seeks social arrangements in which people are 'formally' free – that is, where each is able to choose the best course of action, given his or her opportunity set. But this perspective has little to say about whether people should all enjoy the same opportunity set. It can therefore be taken to justify even egregious levels of inequality.

In contrast, those advancing universal labour standards in trade agreements generally advance internationalist egalitarianism as the appropriate normative foundation for assessing global social arrangements. This perspective holds that just social arrangements are those that ensure that people enjoy equal 'substantive' freedom – that they face the same opportunity sets.[3] To the degree practicable, global policy regimes must seek to achieve this outcome. A just policy regime would be one that seeks to expand the substantive freedom of the relatively impoverished – by increasing their access to resources and consumption goods, to be sure, but also by enhancing their political and economic power so that they can achieve more effective representation and secure the rights to which they are formally entitled.

Labour rights advocates have offered several policy measures to advance the cause of global justice. These include (for instance) the incorporation of labour standards directly into trade agreements, just as these agreements presently comprise strong property rights protections; the adoption of a social charter of labour rights as a precondition for trade; the adoption of corporate codes of conduct that would require a corporation that invests in a country with lower standards to live by the higher standards that obtain in its home country;[4] and the imposition by a high-standard country of 'social tariffs' on imports from countries with lower standards, to offset the cost advantage gained on the basis of these lower standards (Dorman, 1992). In my own work (2000) and in joint work with Stephen Cullenberg (1994) I have advanced a new multilateral approach to trade policy, called the Social Index Tariff Structure (SITS) regime, which would penalise countries for pursuing advantage based on weak standards through social tariffs, while substantially rewarding those countries that take steps to promote worker rights (and human development more generally) through subsidies funded by the social tariffs. The SITS regime advances international equality by inverting the incentive structure that exists under neo-liberalism to erode worker rights. Under SITS, countries achieve open access for their exports in global markets by enhancing worker rights, while the burden for subsidising these measures falls on wealthier countries and on those poorer countries that refuse to promote the substantive freedom of their citizens. On balance, the SITS regime would induce a substantial net flow of resources from the North to the South, with the largest beneficiaries in the South being those countries that most aggressively promote the rights of workers and the dispossessed.

Conclusion

Contrary to the view of most neoclassical economists, global neo-liberalism is not the best imaginable economic system. It is inducing extraordinary inequality, and it threatens to deepen that inequality in the future. Today it is proving to be unsustainable, owing to the insecurity, crises, political backlash and ecological degradation that it is inducing. But even if it does prove to be sustainable, it ought not to be sustained.

Fortunately, those who oppose global neo-liberalism have begun to examine and propose just policy regimes that can and should be built to replace it. I have offered SITS as one possibility, though it surely must be coupled with a range of complementary policy regimes that speak to other facets of global economic integration – such as short-term capital flows (see Grabel, 2003), labour mobility (see Sutcliffe, 1998), and corporate taxation, subsidies and codes of conduct (Rodrik, 1997; DeMartino, 2000, ch. 7). The immediate challenge is to make substantial progress toward realising these initiatives since, if history is any guide, the most likely alternatives to neo-liberalism are apt to be neither internationalist nor egalitarian.

Notes

1. Space precludes an extended examination of neoclassical reductionism here, but I treat this matter at length in DeMartino (2000). See also Wolff and Resnick (1987).
2. See DeMartino (2000, chs. 2 and 3) for an explication of welfarism and a survey of its chief defects.
3. See Sen (1992) for a thorough explication of the 'capabilities' approach to equality, which focuses on substantive freedom. DeMartino (2000, chs. 5–7) examines the global policy implications of capabilities equality.
4. This proposal is reminiscent of the Sullivan Principles, which governed the behaviour of corporations that invested in South Africa during the apartheid era; see Bhagwati (1993), who endorses this approach reluctantly, in order to ameliorate the concerns of labour rights advocates.

References

Bhagwati, J. (1993), 'American rules, Mexican jobs', *New York Times*, 24 March, p. 13.

Bhagwati, J. and T.N. Srinivasan (1996), 'Trade and the environment: does environmental diversity detract from the case for free trade?', in J. Bhagwati and R.E. Hudec (eds), *Fair Trade and Harmonization*, Cambridge, MA: MIT Press.

Bronfenbrenner, K. (1996), *Final Report: The Effects of Plant Closing or Threat of Plant Closing on the Right of Workers to Organize*, submitted to the Labor Secretariat of the North American Commission on Labor Cooperation, 30 September.

Bronfenbrenner, K. (2000), *Uneasy Terrain: The Impact of Capital Mobility on Workers, Wages, and Union Organizing*, submitted to the US Trade Deficit Review Commission, 6 September.

Crocker, D.A. (1992), 'Functioning and capability: the foundations of Sen's and Nussbaum's development ethic', *Political Theory*, **20**(4), 584–612.

DeMartino, G. (2000), *Global Economy, Global Justice: Theoretical Objections and Policy Alternatives to Neoliberalism*, London: Routledge.

DeMartino, G. and S. Cullenberg (1994), 'Beyond the competitiveness debate: an internationalist agenda', *Social Text*, **41**, 11–40.

Dorman, P. (1988), 'Worker rights and international trade: a case for intervention', *Review of Radical Political Economics*, **20**(2&3), 241–6.

Dorman, P. (1992), 'The social tariff approach to international disparities in environmental and worker rights standards: history, theory and some initial evidence', in C. Lehman and R. Moore (eds), *Multinational Culture*, Westport, CT: Greenwood Press, pp. 203–23.

Elster, J. (1982), 'Sour grapes – utilitarianism and the genesis of wants', in A.K. Sen and B. Williams (eds), *Utilitarianism and Beyond*, Cambridge: Cambridge University Press, pp. 219–38.

Goldberg, P.K. and N. Pavcnik (2007), 'Distributional effects of globalization in developing countries', *Journal of Economic Literature*, **45**(1), March, 39–82.

Grabel, I. (2003), 'Averting crisis? Assessing measures to manage financial integration in emerging economies', *Cambridge Journal of Economics*, **27**(3), 317–36.

Hines, C. and J. Oram (2009), 'Time for a progressive protectionism', *World Development Movement Action*, Summer.

Krugman, P. (1997), 'In praise of cheap labor', *Slate Magazine*, 20 March, http://www.slate.com/id/1918/; accessed 21 October 2010.

Krugman, P. (2001), 'Hearts and heads', *New York Times*, 21 April.

Krugman, P. (2007a), 'Divided over trade', *New York Times*, 14 May.

Krugman, P. (2007b), 'Trouble with trade', *New York Times*, 28 December.

Polanyi, K. (1944), *The Great Transformation: The Political and Economic Origins of our Time*, Boston: Beacon Press.

Rodrik, D. (1997), *Has Globalization Gone too Far?*, Washington, DC: Institute for International Economics.

Sen, A.K. (1990), 'Gender and co-operative conflicts', in I. Tinker (ed.), *Persistent Inequalities*, Oxford: Oxford University Press, pp. 123–49.

Sen, A.K. (1992), *Inequality Reexamined*, Cambridge, MA: Harvard University Press.

Sutcliffe, B. (1998), 'Freedom to move in the age of globalization', in D. Baker, G. Epstein and R. Pollin (eds), *Globalization and Progressive Economic Policy*, Cambridge: Cambridge University Press, pp. 325–36.

Wolff, R.D. and S.A. Resnick (1987), *Economics – Marxian Versus Neoclassical*, Baltimore, MD: Johns Hopkins University Press.

27 Global inequality and the global financial crisis: the new transmission mechanism

Photis Lysandrou

According to Marx the root cause of crisis always lies in the inequality of wealth engendered by the commoditisation of labour power. If he was right it follows that the globalisation of commodity relations must lead to a crisis on a corresponding global scale unless the growth in inequality is held in check. The fact that it was not checked but allowed to reach epic proportions by the time the global financial crisis broke out is for many people confirmation that Marx was right. This chapter seeks to give weight to this view by explaining the new mechanism through which the effects of exploitation are transmitted into crisis: prevented from finding expression in an excess supply of products in GDP space, these effects have instead found expression in an excess demand for securities in capital market space. Most economists put the major blame for the financial crisis on the banks because it was they who created the toxic securities that caused the financial system to seize up. My interpretation is different. The banks certainly overreached themselves in creating these securities but the principal reason why they did so was to augment the wealth storage capacity of existing securities stocks in order to accommodate the build-up of private wealth.

1 Background

The financial crisis that began in the US sub-prime mortgage market and then spread to the banking sector has since mutated into the most severe international economic crisis since the Great Depression of the 1930s. As it has done so, popular interest in the theories of Marx has increased in like measure as evidenced by the rate at which his works have been flying off the shelves in Germany and other countries.[1] It is easy to see why. According to Marx, crisis is endemic to capitalism as a commodity-producing system, first, because the commodity form by its very nature gives rise to the possibility of a separation between supply and demand, and, second, because periodic realisation of this separation comes from the fact that the value of the labour capacity is generally less than the value of the output produced by it. In other words, the root cause of crisis in Marx's view is always to be found in the inequality of wealth distribution engendered by the commoditisation of labour power. It follows from this logic that the globalisation of commodity relations, now more or less complete following the end of colonialism and the more recent collapse of communism, must at some point lead to a crisis on a corresponding global scale unless the inequality of wealth distribution is held in check. The fact that it was not, but on the contrary allowed to grow to epic proportions by the time the financial crisis broke out in the US, is for many people confirmation that Marx was right.

This chapter seeks to give analytical weight to this position by directing attention to one key question: how did sub-prime-backed securities get into the financial system and cause it to seize up with such devastating consequences? It will be shown that the answer has exactly to do with wealth inequality and a separation between supply and demand. Faced with an excess of global demand for ordinary ground-level securities (those issued by governments and private corporations the cash flows on which are serviced directly out of their revenue streams), the financial system responded not only by expanding the supply of first-tier securities (those issued by banks the cash flows on which are serviced by the interest payments on various types of loans) but also the supply of second- and higher-order-tier securities (securities backed by pools of securities). The observation that it was the highly complex and opaque nature of these financial instruments that helped to cause the complete breakdown in trust between the large commercial banks in 2007–08 is the single most important reason why the majority of economists put the blame for the ensuing global crisis on the financial system itself. My interpretation is different. The system certainly overreached itself in creating and distributing structured securities that turned out to be highly toxic, but it did so principally because of the external pressures placed upon it to supply those securities and a major source of those pressures can be traced right back to the enormous concentration of wealth ownership.

The structure of this chapter is as follows. Section 2 outlines the major explanations for the global financial crisis. Section 3 explains the reasons behind the emergence of a global excess demand for securities. Section 4 explains the pressures on the financial system to resolve this excess demand problem. Section 5 explains why the crisis transmission mechanism has shifted from the space of material commodities to the space of financial commodities. Section 6 gives some conclusions.

2 Some explanations for the global financial crisis

The global financial crisis originated in the market for collateralised debt obligations (CDOs), structured financial products that were created by pooling mortgage-backed securities (mainly comprising those backed by sub-prime and other non-conforming mortgage loans) with other asset-backed securities as backing collateral. The use of sophisticated credit enhancement techniques in the construction of these products was supposed to have made them safe. However, when the delinquency rate among US sub-prime borrowers began to rise sharply in the wake of the increases in the Federal Reserve rate from late 2005, not only did these sophisticated techniques not prevent a resulting fall in the prices of CDOs, they actually helped to accelerate the rate of that fall by virtue of having helped to make these products too opaque and hence too difficult to value accurately. It was the panic caused by the unexpectedly rapid collapse of the CDO market that led to the breakdown in trust between the large commercial banks (many of whom owned or sponsored investment vehicles that were directly exposed to this market), a breakdown that proved to be catastrophic insofar as it was the catalyst setting in motion a liquidity–solvency crisis spiral that eventually culminated in the paralysis of the whole financial system.

According to the official view, 'the root cause of the crisis was a widespread undervaluation of risk'.[2] As a matter of description, this view is correct in that the crisis would not have occurred in the form that it did had sub-prime-backed securities not entered the financial system and caused it to seize up. But the deeper question is, what led so many financial institutions to undervalue risk on so widespread a scale? The mainstream answer singles out various agency and institutional failures rather than any systemic weaknesses. These failures include: the overzealous quest for fees and commissions and the concomitant over-relaxation of lending standards on the part of the mortgage brokers and banks originating the sub-prime loans; the highly leveraged and chronically under-capitalised positions of the banks and of their investment vehicles; flaws in the risk assessment methods used by the credit rating agencies to rate the various financial products created by the investment banks; and, last but by no means least, the lack of proper oversight of the whole shadow banking system on the part of the regulatory authorities.

The real economy enters into the picture in a somewhat benign way. The period spanning the last decade and a half has generally been characterised by a combination of relatively low and stable inflation with robust output growth, a phenomenon that has led both academics and policy-makers to describe the period as the 'great moderation' or, as in the UK, the 'great stability'.[3] The argument is that this unusually long period of stability gave rise to complacency and lax behaviour all round: on the part of households who over-borrowed, on the part of investors who over-lent, on the part of the banks and other financial institutions who intermediated the whole process and on the part of the authorities who put too much trust in these institutions. The further contention is that what also served to encourage this laxity of behaviour in the Western financial markets was the continued growth of global imbalances:[4] the counterpart to excess liquidity and hence the credit expansion and over-borrowing in many of the developed economies was the 'savings glut' in the Emerging Market Economies (EMEs), principally those of East Asia and the Middle East, a glut allegedly caused by the overcautious, even frugal, behaviour of EME governments, corporations and individuals.

While mainstream economists admit that policy errors played a not insignificant role in the financial crisis, these errors tend to be seen as arising out of gaps in an otherwise sound macroeconomic policy framework. Heterodox economists by contrast put the blame for the crisis squarely on that framework.[5] The contribution to the crisis made by the many agency and institutional failures identified above is not denied; rather, it is that the source of these failures is seen to be the neoclassical theory-inspired dogma that economic resources are allocated most efficiently when the chief responsibility for their allocation is placed with the financial system in general and with the capital markets in particular. This proposition is held to be illusory because capital markets are believed to be inherently speculative in nature, and because short-term speculation is considered to be a poor basis on which to organise resources given its potential conflict with the long-term interests of industry. National economies, it is argued, can only follow a continuously stable and efficient growth path if the capital markets are closely monitored and controlled by governments. On the contrary, if these markets are uncontrolled or too lightly monitored, then speculative interests will take precedence over manufacturing interests with the result that periods of economic stability will be punctuated by episodes of turbulence and instability. What is more, if governments not only do not adequately control the capital markets but also go so far as to give encouragement to the growth in their size and weight in the economy, then it will inevitably be the case that each episode of financial turbulence will be greater in scale and amplitude than the previous one. From this perspective, the global financial crisis that originated in the US mortgage market in 2007 is essentially nothing other than a culminating stage of a process that dates back to the early late 1970s and early 1980s, the point at which the post-war Keynesian macro-policy framework began to give way to the neoliberal framework.

Although there are substantive differences between the mainstream and heterodox explanations for the global financial crisis, there is one issue on which there is common agreement and this is that the cause of the crisis is ultimately to be found in the financial sector itself.[6] This agreement exists because neither camp has ever entertained the possibility of an excess global demand for securities, the effects of which infiltrated the financial system including that part connected with the structured credit products. As a consequence, supply-side factors are unanimously considered to have been the driving force behind the growth of these products, while demand-side factors are seen as having played a largely passive and accommodating role. The reality is that these latter factors played a far more active, one could even say aggressive, role as a result of the pressures spilling over from the government and corporate securities markets. This point is important because the moment that it is brought to the fore, it becomes clear that the reason for the widespread undervaluation of risk that made the financial crisis possible had not merely to do with weaknesses in particular financial institutions and practices, nor merely with the way that the financial system is currently structured, but also with wider problems in the global economy.

3 The excess demand for securities problem

The objection to the idea of demand-side pressures in the global securities markets is based partly on empirical grounds. As shown in Figure 27.1, the rate of growth of the world's financial stock has outstripped that for world GDP over the past three decades. The chief factor responsible for this growth has been the issuance of public and private securities. Subtracting bank deposit money from the total financial stock of \$167 trillion outstanding at end-2006, this left \$111 trillion worth of equities and corporate and government bonds and \$11 trillion worth of asset-backed securities, from which in turn a further \$3 trillion worth of CDOs had been constructed (see Figure 27.2).

Given the extraordinary growth of ordinary debt securities, it is difficult to see how an excess demand for them could have risen to a point where its effects spilled over into the other debt markets. This difficulty begins to disappear, however, when we consider the scale and composition of the global demand for securities. As shown in Table 27.1, the four major sources of this demand in 2006 were: (1) the big institutional investors: the pension funds (PF), mutual funds (MF) and insurance companies (IC); (2) the commercial banks, many of whom, in response to the changes in household saving patterns, have moved into the asset management business; (3) governments, mainly comprising those of EMEs, who not only held substantial amounts of US treasuries as currency

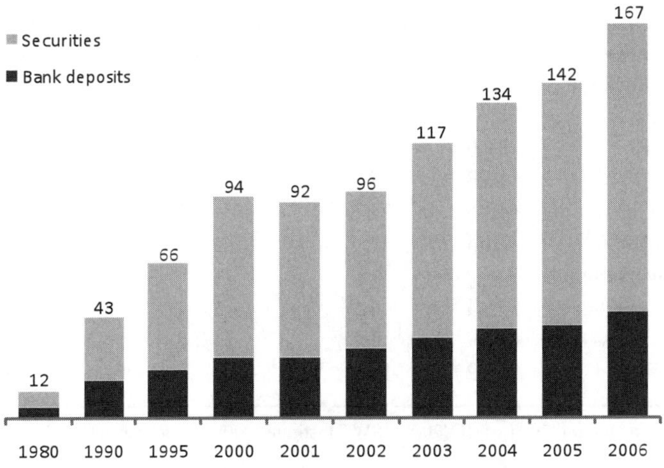

Source: McKinsey Global Institute (2008).

Figure 27.1 Growth of global financial stocks (US\$ trillions)

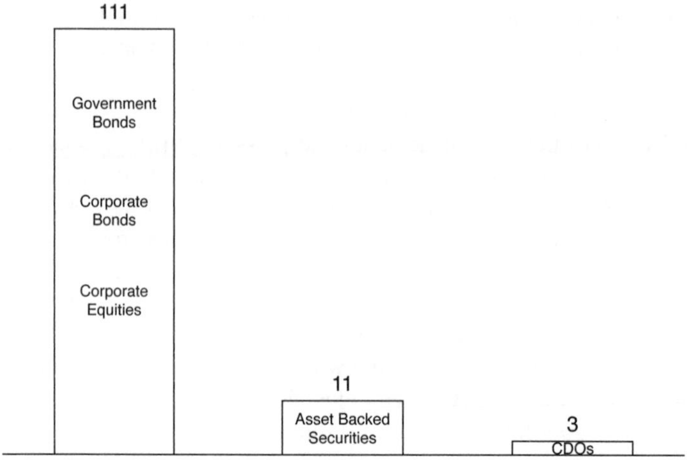

Source: IMF (2008).

Figure 27.2 Composition of global securities stocks, 2006 ($ trillions)

Table 27.1 Major holders of securities, 2006 (US$ trillions)

	Total Assets	Securities	Alternative Investments (inc. hedge funds)	Other Assets (cash, real estate, etc.)
1. Institutional Investors				
PFs	21.6	17.3	1.3	3.0
MFs	19.3	17.4	0.8	1.1
ICs	18.5	14.8	1.1	2.6
2. Banks	74.4	37.2	–	–
3. Governments				
Reserves	5.4	4.9	0	0.5
SWFs	1.9	1.5	0.2	0.2
4. HNWIs	37.2	19.3	3.7	14.1

Source: Capgemini (2007); IMF (2008); SWF Institute (2008); Conference Board (2008).

reserves but were increasingly investing in the securities markets through recently established Sovereign Wealth Funds (SWFs); and (4) high net worth individuals (HNWIs).

Empirics aside, the more important reason why an excess demand for securities is generally considered impossible stems from the idea that the law of supply and demand does not apply in the usual way in the financial markets because prices respond to quantity movements here differently from the way that they respond in the markets for goods and services. To quote from a recent article on the financial crisis published by the Bank for International Settlements, in the real sector:

> an increase in supply tends to reduce the equilibrium price and is hence self-equilibrating. By contrast, in the financial sector, increases in the supply of funds (e.g. credit) will, up to a point, create their own demand, by making financing terms more attractive, boosting asset prices and hence aggregate demand. In a sense, a higher supply (of funding liquidity) ultimately generates its own demand.[7]

This statement of a financial version of Say's Law is put in flow terms; put in stock terms, the argument is that there cannot be an excess demand for securities because there will always be a corresponding level of supply due to the lowering of the cost of capital. This argument helps to explain why the sharp fall in bond yields and the tightening of yield spreads from about 2001[8] were seen as having been largely driven by psychological factors: infected by the general atmosphere of optimism and confidence in the real economy that had been stimulated by the years of the great stability, investors also became over-confident and hence overly willing to accept lower-risk premiums.[9]

Implicit in this argument is the assumption that investors basically view governments and corporations in the way that the latter view themselves, namely, as organisations whose function is to provide certain goods or services and who resort to external funding to help execute that function. This assumption has become an anachronism. Most investors today, if by no means all of them, view governments and corporations as organisations whose chief function is to supply securities that can serve as wealth containers, and whose ability to provide goods and services is the necessary means by which the tangibility of these wealth containers is maintained. From this standpoint, the recent developments in the global securities markets can be interpreted in a way that identifies them with those that typically occur in the product markets: just as prices of goods or services rise when the physical constraints on organisations prevent them from supplying enough quantities to match demand, so did the prices of securities rise (and yields fall) after 2001 because there were constraints on organisations preventing them from supplying securities with a sufficient enough wealth storage capacity to accommodate the build-up of global wealth.

The major source of these constraints can be traced to the recent organisational changes in institutional asset management.[10] It is a general rule that whenever a particular industry expands in scale, there is a corresponding shift towards more standardised forms of provision and the asset management industry is no exception. In place of the broad-based and discretionally managed portfolio that was previously the norm, more typical today is the narrow portfolio managed to a target risk–return ratio. Most of the big institutions now run hundreds of portfolios arranged along a risk–return continuum that begins with the giant beta factory portfolios that combine average market return with an average level of risk, while all other portfolios seek to add an extra amount of return at the cost of accepting a corresponding extra amount of risk. Through the strict separation of portfolios and their benchmarking against market indexes, the pension funds and other institutions can contain portfolio costs by matching the rewards given to individual managers to their performance; thus beta factory managers, for example, are paid substantially less than are the genuine alpha creators. As regards the retail sector, the new approach to asset management represents a cost-efficient way of allowing popular access to its benefits on affordable terms; rather than personally advise retail clients on how best to invest their money, what the mutual funds now do is to make available various off-the-peg investment products and invite clients to choose the product that suits their particular risk appetite.

The increasing standardisation and commoditisation of investment portfolios help to put into context the recent changes spearheaded by the institutional investors in the areas of transparency and disclosure, ratings metrics, accountancy standards, corporate law and corporate governance. Many of these changes have aroused a great deal of opposition on the grounds that the balance of power has swung too far in the direction of the investors holding securities and away from the organisations issuing them. While this reaction is understandable, it is also to some extent misplaced because it fails to take proper account of the recent change in the investor base and thus of the change in the way that securities are perceived. Where previously the typical investor was a small individual, a bank, or another corporation, none of whom had cause to see securities as anything but a means of financing the production of goods or services because none of them had cause to treat their investment portfolios as 'products' to be marketed to the public, the typical investor now dominating the world's capital markets is a pension or mutual fund or an insurance company and these investors on the contrary do have good cause to treat their portfolios as marketable products. Since the risk profiles of these products depend on the risk characteristics of their constituent securities, it follows that asset managers have to impose far stricter transparency and governance rules on security issuers if they are to carry out their basic function. This imposition is in principle no different from what goes on in other product markets: just as households and firms buying goods or services for consumption or production purposes expect them to meet with certain standards regarding material quality, so institutional investors buying securities for portfolio management purposes expect these to meet with well-defined standards regarding risk quality.

The problem with these new governance standards is that, while necessary to the commoditisation of securities, they at the same time exert a restraining effect on their global supply. There are two routes through which this happens. The first is through the impact on the behaviour of individual governments and corporations. There have always been certain norms regarding the amounts of securities that governments and corporations can safely issue, and these norms have always been violated to one degree or other. However, what is different today is that not only has there been a certain hardening of these norms (a process that also reflects their convergence at the global level) but also, and more importantly, that any transgression, no matter how small or trivial, can be instantly picked up and measured with forensic precision. Now when security issuers know that any idiosyncrasy on their part is certain to be factored into their ratings and thus into their capital raising costs, the more likely are they to try to conform in order to limit the costs of idiosyncrasy and this conformity includes keeping a tight rein on their external financial obligations. The second route is through the impact on regional capital market development. As shown in Figure 27.3, the size differences across countries and regions in capital market terms are far higher than are their differences in GDP terms. It is particularly noteworthy that in 2006 the EMEs as a whole only accounted for 14 per cent of the global stock of securities as compared with 30 per cent of world output. Part of the story behind this is that the policy-makers in these regions have deliberately held capital market growth in check because of a continuing preference for alternative, relation-based forms of finance. However, another part of the story is that the establishment of a market for securities that is genuinely deep and liquid requires a legal, accountancy and governance framework that is orders of magnitude stronger and more transparent than that required for the material product markets.

The differences in capital market size help to put into perspective the reasons why the greater part of the assets managed by US and European institutional investors continue to be assigned to domestic securities. This practice is often construed as evidence of a continuing home or regional bias in institutional asset management, but the word 'bias' implies that institutional investors have the option to diversify their portfolios along geographical lines to a far greater extent than they do but choose not to exercise that option.[11] The truth is that they have no such option. Faced with severe limits on the amounts of transparent and reliable securities that are available outside of the core capital markets, US and European institutional investors have of necessity to concentrate their asset holdings in these core markets. This is problem enough, but what greatly adds to it is that these investors face increased competition in these core markets not only from other types of domestic investor but also from foreign institutions and individuals. The scale of the increase in competition from this direction became particularly marked in the period between 2001 and 2006 as was evident

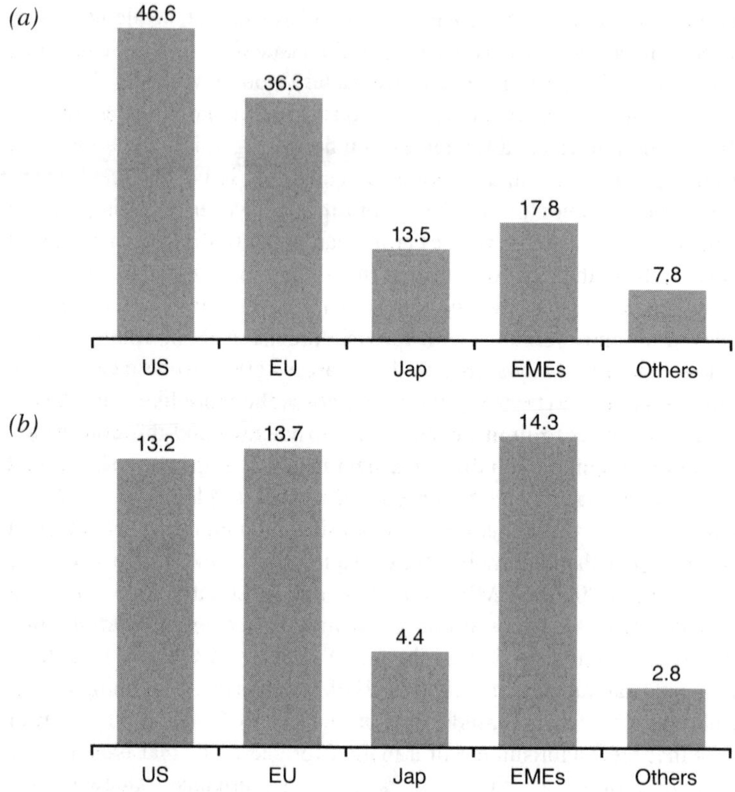

Source: IMF (2008).

Figure 27.3 *(a) World capital markets: 2006 (US$ trillion); (b) world GDP: 2006 (US$ trillion)*

in the volume of net capital outflows from the EMEs (see Figure 27.4a), the majority part of which was directed into the US markets (see Figure 27.4b). As foreign investors pushed into these markets thus putting more downward pressure on treasury yields and also helping to tighten yield spreads, the greater was the corresponding pressure on institutional investors to search for new sources of yield.

While these capital flows in the period up to 2006 were certainly evidence of imbalances in the global economy as has been pointed out by a number of commentators, there are problems with the claim that these imbalances were symptomatic of differences in regional behavioural patterns, notably, that the Americans were not saving enough and the Asians for their part were saving

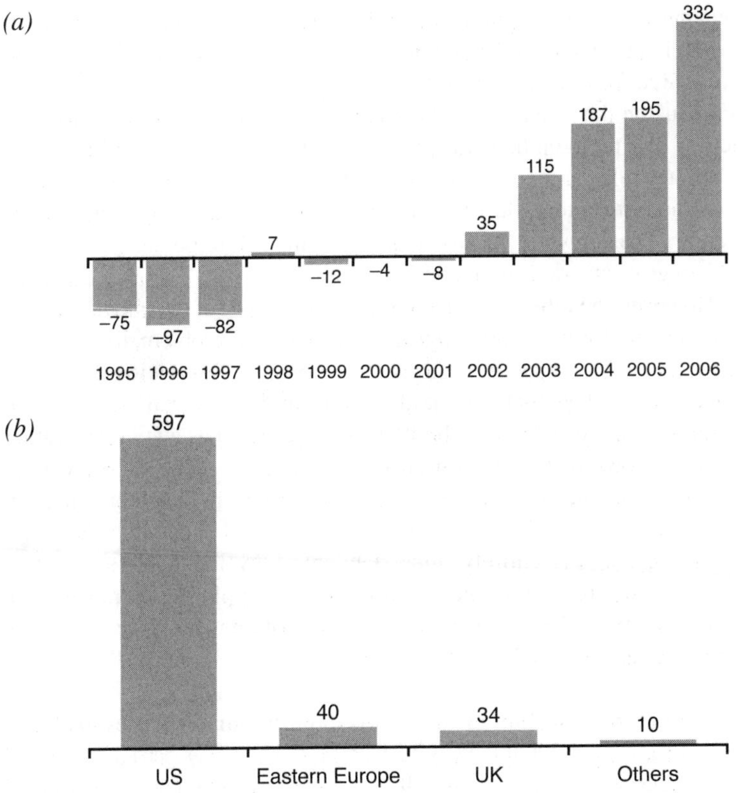

Source: McKinsey Global Institute (2008).

Figure 27.4 (a) EME net capital flows; (b) net capital inflows (av. 2001–06)

too much. It hardly makes sense to single out for special attention a 'savings glut' in the Asian and other EMEs just before the outbreak of the crisis, when at that same time the greater part of the surplus pools of capital in the world were held by US and European institutional investors, banks and wealthy individuals. In retrospect, the observed global imbalances had less to do with behavioural differences than with capital market asymmetries. These asymmetries are substantive but they become even more so when capital market size is measured in currency terms for while the US dollar market remains the same, the eurozone market shrinks in size in the absence of the UK sterling market and the EME markets simply disintegrate into fragments. Given the preponderant size of the dollar market, it was inevitable that EME governments and private investors would try to squeeze into this market for reserve currency and other investment purposes thereby putting more downward pressure on treasury yields and also helping to tighten yield spreads, and thus in turn forcing domestic investors to search for new sources of yield.

The conclusion that falls out of the above is that the institutional investors were victims of a problem that was partly of their own making: having forced through stricter rules and codes of conduct for security issuers in the closing decades of the last century, they then found themselves in the opening decade of this century chasing yield because these rules made it impossible for securities stocks to grow at a rate commensurate with the growth of global aggregate demand. However, the other conclusion that also falls out of the above is that if the excess demand for investable securities was a global problem, the attempts at solving it had to have a more localised character. The observation that it was the US financial markets that were at the centre of the financial crisis has led some commentators to say that it should be characterised as a US crisis rather than as a truly global one.[12] This inference is in my view quite simply wrong. Given the preponderant weight of the US capital markets in the global financial system, and the corresponding international status of the US dollar as the major reserve currency, it was entirely understandable why the world's investors looked to US financial institutions in particular to supply the extra financial products that were needed to absorb the overflow of demand. These were the asset-backed securities (ABS).

4 The attempted resolution of the excess demand for securities problem

Explanations for the growth of the US ABS market, which was particularly rapid in the last decade (see Figure 27.5), usually concentrate attention on the household demand for credit. Some commentators present the expansion in this demand in terms of cultural factors: US households, it is said, became too consumer-oriented, and thus addicted to living on credit.[13] Others give a more plausible story that concentrates on the material effects of globalisation, specifically those arising out of the increasing relocation of manufacturing jobs to the relatively low-wage areas of Asia and China in particular: while helping to keep down wages and hence inflationary pressures in the US, this relocation also meant that US low- to mid-income households had increasingly to rely on credit as a means of survival.[14] From whatever angle the story of consumer credit expansion is told, what tends to be backgrounded is the role played by the global demand for asset-backed securities. However, from the evidence showing a tightening of yield spreads in the US ABS market from 2001[15] there is good reason to believe that the demand for these securities from institutional investors, both US and foreign, was in effect outstripping the rate of growth in their supply. This rate, while impressive when compared with the rate for previous periods, was still not high enough to satisfy expanding demand, and it could not be because the bulk of the loans servicing these securities were given according to conventional lending criteria.

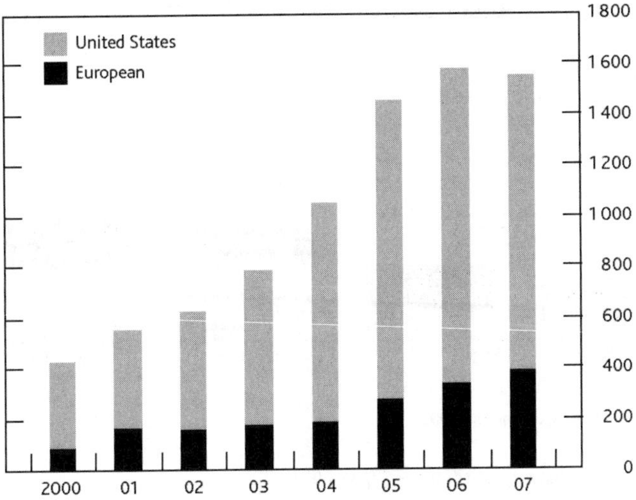

Source: Bank of England (2008).

Figure 27.5 Asset-backed securities issuance (US$ billions)

It is here that we come to the sub-prime products. Of the $11 trillion worth of asset-backed securities in 2006, about $6.5 trillion consisted of residential mortgage-backed securities, of which approximately a third consisted of securities backed by various non-conforming loans.[16] The standard explanation for the growth of this part of the mortgage market starts with the mortgage brokers and banks, who, in order to make commission, gave loans to sub-prime borrowers on terms that were far too easy and then moves on to the role of the investment banks and credit rating agencies who, also eager to make commission, were more than ready to create the sophisticated credit products. This standard explanation then finally ends with a discussion of how trusting and gullible investors were seduced into buying these products. This is not quite accurate. The more accurate explanation is one that runs this story in the reverse direction: in the frantic search for yield, investors put pressure on the investment banks to supply structured credit products in ever greater quantities, and, in order to be able to do this, these banks needed the mortgage originators to take whatever steps were necessary to induce as many sub-prime borrowers as was possible to take out mortgage loans.

The vital clue that this reverse story is the more plausible explanation for the sudden steep rise in sub-prime mortgage loans after 2001 is given by the composition of the demand for CDOs (see Figure 27.6). Banks, asset managers and insurance companies held approximately 52 per cent of the CDOs outstanding

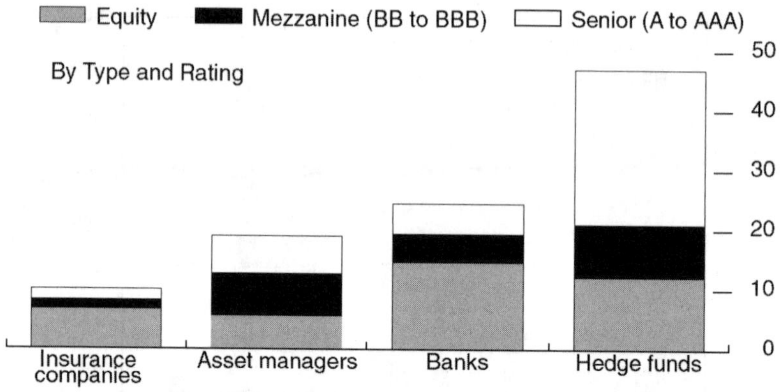

Source: House of Commons (2008).

Figure 27.6 Buyers of CDOs: 2006 (%)

at end-2006, while the hedge funds held the other 48 per cent. This ratio at first seems curious because at that same time the hedge funds as a group held just over 1 per cent of the world's total stock of securities of $122 trillion. The disparity, however, is easily explained. The basic task of hedge funds is to generate for their clients (chief among whom were the high net worth individuals)[17] above average returns for which they get paid above average fees. This task became increasingly difficult in the low-yield macro-environment of the early to mid-2000s because no matter how sophisticated the investment strategies used by the hedge funds to generate yield, there were limits to how much could in fact be sweated and squeezed out of the existing securities and other asset classes.

Thus, the hedge funds found themselves in a dilemma: on the one hand, more and more assets were being placed under their management because other investors were finding it difficult to generate yield (see Figure 27.7); on the other hand, the hedge funds were themselves finding it difficult to generate yield. It was because hedge funds needed to resolve this dilemma that helps to explain why it was they who led the search for alternative financial products that could give higher yields, and, when finding that the structured credit products fitted this description, why it was they who led the demand for them. Far from passively accepting the products provided by suppliers, the hedge funds on the contrary pushed and prodded the suppliers into providing these products at an ever-increasing rate. To quote from testimony given by Gerald Corrigan of Goldman Sachs at a House of Commons hearing on the financial crisis: 'To a significant degree it has been the reach for yield on the part of institutional investors in particular that goes a considerable distance in explaining this very rapid growth of structured credit products'.[18]

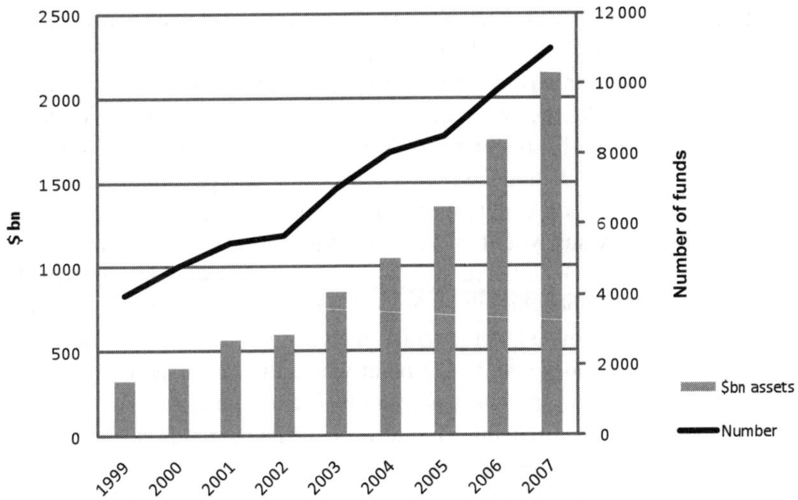

Source: Bank of England (2008).

Figure 27.7 Growth of hedge funds

The growth of these products may have been very rapid, but apparently not rapid enough to keep up with the demand for them and so the investment banks had to find other ways of making up the shortfall. One way was by resecuritising unsold mezzanine and other lower-rated tranches of securities to create CDOs-squared, and resecuritising any unsold mezzanine tranches of these instruments to create CDOs-cubed. According to a recent IMF report, 'These CDOs-squared and structured finance CDOs were created almost solely to resecuritize MBS and CDO mezzanine tranches, for which there was not sufficient demand from investors. Therefore their value added in transferring risk is questionable'.[19] In my opinion, what is more questionable here is the assumption that the CDOs-squared and cubed were created purely to transfer credit risk. This may have been part of their function, but their chief purpose was to serve as wealth containers of a particular risk–return vintage. In the universe of debt securities there are only a handful of banks and corporations and about 20 to 30 governments that have a triple A rating. The rest is filled with lower-rated matter. So when the banks found a way of creating thousands of extra AAA-rated products,[20] it was only logical that investor demand would be concentrated on these products, and it was equally logical that, rather than waste any unsold mezzanine and equity tranches, the banks would collect all of these together to create the additional senior tranches demanded by investors.

A further way of satisfying investor demand was through the supply of 'synthetic' CDOs, products created by the investment banks by taking a cash CDO as a reference entity for two credit default swaps (CDSs) entered into simultaneously: on the one side, the synthetic CDO creator would sell protection to the counterparty in return for payments of interest and principal; on the other, the creator would buy protection from the counterparty and pay interest and principal. There were several variations on this theme. For example, cash flows in the credit default swaps would only involve the payment of interest: the 'unfunded' synthetic CDO. Or the reference entity for CDSs would be a particular tranche of a CDO rather than the whole CDO: the 'single tranche' synthetic CDO. It has been estimated that by 2006, the year before the crash, the supply of synthetic CDOs had grown to the point where they matched the supply of cash CDOs and what is particularly noteworthy is that among the leading institutions that had helped to drive this growth were the hedge funds, second only to the banks in the buying and selling of protection.[21]

If the hedge funds were one of the principal conduits through which flowed the external pressures on the financial system to create the structured credit products, a principal source of those pressures in turn had to be the huge concentration of wealth ownership. Ultimately, it all comes down to simple arithmetic. Recall that on the eve of the crisis the global aggregate demand for securities came from four major groups: institutional investors, banks, governments and high net worth individuals. As regards the first three of these groups, there is some justification, or, at the very least, some plausible explanation, for the size of the demand for securities that was exercised. This hardly applies to the high net worth individuals who in 2006 numbered 9.5 million (a figure that represents just over 0.01 per cent of the world's population of 6.8 billion) and who had a combined wealth of $37 trillion, more than half of which, $19 trillion, was in securities (a figure that represents just under 10 per cent of the total financial claims on the world's governments and large corporations).[22] Taking these figures in conjunction with the observation that the high net worth individuals were by far the most important suppliers of finance to the hedge funds who in turn were the chief buyers of CDOs, it follows that had the wealth of these individuals been more evenly dispersed in the global economy the pressures on the financial system to augment the wealth storage capacity of existing securities stocks would have eased sufficiently so as not to force it into creating the toxic securities on the scale that it did and the financial crisis would not have occurred when it did.

5 The new crisis transmission mechanism

Marx was right. Exploitation and wealth inequality are usually at the root of crises in a commodity producing system, and so also were they at the root of this global financial crisis. To put forward this argument is neither to ignore nor to excuse the many failings and errors on the part of the various financial institutions that supplied the structured credit products that were at the epicentre of the crisis. The point is that important as these factors were, they were facilitating factors nonetheless, factors that helped to bring the crisis to fruition and give it amplification. The causal factors lay outside of the financial sector, in the growth of wealth inequality that had been allowed to reach unsupportable proportions by the early part of this century. If the majority of economists refuse to give credence to this idea, it is because there appear to be insuperable difficulties with Marx's insights into capitalist crises and exploitation that prevent them from serving as a useful framework for understanding contemporary developments. However, these difficulties are only insuperable on the assumption that Marx's insights are inseparable from the traditional theoretical form into which they have been cast and this assumption is wrong.

Consider first the crisis transmission mechanism. The standard Marxian construction of this mechanism is basically as follows:[23] the payment of wages at the value of the labour capacity is at once the primary source of profits and the source of constraints on their realisation; these constraints can never be eliminated but they can be temporarily suspended by various means, including the expansion of credit; when these means are finally exhausted and the constraints on profits again begin to tighten, the resulting cutbacks in capital investment and accompanying rise in lay-offs trigger an economic crisis. Now the opening part of this sequence does accord reasonably well with what has been happening in the global economy: the share of wages in the national incomes of the most advanced economies have been falling since the 1970s,[24] a trend that has been reinforced by the massive influx of labour into the global labour pool following the collapse of the communist systems and the integration of China into the world market,[25] and realisation problems have accordingly become more pressing as attested by the chequered performance of profit rates in the core regions of the world capitalist system[26] and by periodic crises in its peripheral regions. By contrast, the latter part of the sequence does not accord so well with recent events. Although the realisation constraints on profits were never eliminated, they continued to be eased to a sufficient enough extent as to prevent them from being the catalyst triggering a global economic crisis. When this crisis did eventually break out, its origins lay not in the market for corporate debt or in the market for corporate equity, but in the market for mortgage-backed securities, that is to say, in that part of the financial sector that had the least connection with corporate profitability. Although a number of writers have tried to get round this peculiarity in their explanations of the global financial crisis by adding various supplementary stories to the orthodox Marxian theory of crisis (stories that essentially boil down to the same critique of financial institutions and practices as has been given by others) the fact that these explanations remain centrally focussed on corporate profitability means that it is unlikely they will command much support.[27]

The reality is that a new crisis transmission mechanism has emerged following the recent changes in the size and structure of the capital markets. At the time that Marx was writing these markets were still in their infancy. In fact, they remained relatively underdeveloped until about 1980, for at no time prior to that date were the global stocks of securities anywhere near comparable to the level of world output. Since that date the reverse has been true. The world's governments and large bank and non-bank corporations have been colonising the future to escape the constraints of the present and, as a consequence of this colonisation, the effects of global exploitation and wealth inequality have been forced to find a different form of expression: prevented from surfacing in GDP space in the form of an excess supply of material products – because the demand for these products had successfully been propped up by a number of supports that included high levels of public expenditure on the one hand and increased credit to the private sector on the other – these effects have surfaced instead in capital market space in the form of an excess demand for securities. That they did so ultimately comes down to the ambivalent impact of the institutional asset management industry on securities stocks: although the growth of this industry has helped to drive the expansion in the demand for securities, thereby helping governments and corporations to transcend current income constraints on their operations to a far greater degree than would otherwise have been possible, the accompanying shift towards the commoditisation of investment portfolios has necessitated the imposition of certain rules and obligations on security issuers that, while needed to concretise the risk characteristics of portfolios, served to restrain the rate of security issuance. This restraining effect did not become a problem as long as the overall global demand for securities grew at a pace the global supply could keep up with. However, it did become a problem after 2001 when the demand for securities began to accelerate due to the rapid accumulation of wealth seeking a suitable form of wealth storage.

As already noted, the financial sector responded to this pressure of demand by creating structured credit products that were difficult to price and trade against market standards; and, as also noted, when this difficulty proved to be a critical factor in the breakdown of trust between the banks that was in turn responsible for the mutation of the sub-prime crisis into a global financial crisis, the banks took the major blame for causing the crisis. Although not without foundation, this criticism misses the essential point that had the banks stuck to the established rules for giving mortgage loans and to the conventional methods for securitising these loans, they could never have created the extra securities in the amounts needed to absorb the overspill of global demand. The only way that they could even begin to achieve this objective was precisely by breaking the established rules of lending and by resorting to highly unconventional methods of securitisation.[28] It is of course true that a great deal of money was made out of the millions of sub-prime and other non-conforming borrowers whose mortgages provided the raw material from which the CDOs were constructed; but in the final analysis it was not greed, nor complacency, nor even hubris, that drove the banks and their associates to break the rules of commodity exchange so much as the attempt to outstep the limits of the commodity system.

Consider next the process of capitalist exploitation. The orthodox Marxian theory construes this process as a class-based one: the working class produces the surplus, while the capitalist appropriates this surplus and then distributes it within its ranks. Given the sheer diversity of today's high net worth individuals in terms of occupation, background and social status, it is simply impossible to apply this orthodox view of exploitation as an explanation for the observed global inequality of wealth distribution. Indeed, any attempt to do so only serves to reinforce the contrary position that exploitation does not exist or that, if it does, it takes place in a way that is entirely unconnected with anything that Marx had to say. The truth of the matter is that in Marx's own analysis of capitalism the locus of exploitation is to be found in the relation between commodities rather than in the relation between classes.

Marx begins his major work *Capital* with the single commodity.[29] He took the commodity to be the representative unit of analysis because capitalism was the first system in history to be based on generalised commodity production, and it came to be so because the commodity principle was for the first time stretched to encompass labour power. With this unique development, all previous relations of exploitation now began to be dissolved into the relations of market exchange: while the differences between capitalists and workers in terms of their respective positions and powers are necessary to the extraction of a surplus, the sufficient condition for this extraction lies in the pricing of the different capacities possessed by these opposing groups against market standards.[30] Since Marx's time, the commodity principle has been further stretched and deepened so that it now encompasses every possible entity in the world; not only every good or service produced in it, or even every capacity that is used to produce them, but also every financial claim on those capacities.[31] Along with the globalisation of the commodity principle there has been a corresponding dissolution of all parochial relations of exploitation into the exchange relations of the global market. In effect, a global commodity system has come into operation and every individual on the planet occupies a point somewhere in that system. Most individuals do so merely as possessors of a capacity for labour; others do so as possessors of other capacities and/or of various claims on capacities. The majority of individuals put more into the global commodity system than they take out, while a minority of individuals take out more than they put in, and a tiny minority of this minority take out far, far more than they put in. The problem is that, having taken out far more than they can possibly spend on themselves in current consumption, this tiny minority of individuals then seek to put the surplus back into the system in the form of claims on the future income streams created by others so as to secure their own future consumption.

6 Conclusions

The global financial crisis was not caused simply because toxic assets had got into the global financial system, but because the volume of those assets had grown to the point where the system could no longer cope. This point of critical mass was only reached because of the pressure of demand, and a principle source of that pressure was the huge concentration of wealth ownership. The clear implication that falls out of this line of argument is that the world's wealth has to be more equitably distributed if global financial crises are to be avoided. To give priority to this policy is not to exclude the many other proposals that have been suggested for making the banking sector and entire financial system more transparent, more efficient and, above all, more accountable. On their own, however, these proposals are insufficient. No matter how radically the financial system is reformed or restructured, as long as there remain external pressures on it to create products or to indulge in practices that are harmful to it, such products and practices will continue to be introduced and financial crises will continue to occur. These external pressures will only be removed when there is a significant redistribution of wealth, and what this entails as a first step is globally coordinated action in key areas of tax policy that should include the closure of tax havens to prevent tax avoidance, the harmonisation of national tax structures to prevent the exploitation of differences between them and the realignment of tax rates to ensure that the tax burden is again distributed on a progressive basis. In short, what is needed is a globalised version of Keynesianism.

This proposal may seem paradoxical in the context of a paper that purports to give a Marxist analysis of the financial crisis. There is no paradox, however, because there is no Marxist solution to capitalist crises that is essentially different from a radical form of Keynesianism. It used to be widely believed that there was such a solution, namely that as put into practice in the communist systems between 1917 and 1989. As it turned out, this proved to be no solution at all because far from progressing beyond capitalism these systems actually regressed back to a form of feudalism albeit with twentieth-century structures and trappings. The cardinal lesson arising out of this regression is that simply suspending or suppressing the commodity principle will not solve the problems of capitalism. In the final analysis, only three types of social system are possible: pre-commodity systems, the commodity system and a post-commodity system. Humanity will one day move to a stage of development where it will no longer have to rely on markets to allocate resources. However, to get to that stage it is necessary to work with the present commodity system and tap its potential for generating material growth while at the same time bringing it under democratic control so as to contain its other potential for generating wealth inequality. If there is any one positive thing that may come out of this global financial crisis, it is that it can possibly open the way to establishing that democratic control.

Notes

1. Connolly (2008).
2. Jean Claude Trichet, President of the European Central Bank, *Financial Times*, 13 November 2008. See also Goodhart (2008), the IMF (2008) and the Bank of England (2008) for similar statements.
3. See Bernanke (2004); Goodhart (2008).
4. See Bernanke (2005); Wolf (2009).
5. See, for example, Blackburn (2008); Wade (2008); Kregel (2008); Randall Wray (2008); Dore (2008).
6. This agreement is exemplified by the following statement by Kregel (2008): 'In the current crisis, the cushions of safety have been insufficient from the beginning – they are a structural result of how creditworthiness is assessed in the new "originate and distribute" financial system sanctioned by the modernisation of financial services. The crisis has simply revealed the systemic inadequacy of the evaluation of credit – or, what is the same thing, the undervaluation and mispricing of risk' (p. 21). Where the first half of this statement encapsulates the Minskyan critique of current financial developments, the second half gives a characterisation of the root cause of the financial crisis that is indistinguishable from that given by mainstream economists.
7. Borio (2008) p. 13.
8. High yield corporate bond spreads over US treasuries fell from 1200 basis points in 2001 to under 300 basis points in 2007 while Emerging Market bond spreads fell from 900 basis points to under 200 basis points over the same period (Borio, 2008).
9. Goodhart (2008), for example, argues that the 'serious under-pricing of risk' at the root of the financial crisis was in large part induced by the way that 'persistent macro-economic stability led many to believe that macro-economic risks had been significantly reduced. The implication was that investment generally, and financial conditions in particular, were subject to less aggregate, macro-economic risk than in the past' (p. 3).
10. For a more detailed account of these changes see Grahl and Lysandrou (2006).
11. The observed regional 'bias' in institutionally held portfolios was one of the principal arguments used by Hirst and Thompson (1999) to reject the idea of financial globalisation.
12. See Nesvetailova and Palan (2009) and Thompson (2010).
13. See Manning (2000) and Langley (2006).
14. See Boushey and Weller (2006).
15. The ABS spread on US treasuries fell from 150 basis points in 2001 to under 50 basis points in 2006–07 (IMF, 2008).
16. These broadly divided into jumbo loans (so-called because they had an above average loan to property value ratio), alternative-A loans (alt-A borrowers are just below prime borrowers in that, while having no income documentation, they have a good credit history) and sub-prime loans (borrowers belonging to the sub-prime category either have no credit history or an extremely poor one and include NINAs, those with no income and no assets, and NINJAs, those with no income, no job and no assets).
17. According to the Bank of England (2008) in the period 2001–07 wealthy individuals on average accounted for about 50 per cent of the assets placed with hedge funds, while banks, institutional investors and sovereign wealth funds accounted for the other 50 per cent.
18. House of Commons (2008), p. 16.
19. IMF (2008), p. 59.
20. In a statement to the Council of Institutional Investors in April 2009, Lloyd Blankfein of Goldman Sachs pointed out that 'In January 2008, there were 12 triple A-rated companies in the world. At the same time, there were 64,000 structured finance instruments, like CDO tranches, rated triple A'.

21. The hedge funds' share of protection buying went from 16 per cent of the total in 2004 to 28 per cent in 2006, while their share of protection selling went from 15 per cent to 31 per cent in the same period, (IMF, 2008).
22. This figure understates the degree of wealth concentration because to qualify as an HNWI one only needs assets to exceed liabilities by $1 million, which is not a high hurdle in this age. The truth is that the bulk of wealth is held by what are labelled as 'ultra' HNWIs, those with net assets in excess of $30 million.
23. For a lucid summary of the different versions of the Marxian theory of crisis see Evans (2004).
24. See Glyn (2007).
25. For estimates of the size of this influx see IMF (2007).
26. See Brenner (2006) and Glyn (2006).
27. Explanations for the financial crisis given from an orthodox Marxian standpoint can be found in *Monthly Review, International Socialism* and in a host of other left wing periodicals.
28. Goodhart (2008) has stated that 'the trigger for the crisis was, as everyone knows, the rising defaults in the US sub-prime mortgage market, but … the trigger could have been almost anywhere else. It was … an accident waiting and ready to happen'. I strongly disagree with this statement. The crisis was not an 'accident' but an inevitability given the accumulation of wealth seeking a suitable form of storage, and the trigger could not have been anywhere other than in the US sub-prime mortgage market, first, because all other markets had already been tapped to the full for the material needed to create the securities with extra storage capacity, second, because this market was the one market that required breaking the usual rules of transparency and risk evaluation if it too was to be tapped for the necessary security building material, and, third, because had these rules not been broken the trust between the banks would have remained intact and the problems in the mortgage sector would not have led to a crisis of the whole financial system.
29. For a more detailed account of the microfoundations of Marx's economic theory see Lysandrou (1996).
30. This argument is developed in Lysandrou (2000).
31. This argument is developed in Lysandrou (2005).

References

Bank of England (2008), *Financial Stability Report*, October.

Bernanke, B. (2004), 'The great moderation', remarks to Easter Economic Association, Washington DC, February.

Bernanke, B. (2005), 'The global saving glut and the US current account deficit', The Sandridge Lecture, Virginia Association of Economics, Richmond, Virginia.

Blackburn, R. (2008) 'The subprime crisis', *New Left Review*, No. 50.

Blankfein, Lloyd C. (2009), Remarks to the Council of Institutional Investors, April.

Borio, C. (2008), 'The financial turmoil of 2007–?: a preliminary assessment and some policy considerations', BIS Working Papers No. 251, March.

Boushey, H. and Weller, Christian E. (2006), 'Inequality and economic hardship in the United States of America', DESA Working Paper No. 18, April.

Brenner, R. (2006), *The Economics of Global Turbulence*, London: Verso.

Capgemini (2007), *11th World Wealth Report*, June.

Conference Board (2008), *Institutional Investment Report*, September.

Connolly, K. (2008), 'Booklovers turn to Karl Marx as financial crisis bites in Germany', available at http://www.pragoti.org/node/2241; accessed 21 October 2010.

Dore, R. (2008) 'Financialisation of the global economy', *Industrial and Corporate Change*, **17**(6).

Evans, T. (2004), 'Marxian and post-Keynesian theories of finance and the business cycle', *Capital and Class*, **28**(2).

Glyn, A. (2006), *Capitalism Unleashed: Finance, Globalization and Welfare*, New York: Oxford University Press.

Glyn, A. (2007), *Explaining Labour's Declining Share in National Incomes*, G-24 Policy Brief No. 4.

Goodhart, C.A.E (2008), 'The background to the 2007 financial crisis', London School of Economics.

Grahl, J. and Lysandrou, P. (2006), 'Capital market trading volume: an overview and some preliminary conclusions', *Cambridge Journal of Economics*, **30**(6).

Hirst, P. and Thompson, G. (1999), *Globalisation in Question*, Cambridge: Polity.

House of Commons (2008), *Treasury Committee, Report on Financial Stability and Transparency*, 26 February.

International Monetary Fund (2007), *World Economic Outlook*, April.

International Monetary Fund (2008), *Global Financial Stability Report*, April.

Kregel, J (2008), *Minsky's Cushions of Safety, Systemic Risk and the Crisis in the US Subprime Mortgage Market*, Policy Brief No. 93, Levy Economics Institute.

Langley, P. (2006), 'Securitising suburbia: the transformation of Anglo-American mortgage finance', *Competition and Change*, **10**(3).

Lysandrou, P. (1996), 'Methodological dualism and the microfoundations of Marx's economic theory', *Cambridge Journal of Economics*, **20**(5).

Lysandrou, P. (2000), 'The market and exploitation in Marx's economic theory: a reinterpretation', *Cambridge Journal of Economics*, **24**(3).

Lysandrou, P (2005), 'Globalisation as commodification', *Cambridge Journal of Economics*, **29**(5).

Manning, R.D. (2000), *Credit Card Nation: The Consequences of America's Addiction to Credit*, New York: Basic Books.

McKinsey Global Institute (2008), *Mapping Global Capital Markets: Fourth Annual Report*, January.

Nesvetailova, A. and Palan, R. (2009), 'A very North Atlantic credit crunch: geopolitical implications of the global liquidity crisis', *International Affairs*, Autumn 2008/Winter 2009.

Randall Wray, L. (2008), *Financial Markets Meltdown: What Can We Learn From Minsky*, Public Policy Brief No. 99, Levy Economics Institute.

Sovereign Wealth Fund (SWF) Institute (2008), *Asset Comparison – Investor Classes and Asset Classifications*, August.

Thompson, G. (2010), 'Financial globalization and the crisis: a critical assessment and what is to be done?', *New Political Economy*, **15**(1).

Wade, R. (2008), 'Financial regime change?', *New Left Review*, No. 53.

Wolf, M. (2009), *Fixing Global Finance*, New Haven: Yale University Press.

28 The great crash of 2008 and the reform of economics*

*Geoffrey M. Hodgson***

Preface

The 2008 economic crash led to remarkable shifts of opinion among world leaders. Does this crisis create favourable conditions for the reform and revitalisation of economics itself – from a subject dominated by mathematical techniques to a discipline more oriented to understanding real-world institutions and actors? And why were warnings of financial collapse not heeded? Recent shortcomings are partly related to the global triumph of market individualist ideology and partly to the exaggerated roles of modelling and quantification. These failures of economics are partly peculiar to the discipline and also a result of other wider institutional and cultural forces.

1 Introduction

The world financial crash of 2008 signalled the most serious global economic crisis since the Great Depression of the 1930s. Just as John Maynard Keynes is remembered for his critique of the economic theories and policies of his day, critics of mainstream economics may wonder if the latest crisis will help to revive the discipline by exposing the limitations of current economic theory and policy. This article assesses the prospects of such a renewal. It is argued that the possibility of redirecting economics into more constructive and relevant channels is less hopeful than it may appear at first sight, because of major institutional and cultural barriers to the reform of the profession. Among these are obsolete disciplinary boundaries, deep specialisation at the cost of synthetic vision and a cult of metrication and formalisation.

While economics as a discipline evolves slowly, the ideological mood has changed rapidly. The financial crisis of 2008 led to remarkable retractions among world leaders of previous commitments to lightly-regulated financial markets. The market is no longer seen as the solution to every problem. Contrary to his Republican pedigree, the then US President, George W. Bush, became the exponent of a huge state bale-out of the banks with a massive extension of state ownership within the financial system.

Alan Greenspan, former chairman of the US Federal Reserve, belatedly declared that he had 'made a mistake in presuming that the self-interest of organizations, specifically banks' would protect 'shareholders and equity in the firms'. He had 'discovered a flaw in the model' of liberalisation and self-regulation.[1]

All UK Prime Ministers and Chancellors of the Exchequer since 1979 have promoted market liberalisation. As late as 8 November 2005 the then Labour Chancellor, Gordon Brown, spoke to the Confederation of British Industry and explained his policy on financial regulation as 'not just a light touch but a limited touch'.[2]

Yet everything changed with the global financial crisis. Prime Minister Brown adopted a package of measures including partial state ownership of banks. On 19 October 2008 the Chancellor of the Exchequer, Alistair Darling, announced massive government borrowing to kick-start the British economy. He said that Keynes's ideas were coming back into vogue.[3]

These changes in ideology among world politicians create a different environment for economists. But as yet there are no strong shifts of opinion or practice among academic leaders of our profession. We search in vain for similar conversions or recantations. The signs are of 'business as usual' (Cohen, 2009).

This essay discusses the relationship between the economics profession and the 2008 crash. Section 2 considers some economists who warned of the crisis. Section 3 compares the new affection for Keynes among some politicians and journalists with the declining interest by economists not only in the economics of Keynes but also in other classic economics texts. Sections 4 and 5 consider the priority of technique over substance in modern economics, and whether earlier economic crises provide evidence that this priority is likely to be reversed. Section 6 considers why warnings of the crisis were ignored. Section 7 diagnoses the malady of technique-fixation in economics. Section 8 concludes the chapter.

2 Prophets of doom

Who were the prophets of the crash of 2008? On 7 September 2006, Nouriel Roubini, an economics professor at New York University, told International Monetary Fund economists that the USA was facing a collapse in housing prices, sharply declining consumer confidence and a recession. Homeowners would default on mortgages, the mortgage-backed securities market would unravel and the global financial system would seize up. These developments could destroy hedge funds, investment banks and other major financial institutions. Economist Anirvan Banerji responded that Roubini's predictions did not make use of mathematical models and dismissed his warnings as those of a habitual pessimist.[4]

The British sociologist Laurie Taylor asked listeners of his weekly BBC radio programme to find an economist who had predicted the 2008 credit crunch. On 15 October 2008 the radio host announced that the most prescient prophet of the outcome of international financial deregulation since 1980 was the relatively obscure British financial economist Richard S. Dale. In his book on *International Banking Deregulation*, Dale (1992) had argued that the entry of banks into speculation on securities has precipitated the 1929 crash, and that growing involvement of banks in securities activities resulting from incremental deregulation since 1980 might precipitate another financial collapse. Dale's book received a mixed review in the *Journal of Finance* in 1993 and slipped off the citation rankings.

In early 2008, at a time when many leading economists thought that the bank troubles of 2007 would not lead to a downturn, Professor David Blanchflower came to the conclusion that the unfolding credit crisis would tip the British economy into a recession. As late as June 2008, Federal Reserve Chairman Ben S. Bernanke was confident that the risk of a US recession had diminished.[5] But Blanchflower, as a member of the Bank of England Monetary Policy Committee, had been arguing for months that not only was the USA moving into negative growth but that the same was in prospect for the UK. His view did not prevail on that Committee until September 2008. On what did he base his prognosis? According to Blanchflower (2009) the key evidence of an impending recession in both the USA and the UK included 'declines in soft surveys such as consumer confidence, and people's views on the job market'. What led him to his view was not a sophisticated mathematical model but an experienced reading of detailed survey evidence. He remarked: 'The forecasting models were largely useless … forecasters tend to underpredict recessions'.

Several years after his death in 1996, Hyman Minsky has got some credit. In a series of papers, Minsky (1982, 1985, 1992) argued that financial capitalism has an inherent tendency to instability and crisis, due to speculation upon growing debt. He gave a number of warnings about the severe consequences of global financial deregulation after 1980. His ideas were never popular with the mainstream. Yet as early as 4 February 2008 the *New Yorker* noted that references to his financial-instability hypothesis 'have become commonplace on financial websites and in the reports of Wall Street analysts. Minsky's hypothesis is well worth revisiting'.

There are other claimants to the title of Prophet of the Crash. Many post-Keynesians and others have warned since the 1980s of the dangers of expanding derivatives markets, financial deregulation and excessive debt. But we must be wary of extending the list any longer, at least until the criteria involved are clarified. After all, Marxists have been predicting the collapse of capitalism since 1848. Those that habitually predict doom are bound to be right one day. But that does not mean that their wisdom is superior.

The outstanding prophets in this context are those that have added to our understanding of the institutional mechanisms by which massively expanding debt was financed, and who acknowledged its powerful upward trajectory as well as its hidden and growing risk. Essentially, this is not a matter of predicting the timing of a crash, but improving our understanding of the covert structures and forces that pushed the economy over a cliff. It means an appreciation of how the debt-boom unleashed by liberalised financial markets created the preconditions for the collapse.

3 But does anyone read Keynes?

Let us now turn to economics as practised in universities. Politicians, bloggers, newspapers and magazines may have noticed the relevance of such economists as Keynes and Minsky for today, but have they been cherished or rediscovered in departments of economics in the most prestigious universities?

I tried without success to find the work of Keynes or Minsky on any reading list available on the web of any macroeconomics or compulsory economic theory course in any of the top universities in the world. Instead, there is ample evidence of student proficiency requirements in mathematics.

By searching post-1950 leading journals, we can ascertain how many times the aforementioned authors were cited in each decade. Figure 28.1 shows the results. Keynes remains the most highly cited of the four authors, but his visibility in leading journals has declined dramatically. Other authors who warned of the dangers of financial deregulation receive a low level of citations. Notably, while much of Roubini's work is discursive, the majority of his articles in top journals of economics contain models.

Data for 2008 and 2009 were not available and have to be extrapolated from earlier years in the same decade. Of course when this data becomes available, these two years may show a revival of citations to Keynes and others, but so far there is no sign of this. And a return to 1950s levels would be remarkable.

Are academic economists simply citing the wrong people? Such a perception would be mistaken. By citation measures, Keynes's classic antagonists do little better. Take Milton Friedman: from 1950 he was cited by an average of only 344 articles or reviews per decade, in the same list of journals. Friedrich Hayek was cited by only 139 items per decade. Gerard Debreu, a mathematical economist and pioneer of general equilibrium theory, was cited by only 24 items per decade. Mainstream economists seem to have stopped citing anyone, except the most recent pioneers of mathematical technique.

The neglect of the classic texts is dramatically illustrated by the fate of Keyne's own ideas. Keynes's wisdom was quickly bowdlerised and forced into a formal model (Robinson, 1965; Leijonhufvud, 1968; Davidson, 1972; Rotheim, 1998). Even when Keynes's work is acknowledged, it is often in second-hand and suspect terms.

Remarkably, the habit of ignoring past great economists is defended by a professor at the University of Cambridge, in the homeland of Keynes. Partha Dasgupta (2002, p. 61) writes:

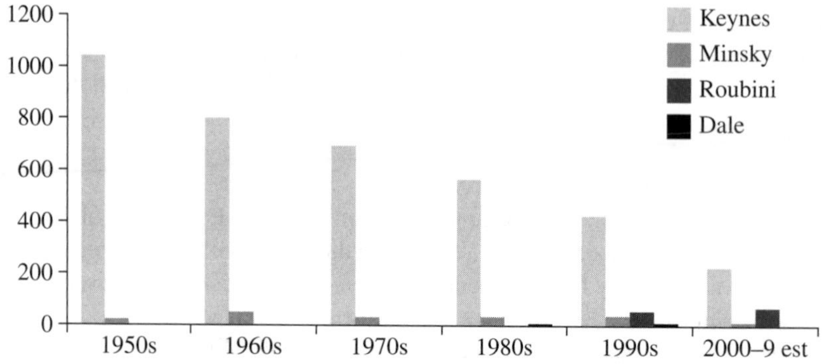

Source: JSTOR. 2008–09 figures are extrapolated from 2000–07 results. Journals used: *American Economic Review*, *Econometrica*, *Economic Journal*, *Economica*, *Journal of Finance*, *Journal of Political Economy*, *Quarterly Journal of Economics*, *Review of Economic Studies*, *Review of Economics and Statistics*.

Figure 28.1 Number of articles or reviews citing Keynes, Minsky, Roubini and Dale in leading journals of economics and finance

> You can emerge from your graduate studies in economics without having read any of the classics, or indeed, without having anything other than a vague notion of what the great thinkers of the past had written. The modern economist doesn't even try to legitimize her inquiry by linking it to questions addressed in the canon; she typically begins her article by referring to something in the literature a few months old.

Dasgupta argues that 'on reflection' it is 'not clear' that 'this is an altogether bad state of affairs'. For him, ignoring the past has important positive compensations:

> In order to do creative work, there is a further advantage in not being knowledgeable about the intellectual concerns and struggles of bygone eras; there would be a lower risk that the past was setting the present's research agenda.

But our research agenda is always set by the past, even if it may address the future. Our concepts and theories come from the past. It can be no other way. Whether we should be 'knowledgeable about the intellectual concerns and struggles of bygone eras' depends largely on whether these issues are of contemporary relevance or not. Sadly, because we are facing an economic crisis on the scale of the Great Depression, we must learn from that distant experience, as we must learn from other recessions caused by bank failures and from the analyses and policies of dead economists. Yet Dasgupta wishes the past away. Great wisdom is given a short consume-by date, and valuable knowledge is neglected.

Despite this, as Mark Blaug (1991, p. x) points out, few inventors of new ideas in economics can resist the temptation to nominate one or two precursors. Yet, as detailed knowledge of the history of economics becomes an unfashionable rarity, the nomination of precursors becomes a shallow ritual. The deeper neglect of past texts undermines habits of careful scrutiny for theoretical precursors, of detailed interrogation of the subtle changes in the meanings of words, of concern for elegant prose and ease of communication, and of attention to careful and precise definition of terms. If anyone bothered to read Keynes then they would find an educated exemplar of these abandoned values – of which we are in dire need today.

4 The dominance of technique

To get published in leading journals in economics today it is unnecessary to read or cite any economist beyond the recent past. Most economists are interested in mathematical models. They are taught tools of analysis rather than the intellectual, historical and institutional contexts in which analytical questions arise. As mathematics has swamped the curricula in leading universities and graduate schools, student economists have become neither equipped nor encouraged to prioritise real world economies and institutions. Treatment of big questions such as the nature and causes of the wealth and poverty of nations brings no accolade, unless one can reduce the analysis to a respectable formalism.

There have been repeated warnings for over 20 years about this elevation of technique over substance, even in the higher echelons of the profession. The problem had become severe by the 1980s. Arjo Klamer and David Colander (1990, p. 18) reported a survey which showed that only 3 per cent of graduate students on top US economics programmes perceived 'having a thorough knowledge of the economy' to be 'very important' for professional success, while 65 per cent thought that 'being smart in the sense of problem-solving' is what matters and 57 per cent believed that 'excellence in mathematics' was very important. Bruno Frey and Reiner Eichenberger (1993, p. 190) likewise remarked that postgraduates are taught 'in a theory-oriented, abstract way and to pay little attention to institutional facts'.

In 1988 the American Economic Association set up a Commission on the state of graduate education in economics in the USA. In a crushing indictment, the Commission expressed its fear that 'graduate programs may be turning out a generation with too many *idiot savants* skilled in technique but innocent of real economic issues' (Krueger et al., 1991, pp. 1044–5). Alan Blinder (1990, p. 445), a member of the Commission, commented:

> Both students and faculty find economics obsessed with technique over substance … the many macro and micro theory exams the Commission examined … tested math-

> ematical puzzle-solving ability, not substantive knowledge about economics ... Only 14 percent of the students report that their core courses put substantial emphasis on 'applying economic theory to real-world problems'.

Since the 1988 Commission there has been a sideline litany of complaints from leading members of the profession. Donald McCloskey (1991, pp. 10–14) wrote:

> To put it rigorously, the procedure of modern economics is too much a search through the hyperspace of conceivable assumptions. ... One economics department after another has been seized by the formalists and marched off to the Gulag of hyperspace searching. Few graduate programs in economics teach economics, especially to first-year students. They teach 'tools', tools which become obsolete every five years or so.

As Blaug (1997, p. 3) put it a few years later:

> Modern economics is sick. Economics has increasingly become an intellectual game played for its own sake and not for its practical consequences for understanding the economic world. Economists have converted the subject into a sort of social mathematics in which analytical rigour is everything and practical relevance is nothing.

At least three Nobel laureates have expressed their concerns. At a very early stage Wassily Leontief (1982, p. 104) objected that models had become more important than data:

> Page after page of professional economic journals are filled with mathematical formulas ... Year after year economic theorists continue to produce scores of mathematical models and to explore in great detail their formal properties; and the econometricians fit algebraic functions of all possible shapes to essentially the same sets of data.

Ronald Coase (1997) complained: 'Existing economics is a theoretical system which floats in the air and which bears little relation to what happens in the real world'. And Milton Friedman (1999, p. 137) observed: 'economics has become increasingly an arcane branch of mathematics rather than dealing with real economic problems'.

What happened after these prestigious complaints? David Colander (2009, p. 6) lamented that none of these prominent warnings 'had any effect on US graduate economic education'. As Mark Blaug (1998, p. 45) wrote pessimistically: 'We have created a monster that is very difficult to stop'.

The problem is not necessarily mathematics per se, but the obsession with technique over substance. Arguably there is a proper place for some limited use of useful heuristics or data-rich models within economics (Hodgson, 2006, ch. 7). But what should determine their adoption is not their technical aesthetics, but their usefulness for helping to explain the real world.[6]

Given the dominance of technique in modern economics, we need to consider how this may have affected the judgement of economists and the advice they gave to policy-makers. This question is addressed later. Before doing so we shall examine whether the current economic crisis is likely to undermine or reinforce this formalistic and technical bias, by looking at precedents such as the 1930s.

5 Did past crises lead economists towards substance rather than technique?

Mathematical technique was well established in the high temples of economics well before the crash of 2008. By contrast, economics in the 1920s was a much more discursive and less technique-obsessed discipline. Economists received training in the history of their discipline and were aware of longstanding problems and changing theoretical approaches. Hence the tasks of reforming economics today differ substantially from those that faced economists after the Great Crash of 1929.

Keynes's (1936) central theoretical argument was that the assumptions behind laisser faire economics were inappropriate for the real world economic system.[7] It was not primarily a battle of economic models or econometric techniques. But ironically the Great Depression helped to provide an impetus for more extensive use of mathematics in economics.

A younger generation of economists, impatient with the failure of the older economists to find solutions, turned to mathematical models as well as the Keynesian doctrine. Gunnar Myrdal once reflected on his own experience in the 1930s, when he had played a role in the initiation of the Econometric Society, which was set up to promote formal methods against the then institutionalist hegemony in the USA, and before he himself turned to institutional economics and became a critic of the neoclassical mainstream. Myrdal (1972, pp. 6–7) wrote:

> Faced with this great calamity, we economists of the 'theoretical' school, accustomed to reason in terms of simplified macro-models, felt we were on the top of the situation ... It was at this stage that economists in the stream of the Keynesian revolution adjusted their theoretical models to the needs of the time, which gave victory much more broadly to our 'theoretical' approach.

Other commentators reached a similar verdict (Hodgson, 2004, pp. 383–6).

Not only had this 'revolution' established a relatively simplified version of Keynesianism but also it was led by a younger generation of economists, including Samuelson and others, which promoted formal economic models. They emphasised only those parts of Keynesianism that could be modelled, and were impatient with the apparently equivocal ruminations of older economists, who had buried themselves in historical facts in their attempts to understand capitalism's laws of motion.

The attraction of this more mathematical approach was partly its technocratic lure, and partly because it proposed apparent solutions to the urgent problem of the day. It appeared that increasing a variable called *G* could alleviate the problem of unemployment. The 'solution' was plain and beguiling and dressed up in mathematical and 'scientific' garb. Although Keynes himself warned of the limitations of mathematical technique in economics (Moggridge, 1992, pp. 621–3), he was championed by a younger generation who saw mathematics as the solution.

A second major impetus towards the formalisation of economics was World War II. The militarisation of scientific activity gave prestige and resources to research involving particular mathematical and statistical techniques. The greatest armed conflict of the twentieth century promoted a central theme of neoclassical economics – the allocation of scarce resources towards the maximisation of a fixed objective function with given institutions and assumed technology (Bernstein, 2001; Mirowski, 2002).

The emergency of war swept away any reservations concerning sustained government budget deficits. The Great Depression had already persuaded many that some deficit-financed public spending was required (Barber, 1988). The war made the conversion total. Anyone who would preach 'balanced budgets' in a sustained wartime emergency could be accused of resisting the war effort. The need for public financing of the war assured the 'Keynesian' victory. Samuelson declared in a 1986 interview: 'By the end of the war the entire academic profession was Keynesian' (Colander and Landreth, 1996, p. 169).

Although the Great Depression established a Keynesian macroeconomics, it also gave impetus to the process of mathematical formalisation that gradually accelerated in the post-war period. The pace and extent of this change can be traced in leading journals such as the *American Economic Review*, the *Economic Journal*, the *Journal of Political Economy* and the *Quarterly Journal of Economics*. Before the 1920s, verbal expositions dominated more than 90 per cent of the articles published in these journals. Verbal exposition became less dominant after 1940, falling steadily to about 33 per cent of articles in the 1960s. By the early 1990s, over 90 per cent of the articles in the leading and enduring journals were dominated by algebra, calculus and econometrics (Stigler et al., 1995, p. 342).[8]

Although Keynes fell out of vogue from about 1975 to 2008, and the character of mainstream economics has changed in other respects in recent decades, its obsession with technique over substance remains. The pressing question is whether the crisis of 2008 will reverse this.

We may remind ourselves of an earlier incident. In 1997 Robert C. Merton and Myron S. Scholes were awarded the Nobel Prize in Economics. Scholes had helped to devise the Black–Scholes equation, upon which a prominent hedge fund was based. However, following the 1997 financial crisis in Russia and East

Asia, the highly leveraged fund lost US$4.6 billion in less than four months in 1998 and failed.[9] Did this lead to significant discussion concerning the limits of models? Alas no.[10]

6 Why were warnings ignored?

A key issue requiring explanation is not the failure of prediction, because (as noted above) crisis predictions of sorts were made. It is more relevant to ask why well-grounded concerns about the nature and extent of bank lending prior to the crisis were ignored.

In a speech on 21 January 2009, the Chairman of the Financial Services Authority, Lord Adair Turner, pointed to the massive failure 'shared by bankers, regulators, central banks, finance ministers and academics across the world … to identify that the whole system was fraught with market wide, systemic risk'.[11] This spreads the blame widely, including to academics, and with some justice. But it fails to explain how such myopia spread simultaneously throughout all these very different political, financial and academic institutions.

The influential economist Richard Posner has addressed the question 'The Financial Crisis: Why Were Warnings Ignored?' on his blog.[12] He cites Roberta Wohlstetter's famous book *Pearl Harbor: Warning and Decision*. Wohlstetter (1962) shows that information pointing to the possibility of a Japanese attack on Pearl Harbor was received by the US military, but by different people who were far from each other. It was difficult to collate relevant information, especially among abundant detail and noise. Consequently, individual bits of intelligence were given low credence or priority and did not reach senior military echelons. Posner thus cites Roubini's warnings of economic collapse and argues that these were similarly thwarted within the bureaucracies of the financial and political system.

Among the factors that caused the warnings to be disregarded are factors that may also have been decisive in the neglect of the advance warnings of the financial crisis now upon us: priors (preconceptions), the cost and difficulty of taking effective defensive measures against an uncertain danger and the absence of a mechanism for aggregating and analysing warning information from many sources.

This argument has insight on how bureaucracies screen out information but it ignores a fundamental difference. Intelligence of existing preparations for attack is not the same thing as a cognitive appraisal of potential but not yet actual crisis. Furthermore, any reported insight that a financial crisis is possible is likely to be met – at least in contemporary bureaucracies – by demands for a quantitative assessment of the risk. But with the degree of complexity and openness of the systems involved, a warranted probability assessment is often difficult or impossible. In current bureaucratic cultures, the absence of quantified risk prevented the warnings from being heeded. Also as noted above, Roubini's warnings were disregarded partly because he lacked a sufficiently respectable backup model. These are important differences between the cases of Pearl Harbor and the 2008 crash. Yet Posner is no straightforward apologist. He singles out economists for special criticism:

> Of all the puzzles about the failure to foresee the financial crisis, the biggest is the failure of foresight of professors of finance and of macroeconomics, with a few exceptions such as Roubini. Some of the media commentary has attributed this to economics professors being overly reliant on abstract mathematical models of the economy. In fact professors of finance, who are found mainly in business schools rather than in economics departments, tend to be deeply involved in the real world of financial markets. They are not armchair theoreticians. They are involved in the financial markets as consultants, investors, and sometimes money managers.

This raises a second argument about the role of mathematical models in diverting economists from reality. Posner denies that they have had an adverse effect and argues that financial economic modellers in business schools were getting their hands dirty in the bustle of money markets. These claims raise still further questions. Why were other professors, in departments of economics, less inclined to be involved in the hurly-burly of market institutions? There is a widespread complaint that we know very little of how market mechanisms actually work (North, 1977, p. 710; Coase, 1988, p. 7; Härdle and Kirman, 1995).

Furthermore, being involved does not mean that one is concerned with the big picture. Most models by financial economists are less concerned with understanding institutional market mechanisms, or even with predicting systemic outcomes, than with providing risk assessment and investment algorithms for client investors. The fallibility of such instrumental models is dramatically illustrated in the Black–Scholes hedge fund scandal. Posner fails to acknowledge that while the financial economists were getting their hands dirty they were ignoring the critical state of the debt-mountain that eventually collapsed.

Warnings were ignored also because an ideology of free markets combined with theoretical claims such as the efficient markets hypothesis and rational expectations. It was widely believed that the markets themselves would regulate and control debt. Overlending would be detected by the market and the stock price of reckless lending institutions would be automatically undermined. Hence government regulation was unnecessary.

The theory of efficient markets claims that prices on traded assets already reflect all known information. This supports light-touch regulation at most.[13] The rational expectations hypothesis 'asserts that outcomes do not differ systematically ... from what people expected them to be. ... In their efforts to forecast prices, investors comb all sources of information' (Sargent, 2008). When economists believe in the informational efficiency of markets and their self-correcting capacity, then warnings of collapse are disregarded because they go against the conventional wisdom.[14]

Also finance professors are attracted to 'the real world of financial markets' partly because of the lucrative consultancy contracts available. Many business schools encourage such consultancy work, and regard it as a mark of relevance and prestige for the school itself. Given the evolution of such vested interests, especially with the global growth of business schools since the 1980s, financial economists had little incentive to call for greater regulation, for restrictions on hedge funds, or raise alarms about the growth of the market for financial derivatives. Vested interests helped to maintain the ideological and policy status quo.

Finally, as noted above, the cult of metrication that prevails in contemporary private and public bureaucracies means that the consultant is pressured to provide a quantitative assessment of any risk. Yet the whole point about complex and open financial markets is that future outcomes are uncertain rather than risky. Uncertainty, at least by the definitions of Knight (1921) and Keynes (1937), applies to circumstances where quantitative calculation of probability is not possible. But few mainstream economists ponder on the difference any more, partly because it is difficult to fit non-quantitative uncertainty into a model. It is a concept banished from mainstream economic theory.[15] Yet it is very difficult to see how advance predictions of financial catastrophes could have been assessed meaningfully in terms of calculated probabilities.[16]

Consequently, when we consider why warnings of the 2008 crash were not heeded, we are not dealing primarily with a Pearl Harbor syndrome of information uncollated or ignored. Instead, premonitions by experienced analysts were ignored by the mainstream economics profession and financial clients alike because they were neither quantified as probabilities nor derived from respectable models.

7 Diagnosing sickonomics

There is now a significant literature on the growth of formalism on economics. Tony Lawson (1997) claims that the use of mathematical models presupposes a 'closed system' ontology that in reality is 'rare'. The details of this argument are controversial (Hodgson, 2006, ch. 7) but they do not bear on the main question here: what are the institutional or cultural conditions that led to the global rise of formalism in economics? It is important to identify underlying assumptions, but it is another task to explain how they became prominent.

The malady that affects economics has peculiar features, but other disciplines are also afflicted with severe problems. For example, after decades when post-Parsonian sociology has failed to establish a consensus over core assumptions, the reputation of sociological theory has declined and sociology has fractured into a variety of different factional preoccupations, including post-modernism, rational choice theory and naive empiricism (Mouzelis, 1995; Somers, 1998).

I suggest that global pressures have impacted on modern universities in the twentieth century and led to significant overall changes in the nature of teaching and research. But the ways in which different disciplines have evolved in response to these pressures reflect varied histories and dynamics. Particularly with formalism in economics, there are strong elements of positive feedback and path dependence. But we also have to understand the general academic context in which these changes take place.

Consider the global change in the nature of university education. In developed countries, before World War II, universities were reserved for a rich or intelligent minority. Despite pressures from business and religious institutions, they managed to dispense a relatively broad education and maintained an ethos for the pursuit of truth. This changed in most developed countries sometime after World War II. Especially since the 1960s, the university has become an institution much more oriented to specialist professional training under the behest of business corporations.

Thorstein Veblen (1918) observed some of the early stages of this evolution within universities long ago. Others (Callahan, 1962; Bloom, 1988; Lutz and Field, 1998; Kirp, 2003; Greenberg, 2007) have charted the post-war decline of broad and questioning inquiry, and the rise of narrower forms of professional training. Students are less encouraged to pursue big questions. They are urged instead to acquire qualifications that signal skills that can be hired on the jobs market.

Behind this process has been the dramatic post-war expansion of systems of higher education in developed capitalist economies, to meet the demands of growing knowledge intensity and relentless specialisation in the sphere of production (Rueschemeyer, 1986; Pryor, 1996). Deep specialisation means that training in any one area takes more time. Renaissance-like figures with a capacity for an informed overview are less likely to emerge, and even less likely to be acknowledged (Hodgson, 1999, pt. 3).

The post-war university expansion had the important benefit of bringing higher learning to a much wider segment of the population. Yet it was impelled by perceived economic needs, and it accelerated the commercialisation of university education. Furthermore, expanded education systems require much more from the public purse, and democratic and other pressures on governments oblige them to account for expenditures in performance terms.

Together these forces eroded enclaves of broad liberal education, vastly expanded specialised professional training, led to explicit requirements to account for the economic value of university research, and promoted the increasing use of league tables and formalised research assessments to pressure academics to publish research in acknowledged outlets.

The cult of quantification has historical sources (Crosby, 1998). But it has also received an impetus through the ideology of market individualism since the 1970s. This formalised individual and organisational contractual obligations and enhanced threats of litigation in the case of failure. Organisations have responded in terms of routinised and quantified risk assessments. Under equivalent if not greater pressures, similar developments are found in business organisations outside academia.[17]

These background institutional and cultural forces have impacted upon disciplines in different ways. Economics suffered in a peculiar way because it had established a type and degree of formalism that allowed research output to be assessed principally in terms of mathematical interest and elegance. Economists were judged and became employable for their aptitudes for statistical analysis or predictive models.

There is a conservative trend in any science. Robert J. Shiller (2008) writes of the herding of economists around conventional views for fear of bucking the trend. This problem is especially severe in a discipline as monolithic as economics, dominated as it is by relatively few theoretical paradigms and approaches, with the control of journals and other resources concentrated in relatively few academic institutions (Hodgson and Rothman, 1999). The oligopolistic distribution of power within the discipline affects both publications and funding. Papers of a less technique-driven nature are more difficult to publish in prestigious journals; grant applications that are bereft of models are unlikely to be approved by refereeing economists; and candidates without a good modelling portfolio are unlikely to be promoted. In a process of cumulative causation, the cult of technique feeds on itself.

Because they are no longer educated to take such issues seriously, mainstream economists care less about the deeper meanings or historical origins of theories or concepts, or about big questions concerning economies and societies.

8 Conclusion: the reform of economics

Neither crises nor failures of prediction necessarily impel economists in the direction of realism. One likely reaction to the current downturn is that we should try harder to develop better models. Perhaps we should. But we must also learn the vital lesson that models on their own are never enough. Economists need to appreciate the limitations of modelling. These limitations are generic and result from the intractabilities of uncertainty, complexity and system openness in the real world. A better understanding of our current predicament must also come from a much fuller appreciation of both economic history and the history of ideas. What is required is a revitalisation of the culture within the economics profession.

Colander (2000) and others have argued that much fuller recognition of the reality and implications of the complexity of reality would be helpful for economics. But existing complexity discourse is no panacea. Its diverse content ranges from playful simulation to social constructivism, and it is sometimes of challengeable coherence or value (Horgan, 1995). Yet recognition of the limits of modelling in the face of complexity is crucial. Even the most sophisticated of models is inadequate to deal with real-world complexities. Rather than look real-world complexity in the face, economists have retreated into an artificial world of much simpler models. Instead of current practice of valuing many models in terms of their intrinsic technical sophistication, economists should judge models in terms of their ability or otherwise to help us understand and engage with the real world.

In dealing with uncertain futures, a business technique known as scenario planning is relevant (Loasby, 1990; Van der Heijden, 1996; Fahey and Randall, 1998). Scenario planning addresses plausible future situations and problems. But no attempt is made to assign a probability to each scenario. Scenario planning prepares organisations collectively for dramatic and uncertain events. Prior to 2008, banks and governments could have asked: 'what happens if buyers default on loans and house prices stop rising?' Scenario planners would then consider policies to either avoid or deal with this policy.

But scenario planning creates problems for organisations. Businesses are typically dominated by routine and find it difficult to deal with uncertain futures. Organisations do not handle uncertainty well, and for this reason scenario planning in its radical and original form is not widely adopted. This makes it all the more important for economists to take uncertainty on board, to understand its significance, to urge its importance upon organisations and governments and help to develop strategies to deal with it.

We have also identified the problem of vested interests. Financial economists are less likely to speak out in favour of regulation when they have lucrative consultancy contracts with firms involved with derivatives, hedge funds and questionable financial innovations. The ideology of market individualism has played havoc with the professional ethics of economists. Mainstream economists declare that everyone is self-interested, so that they cannot be expected to behave ethically in any other sense. The consequence has been a decline in the ethic of professional commitment to truth and some alarming cases of academic plagiarism. The acceptance of a code of ethics for economists may help to reverse this situation and to revive a culture where integrity and professional commitment are valued more highly.[18]

In June 2000 some economics students in leading academic institutions in Paris circulated a petition calling for the reform of their economics curriculum. They complained of a 'disregard for concrete realities' in an approach that 'is supposed to explain everything by means of a purely axiomatic process, as if this were THE economic truth' and called for 'a pluralism of approaches, adapted to the complexity of the objects and to the uncertainty surrounding most of the big questions in economics'. This protest attracted significant global attention and was followed by similar initiatives at the University of Cambridge and elsewhere.[19]

These concerns are as relevant as before. There must be an end to the use of mathematics as 'an end in itself' and to dogmatic teaching styles that leave no place for critical and reflective thought. The teaching of economics must involve an engagement with empirical and concrete economic realities and a comparative plurality of theoretical approaches.

To understand the current economic crisis we have to look at both economic history and the history of economic thought. To understand how markets work we have to dispense with empty proclamations of rationality and delve into psychology and elsewhere. To understand how economics has taken a wrong turn we have to appreciate work in the philosophy of economics and the relationship between economics and ideology. These unfashionable discourses have to be brought back into the centre of the economic curricula and rehabilitated as vital areas of enquiry. Unless mainstream economics takes heed of these warnings and proves its relevance for the understanding of the most severe crisis of the capitalist system since the 1930s, then it will be doomed to irrelevance.

Much greater dialogue is required between economics and the other social sciences. This is not only intrinsically vital, but it has become imperative because both economics and sociology have lost their preceding consensuses concerning the definitions and boundaries of their disciplines (Hodgson, 2008a). This suggests a need for some reorganisation of the social sciences in universities.

The changes of heart among politicians and other leaders noted at the beginning of this essay provide an opportunity to appeal beyond the confines for the profession itself. Opinion leaders should be made aware of the malady within our profession and urged to use their influence for reform. If this fails, then broad-minded real-world economics may well have to reorganise itself separately under another label such as 'political economy' or within a broader social science curriculum.

Notes

* This article uses material from a previous article (Hodgson, 2008b) and historical passages from another (Hodgson, 2004). The author is very grateful to David Blanchflower, Robert Boyer, Alain Caillé, Gerry Epstein, Olivier Favereau, Deirdre McCloskey, Richard Nelson, Pascal Petit, anonymous referees and others for helpful comments and discussions.

** The publisher wishes to thank Oxford University Press, who have kindly given permission for the use of copyright material: Geoffrey M. Hodgson (2009) 'The great crash of 2008 and the reform of economics' in *Cambridge Journal of Economics*, **33**, 1205–21.

1. *Guardian*, 24 October 2008.
2. See http://www.cbi.org.uk/ndbs/press.nsf/0363c1f07c6ca12a8025671c00381cc7/ee59d1c32ce4ec12802570c70041152c?; accessed 22 October 2010.
3. This does not imply that government policies strictly follow those of Keynes (Kregel, 2009) or indeed should do so (Leijonhufvud, 2009).
4. *New York Times*, 15 August 2008. In fact, Roubini had performed some modelling using time-series data on consumer debt and housing prices.
5. http://latimesblogs.latimes.com/money_co/2008/06/tuesday-is-sett.html; accessed 22 October 2010.

6. For useful discussions of the choice, status and explanatory role of models see Sugden (2000) and Mäki (2001, 2005, 2009).
7. Kregel (2009) argues that Keynes's ideas did not take hold until the late 1930s.
8. Blaug (1999, 2003) and Weintraub (2002) argue that the 'formalist revolution' in economics was consolidated in the late 1950s.
9. Source: http://en.wikipedia.org/wiki/Myron_Scholes; accessed 22 October 2010.
10. There is not the space here to discuss the idea that mathematical models themselves may have changed how financial markets work (MacKenzie, 2006). But there is an example of a possible adverse consequence. Mathematical economist David X. Li devised a formula that helped hedge funds assess complex interconnected risks. His formula relies on efficient market valuation and ignores radical uncertainty. In the run-up to the crash it went wildly wrong. See http://www.wired.com/techbiz/it/magazine/17-03/wp_quant?currentPage=all; accessed 22 October 2010.
11. Source: http://www.fsa.gov.uk/pages/Library/Communication/Speeches/2009/0121_at.shtml; accessed 22 October 2010.
12. http://www.becker-posner-blog.com/archives/2008/10/the_financial_crisis_why_were_warnings_ignored_posner.html; accessed 22 October 2010. See also Posner (2009).
13. But this depiction is contestable, partly because costly contract enforcement and irredeemably incomplete markets are neglected. See the empirical evidence and references in Chan et al. (2003) and the powerful critique by Willem Buiter on http://blogs.ft.com/maverecon/2009/03/the-unfortunate-uselessness-of-most-state-of-the-art-academic-monetary-economics/; accessed 23 October 2010.
14. Even now it is easy to find blogs and websites where market individualists blame the collapse not on deregulation, but on too much government intervention in markets, and on incompetent interest rate policy by central banks. Market individualism refers to beliefs in a minimal state, individual private property and competitive free markets. But given that the state is necessary to constitute both money and property rights (Sened, 1997; Ingham, 2004; Hodgson, 2009), we can never in principle reach a utopian market economy where the state plays no role. The diagnostic claims made by market individualists are thus unfalsifiable. Their neglect of large corporations is also a matter of concern (Hodgson, 2005). See also Nelson (2005).
15. Lucas (1981, p. 224) wrote: 'In cases of uncertainty, economic reasoning will be of no value'. This is redolent of Arrow's (1951, p. 417) earlier remark that 'no theory can be formulated in this case'. These two authors upheld that 'economic reasoning' and 'theory' were necessarily quantitative, although Arrow later seemed to modify his view.
16. A similar failure to give weight to non-quantitative factors such as uncertainty has been seen as biasing decision-making at NASA in the years preceding the 2003 Columbia space shuttle disaster: 'an overconfidence in quantitative data went hand-in-hand with a marginalization of nonquantifiable data, leading to an insensitivity to uncertainty and a loss of organizational memory' (Feldman, 2004, p. 691).
17. Hunt (2003) argues that because of growing litigational pressure and media scrutiny, large corporations attempt to quantify and minimise risk. See also Froud et al. (2000) for a discussion of related processes of corporate financialisation, involving attempts to maximise shareholder value and the deployment of insured consultants to outsource advice concerning uncertain decisions.
18. The Association for Integrity and Responsible Leadership in Economics and Related Professions (AIRLEAP) has been formed to campaign on these issues. See http://www.airleap.org/index.htm; accessed 22 October 2010.
19. See http://www.paecon.net/HistoryPAE.htm; accessed 22 October 2010.

References

Arrow, K.J. 1951. Alternative approaches to the theory of choice in risk-taking situations, *Econometrica*, vol. 19, no. 4, 404–37.

Barber, W.J. 1988. *From New Era to New Deal: Herbert Hoover, the Economists, and American Economic Policy, 1921–1933*, Cambridge, Cambridge University Press.

Bernstein, M.A. 2001. *A Perilous Progress: Economists and Public Purpose in Twentieth-Century America*, Princeton, NJ, Princeton University Press.
Blanchflower, D.G. 2009. Email to Geoffrey M. Hodgson of 23 April 2009.
Blaug, M. 1991. Introduction, in Blaug, M. (ed.), *Historiography of Economics*, Aldershot, UK and Brookfield, VT, USA, Edward Elgar.
Blaug, M. 1997. Ugly currents in modern economics, *Options Politiques*, vol. 18, no. 17, 3–8 (reprinted in Mäki, U. (ed.) 2002, *Fact and Fiction in Economics: Models, Realism and Social Construction*, Cambridge and New York, Cambridge University Press.
Blaug, M. 1998. The problems with formalism: interview with Mark Blaug, *Challenge*, vol. 41, no. 3, 35–45.
Blaug, M. 1999. The formalist revolution or what happened to orthodox economics after World War II? pp. 257–80, in Backhouse, R.E. and Creedy, J. (eds), *From Classical Economics to the Theory of the Firm: Essays in Honour of D.P. O'Brien*, Cheltenham, UK and Northampton, MA, USA, Edward Elgar.
Blaug, M. 2003. The formalist revolution of the 1950s, pp. 395–410, in Samuels, W.J. Biddle, J.E. and Davis, J.B. (eds), *A Companion to the History of Economic Thought*, Malden, MA and Oxford, UK, Blackwell.
Blinder, A. 1990. *Discussion, American Economic Review*, vol. 80, 445–7.
Bloom, A. 1988. *The Closing of the American Mind*, New York, Simon and Schuster.
Callahan, R.E. 1962. *Education and the Cult of Efficiency*, Chicago, University of Chicago Press.
Chan, K.C., Gup, B.E. and Pan, M.-S. 2003. International stock market efficiency and integration: a study of eighteen nations, *Journal of Business Finance and Accounting*, vol. 24, no. 6, 803–13.
Coase, R.H. 1988. *The Firm, the Market, and the Law*, Chicago, University of Chicago Press.
Coase, R.H. 1997. Interview with Ronald Coase, 17 September, available at http://www.coase.org/coaseinterview.htm; accessed 22 October 2010.
Cohen, P. 2009. Ivory tower unswayed by crashing economy, New York Times, 5 March, http://www.nytimes.com/2009/03/05/books/05deba.html?_r51&ref5arts; accessed 22 October 2010.
Colander, D.C. (ed.) 2000. *The Complexity Vision and the Teaching of Economics*, Cheltenham, UK and Northampton, MA, USA, Edward Elgar.
Colander, D.C. 2009. *The Making of a European Economist*, Cheltenham, UK and Northampton, MA, USA, Edward Elgar.
Colander, D.C., Landreth, H. (eds) 1996. *The Coming of Keynesianism to America: Conversations with the Founders of Keynesian Economics*, Aldershot, UK and Brookfield, VT, USA, Edward Elgar.
Crosby, A. W. 1998. *The Measure of Reality: Quantification and Western Society, 1250–1600*, Cambridge, Cambridge University Press.
Dale, R.S. 1992. *International Banking Deregulation: The Great Banking Experiment*, Oxford, Blackwell.
Dasgupta, P. 2002. Modern economics and its critics, pp. 57–89, in Mäki, U. (ed.), *Fact and Fiction in Economics: Models, Realism and Social Construction*, Cambridge, Cambridge University Press.
Davidson, P. 1972. *Money and the Real World*, 1st edn. London, Macmillan.
Fahey, L. and Randall, R.M. (eds) 1998. *Learning from the Future: Competitive Foresight Scenarios*, New York, Wiley.
Feldman, S.P. 2004. The culture of objectivity: quantification, uncertainty, and the evaluation of risk at NASA, *Human Relations*, vol. 57, no. 6, 691–718.
Frey, B.S. and Eichenberger, R. 1993. American and European economics and economists, *Journal of Economic Perspectives*, vol. 7, no. 4, 185–93.
Friedman, M. 1999. Conversation with Milton Friedman, pp. 122–44, in Snowdon, B. and Vane, H. (eds), *Conversations with Leading Economists: Interpreting Modern Macroeconomists*, Cheltenham, UK and Northampton, MA, USA, Edward Elgar.
Froud, J., Haslam, C., Johal, S. and Williams, K. 2000. Shareholder value and financialization: consultancy promises, management moves, *Economy and Society*, vol. 29, no. 1, 80–110.
Greenberg, D.S. 2007. *Science for Sale: The Perils, Rewards, and Delusions of Campus Capitalism*, Chicago, University of Chicago Press.

Härdle, W.K. and Kirman, A. P. 1995. Nonclassical demand: a model-free examination of price quantity relations in the Marseille fish market, *Journal of Econometrics*, vol. 67, no. 1, 227–57.

Hodgson, G.M. 1999. *Economics and Utopia: Why the Learning Economy is not the End of History*, London and New York, Routledge.

Hodgson, G.M. 2004. *The Evolution of Institutional Economics: Agency, Structure and Darwinism in American Institutionalism*, London and New York, Routledge.

Hodgson, G.M. 2005. Knowledge at work: some neoliberal anachronisms, *Review of Social Economy*, vol. 63, no. 4, 547–65.

Hodgson, G.M. 2006. *Economics in the Shadows of Darwin and Marx: Essays on Institutional and Evolutionary Themes*, Cheltenham, UK and Northampton, MA, USA, Edward Elgar.

Hodgson, G.M. 2008a. Prospects for economic sociology, *Philosophy of the Social Sciences*, vol. 38, no. 1, 133–49.

Hodgson, G.M. 2008b. After 1929 economics changed: will economists wake up in 2009? *Real-World Economics Review*, no. 48, 6 December, 273–8, available at http://www.paecon.net/PAEReview/issue48/Hodgson48.pdf (date last accessed 31 July 2009).

Hodgson, G.M. 2009. On the institutional foundations of law: the insufficiency of custom and private ordering, *Journal of Economic Issues*, vol. 43, no. 1, 143–66.

Hodgson, G.M. and Rothman, H. 1999. The editors and authors of economics journals: a case of institutional oligopoly? *Economic Journal*, vol. 109, no. 2, F165–86.

Horgan, J. 1995. From complexity to perplexity, *Scientific American*, vol. 272, no. 6, 104–9.

Hunt, B. 2003. *The Timid Corporation: Why Business is Terrified of Taking Risk*, New York, Wiley.

Ingham, G. 2004. *The Nature of Money*, Cambridge, Polity Press.

Keynes, J.M. 1936. *The General Theory of Employment, Interest and Money*, London, Macmillan.

Keynes, J.M. 1937. The General Theory of Employment, *Quarterly Journal of Economics*, vol. 51, no. 1, 209–23.

Kirp, D.L. 2003. *Shakespeare, Einstein, and the Bottom Line: The Marketing of Higher Education*, Cambridge, MA, Harvard University Press.

Knight, F.H. 1921. *Risk, Uncertainty and Profit*, New York, Houghton Mifflin.

Klamer, A. and Colander, D. 1990. *The Making of an Economist*, Boulder, Westview Press.

Kregel, J.A. 2009. Why don't the bailouts work? Design of a new financial system versus a return to normalcy, *Cambridge Journal of Economics*, vol. 33, 653–63.

Krueger, A.O. et al. 1991. Report on the Commission on Graduate Education in Economics, *Journal of Economic Literature*, vol. 29, no. 3, 1035–53.

Lawson, T. 1997. *Economics and Reality*, London and New York, Routledge.

Leijonhufvud, A. 1968. *On Keynesian Economics and the Economics of Keynes: A Study in Monetary Theory*, London, Oxford University Press.

Leijonhufvud, A. 2009. Out of the corridor: Keynes and the crisis, *Cambridge Journal of Economics*, vol. 33, 741–57.

Leontief, W.W. 1982. Letter in *Science*, no. 217, 9 July, 104–7.

Loasby, B.J. 1990. The use of scenarios in business planning, pp. 46–63, in Frowen, S.F. (ed.), *Unknowledge and Choice in Economics*, London, Macmillan.

Lucas, R.E., Jr 1981. *Studies in Business Cycle Theory*, Cambridge, MA and Oxford, UK, MIT Press and Basil Blackwell.

Lutz, F.W. and Field, R.W. 1998. Business valuing in academia: the American university as a center for profit or inquiry? *Higher Education*, vol. 36, no. 4, 383–419.

MacKenzie, D. 2006. *An Engine, Not a Camera*, Cambridge, MA, MIT Press.

Mäki, U. 2001. The way the world works (www): towards an ontology of theory choice, pp. 369–89, in Mäki, U. (ed.), *The Economic World View: Studies in the Ontology of Economics*, Cambridge, Cambridge University Press.

Mäki, U. 2005. Models are experiments, experiments are models, *Journal of Economic Methodology*, vol. 12, no. 2, 303–15.

Mäki, U. 2009. MISSing the world. Models as isolations and credible surrogate systems, *Erkenn*, vol. 70, no. 1, 29–43.

McCloskey, Donald, N. 1991. Economic Science: a search through the hyperspace at assumptions?, *Methodus*, vol. 3, no. 1, June, 6–16.
Minsky, H.P. 1982. Finance and profits: the changing nature of American business cycles, in Hyman Minsky, H.P. (ed.), *Can 'It' Happen Again?: Essays in Instability and Finance*, Armonk, NY, M.E. Sharpe.
Minsky, H. P. 1985. The financial instability hypothesis: a restatement, in Arestis, P. and Skouras, T. (eds), *Post Keynesian Economic Theory*, Armonk, NY, M.E. Sharpe.
Minsky, H. P. 1992. 'The financial instability hypothesis', Working Paper no. 74, Jerome Levy Economics Institute (reprinted in Arestis, P. and Sawyer, M.C. (eds), *Handbook of Radical Political Economy*, Aldershot, UK and Brookfield, VT, USA, Edward Elgar).
Mirowski, P. 2002. *Machine Dreams: Economics Becomes a Cyborg Science*, Cambridge and New York, Cambridge University Press.
Moggridge, D.E. 1992. *Maynard Keynes: An Economist's Biography*, London, Routledge.
Mouzelis, N. 1995. *Sociological Theory: What Went Wrong? Diagnosis and Remedies*, London and New York, Routledge.
Myrdal, G. 1972. *Against the Stream: Critical Essays in Economics*, New York, Pantheon Books.
Nelson, R.R. (ed.) 2005. *The Limits of Market Organization*, New York, Russell Sage Foundation.
North, D.C. 1977. Markets and other allocation systems in history: the challenge of Karl Polanyi, *Journal of European Economic History*, vol. 6, no. 3, 703–16.
Posner, R.A. 2009. *A Failure of Capitalism: The Crisis of '08 and the Descent into Depression*, Cambridge, MA, Harvard University Press.
Pryor, F.L. 1996. *Economic Evolution and Structure: The Impact of Complexity on the U.S. Economic System*, Cambridge and New York, Cambridge University Press.
Robinson, J. 1965. *Collected Economic Papers, Volume Three*, Oxford, Basil Blackwell.
Rotheim, R.J. (ed.) 1998. *New Keynesian Economics/Post Keynesian Alternatives*, London and New York, Routledge.
Rueschemeyer, D. 1986. *Power and the Division of Labor*, Stanford and Cambridge, Stanford University Press and Polity Press.
Sargent, T.J. 2008. Rational expectations, *The Concise Encyclopedia of Economics*, available at http://www.econlib.org/library/Enc/RationalExpectations.html; accessed 22 October 2010.
Sened, I. 1997. *The Political Institution of Private Property*, Cambridge, Cambridge University Press.
Shiller, R.J. 2008. *The Subprime Solution: How Today's Global Financial Crisis Happened, and What to Do about It*, Princeton, NJ, Princeton University Press.
Somers, M.R. 1998. Symposium on Historical Sociology and Rational Choice Theory "We're no angels": realism, rational choice, and relationality in social science, *American Journal of Sociology*, vol. 104, no. 3, 722–84.
Stigler, G.J., Stigler, S.M. and Friedland, C. 1995. The journals of economics, *Journal of Political Economy*, vol. 105, no. 2, 331–59.
Sugden, R. 2000. Credible worlds: the status of theoretical models in economics, *Journal of Economic Methodology*, vol. 7, no. 1, 1–31.
Van der Heijden, K. 1996. *Scenarios: The Art of Strategic Conversation*, Chichester, Wiley.
Veblen, T.B. 1918. *The Higher Learning in America: A Memorandum on the Conduct of Universities by Business Men*, New York, Huebsch.
Weintraub, E.R. 2002. *How Economics Became a Mathematical Science*, Durham, NC, Duke University Press.
Wohlstetter, R. 1962. Pearl Harbor, *Warning and Decision*, Stanford, Stanford University Press.

Index